ANTIQUE TRADER ®

AMERICAN
Pressed Glass
& Bottles

2ND EDITION   PRICE GUIDE

EDITED BY
Kyle Husfloen

Published by
Antique Trader Books, A Division of

krause
publications

700 E. State Street • Iola, WI 54990-0001
Telephone: 715/445-2214

Web: www.krause.com

Please, call or write us for our free catalog of antiques and collectibles publications.
To place an order or receive our free catalog, call 800-258-0929.
For editorial comment and further information,
use our regular business telephone at (715) 445-2214.

Library of Congress Catalog Number: 00-104626
ISBN: 0-87341-897-2

Printed in the United States of America

Introduction

For thirty years The Antique Trader has been publishing a periodical price guide covering the whole realm of antiques and collectibles, first as a semi-annual and then a quarterly publication and then, from 1984 to 1993, a bi-monthly magazine. In 1985 we introduced a single annual edition to compliment the periodical issues and this yearly edition remains a mainstay of our publishing efforts today.

We have now broadened our coverage of specialized collecting interests with price guides such as Antique Trader Books Pottery and Porcelain - Ceramics Guide, now in its third edition. We have also recently prepared the second edition of Antique Trader Books American & European Decorative & Art Glass and the volume you hold is the second edition of the sequel to this guide.

Antique Trader Books American Pressed Glass & Bottles Price Guide, Second Edition offers an in depth guide to all sorts of popular American-made glasswares of the 19th and 20th centuries.

For over seventy years Victorian pressed glass has been a passion for hundreds of collectors and in recent decades a more diverse range of wares has joined the ranks of collectibility. These include Carnival glass, Depression glass, kitchen glasswares and the products of such well known 20th century American manufacturers as Heisey, Cambridge and Imperial, to name a few.

In this volume we are covering all the most popular categories of glassware produced with the use of molds and machines. In general this includes all types of glasswares, both decorative and useful, which were originally marketed to attract the broadest spectrum of middle class consumers possible. Attractive and relatively inexpensive, such glasswares have been widely available to American housewives since the mid-19th century and have served to brighten the tables and sideboards of this country for generations. Today few of the old glass-producing firms are still operating in the U.S. and the wares they marketed to our mothers, grandmothers and great-grandmothers are increasingly collectible.

Over 170 years of American glass manufacture are covered in this volume and I hope it will serve today's glass lover well.

My staff and I have worked diligently to gather a wide spectrum of accurate and in-depth descriptions for this expanded volume on American glass and we have also added a large selection of black and white photographs to highlight our listings. As an added bonus, 16 pages of glass are presented in full-color. To start you off we provide a chapter on "Collecting Guidelines" and a series of sketches of typical forms you may encounter in glass. Our price listings themselves are arranged alphabetically by the name of the type of glass or the producing company and each section begins with a brief introduction to that glassware. Although not many American companies permanently marked their pieces, a few did. So where applicable, we include a sketch of the company marking or label. To round out our text we provide a "Glossary of Terms" relating to pressed and mold-blown glass and bottles as well as Appendices covering various collector clubs, associations and museums. Finally, we have carefully indexed and cross-referenced all of the listings included in this price guide.

We think you'll find this book a useful and informative guide to one of America's most popular collecting fields. It's hoped that our hard work will pay off in your greater understanding and appreciation of America's glassmaking heritage.

In closing I wish to express sincere appreciation to my staff for their hard work and perseverance in producing this book. A special thank you goes to Consulting Editor Dean Six who prepared a number of our categories and offered invaluable insights into how to make this the most comprehensive yet easy-to-use guide available. Dean is well known in glass collecting circles for his wide-ranging knowledge and glass scholarship and as the founder of The West Virginia Museum of American Glass in Weston, West Virginia. Also offering invaluable assistance and help with several important categories was Dr. James S. Measell, another leading writer and researcher in the field of American Glass.

Dr. Measell today works closely with The Fenton Art Glass Company of Williamstown, West Virginia. It was a great pleasure to work with these dedicated glass lovers and all the other kind contributors to this guide.

Enjoy the fruits of our combined efforts and, if you have any comments or suggestions we're always interested in hearing from you. We'll do our best to respond to your inquiries. Sit back now and take an armchair tour of over 200 years of American glassmaking history.

—Kyle Husfloen, Editor

Please note: Though listings have been double-checked and every effort has been made to insure the accuracy, neither the compilers, editors nor publisher can assume responsibility for any losses that might be incurred as a result of consulting this guide, or of errors, typographical or otherwise.

Photography Credits

Photographers who have contributed to this issue include: E.A. Babka, East Dubuque, Illinois; Stanley L. Baker, Minneapolis, Minnesota; Dorothy Beckwith, Platteville, Wisconsin; Johanna Billings, Danielsville, Pennsylvania; Donna Bruun, Galena, Illinois; Herman C. Carter, Tulsa, Oklahoma; J.D. Dalessandro, Cincinnati, Ohio; Ruth Eaves, Marmora, New Jersey; Susan Eberman, Bedford, Indiana; Joe Hallahan, Dubuque, Iowa; Robert G. Jason-Ickes, Olympia, Washington; the late Don Moore, Alameda, California; Louise Paradis, Sparta, Wisconsin; and Tom Wallace, Chicago, Illinois.

For other photographs, artwork, data or permission to photograph in their shops, we sincerely express appreciation to the following auctioneers, galleries, museums, individuals and shops: Tom and Neila Bredehoft, St. Louisville, Ohio; Brown Auctions, Mullenville, Kansas; Charles Casad, Monticello, Illinois; Collector's Auction Services, Oil City, Pennsylvania; Collector's Sales and Service, Middletown, Rhode Island; S. Davis, Williamsburg, Ohio; T. Ermert, Cincinnati, Ohio; Bill Freeman, Smyrna, Georgia; Garth's Auctions, Inc., Delaware, Ohio; Glass-Works Auctions, East Greenville, Pennsylvania; Glick's Antiques, Galena, Illinois; Robert Gordon, San Antonio, Texas; and Grunewald Antiques, Hillsborough, North Carolina.

Also to Vicki Harmon, San Marcos, California; the late William Heacock, Marietta, Ohio; Jackson's Auctioneers, Cedar Falls, Iowa; Jerry's Antiques, Davenport, Iowa; J. Martin, Mt. Orab, Ohio; Randall McKee, Kenosha, Wisconsin; Jim Ludescher, Dubuque, Iowa; Joy Luke Gallery, Bloomington, Illinois; Pacific Glass Auctions, Sacramento, California; Mary M. Wetzel-Romalka, Mishawaka, Indiana; Jane Rosenow, Galva, Illinois; Tammy Roth, East Dubuque, Illinois; Robert W. Skinner, Inc., Bolton, Massachusetts; Doris Spahn, East Dubuque, Illinois; Temples Antiques, Minneapolis, Minnesota; Lee Vines, Hewlett, New York; Lloyd Williams Auctions, Harrisonville, Missouri; Woody Auctions, Douglass, Kansas; and Yesterday's Treasures, Galena, Illinois.

Special Category Contributors

Dean Six
% West Virginia Museum of
American Glass, Ltd.
P.O. Box 574
Weston, WV 26452
Blenko, Bryce, Cambridge, Central,
Fostoria, Imperial, Lotus,
Monongah, Seneca, Dorothy C.
Thorpe, Westmoreland, Weston

Dr. James Measell
% Fenton Art Glass Company
Williamstown, WV
Dugan-Diamond, Greentown,
Northwood

Bruce Dooley
2571 - 7th Ave.
Sweetwater, NJ 08037
(609) 965-2535
Carnival Glass

Robert G. Jason-Ickes
3600 Elizabeth Ave., SE, #19-203
Olympia, WA 98501
Antiqueappraisers@home.com
Car Vases

Kate Trabue
1603 Pine St., #1
Eureka, CA 95501-2280
(707) 444-3326
Kitchen Glassware

Judy Swan
Swan's Showcase
Dubuque, IA 52203
(319) 582-4389
Kitchen Glassware

Frank Chiarenza
National Milk Glass Collectors
Society
80 Crestview
Newington, CT 06111-2405
(860) 666-5576
Milk Glass

John Tutton
1967 Ridgeway Road
Front Royal, VA 22630
(540) 635-7058
e.mail: jtutton@rma.edu
Publications: Udderly Delightful,
three editions and Udderly Beautiful
Milk Bottles

On the Cover:

Front cover: McKee Rock Crystal pattern sugar bowl in ruby, rare; Fenton
Hobnail pattern green opalescent bowl, $30-40; Atterbury milk glass
Rabbit covered dish with original red eyes, $250-300.

Back cover: Blown three mold Baroque pattern decanter in sapphire blue,
$3,000-4,000; Carnival glass Coin Spot green bowl, $25-50.

Collecting Guidelines

It has been over 30 years since I first became enamored with early American glass and I still remember the piece that set my pulse racing - a tall clear pressed whale oil lamp with a large band of hearts encircling the font. "It's Sandwich," my dealer friend informed me, "and quite rare." I thought it was one of the loveliest antiques I'd seen in my budding collecting career and, if my meager allowance had allowed I would have certainly added it to my collection. However, it was priced out of my range so, as an alternative I soon discovered later 19th century pressed glass and began a collection of this much more affordable and available glassware. Today my love of American glass continues unabated and, although I still have to watch my budget, I've been able to add quite a few nice pieces to my collection.

I will admit that when I first got interested in American glass I found it a very daunting prospect...there are so many types available in so many styles and colors. I wasn't sure I'd ever understand all the intricacies of this diverse field. However, year by year and book by book my knowledge and understanding grew. About the time I first discovered pattern glass the interest in Depression era glassware developed, spurred on by Hazel Marie Weatherman's first book. That reference became one of the first in my library. Soon after I discovered the pioneering works on American pressed glass by Ruth Webb Lee who, in the early 1930s, became the moving force behind the collecting mania for 19th century American pressed glass. Other books on glass and other antiques topics have gradually found their way into my library but it's still a long way from complete.

Anyone who collects anything should know that building a good reference library is vital to the success of your collecting forays and an investment which will pay big dividends over the years. Today there are dozens of fine books available on all types of American glass and there's still glass available in a style and price range to fit nearly every pocketbook. If you are fortunate, like I was, to have a knowledgeable antiques dealer who is also a good friend, you're well ahead of the game. Learning first-hand from a dealer or fellow collector can give you many valuable insights into collecting which books alone may not.

Today there are also any number of national glass collecting clubs which anyone is free to join. These groups have become vital links between collectors and serve as a major source of important research information through their newsletters, books and conventions. The National American Glass Club was the first such organization, founded over 60 years ago. It has been joined in the last twenty years by many other groups formed to focus on such popular glasswares as Depression era glass, Heisey, Fostoria, Milk Glass, Cambridge and many others. In a special Appendix at the back of this book we list these clubs for reference.

Although each glass collecting topic has its own specialized vocabulary and methodology for collecting, certain guidelines apply to most glass specialties. First and foremost, as I mentioned above, is to begin building your reference library. Second, make contact with others who share your passion and become an avid student of the field. Finally, start out conservatively and try to specialize in one company, pattern, piece or even color of glass. Focusing your collecting is helpful to the novice collector, no matter what your interest, and this is especially true in a field as broad as American glass.

I have found, over the years, that certain factors will affect the collectibility and value of American glass, and they hold true for all types of glass, from Lacy glass to Depression or Lalique to Venini. The first factor is the condition of a piece. Glass, unlike ceramic wares, can not be easily and invisibly repaired or restored. Once a piece is chipped or cracked it will stay that way and such damages will greatly affect its market value unless it is exceedingly rare or unique. Buy only perfect pieces, especially if you are just starting out, since they will undoubtedly maintain their value and appreciate over time.

A second factor which determines overall value is rarity of form. In glassware very large or very small pieces are often the scarcest, and unusual forms can bring premium prices. For example, in early Lacy glass from the 1820-1850 era, some common clear cup plates can sell for a few dollars since they were produced in such abundance, whereas a rare set of green Cherry Blossom salt and pepper shakers in Depression Glass (ca. 1930s) may bring over $1,000.

It's a matter of the rarity of the piece as well as a third factor of value: color. Over the past two hundred years a vast majority of the glass produced for everyday use was made in clear and, in fact, early manufacturers strove to make the clearest and brightest glass possible. It wasn't until around the 1880s that it became possible to less expensively produce pressed glass in various bright hues. Since then glass tablewares in shades of blue, purple, green, yellow and amber have become more common although clear wares still lead production.

Since it required certain chemicals in the glass batch to produce certain colors, these additives added to the cost of production and some colors, such as a true red, were very difficult to produce. This is still true today and that is why red remains one of the scarcer and most expensive colors to collect in most glass patterns. The popularity of the color blue with the general public has meant that more of it was produced than red, but it is always a choice color for collectors today. The varied hues of purple, green, yellow and amber also have their following, but blue generally leads in collector appeal, no matter the type of glass.

Keep in mind, of course, that certain colors or pieces may be rare in one pattern of glass but common in another pattern of the same vintage. Sorting out what makes one piece or pattern unique and desirable is the challenge of glass collecting. This hunt for hidden treasure is one of the great pleasures in any collecting field and the broad realm of American-made glass means the likelihood of making such a discovery is even greater.

The collecting of American glass, no matter the type or age, is an exciting and fascinating pastime but, unfortunately there are some pitfalls which need to be touched upon. The biggest frustration today for collectors and dealers in glass is dealing with reproductions. This is not a new problem but one that continues to haunt us. Luckily for today's collector it is much easier to share information on troublesome pieces using the numerous trade publications, newsletters and magazines which serve the collecting market. When author Ruth Webb Lee released her book, Antique Fakes and Reproductions, over fifty years ago it was one of the few publications to address the problem, especially as it pertains to American 19th century pressed glass. Although no longer in print, Mrs. Lee's pioneering volume is still an invaluable source of information.

In more recent years many other books have been published which deal with this problem. In my 1992 book, *Collector's Guide to American Pattern Pressed Glass, 1825-1915,* I provided as much detail as possible on what patterns and pieces have been reproduced in pressed glass made before World War I. Other books have added greatly to this field of knowledge including *Identifying Pattern Glass Reproductions,* by Bill Jenks, Jerry Luna and Darryl Reilly (Wallace-Homestead, 1993). Many other glass categories have been covered in reference books which offer some coverage of reproductions to avoid. For the many collectors interested in Depression era glass, *The Collector's Encyclopedia of Depression Glass,* by Gene Florence (Collector Books) is especially helpful in guiding collectors through the repro maze.

Although the thought of being stung by reproductions may at first discourage some new collectors, they should know that it really isn't as big an obstacle to building a fine collection as they may think. Armed with some key reference books and the support and enthusiasm of fellow collectors you can quite easily maneuver your way through that mine field. With the enormous volume of American pressed and mold-blown glass produced in the past 150 years, everyone should be able to find a line of glass that fits their budget and taste. We hope this new edition will help prepare you for an exciting and fulfilling collecting career, an adventure sure to bring you hours of satisfaction and enjoyment.

—Kyle Husfloen

Typical Forms

Bowls in Pressed Glass

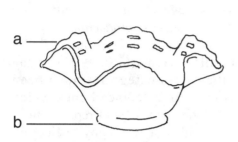

CANDY DISH   6"-8" d.

a. Deeply ruffled openwork (latticework) sides with a lightly scalloped rim
b. Footring

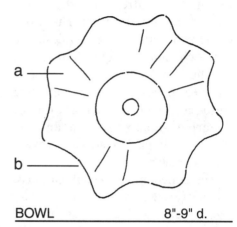

BOWL   8"-9" d.

a. Gently ruffled sides
b. Smooth rim

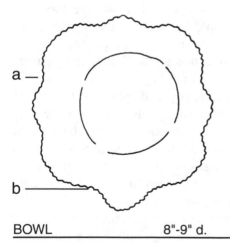

BOWL   8"-9" d.

a. Gently ruffled rim
b. Tiny scallops at the edge. A rim with evenly spaced small crimps is sometimes called a "piecrust" rim, while one with multiple rounded looping crimps is sometimes called a "ribbon candy" rim.

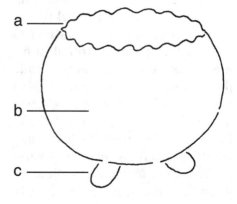

ROSE BOWL   4" d.

a. Incurved (or 'closed') rim with small ruffles
b. Spherical, bulbous body
c. Knob feet

CREAMERS & PITCHERS IN BLOWN & PRESSED GLASS

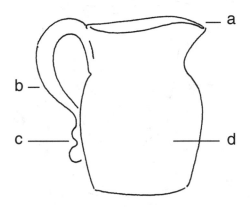

CREAMER & PITCHER

a. Flared rim with pinched spout
b. Early applied strap handle
c. Curlique on base of handle
d. Ovoid body

CREAMER & PITCHER

a. Late applied round handle
b. Bulbous spherical body
c. Footring

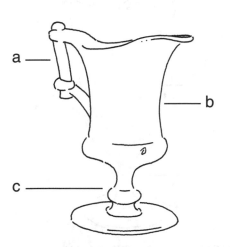

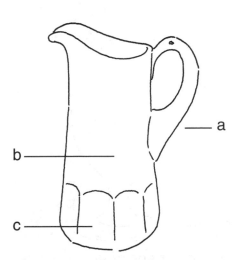

CREAMER & PITCHER

a. Pressed angular handle
b. Flaring cylindrical body
c. Pedestal base with knob or knop

CREAMER & PITCHER

a. Late applied round handle
b. Tall tankard-form body
c. Panelled base

CELERY VASES, SPILLHOLDERS & SPOONERS IN PATTERN GLASS

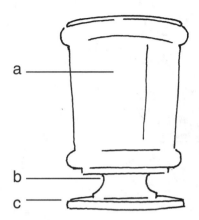

FLINT SPILLHOLDER (SPOONER)
ca. 1850-1860   5"-5 1/2" h.

a. Heavy, thick nearly cylindrical body
b. Short, thick applied pedestal
c. Thick, round applied foot

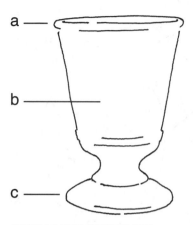

NON-FLINT SPOONER
ca. 1880   4 1/2"-6" h.

a. Flaring, flat rim
b. Tapering cylindrical body
c. Short pressed pedestal and round foot

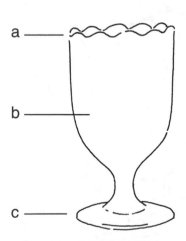

NON-FLINT SPOONER
ca. 1880   4 1/2"-6" h.

a. Scalloped rim
b. Bell-form round body
c. Slender pressed pedestal
    on round foot

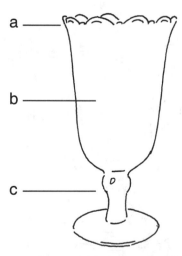

NON-FLINT CELERY VASE
ca. 1885   8"-10" h.

a. Flaring and scalloped rim
b. Tall bell-form body
c. Slender pressed pedestal with
    knob or knop on round foot

ANIMALS

Americans evidently like to collect glass animals. For the past sixty years, American glass manufacturers have turned out a wide variety of animals to please the buying public. Some were produced for long periods and some were later reproduced by other companies, while others were made for only a short period of time and are rare. We have not included late productions in our listings and have attempted to date the productions where possible. Evelyn Zemel's book, American Glass Animals A to Z, will be helpful to the novice collector. Another helpful book is Glass Animals of the Depression Era *by Lee Garmon and Dick Spencer (Collector Books, 1993).*

Asiatic Pheasant, clear, Heisey Glass Co., 7 1/2" l., 10 1/2" h. **$280**

Barnyard Rooster, black, Dalzell/Viking Glass Co. reissue of Paden City Glass Co., 8 3/4" h. 550

Bird, light blue, Paden City Glass Co., 5" h. 165

Borzoi, clear, large, New Martinsville Glass Mfg. Co. 50

Boxer dog, lying down, clear, American Glass Co., 3 7/8" h. 65

Boxer dog, sitting, clear, American Glass Co., 4 3/4" h. 65

Cat, light blue, Fostoria Glass Co., 3 1/4" h. 30

Cat, dark medium blue, No. 1322, 1960s, Viking Glass Co., 8" h. 45

Chanticleer, clear, Fostoria Glass Co., 10 1/4" h. 215

"Chessie" cat, milk glass & black satin finish, Tiffin Glass Company 350

Dog, dark medium blue, No. 1323, 1960s, Viking Glass Co., 8" h. 50

Dragon Swan, clear, Paden City Glass Co., 9 3/4" h. 175

Dragon Swan, pale blue, Paden City Glass Co., 9 3/4" h. 700

Elephant book end, clear, No. 237, New Martinsville Glass Co., 5 1/2" h. 75

Elephant w/long trunk extended, clear, (Mama), Heisey Glass Co., 1944-55, 6 1/2" l., 4" h. 425

Elephant w/trunk raised, clear, (Baby), Heisey Glass Co., 1944-53, 5" l., 4 1/2" h. 225

Fawn, w/flower floater & sockets for three candles, citron green, Tiffin Glass Co., ca. late 1940s, 14 1/2" l., fawn 10" h., ... 325

Fawn, w/flower floater & sockets for three candles, copen blue, Tiffin Glass Co., ca. late 1940s, 14 1/2" l., fawn 10" h. 500

Fighting Rooster, clear, Heisey Glass Co., 1940-46, 7 1/2" h. 145

Fish book end, clear, A.H. Heisey & Co., 1942-52, 6 1/2" h. 145

Fish candleholder, clear, A.H. Heisey & Co., 1941-58, 5" h. 135

Frog, covered dish, green, 1969, Erskine Glass Co. 130

Heisey Giraffe

Giraffe, clear, A.H. Heisey & Co., 1942-52, 3" l., 10 3/4" h. (ILLUS.)............................... 275

Goose, wings down, clear, A.H. Heisey & Co., 1947-55, 4 1/2" l., 4 1/2" h. (small bubble in neck)... 375

Goose, wings half up, clear w/Carleton roses decoration, A.H. Heisey & Co., 1947-55, 5 1/2" l., 5" h.................................. 95

Goose, wings half up, clear, A.H. Heisey & Co., 1947-55, 5 1/2" l., 5" h. 103

Goose, pale blue, Paden City Glass Co., ca. 1940, 5" h... 125

Goose, wings up, clear, A.H. Heisey & Co., 1942-53, 7 1/2" l., 6 1/2" h.......................... 105

Goose (The Fat Goose), clear & frosted, Duncan & Miller Glass Co., 6" l., 6 1/2" h. 195

Heisey Balking Colt

Horse, Colt, balking, clear, A.H. Heisey & Co., 1941-45, 3 1/2" h. (ILLUS.).................. 220

Horse, Plug (Sparky), clear, A.H. Heisey & Co., 1941-46, 3 1/2" l., 4 1/4" h. 125

Horse, Colt, standing, clear, A.H. Heisey & Co., 1940-52, 5" h. 85

Horse Head book ends, A. H. Heisey Co., 1937-55, clear, 6 7/8" h., pr............................ 275

Horse, Head Up, clear, New Martinsville Glass Co., 8" h. 85

Mama Bear, clear, No. 488, New Martinsville Glass Co., 6" l., 4" h. 145

Mama Pig, w/three nursing piglets attached on each side, clear, No. 1, limited edition of approximately 200, New Martinsville Glass Co., 6" l., 3" h. 913

Marmota Sentinel (Woodchuck), caramel slag, Imperial Glass Co., 4" h. 55

"Oscar," 1991 Heisey Club souvenir, sapphire blue opalescent frosted, Fenton Art Glass Co. 45

"Oscar," 1994 Heisey Club souvenir, frosted green, Fenton Art Glass Co. 40

Papa Bear, clear, No. 489, New Martinsville Glass Co., 6 1/2" l., 4" h. 165

Pelican, clear, No. 761, New Martinsville Glass Co., 8" h. 80

Penguin, amber, No. 1319, 1960s, Viking Glass Co., 7" h. 20

Plug Horse, clear, A. H. Heisey & Co., clear, 1941-46, 4" l., 4" h. 125

Polar Bear, clear, Fostoria Glass Co., 4 5/8" h. 65

Polar Bear on ice, clear, No. 611, Paden City Glass Co., 4 1/2" h. 60

Police Dog (German Shepherd), clear, No. 733, New Martinsville Glass Co., 5" h. 55

Porpoise on wave, clear, No. 766, New Martinsville Glass Co., 6" h. 475

Rabbit, large mama, clear, No. 764, New Martinsville Glass Co., 2 1/2" h. 325

Ringneck Pheasant, clear, Heisey Glass Co., 1942-53, 12" l., 5" h. 145

Ringneck Pheasant, clear, A.H. Heisey & Co., 1942-53, 11" l., 4 3/4" h. 115

Rooster (Chanticleer), pale blue, Paden City Glass Co., 9 1/2" h. 175

Rooster Head Stopper, clear, A.H. Heisey & Co., 4 1/2" h. 45

Rooster with Crooked Tail, clear, No. 668, New Martinsville Glass Co., 8" h. 60

Scottie Dog book ends, Cambridge Glass Co., 6 1/2" h., pr. 195

Small Cat, black satin, No. 9446, Tiffin Glass Company.. 250

Sparrow, clear, A.H. Heisey & Co., 1942-45, 4" l., 2 1/4" h. 100

Squirrel, clear, No. 674, New Martinsville Glass Co., 4 1/2" h. (no base) 45

Squirrel on curved log, clear, No. 677, Paden City Glass Co., 5 1/2" h. 50

Swordfish, blue opalescent, Duncan & Miller Glass Co., 5" h............................. 425-450

Swordfish, clear, Duncan & Miller Glass Co., 5" h. 275

Tiger, Head Up, clear, New Martinsville Glass Co., 6 1/2" h. 150

Wolfhound, black, No. 716, Dalzell/Viking Glass Co. reissue of New Martinsville Glass Co., 7" h. 450

Wolfhound, clear, No. 716, New Martinsville Glass Co., 7" h. 78

BLENKO

This company represents one family's story of triumph in the glass industry. The Blenkos developed some of the world's finest glass colors in stained and leaded glass for use in windows around the globe. Tableware and decorative glass were added to their line later to supplement their flat glass production. Begun in Milton, West Virginia in 1931 it continues in operation today.

Basket, "opaline" - opaque yellow, No. 8628, 8 3/4".. $74

Book ends, model of an elephant, green, pr... 28

Book ends, model of an owl, clear, pr. 22

Bottle w/original cap, mushroom-shaped, red w/a multicolored cap, No. 7022, 8 1/2" h.. 54

Bowl, tri-lobed form, green, blue & red leaves.. 210

Bowl, 10 1/4" d., salad, petal-form, amber......... 19

Candleholder, paperweight-form w/airtwist spiral blue core, 6 1/2" h., each.................... 48

Cigarette lighter, footed, blue, No. 6943, 7 1/2" h... 32

Cigarette lighter, lemon yellow, No. 644, 11" h... 28

Decanter w/figural animal stopper, clear bottle w/a ruby figural steer stopper, No. 7050 65

Decanter w/figural animal stopper, clear bottle w/figural green owl stopper, No. 7050 48

Blenko Human-form Decanter

Decanter w/original stopper, bottle molded as a human form w/applied arms, stopper molded w/a face, No. 6525, 13 1/4" h. (ILLUS.)............................. 140

Decanter w/original stopper, cased blue over clear bottle w/airtrap stopper, No. 6724, 14" h. 74

Decanter w/original stopper, Crackle glass w/applied amber rosettes on the shoulder, Crackle clear stopper, No. 6821 42

Decanter w/original stopper, molded as a loaf of bread, ruby, No. 6316 64

Decanter w/original stopper, the bottle molded as a human face, w/a tall spire-form stopper, blue, No. 6218, 22" h. 58

Decanter w/original stopper, the bottle & stopper in Tangerine/Amberina w/applied red threading around the middle of each, No. 6739, 28 1/2" h. 134

Epergne, single-lily, a fluted lemon yellow bowl w/red threading & a matching upright lily vase, No. 6830, 15 1/2" h. 120

Goblet, Citron/yellow, No. 489, ornamental twisted airtrap stem, 13" h. 164

Blenko Williamsburg Goblet

Goblet, water, Williamsburg, airtwist stem, clear, 8" h. (ILLUS.) 36

Goblet, water, Williamsburg, teardrop stem, clear 30

Ice bucket, model of a tall cowboy hat, dark green, 8 1/2" h. 128

Ice bucket, model of a top hat, clear w/pink band, 8" h. 78

Model of a fish, blue, No. 5433, 10" l. 60

Model of a fish, Tangerine/Amberina, No. 971, 25" l. 120

Model of a penguin, pulled form, clear & blue, No. 8020, 14" h. 86

Paperweight, clear top, spiral airtwist w/amber core 30

Paperweight, round, airtrap blue core, No. 68 28

Paperweight, round, spiral airtrap green core, No. 68 35

Pitcher, 17 1/2" h., crackle glass, green w/blue threading near the top, blue handle, No. 6835 74

Pitcher, 9 3/4" h., pinched-in sides, Tangerine/Amberina, No. 6714 65

Pitcher, double-lipped, handleless, impressed sides, amber 18

Pitcher, double-lipped, handleless, impressed sides, Tangerine/Amberina 32

Pitcher, figural, model of a cat w/applied tail & features in blue & clear 260

Pitcher, footed, amber, No. 6726 48

Plate, 8" d., luncheon, petal-form, seeded texture, blue 18

Punch set: 10" d. lipped ruby bowl No. 925, a ladle & 12 cups; the set 360

Punch set: punch bowl, ladle & 12 cups; Crackle glass, green, ladle w/seeded texture, the set 450

Tumbler, pinched sides, blue Crackle glass, No. 418, 6" h. 16

Tumbler, pinched sides, ruby Crackle glass, No. 418, 6" h. 22

Tumbler, pinched sides, Tangerine/Amberina, No. 418, 4 1/2" h. 12

Tumbler, pinched sides, Tangerine/Amberina, No. 418, 6" h. 18

Vase, cylindrical, clear w/applied turquoise & olive green spiral bands, No. 6710 42

Vase, 6 1/2" h., round w/sheared folded-back lip, green Crackle glass, No. 6621 45

Vase, 7" h., flip-style, Crackle glass w/applied red leaves, No. 366 38

Vase, 11" h., figural human form in clear w/applied colored arms & breasts, crimped top forming hair 134

Vase, 11" h., hat-form, olive green, No. 3715 78

Vase, 12" h., figural, silhouetted human face, cobalt blue 110

Vase, 12" h., flip-style, Crackle glass w/applied blue leaves, No. 366 58

Vase, cov., 14 1/2" h., bamboo-style, green w/red cover, signed "Driesbeck" 475

Vase, 24" h., extreme bud-form, Tangerine/Amberina 55

Wall pocket, figural, model of a steer head w/horns, blue & amber, 13" w. point to point 120

Wine, Williamsburg, clear, airtwist stem, 6 1/2" h. 38

BLOWN THREE MOLD

This type of glass was entirely or partially blown in a mold and was popular from about 1820 to 1840. The object was formed and the decoration impressed upon it by blowing the glass into a metal mold, usually of three—but sometimes more—sections hinged together. Mold-blown glass actually dates back to ancient times. Recent research reveals that certain geometric patterns were reproduced in the 1920s; some new pieces, usually sold through museum gift shops, are still available. Collectors are urged to read all recent information available. Reference numbers are from George L. and Helen McKearin's book, American Glass.

Pieces are clear unless otherwise noted.

Creamer, geometric, ovoid body tapering to a wide flared neck w/pinched spout, applied strap handle w/end curl, 3 1/4" h. (GIII-26) $550

Creamer, miniature, geometric, applied handle, 2 7/8" h., GII-18 (chip at handle tip) 110

Decanter w/bar lip, Baroque, pontiled base, rare applied bar lip, clear, 7 1/4" h. (GV-8) 495

Decanter w/flattened unpatterned stopper, geometric, miniature, ovoid body tapering to a plain neck w/flared rim, clear, 3 1/2" h. (GIII-12) **495**

Decanter w/hollow blown stopper, geometric, molded in relief w/"Rum" on the front, 8 1/4" h., GIII-2 (minor stain) **303**

Decanter w/plain flat teardrop stopper, geometric, cylindrical ribbed sides below the tapering ringed neck w/flared lip, overall 6 3/4" h., GI-15 (minor stains) **220**

Decanter w/pressed wheel stopper, geometric, ovoid body tapering to double-ringed neck w/flattened flared rim, slightly oversized stopper, clear, 1/2 pt., 7 1/2" h., GII-33 (ILLUS. right below) **209**

Decanter w/stopper, Baroque patt., probably original hollow blown ribbed stopper, clear, 11 1/2" h., GV-9 (some light interior residue) **209**

Decanter w/stopper, geometric, flared mouth, rayed base, possibly original hollow blown stopper, clear, 10 1/2" h., GIII-24 (slight light mold impression) **142**

Decanter w/stopper, geometric, large star in ring design around sides w/rows of short ribs above & below, flared folded lip & original hollow blown stopper, clear, 11 1/4" h. (GV-10) **550**

Blown Three Mold Decanters

Decanter w/stopper, geometric, ovoid body tapering to a plain neck w/flattened flared rim, original hollow patterned ball stopper, clear, 10 1/2" h., GIII-5 (ILLUS. left) **176**

Decanter w/stopper, Gothic arch design, bands of Gothic arches above & below a central reserve molded w/"RUM," flared rim w/original compressed hollow blown stopper, clear, 10 3/4" h., GIV-7 (some light amber residue) **220**

Decanter w/wheel stopper, geometric, barrel-shaped body w/tapering shoulder to a short neck w/pinched spout, polished pontil, slightly frosted interior, probably Keene, New Hampshire, 8 3/4" h., GII-7 (ILLUS. top next column) **204**

Dish, geometric, shallow round form w/folded rim, clear, 5 5/16" d., 1 1/8" h. (GII-22) **99**

Dish, geometric, shallow round form w/rolled rim, rough pontil, clear, 6" d. (GIII-5) **187**

Barrel-Shaped Decanter with Stopper

Model of a top hat, miniature, geometric, tapering cylindrical sides w/deeply rolled rim, Boston & Sandwich Glass Co., 1 3/4" h. (GII-16) **330**

Model of a top hat, geometric, tapering cylindrical sides w/narrow flared & folded rim, probably Boston & Sandwich Glass Co., cobalt blue, 2" h. (GII-18) **715**

Model of a top hat, geometric, cylindrical sides w/wide rolled rim, probably Boston & Sandwich Glass Co., 1825-40, 2 1/2" h. (GIII-8) **143**

Model of a top hat, geometric, folded rim, deep sapphire-violet blue, unlisted, 2 3/4" h. (GI-6) **1,320**

Pan, geometric, wide shallow round dish w/folded rim, pontiled, slightly weak impression, 8 1/2" d., 1 1/2" h. (GIII-15) **550**

Pitcher, 3 1/8", miniature, geometric, squatty bulbous body w/widely flaring rim & pinched spout, applied handle, clear, GII-18 (hard to see line in handle) **132**

Quality Blown Three Mold Pitcher

Pitcher, geometric, bulbous ovoid body tapering to a flaring neck w/pinched spout, applied strap handle w/end curl, pontil, 6 3/4" h., GIII-5 (ILLUS.) **935**

Salt dip, cylindrical sides w/deeply rolled rim, fifteen-diamond base w/pontil, probably Boston & Sandwich Glass Co., cobalt blue, ca. 1825-40, 2 1/4" d., 2" h. (GII-21)............ **2,750**

Salt dip, geometric, cushion foot & flaring squatty body w/low flared rim, clear, 2 1/2" d., 2 1/8" h. (GIII-25) **143**

Salt dip, geometric, wide bell-form top w/flared rim raised on a short flaring pedestal foot, clear, unseen pontil chip, 2 1/4" h. (GII-21).. **468**

Salt dip, geometric, wide tulip-form bowl w/rolled rim on a short applied pedestal foot, 2 3/8" h., GII-21 (pinpoint lip flakes)..... **165**

Shakers w/original brass lids, geometric, cylindrical body tapering slightly toward top, ringed base w/pontil, loose lids, clear, 4 1/2" h., GIII-27 (one w/chip under lid), pr. **143**

Tumbler, miniature, geometric, cylindrical, ringed base, clear, 1 3/4" h. (GII-16)........... **275**

Tumbler, geometric, cylindrical w/diamond point band, 3 1/4" h. (GII-18)...................... **171**

Tumbler, geometric, cylindrical w/fine ribbing around lower half, clear, McKearin Collection sticker, 3 1/4" h. (GI-?) **303**

Blown Three Mold Tumbler

Tumbler, geometric, slightly tapering cylindrical form, 5 3/4" h., GII-18 (ILLUS.)........... **259**

Wine, geometric, flaring cylindrical bowl w/applied bladed stem & pontiled foot, clear, 4" h. (GII-19)...................................... **330**

BOTTLES

BITTERS

(Numbers with some listings below refer to those used in Carlyn Ring's For Bitters Only.)

African Stomach Bitters, cylindrical w/applied top, smooth base, dark amber, 9 5/8" h. **$88**

African Stomach Bitters - Spruance, Stanley & Co., cylindrical w/applied mouth, dark amber, 9 5/8" h. (cleaned)........ **132**

Allen's (Dr.) Stomach Bitters - Pittsburgh, PA, cylindrical w/tall neck & applied mouth, aqua, 12 1/4" h. **330**

American Life Bitters - P.E. ller, Manufacturer, Tiffin, Ohio - American Life Bitters, cabin-shaped w/rounded shoulder & pointed lower doors & windows, applied sloping collar mouth, smooth base, ca. 1865-75, medium amber, 9" h. (ILLUS. top of next column) **9,625**

Rare American Life Cabin-form Bottle

Appentine Bitters (under) Geo. Benz & Sons, St. Paul, Minn., w/"Pat. Nov. 23, 1897" on base, square, scrolls along sides of label panel, medium amber, 8 1/4" h. (ILLUS. bottom of column)............. **385**

Arabian Bitters - Lawrence & Weichsel-baum, Savannah, Ga., rectangular w/paneled sides & applied sloping collar, ca. 1870, medium amber, 9 3/4" h. (some light inside stain) **242**

Baker's - Orange Grove - Bitters, square w/ropetwist corners, applied sloping collar mouth, ca. 1865-75, cherry puce, 9 3/8" h. **1,265**

Bell's (Dr.) - Golden Tonic - Bitters, figural bell w/tall neck & applied mouth, red iron pontil, ca. 1870-75, medium amber, 10" h. **12,650**

Appentine Bitters Bottle

Dr. Bell's Liver - Kidney Bitters

Bell's (Dr.) Liver - Kidney Bitters, square w/beveled corners, applied sloping collar mouth, pale greenish aqua, 9" h. (ILLUS.).. **105**

Berkshire Bitters Pig Bottle

Berkshire Bitters - Amann. Co. Cincinnati. O., figural pig, applied mouth, ca. 1865-76, amber, 10" l. (ILLUS.) **1,540**
Big Bill Best Bitters, tapering square, golden amber, ca. 1870-90, 12 1/8" h. **154**

Rare Dr. Birmingham's Bitters Bottle

Birmingham's (Dr.) Anti Bilious Blood Purifying Bitters - This Bottle Not Sold, cylindrical w/narrow panels up the sides, applied sloping collar mouth, smooth base, ca. 1855-65, some overall inside stain, medium blue green, 8 7/8" h. (ILLUS.)...................................... **4,180**

Brown (F.) Boston - Sarsaparilla - & Tomato - Bitters, cylindrical w/applied sloping double collar mouth, pontiled base, ca. 1845-55, aqua, 9 1/4" h. **303**
Brown's Celebrated Indian Herb Bitters - Patented 1867, figural Indian Queen, rolled lip, light yellow, 12 1/8" h. **3,300**
Brown's Celebrated Indian Herb Bitters - Patented 1868, figural Indian Queen, golden amber, rolled lip, 12 1/8" h. (area of lip unrolled w/minor roughness) **578**
Brown's Celebrated Indian Herb Bitters - Patented 1868, figural Indian Queen, yellowish amber, rolled lip, 12 1/8" h. **688**
Brown's Celebrated Indian Herb Bitters - Patented Feb. 11 1868, figural Indian Queen, rolled lip, medium to deep amber w/some red, 12 1/8" h. **715**
Bryant's Stomach - Bitters, octagonal w/lady's leg neck w/applied sloping double collar mouth, ca. 1860-70, deep olive green, 12" h.. **7,975**

Very Rare Cassin,s Bitters Bottle

Cassin,s Grape Brandy Bitters, nearly square w/violin-shaped sides, applied lip, ca. 1871-75, medium golden amber, tiny flakes on lip, very rare, 10" h. (ILLUS.).. **44,000**
Clarke's Sherry Wine Bitters, rectangular, most original label & tax stamp, aqua, 8" h. **88**
Cock's Celebrated Stomach Bitters (label only), square, tooled top, medium to light amber **66**
Corwitz - Stomach Bitters, rectangular w/paneled sides, tooled mouth, ca. 1880-90, deep bluish aqua, 7 5/8" h. **264**
Crooke's (H.M.) Stomach Bitters, cylindrical w/bulbed lady's leg neck, applied sloping collar mouth, smooth base, ca. 1850-60, olive amber, 10 3/8" h. (ILLUS. top next page) **1,595**
Curtis - Cordial - Calisaya - The Great - Stomach - Bitters - 1 - 8 - 6 - 6 -C - C - C -1- 9 - 0 - 0, cylindrical w/tall tapering paneled shoulder, cylindrical short neck w/applied mouth, ca. 1866-75, deep root beer amber, dug, 11 1/2" h. (some minor scratches).. **1,018**

H.M. Crooke's Stomach Bitters Bottle

Davis's Kidney and - Liver Bitters - Best Invigorator - and Cathartic, square w/paneled sides, tooled mouth, ca. 1880-90, medium golden amber, 10" h. **143**

Digestine Bitters, rectangular, sample size, ringed lower neck & tooled mouth, medium amber, 3 1/2" h. (lightly cleaned) **853**

Doyle's - Hop - Bitters - 1872, around sides of sloping shoulder, square w/paneled sides w/raised clusters of hop berries & leaves, applied sloping double collar mouth, partial paper labels, ca. 1872-80, amber, 9 7/8" h. **66**

Doyle's - Hop - Bitters - 1872, around sides of sloping shoulder, square w/paneled sides w/raised clusters of hop berries & leaves, yellow w/green tone, 9 5/8" h. **275**

Doyle's - Hop - Bitters - 1872, around sides of sloping shoulder, square w/paneled sides w/raised clusters of hop berries & leaves, applied sloping double collar mouth, ca. 1872-80, yellowish green, 9 7/8" h. (very shallow flake at one base corner) **413**

Drake's Plantation Bitters - Patented 1862, cabin-shaped, five-log, deep chocolate amber, 10" h., D-109 (ILLUS. top of next column)... **220**

Drake's (S T) - 1860 - Plantation - X - Bitters - Patented - 1862, cabin-shaped, four-log, applied sloping collar mouth, 95% original paper labels, ca. 1862-70, amber, 10" h. (D-110)................................. **264**

Drake's (S T) - 1860 - Plantation - X - Bitters - Patented - 1862, cabin-shaped, four-log, applied sloping collar mouth, ca. 1862-70, amber, 10" h. (D-110) **88**

Drake's (S T) - 1860 - Plantation - X - Bitters - Patented - 1862, cabin-shaped, four-log, applied sloping collar mouth, ca. 1862-70, yellowish amber, 10 1/8" h. (D-110)................................ **264**

Drake's Plantation Bitters Bottle

Drake's (S T) - 1860 - Plantation - X - Bitters - Patented - 1862, cabin-shaped, six-log, ca. 1862-70, deep cherry puce, 10" h. (D-105)... **220**

Drake's (S T) - 1860 - Plantation - X - Bitters - Patented - 1862, cabin-shaped, six-log, ca.1862-70, medium grape puce, 9 7/8" h. (D-106) **1,650**

Drake's (S T) - 1860 - Plantation - X - Bitters - Patented - 1862, cabin-shaped, six-log, golden honey amber, 10" h. (D-105).. **116**

Rare Drake's Plantation Bitters

Drake's (S T) 1860 Plantation X Bitters - Patented 1862, cabin-shaped, six-log, light to medium yellowish olive, 10" h., D-108 (ILLUS.) **3,080**

Drake's (S T) - 1860 - Plantation - X - Bitters - Patented - 1862, cabin-shaped, six-log, medium copper puce, 10" h. (D-105) **231**

Drake's (S T) 1860 Plantation X Bitters - Patented 1862, cabin-shaped, six-log, medium reddish puce, 10" h. (D-105) **156**

Drake's (S T) - 1860 - Plantation - X - Bitters - Patented - 1862, cabin-shaped, six-log, strawberry puce, 10" h. (D-105) **251**

Drakes Plantation Bitters Bottle

Drakes (arabesque) - Plantation (arabesque) - Bitters - Patented 1862, cabin-shaped, six-log, three-tier roof, square, applied sloping collar mouth, smooth base, ca. 1865-75, medium apricot puce, 9 7/8" h., D-102 (ILLUS.) **743**

Electric Bitters (on front & back labels), square, light amber, pt. **44**

Fenner's (Dr. M.M.) - Capitol Bitters - Fredonia, N.Y., rectangular, applied top, original paper label & tax stamp, aqua, 10 1/2" h. **66**

Fish (The) Bitters - W.H. Ware, Patented 1866, figural fish, dark amber, 11 1/2" h. **225**

Gates (C.) & Cos - Life of Man - Bitters, rectangular w/short neck & tooled mouth, 95% of paper label, Canada, ca. 1890-1900, pale green, 8" h. **55**

Rare German Balsam Bitters Bottle

German Balsam Bitters, W.M. Watson & Co., Sole Agents for U.S., square w/applied tapering collar, rare opaque blue, 9" h. (ILLUS.) **825**

The Globe Tonic Bitters

Globe (The) Tonic Bitters, square w/paneled sides, applied sloping collar mouth, smooth base, 98% original paper label, ca. 1865-75, thin cooling check in shoulder, yellow amber, 9 7/8" h. (ILLUS.) **660**

Great Tonic (The) - Caldwell's - Herb Bitters, triangular w/tall neck & applied sloping collar mouth, iron pontil, ca. 1870-80, medium golden amber, 12 3/4" h. **209**

Greeley's Bourbon Bitters

Greeley's Bourbon Bitters, barrel-shaped, ten rings above & below center band, medium smoky olive green, 9 3/8", G-101 (ILLUS.) **1,155**

Hall's Bitters - E.E. Hall New Haven - Established 1842, barrel-shaped, applied square collar top, smooth base, light yellow olive, 9 1/8" h. **825**

Hartwig - Kantorowicz - (Star of David) - Posen - Berlin - Hamburg, tall lobed form w/tall slender neck & applied mouth, Germany, ca. 1880-95, bright grass green, 13" h. **3,960**

Henley's (Dr.) California IXL Bitters, cylindrical w/applied lip ring, open pontil, ca. 1870s, light sapphire blue, 12" h. (some interior stain, tiny ding on inside lip) **275**

Henley's (Dr.) Wild Grape Root IXL Bitters, cylindrical w/applied rim, aqua, 12" h. (slight haze) **121**

Henley's (Dr.) Wild Grape Root IXL Bitters, cylindrical w/applied rim, dark aqua, 12" h. (some scratching, tiny potstone) **523**

Henley's (Dr.) Wild Grape Root IXL Bitters, cylindrical w/applied rim, light green, 12" h. (some minor interior haze)...... **413**

Henley's (Dr.) Wild Grape Root IXL Bitters, cylindrical w/applied rim, teal blue, 12" h. (minor interior stain) **1,100**

Henley's (Dr.) Wild Grape Root IXL Bitters, cylindrical w/applied rim, yellowish green, 12" h. (minor interior stain) **2,090**

Henley's (Dr.) Wild Grape Root - IXL (in oval) Bitters, cylindrical w/tall neck & applied mouth, smooth base, deep aqua, ca. 1870, 12 1/8" h. (light spots of stain) **88**

Rare H.P. Herb Wild Cherry Bitters

Herb (H.P.) Wild Cherry Bitters, Reading, Pa., cabin-shaped, square w/cherry tree motif & roped corners, paper label reading "H.P. Herb Wild Cherry Bark Bitters," 99% of label, medium 7-Up green, 8 7/8" h. (ILLUS.)..................................... **5,060**

Hertrichs Bitter, Einziger Fabrikant, Hans Hertrich Hof Gesetzlich Geschutzt, footed ball-shaped w/tall ringed neck, applied double collar, deep olive green, 9" h.. **385**

Holtzermann's - Patent - Stomach - Bitters, cabin-shaped, four-roof, tooled mouth, ca. 1880-1895, medium amber, 9 3/4" h. **209**

Holtzermann's - Patent - Stomach - Bitters, cabin-shaped, four-roof, tooled mouth, ca. 1880-1895, reddish amber, 9 3/4" h. **253**

Hopkins (Dr. A.S.) - Union Stomach Bitters - F.S. Amidon, Sole Prop. - Hartford, Conn U.S.A., rectangular w/paneled sides, tooled mouth, ca. 1880-1900, medium golden amber, 9 1/2" h. **71**

Hostetter's (Dr. J.) - Stomach Bitters, square w/beveled corners, short neck w/applied sloping collar mouth, ca. 1860-70, deep olive green w/amber tone, 9 1/4" h............................... **231**

Keystone Bitters Barrel-shaped Bottle

Keystone Bitters, barrel-shaped w/ribs, applied sloping collar mouth, smooth base, ca. 1870-80, golden amber, 9 3/4" h. (ILLUS.)... **743**

Kuyper's (D) Orange Bitters, short cylindrical body w/rounded shoulder to tall neck, ABM, complete original labels, 1920s, dark green **44**

Lacour's Bitters - Sarsapariphere, cylindrical w/ringed rim & sunken side panels, amber, 9" h. **935**

Lacour's Bitters Sarsapariphere, cylindrical w/sunken side panels & ringed rim & base, applied mouth, ca. 1866-79, deep green, 9 3/8" h. (ILLUS. top next page)... **11,000**

Langley's (Dr.) - Root & Herb - Bitters - 99 Union St. - Boston, cylindrical w/short neck & flattened applied mouth, ca. 1855-65, yellowish amber, 7" h. **330**

Langley's (Dr.) Root & Herb Bitters, J.O. Langley, proprietor, cylindrical, deep amber, 6" h.. **121**

Lash's Kidney and Liver Bitters - The Best Cathartic and Blood Purifier, square w/paneled sides & applied sloping collar, deep red amber, 8 3/4" h. (few haze spots).. **187**

Rare Lacour's Bitters Bottle

Lediard's Celebrated Stomach Bitters, square w/beveled corners, applied sloping double collar mouth, medium bluish green, ca. 1865-70, 9 1/2" h. (lightly cleaned) 743

Litthauer Stomach Bitters (paper label), Hartwig, Kantorowicz, Posen, Germany, square case gin shape, milk glass, 99% of label, 9 1/2" h. 132

Mishler's Herb Bitters - Table Spoon Graduation (ruler marker) - Dr. S.B. Hartman & Co. - 40 Med. Doses, embossed on base "Stoeckels Grad. Pat. Feb. 6 '66W. McC. & Co. No. 2," square, strawberry, 9" h. (lightly cleaned) 385

Mishler's Herb Bitters - Table Spoon Graduation (ruler marker) - Dr. S.B. Hartman & Co. - 40 Med. Doses, embossed on base "Stoeckels Grad. Pat. Feb. 6 '66W. McC. & Co. No. 2," square, medium peach or topaz, 9" h. 523

Moffat Phoenix Bitters

Moffat (John) - Phoenix Bitters - New York - 1-Dollar, rectangular w/beveled corners, medium olive amber, 1/2 pt., 5 3/8" h. (ILLUS.) 908

Morning (design of star) Bitters - Inceptum 5869 - Patented - 5869, triangular slender form w/slanted ridges on neck, applied sloping collar mouth, iron pontil, ca. 1870-80, medium amber, 12 1/2" h. 198

National Bitters, figural ear of corn, medium yellowish amber, "Patent 1867" on base, applied mouth, 12 1/2" h. 550

National Bitters Ear of Corn Bottle

National Bitters - Patent 1867, figural ear of corn, "Patent 1867" on base, applied mouth, medium amber, 12 5/8" h. (ILLUS.) 303

National Bitters - Patent 1867, figural ear of corn, "Patent 1867" on base, applied mouth, medium amber w/hint of puce, 95% of original paper label, 12 5/8" h. 770

Nibol Kidney and Liver Bitters

Nibol Kidney and Liver Bitters, square, 100% paper label reading "Nibol Tonic Laxative," w/contents, amber, 9 1/2" h. (ILLUS.).. 176

Old - Homestead - Wild Cherry - Bitters - Patent, cabin-shaped, scalloped shingles on four-sided roof, applied sloping collar mouth, ca. 1865-80, golden yellow amber, 9 3/8" h. (partially open bubble on inside of lip) 385

Old Sachem - Bitters - and - Wigwam Tonic, barrel-shaped, ten-rib, applied mouth, ca. 1855-70, deep strawberry puce, 9 1/2" h. (shallow flake on side of lip) 633

Old Sachem Bitters Bottle

Old Sachem - Bitters - and - Wigwam Tonic, barrel-shaped, ten-rib, applied mouth, smooth base, ca. 1855-70, peach puce, 9 1/4" h. (ILLUS.)..................... 770

Old Sachem - Bitters - and - Wigwam Tonic, barrel-shaped, ten-rib, deep cherry puce, 9 1/2" h. 660

Old Sachem - Bitters - and - Wigwam Tonic, barrel-shaped, ten-rib, deep reddish puce, 9 1/2" h.. 440

Rare Original Pocahontas Bitters

Original Pocahontas Bitters - Y. Ferguson, barrel-shaped w/ten horizontal ribs above & below embossing, applied mouth, smooth base, ca. 1855-65, deep bluish aqua, 9 1/4" h. (ILLUS.) 5,500

Owen (Garry.) Strengthening Bitters - Ball & Lyons New Orleans, LA Sole Proprietors, square, applied top, amber, 9" h.. 132

Oxygenated - For Dyspepsia - Asthma & - General Debility - Bitters, rectangular w/paneled sides, applied sloping collar mouth, pontiled base, ca. 1845-55, aqua, 7 1/2" h.. 132

P.D. H. & Co. (monogram on shoulder) - Sazerac Aromatic Bitters, cylindrical w/tall lady's leg neck & applied mouth, ca. 1865-75, milk glass, 12 1/8" h.. 303

Peruvian Bitters with Monogram

Peruvian Bitters - "W & K" monogram in shield, applied top, smooth base, orangish red amber, 9 1/8" h. (ILLUS.)................. 231

Petzold's (Dr.) Genuine German Bitters Incept. 1862, oval w/twenty side ribs, tooled top, amber, 10 5/8" h. (potstone w/ding on base) 110

Pharazyn (H.) Phila. Rights Secured, figural Indian Queen w/raised shield, golden amber 990

Pineapple figural, embossed diamond-shaped panel, applied top, amber, 8 7/8" h. 187

Rising Sun Bitters - John C. Hurst, Philada., square, applied top, amber, 9 3/8" h. 143

Roback's (Dr. C.W.) - Stomach Bitters - Cincinnati, O., barrel-shaped, applied sloping collar mouth, iron pontil, ca. 1855-65, medium amber, 9 7/8" h. 495

Roback's (Dr. C.W.) - Stomach Bitters - Cincinnati, O., barrel-shaped, applied sloping collar mouth, smooth base, ca. 1860-70, golden yellow w/olive tone, 9 1/4" h... 1,100

Roback's Stomach Bitters

Roback's (Dr. C.W.) - Stomach Bitters - Cincinnati, O., barrel-shaped, yellow amber w/olive tone, some light inside haze, minor scratches on label panel, 9 3/8" h. (ILLUS.).. **743**

Rose's (E.J.) Magador Bitters For Stomach, Kidney & Liver - Superior Tonic, Cathartic and Blood Purifier, rectangular w/beveled corners & tooled lip, medium amber, ca. 1900, 8 3/4" h. **83**

Rare Royce's Sherry Wine Bitters

Royce's Sherry Wine Bitters, rectangular w/beveled corners & rounded shoulders, applied sloping collar, aqua, 8" h. (ILLUS.)... **1,705**

Sahl'burgh, PA, rectangular w/indented side panels, rounded shoulders, applied sloping collar, root beer amber, 10 1/4" h. **3,960**

Smith (Dr. A.H.) Celebrated Old Style Bitters - O.S. 2781 The Standard Tonic and Blood Purifier, square w/beveled corners, applied sloping collar mouth, ca. 1875-85, deep chocolate amber, 8 7/8" h. (ILLUS. top of next column).. **143**

Solomon's Strengthening & Invigorating Bitters - Savannah, Georgia, square, crudely applied top, cobalt blue, 9 5/8" h. (lightly cleaned, tiny potstone in side) **715**

Dr. A.H. Smith Old Style Bitters

Soule (Dr.) - Hop - Bitters - 1872 (on shoulders), square w/embossed hop flowers & leaves design on one side, crooked neck, amber, 9 1/4" h. **176**

Southern Aromatic - Cock Tail - Bitters - J. Grossman - New Orleans - Sole Manufacturer, cylindrical w/tall lady's leg neck & tooled mouth, ca. 1880-90, yellow w/amber tone, 12 5/8" h. (some spotty inside stain) **1,430**

Sun Kidney and Liver Bitters - Vegetable Laxative, Bowel Regulator and Blood Purifier (one front & back paper labels), square, amber, 95% of labels, 9 1/2" h. **66**

Tippecanoe (birch bark & canoe design), H.H. Warner & Co., cylindrical, "Rochestr N.Y." on base, applied disc mouth, amber, 9 1/4" h... **121**

Toneco Stomach Bitters - Appetizer & Tonic (one front & back labels), square, clear, 9" h. **66**

Rare Old Dr. Townsend's Bitters Flask

Townsend's - (Old Dr.) - Celebrated - Stomach - Bitters, chestnut flask-shaped w/applied mouth & applied handle, open pontil, ca. 1860-70, golden yellow amber, 8 3/4" h. (ILLUS.) **12,000-14,300**

Townsend's (Old Dr.) Magic Stomach Bitters, New York, rectangular w/indented panels, applied sloping collar, medium bluish green, 10" h. (shallow chip on side of lip) 963

Traudt's Alterative Bitters (label only), over embossed Dr. J. Hostetter's Stomach Bitters, square, amber, 10 1/2" h. 143

Uhler's Purifying & Strengthening Bitters, Philada., rectangular w/indented side panels, applied sloping mouth, aqua, 7 7/8" h. (overall stain, spider crack) 143

Von Hopf's (Dr. E.R.) Curacoa Bitters - Chamberlain & Co. Des Moines Iowa, rectangular, w/100% original paper label, amber, 7 1/2" h. 99

Von Koster - Stomach - Bitters - Fairfield - Conn., rectangular w/beveled corners, short neck w/tooled mouth, ca. 1880-1900, amber, 9" h. 99

Wahoo & Calisaya Bitters Semi-Cabin

Wahoo - & - Calisaya - Bitters - Jacob Pinkerton - Y!! - O.K. - I.M. - Y!!!, semi-cabin w/paneled sides, applied sloping collar mouth, ca. 1865-75, amber, 10 3/8" h. (ILLUS.)...................................... 660

Wallace's Tonic Stomach Bitters, square, applied top, full front & rear labels w/a peacock, amber, 9 1/4" h. 440

Warner's (Dr. C.D.) German Hop Bitters - 1880 - Reading, Mich., square, tooled top, amber, 9 1/2" h. 143

Warner's Safe Bitters (design of safe), Rochester, N.Y., "A. & D. H.C." on base, rectangular w/rounded shoulders, applied mouth, medium amber, 7 1/2" h. 605

Wheeler's - Berlin - Bitters - Baltimore, hexagonal, applied mouth, pontil, yellowish green citron, 9 1/2" h. (light exterior cleaning)................................... 5,500

Wilder's (Edw) - Stomach Bitters - (design of a building) - Edw. Wilder's - Wholesale Druggists - Louisville, KY., square semi-cabin w/paneled sides & beaded corners, tooled mouth, ca. 1885-95, clear, 9 3/4" h. 148

Rare Dr. Wonser's Bitters Bottle

Wonser's (Dr.) U.S.A. , Indian Root Bitters, cylindrical w/applied mouth, ringed neck, ribbed shoulder, amber, 3/4 qt., 11" h. (ILLUS.)... 6,600

Wood's (Dr.) - Sarsaparilla - & - Wild Cherry - Bitters, rectangular w/beveled edges, applied sloping collar mouth, ca. 1845-55, aqua, 8 3/4" h. (lightly cleaned)..... 308

Woodcock Pepsin Bitters, Joseph C. Schroeder Co., St. Louis, MO. U.S.A., wide rectangular form w/rounded shoulders, 90% original paper labels on front & back, clear, ca. 1900, 8" h. 187

Zingari Bitters - F. Rahter, round, lady's leg neck, amber, 12" h. 468

FIGURALS

Figural Kummel Bear Bottle

Bear, "Kummel," seated on haunches w/shaped base, applied mouth, black olive amber, ca. 1880-95, 11 1/8" h. (ILLUS.)... 39

Clam Flask with Metal Cap

Clam, ground lip, smooth base, original metal screw cap, ca. 1885-95, medium amber, 5 1/4" h. (ILLUS.) **121**

Coachman, three-quarters length bust w/top hat & holding pipe & glass, ground lip, smooth base, milk glass, ca. 1880-95, 10 1/4" h. (slight chip on side of lip) **1,650**

Duck, upright position w/neck extending from bird's beak, Atterbury Glass Co., ca. 1865-75, milk glass, 11 5/8" h. (shallow chip on top of lip) **187**

Harrison Monument, frosted clear bust of Benjamin Harrison atop tall reeded black glass column, ground lip, smooth base, ca. 1888, 11 1/4" h. **1,073**

Belgian Bear Bottle

Bear, seated w/shield in front, embossed on back "Distrie 'Mercator' SA - Anvers Belgique - Deposé," tooled mouth, smooth base, ca. 1890-1910, Belgium, clear, 9 7/8" h. (ILLUS.) **181**

Rare Man in the Moon Bottle

Man in the Moon, milk glass crescent moon face w/original red, blue, black & pink facial paint, original embossed metal wire stand & end spigot, early 20th c., 9 7/8" h. (ILLUS.) **4,510**

Man standing leaning on stump, wearing 18th c. costume, flared lip, pontil, ca. 1870-90, Europe, cobalt blue, 7 1/8" h. **578**

Cherub and Clock Bottle

Cherub holding clock, kneeling figure holding a round clock on one shoulder, short cylindrical neck w/flared lip, ca. 1900-20, yellowish topaz, 13 3/8" h. (ILLUS.) **154**

Octopus & Silver Dollar Bottle

Octopus on silver dollar, relief-molded design w/short cylindrical neck & ground lip, dollar dated "1901," milk glass, 4 1/2" h. (ILLUS.)... **413**

French Orange-shaped Bottle

Orange or tangerine, "P. Bardinet Bordeaux," oblong w/ground lip & smooth base, center band w/wording, ca. 1900-20, straw yellow w/orange tone, probably French, 4 1/8" h. (ILLUS.)........................ **44**

Fine Figural of Standing Woman

Woman standing wearing peasant dress, rolled lip, pontil, base of back embossed "Deposé," ca. 1890-1910, France, medium green, 13 1/8" h. (ILLUS.)... **1,265**

FLASKS
Flasks are listed according to the numbers provided in American Bottles & Flasks and Their Ancestry by Helen McKearin and Kenneth M. Wilson.

Chestnut, eighteen ribs swirled to the right, short flared neck, cobalt blue, 6" h. **715**

Chestnut, fifteen vertical ribs, attributed to Mantua, Ohio, early 19th c., citron, 1/2 pt., 5 1/8" h. **605**

Chestnut, "grandfather" type, twenty-four broken ribs swirled to the right, sheared lip, deep reddish amber, Midwestern, ca. 1820-30, 8 1/4" h. (some milky inside stain) **990**

Rare Chestnut Flask

Chestnut, "grandfather" type, twenty-four ribs swirled to the left, sheared lip, golden amber, Midwestern, ca. 1820-30, few spots of inside haze, 8 3/8" h. (ILLUS.)... **3,850**

Chestnut, mold-blown, twenty-four vertical ribs, Zanesville, Ohio, golden amber, 5 1/4" h. (wear, scratches) **275**

Chestnut, plain body, sheared lip, brilliant yellow green, Midwestern, ca. 1820-30, 5 1/2" h. (small patch of exterior wear)......... **358**

Chestnut, twenty broken ribs swirled to the left, small slender neck w/sheared lip, yellow olive, Midwestern, ca. 1820-30, 7 3/8" h. **3,850**

Early Chestnut Flask

Chestnut, twenty ribs swirled to the right, tooled & flared lip, open pontil, deep cobalt blue, 3 3/4" h. (ILLUS.) **633**

Chestnut, twenty-four vertical ribs, grand-father-size, sheared top, open pontil, medium to light amber, Zanesville, Ohio (interior haze) 440

Chestnut, twenty-four vertical ribs, sheared & inward-rolled rim, medium amber, Midwestern, ca. 1820-30, 5 1/2" h............... 330

Chestnut, twenty-four vertical ribs, sheared lip, open pontil, medium to deep amber, Zanesville, Ohio (some scratches)............... 187

GI-2 - Washington bust below "General Washington" - American Eagle w/shield w/seven bars on breast, head turned to right, edges w/horizontal beading w/vertical medial rib, sheared lip, open pontil, pale greenish aqua, pt................................. 187

GI-11 - Washington bust below branches - American eagle w/head turned right & body curving, sunrays above eagle's head & 13 small stars, horizontal beading w/vertical medial rib, deep bluish aqua, pt. 550

GI-20 - Washington bust facing left w/"Fells" above & "Point" below - Monument without statue above "Balto.," vertical medial rib, light to medium pink amethyst, pt.. 1,760

GI-24 - "Washington" above bust - Taylor bust below "Bridgeton" [star] New Jersey," vertically ribbed sides, pale greenish aqua, pt... 110

GI-26 - Washington bust - American Eagle w/shield w/eight vertical & two horizontal bars on breast, head turned to right, aqua, qt. (highpoint wear, spotty inside stain) 105

GI-28 - Washington bust below "Albany Glass Works," "Albany NY" below bust - full-rigged ship sailing to right, applied tapering top, open pontil, vertically ribbed edges, aqua, pt. 253

GI-31 - "Washington" above bust - "Jackson" above bust, yellow amber w/olive tone, pt. 176

"Washington" - "Jackson" Flask

GI-34 - "Washington" above bust - "Jackson" above bust, vertically ribbed edges w/heavy medial rib, yellowish amber w/slight olive tone, pinhead flake on outer lip, bold impression, 1/2 pt. ILLUS.) 385

GI-40a - Washington bust below "The Father of His Country" - Taylor bust, "Gen Taylor Never Surrenders," smooth edges, applied double collared lip, aqua, pt. 66

Washington - Taylor Flask

GI-42 - Washington bust below "The Father of His Country" - Taylor bust below "A Little More Grape Captain Bragg, Dyottville Glass Works, Philad.a," smooth edges, sheared lip, open pontil, light teal blue, qt. (ILLUS.)....................... 413

GI-47 - Washington bust below "The Father of His Country" - plain reverse, applied collar mouth, iron pontil, medium bluish green, qt... 330

GI-54 - Washington bust without queue - Taylor bust in uniform, open pontil, applied sloping double collar mouth, deep yellowish olive green, qt. 605

GI-55 - Washington bust w/short queue & plain toga - Taylor bust w/collar decoration missing, smooth edges, medium pale bluish green, pt.................................. 440

GI-71 - Taylor bust (facing left) w/"Rough and Ready" below - Ringgold bust (facing left) w/"Major" in semicircle above bust & "Ringgold" below bust, heavy vertical ribbing, aqua, pt. 165

GI-79 - Grant bust in medallion - American Eagle on shield & carrying ribbon in beak all above oval framed w/"Union," smooth edges, applied mouth, smooth base, deep aqua, pt. (tiny flake on edge of lip) 231

GI-80 - "Lafayette" above bust & "T.S." & bar below - "DeWitt Clinton" above bust & "Coventy C-T" below, horizontally corrugated edges, medium yellow olive w/amber tone, pt. 605

GI-94 - "Where Liberty Dwells is My Country - Benjamin Franklin" over bust of Franklin - "Dyottville Glass Works Philadelphia - T.W. Dyott, M.D." over bust of Dyott, aqua, pt... 385

GI-95 - Franklin bust below "Benjamin Franklin" - Dyott bust below "T.W. Dyott, M.D.," three vertical ribs w/heavy medial rib, sheared lip, open pontil, aqua, pt. 358

GI-97 - Franklin bust obverse & reverse, vertical ribbing, pale greenish aqua, qt. **160**

GI-99 - "Jenny Lind" above bust - View of Glasshouse w/"Glass Works" above & "Huffsey" below, calabash, smooth sides, broad sloping shoulder, pale bluish green, qt. **77**

Jenny Lind - Kossuth Calabash Flask

GI-100 - "Jenny Lind" above bust of Jenny Lind within wreath - "Kossuth" above bust of Kossuth, calabash, applied ringed mouth, open pontil, aqua, qt. (ILLUS.)...................... **176**

GI-103 - "Jeny. Lind (sic)" above bust within wreath - View of Glasshouse, no wording, vertically ribbed sides, calabash, aqua, qt. **80**

GI-111 - Kossuth bust facing right w/heavy beard, "Bridgeton." at right & "New Jersey" at left - Sloop sailing left w/flying pennant, sheared lip, open pontil, aqua, pt. **242**

Kossuth & Frigate Flask

GI-112 - "Louis Kossuth" above full-faced bust of Kossuth in uniform above crossed flags - Frigate sailing left flying flags above "U.S. Steam Frigate Mississippi S. Huffsey," "Ph. Doflein Mould Maker Nth.5t St 84" on base, calabash, applied sloping collar, iron pontil, bluish aqua, qt. (ILLUS.)........................ **275**

GI-114 - Classical bust obverse & reverse, sheared lip, open pontil, olive green, 1/2 pt. **303**

GI-114 - Draped bust of Byron facing left - Draped bust of Scott facing right, vertically ribbed edges, dark amber, 1/2 pt. (some inside stain) **176**

GI-114 - Draped bust of Byron facing left - Draped bust of Scott facing right, vertically ribbed edges, medium olive green, 1/2 pt.(some highpoint wear) **253**

GII-1 - American Eagle on oval, head turned to right obverse & reverse, horizontally beaded edges w/narrow vertical medial rib, sheared lip, open pontil, aqua, pt. **275**

GII-10 - American Eagle w/"W. Ihmsen's" above "Glass" below - Sheaf of Rye w/"Agriculture" above & farm implements below, vertically ribbed edges, sheared lip, open pontil, aqua, pt. **440**

GII-11 - American Eagle facing left w/eleven stars above, standing on plain oval - Cornucopia with Produce vertically ribbed edges, plain lip, pontil, yellowish amber, 1/2 pt. **88**

GII-11 - American Eagle facing left w/eleven stars above, standing on plain oval - Cornucopia with Produce vertically ribbed edges, plain lip, pontil, aqua, 1/2 pt. (small lip flake) **231**

GII-13 - American Eagle w/head turned to left & w/large beak & no shield above an oval frame cut-off at the bottom & enclosing ten large pearls, a semicircle of eighteen stars above eagle - Cornucopia inverted & coiled to left filled w/produce, horizontally beaded border w/medial rib, light to medium yellowish green, 1/2 pt. (lightly cleaned) **5,500**

GII-15 - American Eagle with head to the right & surrounded by sunrays, shield on breast, on oval beaded panel w/"F.L." - Cornucopia filled w/produce, sheared lip, open pontil, aqua, 1/2 pt............................. **330**

Eagle - Lyre Flask

GII-22 - American Eagle w/head turned to left holding a banner reading "Union" w/two rows of stars above & an oval frame enclosing an eight-point star below - Lyre below two rows of fourteen stars, corrugated edges, sheared lip, open pontil, deep aqua, pt. (ILLUS. of back & front)................................. **1,100**

GII-26 - American Eagle above stellar motif obverse & reverse, horizontally corrugated edges, plain lip, smooth base, aqua, 1/2 pt. **55**

GII-26 - American Eagle above stellar motif obverse & reverse, horizontally corrugated edges, plain lip, open pontil, medium to deep bluish green, 1/2 pt. **2,145**

GII-45 - American Eagle facing right w/wings spread, shield on breast, within an oval border & standing on a plain oval - Cornucopia filled with produce, sheared lip, open pontil, aqua, 1/2 pt. **198**

GII-53 - American Eagle w/shield & furled flag - "For Our Country," wide bands of vertical edge ribbing, aqua, pt. **143**

Rare Eagle & Furled Flag Flask

GII-54 - American Eagle facing left on large shield, sunrays around head - U.S. flag furled on standard above "For Our Country," sheared lip, open pontil, chocolate tobacco amber, pt. (ILLUS.) **5,280**

GII-56 - American Eagle facing left within oval panels, larger shield on breast, thirteen small stars above - Large cluster of grapes, sheared lip, open pontil, aqua, 1/2 pt. **209**

GII-60 - American Eagle in oval beaded medallion - "Liberty" in scroll above beaded medallion around leafy tree, sheared lip, open pontil, aqua, 1/2 pt. **413**

GII-63 - American Eagle below "Liberty" - inscription in five lines "Willington - Glass - Co - West Willington - Conn.," smooth edges, deep amber w/olive tone, 1/2 pt. **231**

GII-63 - American Eagle below "Liberty" - inscription in five lines "Willington - Glass - Co - West Willington - Conn.," smooth edges, deep bluish green, 1/2 pt. **1,540**

GII-63 - American Eagle below "Liberty" - Willington Glass Co., smooth edges, applied lip, dark amber, 1/2 pt. **143**

GII-64 - "Liberty" above American Eagle w/shield facing left on leafy branch - "Willington - Glass - Co - West Willington - Conn," smooth sides, olive green, pt. (tiny lip flake) **121**

GII-72 - American Eagle w/head turned right & standing on rocks - Cornucopia w/produce, vertically ribbed edges, sheared neck, open pontil, yellowish olive amber, pt. **165**

Eagle - Cornucopia Flask

GII-73 - American Eagle w/head turned right & standing on rocks - Cornucopia w/produce & X to the left, vertically ribbed edges, sheared neck, open pontil, yellow amber, pt. (ILLUS.) **176**

American Eagle Flask

GII-79 - American Eagle above oval obverse & reverse, edges w/single vertical rib, deep olive amber, qt. (ILLUS.) **275**

GII-81 - American Eagle above oval inscribed "Granite - Glass Co." obverse - reverse the same except inscription "Stoddard - NY," narrow vertical edge rib, sheared lip, tubular pontil, olive amber, pt. **209**

GII-86 - American Eagle above oval obverse & reverse, vertically ribbed edges, medium olive amber, 1/2 pt. **143**

GII-106 - American Eagle above oval obverse & reverse, w/"Pittsburgh, PA" in oval on obverse, narrow vertical rib on edges, deep green, pt. (small lip ding) **176**

GII-126 - American Eagle w/shield above laurel wreath, obverse & reverse, smooth edges, light pink amethyst, 1/2 pt. **715**

GII-143 - American Eagle w/plain shield in talons & pennants in beak, calabash, four-flute edges, medium green, qt. **495**

GIII-4 - Cornucopia with Produce - Urn with Produce, vertically ribbed edges, plain lip, pontil, dark olive green, pt. **77**

GIII-4 - Cornucopia with Produce - Urn with Produce, vertically ribbed edges, plain lip, pontil, dark amber, pt. **88**

Cornucopia - Urn Flask

GIII-4 - Cornucopia with Produce - Urn with Produce, vertically ribbed edges, tooled lip, pontil, olive green, pt. (ILLUS.) **104**

GIII-4 - Cornucopia with Produce - Urn with Produce, vertically ribbed edges, plain lip, pontil, dark emerald green, pt. **468**

GIII-8 - Cornucopia with Produce & large pearl at left - Urn with Produce, vertically ribbed sides, sheared lip, pontil, amber, 1/2 pt. (slight interior stain) **88**

GIII-14 - Cornucopia with Produce & curled to right - Urn with Produce, vertically ribbed edges, deep bluish green, 1/2 pt. **358**

GIV-1 - Masonic Emblems - American Eagle w/ribbon reading "E Pluribus Unum" above & "P" (old-fashioned J) below in oval frame, sheared lip, open pontil, aqua, pt. **413**

GIV-2 - Masonic Emblems - American Eagle w/ribbon reading "E Pluribus Unum" above & "HS" below in oval frame, rolled lip, open pontil, light bluish green, pt. **385**

GIV-3 - Masonic Emblems - American Eagle w/heavily crimped ribbon above &

"J.K. - B." below in oval frame, thick rolled lip, open pontil, yellowish topaz shading to yellowish green, pt. **4,510**

GIV-18 - Masonic Arch, pillars & pavement w/Masonic emblems - American Eagle without shield on breast, plain oval frame below "KCCNE" inside, smooth edges w/single rib, medium yellowish amber, pt. **220**

GIV-18 - Masonic Arch w/pillars & pavement & six stars around quarter moon - American Eagle over plain oval frame w/"KCCNC," light yellow amber, pt. **220**

GIV-19 - Masonic Arch, pillars & pavement w/Masonic emblems - American Eagle without shield on breast, plain oval frame below "KCCNE" inside, smooth edges w/single rib, some design elements such as trowel, skull & beehive missing, yellowish amber green, pt. **204**

GIV-19 - Masonic Arch w/pillars & pavement - American Eagle above oval frame w/"KCCNC," sheared lip, open pontil, dark olive green, pt. (minor interior stain) **176**

GIV-20 - Masonic arch, pillars & pavement w/Masonic emblems - American Eagle w/"KCCNC" in oval frame below, single vertical edge rib, medium yellowish amber, lots of seed bubbles, pt. **176**

GIV-43 - Masonic six-point star w/eye of God in center all above "A D" - six-point star w/arm in center all above "GRJA," sheared lip, vertical edge ribs, olive amber, pt. **198**

GV-1 - "Success to the Railroad" around embossed locomotive - similar reverse, sheared lip, open pontil, yellow-amber, pt. **3,740**

GV-3 - "Success to the Railroad" around embossed horse pulling cart - similar reverse, sheared lip, open pontil, olive green, pt. **209**

GV-3 - "Success to the Railroad" around embossed horse pulling cart - similar reverse, sheared lip, open pontil, yellow amber, pt. **303**

"Success to the Railroad" Flask

GV-5 - "Success to the Railroad" around embossed horse pulling cart - similar reverse, plain lip, vertically ribbed edges, medium moss green, light inside stain, pt. (ILLUS.)... **385**

GV-6 - "Success to the Railroad" around embossed horse pulling cart obverse & reverse, w/"Success" above scene, sheared lip, pontil, olive green w/dark striations, pt... **242**

Horse Pulling Cart Flask

GV-7 - Horse pulling loaded cart obverse & reverse, no inscription, applied mouth, open pontil, deep olive green, pt. (ILLUS.).. **880**

GV-10 - "Railroad" above horse-drawn cart on rail & "Lowell" below - American Eagle lengthwise & 13 five-point stars, vertically ribbed edges, plain lip, pontil, olive green, 1/2 pt....................................... **237**

GVI-4 - "Baltimore" below monument - "Corn For The World" in semicircle above ear of corn, smooth edges, applied lip band, open pontil, copper puce, qt. **1,320**

Corn For The World Flask

GVI-4 - "Baltimore" below monument - "Corn For The World" in semicircle above ear of corn, smooth edges, applied lip band, open pontil, golden yellow amber, qt. (ILLUS.) **1,375**

"Corn for the World" Flask

GVI-5 - "Corn for the World" above large ear of corn - Monument w/"Baltimore," crude pebbly glass, golden yellowish amber, qt. (ILLUS.)................................... **1,600**

GVI-6 - "Baltimore" below monument - "Corn For The World" in semicircle above ear of corn, sheared & tooled lip, open pontil, bright yellow green, pt. **6,875**

Rare Sunburst Flask

GVIII-7 - Sunburst w/twenty-four rounded rays flanked by a small circle on each side, obverse & reverse, horizontal corrugated edges & stepped lower neck, yellowish olive amber, pt. (ILLUS.)............ **1,380**

GVIII-8 - Sunburst w/twenty-eight triangular sectioned rays, obverse & reverse, center raised oval w/"KEEN" on obverse & w/"P & W" on reverse, yellowish olive amber, pt. **440**

GVIII-8 - Sunburst w/twenty-eight triangular sectioned rays obverse & reverse, center raised oval w/"KEEN" reading from top to bottom on obverse & "P & W" on reverse, sheared lip, open pontil, dark olive green, pt. **440**

GVIII-8 - Sunburst w/twenty-eight triangular sectioned rays, obverse & reverse, center raised oval w/"KEEN" on obverse & w/"P & W" on reverse, olive amber, pt. **523**

GVIII-10 - Sunburst w/twenty-nine triangular sectioned rays, center raised oval w/"Keen" reading from top to bottom on obverse & reverse, yellowish olive green w/amber tone, 1/2 pt. (some heavy highpoint wear) **231**

GVIII-14 - Sunburst w/twenty-one triangular sectioned rays, obverse & reverse, sunburst centered by ring w/a dot in middle, deep yellowish green, 1/2 pt. (small iridescent inside lip bruise) **413**

GVIII-16 - Sunburst w/twenty-one triangular sectioned rays obverse & reverse, sheared & tooled lip, open pontil, olive amber, 1/2 pt. **385**

Moss Green Sunburst Flask

GVIII-16 - Sunburst w/twenty-one triangular sectioned rays obverse & reverse, sheared & tooled lip, open pontil, moss green, 1/2 pt. (ILLUS.) **935**

GVIII-18 - Sunburst w/twenty-four rounded rays obverse & reverse, horizontal corrugated edges, open pontil, sheared lip, light olive green, 1/2 pt. **440**

GVIII-20 - Sunburst w/thirty-six slender rays forming a scalloped ellipse w/five small oval ornaments in center - similar but variations in size of center oval ornaments, sheared lip, open pontil, aqua, pt...... **220**

GVIII-27 - Sunburst w/sixteen rays obverse & reverse, rays converging to a definite point at center & covering entire side of flask horizontally, ribbed edges, sheared lip, open pontil, light blue, 1/2 pt.................. **358**

GVIII-28 - Sunburst w/sixteen rays obverse & reverse, rays converging to a definite point at center & covering entire sides, horizontally corrugated edges, light yellow green, 1/2 pt. (some wear).................... **413**

GVIII-29 - Sunburst in small sunken oval w/twelve rays obverse & reverse, panel w/band of tiny ornaments around inner edge, sides around panels w/narrow spaced vertical ribbing, light bluish green, 3/4 pt. **259**

GIX-1 - Scroll w/two six-point stars obverse & reverse, vertical medial rib, long neck w/sheared lip, graphite pontil, deep yellowish green, qt. (slight inside stain, small spot of interior lip roughness) **825**

GIX-10b - Scroll w/six-point stars, a small one in upper space & medium sized one in lower space obverse & reverse, vertical medial rib, dark olive amber, pt. **660**

GIX-11 - Scroll w/two eight-point stars obverse & reverse, tubular pontil, aqua, pt. (slight inside haze) **88**

GIX-48 - "M'Carty & Torreyson" arched above a star w/"Manufacturers, Wellsburg, Va." below - Large sunburst w/twenty-four rays in circular frame, fiddle-shaped w/sheared & tooled lip, open pontil, deep aqua, pt.................................. **1,073**

GX-4 - Cannon framed by "Genl Taylor Never Surrenders," grapevine frame around "A Little More Grape Capt Bragg," vertically ribbed sides, copper color, pt. **4,950**

GX-15 - Summer Tree - Winter Tree, smooth edges, applied double lip, smooth base, deep aqua, pt. (inside haze) **66**

Spring Tree - Summer Tree Flask

GX-18 - Spring Tree (leaves & buds) - Summer Tree, smooth edges, light inside haze, deep bluish green, qt. (ILLUS.)... **1,705**

GX-18 - Spring Tree (leaves & buds) - Summer Tree, smooth edges, smoky ice blue, qt. **413**

GX-19 - Summer Tree - Winter Tree, smooth edges, deep bluish aqua, qt. **110**

GX-19 - Summer Tree - Winter Tree, smooth edges, yellow w/olive tone, qt....... **1,540**

GXI-26 - "For Pike's Peak" above a small miner w/tools above oval reserve - American Eagle above oval reserve, aqua, 1/2 pt. **143**

GXI-27 - "For Pike's Peak" above prospector w/knapsack on shoulder & walking w/a cane above an oval - American Eagle w/shield & banner above oval, aqua, pt. 88

GXI-34 - "For Pike's Peak" above prospector w/tools & cane standing on oblong frame - American Eagle w/pennant above frame "Ceredo," crude square band lip, aqua, qt.. 88

GXI-50 - "For Pike's Peak" above prospector w/tools & cane - Hunter shooting stag, plain edges, root beer amber, pt. 990

GXII-13 - Clasped hands above oval w/"L.F. & Co." all inside shield w/"UNION" above - American Eagle above frame w/"Pittsburgh Pa.," yellow w/strong olive tone, qt. 1,210

GXII-18 - Clasped hands above oval, all inside shield - American Eagle w/plain shield above oval frame, base w/"L & W" inside disc-shaped frame, medium amber, pt. 187

GXII-30 - Clasped hands above oval, all inside large shield w/"Union" above - American Eagle w/shield w/bars above oval frame, amber, 1/2 pt. 176

GXII-41 - Clasped hands above oval all inside shield w/"Union" above shield - Cannon, medium lime green, pt. (some overall inside milky stain) 798

GXII-43 - Clasped hands above square & compass above oval w/"Union" all inside shield - American Eagle, calabash, greenish aqua, qt. 138

GXII-43 - Clasped hands above square & compass above oval w/"Union" all inside shield - American Eagle, calabash, amber, qt. 385

GXIII-4 - Hunter facing left wearing flat-top stovepipe hat, short coat & full trousers, game bag hanging at left side, firing gun at two birds flying upward at left, large puff of smoke from muzzle, two dogs running to left toward section of rail fence - Fisherman standing on shore near large rock, wearing round-top stovepipe hat, V-neck jacket, full trousers, fishing rod held in left hand w/end resting on ground, right hand holding large fish, creel below left arm, mill w/bushes & tree in left background, calabash, edged w/wide flutes, open pontil, aqua, qt. 88

GXIII-17 - Horseman wearing cap & short tight coat on a racing horse w/flying tail - Hound walking to the right, aqua, pt............. 105

GXIII-21 - "Flora Temple" above figure of a horse over "Harness Trot 219 3/4," plain reverse w/original round paper label reading "Salt River Bourbon Whiskey Distilleries, Jefferson County Kent'y...," rare w/label, applied shoulder handle, smoky copper, pt. (ILLUS. top next column) 1,925

GXIII-23 - Flora Temple obverse, plain reverse, smooth edges w/beads at lower neck & shoulder, blue green, pt. 105

Rare "Flora Temple" Flask

GXIII-35 - Sheaf of Grain w/rake & pitchfork crossed behind sheaf - "Westford Glass Co., Westford Conn," smooth edges, olive green, pt................................... 121

GXIII-35 - Sheaf of Grain w/rake & pitchfork crossed behind sheaf - "Westford Glass Co., Westford Conn," smooth edges, applied double collar w/large spillover, olive amber, pt. (slight inside stain) 143

GXIII-35 - Sheaf of Grain w/rake & pitchfork crossed behind sheaf - "Westford Glass Co., Westford Conn," smooth edges, reddish amber, 1/2 pt. 165

Sheaf of Grain - Westford Glass Flask

GXIII-37 - Sheaf of grain on crossed rack & pitchfork - "Westford Glass Co., Westford, Conn.," applied double collar mouth, smooth base, tobacco amber, 1/2 pt. (ILLUS.)................................. 132

GXIII-38 - Sheaf of Wheat w/rake & pitchfork crossed behind it - star, yellowish
olive, qt. (minor inside content stain)............ **688**

GXIII-39 - Sheaf of Grain above crossed
rake & pitchfork - large five-pointed star,
smooth edges, applied double lip, deep
green, pt. **1,210**

GXIII-41 - Sheaf of Grain on rake & pitchfork below arched laurel branches -
eight-petal ornament below "Sheets &
Duffy," calabash, ribbed edges, tapering
lip, open pontil, deep bluish aqua, qt........... **165**

GXIII-42 Sheaf of Grain in front of rake &
pitchfork, two laurel branches above -
eight-petal ornament w/no inscription,
calabash, tapered lip, open pontil, aqua,
qt. **77**

GXIII-46 - Sheaf of Grain above crossed
rake & pitchfork - Tree & foliage, calabash, vertically ribbed, applied mouth,
open pontil, dark claret, qt............................ **825**

GXIII-48 - Anchor between fork-ended
pennants inscribed "Baltimore" & "Glass
Works" - Sheaf of Grain w/crossed rake
& pitchfork, yellowish amber, qt. **935**

GXIV-7 - "Traveler's Companion" arched
above & below stylized duck - eight-
pointed star, smooth sides, medium
amber, 1/2 pt. **578**

GXV-19 - "Geo. W. Robinson" in an arc &
"Main St. W. V.A" in a reverse arc on
obverse, plain reverse, strapside flask,
smooth base, applied mouth, deep blu-
ish aqua, pt.. **198**

Pitkin sixteen broken ribs swirled to the
right, Midwestern, light green, 5 1/4" h.
(exterior worn) **413**

Pitkin, thirty-six broken ribs swirled to the
left, sheared lip, deep root beer
amber, ca. 1820-30, 6 1/4" h........................ **413**

Pitkin, thirty-two ribs swirled to the right,
sheared lip, olive green, ca. 1790-1810,
7 1/4" h. **853**

Pumpkinseed, picnic-type, tooled lip,
amber, 1/2 pt. (some interior stain) **121**

INKS

Cathedral, master-size, six Gothic arch
panels, cobalt blue, ABM lip, smooth
base marked "Carter's," ca. 1920, some
inside stain, 9 3/4" h. (ILLUS. top of next
column) **99**

Cone-shaped, amber, bubbly **55**

Cone-shaped, "Carters" on the base,
cobalt blue.. **66**

Cone-shaped, light blue................................... **66**

Cone-shaped, light green, some bubbles.......... **66**

Cone-shaped, marked "Sanford's" on
base, deep purple **55**

Carter's "Cathedral" Master Ink

Cylindrical, light to medium green w/olive
tone, thin flared lip, open pontil,
embossed "Hover - Phila," ca. 1845-55,
2 5/8" h. (several tiny flakes off lip) **165**

Master "Carter's" Ink Bottle

Cylindrical, master-size, deep bluish
green, applied sloping double collar
w/pour spout, smooth base, 98% front &
back original illustrated Carter's paper
labels, ca. 1870-80, 8" h. (ILLUS.) **358**

Hover Master Ink Bottle with Spout

Cylindrical, master-size, medium emerald green, applied sloping double-collar mouth w/crimped pour spout, open pontil, embossed around shoulder "Hover - Phila," ca. 1845-55, 7 1/2" h. (ILLUS.) **358**

Cylindrical, medium green, rolled lip, open pontil, embossed "S. Fine Blk. Ink," ca. 1845-55, 3" h. (some faint scratches) **176**

Domed w/central neck, 12-sided form, deep olive amber, sheared lip, base pontil, 2" h. **660**

Scarce Harrison' Columbian Ink

Eight-sided w/central neck, light to medium bluish green, rolled lip, pontil, embossed "Harrison' Columbian Ink," ca. 1845-55, 1 7/8" h. (ILLUS.)............. **633**

Eight-sided w/central neck, master-size, medium bluish green, applied mouth, open pontil, embossed "Estes - N.Y. - Ink," ca. 1845-55, 6 1/4" h. **715**

Eight-sided w/central neck, medium apple green, rolled lip, pontil, embossed "Harrison' Columbian Ink," ca. 1845-55, 2" h. **990**

Very Rare Farley's Ink

Eight-sided w/central neck, yellowish amber, thin flared lip, open pontil, embossed "Farley's Ink," ca. 1845-55, very faint content haze, 3 3/4" h. (ILLUS.)... **1,760**

Figural, blown-molded head of Ben Franklin w/neck curving upward, aqua, sheared lip, smooth base, 2 3/4" h. (small flake on edge of base) **209**

Rare Train Engine Inkwell

Figural, model of an early train engine, aqua glass, marked "Trademark Pat. Oct. 1874," 2 1/8" l. (ILLUS.) **1,320**

House-shaped w/central neck, aqua, marked "S.I. - Comp.," tooled mouth, smooth base, 2 3/4" h. **132**

Igloo-form w/side neck, deep purple, sheared lip, smooth base, 2" h. **1,375**

Igloo-form w/side neck, reddish amber, ground lip, smooth base, 2" h. **242**

Rectangular, flared lip, open pontil, "J Kidd Improved Indelible Ink," clear **143**

Rare "Teakettle" Inkwell

Teakettle-type fountain inkwell w/neck extending at angle from base, deep cobalt blue, ground lip, smooth base, original brass neck ring & hinged lid, 2" h. (ILLUS.)... **660**

Teakettle-type fountain inkwell w/neck extending at angle from base, double dome-form body, lime green opaque, polished lip & base, possibly Boston & Sandwich Glass Co., 2" h. **880**

Teakettle-type fountain inkwell w/neck extending up at angle from base, black amethyst glass, sheared lip, smooth base, ribbed & slightly domed tapering sides, probably Europe, ca. 1880-1900, 2 1/8" h. (tiny chip on lid & flake on edge of top) **440**

Teakettle-type fountain inkwell w/neck extending up at angle from base, cut overlay glass, cobalt blue cut to clear w/a bold cross & punty design, polished lip, cut base, ca. 1880-95, 2 1/4" h. **688**

Teakettle-type fountain inkwell w/neck extending up at angle from base, cut overlay glass, cobalt cut to clear w/clear polished ribs, lip w/original brass press-on cap, polished pontil, ca. 1880-95, 1 1/2" h. **633**

Teakettle-type fountain inkwell w/neck extending up at angle from base, cut overlay glass, jade green cut to clear in a tiered scallop design, cut starburst on base, ground lip w/original brass neck ring, ca. 1880-95, 2 1/8" h. (missing hinged lid)... **743**

Teakettle-type fountain inkwell w/neck extending up at angle from base, deep cobalt blue glass, eight-sided, sheared lip, smooth base, ca. 1880-90, 2" h. (needs cleaning)... **165**

Teakettle-type fountain inkwell w/neck extending up at angle from base, deep cobalt blue glass, four-sided w/beveled corner panels, sheared & ground lip, smooth base, ca. 1870-90, 1 5/8" h. **358**

Blue English Teakettle Ink

Teakettle-type fountain inkwell w/neck extending up at angle from base, deep cobalt blue glass, polished pontil & original silver hinged lid, applied top brass medal reading "G. Riddle London," England, ca. 1870-90, 2" h. (ILLUS.) **523**

Teakettle-type fountain inkwell w/neck extending up at angle from base, deep emerald green glass, eight-sides, ground lip, smooth base, ca. 1875-95, 2" h. (small chip along one panel edge)....... **143**

Teakettle-type fountain inkwell w/neck extending up at angle from base, milk glass w/embossed flowers & leaves, rounded tapering form, original sterling silver neck ring, smooth base, ca. 1875-95, 2 1/2" h. **303**

Teakettle-type fountain inkwell w/neck extending up at angle from base, opalescent milk glass, eight-sided, ground lip w/original brass neck ring & hinged lid, smooth base, original gold & yellow paint on the embossed floral decoration, ca. 1875-95, 3" h. (ILLUS. top of next column)..... **578**

Teakettle-type fountain inkwell w/neck extending up at angle from base, stoneware pottery, unglazed greyish brown, five-sided, impressed on base "Boss Brothers Middlebury," ca. 1875-90, 1 5/8" h. **121**

Fine Decorated Teakettle Ink

Teakettle-type fountain inkwell w/neck extending up at angle from base, white porcelain w/multi-colored floral decoration on each panel, original brass hinged lid, 2 3/8" h.. **633**

Rare "Turtle" Ink Bottle

Turtle-form, paneled sides, light yellow w/green tint, embossed letters on panels "J - & - I - E - M," sheared lip, smooth base, 1 3/4" h. (ILLUS.)................................. **825**

Unusual "J.S. Dunham" Ink

Twelve-sided w/central neck, aqua, embossed around panels "J.S. Dunham - St. Louis," rolled lip, open pontil, 2 7/8" h. (ILLUS.).. **385**

Twelve-sided w/central neck, light ice blue, embossed around sides "Titcomb's Ink Cin.," rolled lip, base pontil, 2 7/8" h. (lightly cleaned) **358**

Small Hover - Phila. Umbrella Ink

Umbrella-type (12-panel cone shape), medium bluish green, rolled lip, open pontil, embossed "Hover - Phila," ca. 1845-55, light overall stain, 2" h. (ILLUS.) **220**

Umbrella-type (16-panel cone shape), deep yellowish root beer amber, rolled lip, open pontil, possibly Stoddard glassworks, 2 1/4" h **440**

Umbrella-type (6-panel cone shape), aqua, rounded sides w/rolled lip & open pontil, embossed "Waters - Ink - Troy N.Y.," ca. 1845-55, 2 7/8" h. (overall stain, some minor ground wear) **660**

Umbrella-type (6-panel cone shape), light bluish green, rolled lip, open pontil, 2 1/2" h. **149**

Umbrella-type (6-panel cone shape), pale apple green, waisted base & rounded shoulders to rolled lip, open pontil, embossed "Boss - Patent," ca. 1845-55, 2 3/4" h. (lightly cleaned) **358**

Umbrella-type (8-panel cone shape), aqua, rolled lip, open pontil, embossed "S.O. Dunbar - Taunton," ca. 1845-55, 2 1/2" h. (overall stain) **105**

Umbrella-type (8-panel cone shape), bluish aqua, rolled lip, pontil, ca. 1845-55, 3 1/8" h. **121**

Umbrella-type (8-panel cone shape), bright lime green, rolled lip, smooth base, 2 5/8" h. (lightly cleaned) **468**

Umbrella-type (8-panel cone shape), deep amber, sheared lip, smooth base w/pontil, probably New Hampshire, 2 1/2" h **187**

Umbrella-type (8-panel cone shape), deep cobalt blue, tooled lip, "N.Y." on smooth base, ca. 1870-80, 2 5/8" h. (lightly cleaned) **495**

Umbrella-type (8-panel cone shape), deep olive amber, sheared lip, base pontil, New England, 2 1/2" h. **132**

Rare Purple Umbrella Ink

Umbrella-type (8-panel cone shape), deep purple, rolled lip, open pontil, ca. 1845-55, shallow chip off flat base, 2 5/8" h. (ILLUS.) **358**

Umbrella-type (8-panel cone shape), medium emerald green, rolled lip, base pontil, 2 1/2" h. **209**

Rare Umbrella Ink

Umbrella-type (8-panel cone shape), medium orangey puce glass, rolled lip, open pontil, some roughness on lip, late 19th c. (ILLUS.) **605**

Umbrella-type (8-panel cone shape), medium yellowish olive amber, rolled lip, pontil, ca. 1845-55, crude, 2 3/8" h. **187**

Umbrella-type (8-panel cone shape), sapphire blue, molded on four panels "B - B - & - Co.," deep olive amber, sheared lip, base pontil, New England, 2 1/2" h. rolled lip, base pontil, 1 3/4" h. (overall light haze) **770**

Umbrella-type (8-panel cone shape), straight lower panels, aqua, marked "Harrison's Columbian Ink," rolled lip, base pontil, 2" h **154**

Umbrella-type (8-panel cone shape), yellowish olive w/amber tone, rolled lip, open pontil, 2 3/8" h. **330**

MEDICINES

Allan's Anti-Fat - Botanic Medicine Co. - Buffalo, N.Y., rectangular w/indented panels, applied sloping collar, medium sapphire or peacock blue, 7 5/8" h. 358

Arnold's (Dr. S.) Balsam, eight-sided, flared lip, open pontil, ca. 1845-55, pale aqua, 2 3/8" h. 176

Baker's Vegetable Blood & Liver Cure

Baker's Vegetable Blood & Liver Cure, Lookout Mountain Medicine Co. Manufacturers & Proprietors, Greenville, Tenn., oval w/tooled mouth & smooth base, ca. 1880-90, reddish amber, minor content stain, 9 7/8" h. (ILLUS.) 385

Balm of Thousand Flowers - Fetridge & Co., New York, curved rectangular form w/beveled rim, applied rim, open pontil, crude, aqua, 4 3/4" h. 77

Birmingham's (Dr.) Antibilous Blood Purifier, paneled cylinder, applied mouth, teal blue green, 8 5/8" h. 688

Bonpland's Fever and Ague Remedy, New York, rectangular w/applied top & open pontil, aqua, 5 1/8" h. 44

Brown's Blood Cure

Brown's Blood Cure, Philadelphia, base marked "M.B.W. - U.S.A.," square w/beveled corners, tooled mouth, some milky stain inside, bright 7-Up green, 6 1/4" h. (ILLUS.)... 121

Buckhout's (E.A.) Dutch Liniment (design of standing man) - Prepared at Mechanicville Saratoga Co. N.Y., flattened rectangle w/rounded shoulders & rolled lip, ca. 1845-55, deep bluish aqua, 4 3/4" h. 440

Budwell's Emulsion of Cod Liver Oil No. 2 with Guaiacol and Creosote Carbonate - Budwell Pharmacal Co., Lynchburg, Va., oval w/tooled mouth & "W.T. & Co. U.S.A. Pat Jan 18 1898" on smooth base, ca. 1890-1900, deep cobalt blue, 8" h. (dug) 187

Cook's Balm of Life, oval w/strap sides, tooled mouth smooth base, ca. 1880-90, light cobalt blue, 8 1/4" h. 176

Copper's (Dr.) Ethereal Oil For Deafness, rectangular, rolled lip, deep bluish aqua, ca. 1840-55, 2 5/8" h. 242

Cure (The) for Fits - Dr. Chas. T. Price - 67 William St. New York, oval w/tooled mouth & smooth base, ca. 1880-95, clear, 8 1/2" h. (lightly cleaned) 330

Curtis & Perkin's Cramp and Pain Killer, cylindrical w/rolled lip & open pontil, aqua, 4 7/8" h. 77

Curtis & Perkins Wild Cherry Bitters, cylindrical w/applied mouth, open pontil, greenish aqua (slight mouth ding) 99

Davis Vegetable Pain Killer, rectangular w/applied top & open pontil, aqua, 4 5/8" h. 77

Davis's (Dr.) - Depurative - Phila., square w/beveled corners, applied sloping collar mouth, iron pontil, ca. 1845-55, medium bluish green, 9 3/4" h. 2,970

Drink Dr. Radam's Microbe Killer (around shoulder), square w/rounded shoulder & tooled mouth, 45% original paper label, ca. 1890, medium amber, 10 3/8" h. 121

Duffy's Tower Mint (below) - Est. (castle moftif) 184 Trade Mark, tall tapering three-story building-shaped, applied mouth, smooth base, ca. 1875-85, medium amber, 9" h. 578

Duffy's Tower Mint Cure

Duffy's Tower Mint Cure (below) - Est. (castle motif) 184 Trade Mark, tall tapering three-story building-shaped, applied mouth, smooth base, ca. 1875-85, yellowish amber, partially polished small chip on lid, cleaned, 9" h. (ILLUS.) .. **1,073**

Fenner's (Dr. M.M.) Peoples Remedies - Fredonia N.Y. U.S.A. - Kidney & Backache Cure 1872-1898, oval w/tooled mouth & smooth base, ca. 1890-1900, 98% original label, contents, tax stamp & box, medium amber, 10" h. **385**

Foster's (Dr.) Anti-Catarrh, eight-sided bullet-shape, tooled mouth, smooth base, ca. 1890-1900, deep teal green, 3 3/4" l. **149**

Gargling Oil, Lockport, N.Y., rectangular w/ABM lip & smooth base, 99% of original paper label, ca. 1910-15, cobalt blue, 5 1/8" h. **143**

Ginseng - Panacea, rectangular w/paneled sides, rolled lip, ca. 1845-55, deep aqua, 4 1/2" h. **176**

Rare Gleet Gonorrhea Bottle

Gleet Seven-Days Gonorrhea, rectangular w/tooled mouth & "M.B.W. Millville" on smooth base, ca. 1890-1910, some inside & outside milky stain, deep cobalt blue, 5" h. (ILLUS.)...................................... **798**

Gogings Wild Cherry Tonic, square w/beveled corners, tooled mouth, smooth base, ca. 1890-1900, medium amber, 8 3/4" h.............................. **66**

Graefenberg & Co. - Dysentery Syrup - New York, rectangular w/beveled corners & paneled sides, applied sloping collar mouth, open pontil, ca. 1845-55, aqua, 6" h. **77**

Ham's (Dr.) Aromatic Invigorating Spirit, N.Y., cylindrical w/applied mouth & smooth base, ca. 1875-85, orangish amber, 8 1/2" h. **61**

Heimstreet (C.) & Co. - Troy, N.Y., tall octagonal shape w/applied double collar mouth & open pontil, ca. 1845-55, medium sapphire blue, 7 1/8" h.................... **303**

Houcks Vegetable Pancea - Goodletsville Tenn., rectangular w/beveled corners, applied double collar mouth, smooth base, ca. 1855-60, deep bluish aqua, 7 1/8" h.. **688**

Hyatt's - Infallible - Life Balsam, N.Y., rectangular w/paneled sides & beveled corners, applied sloping double collar, medium bluish green, 9 3/4" h..................... **303**

Hyatt's - Pulmonic - Life Balsam - N-Y, rectangular w/paneled sides & sloping double collar mouth, ca. 1845-55, aqua, 9 3/4" h. (spots of faint inside haze)............ **468**

Rare Western Medicine Bottle

Indian Tla-Quillaugh's Balsam - Dr. R. Parker, S.F., cylindrical w/applied mouth & smooth base, ca. 1864-67, copper shading light to dark from shoulder, rare, 8 1/2" h. (ILLUS.)..................................... **11,650**

James (Dr. H.) Cannabis Indica, Crabbock & Co., Proprietors, Phila., Pa., cylindrical w/tooled mouth, clear, 7 3/4" h. (some minor stain) **209**

Kennedy's (Dr.) - Medical Discovery - Roxbury, Mass., rectangular w/paneled sides, applied mouth, open pontil, aqua, 8 1/2" h... **88**

Kilmer's (Dr.) Cough Cure - Consumption Oil - Cartarrh Specific, rectangular w/tooled mouth, aqua, 8 1/2" h.................... **715**

Lahnstoks (Dr.) Vermifuge, cylindrical vial-form w/rolled lip & open pontil, aqua, small... **110**

Liquid Opodeldoc, cylindrical, thin flared lip, pontil, aqua, 4 1/2" h.............................. **55**

Log Cabin - Hops and Buchu - Remedy, paneled cylinder, applied mouth, base marked "Pat Sept 6/87," deep root beer amber, lightly cleaned, 10" h. (ILLUS. top of next page) **198**

McBride (Dr. J.J.) - King of Pain, rectangular w/paneled sides, applied top, deep aqua, 6 1/4" h. **88**

Mintie's (Dr.) Dephreticum, San Francisco, rectangular w/paneled sides, applied mouth, smooth base, aqua **209**

Log Cabin Hops and Buchu Remedy

River Swamp Chill & Fever Cure

Mitchell's - Liniment - Pittsburgh, PA, rectangular w/paneled sides, rolled lip, ca. 1845-55, aqua, 4 7/8" h. 358

Mother Putnam's Blackberry Cordial - Rheinstrom Bros. Proprietors, rectangular w/paneled sides, applied mouth on tall ringed neck, smooth base, ca. 1880-90, medium amber, 10 7/8" h. (tiny chip off lip) 220

Murray's (Dr.) Magic Oil, S.F. - Cal., rectangular w/paneled sides, tooled top, aqua, 6" h. (tiny potstone in neck) 121

N.Y. Medical - University, rectangular w/tooled mouth & smooth base, 100% original paper label w/"Compound Fluid Extract of Cancer-Plant," ca. 1885-95, deep cobalt blue, 7 3/8" h............................ 798

Newell's - Pulmonary Syrup - Redington & Co., rectangular w/paneled sides, applied top, smooth base, aqua, 7 5/8" h. 88

Orcutt's Sure Rheumatic Cure, rectangular w/paneled sides, tooled lip, smooth base, ca. 1885-95, deep cobalt blue, 6 1/8" h. 633

Pearl's White Glycerine, rectangular w/sunken panel, tooled mouth, smooth base, ca. 1880-90, deep cobalt blue, 6 3/8" h.. 143

Perkinson's (Dr.) Pain Killer - Balt., rectangular, rolled lip, ca. 1845-55, aqua, 3 7/8" h. (overall stain) 330

Perry's Magnetic Wine of Iron - Manchester, N.H., rectangular w/paneled sides & applied mouth, deep cobalt blue, 7" h. 231

Pratt's Abolition Oil for Abolishing Pain, rectangular w/paneled sides, flared lip, smooth base, aqua, 5 7/8" h. (tiny lip flakes).. 55

Radam's (Wm.) Microbe Killer, Germ, Bacteria or Fungus Destroyer, (design of man beating a skeleton), Registered Trade Mark Dec. 13, 1887, Cures All Diseases, square w/rounded shoulders, tooled mouth, medium amber, 10 1/4" h.. 132

River Swamp (The) Chill and Fever Cure, Augusta, GA (center design of alligator), rectangular w/beveled corners & rounded shoulders, tooled mouth, medium amber, light overall haze & scratches, ca. 1880, 6 1/4" h. (ILLUS.) 660

Sanford's Extract of Hamamelis or Witch Hazel, round w/sunken panel, tooled mouth, smooth base, ca. 1885-95, deep cobalt blue, 10 1/4" h.................................. 330

Sanford's Radical Cure, rectangular w/tooled mouth & smooth base, 95% of original paper label w/"Sandford's Radical Cure for Catarrh," ca. 1870-80, deep cobalt blue, 7 5/8" h..................................... 165

Shaker (The) Family Pills - Dose 2 to 4 - A.J. White, rectangular w/paneled sides, sheared lip, smooth base, ca. 1890-1900, medium amber, 2 1/4" h. 94

Sparks Perfect Health (below Trade Mark) - bust of man - for Kidney & Liver Diseases, rectangular w/beveled corners, tooled mouth, smooth base, ca. 1880-95, medium amber, 9 1/2" h. 275

Rare Stone's Liquid Cathartic Bottle

Stone's (G.W.) Liquid Cathartic & Family
Physic, Lowell Mass., rectangular
w/beveled corners & three indented panels, applied double collar mouth, smooth
base, ca. 1850-60, tobacco or root beer
amber, 8 7/8" h. (ILLUS.) 9,625

Swaim's Panacea - Genuine - Philadelphia, rectangular w/applied sloping collar mouth & open pontil, ca. 1840-50,
aqua, 7 3/4" h. 853

Swaim's - Panacea - Philada, paneled cylinder, applied sloping double collar,
medium to deep olive green, 8" h. 253

Dr. Urban's Anti-Bacchanalian Elixir

Urban's (Dr.) - Anti - Bacchanalian Elixir
- Louisville, KY, rectangular w/paneled
sides, applied mouth, ca. 1845-55, deep
bluish aqua, lightly cleaned, 7 1/4" h.
(ILLUS.) 990

Vanvleck & Johnsons (Drs. H. & W.G.)
Ague Conqueror, rectangular
w/rounded shoulders & rolled lip, ca.
1845-55, deep bluish aqua (lightly
cleaned) 176

(Warner's) Log Cabin Extract - Rochester, N.Y., three indented panels on front,
flat back, smooth base, tooled
mouth, ca. 1880-90, w/original box &
directions, medium amber, 6 3/8" h. 264

Fine Swaim's Panacea Bottle

Swaim's - Panacea - Philada, paneled cylinder, applied sloping double collar,
open pontil, ca. 1840-50, medium yel-
lowish olive, 7 3/4" h. (ILLUS.) 853

Swayne's (Dr.) Compound Syrup of Wild
Cherry, squared w/indented side panels, flared lip & open pontil, aqua, 6" h.
(some staining).. 77

Swift's Syphilitic Specific, strap-side flask
form, applied mouth, smooth base, ca.
1870-80, deep cobalt blue, 9 1/8" h.
(spot of roughness on one strap edge) 633

U.S.A. - Hosp. Dept., cylindrical w/applied
double collar, base marked "S.D.S.,"
reportedly dug, apricot yellow, ca. 1860-
70, 9 3/8" h. 688

U.S.A. - Hosp. Dept., cylindrical w/applied
double collar, yellow w/olive tone, ca.
1860-70, 9 1/4" h. 660

U.S.A. - Hosp. Dept., cylindrical w/rounded
shoulder, tooled mouth, medium cobalt
blue, ca. 1865-80, 7 1/4" h. 1,650

U.S.A. - Hosp. Dept., oval w/rounded
shoulder, tooled mouth, deep cobalt
blue, ca. 1865-80, 2 1/2" h. 688

U.S.A.- Hosp. Dept. (in oval), cylindrical
w/applied mouth & smooth base, ca.
1860-75, deep cobalt blue, rare size,
6 1/4" h. 6,160

Warner's Safe Cure - Frankfurt

Warner's Safe Cure (motif of safe)
Frankfurt A/M, oval w/applied mouth &
smooth base, ca. 1890-1900, deep olive
green, 9" h. (ILLUS.) 358

Warner's Safe Cure (motif of safe) Mel-
bourne, Aus - London, Eng - Toronto,
Can - Rochester, N.Y. U.S.A., oval
w/applied blob top & smooth base, late
19th c., medium copper, 9 5/8" h. (shal-
low open bubble).. 176

Warner's Safe Cure (motif of safe) Mel-
bourne, Aus - London, Eng - Toronto,
Can - Rochester, N.Y. U.S.A., oval
w/applied double collar mouth & smooth
base, late 19th c., reddish amber,
9 5/8" h. 99

Warners Safe Nervine (above design of a
safe), Rochester, N.Y., flattened rectangle w/rounded shoulder & tooled mouth,
golden honey amber, 7 3/8" h. 66

Wishart's Pine Tree Tar Cordial

Wistar's (Dr.) Balsam of Wild Cherry -
Sanford & Park - Cincinnati, O., eight-
sided w/applied sloping collar mouth &
iron pontil, ca. 1845-55, deep ice blue,
6 3/8" h. (some light haze) 159

Wood's (Dr. J.S.) Elixir, Albany , N.Y.,
rectangular w/deeply cut corners &
tombstone shoulders, applied sloping
collar mouth, iron pontil, ca. 1845-55,
deep bluish green, 8 3/4" h. (tiny flake
on front panel) 4,400

Wright (P.T.) & Co. Pectoral Syrup,
Philada., rectangular w/applied top &
open pontil, aqua, 6 1/4" h. (light stain) 110

Dr. Weaver's Canker Syrup Bottle

Weaver's (Dr. S.A.) Canker & Salt Rheum
Syrup, oval w/applied mouth & iron
pontil, ca. 1845-55, aqua, 9 3/8" h.
(ILLUS.).. 66

Westmoreland's - Calisaya Tonic, rectangular w/paneled sides & tooled mouth,
base marked "A.G. Co.," golden yellow
amber, 8 1/4" h... 88

Wheatley's (J.B.) Compound Syrup, Dal-
lasburgh, NY, cylindrical w/applied dou-
ble collar, aqua, 6" h..................................... 121

Wilder's (Edward) Compound Extract of
Wild Cherry (motif of five-story building) - Edward Wilder & Co. Wholesale
Druggists Louisville, KY., semi-cabin
shaped w/paneled sides, tooled mouth,
smooth base, ca. 1885-95, clear,
7 1/2" h. 121

Wishart's (L.Q.C.) - Pine Tree Tar Cordial, Phila. - Patent (design of pine
tree) 1859, square w/beveled corners,
applied sloping collar, emerald green,
milky inside base stain, 9 3/8" h.(ILLUS.
top of next column).................................... 231

Wishart's (L.Q.C.) - Pine Tree Tar Cordial, Phila. - Patent (design of pine
tree) 1859, square w/beveled corners,
applied sloping collar, medium bluish
green, 9 3/4" h... 187

Wishart's (L.Q.C.) - Pine Tree Tar Cordial, Phila. - Patent (design of pine
tree) 1859, square w/beveled corners,
applied sloping collar, smooth base, ca.
1859-70, medium emerald green,
9 1/2" h. 220

Rare Wynkoop's Medicine Bottle

Wynkoop's Katharismic Sarsaparilla - New York, rectangular w/sunken panels, applied sloping collar mouth, iron pontil, ca. 1845-55, medium cobalt blue, 10" h. (ILLUS.).. **7,975**

Yerba Santa (in cross) - San Francisco, California, rectangular w/paneled sides, tooled mouth, aqua, large (some milkiness on lip).. **198**

MILK

The milk bottles in this listing are all glass with dairy names. Milk bottles were patented in 1886 and handmade until the introduction of the Owens semi-automatic bottle machine. The turn-of-the-century saw a large increase in the use of milk bottles by small dairies in most every town in America. These lowly utilitarian glass bottles have become a prized collectable because of the pride of the farmer who produced the milk and the way he promoted the sale of milk through these bottles. Also nearly all folks have ties to a family farm, some close, some far, which causes us to want part of the past. Our listing will note size, square or round, embossed (raised glass lettering) or pyro (painted label). All pricing is for milk bottles in good plus condition, meaning free from cracks, chips, stain or paint wear or fading.

Aldrich Dairy Milk Bottle

Aldrich Dairy - Norwich, NY, quart, round, pyro (ILLUS.).. **35**

Baxter's Dairy - Watkins Glen, NY, quart, square, pyro **8**

Birch Lawn Dairy J.M. Leighty - Tarrs, Pa., quart, round, pyro, farm scene................ **55**

Branglebrink Farm - St. James, N.Y., half-pint, round, embossed.............................. **6**

Brookefield Dairy - Hellerstown, Pa., half-pint, round, embossed, baby top............. **35**

C.N. Baker - Charlotte, N.C., pint, round, embossed... **16**

Chapman's Dairy - Greenville, S.C., quart, round, pyro.. **40**

Chestnut Farm Chevy Chase Dairy - Washington, DC, quart, round, embossed, carton.. **30**

Churchill's Dairy Quart Milk Bottle

Churchill's Dairy - Bethlehem, NH, quart, round, pyro (ILLUS.)....................................... **35**

Clay County Farms - Middleburg, Fl., jersey cow **50**

Coop Golden Crust Bread Milk Bottle

Coop Golden Crust Bread, quart, round,
  pyro (ILLUS.) 50
Cream Valley Dairy - Woodstown, N.J.,
  quart, square, pyro 10

Dairy Gold Milk Bottle

Dairy Gold, quart, round, pyro, 2 color
  (ILLUS.) 60
Dairylea, quart, round, pyro, 2 color, eagle,
  girl/hoop, family 30
**Damascus Cream Top Milk - Portland,
  Ore.,** quart, round, pyro, cream top 35
David Fiske Warehouse - Point, Conn.,
  quart, round, embossed 18
Dellinger Dairy - Jeffersonville, IN, quart,
  round, pyro, 2 color, gold medal herd 55
Dykes Dairy - Warren/Youngstown, Pa.,
  quart, round, pyro, 2 color, "United
  States is a Sound Investment Buy War
  Bonds & Stamps," Statue of Liberty 75
**Earl Lapan's Dairy - South Burlington,
  Vt.,** half-pint, round, pyro 12
Eveleth Creamery - Eveleth, Minn., quart,
  round, pyro, cream top 45
**Franz Dairy Knox Clarion - Emlenton,
  PA,** quart, round, pyro (ILLUS. top of
  next column) 45
Frasure & Brown Dairy - Logan, OH,
  quart, square, pyro 10
**Frink Serving Denver Make America
  Strong,** quart, round, pyro, eagle,
  girl/hoop 60
Fryes Dairy - Leominster, Mass., quart,
  square, pyro, baby top 75
Furman Bros. - Ithaca, N.Y., quart, round,
  pyro, cop the cream 200
G.C. Kaufman - Kingston, N.Y., half-pint,
  round, embossed, tin top 50
Gayoso Farms - Horn Lake, Miss., quart,
  round, pyro 55

Franz Dairy Knox Clarion Milk Bottle

George Godin - Richfort, Vt., quart,
  round, pyro 60
Greenhill Dairy - Wilmington, Del., quart,
  round, embossed 35
H.E. Larrimore's Dairy - Seaford, Del.,
  quart, round, pyro 50
H & L Hometown Dairy - Keokuk, Ia.,
  quart, round, pyro 45

Harris Dairy Quart Milk Bottle

Harris Dairy - St. Joseph, MO, quart,
  round, pyro squat (ILLUS.) 30

Homecroft Dairy Quart Milk Bottle

Homecroft Dairy - Bessember, PA, quart,
round, pyro (ILLUS.)...................................... 40
**Independent Riviera Dairy - Santa Bar-
bara, Calif.,** quart, round, pyro 35
Julius Heretick Dairy - Hopewell, Va.,
pint, round, embossed................................... 10
Kilfasset Farms - Passumpsic, Vt., quart,
square, pyro 10

Lackrone Dairy Milk Bottle

Lackrone Dairy - Salem, IL, quart, round,
pyro (ILLUS.)... 45
Leadbelt Dairy - Bonne Terre, Mo., quart,
round, pyro 45

Leake Bros. Dairy Fountain Inn, half-pint,
round, pyro, stork 18
M.H. Williams Ayrshire Dairy, quart,
round, pyro, four Ayrshire cows 45
Maple Farm - Boston, Mass., quart,
round, embossed, store bottle....................... 25
Meadowsweet Dairies - Tacoma, Wash.,
quart, round, embossed 22
**Midland Creamery - Colorado Springs,
Colo.,** pint, round, pyro, two-color................. 40

Midwest Dairy Bottle

Midwest Dairy - St. Louis, MO, quart,
round, pyro, war slogan (ILLUS.) 65
Mohawk Farms - Staten Island, N.Y.,
quart, round, embossed, Indian 50
Newton Farm Dairy - Ellicott City, Md.,
quart, round, embossed 35
Oak Grove Dairy - Windsor, N.C., quart,
round, embossed 30
Peapack Gladstone Dairy, quart, round,
embossed.. 15
Pet Milk Company, quart, round, pyro.............. 30
Quality Coughlin Dairy - Pierre, S.D.,
quart, round, pyro.. 60
Quality Dairy W. Fudge - El Dorado, Ark.,
quart, round, embossed 30
**Redford Farm D. Cardillo - Stockbridge,
Mass.,** quart, round, pyro.............................. 35
**Rices Dairy Benzie County - Benzonia,
Mich.,** quart, round, pyro............................... 45
Riverview Farms - Frankfort, Ky., pint,
round, pyro 18
Sanitary Dairy - Fort Dodge, Ia., quart,
round, pyro, cream top 35
Sawyer Farms - Gilford, N.H., quart,
round, pyro, baby top 125
**Silver Leaf Dairy Guernsey - Ironwood,
Mich.,** pint, round, pyro ....
Southern Dairy Farm - Tuscaloosa, Ala.,
quart, round, pyro.. 70
Southside Dairy - Oneonta, N.Y., quart,
round, pyro, large tree................................... 40

Sunny Brook Farm - Alhambra, Calif.,
half-pint, round, pyro 15
Sweet's Dairy - Fredonia, N.Y., quart,
round, pyro, cop the cream 200
The Dell Newtown Bucks Co. - PA, quart,
round, pyro 125
Tyoga Farms Dairy, quart, square, pyro,
bulk milk truck 15

Walthours Dairy Milk Bottle

Walthours Dairy - Greensburg, PA, quart,
round, pyro, 2 color (ILLUS.) 75
Winchester Creamery - Winchester, Va.,
half-pint, round, pyro 40

Winona Quart Milk Bottle

Winona - Winona Lake, IN, quart, round,
pyro (ILLUS.) 95

MINERAL WATERS, SODAS & SARSAPARILLAS

Adirondack Spring - Westport, N.Y.,
cylindrical w/applied sloping double collar mouth, ca. 1865-80, deep emerald
green, qt. 242

Rare Alfs Soda Water Bottle

**Alfs (C.) - Soda Water - Charleston - This
Bottle To Be Returned,** 8-paneled ten-
pin shape, yellowish olive green, applied
sloping collar mouth, iron pontil, ca.
1845-55, cleaned, 7 1/4" h. (ILLUS.) **8,525**
Andrae (C.) Port Huron, Michigan, Hutchinson stopper w/applied top, cobalt blue
(some wear & scratches, needs clean-
ing) 550

Artesian Spring Co. Bottle

**Artesian Spring Co. "AS" (monogram)
Ballston N.Y. - Ballston Spa "AS"
(monogram) Mineral Water,** cylindrical
w/applied sloping double collar, ca.
1865-75, green, pt., 7 5/8" h. (ILLUS.) 83
Aufrecht (J.), Philada (in slug plate) cylindrical w/applied sloping double collar, ca.
1845-55, deep bluish green, 7 1/4" h. 77

B.B.W. San Rafael, Hutchinson stopper w/tooled top, California, late 19th c., light aqua (some wear) 33

B&G San Francisco Superior Mineral Water, cylindrical w/ten-sided base, applied flattened blob top, iron pontil, cobalt blue, ca. 1852-56 (never cleaned, typical wear)... 358

B&G Soda San Francisco "Superior Mineral Water," cylindrical w/ten-sided base & applied blob top, iron pontil, dark blue, 1850s (some scratching, little roughness, lightly cleaned) 253

Blaffer (J.A.) & Co. - New Orleans, cylindrical w/tall neck & applied double collar mouth, ca. 1865-75, deep golden amber, 6 3/8" h. (some scratching) 242

Blue Lick Water Co., KY, cylindrical w/applied sloping double collar, ca. 1855-65, deep bluish green, pt., 8" h. (minor iridescent bruise).............................. 688

Boley & Co. Sac City Cal. Union Glass Works, Philad., cylindrical w/applied blob top, iron pontil, small "c" variety, cobalt blue, 1850-52 (cleaned, small ding near base) 220

Rare Ten Pin-Shaped Mineral Water

Borcman (H.) Mineral Water Manufacturer - Cumberland, MD., ten pinshaped, applied mouth, iron pontil, ca. 1845-55, pinhead flake on lip, deep cobalt blue, 8 1/4" h. (ILLUS.) 3,850

Burt (W.H.) San Francisco, cylindrical w/applied blob top, iron pontil, deep green,... 165

Burt (W.H.) San Francisco, cylindrical w/applied blob top, iron pontil, emerald green, 1852 (cleaned) 165

C & K Eagle Works Sac. City, applied top, smooth base, California, 1858-66, light cobalt blue (polished) 66

Owen Casey Soda Water Bottle

Casey (Owen) Eagle Soda Works - Sac City, cylindrical w/applied mouth & smooth base, ca. 1860-70, medium cobalt blue, 7 1/8" h. (ILLUS.) 143

Rare Catell's Superior Mineral Water

Catell's Superior Mineral Water, tensided cylinder w/applied sloping mouth, some light outside stain, small bruise & chip on contour of lip, ca. 1845-55, sapphire blue, 6 7/8" h. (ILLUS.).................... **1,595**

Chalybeate Water Bottle

Chalybeate Water of the American Spa Spring Co. N.J., cylindrical w/applied mouth, light to medium bluish green, ca. 1865-75, pt. (ILLUS.)................................... 495

Champion Spouting Spring - Saratoga Mineral - Spring - (superimposed over) C.S.S. Co. (monogram) - Limited - Saratoga N.Y. - Champion - Water, cylindrical w/applied sloping double collar mouth, bluish aqua, ca. 1865-80, pt. 72

Clark (C.), Charleston (in slug plate),
cylindrical, deep grass green, applied
sloping collar, iron pontil, ca. 1845-55,
7 1/2" h. (lightly cleaned) 303
Clark (C.) Mineral Water, cylindrical
w/applied sloping collar, iron pontil, deep
emerald green, ca. 1845-55, 7 1/4" h.
(cleaned) 231
Clark (Charles) - Charleston - SC - Soda -
Water, cylindrical w/applied sloping collar mouth, iron pontil, ca. 1845-55,
medium green, 7 7/8" h. (some overall
stain & ground lines) 143

Clarke & Co. Mineral Water Bottle

Clarke & Co. - New-York, cylindrical
w/applied ringed mouth & smooth
base, ca. 1855-65, black olive amber,
7 5/8" h. (ILLUS.) 440
Clarke (John) - New York (around shoul-
der), cylindrical w/applied sloping double
collar mouth, pontiled base, ca. 1855-60,
medium yellowish olive amber, qt. 176
Clarke & White - New York, cylindrical
w/applied sloping double collar
mouth, ca. 1860-75, deep forest green,
pt. 55
Clarke & White - New York, cylindrical
w/applied sloping double collar
mouth, ca. 1860-75, deep emerald or
forest green, qt. 66
Clarke & White - New York, cylindrical
w/applied sloping double collar
mouth, ca. 1860-75, deep emerald
green, pt. 77
Classen & Co. - design of crossed
anchors - Sparkling, cylindrical
w/applied mouth, sapphire blue, dug,
7 5/8" h. 330
Coca-Cola Bottling Co. In Binghamton,
cylindrical w/tall tapering neck & tooled
crown top, ca. 1900-10, medium olive
yellow, 7 3/4" h. 176
Coca-Cola Bottling Co., Inc. Bingham-
ton, cylindrical machine-made w/crown
top, ca. 1900-10, yellow olive, 7 3/4" h.
(ILLUS. top of next column) 105

Early Coca-Cola Bottle

Congress & Empire - Spring (C in frame)
- Saratoga. N.Y. - Congress - Water,
cylindrical w/applied sloping double collar mouth, deep emerald green, ca.
1865-75, dug, pt. 853
Congress & Empire Spring - C -
Saratoga, N.Y. - Congress - Water,
cylindrical w/applied sloping double collar mouth, deep emerald green,
crude, ca. 1860-75, pt. 143
Congress & Empire Spring Co. E
Saratoga, N.Y., cylindrical w/tall neck &
applied sloping double collar, ca. 1865-
75, deep olive green, qt., 9 3/8" h. (small
flake inside lip) 55
Congress & Empire Spring Co. - Hotch-
kiss' Sons - C - New-York - Saratoga,
N.Y., cylindrical w/applied sloping double collar mouth, ca. 1865-75, deep
emerald green, qt. 116
Cooper's Well Water - Miss. - B.B. Co.,
cylindrical w/applied straight double collar mouth, heavy overall ground
stain, ca. 1875-85, amber, qt. 121
Cosgrove (J.) Charleston 1866, cylindrical
w/applied blob top, smooth base,
aqua, ca. 1855-70, 7 1/4" h. (overall
stain & dullness) 99
D.S. & Co. San Francisco, applied top,
smooth base, 1861-64, dark cobalt blue
(lightly cleaned) 231
Dawson & Blackman, Charleston, S.C. -
Union Glass Works Philad Superior
Mineral Water, cylindrical w/applied
blob top, paneled mug base, deep cobalt
blue, ca. 1845-55, 7 1/2" h. (staining,
small iridescent bruise) 550
Dawson & Blackman, Charleston, S.C. -
Union Glass Works Philad Superior
Mineral Water, cylindrical w/applied
blob top, paneled mug base, peacock
blue, ca. 1845-55, 7 5/8" h. (overall
stain, small iridescent bruise inside edge
of base) 825

Deep Rock Spring - Trade - Deep Rock - Mark - Oswego N.Y. - DRS (monogram), cylindrical w/applied sloping double collar, aqua, 1870-80, pt. **231**

Dewer (James). Elko, Nevada, Hutchinson stopper, 1892-95, clear **1,870**

Eagle (Geo.), cylindrical w/spiral ribbed design on lower body w/plain band w/the name, applied sloping collar, ca. 1845-55, medium bluish green, 6 7/8" h............... **935**

Eagle (W.) - New-York - Union Glass Works Phila. - Superior - Mineral Water, cylindrical w/paneled base & applied sloping collar mouth, iron pontil, ca. 1845-55, medium sapphire blue, 7 1/2" h. (lightly cleaned, faint bruise on lip)................................. **385**

Eastern Cider Co., cylindrical w/applied blob top & smooth base, medium golden amber, 1877-82... **165**

Empire Soda Works - Vallejo (design of eagle), cylindrical w/applied mouth, ca. 1860-70, bluish green, 7 3/8" h. **110**

Eureka - California Soda Water Co. S.F., w/eagle design, Hutchinson stopper w/tooled mouth, aqua (minor case wear) **88**

Excelsior Spring, Saratoga, N.Y., cylindrical w/applied sloping double collar, ca. 1870-80, deep yellowish olive amber, pt., 7 3/4" h. (minor inside stain)................... **121**

Excelsior Spring - Saratoga, N.Y., cylindrical w/applied sloping double collar, ca. 1870-80, deep bluish green, qt. (minor scratches) **121**

Excelsior Spring - Saratoga, N.Y., cylindrical w/applied sloping double collar, ca. 1870-80, teal blue, pt., 7 3/4" h. **193**

Farrel & Co. Mineral Water, Evansville, I.A. - F. & Co., cylindrical w/applied blob mouth, ca. 1845-55, ice blue, 7 3/8" h......... **798**

Fehr (John) - Reading, wide cylindrical form w/applied sloping double collar mouth, iron pontil, ca. 1845-55, medium bluish green, 7" h. (lightly cleaned) **198**

Fields - Superior - Soda Water - Charleston, S.C., eight-sided ten-pin shape, cobalt blue, applied sloping collar, iron pontil, ca. 1845-55, 7 5/8" h. (some overall ground lines & imperfections) **413**

Fields - Superior - Soda Water - Charleston - S. C., octagonal w/applied sloping collar mouth, iron pontil, ca. 1845-55, deep cobalt blue, 7 5/8" h. (two tiny under collar flakes, interior & exterior stain) **358**

Gardner (John H.) & Son - Sharon Springs - N.Y., cylindrical w/rounded shoulder & applied sloping double collar mouth, medium teal blue, ca. 1865-75, pt. **303**

Gettysburg Katalysine Water, cylindrical w/tall neck & applied sloping double collar, ca. 1865-80, medium emerald green, qt., 9 5/8" h. **61**

Gettysburg Katalysine Water, cylindrical w/tall neck & applied sloping double collar, ca. 1865-80, lots of bubbles, emerald green, qt., 9 5/8" h. **88**

Gettysburg Katalysine Water, cylindrical w/tall neck & applied sloping double collar, ca. 1865-80, olive green, qt., 9 5/8" h. **132**

Geyser Spring, Saratoga Spring, State of New York- The Saratoga Spouting Spring, cylindrical w/applied sloping double collar, ca. 1865-75, bluish aqua, pt., 7 5/8" h. **61**

Geyser Spring - Saratoga Springs - State of New York - The Saratoga Spouting Spring, cylindrical w/applied sloping double collar, ca. 1865-75, deep bluish aqua, pt., 7 3/4" h...................... **53**

Guilford Mineral - GMWS (inside circle) - Guilford - VT - Spring Water, cylindrical w/tall tapering neck & applied sloping double collar mouth, deep bluish green, ca. 1870-80, qt. **159**

Guilford Mineral - GMWS (inside circle) - Guilford - VT - Spring Water, cylindrical w/tall tapering neck & applied sloping double collar mouth, 99% original paper labels, deep teal green, ca. 1870-80, qt. (potstone w/small stress crack)................... **209**

Haas Bros - Natural - Mineral Water - Napa - Soda, cylindrical w/applied mouth, ca. 1860-70, deep sapphire blue, lightly cleaned, 7 3/8" h. **121**

Harris (J.W.) Soda New Haven, Conn., applied top, iron pontil, cobalt blue............... **440**

Harris Lithia Water - Harris Springs - S.C., cylindrical w/short neck & tooled mouth, ca. 1890-1910, greenish aqua, 1/2 gal. **66**

Highrock Congress Spring- 1767- (design of a rock), C. & W. Saratoga N.Y., cylindrical w/applied sloping double collar mouth, deep chocolate amber, ca. 1865-75, qt. **242**

Highrock Congress Spring (design of a rock), C. & W. Saratoga N.Y., cylindrical w/applied sloping double collar, ca. 1865-75, medium root beer amber, pt. **198**

Highrock Congress Spring Bottle

Highrock Congress Spring (design of a rock), C. & W. Saratoga N.Y., cylindrical w/applied sloping double collar, ca. 1865-75, medium yellowish amber, pt. (ILLUS.) **248**

Highrock Congress Spring (variant design of a rock), C. & W. Saratoga N.Y., cylindrical w/applied sloping double collar, ca. 1865-75, medium root beer amber, pt. **358**

Humboldt Mineral Water Bottle

Humboldt Artesian Mineral Water - Eureka, Cal., cylindrical w/tooled lip, numerous seed bubbles, dark aqua, ca. 1895, 6 7/8" h. (ILLUS.) **66**

Italian Soda Water Manufactory San Francisco, cylindrical w/applied blob top, dark green, late 1850s (cleaned, some superficial crazing) **143**

Jackson's Napa Soda, applied top, 1873-85, cobalt blue (minor interior stain) **605**

Kensington - Glassworks, wide cylindrical form w/applied sloping double collar mouth, iron pontil, ca. 1845-55, medium emerald green, 7 1/4" h. (inside stain) **187**

Ketner (M.M.) and Aulenbach (J.) Pottsville - Union Glass Works, Phila., cylindrical w/applied blob mouth, ca. 1845-55, deep bluish aqua, 7 1/4" h. **605**

Kissingen Water - Patterson & Brazeau, cylindrical w/applied sloping collar mouth, yellowish lime green, ca. 1870-85, pt. **143**

Knowlton (D.A.) - Saratoga - N.Y., cylindrical w/applied sloping double collar mouth, deep olive green, ca. 1855-70, dug, pt. **154**

L. & Cochcrane - Selzer (on shoulder), bulbous cylindrical w/slender neck & applied blob top, ca. 1865-75, English, medium pinkish puce w/wisps of darker color, 7" h. (lightly cleaned, illegible words on back) **187**

Lappeus Soda Water Bottle

Lappeus (Wm. W.) Premium Soda & Mineral Water - Albany, ten-sided w/applied blob top & iron pontil, ca. 1845-55, cobalt blue, 7" h. (ILLUS.) **1,073**

Ledic (A.) - Utica - Bottling Establishment - Superior - Water - Mineral, cylindrical 24-sided 'teepee' form w/applied mouth, iron pontil, ca. 1845-55, deep cobalt blue, 7 5/8" h. **1,165**

Lithia Mineral Spring Co. Gloversville, cylindrical w/applied sloping collar, ca. 1865-80, bluish aqua, pt., 7 3/4" h. (very light haze, tiny flake on underside of collar) **825**

Litton's Mineral Water Healdsburg, cylindrical w/applied mouth & smooth base, dark aqua, ca. 1870s (small ding on base) **358**

Lynde & Putnam Mineral Waters San Francisco Cala. Union Glass Works, Philad., cylindrical w/applied blob top & iron pontil, shaded cobalt blue, 1850-51 (cleaned) **303**

Rare M.R. 'Sacrimento' Soda Bottle

M.R. Sacrimento (sic) Union Glass Works, Phila., cylindrical w/applied blob top & iron pontil, teal green, open bubble above the "R," 1850s (ILLUS.) **1,430**

Massena Spring - (monogram in frame above bird) - Water, cylindrical w/applied sloping double collar mouth, ca. 1870-80, medium amber, qt. **132**

Massena Spring - (monogram in frame above bird) - Water, cylindrical w/applied sloping double collar mouth, ca. 1870-80, medium teal blue, qt. **165**

McIntire (E.) - Mineral - Patent, cylindrical w/applied sloping collar mouth, iron pontil, ca. 1835-45, medium green, 6 3/4" h. (minor case wear) **495**

McKinney Mineral Water Bottle

McKinney Philada - Rice & Mineral Water, cylindrical w/applied blob mouth, ca. 1845-55, medium teal blue, 7" h. (ILLUS.) **121**

Middletown Healing Springs, Grays & Clark, Middletown, Vt., cylindrical w/tall neck & applied sloping double collar, ca. 1865-75, amber w/olive tone, qt. **154**

Missisquoi - A - Springs, cylindrical w/applied sloping double collar mouth, ca. 1865-80, deep emerald amber, qt. (in-making chip from under applied collar) **99**

Naturliches - Miner Wasser - Doppelkohlens. - Fullung - Des - Apollinaris - Brunnen, cylindrical w/tall neck & applied mouth, ca. 1865-75, Germany, olive green, crude, dug, 10" h. **121**

Nevada City Soda Works - L. Seibert, applied top, smooth base, 1880s, aqua **66**

New Liberty - Soda W. Co. - Trade (design of Liberty head) Mark - S.F., cylindrical w/short neck & tooled mouth, Hutchinson closure-type, ca. 1890-1900, aqua, 6 3/4" h. (very minor ground pecks) **66**

O'Kane & Maginnis C. May, N.J., cylindrical w/applied sloping double collar, ca. 1855-70, medium teal blue, 6 7/8" h. (light scratching) **88**

Oak Orchard Acid Springs, Address G.W. Merchant, Lockport, N.Y., cylindrical w/applied sloping collar, ca. 1865-75, Lockport green, qt., 9" h. **83**

Oak Orchard - Acid Springs - Alabama - Genesee Co. N.Y. (around shoulder), cylindrical w/applied sloping double collar mouth, ca. 1865-80, deep bluish green, qt. **200**

Oak Orchard - Acid Springs - H.W. Bostwick - Agt. No. 574 - Broadway, New York, cylindrical w/applied sloping double collar mouth, embossed on smooth base "Glass From F. Hitchins Factory - Lockport, N.Y.," deep root beer amber, qt. **154**

Rare Townsend's Sarsaparilla Bottle

Old Dr. Townsend's Sarsaparilla - New York, square w/beveled corners, applied sloping collar mouth, open pontil, ca. 1845-55, tiny flake on lip, deep tobacco amber, 9 1/2" h. (ILLUS.) **2,530**

Ormsby Soda Water Bottle

Ormsby (D.L.) New York Union Glass Works - Phila., cylindrical w/applied blob top & iron pontil, ca. 1845-55, deep vivid cobalt blue, 7 3/8" h. (ILLUS.) **605**

Owen Casey Eagle Soda Works Sac City, cylindrical w/applied blob top & smooth base, medium green, 1867-71 176

Owen Casey Eagle Soda Works Sac City, cylindrical w/applied blob top & smooth base, sapphire blue w/green streaks, 1867-71 88

Pacific Congress Water, cylindrical w/applied blob top & smooth base, deep aqua, 1869-76 66

Pavilion & United States Spring Co. - Saratoga, N.Y. - Pavilion Water - Aperient, cylindrical w/rounded shoulder & applied sloping double collar mouth, deep Lockport green, ca. 1865-80, pt. 242

Pavilion & United States Spring Co. - Saratoga, N.Y. - Pavilion Water - Aperient, cylindrical w/rounded shoulder & applied sloping double collar mouth, yellowish olive amber, ca. 1865-80, pt. 330

Scarce Clear Poland Water Bottle

Poland - Water - Poland Mineral Spring Water (around monogram) - H. Ricker & Sons Proprietors, figural, seated Moses Poland, applied sloping collar mouth, unusual pontil-scarred base, lightly cleaned, ca. 1880-90, clear, 11 1/2" h. (ILLUS.) 303

Rare Florida Mineral Water Bottle

Ponce de Leon Spring (monogram) Water - St. Augustine, Fl., cylindrical w/applied ringed mouth, smooth base, very minor imperfections, ca. 1870-80, yellowish olive green, pt., 7 1/2" h. (ILLUS.) 4,070

Post (E.A.) Portland, Ogn., w/eagle motif, applied top, smooth base, 1881-83, clear 560

Cobalt Blue Ginger Ale Bottle

Ray (James) Savannah, Geo. - Ginger Ale, Hutchinson stopper, cylindrical w/tooled mouth & smooth base, ca. 1870-80, lightly cleaned, deep cobalt blue, 8" h. (ILLUS.) 468

Saint Leon - Spring Water (inside diamond enclosing) - Earl W. Johnson - 27 - Congress St. - Boston - Mass., cylindrical w/applied sloping double collar mouth, medium emerald green, ca. 1870-80, pt. (faint bruise inside lip) 148

Saratoga (design of star) Spring, cylindrical w/tall neck & applied sloping double collar, ca. 1865-75, medium orangish amber, qt., 9 3/8" h. 138

Saratoga (design of star) Spring, cylindrical w/tall neck & applied sloping double collar, ca. 1865-75, deep olive green, qt., 9 1/2" h. 143

Saratoga (design of star) Spring (backwards S), cylindrical w/applied sloping double collar mouth, deep yellowish olive green, ca. 1865-80, qt. 121

Saratoga Red Spring, cylindrical w/applied sloping double collar, ca. 1865-75, deep bluish green, qt., 9 5/8" h. 110

Seedorff (J.) - Charleston - S.C., cylindrical w/applied blob top, ca. 1855-70, medium bluish green, 7" h. (light scratching) 330

Seedorff (John) - Charleston, S.C. (in slug plate), cylindrical w/applied blob top, iron pontil, ca. 1845-55, deep sapphire blue, 7 1/8" h. 253

Seedorff (John) - Charleston, S.C. (in slug plate), cylindrical w/applied mouth, iron pontil, ca. 1845-55, medium sapphire blue, 6 7/8" h. (tiny open shoulder bubble, minor stain & wear) 154

Smith (A.P.) - Charleston, S.C., cylindrical w/applied sloping collar & iron pontil, deep sapphire blue, ca. 1845-55, 7 1/2" h. (overall heavy stain, pick bruise inside lip) 264

Smith (A.P.) - Charleston, S.C. (arched embossing variant), cylindrical w/applied sloping collar & iron pontil, deep cobalt blue, ca. 1845-55, 7 5/8" h. 413

Smith (A.P.) - Charleston (slug plate variant), cylindrical w/applied sloping collar mouth, iron pontil, ca. 1845-55, deep cobalt blue, 7 3/8" h. (lightly cleaned) 242

Smith & Co. Soda Water Bottle

Smith & Co. - Premium - Soda Water - Charleston, eight-sided ten-pin shape, deep green, applied blob top, iron pontil, ca. 1845-55, cleaned, 7 1/2" h. (ILLUS.).. 468

Smith & - Fotheringham - Soda Water - St. Louis - This Bottle - Is Never Sold, ten-sided w/applied sloping collar mouth, iron pontil, ca. 1845-55, deep sapphire blue, 7 1/2" h. (light stain, some case wear) 605

Southwick & Tupper Soda Bottle

Southwick & G.O. Tupper - New York - Adna - H, ten-sided w/applied sloping collar mouth, iron pontil, ca. 1845-55, cobalt blue, 7 3/8" h. (ILLUS.) 550

Southwick & Tupper New York, applied top, iron pontil, early, dark cobalt blue (some resin repair in top) 132

Unlisted Mineral Water Bottle

St. Louis Artesian Mineral Water by W.H. Stevens & Co., cylindrical w/ringed applied mouth, smooth base, ca. 1865-75, unlisted, tiny cooling crack & lip flake, deep bluish aqua, 9 1/2" h. (ILLUS.).. 2,640

St. Regis - Water - Massena Springs, cylindrical w/tall tapering neck & applied sloping double collar mouth, ca. 1870-80, medium teal blue, qt. 176

Star Spring Co. (design of star) Saratoga, N.Y., cylindrical w/applied sloping double collar, ca. 1865-75, deep chocolate amber, pt., 7 3/4" h. 358

Star Spring Co. Bottle

Star Spring Co. (design of star) Saratoga, N.Y., cylindrical w/applied sloping double collar, ca. 1865-75, medium yellowish olive amber, pt., 7 5/8" h. (ILLUS.).................................. 209

Star Spring Co. (design of star) Saratoga, N.Y., cylindrical w/applied sloping double collar, ca. 1865-75, root beer amber, pt., 7 5/8" h.............................. 121

Star Spring Co. (design of star) Saratoga, N.Y., cylindrical w/applied sloping double collar, ca. 1865-80, deep reddish amber, pt., 7 5/8" h. (faint bruise inside lip) 61

Steinke & Kornahrens - Soda Water - Return This Bottle - Charleston, S.C., eight-sided ten-pin shape, deep cobalt blue, applied sloping collar, ca. 1845-55, 8 1/4" h. (two shallow lip chips) 154

Stenson (James) Chicago, Ills., wide cylindrical body w/rounded shoulder tapering to applied ringed top, amber 121

Superior Soda Water - design of a spread-winged eagle & shield, cylindrical w/applied sloping collar, iron pontil, grass green, 7 3/4" h. (overall stain, several chips & bruises around lip)................... 275

Superior Soda Water - design of a spread-winged eagle & shield, cylindrical w/applied sloping collar, iron pontil, medium sapphire blue, 7 7/8" h. (iridescent bruise on inside of lip, some scratching & stain)...................................... 154

Taylor & Co. Soda Waters San Francisco, Eureka, cylindrical w/applied blob top & iron pontil, dark sapphire blue, 1850s (wear, uncleaned)............................ 341

Thomas (C.) - Truckee, Hutchinson stopper four-piece tooled top, California, ca. 1890s, aqua 330

Townsend's (Dr.) - Sarsaparilla - Albany, N.Y., square w/beveled corners & applied sloping collar, ca. 1845-55, deep forest green, 9 1/2" h.................................. 385

Townsend's (Dr.) - Sarsaparilla - Albany, N.Y., square w/beveled corners & applied sloping collar, ca. 1845-55, deep emerald green, 9 1/2" h.............................. 495

Townsend's (Dr.) - Sarsaparilla - Albany, N.Y., square w/beveled corners & applied sloping collar, iron pontil, ca. 1845-55, sapphire blue, 9 1/2" h. (repair in base) 523

Townsend's (Dr.) - Sarsaparilla - Albany, N.Y., - IIII, square w/beveled corners & applied sloping collar, ca. 1845-55, deep olive green, 9 1/2" h. 413

Tweddale's - Mineral Waters, cylindrical w/applied sloping collar mouth, open pontil, ca. 1840-50, medium emerald green, 6 1/8" h. (chip off side of lip)............. 303

Tweddle's Celebrated Soda or Mineral Water - Courtland Street - 38 New York, cylindrical w/applied blob top & iron pontil, very minor ground imperfections, ca. 1845-55, cobalt blue, 7 1/4" h. (ILLUS. top next column) 209

Tweddle's Soda Water Bottle

Twedles' Celebrated Soda or Mineral Waters - Courtland Street 38 New York, cylindrical w/applied sloping collar, ca. 1845-55, medium bluish green, 7" h. (tiny lip flake)............................... 66

Vincent & Hathaway Soda Bottle

V - Vincent & Hathaway - Boston - H - A.B.C. Co. - New Haven Ct - Pat. Jan. 5th 1864, cylindrical w/applied mouth & smooth base, ca. 1864-70, cobalt blue, 6 1/2" h. (ILLUS.)... 275

Vermont Spring - Saxe & Co. - Sheldon Vt., cylindrical w/a tall tapering neck & applied sloping double collar mouth, olive green, ca. 1870-80, qt. 99

Vermont Spring - Saxe & Co. - Sheldon Vt., cylindrical w/a tall tapering neck & applied sloping double collar mouth, peach puce, ca. 1870-80, qt. (faint bruise on shoulder) 330

Voelker and Bro. Cleveland, O, w/"V&B"
on base, applied top, smooth base, light
cobalt blue (needs cleaning) 77

Wagner (A.) & Co., Philada - W, cylindrical
w/applied blob mouth, ca. 1855-65, deep
emerald green, 7 1/4" h. 72

Washington Lithia Well Bottle

Washington Lithia Well Mineral Water,
Ballston Spa, N.Y., cylindrical w/applied
sloping double collar, ca. 1865-75, deep
bluish aqua, pt., 7 3/4" h. (ILLUS.) 468

Washington Spring - Saratoga - N.Y.,
cylindrical w/rounded shoulder, applied
sloping double collar mouth, medium
emerald green, ca. 1865-80, pt. 198

Washington Spring - Saratoga - N.Y.,
cylindrical w/rounded shoulder, applied
sloping double collar mouth, deep emer-
ald green, ca. 1865-80, pt. 231

Williams & Severance, cylindrical
w/applied blob top, iron pontil, sapphire
blue, ca. 1852-54 303

Williams & Severance San Francisco,
Cal. Soda and Mineral Waters, cylindrical w/applied blob top, iron pontil, dark
green, ca. 1852-54 198

Winkle (Henry) Sac. City, applied top, iron
pontil, California, 1852-54, greenish
aqua (minor haze) 209

Wise (J.) - Allentown - PA - This Bottle -
Belongs To - James Wise, cylindrical
w/long neck & applied sloping double
collar, ca. 1855-65, deep cobalt blue,
7" h. 121

Young (Philip) & Co., Savannah, Ga. -
design of spread-winged eagle &
shield, cylindrical w/applied mouth,
smooth base, medium teal blue,
7 3/8" h. (lightly cleaned) 550

PICKLE BOTTLES & JARS

Amber, six-sided cathedral-type, tooled
mouth, smooth base, ca. 1880-1890,
13 3/8" h. 1,265

Apple green, four-sided cathedral-type
w/Gothic windows, applied mouth,
smooth base, ca. 1855-1865, light to
medium apple green, 10 7/8" h. 440

Aqua, four-sided cathedral-type, double-
ring tooled mouth, smooth base, "S.J.G."
on one panel, ca. 1855-65, 7 1/4" h. 209

Aqua, four-sided cathedral-type, rolled lip,
double neck ring, graphite pontil,
8 1/4" h. (lightly cleaned) 358

Aqua, lobe-sided, iron pontil, "W.K. Lewis &
Co." 475

Aqua, square w/applied top, double neck
ring & shoulder scrolling, iron pontil,
embossed "W. D. Smith, N.Y.," lots of
whittle 750

Aqua, cathedral-type, rolled lip, double
neck ring tapering to fishtail shoulder
scroll, iron pontil, embossed "Albany
Glass Works," ca. 1850-1860, 8 5/8" h. 990

Aqua, square w/double neck ring, shoulder
scrolling, obverse & reverse diamond
panel embossing, W. D. Smith, N.Y., ca.
1839-1959, 8 3/4" h. 700

Aqua, six-sided cathedral-type w/Gothic
windows, rolled lip, open pontil, marked
"T. Smith & Co." around shoulder, ca.
1850-1860, 9 1/2" h. 688

Aqua, square, rolled lip w/tapering shoul-
der collar, iron pontil, embossed "64 oz.
William - Underwood - & Company -
Boston," ca. 1850-1860, 12 1/2" h. 187

Bluish-green, four-sided cathedral-type
w/Gothic windows, rolled lip, iron
pontil, ca. 1855-1865, 11 3/4" h. 1,265

Cathedral-type Pickle Jar

Citron, four-sided cathedral-type, four
Gothic arches, ringed wide applied
neck, ca. 1855-65, 11 5/8" h. (ILLUS.) 468

Deep aqua, cathedral-type, four Gothic arches w/ornate finials, wide ringed neck w/rolled lip, ca. 1855-65, 11 3/4" h. **253**

Deep bluish aqua, four-sided cathedral-type, diamond lattice design in windows, double-ringed molded mouth, smooth base, 7 3/8" h. **193**

Deep bluish aqua, rectangular w/paneled sides & wide applied mouth, marked "Anchor Pickle And Vinegar Works," smooth base marked "H.N. & Co.," ca. 1880, 8" h. (potstone on one side w/small radiations) **44**

Deep greenish aqua, four-sided cathedral-type, double-ringed tooled neck, smooth base, crude, 11 1/2" h. **220**

Deep purple, four-sided w/rounded panels, double-ringed tooled neck, 7" h...................... **77**

Emerald green, four-sided cathedral-type w/Gothic arch windows, rolled lip, iron pontil, ca. 1850-1860, 11 1/2" h. **2,530**

Emerald green, four-sided cathedral-type w/Gothic arch windows, rolled lip, smooth base, ca. 1860-1870, 13 3/4" h. **143**

Early Sanborn Boston Pickle Bottle

Greenish-aqua, paneled body w/petal-style embossing on shoulder & base, rolled lip, ca. 1855-1865, 10 5/8" h............... **330**

Golden Amber Early Pickle Bottle

Golden amber, four-sided w/rounded panels, double-ringed tooled neck, 8" h. (ILLUS.)... **121**

Golden yellow amber, tapering cylindrical form w/molded ground lip & smooth base, embossed on the side w/"G.P. Sanborn & Son - Union (inside shield & star) - Boston Pickle," ground lip, smooth base, 5 1/8" h. (ILLUS. top of next column) **143**

Green aqua, four-sided cathedral-type w/star & diamond design in windows & molded shoulders, double-ringed molded mouth, smooth base, ca. 1860-70, 11 1/2" h. **242**

Green (deep to medium), square w/applied top, two neck rings & vertically ribbed, open pontil, ca. 1839-1859, 7 1/2" h... **1,700**

Greenish aqua, square w/two rings & vertical ribs on neck, rolled lip, iron pontil, embossed "W.D.S. N.Y.," ca. 1855-1865, 7 3/4" h. **198**

Ribbed Amber Pickle Jar

Medium amber, square heavily ribbed sides w/rounded corners & wide applied mouth, tiny flake inside lip, ca. 1855-70, 8 1/4" h. (ILLUS.).. **231**

Four-sided Cathedral Pickle

Medium blue green, four-sided cathedral-type, double-ringed molded mouth, iron pontil, ca. 1855-65, small bruise inside lip, some minor grinding, 11 3/8" h. (ILLUS.) **468**

Rare Cylindrical Pickle Bottle

Medium green, cylindrical w/top & base rings & paneled rounded shoulder, applied mouth, iron pontil, ca. 1855-65, some milky inside stain, 12 1/4" h. (ILLUS.) **1,705**

Pale blue aqua, six-sided cathedral-type, double-ring tooled neck, embossed "I.C. CO." on base, one gal., 13" h. (some scratches) **165**

Early Reddish Amber Pickle Bottle

Red amber, four-sided w/recessed ribbing & outset columnar corners, applied top, smooth base, ca. 1860-75, lightly cleaned, 8 1/4" h. (ILLUS.) **358**

Teal blue, cathedral-type, rolled lip, double neck ring tapering to fishtail shoulder scroll, iron pontil, embossed "J McCollick & Co New York," ca. 1850-1860, 8 5/8" h. **1,650**

Yellow green, round, rolled lip, pontil-scarred base, ca. 1850-1860, embossed "Wm. Numsen & Sons Baltimore," 9 1/4" h. **330**

Yellow olive, round w/tooled mouth, smooth base, embossed "Skilton Foote & Co. S Trade [motif of monument] Mark Bunker Hill Pickles" on body, "Onions, from Skilton, Foote & Co., Bunker Hill Pickles" on 100% original label, 7 3/8" h. **176**

Yellow w/amber tone, square w/cathedral panels, tooled mouth, smooth base, 98% original label marked "Arrow Brand Pickles, J. J. Wilson Chicago," ca. 1880-1900, 8 5/8" h. **358**

Yellow w/olive amber tone, "Bunker Hill Pickles" w/embossed monument, 6 1/2" h., Twilight Rose patt. **140**

Skilton Foote & Cos. Pickle Bottle

Yellowish amber, cylindrical w/wide applied mouth, "Skilton Foote & Cos Bunker Hill Pickles" w/trademark, professionally cleaned, 7 3/4" h. (ILLUS.) **55**

POISONS

Amber, cylindrical embossed "Poison - Wyeth," 100% of original front & back paper labels, ABM lip, smooth base, ca. 1890-1910, 2 1/4" h. **220**

Clear, cylindrical w/tooled top & some exterior striations, embossed "Strychinia Poison," 2 1/2" h. **44**

Clear, flask-form, flattened round body w/mold-blown swirled broken-rib design, base pontil, probably Europe, ca. 1800-40, 6 1/2" h. **94**

Clear, flask-shaped w/overall mold-blown Hobnail patt., sheared lip, pontil, ca. 1845-55, 4 3/8" h. **110**

Large Diamond Lattice Poison Bottle

Cobalt blue, cylindrical w/overall embossed diamond lattice design, tooled lip, smooth base, ca. 1890-1910, 11 1/4" h. (ILLUS.).. **413**

Cobalt blue, rectangular w/beveled ribbed corners, "Poison" down the side, 4 1/4" h.. **44**

Rare Skull Poison Bottle

Cobalt blue, small figural skull, marked "Poison - Pat. Appl'd for," base marked "Pat June 26th 1894," light milky overall haze & crazing lines, 2 7/8" h. (ILLUS.) **1,925**

Cobalt blue, square w/beveled corners, tooled mouth, marked "Poison (skull & crossbones) Demert Drug & Chemical Co. Spokane," smooth bottom marked "W.T. Co, U.S.A.," ca. 1890, 5 5/8" h. (ILLUS. top of next column) **2,750**

Cobalt blue, square w/beveled corners w/"Poison," embossed stars & skull & crossbones on sides, w/original paper label, ABM, probably ca. 1915, small........... **143**

Rare Demert Poison Bottle

Cobalt blue, square w/ribbed sides w/tooled lip & original sawtooth-edged stopper, plain front panel & side panels w/"Poison," smooth base marked "E.R.S. & S.," ca. 1890, 4 5/8" h. (edge of stopper chipped) **440**

Cobalt blue, three-sided w/embossed "Poison" on one side, design of owl & mortar & pestle on second & "The Owl Drug Co." on third, tooled lip, smooth base, ca. 1900-1910, 4 7/8" h. **88**

Cobalt blue, triangular w/rounded shoulder & tooled mouth, marked "Poison - [molded design of owl on mortar & pestle] - The Owl Drug Co.," 8" h. **385**

Green, rectangular w/ribbed beveled corners w/"Poison" & "The Sun Drug Company" on the front, 4" h............................... **231**

Medium moss green, three-sided embossed w/skull & crossbones & "De-Dro Gift Flasche Der Deutscher Drogisten Verbandes," ABM lip, smooth base, ca. 1910-20, Germany, 4 3/8" h. **605**

German Green Poison Bottle

Olive green, six-sided w/embossed skull & crossbones panels alternating w/"Poison - Gift" on panels, ABM lip, smooth base, Germany, ca.   1910-20,   9 3/4" h. (ILLUS.) **358**

Turquoise blue overlay, three-sided w/diamond lattice design & "Poison - Poison," tooled mouth, smooth base, w/original coffin-shaped pills each marked "Poison," ca. 1890-1910, slight wear, 5 1/4" h. **132**

Small Amber Poison Bottle

Yellowish amber, cylindrical w/tooled mouth, overall latticework design w/a central panel w/"Poison" on each side of a skull & crossbones, a five-point star above & below the skull, ca. 1890, 4 3/4" h. (ILLUS.).. **550**

WHISKEY & OTHER SPIRITS

Beer, "Bay View Brewing Co., Seattle, Wash. - Not To Be Sold," cylindrical w/applied mouth & original marked porcelain stopper & wire bail, medium olive green, ca. 1890, 11 3/4" h. (wire bail broken) **303**

Beer, "C. Conrad & Co's Original Budweiser U.S. Patent No. 6376," cylindrical w/lady's-leg neck & applied mouth, aqua, 9 1/4" h. (lightly cleaned)...................... **99**

Beer, "Capitol Bottling Works Petaluma, Cal." w/monogram, "P.C.G.W." on base, cylindrical w/tall neck, amber, qt. (minor stain) **44**

Beer, "Fredericksburg Bottling Co. S.F." in ring w/shield & monogram, cylindrical w/tall neck & wire & porcelain stopper, green, qt. **44**

Gambrinus Brewing Co. Bottle

Beer, "Gambrinus Brewing Co., G.B. Co., Portland, Or.," cylindrical w/lady's-leg neck & tooled mouth, "S.B. & G. Co." on smooth base, amber, ca. 1890, some inside stain, tiny "peck" mark on shoulder, 11 1/4" h. (ILLUS.) **33**

Golden Gate Beer Bottle

Beer, "Golden Gate Bottling Works, Trade (design of bear drinking from stein) Mark, San Francisco," cylindrical w/tooled top & original wire bail & porcelain stopper, medium yellow amber, ca. 1900, 7 3/4" h. (ILLUS.).................................. **55**

Unique Beer Bottle with Seal

Beer, "Phoenix Bott'g Phila This Bottle Not To Be Sold" on applied shoulder seal, cylindrical w/applied mouth & smooth base, original lightning-type closure, ca. 1885-95, olive green, chip on lower edge of seal, 9 3/8" h. (ILLUS.) **413**

Early Rainier Beer Bottle

Beer, "Rainier Beer, Seattle, U.S.A.," cylindrical w/lady's-leg neck & tooled lip, amber, fragments of original foil wrapper on neck, ca. 1900, 5 1/2" h. (ILLUS.) **66**

Beer, "Richmond Bottling Works," cylindrical w/tall neck & wire & porcelain stopper, amber, qt. (some interior haze) **77**

Beer, "The Phoenix Brewery Co. Victoria B.C." w/embossed phoenix, cylindrical w/pontiled base & applied top, dark olive green, qt. (cleaned, some scratches) **154**

Beer, "Tivoli Brewing Co. Registered Detroit Mich." in seal on shoulder, cylindrical w/tall neck, dark amber, qt. (few scratches) **33**

Beer, "Wreden's Lager Oakland Cal.," cylindrical w/tall neck, amber, qt. **44**

Red Wing Brewing Co. Beer Bottle

Beer, "Red Wing Brewing Co., Red Wing, Minn.," embossed wording, attached porcelain stopper, amber, rare, 15" h. (ILLUS.) **95**

Bourbon, "Cutter (J.H.) Old Bourbon A.P. Hotaling & Co., Portland, O.," tapering flask form w/applied mouth, smoky clear, pt. (small pressure ding on top, stained) **330**

Rare Dallimores Brandy Bottle

Brandy, "Dallimores - Celebrated - Brandy - 130 Broome St. - N.R. Broadway - New York," paneled cylinder w/applied straight double collar, small flake at base of one panel, ca. 1845-55, deep olive green, 7 1/8" h. (ILLUS.) **2,860**

Case gin, free-blown square tapering shape w/small crude applied top, open pontil, 1770-1830, light olive green **143**

Case gin, free-blown tall slender square tapering shape w/applied flared lip, large open pontil, possibly 17th c., medium olive green, 9 1/2" h. **66**

Cognac, "Cognac - W. & Co." (in seal), squatty bulbous tapering to a cylindrical neck w/applied mouth & neck handle, ca. 1860-70, medium amber, 5 3/4" h. **660**

Gin, "Cosmopoliet J.J. Melchers W.Z. Schiedam," tall square tapering form, dark green, 1850-70, 11" h. **121**

Kiderlen Celebrated Old Gin

Gin, "Kiderlen Rotterdam Celebrated Old Gin," barrel-shaped, tooled mouth, light olive green, crack down from lip, 8 1/2" h. (ILLUS.).. **176**

Gin, "London - Jockey - Club House - Gin" w/design of jockey on horse, square w/rounded shoulder & short neck w/applied sloping collar, iron pontil, ca. 1855-70, amber, 9 5/8" h. (tiny collar flake) **523**

Mead, "Champagne Mead," eight-sided cylinder w/applied blob top, smooth base, greenish blue (few dings at bottom corners) **110**

Schnapps, "Burke's (E. & J.) Schiedam Schnapps," square w/beveled corners, applied sloping collar mouth, smooth base, ca. 1880-1900, deep olive amber, 8" h. **77**

Schnapps, "Gayen (J.T.) Schiedam Schnapps," square w/beveled corners, applied mouth, smooth base, ca. 1880-90, medium yellow olive green, 7 5/8" h. **54**

Schnapps, "Nolet (A.C.A.) Schiedam Aromatic Schnapps," square w/beveled corners, applied sloping collar mouth, smooth base, ca. 1875-90, bright yellow olive, 9 3/8" h. **94**

Schnapps, "Royal Club - Schnapps - Schiedam," square w/beveled corners, applied sloping collar mouth, smooth base, ca. 1880-1900, yellowish olive green, 7 3/4" h. **54**

Schade & Buysing's Schnapps Bottle

Schnapps, "Schade & Buysing's - Schiedam - Aromatic Schnapps," square w/beveled corners, applied sloping collar mouth, smooth base, 80% paper label w/"Sparrow Schiedam," ca. 1885-1900, medium olive green, 9" h. (ILLUS.) **88**

Schnapps, "Schiedam Schnapps - Aromatico," square w/beveled corners, applied sloping collar, smooth base, ca. 1855-65, deep olive amber, 9 1/4" h. **55**

Silver Stream Schnapps Bottle

Schnapps, "Silver Stream Schnapps - W & A Gilbey," tall square form w/beveled corners, applied sloping collar mouth, smooth base, ca. 1880-90, olive green w/amber tone, 8 3/8" h. (ILLUS.)................... **77**

Schnapps, "Udolpho Wolfe's Aromatic Schnapps, Schiedam," rectangular w/beveled corners, applied sloping collar mouth, dark green w/yellow tone, 9 3/8" h. **55**

Schnapps, "Udolpho Wolfe's Aromatic Schnapps, Schiedam," rectangular w/beveled corners, applied sloping collar mouth, olive green w/amber tone, 9 3/8" h. **77**

Schnapps, "Udolpho Wolfe's Aromatic Schnapps, Schiedam," rectangular w/beveled corners, applied sloping collar mouth, ca. 1880-90, medium olive green, 3 1/2" h.. **198**

Udolpho Wolfe's Schnapps Bottle

Schnapps, "Udolpho Wolfe's Aromatic Schnapps, Schiedam," rectangular w/beveled corners, applied sloping collar mouth, smooth base, ca. 1860-70, medium apricot puce, 8 1/4" h. (ILLUS.) **220**

Schnapps, "Udolpho Wolfe's Aromatic Schnapps, Schiedam," rectangular w/beveled corners, applied sloping collar mouth, smooth base, ca. 1885-90, medium blue green, 9" h. **275**

Schnapps, "Van Brunt's Aromatic Schnapps, Schiedam," square w/beveled corners, applied sloping collar, deep olive green, some inside stain, 10" h. (ILLUS. top of next column) **132**

Schnapps, "Voldner's Aromatic Schnapps Schiedam," applied top, smooth base, bright medium lime green (minor scratches)..................................... **88**

Schnapps, "Vollmar Schnapps," square w/beveled corners, tooled mouth, smooth base, ca. 1890-1900, bluish aqua, 8" h. **39**

Van Brunt's Aromatic Schnapps

Schnapps, "Wolfe's (Hudson G.) - large embossed bell - Bell Schnapps," square w/beveled corners, applied mouth, smooth base, ca. 1870-80, medium amber, 9 7/8" h. (cleaned) **99**

Spirits, club-form, tall neck w/applied rim, swirled broken-rib design, yellow olive, Midwestern, ca. 1820-30, 8 1/8" h............. **4,400**

Spirits, club-shaped, twenty-four swirled ribs, aqua, early 19th c., 7 3/8" h. (minor wear) **94**

Spirits, free-blown, globular, amber, 11 3/4" h. (broken surface blisters, light stain) **303**

Spirits, free-blown mallet-form, pontil w/deep kick-up, applied string lip, deep olive amber, England, ca. 1730-45, 8" h. **440**

Spirits, free-blown onion-form w/tall neck & applied string lip, pontilled base, medium yellowish olive green, Europe, ca. 1715-30, 6 7/8" h. **143**

Spirits, globular, mold-blown, twenty-four swirled ribs, good impression, aqua, 7 1/2" h. (stain, lip chips) **154**

Rare Early English Seal Bottle

Spirits, "Greive (B) - 1727" seal bottle, bulbous cylindrical body tapering to a tall neck w/applied string lip & applied seal, open pontil, England, ca.1727, medium olive green, 4 1/2" d. base, 6 1/4" h. (ILLUS.) **5,720**

Spirits, mold-blown, globular, twenty-four swirled ribs, Zanesville, Ohio, amber, 7 1/2" h. (stain, wear) **220**

Spirits, mold-blown, globular, twenty-four swirled ribs, Zanesville, Ohio, amber, 7 1/2" h. (stain) **385**

Spirits, squat bulbous form w/tall tapering neck w/applied ring, free-blown open pontil, deep emerald green-black, ca. 1650, 7 1/4" h. (chipping on lip in making) **1,210**

Spirits, squatty onion-form, free-blown, tall tapering neck w/applied ring, open pontil, Holland, 1720-35, emerald green **198**

Early Dated Onion-shaped Bottle

Spirits, "Watt (Nath) - 1718" seal bottle, squatty bulbous onion shape, tall tapering neck w/silver mouth band & applied seal, open pontil, minor content stain, England, ca. 1718, 5 3/4" d. base, 6 7/8" h. (ILLUS.) **3,630**

Early Zanesville Bottle with Handle

Spirits, globular, short neck w/rolled rim, applied strap handle w/end crimp, twenty-four ribs swirled to the left, medium amber, Zanesville, Ohio, ca. 1820-30, V-shaped stress crack from end of handle, 6 1/2" h. (ILLUS.) **4,620**

Spirits, globular, tall neck w/rolled rim, twenty-four ribs swirled to the left, unusual wide neck, yellow w/strong olive tone, Midwestern, ca. 1820-30, 7 3/8" h.... **1,018**

Spirits, globular, tall ribbed neck, broken-rib patt., rolled lip, Midwestern, ca, 1820, medium amber, 7 1/2" h. (some milky inside stain) **8,250**

Spirits, globular, plain body w/tall neck, rolled rim, medium yellowish amber, Midwestern, ca. 1820-30, 7 7/8" h............... **275**

Spirits, globular, tall neck w/rolled rim, twenty-four ribs swirled to the left, medium amber, Midwestern, ca. 1820-30, 8" h. **468**

Spirits, club-form, tall neck w/applied rim, twenty-four broken ribs swirled to the right, medium sapphire blue, Midwestern, ca. 1820-30, 8 1/4" h............. **8,525**

Spirits, globular, tall neck w/rolled lip, twenty-four ribs swirled to the left, lots of bubbles, yellowish amber, Midwestern, ca. 1820-30, 9 5/8" h................ **577**

Ambrosial Sealed Chestnut Flask

Whiskey, "Ambrosial - B.M. & E.A.W. & Co." on seal, chestnut flask-shaped w/applied mouth, handle & seal, open pontil, ca. 1860-70, yellowish amber, 9 1/2" h. (ILLUS.) **413**

Rare Bininger Cannon Bottle

Whiskey, "Bininger (A.M.) & Co. - 19 Broad St. - N.Y.," cannon-shaped, sheared lip, smooth base, 60% original paper label w/"Great Gun Bourbon," ca. 1855-70, medium amber, 12 1/2" h. (ILLUS. front & back) 585

Bininger Barrel-shaped Bottle

Whiskey, "Bininger (A.M.) & Co. 19 Broad St. N.Y. - Distilled in 1848 - Old Kentucky - Bourbon - 1849 Reserve" w/embossed clock face, ringed barrel shape w/applied double collar mouth, open pontil, ca. 1855-65, medium amber, 8 1/8" h. (ILLUS.) 253

Whiskey, "Bininger (A.M.) & Co 338 Broadway N.Y. - Distilled in 1848 - Old Kentucky - 1849 Reserve Bourbon," ringed barrel shape w/applied double collar mouth, open pontil, ca. 1855-65, medium amber, 8" h. 204

Whiskey, "Bininger (A.M.) & Co. New York," square w/beveled corners, applied sloping collar mouth, smooth base, ca. 1855-70, medium amber, 9 3/4" h. 94

Whiskey, "Bininger's (clock face) Regulator 19 Broad St. New York," round flat shape w/faint clock face, applied double collar mouth, open pontil, ca. 1855-65, yellow amber, 6" h. 495

Whiskey, "Binninger's Night Cap No. 19 Broad St. N.Y.," flattened rectangular form w/short neck & applied mouth w/internal screw threads, smooth base, ca. 1855-70, medium amber, 8 1/4" h. (stopper missing) 209

Whiskey, "Binninger's Regulator, 19 Broad St., New York" around molded clock face, 100% paper label on reverse w/printed clock face & same inscription, applied double collar, medium amber, 6" h. 2,315

Whiskey, "Brent. Warder & Co. - Louisville, KY," ringed barrel-shape w/applied mouth, smooth base, ca. 1865-75, medium copper puce, 6 7/8" h. (light content stain)... 2,255

Whiskey, "Buffalo Old Bourbon (design of buffalo) Geo. E. Dierssen & Co. Sacramento, Cal.," cylindrical w/tall neck & tooled mouth, smooth base, ca. 1890-1910, clear, 11 7/8" h. 605

Whiskey, "C.A. Richards & Co., 99 Washington St., Boston," square w/beveled corners, reversed "Ns" in molded text, applied sloping collar, deep reddish amber, 9 1/2" h.. 94

Whiskey, "Carhart & Brother N.Y." on applied seal, handled chestnut flask-shape, applied mouth & handle, iron pontil, ca.1855-70, deep puce, 9" h........... 1,705

Rare Carhart Chestnut Flask Whiskey

Whiskey, "Carhart & Brother N.Y." on applied seal, handled chestnut flask-shape, applied mouth & handle, iron pontil, ca.1855-70, medium smoky topaz puce, 8 3/4" h. (ILLUS.)............................ 2,035

Whiskey, "Caspers Whiskey - Made by Honest - North - Carolina People," cylindrical w/long lappets w/dots around the shoulder & a reeded neck w/a tooled mouth, smooth base, ca. 1880-90, deep cobalt blue, 12 3/8" h................................. 523

Rare Caspers Whiskey Clear Bottle

Whiskey, "Caspers Whiskey - Made by Honest - North - Carolina People," cylindrical w/long lappets w/dots around the shoulder & a reeded neck w/a tooled mouth, smooth base, ca. 1880-90, clear w/amethystine tint, 12" h. (ILLUS.).............. **578**

Whiskey, "Ce Tooraen Bayou Sara, La." embossed around shoulder, cylindrical w/tall neck & applied collar, stepped base, dark olive green, early rare Louisiana bottle, 11 1/2" h. **3,520**

Chestnut Grove Whiskey Flask

Whiskey, "Chestnut Grove Whiskey, C.W.," chestnut flask-shaped w/applied neck handle, applied mouth, medium amber, 8 7/8" h. (ILLUS.) **154**

Whiskey, "Chestnut Grove Whiskey, C.W." on applied seal, chestnut flask-shaped w/applied mouth w/spout & applied handle, open pontil, medium root beer amber, 8 1/2" h... **209**

Whiskey, "Chestnut Grove Whiskey, C.W." on applied seal, chestnut flask-shaped w/applied mouth w/spout & applied handle, open pontil, ca. 1860-70, yellow olive, 8 5/8" h... **2,090**

Whiskey, "Clinch & Co. Liquor Dealers, Grass Valley," coffin flask, applied sloping mouth, clear, half pint **303**

Whiskey, "Crown Distilleries Company," cylindrical w/tall neck w/tooled lip & inside screw threads, amber, pt. (half-open bubble on shoulder) **55**

Whiskey, "Cutter (R.B.), Louisville, KY," ovoid w/applied mouth & handle, partial paper label on reverse w/"Woodbury, New Jersey," golden amber, 8 3/4" h. **413**

R.B. Cutter Pure Bourbon Bottle

Whiskey, "Cutter (R.B.) Pure Bourbon," ovoid body w/applied mouth & handle, iron pontil, ca. 1855-65, two small stress cracks at handle, strawberry puce, 8 3/4" h. (ILLUS.)... **303**

Whiskey, "Davy Crocket Pure Old Bourbon, Hey, Grauderholz & Co., S.F. Sole Agents," cylindrical w/tall neck & tooled mouth, ca. 1900, medium orangish amber, 12" h... **110**

Whiskey, "Duffy' Formula" embossed on one side, original intact paper label on other side, tall slender cylindrical shape w/applied mouth & smooth base, ca. 1880-90, medium amber, 9 7/8" h............... **242**

Whiskey, "Duffy's Malt Whiskey Company - D.M.W. Co. (monogram) - Rochester, N.Y. U.S.A.," on base "Patd. Aug. 24 - 1886," cylindrical w/tooled mouth & smooth base, 85% original front & back paper labels, ca. 1890-1910, amber, 8 1/4" h. **44**

Rare E.G. Booz Whiskey Bottle

Whiskey, "E.G. Booz's Old Cabin Whiskey
- 1840 - E.G. Booz's Old Cabin Whiskey
- 120 Walnut St., Philadelphia," cabin-
shaped, straight roof, overall milky inside
stain, deep amber, 7 5/8" h. (ILLUS.) **3,300**

Forest Lawn Whiskey Bottle

Whiskey, "Forest Lawn - J.V.H.," spherical
body w/tall neck & applied mouth, iron
pontil, ca. 1855-65, deep olive green,
7 1/2" h. (ILLUS.) **440**

Whiskey, "From Wine House Liquors &
Cigars Reno, Nev.," pumpkinseed flask,
clear, half pint **1,540**

Whiskey, "G.D. & M. Baltimore" on applied
shoulder seal, wide cylindrical body
w/rounded shoulder & tall neck
w/applied sloping double collar
mouth, ca. 1870-85, medium amber,
9 1/2" h. **303**

Whiskey, "G.W. Huntington" (on applied
seal), cylindrical w/wide rounded shoulder w/seal, applied sloping collar, ca.
1855-65, medium bluish green,
11 3/4" h. **468**

Whiskey, "Gaines (W.A.) Old Crow Whiskey, The Capital, Cheyenne, Wyo.,"
flask-shaped w/neck screw threads,
clear, half pint **264**

Whiskey, "Gilmor & Gibson, Importers,
Baltimore" (on applied seal), cylindrical
w/wide rounded shoulder, tall neck &
applied sloping collar, ca. 1870-80, red
amber, 9 3/4" h. **303**

Whiskey, "Good Old Bourbon - In A Hogs"
w/arrow, pig-shaped, ca. 1885-1900,
clear, 6 7/8" l. **99**

Whiskey, "Graves (Jno.H.) Old Kentucky
Whiskey San Jose Cal.," w/full paper
label 90% intact, cylindrical w/tall neck &
tooled top, amber, 1910-15, fifth **88**

Whiskey, "Griffith Hyatt & Co. - Baltimore,"
bulbous ovoid shape tapering to neck
w/applied mouth & applied handle, open
pontil, ca. 1860-70, medium tobacco
amber, 7 1/8" h. **523**

Whiskey, "Lilienthal and Co. Distillers"
w/embossed crown in circular slug plate,
coffin flask-form, amber, 1885-90, pt. **2,090**

Whiskey, "McFarlane & Co. Honolulu"
w/monogram, cylindrical w/tall tapering
neck & applied collar, amber, fifth **99**

Whiskey, "Melczer & Co. (Jos.) Wholesale
Liquor Dealers San Francisco, Cal.,"
flask w/applied tapering mouth, clear,
half pint **99**

Whiskey, "Miller's Extra Trade Mark - E.
Martin & Co. Old Bourbon," flask-shaped
w/applied mouth & smooth base, small
letter variant, ca. 1875-80, rich yellow
olive, 7 1/2" h. (small stress crack in
neck) **1,540**

Whiskey, "Mohawk Pure Rye Whiskey,
Patented Feb. 11, 1868," figural Indian
queen w/shield, rolled lip, golden amber,
12 5/8" h. **2,315**

Rare Moore Western Whiskey Flask

Whiskey, "Moore (Jesse) and Co. Louisville KY. Trademark Moore Hunt and
Co.," flask-shaped w/double applied collar mouth, w/monogram & deer antlers,
deep olive amber, minor imperfections,
cleaned (ILLUS.) **6,050**

Whiskey, "Old Bourbon Castle Whiskey -
F. Chevalier & Co., Sole Agents," cylindrical w/tall neck & tooled lip, medium
orangish amber, 12" h. **231**

Whiskey, "Old Monongahela, C (sheaf of
wheat) H, Rye Whiskey," cylindrical
w/wide rounded shoulder w/seal, applied
sloping collar, ca.1865-75, olive amber,
9 1/2" h. (ILLUS. top of next page) **330**

Whiskey, "Old Velvet Brandy, S.M. & Co."
(on applied seal w/necklace), conical
w/tall neck & applied double collar, inter-
nally ribbed, ca. 1855-70, medium
amber, 9 7/8" h. **688**

Whiskey, "Patent" on shoulder, "Wm.
McCully & Co. Pittsburgh" (on base),
cylindrical w/lady's leg neck, applied
double collar mouth, smooth base, ca.
1860-70, yellowish beer amber,
11 1/2" h. **121**

Old Monongahela Rye Whiskey

Whiskey, "Peerless (in script) Whiskey [in banner], Wolf, Wreden Co. Sole Agents, S.F.," cylindrical w/tall neck & tooled lip, medium orangish gold, 11 7/8" h. **440**

Whiskey, "Potts & Potts - Atlanta, Ga." (on applied seal), cylindrical w/tall neck w/applied sloping double collar, medium amber, ca. 1870, 9 1/2" h. **264**

Whiskey, "R. & S. (monogram) - Roehling & Schutz, Inc. - Chicago," four-roof cabin-shape, smooth base, tooled mouth, ca. 1880-1890, amber, 9 3/4" h. (small flake on edge of one roof panel) **242**

Whiskey, "Rothenberg (D.) Co. Old Judge Kentucky Whiskey," w/picture of the judge drinking, cylindrical w/tall tapering neck w/applied collar, amber, fifth **33**

Whiskey, "Sacken Belcher & Co. 26 Pearl St. N.Y." on applied seal, chestnut flask-shaped w/applied mouth & handle, open pontil, ca. 1860-70, amber, 9" h. **1,650**

Silkwood Whiskey Bottle

Whiskey, "Silkwood Whiskey, Laventhal Bros., San Francisco, Cal.," cylindrical w/swirled ribs at base of the tall neck w/tooled lip, amber, ca. 1900, 11 3/8" h. (ILLUS.) **154**

Scarce Clear Nabob Whiskey Bottle

Whiskey, "Simmond's Nabob Pure KY Bourbon Whiskey," cylindrical w/embossed scene of nabob, tooled neck, small annealing check in neck, open bubble on top, cleaned, clear (ILLUS.) **523**

Rare Semi-Cabin Whiskey Bottle

Whiskey, "Smith (S.S.) & Co. - Cincinnati," semi-cabin shape, applied sloping collar mouth, smooth base, ca. 1860-70, medium cobalt blue, 9 5/8" h. (ILLUS.) **3,190**

Whiskey, "Sontaw's Old Cabinet Whiskey" (one applied seal), cylindrical w/sloping applied mouth, medium amber, 8 3/8" h. (cleaned) **183**

Star Whiskey Handled Bottle

Whiskey, "Star Whiskey New York W.B. Growell Jr." in oval, conical body w/applied mouth w/spout & applied handle w/tip of finial missing, large open pontil, ca. 1865-75, medium yellowish amber, 8" h. (ILLUS.) 242

Whiskey, "Taylor (G.O.)" on base, paper label w/"G.O. Taylor Pure Rye," cylindrical w/tall neck & tooled top, amber, fifth......... 44

Whiskey, "Teakettle Old Bourbon Shea, Bocqueraz & McKee Agents San Francisco" w/embossed teakettle, cylindrical w/tall neck & applied collar, bright amber, fifth (pressure ding on lip, open bubble on front) 385

Whiskey, "Warranted Flask From The Culpepper Liquor Co Culpeper, VA," flattened strap-sided flask, smooth base, tooled mouth, ca. 1890-1900, clear 413

Whiskey, "Wertz (S.A.) Phila Superior Old Rye Whiskey" on applied shoulder seal, wide cylindrical body w/rounded shoulder & neck w/applied sloping double collar mouth, smooth base, ca. 1870-80, yellow amber, 9 1/2" h. (tiny potstone on back) 94

Whiskey, "Wolters Bros. & Co. 115 & 117 Front Street SF," cylindrical w/tall neck & applied collar, brownish amber, fifth (minor dirt inside) 285

Wine, "Heller (A.) & Bro." under crest on applied neck seal, tall slender tapering cylindrical body w/applied mouth, smooth base, ca. 1880-90, reddish amber, 14" h.. 121

Wine, "Kohler & Van Bergen San Francisco" w/monogram & "1883," cylindrical w/slender neck & ringed mouth, seal on shoulder, dark green, qt. 143

Wine, "Napa Valley Wine Co. SF 1890" in seal on shoulder, cylindrical w/slender neck & ringed mouth, very dark green, qt. 55

Wine, "Paul O. Burns Wine Co. Proprietors Yerba Buena San Jose Cal. U.S." on shoulder seal, cylindrical w/lady's leg neck, applied collar, medium to deep olive green, ca. 1890s, qt. 143

BRYCE

From its factory in Mt. Pleasant, Pennsylvania Bryce produced lines of hand-crafted, mouth-blown glass until it became a part of Lenox circa 1965. Bryce produced a diverse number of stemware lines including many that incorporated two colors and exaggerated shaped stems. Colors include milk glass, Amberina, ruby, dark green, amethyst, light blue, cobalt blue, amber and others. Today it operates as Lenox Crystal

Basket, No. 1, rimmed edge, arched handle, 6" h. $42
Basket, No. 3, rimmed edge, arched handle, 10" h. 48
Bell, No. 1, dinner, twisted rope handle 38
Bowl, finger, Aquarius, Flame/ruby 32
Bowl, fruit, El Rancho, amber............................ 14
Candy jar, cov., low, no stem, "Turnabout," El Rancho, pink 36
Candy jar, cov., stemmed, El Rancho, blue....... 38
Cocktail, liquor contour, clear bowl & foot w/light blue marble stem 19
Goblet, water, amethyst bowl, clear foot & stem, inverted cone stem, No. 894 34
Goblet, water, Aquarius, blue bowl, cut stem No. 961 28
Goblet, water, Aquarius, ruby bowl, cut stem No. 961 32
Goblet, water, Carnation No. 366 plate etching.. 24
Goblet, water, clear w/green twist stem, No. 325.. 34
Goblet, water, El Rancho, amber...................... 12
Goblet, water, El Rancho, amethyst................... 14
Goblet, water, El Rancho, Flame/ruby 26
Goblet, water, El Rancho, milk glass 14

Bryce Laurel Cut Goblet

Goblet, water, Laurel cut, two wafer stem, clear, No. 575 (ILLUS.) 16
Pitcher, El Rancho, blue 62
Pitcher, El Rancho patt., Flame/ruby 84
Plate, El Rancho, Fame/ruby 27
Plate, 8" d., Kingsley floral spray cut No. 298 22

Plate, 8 1/4" d., Aquarius, amber....................... 20
Salt & pepper shakers, El Rancho,
Flame/ruby, pr. 38
Sherbet/champagne, Aquarius, dark
green bowl & foot, clear block stem 26
Sherbet/champagne, Delhi, chartreuse
bowl, clear stem & foot, bulging ribbed
stem 22
Sherbet/champagne, Delhi, dark green
bowl, clear stem & foot, bulging ribbed
stem 32
Teapot, cov., 56 oz.. 110
Tumbler, Carousel No. 603, Amberina
striped 36
Tumbler, flat, El Rancho, amber 9
Tumbler, flat, El Rancho, smoke...................... 12
Tumbler, footed, El Rancho, smoke 12
Tumbler, highball, Turkey Eagle applied
blue medallion, 5 1/4" h................................. 22
Tumbler, iced tea, Aquarius, blue bowl, cut
stem No. 961... 22
Tumbler, iced tea, El Rancho, Flame/ruby 22
Tumbler, juice, El Rancho, Flame/ruby.............. 16
Tumbler, Old Fashion, Indian Head applied
amber medallion... 18
Vase, 6" h., El Rancho, crimped top, milk
glass... 22
Vase, 15" h., El Rancho, crimped top, milk
glass... 36
Vase, "toddy," El Rancho, milk glass................. 28
Wine, amethyst bowl, colorless foot &
stem, four disk stem No. 657 32
Wine, Aquarius, blue bowl, cut stem No.
961 24
Wine, ruby bowl, clear foot & stem, three
knop & three wafer stem No. 625................... 38

CAMBRIDGE

*Cambridge Glass operated from 1902 until 1954
in Cambridge, Ohio. Early wares included numerous pressed glass in imitation of cut glass, often
clear and bearing an impressed mark of "NEAR
CUT" in the inside center of the object. Later products included color, stylized shapes, animals and
hand-cut and decorated tableware. Particularly
popular with collectors today are the Statuesque
line, popularly called Nude Stems, and a pink
opaque color called Crown Tuscan. When marked,
which is infrequently, the Cambridge mark is the
letter "C" in a triangle. Other authors have been
wise to remind us not to confuse this 20th century
company with the earlier New England Glass Company of Cambridge, Massachusetts, at times called
"Cambridge Glass."*

NEAR
CUT

TUSCAN

Cambridge Marks

ETCHED ROSE POINT PATTERN
Ashtray, clear, 4 1/2" $59
Bell, clear 148
Bowl, 13" d., 12" l., No. 3400/1, clear 85
Butter dish, cov., round, clear, 5 1/2" 200

Cake plate, handled, No. 3500, clear,
13 1/2" d.. 74
Cake plate, handled, No. 3900, clear,
14" d. 89
Candlestick, single-light, No. 3400, clear,
5 1/4" h. 42
Candlestick, single-light, No. 3900, clear,
4 1/2" h. 37
Candlestick, two-light, No. 3400, clear............. 59
Candy dish, cov., No. 3500/57, clear............... 125
Celery tray, No. 3500, clear, 11 1/2" l............... 54
Champagne, No. 3121, clear............................ 27

Rose Point Cocktail and Sherbet

Cocktail, No. 3500, clear, 3 oz. (ILLUS.
right) 35
Cordial, clear, 5 1/2" h. 82
Cordial, No. 3106, clear 250
Cordial, No. 7966, clear 165
Cup & saucer, No. 3400, clear 48
Cup & saucer, No. 3900, clear 42
Decanter w/stopper, No. 1320, clear 410
Goblet, water, clear, 8 3/4" h............................. 48
Lamp globe, hurricane-type, clear, 6" h.......... 190
Mayonnaise bowl, ladle & underplate,
No. 3400, clear, the set................................. 70
Nappy, No. 3500, 6 3/4" d. 39
Oyster cocktail, No. 3121, clear....................... 65
Pitcher, 7" h., No. 3400, clear 420
Pitcher, 8" h., No. 3400, Doulton-style,
clear 290
Plate, 8 1/2" d., No. 3500, clear......................... 27
Plate, 9 1/2" d., No. 3400, clear......................... 48
Plate, 10 1/4" d., No. 3400, clear..................... 160
Plate, 10 1/2" d., No. 3900, clear..................... 174
Relish dish, No. 3400, clear, 8" 56
Relish dish, two-part, No. 3400/1093, clear....... 85
Relish dish, two-part, No. 3500, clear,
8 1/2"... 48
Salt & pepper shakers, No. 3400, clear,
pr. 68
Sherbet, No. 3500, clear, tall 7 oz. (ILLUS.
left) 25
Tumbler, flat, No. 3400, clear, 2" h. 100

Tumbler, flat, No. 3400, clear, 4" h. 68
Tumbler, footed, clear, 7" h. 29
Tumbler, iced tea, clear, 7 1/2" h. 36
Tumbler, No. 497, clear, 8 oz. 125
Tumbler, No. 3400/38, clear, 12 oz. 85
Vase, bud, 8 1/2" h., clear 64
Wine, clear, 5 7/8" h. 94
Wine, clear, 6 1/4" h. 115

MISCELLANEOUS PATTERNS

Almond dish, individual, etched Cleo patt.,
pink, 2 1/2" 64
Ashtray, etched Minerva patt., clear 55
Ashtray, pressed Caprice patt., clear, 4" 10
Ashtray, Silhouette line, Royal Blue bowl
on clear Nude Lady stem 325
Ashtray/match holder, pressed Caprice
patt., Moonlight (light blue) 12
Basket, footed, two-handled, etched Diane
patt., clear, 6" h. 26
Basket, Janice patt., ruby w/clear handle 195
Basket, reeded handle, No. 3500/52, clear,
6" h. 550
Bonbon, footed, two handled, etched Can-
dlelight patt., clear 42
Bonbon, pressed Caprice patt., clear, 6" 20
Bowl, 5" sq., jelly, two-handled, pressed
Caprice patt., No. 151, clear 15
Bowl, 7 1/2" d., footed, Azurite 40
Bowl, 9" d., four-footed, pressed Caprice
patt., Moonlight 125
Bowl, 10" d., etched Chantilly patt., three-
part, on silvered metal base, clear 89
Bowl, 10" d., shallow, four-footed, pressed
Caprice patt., clear 45
Bowl, 10 1/2" d., No. 1359, clear 125
Bowl, 11" d., etched Apple Blossom patt.,
low footed, gold-encrusted, Mandarin
Gold (light yellow) 125
Bowl, 11" d., four-footed, No. 3400/45,
clear 118
Bowl, 11" d., No. 3400/48, clear 135
Bowl, 12" d., etched Chantilly patt., Martha
line blank, four-footed, clear 275
Bowl, 12" d., etched Wildflower patt., No.
3400/4, four-footed, flared, gold-
encrusted clear 115
Bowl, 12" d., pressed Caprice patt., Deca-
gon line, pink 68
Bowl, 12" l., etched Wildflower patt.,
oblong, fancy edge, No. 3900/160, clear 125
Bowl, 12" l., four-footed, oblong, fancy rim,
No. 3400/160, clear 150
Bowl, 12 1/2" d., 5 1/2" h., crimped rim,
footed, pressed Caprice patt., Moonlight,
No. 61 139
Bowl, salad, 13 1/2" d., Caprice patt., No.
82, Moonlight 325
Bowl, etched Diane patt., four-footed,
square, clear 75
Bowl, etched Diane patt., Tally-Ho line,
clear 155
Butter dish, cov., etched Diane patt., clear 195
Candelabra, three-light, No. 1338, clear,
pr. 200
Candleholder, Martha Washington line,
Ebony (black), 4" h. 20
Candlestick, three-light, Cambridge Arms
patt., clear, 5 1/4" h. 42

Candlestick, three-light, keyhole shape,
pressed Caprice patt., clear 35
Candlestick, three-light, pressed Caprice
patt., clear, 6" h. 40
Candlestick, two-light, etched Wildflower
patt., No. 647, clear 55
Candlestick, two-light, keyhole stem, gold-
encrusted, No. 3400/647, clear, 6" h. 95
Candlesticks, etched Diane patt., Martha
line blank, No. 497, clear, pr. 350
Candlesticks, figural dolphin stem, domed
base, clear, 8 1/4" h., pr. 125
Candlesticks, Gadroon (No. 3500) line,
molded ram's heads on the socket,
Amber, 4 1/2" h., pr. 149
Candlesticks, Martha line blank, No. 497,
w/prisms, clear, 7 1/2" h., pr. 550
Candlesticks, one-light, etched Apple
Blossom patt., Topaz, pr. 48
Candlesticks, three-light, pressed Caprice
patt., No. 1338, Mandarin Gold, 6" h., pr. 135
Candlesticks, two-light, etched Portia patt.,
cornucopia-stem, Mandarin Gold, pr. 229
Candlesticks, two-light, etched Wildflower
patt., fleur-de-lis stem, No. 3400/647,
gold-encrusted clear, 6" h., pr. 125
Candlesticks, two-light, keyhole stem,
gold-encrusted, No. 3400/647, clear,
6" h., pr. 150
Candlesticks, pressed Caprice patt., No.
67, Moonlight, 2 1/2" h., pr. 55
Candlesticks, three-light, pressed Caprice
patt., clear, 6" h., pr. 80
Candlesticks, pressed Caprice patt., No.
69, Moonlight, 7" h., pr. 160
Candy box, cov., etched Chantilly patt.,
footed, clear 135
Candy box, cov., etched Wildflower patt.,
No. 3900/165, clear 100
Candy dish, cov., three-footed, pressed
Caprice patt., clear 45
Candy dish, cov., etched Diane patt., clear 130
Center bowl, Gadroon (No. 3400) line,
footed, scalloped rim, ram's head han-
dles, Amber, 9" d. 129
Cigarette box, cov., footed, etched Gloria
patt., gold encrusted Crown Tuscan 220
Cigarette urn, etched Diane patt., clear 38
Claret, pressed Caprice patt., Moonlight,
No. 5, 4 1/2 oz. 195
Claret, Statuesque line, Carmen bowl,
clear Nude Lady stem, 7 5/8" h. 275
Claret, pressed Caprice patt., Moonlight,
Alpine etching 165
Cocktail, blown Caprice patt., No. 301,
Moonlight, 3 oz. 45
Cocktail, etched Portia patt., No. 3121,
clear, 3 oz. 122
Cocktail, Mt. Vernon line, footed, clear, No.
26, 3 1/2 oz. 6
Cocktail, Statuesque line, Mandarin Gold
bowl, clear Nude Lady stem (ILLUS. top
of next page) 80
Cocktail, Statuesque (No. 3011) line, Ame-
thyst bowl, clear Nude Lady stem, 4 1/2
oz., 6 1/2" h. 110
Cocktail, Statuesque (No. 3011) line,
Emerald (light green) bowl, clear Nude
Lady stem, 4 1/2 oz., 6 1/2" h. 110

Statuesque Line Cocktail

Cocktail, clear, 3 oz., 6" h. 30
Cocktail icer, etched Diane patt., clear 78
Cocktail & icer, No. 3600, clear, 2 pcs. 110
Cocktail & icer, No. 968, clear, 2 pcs. 110
Cocktail shaker, No. 3400/175, clear 200
Cocktail shaker, No. 98, clear 210
Comport, two-handled, Mt. Vernon line,
 Emerald green 65
Compote, blown, No. 3121 stem, clear,
 5 3/8" h. 175

Compote on Chrome Nude Lady Base

Compote, open, chrome Farberware Nude
 Lady stem w/Amethyst bowl insert
 (ILLUS.) 62
Compote, open, 7" d., low, footed, pressed
 Caprice patt., clear 24
Compote, open, 8" d., Mt. Vernon line,
 clear 25
Compote, open, Statuesque line, Cobalt,
 clear Nude Lady stem 425

Console bowl, etched Apple Blossom
 patt., rolled edge, Gold Krystol,
 12 1/2" d. 125
Cordial, etched Chantilly patt., No. 3625,
 clear, 1 oz. 65
Cordial, etched Diane patt., clear 42
Cordial, etched Portia patt., No. 3130,
 clear, 1 oz. 60
Cordial, Line 1341, mushroom-style,
 Amber 7
Cordial, Line 1341, mushroom-style, Car-
 men (bright red) 25
Cordial, Line No. 3500, Carmen 90
Cordial, Mt. Vernon line, footed, clear, 1
 oz. 22
Cordial, No. 3121, clear, 1 oz. 93
Cordial, pressed Cambridge Square patt.,
 clear, 2 1/8" h. 28
Cordial, pressed Caprice patt., Moonlight,
 4 1/2" h. 115
Cordial, pressed Pristine patt., No. 1936,
 clear, 4 1/2" h. 52
Cordial, Tally-Ho line, forest green, 5" h. 74
Creamer & sugar bowl, English Hobnail
 patt., clear, pr. 32
Crown Tuscan candy dish, cov., shell-
 shaped, gold decoration, 6" w. 70
Crown Tuscan candy dish, cov., three-
 part 95
Crown Tuscan cigarette box, cov. 55
Crown Tuscan cocktail, topaz bowl
 w/Nude Lady stem, 6 1/2" h. 150
Crown Tuscan compote, 6" d., Nude Lady
 stem, gold-encrusted 200

Crown Tuscan Plate

Crown Tuscan plate, 7" d. (ILLUS.) 45
Crown Tuscan plate, 8" d., pressed
 Caprice patt. 35
Crown Tuscan plate, torte, 14" d. 125
Crown Tuscan urn, cov., 8" h. 140
Crown Tuscan vase, 10" h., Sea Shell
 patt., pedestal base 43
Cruet w/original stopper, No. 3900/100,
 clear, 6 oz. 145
Cruet w/original stopper, pressed Caprice
 patt., oil, No. 101, clear, 3 oz. 50
Cruet w/original stopper & metal holder,
 No. 3400 line, oil, Emerald 40

Cup, pressed Caprice patt., No. 17, clear 14
Cup & saucer, demitasse, No. 3400 line, clear 15
Cup & saucer, Mt. Vernon line, clear 14
Cup & saucer, pressed Caprice patt., midnight blue 48
Cup & saucer, pressed Caprice patt., Moonlight.............. 40
Cup & saucer, pressed Cascade patt., clear 22
Cup & saucer, Tally-Ho line, Royal/cobalt blue 64
Decanter w/stopper, etched Portia patt., No. 1321, clear, 28 oz. 325
Decanter w/stopper, etched Portia patt., No. 3400/92, clear, 32 oz. 375
Decanter w/stopper, No. 1372, cut neck & stopper, clear 1,950
Figural flower frog/holder, "Draped Lady," clear, 13" h. 125
Figure flower frog/holder, "Bashful Charlotte," Emerald green, 13" h. 295
Figure flower holder, "Draped Lady," Emerald green, 8 1/2" h. 295
Figure flower holder, "Draped Lady," Ritz blue, 8 1/2" h. 325
Goblet, etched Apple Blossom patt., clear, 9 oz. 20
Goblet, etched Candlelight patt., clear, 6 1/4" h. 58
Goblet, etched Diane patt., No. 3122, clear, 9 oz. 30
Goblet, etched Diane patt., Regency line, clear 65
Goblet, etched Elaine patt., water, clear 25
Goblet, Mt. Vernon line, clear, 10 oz................ 15
Goblet, Mt. Vernon line, clear, 12 oz. 12
Goblet, Statuesque line, banquet-size, Emerald green bowl, clear Nude Lady stem, 10" h. 375
Goblet, Statuesque line, table-size, Carmen bowl, clear Nude Lady stem, 9 1/2" h. 275
Goblet, water, Cambridge Square patt., clear, 5" h. 26
Goblet, water, Gadroon (No. 3500 line), royal/cobalt blue, 8 3/8" h. 49
Goblet, water, hand blown Caprice patt., clear, 5 7/8" h. 34
Goblet, water, pressed Caprice patt., clear, 6 3/4" h. 30
Goblet, water, pressed Caprice patt., midnight blue, 6 1/2" h. 48
Goblet, water, pressed Caprice patt., No. 300, clear, 9 oz................ 16
Goblet, water, pressed Cascade patt., clear, 5 1/2" h. 18
Honey jar, No. 3500/139, clear 500
Ice bucket, etched Candlelight patt., No. 3900, clear 135
Lamp, table model, etched Diane patt., gold-encrusted, slender ovoid body, metal fittings, Carmen, 14 1/2" h. 585
Martini pitcher, etched Diane patt., clear, 60 oz. 1,995
Mayonnaise bowl & ladle, etched Portia patt., clear, 2 pcs. 40

Mayonnaise set: bowl, underplate & ladle; etched Wildflower patt., No. 3900/129, gold-encrusted clear, the set 125
Model of a swan, Crown Tuscan, 6" h. 150
Model of a swan, Emerald green, No. 1040, 3" l. 50
Mug, Mt. Vernon line, stein-type, No. 84, Amber, 14 oz. 38
Nut dish, low, divided, pressed Caprice patt., Moonlight, No. 94, 7 1/2" d. 52
Nut dish, pressed Caprice patt., yellow 38
Parfait, pressed Caprice patt., midnight blue, 6 1/2" h. 154
Pitcher, Caprice patt., ball-shaped, Moonlight, 80 oz. 360
Pitcher, etched Apple Blossom patt., ball-shaped, clear, 80 oz. 175
Pitcher, etched Cleo patt., No. 955, Amber, 62 oz. 268
Pitcher, etched Diane patt., ball-shaped, clear 295
Pitcher, etched Elaine patt., jug-form, clear 295
Pitcher, etched Portia patt., ball-shaped, gold-encrusted, Mandarin Gold 179
Pitcher, pressed Caprice patt., ball-shaped, No. 183, clear, 80 oz. 150
Pitcher, pressed Caprice patt., Moonlight, 32 oz. 375
Plate, 6 1/2" d., bread & butter, etched Portia patt., clear.............. 9
Plate, 7" d., etched Cleo patt., Decagon line, Moonlight 20
Plate, 7" d., pressed Caprice patt., clear 15
Plate, 8" d., No. 739 line, Mandarin Gold 11
Plate, 8" d., pressed Caprice patt., clear 14
Plate, 8 1/2" d., Everglade patt., clear 36
Plate, 9" d., pressed Caprice patt., clear (slight wear) 20
Plate, 10" d., two-handled, etched Martha patt., clear 19
Plate, 10 1/2" d., dinner, etched Portia patt., clear 70
Plate, 11" d., three-footed, pressed Caprice patt., clear 26
Plate, 14" d., four-footed, pressed Caprice patt., Moonlight, No. 28 98
Plate, 14" d., three-footed, pressed Caprice patt., clear 38
Plate, cabaret, pressed Caprice patt., Moonlight.............. 55
Platter, 13 1/2" l., etched Apple Blossom patt., rectangular w/tab handles, Mandarin Gold 110
Relish dish, divided, pressed Caprice patt., clear, 6" l. 25
Relish dish, three-part, etched Candlelight patt., No. 3400, clear, 8" 38
Relish dish, two-part, etched Diane patt., clear, 6" l. 27
Relish dish, three-part, No. 3400 line, Emerald green, 7" l. 28
Relish dish, three-part, No. 3900/125, gold-encrusted, clear, 9" d. 65
Relish dish, three-part, pressed Caprice patt., No. 124, clear, 8" l. 25
Relish dish, five-part, pressed Caprice patt. 375
Relish dish, etched Elaine patt., No. 3500/67, clear, 6 pcs. 250

Caprice Rose Bowl

Rose bowl, pressed Caprice patt., Moonlight, large (ILLUS.) **125-160**

Rose bowl & flower frog, pressed Caprice patt., footed, No. 235, Moonlight, 6" d., 2 pcs.. **450**

Salt dip, No. 3400 line, Amethyst...................... **15**

Salt & pepper shakers, etched Elaine patt., clear, pr. (one glass lid)........................ **40**

Salt & pepper shakers, footed, etched Chantilly patt., clear, pr. **36**

Salt & pepper shakers w/glass tops, etched Gloria patt., tall, Mandarin Gold, pr.. **120**

Salt shaker w/original chrome top, No. 3400 line, Cobalt (dark blue) **30**

Salt shaker w/original top, etched Apple Blossom patt., Moonlight.............................. **130**

Salt shaker w/original top, etched Wildflower patt., No. 3900/1177, clear **20**

Salt shaker w/original top, pressed Caprice patt., Moonlight, No. 96.................. **50**

Saucer, pressed Caprice patt., No. 17, clear **3**

Sherbet, blown Caprice patt., tall, No. 300, clear, 6 oz. **14**

Sherbet, etched Apple Blossom patt., Mandarin Gold, tall, No. 3130, 6 oz...................... **20**

Sherbet, Mt. Vernon line, clear, 6 1/2 oz............ **10**

Sherbet, No. 3500, clear, tall **24**

Sherbet, pressed Caprice patt., midnight blue, 4 1/2" h. **38**

Sherbet, pressed Caprice patt., No. 301, clear, 4 1/4" h. **12**

Sherbet, pressed Caprice patt., No. 301, clear, 5 3/4" h. **18**

Sherbet, etched Elaine patt., clear, No. 3035 .... **18**

Smoke set, pressed Caprice patt., Moonlight, shell-footed, six pieces in original box, the set... **110**

Sugar bowl, individual, pressed Caprice patt., clear **12**

Sugar bowl, pressed Caprice patt., clear, No. 38, medium.. **11**

Sugar bowl, pressed Caprice patt., clear, No. 41, large.. **13**

Sugar sifter w/lid, etched Cleo patt., footed, Moonlight, 6 3/4" h. **1,500**

Tray, for individual creamer & sugar bowl, pressed Caprice patt., clear **18**

Tray, oval, pressed Caprice patt., clear, 9" l. **22**

Tray, wafer, etched Cleo patt., Emerald green **365**

Tumbler, etched Apple Blossom patt., footed, No. 3135, clear, 12 oz. **22**

Tumbler, etched Apple Blossom patt., No. 3130, footed, Mandarin Gold, 12 oz. **40**

Tumbler, etched Cleo patt., Amber, 8 oz. **22**

Tumbler, etched Portia patt., footed, No. 3077, clear, 12 oz. **25**

Tumbler, footed, pressed Caprice patt., No. 10, Moonlight, 10 oz. **50**

Tumbler, footed, pressed Caprice patt., No. 180, Moonlight, 5 oz. **55**

Tumbler, footed, pressed Caprice patt., No. 184, Moonlight, 12 oz. **60**

Tumbler, footed, pressed Caprice patt., No. 184, pink, 12 oz. **50**

Tumbler, footed, pressed Caprice patt., No. 300, Moonlight, 10 oz. **40**

Tumbler, footed, pressed Caprice patt., No. 300, Moonlight, 12 oz. **40**

Tumbler, footed, pressed Caprice patt., No. 300, Moonlight, 5 oz. **40**

Tumbler, footed, pressed Caprice patt., No. 310, Moonlight, 5 oz. **85**

Tumbler, footed, pressed Cascade patt., clear, 5 1/8" h. **20**

Tumbler, iced tea, Caprice patt., No. 300, clear, 6 1/8" h. **36**

Tumbler, iced tea, etched Elaine patt., clear, 12 oz... **25**

Tumbler, juice, Cambridge Square patt., clear, 4" h. **14**

Tumbler, Old Fashion, pressed Caprice patt., Moonlight, No. 310, 7 oz. **130**

Tumbler, pressed Caprice patt., No. 184, Moonlight, 12 oz.. **55**

Tumbler, Square Line, No. 3797, clear.............. **13**

Tumbler, iced tea, pressed Caprice patt., flat, Moonlight.. **115**

Tumbler, iced tea, pressed Caprice patt., No. 310, clear, 5 1/4" h.. **115**

Vase, 6" h., etched Apple Blossom patt., No. 1308, Emerald green **600**

Vase, bud, 6" h., pressed Caprice patt., midnight blue.. **68**

Vase, 6 1/2" h., etched Wildflower patt., globe-shaped, No. 3400/103, Mandarin Gold... **375**

Vase, 8" h., flip, No. 3500/139, clear **125**

Vase, 8 1/2" h., ball-shaped, pressed Caprice patt., three ring, Moonlight **450**

Vase, 9" h., etched Candlelight patt., keyhole shape, clear.. **74**

Vase, 11" h., etched Cleo patt., Emerald green **130**

Vase, bud, Statuesque line, Amber, clear Nude Lady stem **775**

Vegetable bowl, cov., etched Cleo patt., Amber, 9" **190**

Water set: Doulton-style 80 oz. pitcher & five flat tumblers; No. 3400, Cobalt (dark blue), the set **275**

Water set: pitcher & four tumblers; Gyro Optic line, Amber, the set.............................. **68**

Water tray, etched Cleo patt., Amber.............. **225**

Wine, pressed Caprice patt., clear **38**

Wine, pressed Caprice patt., No. 300,
clear, 4 1/2" h. **44**
Wine, pressed Caprice patt., No. 302,
clear, 5 5/8" h. **21**
Wine, Tally-Ho line, No. 1420, clear,
4 1/2" h. **58**

CAR VASES

Carnival Six-sided Car Vases

Carnival, marigold, six-sided trumpet-form
w/scalloped rim, 7 1/4" l., pr. (ILLUS.) **$155**

Blossoms & Band Pattern Car Vases

Carnival, marigold, trumpet-form, Blossoms & Band patt., 7 1/2" l., pr. (ILLUS.) **185**

Eight-sided Clear Car Vase

Clear, trumpet-form, eight-sided w/wide
flared & scalloped mouth, sterling silver
tip, 8 1/2" l. (ILLUS.) **105**

Clear Crystal Six-sided Car Vase

Clear, trumpet-form, six-sided w/scalloped
rim & sterling silver tip, Model T fitting,
8 1/2" l. (ILLUS.) **85**

Clear Car Vases w/Floral & Fern Etching

Clear, trumpet-form w/incurved mouth, Floral & Fern etching, 7 1/2" l., pr. (ILLUS.) **175**

Green Car Vase w/Model T Fitting

Frosted green, trumpet-form w/flared
mouth & Model T fitting, 8" l. (ILLUS.) **135**

Frosted Yellow Tulip Style Car Vase

Frosted yellow, tulip style w/Model T fit-
ting, 8 1/4" l. (ILLUS.) **135**

CARNIVAL

Earlier called Taffeta glass, the Carnival glass now being collected was introduced early in this century. Its producers gave it an iridescence that attempted to imitate that of some Tiffany glass. Collectors will find available books by leading authorities Donald E. Moore, Sherman Hand, Marion T. Hartung, Rose M. Presznick, and Bill Edwards.

ACORN BURRS (Northwood)

Berry set: master bowl & 4 sauce dishes; purple, 5 pcs.................................... **$395-425**
Berry set: master bowl & 5 sauce dishes; purple, 6 pcs............................... **450-500**
Berry set: master bowl & 6 sauce dishes; marigold, 7 pcs............................ **250-260**
Berry set: master bowl & 6 sauce dishes; purple, 7 pcs.................................... **525**
Butter dish, cov., green **750**
Butter dish, cov., marigold **150**

Acorn Burrs Butter Dish

Butter dish, cov., purple (ILLUS.)............. **350-400**
Creamer, marigold **150**
Creamer, purple **150**
Pitcher, water, green......................... **400**
Pitcher, water, marigold **425**
Pitcher, water, purple..................... **425-500**
Punch bowl base, green **125**
Punch cup, green **55-60**
Punch cup, ice green...................... **100-150**
Punch cup, marigold......................... **35**
Punch cup, purple **45**
Punch set: bowl, base & 6 cups; purple, 8 pcs.................................... **1,250-1,400**
Sauce dish, green............................. **60**
Sauce dish, marigold **30**
Sauce dish, purple............................ **40-50**
Spooner, green **170-180**
Spooner, marigold **100**
Spooner, purple **255**
Sugar bowl, cov., marigold............... **160**
Sugar bowl, cov., purple................... **290**
Sugar bowl, open, purple **220**
Tumbler, green **60**
Tumbler, marigold **45-50**
Tumbler, purple **80**
Water set: pitcher & 6 tumblers; purple, 7 pcs.................................... **955-975**

ACORN (Fenton)

Bowl, 6" d., vaseline........................ **113**
Bowl, 7" d., amber, ruffled.................. **105-115**
Bowl, 7" d., aqua **84**
Bowl, 7" d., blue **65-70**
Bowl, 7" d., marigold **49**

Bowl, 7" d., red.............................. **615**
Bowl, 7" d., red, ice cream shape **300**
Bowl, 7" d., sapphire blue, ice cream shape **400**
Bowl, 7" d., vaseline, ruffled............. **105**
Bowl, 7 1/2" d., blue........................ **48**
Bowl, 7 1/2" d., blue, ruffled **105**
Bowl, 7 1/2" d., marigold **43**
Bowl, 7 1/2" d., purple **140**
Bowl, 8" d., amber........................... **165**
Bowl, 8" to 9" d., blue...................... **55**
Bowl, 8" to 9" d., marigold **42**
Bowl, 8" to 9" d., purple, ribbon candy rim **110-115**

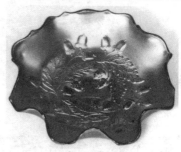

Acorn Bowl

Bowl, 8" to 9" d., red, ruffled (ILLUS.) **675-725**
Bowl, ice cream shape, aqua................... **165-175**
Bowl, ice cream shape, blue **48**
Bowl, ice cream shape, green........................ **105**
Bowl, ice cream shape, vaseline..................... **195**
Bowl, red, deep **428**
Bowl, red, flat **950**
Bowl, ruffled, aqua opalescent......................... **130**
Bowl, ruffled, sapphire blue.......................... **675**
Bowl, white................................ **185**

ADVERTISING & SOUVENIR ITEMS

Basket, "Feldman Bros. Furniture, Salisbury, Md.," open edge, marigold **68**
Basket, "Miller's Furniture," marigold **88**
Bell, souvenir, BPOE Elks, "Atlantic City, 1911," blue **2,200**
Bell, souvenir, BPOE Elks, "Parkersburg, 1914," blue **2,000**
Bowl, "E. A. Hudson Furniture Co.," ruffled, purple **850**
Bowl, "Gervitz Bros.," ruffled, purple (Northwood) **500**

"Great House of Isaac Benesch" Bowl

Bowl, "Isaac Benesch," 6 1/4" d., purple, Millersburg (ILLUS.) **325**

Bowl, "H. Mayday & Co., 1910," 8 1/2" d.,
Wild Blackberry patt., purple **190-350**
Bowl, "Dreibus Parfait Sweets," smoky lavender, ruffled **567**
Bowl, "Horlacher," green, Peacock Tail
patt. **100-115**
Bowl, "Horlacher," green, Thistle patt. **175**
Bowl, "Horlacher," marigold, Vintage patt. **120**
Bowl, "Morris Smith," purple, ruffled.............. **1,250**
Bowl, souvenir, BPOE Elks, "Atlantic City,
1911," blue, one-eyed Elk **1,298**
Bowl, souvenir, BPOE Elks, "Detroit,
1910," blue, one-eyed Elk **900**
Bowl, souvenir, BPOE Elks, "Detroit,
1910," green, one-eyed Elk....................... **1,250**
Bowl, souvenir, BPOE Elks, "Detroit, 1910"
purple, one-eyed Elk **600**
Bowl, souvenir, BPOE Elks, "Detroit,
1910," purple, two-eyed Elk (Millersburg).. **1,900**
Bowl, souvenir, "Brooklyn Bridge," marigold **250-350**
Bowl, souvenir, "Millersburg Courthouse,"
purple **850**
Bowl, souvenir, "Millersburg Courthouse,"
purple, unlettered **2,000-2,500**
Card tray, "Fern Brand Chocolates,"
turned-up sides, purple, 6 1/4" d. **600**
Card tray, "Isaac Benesch," marigold, Holly
Whirl patt. **106**
Hat, "Miller's Furniture - Harrisburg," marigold, basketweave **125**
Paperweight, souvenir, BPOE Elks, green... **3,500**
Plate, "Brazier Candies," w/handgrip, 6" d.,
purple **1,050**
Plate, "Central Shoe," purple, flat **1,200**
Plate, "Davidson Chocolate Society,"
6 1/4" d., purple.. **1,100**
Plate, "Dreibus Parfait Sweets," 6 1/4" d.,
purple **385-400**
Plate, "Fern Brand Chocolates," 6" d.,
purple **700**
Plate, "Gervitz Bros., Furniture & Clothing,"
w/handgrip, 6" d., purple **1,690**
Plate, "Hudson, E. A.," w/handgrip, purple **1,450**
Plate, "Old Rose Distillery," green, Grape &
Cable patt., stippled, 9" d. **614**
Plate, "Season's Greetings - Eat Paradise
Soda Candies," 6" d., purple **500**
Plate, souvenir, BPOE Elks, "Atlantic City,
1911," blue **1,600**
Plate, souvenir, BPOE Elks, "Parkersburg,
1914," 7 1/2" d., blue **1,225**
Plate, "Spector's Department Store," marigold, Heart & Vine patt., 9" d.................... **1,000**
Vase, "Howard Furniture," green, Four Pillars patt., green **65**

APPLE BLOSSOMS
Bowl, 5" d., marigold **40**
Bowl, 6" d., marigold **22**
Bowl, 7" d., marigold, collared base
(ILLUS. top of next column) **34**
Bowl, 7" d., purple, collared base....................... **78**
Bowl, 7" d., marigold, ribbon candy rim......... **30-45**
Bowl, 9" d., peach opalescent, three-in-one
edge **130**
Rose bowl, marigold **65**
Tumbler, blue, enameled **85**
Water set: pitcher & 1 tumbler; blue, enameled, 2 pcs. **300**

Apple Blossoms Bowl

APRIL SHOWERS (Fenton)
Vase, teal.. **225**
Vase, white **200**
Vase, 7 1/2" h., purple **55**
Vase, 8" h., green **70**
Vase, 8" h., marigold **45**
Vase, 9" h., blue, pie crust edge **80**
Vase, 9 3/4" h., green, Peacock Tail interior....... **95**
Vase, 10" h., blue **50**

April Showers Vase

Vase, 10" h., purple (ILLUS.).............................. **48**
Vase, 10" h., teal **70**
Vase, 10 1/2" h., purple, Peacock Tail interior **75-80**
Vase, 11" h., blue **80-90**
Vase, 11" h., green, Peacock Tail interior **90**
Vase, 11" h., purple, Peacock Tail interior......... **70**
Vase, 11" h., ribbon candy rim, purple.............. **175**
Vase, 11 1/2" h., green, Peacock Tail interior **150**
Vase, 11 1/2" h., marigold **57**
Vase, 12" h., blue **57**
Vase, 12" h., green **65**
Vase, 12" h., marigold, Peacock Tail interior **40**
Vase, 12" h., purple, Peacock Tail interior......... **90**
Vase, 12" h., vaseline **175**
Vase, 13" h., green **35**
Vase, 13 1/2" h., marigold **46**
Vase, purple opalescent **700-750**

AUSTRALIAN

Bowl, 9" to 10" d., Emu, marigold 175
Bowl, 9" to 10" d., Emu, purple 600
Bowl, 9" to 10" d., Kangaroo, black amethyst........................... 650
Bowl, 9" to 10" d., Kangaroo, purple **250-275**
Bowl, 9" to 10" d., Kingfisher, purple......... **150-200**
Bowl, 9" to 10" d., Kiwi, marigold, ruffled .. **240-250**
Bowl, 9" to 10" d., Kookaburra, purple 188
Bowl, 9" to 10" d., Magpie, marigold 185
Bowl, 9" to 10" d., Swan, marigold................... 138

Australian Swan Bowl

Bowl, 9" to 10" d., Swan, purple (ILLUS.) ... **140-150**
Bowl, 9" to 10" d., Thunderbird, marigold......... 215
Bowl, 11" d., Kookaburra, marigold, ice cream shape **185-200**
Compote, Butterflies & Waratah, marigold 200
Sauce dish, Kangaroo, purple 57
Sauce dish, Magpie, purple 300

BASKET or BUSHEL BASKET (Northwood)

Aqua, 4 1/2" d., 4 3/4" h. **800-850**
Aqua opalescent, 4 1/2" d., 4 3/4" h. 375
Blue 123
Blue opalescent 220
Green **375-400**
Horehound, variant.. 650
Horehound, variant **525-625**
Ice blue, ... 450
Ice green 175
Lavender, ... 250
Lavender 340
Lime green, ... 438
Lime green 450
Lime green opalescent **1,825**

Marigold Basket

Marigold (ILLUS.) **165-185**
Purple 95
Sapphire blue **1,700**
Smoky 800
White **225-350**

BEADED SHELL (Dugan or Diamond Glass Co.)

Butter dish, cov., purple 160
Mug, blue.. **140-150**
Mug, marigold.. **105-115**

Beaded Shell Mug

Mug, purple (ILLUS.) 50
Mug, white... 700
Sauce dish, purple 42
Spooner, footed, marigold 40
Sugar bowl, cov., marigold 55
Tumbler, blue.. **190-225**
Tumbler, lavender... 80
Tumbler, marigold...................................... **55-65**
Tumbler, purple.. **75-80**

BIG FISH BOWL (Millersburg)

Green 675
Green, ice cream shape **1,000**
Green, square **900-1,000**
Marigold 625
Marigold, ice cream shape............................. 800

Big Fish Bowl

Marigold, ruffled (ILLUS.)................................ 550
Marigold, square.. **1,500**
Purple, ice cream shape 900
Purple, ruffled... 535
Purple, square.. **1,200**

BLACKBERRY (Fenton)

Basket, blue 65-75
Basket, green.. 155
Basket, marigold 45
Basket, purple 95-120
Basket, red... 250-375
Bowl, 7" d., purple... 80
Bowl, 8" to 9" d., green, ruffled 95

Blackberry Plate

Plate, marigold, openwork rim (ILLUS.) 500-525

BLACKBERRY MINIATURE COMPOTE

Blackberry Miniature Compote

Blue (ILLUS.).. 75-85
Green 200-350
Marigold 85
Purple 75

BLACKBERRY WREATH (Millersburg)

Bowl, 5" d., green....................................... 80-100
Bowl, 5" d., marigold 35
Bowl, 5" d., marigold, ruffled 80
Bowl, 5" d., marigold variant, fluted.................. 100
Bowl, 5" d., purple... 70
Bowl, 5" d., purple, candy ribbon edge 100
Bowl, 5" d., purple variant, ice cream
   shape, fluted.. 200-215
Bowl, 6" d., green, three-in-one edge 124
Bowl, 6" d., marigold, ruffled 63
Bowl, 6" d., purple, three-in-one edge.............. 137
Bowl, 7" d., green.. 110
Bowl, 7" d., marigold 60-70
Bowl, 7" d., purple... 85
Bowl, 7" d., three-in-one edge, purple............... 78

Bowl, 7 1/2" d., clambroth, three-in-one
   edge 75
Bowl, 7 1/2" d., purple, ruffled 100
Bowl, 8" d., green, ruffled.................................. 59
Bowl, 8" d., marigold, three-in-one edge.......... 103
Bowl, 8" to 9" d., green...................................... 197
Bowl, 8" to 9" d., marigold 88
Bowl, 8" to 9" d., purple............................. 100-115
Bowl, 8 1/2" d., ice cream shape, green 130
Bowl, 9" d., green, crimped rim 125-175
Bowl, 9" d., three-in-one edge, green 165
Bowl, 9" d., three-in-one edge, purple............. 113
Bowl, 10" d., blue 925-1,500
Bowl, 10" d., green................................... 100-120
Bowl, 10" d., green, ice cream shape 245
Bowl, 10" d., marigold 125-150
Bowl, blue, ice cream, large............................ 750
Bowl, green, ice cream, large.................... 80-100
Bowl, marigold, ice cream, large.................. 65-70
Bowl, purple, ice cream, large......................... 213
Bowl, marigold, triangular, large..................... 110
Plate, 6" to 7 1/2" d., marigold......................... 750

BROKEN ARCHES (Imperial)

Punch bowl & base, marigold, 12" d., 2
   pcs... 350-550
Punch cup, marigold.. 25
Punch cup, purple 45

Broken Arches Punch Set

Punch set: bowl, base & 6 cups, marigold,
   8 pcs. (ILLUS.) 437
Punch set: bowl, base & 6 cups; purple, 8
   pcs... 725

BUTTERFLY & BERRY (Fenton)

Berry set: master bowl & 5 sauce dishes;
   marigold, 6 pcs...................................... 150-250
Bowl, 8" to 9" d., blue, master berry, four-
   footed 175-200
Bowl, 8" to 9" d., green, master berry, four-
   footed 230-250
Bowl, 8" to 9" d., marigold, master berry,
   four-footed 65
Bowl, 8" to 9" d., purple, master berry, four-
   footed 165-275
Bowl, 8" to 9" d., white, master berry, four-
   footed 500-750
Butter dish, cov., blue 250
Butter dish, cov., green 750-1,000
Butter dish, cov., marigold.............................. 160
Creamer, marigold 75-85
Hatpin holder, blue...................................... 1,900
Hatpin holder, marigold................................ 1,600
Pitcher, water, green...................................... 595

Butterfly & Berry Pitcher

Pitcher, water, marigold (ILLUS.)............. **240-275**
Sauce dish, blue **50-75**
Sauce dish, green.................................... **100-125**
Sauce dish, marigold **30**
Sauce dish, purple...................................... **65-85**
Spooner, marigold **50**
Spooner, purple **140**
Sugar bowl, cov., marigold **75**
Table set, marigold, 4 pcs....................... **350-400**
Tumbler, blue.. **45-60**
Tumbler, green **150**
Tumbler, marigold **30-40**
Tumbler, purple.. **125-150**
Vase, 6" to 10" h., amber......................... **150-175**
Vase, 6" to 10" h., blue **75-85**
Vase, 6" to 10" h., green.......................... **155-165**
Vase, 6" to 10" h., marigold **40-50**
Vase, 6" to 10" h., purple........................ **125-150**
Water set: pitcher & 6 tumblers; marigold,
   7 pcs.. **450-500**
Water set: pitcher & 6 tumblers; purple, 7
   pcs.. **1,050**

BUTTERFLY (Northwood)

Butterfly Bonbon

Bonbon, blue, threaded exterior (ILLUS.)... **250-270**
Bonbon, blue w/electric iridescence,
   threaded exterior **450-500**
Bonbon, emerald green, threaded exterior...... **575**
Bonbon, green **125-150**
Bonbon, ice blue, threaded exterior.............. **2,850**
Bonbon, marigold **48**
Bonbon, purple **67**
Bonbon, purple, threaded exterior **200-250**

BUTTERFLY & TULIP

Bowl, square, marigold **275**
Bowl, 9" w., 5 1/2" h., marigold, footed
   (ILLUS. top of next column) **275-350**
Bowl, 10 1/2", marigold, square flat shape,
   footed **275**

Butterfly & Tulip Bowl

Bowl, 10 1/2", purple, square flat shape,
   footed **1,900**
Bowl, 12" d., marigold, upturned sides,
   footed **354**

CAPTIVE ROSE

Bonbon, blue, two-handled, 7 1/2" d............ **80-90**
Bonbon, green, two-handled, 7 1/2" d. **75**
Bowl, 8" d., blue, three-in-one edge............... **108**
Bowl, 8" d., purple, three-in-one edge............ **106**
Bowl, 8" to 9" d., blue.................................... **102**
Bowl, 8" to 9" d., green.................................... **75**
Bowl, 8" to 9" d., marigold **90-95**
Bowl, 8" to 9" d., purple.................................. **65**
Bowl, 8" to 9" d., blue, candy ribbon edge **75**
Bowl, 8" to 9" d., green, candy ribbon edge..... **122**
Bowl, 8" to 9" d., marigold, candy ribbon
   edge **60**

Captive Rose Bowl

Bowl, 8" to 9" d., purple, candy ribbon edge
   (ILLUS.).. **121**
Compote, blue **75**
Compote, green **58**
Compote, ice blue **125-150**
Compote, marigold....................................... **70-80**
Compote, purple **100**
Compote, purple, candy ribbon edge.............. **130**
Compote, white.. **149**
Plate, 7" d., blue **250**
Plate, 7" d., purple **250**
Plate, 9" d., blue **475-525**
Plate, 9" d., green.. **400**
Plate, 9" d., marigold **400**
Plate, 9" d., purple **525-575**

CATTAILS & WATER LILY - See Water Lily & Cattails Pattern

CHATELAINE

Pitcher, purple.. **2,500**
Tumbler, purple (ILLUS. top of next
   page).. **200-225**

Chatelaine Tumbler

Cherry Pitcher & Tumbler

Water set: pitcher & 4 tumblers; marigold,
5 pcs. (ILLUS. of part) 950

CHERRY or HANGING CHERRIES (Millersburg)

Banana compote (whimsey), purple 2,700
Berry set: master bowl & 4 sauce dishes;
  purple, 5 pcs. 750
Bowl, 5" d., blue 825
Bowl, 5" d., green satin, ruffled 145
Bowl, 5" d., marigold satin, ruffled................... 130
Bowl, 6" d., purple, crimped 190
Bowl, 7" d., ice cream shape, green 140
Bowl, 7" d., lavender 450
Bowl, 7" d., marigold 175
Bowl, 7" d., marigold, ice cream shape..... 125-150
Bowl, 8" to 9" d., purple................................... 98
Bowl, 10" d., green, ice cream shape 450
Bowl, 10" d., green, ruffled, Wide Panel
  exterior 125
Bowl, 10" d., marigold, ice cream shape.......... 150
Bowl, 10" d., marigold, ruffled, Hobnail
  exterior 650-750
Bowl, 10" d., marigold, three-in-one rim........... 195
Bowl, 10" d., purple, ice cream shape.............. 275
Bowl, 10" d., purple, ruffled, Hobnail exte-
  rior 875
Bowl, 10 1/2" d., white, ruffled......................... 125
Butter dish, cov., purple 200-225
Compote, purple 3,500
Creamer, green 100-125
Creamer, marigold 100-125
Creamer, purple 100-125
Pitcher, water, green............................... 500-600
Pitcher, water, purple.............................. 600-650
Spooner, green 77
Spooner, marigold 65
Spooner, pastel marigold............................... 100
Spooner, purple 100-125
Sugar bowl, cov., green.................................... 95
Sugar bowl, cov., marigold 85
Table set, marigold, 4 pcs. 415

CHRISTMAS COMPOTE

Marigold 3,250
Purple 2,800-3,000

CHRYSANTHEMUM or WINDMILL & MUMS

Bowl, 8" to 9" d., blue, three-footed................. 145
Bowl, 9" d., blue, ruffled 113
Bowl, 9" d., green, ruffled................................ 100
Bowl, 9" d., marigold, ruffled 58
Bowl, 9" d., purple, ruffled............................... 150
Bowl, 9" d., red w/amber center 1,500-2,500
Bowl, 9" d., ruffled, red................................. 4,500
Bowl, 10" d., blue, three-footed....................... 210
Bowl, 10" d., green, three-footed 350

Chrysanthemum Bowl

Bowl, 10" d., marigold, three-footed
  (ILLUS)... 80-100
Bowl, 10" d., red, collared base 2,000-2,500
Bowl, 11" d., blue, ice cream shape, footed..... 120
Bowl, 11" d., blue, three-footed....................... 220
Bowl, 11" d., marigold, three-footed.................. 55
Bowl, 11" d., purple, three-footed.................... 250
Bowl, 12" d., vaseline, three-footed 260
Bowl, marigold, collared base 63

COIN DOT

Bowl, 6" d., green.. 48
Bowl, 6" d., red, ice cream shape 1,000-1,500
Bowl, 6 1/2" d., purple, stippled........................ 50
Bowl, 7" d., green... 50

Coin Dot Bowl

Bowl, 7" d., green, candy ribbon edge
(ILLUS.).. 50
Bowl, 7" d., purple, candy ribbon edge 35
Bowl, 7" d., red... 1,450
Bowl, 7 1/2" d., blue 55
Bowl, 8" d., purple, pie crust rim 20
Bowl, 8" to 9" d., green 25-50
Bowl, 8" to 9" d., green, stippled 25
Bowl, 8" to 9" d., marigold............................. 35-40
Bowl, 8" to 9" d., peach opalescent 149
Bowl, 8" to 9" d., purple..................................... 43
Bowl, 9" d., purple, three-in-one edge............... 97
Bowl, 9 1/2" d., purple, ruffled 60-65
Bowl 10" d., peach opalescent, ruffled............. 158
Bowl, green 70
Bowl, marigold, ruffled 15
Bowl, purple 77
Compote, celeste blue opalescent................... 850
Compote, purple 60
Rose bowl, green.. 70-75
Rose bowl, marigold 45
Rose bowl, marigold, stippled............................ 60
Rose bowl, purple, stippled 65-70
Rose bowl, vaseline... 100

COMET or RIBBON TIE (Fenton)
Bowl, 8" d., green, ice cream shape 125
Bowl, 8" to 9" d., blue...................................... 65
Bowl, 8" to 9" d., lavender, candy ribbon
edge 88

Comet Bowl

Bowl, 8" to 9" d., marigold (ILLUS.)..................... 60
Bowl, 8" to 9" d., purple...................................... 80
Bowl, 9" d., blue w/electric iridescence,
three-in-one edge................................. 175-200

Bowl, green, candy ribbon edge 95
Bowl, green, ruffled 125
Plate, 9" d., blue, ruffled 250-300
Plate, 9" d., marigold, ruffled 142
Plate, 9" d., purple, ruffled............................... 190

CONCORD (Fenton)
Bowl, 8 1/2" d., piecrust rim, marigold.............. 125
Bowl, ruffled, purple 400
Bowl, 8 1/2" d., marigold, piecrust rim.............. 125
Bowl, 9" d., blue, ruffled 363
Bowl, 9" d., green, three-in-one edge 800
Bowl, blue, candy ribbon edge......................... 225
Bowl, green 325
Bowl, ice cream shape, green.......................... 475

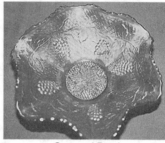

Concord Bowl

Bowl, marigold (ILLUS.) 102
Bowl, marigold, ruffled 310
Bowl, marigold, three-in-one edge 300
Bowl, purple 163
Bowl, purple, three-in-one edge.............. 425-500
Plate, green 3,500-5,000
Plate, marigold 1,250-2,000
Plate, purple 1,100

CONSTELLATION (Dugan)
Compote, clambroth... 150
Compote, marigold.. 85
Compote, purple 310
Compote, white... 95-125

CORN BOTTLE
Green 250
Marigold 250-300

Corn Bottle

Smoky (ILLUS.)... 275

CORN VASE (Northwood)

Black amethyst 3,000
Emerald green 2,700

Corn Vase

Green (ILLUS.) 650
Ice blue 1,750
Ice green 375-400
Marigold 956
Purple 500-575
Purple, electric 1,850
White 290-300

COSMOS

Bowl, 5" d., green, ice cream shape 59
Bowl, 8" d., ruffled, blue 125
Bowl, 9" d., blue 80

Cosmos Bowl

Bowl, 9" d., green (ILLUS.) 50
Bowl, 9" d., marigold 50-60
Bowl, 10" d., ruffled, marigold 47
Bowl, 10 1/2" d., blue, ice cream shape...... 80-100
Bowl, 10 1/2" d., green, ice cream shape 80
Plate, 6" d., green... 62
Plate, chop, 10 1/2" d., marigold 165-175

DAHLIA (Dugan or Diamond Glass Co.)

Bowl, master berry, 10" d., white, footed .. 185-195
Butter dish, cov., marigold 163
Creamer, marigold 73
Creamer, white.. 177
Creamer & cov. sugar bowl, white, pr............ 325
Pitcher, water, purple.................................. 800-900
Pitcher, water, white 900-1,000
Sauce dish, purple... 55

Sauce dish, white 60-75
Spooner, white.. 200
Tumbler, marigold..................................... 130-150

Dahlia Tumbler

Tumbler, purple (ILLUS) 150-175
Water set: pitcher & 6 tumblers, purple, 7
    pcs.. 1,600-1,700

DAISY CUT BELL

Daisy Cut Bell

Marigold (ILLUS.) 425

DAISY & PLUME

Bowl, 8" to 9" d., marigold, three-footed............. 75
Candy dish, green, footed 70
Candy dish, ice blue, footed 875
Candy dish, ice green, footed.......................... 750
Candy dish, lime green, footed........................ 700
Candy dish, marigold, footed............................ 85

Candy dish, purple, footed 100-110
Compote, green 60
Compote, purple 73
Rose bowl, blue, three-footed, Blackberry
   interior 475
Rose bowl, green, three-footed, Blackberry
   interior 200-250

Daisy & Plume Rose Bowl

Rose bowl, green, three-footed (ILLUS.) 60
Rose bowl, green, three-footed, Stippled
   Rays interior 95
Rose bowl, ice blue, three-footed, Black-
   berry interior 1,100
Rose bowl, ice green, three-footed................. 950
Rose bowl, marigold, three-footed................. 55
Rose bowl, marigold, three-footed, Black-
   berry interior 110
Rose bowl, purple, three-footed 85
Rose bowl, white, three-footed 850-900
Rose bowl, white, three-footed, Black-
   berry interior 750

DANDELION (Northwood)
Mug, aqua 365
Mug, aqua opalescent 400
Mug, blue 500-550

Dandelion Mug

Mug, ice blue opalescent (ILLUS.) 750
Mug, marigold.. 300
Mug, purple 225-275
Mug, Knights Templar, marigold....................... 513
Pitcher, water, tankard, green............ 1,000-1,200
Pitcher, water, tankard, marigold 350-400
Tumbler, green 150
Tumbler, ice blue 100-150
Tumbler, marigold.. 80
Tumbler, purple... 100
Tumbler, white 100
Water set: pitcher & 6 tumblers; marigold,
   7 pcs.. 1,110

DIAMOND LACE (Imperial)
Bowl, 8" to 9" d., marigold 55
Bowl, 8" to 9" d., purple.................................... 70

Diamond Lace Pitcher

Pitcher, water, purple (ILLUS.)...................... 400
Sauce dish, green, 5" d. 40
Sauce dish, marigold, 5" d........................... 20-25
Sauce dish, purple, 5" d................................ 35-40
Tumbler, purple.. 75

DIAMOND POINT COLUMNS
Vase, ice blue.. 450
Vase, ice green... 475
Vase, 6" h., marigold 60
Vase, 7" h., green 130-135
Vase, 7" h., marigold 40
Vase, 7" h., purple 80
Vase, 7 1/2" h., white.. 165
Vase, 8" h., blue w/electric iridescence 325
Vase, 8" h., green (ILLUS. top of next
   page) 43
Vase, 9" h., green 90
Vase, 9" h., purple 65
Vase, 9 1/2" h., purple 185
Vase, 10" h., blue opalescent 900
Vase, 10" h., green 73
Vase, 10" h., marigold 51
Vase, 10" h., purple 85
Vase, 10" h., sapphire blue............................. 800
Vase, 11" h., blue 70
Vase, 11" h., green 65
Vase, 11" h., marigold 45-50
Vase, 11" h., purple 120
Vase, 11" h., white 190
Vase, 12" h., marigold 28
Vase, 12" h., purple 75
Vase, 13" h., green 78

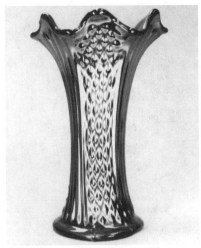

Diamond Point Columns Vase

Vase, 13" h., purple 50
Vase, 16" h., blue 275
Vase, 16" h., ribbon candy rim, white 325
Vase, teal.. 320

DIAMOND RING (Imperial)
Bowl, 8" to 9" d., marigold............................. 40-45
Bowl, 8" to 9" d., purple.................................... 200

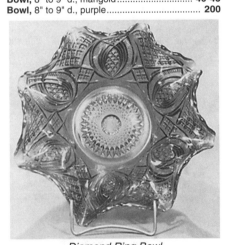

Diamond Ring Bowl

Bowl, 8" to 9" d., smoky (ILLUS.)................... 40-45
Rose bowl, marigold 400

DOGWOOD SPRAYS
Bowl, purple, tricornered 200
Bowl, 8" to 9" d., marigold, dome-footed............ 34
Bowl, 8" to 9" d., peach opalescent, dome-
footed 150
Bowl, 8" to 9" d., purple, dome-footed 174
Bowl, blue opalescent 300

DOLPHINS COMPOTE (Millersburg)
Blue, Rosalind interior 5,250
Green, Rosalind interior 4,500
Purple, Rosalind interior.............................. 1,900

DRAGON & LOTUS (Fenton)
Bowl, 7" to 9" d., blue, three-footed................... 65
Bowl, 7" to 9" d., green, three-footed 90-95
Bowl, 7" to 9" d., lime green opalescent,
three-footed.. 550
Bowl, 7" to 9" d., marigold, three-footed............ 55
Bowl, 7" to 9" d., purple, three-footed 70
Bowl, 8" to 9" d., amber, collared base 200-225
Bowl, 8" to 9" d., blue, collared base........... 95-125
Bowl, 8" to 9" d., green, collared base 82
Bowl, 8" to 9" d., lime green opalescent,
collared base 500-550
Bowl, 8" to 9" d., marigold, collared base.... 85-100
Bowl, 8" to 9" d., moonstone, collared base.. 1,100
Bowl, 8" to 9" d., peach opalescent, col-
lared base 500
Bowl, 8" to 9" d., purple, collared base 160-165
Bowl, 8" to 9" d., red (ILLUS.) 1,485
Bowl, 9" d., amber, ice cream shape, col-
lared base 166
Bowl, 9" d., amber opalescent. ice cream
shape, collared base 300
Bowl, 9" d., aqua opalescent, ice cream
shape, collared base 2,400
Bowl, 9" d., blue, ice cream shape, collared
base 85
Bowl, 9" d., green, three-in-one edge 185
Bowl, 9" d., marigold 95
Bowl, 9" d., marigold, ice cream shape,
collared base.. 60-65
Bowl, 9" d., marigold, scalloped 185
Bowl, 9" d., moonstone w/peach marigold
overlay, ice cream shape, collared base ... 1,375
Bowl, 9" d., purple, ice cream shape, col-
lared base 199

Dragon & Lotus Ice Cream Bowl

Bowl, 9" d., red, ice cream shape, collared
base (ILLUS.).. 2,553
Bowl, 9" d., Reverse Amberina, ice cream
shape, collared base 1,125
Bowl, amber, ruffled, Bearded Berry exte-
rior.. 195
Bowl, blue, ruffled 143
Bowl, green, ruffled, spatula-footed 183
Bowl, ice cream shape, red............................. 800
Bowl, lavender, ruffled 195
Bowl, lavender, three-in-one edge 295
Bowl, marigold opalescent, ruffled 675
Bowl, marigold, ruffled 150
Bowl, marigold w/vaseline base 200-225

Bowl, moonstone **1,700**
Bowl, peach opalescent, low, ruffled, three-
in-one edge **293**
Bowl, peach opalescent, ruffled, flat **375**
Bowl, peach opalescent, ruffled, spatula-
footed **350**
Bowl, purple, ice cream shape, spade-
footed **105**
Bowl, purple, ruffled **70**
Bowl, red, ruffled **1,900**
Bowl, smoky.. **425**
Bowl, vaseline **200**
Bowl, violet opalescent, three-in-one edge **800**
Nut bowl, blue, spatula-footed **205**
Nut bowl, marigold, spatula-footed **225**
Plate, 9" d., blue **1,975**
Plate, blue, collared base **1,750**
Plate, blue, edge turned up **250**
Plate, marigold, collared base, ruffled **2,200**
Plate, marigold, spatula-footed........................ **638**
Plate, 9" d., marigold **2,600**

EMBROIDERED MUMS (Northwood)
Bonbon, white, stemmed **1,025-1,075**
Bowl, 8" to 9" d., blue **495**
Bowl, 8" to 9" d., blue, ruffled **1,000**
Bowl, 8" to 9" d., blue w/electric irides-
cence.. **738**
Bowl, 8" to 9" d., ice blue **785**
Bowl, 8" to 9" d., ice green **875**
Bowl, 8" to 9" d., marigold........................ **475-500**
Bowl, 8" to 9" d., marigold, ruffled................... **285**

Embroidered Mums Bowl

Bowl, 8" to 9" d., purple (ILLUS.) **400**
Bowl, lavender **975-1,000**
Bowl, purple, ruffled **275**
Bowl, purple, ruffled, ribbed exterior **612**
Bowl, sapphire blue, piecrust rim **2,850**
Plate, ice green **3,100**

FANCIFUL (Dugan)
Bowl, 8" to 9" d., blue, ruffled **165**
Bowl, 8" to 9" d., marigold............................ **50-75**
Bowl, 8" to 9" d., marigold, piecrust rim **100-125**
Bowl, 8" to 9" d., peach opalescent **200-225**
Bowl, 8" to 9" d., purple, ruffled (ILLUS. top
of next column)....................................... **155-175**
Bowl, 8" to 9" d., white, ruffled **155**
Bowl, 9" d., white, three-in-one edge **225**
Bowl, 10" d., white, ruffled.............................. **165**
Bowl, ice cream shape, marigold **130**
Bowl, peach opalescent, ice cream shape....... **127**
Bowl, purple, ice cream shape......................... **255**

Fanciful Bowl

Bowl, white, ice cream shape........................... **190**
Plate, 9" d., blue **320**
Plate, 9" d., marigold **110**
Plate, 9" d., peach opalescent.................. **275-300**
Plate, 9" d., purple.................................. **200-250**
Plate, 9" d., white.................................... **200-250**
Plate, 9 1/2" d., white, ruffled........................... **140**

FANTAIL
Bowl, ice cream shape, blue (buffed point)...... **270**
Bowl, 9" d., blue, footed **185-200**
Bowl, 9" d., blue, shallow, footed, w/Butter-
fly & Berry exterior....................................... **175**
Bowl, 9" d., marigold, footed **90**
Bowl, 9" d., marigold, ice cream shape,
w/Butterfly & Berry exterior **163**
Bowl, blue, low, ruffled, footed **285-300**

FARMYARD (Dugan)

Farmyard Bowl

Bowl, purple, candy ribbon edge
(ILLUS.).. **4,000-4,500**
Bowl, three-in-one edge, purple.................. **7,000**

FASHION (Imperial)
Bowl, 9" d., clambroth **40**
Bowl, 9" d., marigold **25**
Bowl, 9" d., smoky, ruffled............................... **175**
Breakfast set: small size creamer & sugar
bowl, smoky, pr. **175**
Creamer, purple, breakfast size **225**
Creamer, smoky **85**

Fashion Pitcher

Pitcher, water, marigold (ILLUS.)............. 100-125
Pitcher, water, purple........................... 900-1,000
Punch bowl & base, marigold, 12" d., 2
   pcs.. 125-150
Punch cup, marigold.................................... 21
Punch cup, smoky.. 40
Rose bowl, purple, large........................... 2,050
Sugar bowl, smoky....................................... 90
Tumbler, marigold....................................... 30
Tumbler, purple.. 200
Tumbler, smoky..................................... 95-115

FEATHER & HEART
Pitcher, water, green.............................. 400-500
Tumbler, green.. 225
Tumbler, marigold...................................... 70

Feather & Heart Tumbler

Tumbler, purple (ILLUS.) 125
Water set: pitcher & 4 tumblers; purple, 5
   pcs.. 975

FENTON'S FLOWERS ROSE BOWL - See Orange Tree Pattern

FENTONIA
Berry set: master bowl & 4 sauce dishes;
   marigold, 5 pcs.................................. 145-165
Bowl, master berry, blue 263
Bowl, master berry, marigold 55

Butter dish, cov., blue, footed 150-200
Butter dish, cov., marigold, footed................. 350
Creamer, blue 100
Creamer, marigold 60
Pitcher, water, blue 695
Sauce dish, blue, claw feet.......................... 35
Sauce dish, marigold, claw feet...................... 22
Spooner, marigold 75-100
Tumbler, blue..................................... 60-65
Tumbler, marigold.................................... 47

Fentonia Water Set

Water set: pitcher & 6 tumblers; marigold,
   7 pcs. (ILLUS.) 500

FERN
Compote, green, w/Daisy & Plume exterior
   (Northwood) 160-180
Compote, purple, w/Daisy & Plume exterior (Northwood) 100-125
Dish, hat-shaped, marigold (Fenton)................. 34

FIELD FLOWER (Imperial)
Pitcher, water, amber.................................. 425
Pitcher, water, green............................. 250-300
Pitcher, water, marigold 230
Pitcher, water, purple 425-500
Tumbler, blue... 85
Tumbler, green 70
Tumbler, marigold................................. 25-35
Tumbler, purple....................................... 55
Water set: pitcher & 1 tumbler; green, 2
   pcs... 300-350
Water set: pitcher & 1 tumbler; marigold, 2
   pcs... 250-275

FILE & FAN
Compote, blue opalescent............................ 250
Compote, milk white w/marigold overlay.......... 200
Compote, peach opalescent 140

FILE (Imperial)
Bowl, 8" d., marigold 40
Spooner, marigold 60
Sugar bowl, marigold................................ 115
Vase, marigold....................................... 315
Water set: pitcher & 3 tumblers; marigold,
   4 pcs.. 950

FINE RIB (Northwood & Fenton)
Bowl, 7" d., white..................................... 33
Bowl, master berry, 9" d., marigold.................. 35
Compote, green, ruffled 45
Vase, 5 1/2" h., footed, jack-in-the-pulpit,
   blue 175
Vase, 6 1/2" to 12" h., aqua......................... 75

Large Fine Rib Vase

Vase, 6 1/2" to 12" h., blue (ILLUS.).............. 55-75
Vase, 6 1/2" to 12" h., green............................. 60
Vase, 6 1/2" to 12" h., ice blue 210
Vase, 6 1/2" to 12" h., marigold 32
Vase, 6 1/2" to 12", purple 55-75
Vase, 6 1/2" to 12", red (Fenton) 275-375
Vase, 6 1/2" to 12", vaseline (Fenton) 75-100
Vase, 14" to 17", blue 60-80
Vase, 14" to 17", marigold 50-75
Vase, 14" to 17", purple 80-100

FISHERMAN'S MUG
Marigold 300
Pastel marigold 200-250
Peach opalescent 600-800

Fisherman's Mug

Purple (ILLUS.) 105
Purple, w/advertising................................. 150-175

FLEUR DE LIS (Millersburg)
Bowl, 8" to 9" d., marigold, dome-footed.......... 200

Fleur De Lis Bowl

Bowl, 8" to 9" d., purple, dome-footed
(ILLUS.)... 275-300
Bowl, 10" d., green................................... 250-300
Bowl, 10" d., marigold 210
Bowl, 10" d., purple 450-500
Bowl, marigold, dome-footed, ruffled 150-250
Bowl, purple, dome-footed 425
Bowl, marigold, tricornered, footed 300
Bowl, purple, dome-footed, ruffled 425
Bowl, purple, tricornered, footed 650
Bowl, three-in-one edge, green....................... 525

FLORAL & GRAPE (Dugan or Diamond Glass Co.)
Pitcher, water, blue 300-350
Pitcher, water, dark marigold 250
Pitcher, water, marigold 180
Pitcher, water, purple..................................... 233
Pitcher, water, white 475
Tumbler, blue 35-40
Tumbler, purple... 27
Tumbler, white 80
Tumblers, purple, set of 4.............................. 180
Water set: pitcher & 4 tumblers; blue, 5
pcs... 450

FLOWERS & FRAMES
Bowl, 7" d., peach opalescent.................. 100-175

Flowers & Frames Bowl

Bowl, 7" d., purple, dome-footed (ILLUS.) 350
Bowl, 9" d., green, dome-footed...................... 275

Bowl, 9" d., peach opalescent, dome-
footed **150-200**
Bowl, peach opalescent, tricornered **150**
Bowl, purple, tricornered, dome-footed **200-250**

FLUFFY PEACOCK - See Peacock, Fluffy Pattern (Fenton)

FLUTE (Imperial)
Berry set: master bowl & 6 sauce dishes;
marigold, 7 pcs. **135**
Bowl, 8" d., teal green **200**
Bowl, 8" to 9" d., marigold **31**
Butter dish, cov., marigold **95-125**
Celery vase, purple, 5 1/2" **400**
Compote, green **25**
Compote, marigold, 11" d., 7" h. **100**
Creamer, green, breakfast size **50**
Creamer, marigold, breakfast size **50**
Creamer, purple, breakfast size **65-70**
Creamer & open sugar bowl, purple,
breakfast size, pr. **100-115**

Flute Matchbox Holder

Matchbox holder, purple (ILLUS.) **900**
Pitcher, water, marigold **275**
Pitcher, water, purple **575**
Punch cup, marigold **37**
Punch set: bowl, base & 5 cups; marigold,
7 pcs. **495**
Sauce dish, marigold **15-20**
Sauce dish, purple **40-45**
Sugar bowl, open, purple, breakfast size **60**
Toothpick holder, blue **225**
Toothpick holder, green **50**
Toothpick holder, lavender **75-100**
Toothpick holder, marigold **65-75**
Toothpick holder, purple **55**
Toothpick holder, vaseline **200-250**
Tumbler, marigold **40**
Tumbler, purple **90**
Vase, 9" h., marigold **30**
Vase, 13" h., green **150**
Vase, 13" h., marigold, funeral **275**

FORMAL
Hatpin holder, marigold **675**
Hatpin holder, purple **925**
Vase, marigold, jack-in-the-pulpit **310**
Vase, purple, jack-in-the-pulpit **625**

FOUR SEVENTY FOUR (Imperial)
Compote, marigold **185**
Goblet, water, marigold **50-55**
Pitcher, milk, green **365-400**
Pitcher, milk, marigold **155**

Four Seventy Four Pitcher

Pitcher, water, green (ILLUS.) **400-450**
Pitcher, water, marigold **175-225**
Pitcher, water, purple, mid-size.................... **3,000**
Punch bowl & base, marigold, 2 pcs.............. **168**
Punch cup, green **40**
Punch cup, marigold.................................... **20-25**
Punch set: bowl, base & 6 cups; marigold,
8 pcs. **375**
Tumbler, green **125**

FRUITS & FLOWERS (Northwood)
Bonbon, aqua opalescent, stemmed, two-
handled **550**
Bonbon, blue, stemmed, two-handled **200**
Bonbon, blue, stippled **550**
Bonbon, blue w/electric iridescence,
stemmed, two-handled................................ **208**
Bonbon, green, stemmed, two-handled.......... **105**
Bonbon, green, stippled.................................. **650**
Bonbon, ice blue opalescent, stemmed,
two-handled.. **875**
Bonbon, ice blue, stemmed, two-handle.......... **750**
Bonbon, ice green, stemmed, two-handled **750**
Bonbon, lavender, stemmed, two-handled **800**

Fruits & Flowers Bonbon

Bonbon, marigold, stemmed, two-handled
(ILLUS.).. **95**
Bonbon, marigold, stippled **200**

Bonbon, purple, stemmed, two-handled **135**
Bonbon, sapphire blue, two-handled **1,100**
Bonbon, teal **3,000**
Bonbon, white, stemmed, two-handled **300-350**
Bowl, 6" d., green, ruffled **55-65**
Bowl, 6" d., purple, ruffled **40**
Bowl, 7" d., blue w/electric iridescence **275-300**
Bowl, 7" d., green, ruffled, Basketweave
exterior **105**
Bowl, 7" d., green, stippled **325**
Bowl, 7" d., ice green, ruffled **350**
Bowl, 7" d., purple **60**
Bowl, 9 1/2" d., green, ruffled, Bas-
ketweave exterior **70**
Bowl, 9 1/2" d., marigold, ruffled, Bas-
ketweave exterior **75**
Bowl, 10" d., ice green, ruffled **475**
Bowl, 10" d., purple, ruffled **250**
Bowl, master berry, 10" d., green **100-125**
Bowl, master berry, 10" d., ice green **450**
Bowl, master berry, 10" d., marigold **75**
Bowl, marigold, ruffled, stippled **50**
Plate, 7" d., blue **320**
Plate, 7" d., marigold **178**
Plate, 7" d., purple **170**
Plate, 7 1/2" d., purple, handgrip **175**
Plate, 9 1/2" d., marigold **250**
Sauce dish, marigold **30**
Sauce dish, purple **30-35**

GARDEN PATH
Bowl, 8" to 9" d., marigold **68**
Bowl, 9" d., marigold, ice cream shape **75**
Bowl, 9" d., marigold, variant, Soda Gold
exterior **35-45**
Bowl, 9" d., purple, ice cream shape **750**
Bowl, 10" d., marigold, ruffled **95**
Bowl, 10" d., purple, ice cream shape **1,300**
Bowl, 10" d., white, ruffled **300-325**
Hatpin, purple **150**
Plate, 6" d., white, variant **525**
Plate, 6 1/2" d., white **375**

Garden Path Plate

Plate, chop, 11" d., purple (ILLUS.) **6,250**

GARLAND ROSE BOWL (Fenton)

Garland Rose Bowl

Blue (ILLUS.) **185**
Green **195**
Marigold **55**

GOD & HOME
Pitcher, blue **2,000-2,250**
Tumbler, blue **225-250**

God & Home Water Set

Water set: pitcher & 6 tumblers; blue, 7
pcs. (ILLUS.) **3,800**

GOOD LUCK (Northwood)
Bowl, 8" d., blue, ruffled **312**
Bowl, 8" d., blue, ruffled, stippled **375**
Bowl, 8" d., blue w/electric iridescence, ruf-
fled **410**
Bowl, 8" d., green, ruffled **250**
Bowl, 8" d., green, ruffled, Basketweave
exterior **275**
Bowl, 8" d., lavender, ruffled **350**
Bowl, 8" d., marigold, ruffled **152**
Bowl, 8" d., marigold, ruffled, Basketweave
exterior **255**
Bowl, 8" d., marigold, ruffled, stippled **190**
Bowl, 8" d., purple, ruffled **265**
Bowl, 8" d., purple, ruffled, Basketweave
exterior **280**
Bowl, 8" to 9" d., aqua opalescent, piecrust
rim **2,900**
Bowl, 8" to 9" d., blue, piecrust rim (ILLUS.
top of next page) **425-450**
Bowl, 8" to 9" d., blue w/electric irides-
cence, piecrust rim **585**
Bowl, 8" to 9" d., green, piecrust rim **365**
Bowl, 8" to 9" d., marigold, piecrust rim **275-325**
Bowl, 8" to 9" d.,marigold, piecrust rim,
Basketweave exterior **250-300**

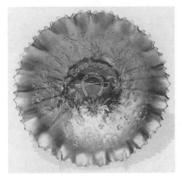

Good Luck Bowl

Bowl, 8" to 9" d., marigold, piecrust rim,
   stippled 325-375
Bowl, 8" to 9" d., purple, piecrust rim 275
Bowl, 8" to 9" d., teal blue, piecrust rim 2,750
Bowl, 8" to 9" d., aqua opalescent, ruffled 1,025
Bowl, 8" to 9" d., blue, ruffled 475
Bowl, 8" to 9" d., green, ruffled 650
Bowl, 8" to 9" d., ice blue, ruffled 3,700
Bowl, 8" to 9" d., lavender, ruffled 225
Bowl, 8" to 9" d., marigold, ruffled 170
Bowl, 8" to 9" d., marigold, ruffled,
   stippled 425-450
Bowl, 8" to 9" d., teal blue, ruffled 1,350
Bowl, 9" d., aqua opalescent, ruffled,
   ribbed exterior 2,425
Bowl, blue w/electric iridescence, piecrust
   rim, stippled, ribbed exterior 642
Bowl, emerald green, piecrust rim 1,500
Bowl, ice blue, piecrust rim 5,000
Bowl, ice green, ruffled 4,500
Bowl, marigold iridescence, stippled 380
Bowl, pastel marigold, piecrust rim, stip-
   pled 410
Bowl, purple, piecrust rim, ribbed exterior 337
Bowl, purple, ruffled, Basketweave exterior 378
Plate, 9" d., green 1,650
Plate, 9" d., green, Basketweave exterior 650
Plate, 9" d., marigold 375
Plate, 9" d., marigold, stippled 2,000
Plate, 9" d., purple 500
Plate, 9" d., purple, Basketweave exterior. 600-650
Plate, 9" d., purple, stippled 700

GRAPE ARBOR (Northwood)
Bowl, 10" d., purple, footed (Dugan) 350-375
Hat shape, blue 87
Hat shape, ice green 350
Hat shape, marigold 75-100
Hat shape, purple 195
Hat shape, white 100
Pitcher, tankard, ice blue (ILLUS. top of
   next column) 1,500
Pitcher, tankard, marigold 250-300
Pitcher, tankard, purple 550-600
Tumbler, blue 175-225
Tumbler, blue w/electric iridescence 200
Tumbler, ice blue 250
Tumbler, ice green 375-400
Tumbler, marigold 45-55
Tumbler, pastel marigold 40
Tumbler, purple 63
Tumbler, white 125

Grape Arbor Pitcher

Water set: tankard pitcher & 4 tumblers;
   marigold, 5 pcs. 525-550
Water set: tankard pitcher & 4 tumblers;
   purple, 5 pcs. 800
Water set: tankard pitcher & 4 tumblers;
   white, 5 pcs. 1,000-1,050
Water set: tankard pitcher & 6 tumblers;
   ice blue, 7 pcs. 3,000-3,500
Water set: tankard pitcher & 6 tumblers;
   marigold, 7 pcs. 500-575

GRAPE & CABLE (Northwood)
Banana boat, banded rim, stippled, aqua 575
Banana boat, blue 425-500
Banana boat, blue, banded rim 550-600
Banana boat, blue, banded rim,
   stippled 1,000-1,200
Banana boat, green 400
Banana boat, green, banded rim, stippled 550-600
Banana boat, green, stippled 300-325
Banana boat, ice blue 700
Banana boat, ice green 750
Banana boat, marigold 150-200
Banana boat, marigold, stippled 200-250
Banana boat, purple 335
Berry set: master bowl & 4 sauce dishes;
   purple, 5 pcs. 375
Bonbon, two-handled, blue 148
Bonbon, two-handled, green 75-100
Bonbon, two-handled, horehound 375
Bonbon, two-handled, marigold 75
Bonbon, two-handled, purple 75-100
Bonbon, two-handled, stippled, blue 175-200
Bonbon, two-handled, stippled, green 165
Bonbon, two-handled, stippled, marigold 60-70
Bonbon, two-handled, white 500-550
Bowl, 5" d., blue (Fenton) 60
Bowl, 5" d., green 60
Bowl, 5" d., marigold 30
Bowl, 5" d., purple 60
Bowl, 6" d., three-in-one edge, marigold
   variant 160
Bowl, 6 1/2" d., Amberina (Fenton) 650
Bowl, 6 1/2" d., marigold 38

Bowl, 7" d., ice cream shape, marigold
(Fenton).. 35
Bowl, 7" d., ice cream shape, milk white
w/marigold overlay (Fenton) 250
Bowl, 7" d., ice cream shape, purple (Fen-
ton) 55
Bowl, 7" d., ice cream shape, vaseline
(Fenton).. 45
Bowl, 7" d., ruffled, green (Fenton) 58
Bowl, 7" d., ruffled, marigold 25
Bowl, 7" d., ruffled, red.............................. 800
Bowl, 7" d., spatula-footed, green (Fenton) 85
Bowl, 7 1/2" d., ball-footed, aqua (Fenton).... 80-85
Bowl, 7 1/2" d., ball-footed, blue (Fenton)... 75-100
Bowl, 7 1/2" d., ball-footed, marigold (Fen-
ton).. 55
Bowl, 7 1/2" d., ball-footed, purple (Fenton)....... 89
Bowl, 7 1/2" d., ball-footed, red (Fenton) 575
Bowl, 7 1/2" d., ruffled, green............................ 85
Bowl, 7 1/2" d., ruffled, red...................... 800-825
Bowl, 7 1/2" d., ruffled, vaseline,.................... 100
Bowl, 7 1/2" d., spatula-footed, green
(Northwood) 100
Bowl, 7 1/2" d., spatula-footed, purple
(Northwood) 63
Bowl, 8" d., ice cream shape, footed, blue
(Fenton).. 60-65
Bowl, 8" d., ruffled, green............................ 65
Bowl, 8" d., ruffled, red (Fenton) 800
Bowl, 8" to 9" d., ball-footed, celeste blue
(Fenton).. 1,200
Bowl, 8" to 9" d., ball-footed, green (Fen-
ton) 76
Bowl, 8" to 9" d., ball-footed, pastel mari-
gold (Fenton)...................................... 55
Bowl, 8" to 9" d., piecrust rim, aqua opales-
cent (Northwood).............................. 3,450
Bowl, 8" to 9" d., piecrust rim, blue,
stippled... 375-425
Bowl, 8" to 9" d., piecrust rim, blue w/elec-
tric iridescence 300-350
Bowl, 8" to 9" d., piecrust rim, green........ 100-110
Bowl, 8" to 9" d., piecrust rim, green, Bas-
ketweave exterior 250-300
Bowl, 8" to 9" d., piecrust rim, ice blue 1,300
Bowl, 8" to 9" d., piecrust rim, marigold 85
Bowl, 8" to 9" d., piecrust rim, marigold,
Basketweave exterior.............................. 40-45
Bowl, 8" to 9" d., piecrust rim, marigold,
stippled... 185
Bowl, 8" to 9" d., piecrust rim, pastel mari-
gold 90
Bowl, 8" to 9" d., piecrust rim, purple 135-150
Bowl, 8" to 9" d., piecrust rim, purple, Bas-
ketweave exterior 150-175
Bowl, 8" to 9" d., spatula-footed, blue
(Northwood) 250
Bowl, 8" to 9" d., spatula-footed, green
(Northwood) 90
Bowl, 8" to 9" d., spatula-footed, lavender 250
Bowl, 8" to 9" d., spatula-footed, marigold
(Northwood) 65
Bowl, 8" to 9" d., spatula-footed, ruffled,
purple (Northwood) 85-90
Bowl, 8" to 9" d., stippled, blue 388
Bowl, 8" to 9" d., stippled, green, ruffled 275
Bowl, 8" to 9" d., stippled, marigold, ruffled,
Basketweave exterior................................ 300
Bowl, 8 1/2" d., scalloped, marigold.................. 85

Bowl, 8 1/2" d., scalloped, purple (North-
wood) 95
Bowl, 8 12" d., ruffled, stippled, green 270
Bowl, 9" d., Basketweave exterior, green 78
Bowl, 9" d., ruffled, Basketweave exterior,
marigold 40
Bowl, berry, 9" d., clambroth 88
Bowl, berry, 9" d., green............................... 188
Bowl, berry, 9" d., ice green 838
Bowl, berry, 9" d., marigold 135
Bowl, berry, 9" d., purple.............................. 80
Bowl, 10" d., ruffled, stippled, Bas-
ketweave exterior, marigold 225
Bowl, 10 1/2" d., ruffled, Basketweave
exterior, marigold 70
Bowl, 10 1/2" d., ruffled, Basketweave
exterior, purple 125
Bowl, 10 1/2" d., ruffled, white...................... 150
Bowl, orange, 10 1/2" d., blue, footed 475
Bowl, orange, 10 1/2" d., blue, footed, Per-
sian Medallion interior (Fenton)................... 350
Bowl, orange, 10 1/2" d., blue w/electric iri-
descence, footed, stippled (Northwood)....... 650
Bowl, orange, 10 1/2" d., green, footed 325
Bowl, orange, 10 1/2" d., green, footed,
Persian Medallion interior (Fenton) 225-250
Bowl, orange, 10 1/2" d., ice green, footed ... 1,050
Bowl, orange, 10 1/2" d., marigold, banded 413
Bowl, orange, 10 1/2" d., marigold, footed ... 188
Bowl, orange, 10 1/2" d., marigold, footed,
Persian Medallion interior (Fenton) 125-150
Bowl, orange, 10 1/2" d., marigold, footed,
stippled.. 400
Bowl, orange, 10 1/2" d., purple, footed.......... 450
Bowl, orange, 10 1/2" d., purple, footed,
Persian Medallion interior (Fenton) 500
Bowl, orange, 10 1/2" d., white, footed 1,538
Bowl, 11" d., ice cream shape, blue.............. 1,200
Bowl, 11" d., ice cream shape, green 600
Bowl, 11" d., ice cream shape, green, Bas-
ketweave exterior 750
Bowl, 11" d., ice cream shape, ice blue 2,425
Bowl, 11" d., ice cream shape, ice green 1,350
Bowl, 11" d., ice cream shape, marigold.......... 375
Bowl, 11" d., ice cream shape, purple....... 350-400
Bowl, 11" d., ice cream shape, purple, Bas-
ketweave exterior 400
Bowl, 11" d., ice cream shape, white 375
Bowl, 11" d., ice cream shape, white, Bas-
ketweave exterior 300-325
Bowl, 11" d., ruffled, green.............................. 195
Bowl, fruit, blue 438
Bowl, fruit, green 488
Bowl, fruit, purple 750
Bowl, ruffled, marigold (Fenton) 45
Breakfast set: individual size creamer &
sugar bowl; green, pr. 172
Breakfast set: individual size creamer &
sugar bowl; marigold, pr. 140
Breakfast set: individual size creamer &
sugar bowl; purple, pr.............................. 188
Butter dish, cov., amber 115
Butter dish, cov., blue 350
Butter dish, cov., green 200-250
Butter dish, cov., ice blue 350
Butter dish, cov., marigold....................... 125-150
Butter dish, cov., purple 150-225
Candle lamp, green 1,000
Candle lamp, marigold................................ 1,100

Candle lamp, purple 850
Candle lamp shade, green............................. 575
Candle lamp shade, marigold 750
Candlestick, green 135
Candlestick, marigold...................................... 75
Candlestick, purple 115
Candlesticks, green, pr. 223
Candlesticks, purple, pr. 225-250
Centerpiece bowl, marigold 250-300
Centerpiece bowl, purple 375-425
Cologne bottle w/stopper, green 250-275
Cologne bottle w/stopper, ice blue 725-775
Cologne bottle w/stopper, marigold.............. 275
Cologne bottle w/stopper, purple............ 250-300
Cologne bottle w/stopper, white 625-650
Compote, cov., purple, large 550-600
Compote, cov., purple, small 375
Compote, open, green, large 925-1,100
Compote, open, marigold, large 425
Compote, open, purple, large 475
Compote, open, purple, small 275-300
Cracker jar, cov., marigold............................. 450
Cracker jar, cov., purple 375-425
Creamer, green 125
Creamer, marigold 75-80
Creamer, purple 86
Creamer, green, individual size.................... 75-80
Creamer, marigold, individual size 65
Creamer, purple, individual size.................. 75-85
Cup & saucer, purple.............................. 250-300
Cuspidor, purple 3,000-4,000

Grape & Cable Whiskey Decanter

Decanter w/stopper, whiskey, marigold
  (ILLUS.).. 175
Dresser set, purple, 7 pcs............................ 1,500
Dresser tray, green.................................. 250-275
Dresser tray, ice blue 1,500
Dresser tray, marigold 200
Dresser tray, purple 225
Fernery, purple... 725-775
Hat shape, green 75
Hat shape, marigold 55
Hat shape, purple 50-60
Hatpin holder, marigold........................... 300-375
Hatpin holder, purple............................... 300-350
Humidor, cov., marigold........................... 300-375
Humidor, cov., purple 550-600
Nappy, green, single handle 80

Nappy, marigold, single handle.................... 50-60
Pin tray, green 350
Pin tray, ice blue 900-950
Pin tray, marigold...................................... 125-175
Pitcher, tankard, 9 3/4" h., green 1,500
Pitcher, water, 8 1/4" h., green 475
Pitcher, water, 8 1/4" h., marigold.................... 275
Pitcher, water, 8 1/4" h., purple................ 185-275
Pitcher, tankard, 9 3/4" h., ice green............. 8,000
Pitcher, smoky 800
Plate, 5" to 6" d., marigold, two sides up......... 125
Plate, 5" to 6" d., purple (Northwood).............. 125
Plate, 8" d., clambroth 125-150
Plate, 8" d., marigold, flat, spatula-footed......... 175
Plate, 8" d., marigold, footed 95
Plate, 8" d., purple................................... 200-225
Plate, 9" d., Basketweave exterior, green 350
Plate, 9" d., Basketweave exterior, mari-
  gold 130-140
Plate, 9" d., Basketweave exterior, purple ... 175-200
Plate, 9" d., blue, spatula-footed 145-150
Plate, 9" d., blue, stippled........................... 1,200
Plate, 9" d., clambroth 165
Plate, 9" d., green... 400
Plate, 9" d., green, spatula-footed 200
Plate, 9" d., ice green, spatula-footed 850-875
Plate, 9" d., marigold, spatula-footed 95-115
Plate, 9" d., purple 195
Plate, 9" d., purple, spatula-footed 135
Plate, 9" d., stippled, green 725
Plate, 9" d., stippled, marigold........................ 700
Plate, 9" d., stippled, marigold, variant...... 175-300
Plate, 9" d., stippled, purple........................... 450
Plate, 9" d., stippled, sapphire blue 3,300-3,500
Powder jar, cov., green.................................. 335
Powder jar, cov., marigold 175
Powder jar, cov., purple 155
Punch bowl & base, horehound, 11" d., 2
  pcs.. 2,450
Punch bowl & base, purple, 14" d., 2 pcs. 575
Punch bowl & base, marigold, 17" d., 2
  pcs.. 1,000
Punch cup, marigold.. 28
Punch cup, purple 25-30
Punch set: 11" bowl, base & 6 cups; pur-
  ple, 8 pcs. 575
Punch set: 14" bowl, base & 6 cups; pur-
  ple, 8 pcs. 1,375

Grape & Cable Punch Set

Punch set: 14" bowl, base & 6 cups; white,
  8 pcs. (ILLUS.) 5,500
Punch set, master: 17" bowl, base & 6
  cups; purple, 8 pcs. 3,200
Punch set, master: 17" bowl, base & 8
  cups; marigold, 10 pcs. 2,450
Punch set, master: 17" bowl, base & 12
  cups; marigold, 14 pcs. 3,100

Sauce dish, green... 25
Sauce dish, marigold 45
Sauce dish, purple....................................... 25-30
Sherbet or individual ice cream dish,
  marigold 30
Sherbet or individual ice cream dish,
  purple 55-65
Sherbet or individual ice cream dish,
  white... 160-170
Spooner green 100
Spooner marigold 68
Spooner purple 85
Sugar bowl, cov., marigold 85
Sugar bowl, cov., purple......................... 145-175
Sugar bowl, individual size, purple 60-70
Sweetmeat jar, cov., purple 300
Table set: cov. sugar bowl, creamer, cov.
  butter dish & spooner; green, 4 pcs. 450
Tumbler, green 55-65
Tumbler, ice green.................................. 375-400
Tumbler, marigold................................... 50-75
Tumbler, purple... 40
Water set: pitcher & 6 tumblers; purple, 7
  pcs.. 600
Water set: pitcher & 8 tumblers; purple, 9
  pcs... 600-625
Whiskey set: whiskey decanter w/stopper
  & 6 shot glasses; marigold, 7 pcs. 1,100
Whiskey shot glass, marigold................. 125-150
Whiskey shot glass, purple 155

GRAPE DELIGHT
Nut bowl, six-footed, blue 100-125
Nut bowl, six-footed, ice blue........................... 60
Nut bowl, six-footed, ice green 88

Grape Delight Nut Bowl

Nut bowl, six-footed, purple (ILLUS.).......... 80-100
Nut bowl, six-footed, white........................... 70-90
Rose bowl, six-footed, amber 70
Rose bowl, six-footed, blue 120
Rose bowl, six-footed, marigold 60
Rose bowl, six-footed, purple 95-100
Rose bowl, six-footed, white 100-120

GRAPEVINE LATTICE
Bowl, 7" d., purple, ruffled.............................. 75
Bowl, 7" d., white, ruffled............................ 50-60
Bowl, white, fluted... 85
Pitcher, water, purple.............................. 700-800
Plate, 6" to 7" d., marigold............................... 55

Grapevine Lattice Plate

Plate, 6" to 7" d., purple (ILLUS.) 200-250
Plate, 6" to 7" d., white 75-85
Plate, 8" d., marigold, ruffled 110
Plate, 8" d., white... 150
Tumbler, marigold.. 20-30
Tumbler, purple.. 60

GREEK KEY (Northwood)
Bowl, 8" to 9" d., blue.................................... 255
Bowl, 8" to 9" d., green, fluted........................ 275
Bowl, 8" to 9" d., marigold, ruffled............. 150-200
Bowl, 8" to 9" d., purple.................................. 325
Bowl, 8" to 9" d., purple, ruffled...................... 145
Bowl, blue, ribbed exterior 700
Bowl, green, dome-footed 75
Bowl, green, piecrust rim................................. 900
Bowl, purple, piecrust rim................................ 200
Pitcher, water, green......................... 1,300-1,350
Pitcher, water, marigold 750

Greek Key Plate

Plate, 9" d., green (ILLUS.) 475
Plate, 9" d., marigold 525
Tumbler, green 145
Tumbler, marigold...................................... 90-100
Tumbler, purple.. 120-140

HATTIE (Imperial)
Bowl, 7 1/4" d., blue 60
Bowl, 8" to 9" d., green.................................... 69
Bowl, 8" to 9" d., marigold 48
Bowl, 8" to 9" d., purple................................... 90

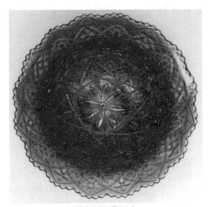

Hattie Bowl

Bowl, 8" to 9" d., smoky (ILLUS.) **75-85**
Plate, 10" d., green 400
Plate, chop, 10 1/2" d., amber 3,250
Plate, chop, green 675
Plate, chop, marigold 538
Plate, chop, purple 2,188
Rose bowl, marigold 500

HEART & VINE (Fenton)
Bowl, 8" to 9" d., blue **90-100**
Bowl, 8" to 9" d., blue, candy ribbon edge ... **100-125**
Bowl, 8" to 9" d., green 83

Heart & Vine Bowl

Bowl, 8" to 9" d., green, candy ribbon edge
(ILLUS.) 80
Bowl, 8" to 9" d., marigold, candy ribbon
edge 70
Bowl, 8" to 9" d., purple 95
Bowl, 8 1/2" d., purple, candy ribbon
edge 100-120
Plate, 9" d., blue 725
Plate, 9" d., marigold 250
Plate, 9" d., purple 395-425

HEARTS & FLOWERS (Northwood)
Bowl, 8" d., white 350-400
Bowl, 8" to 9" d., aqua opalescent 1,500-2,000
Bowl, 8" to 9" d., blue 600
Bowl, 8" to 9" d., piecrust rim, blue 900

Bowl, 8" to 9" d., piecrust rim, blue w/electric iridescence 2,300
Bowl, 8" to 9" d., piecrust rim, green 2,000
Bowl, 8" to 9" d., piecrust rim, ice blue 1,000
Bowl, 8" to 9" d., piecrust rim, ice green 2,600
Bowl, 8" to 9" d., piecrust rim, lime green 2,750
Bowl, 8" to 9" d., piecrust rim, marigold 450-500
Bowl, 8" to 9" d., piecrust rim, purple 700-725
Bowl, 8" to 9" d., ruffled, aqua 1,575
Bowl, 8" to 9" d., ruffled, blue 402
Bowl, 8" to 9" d., ruffled, green 1,275-1,300
Bowl, 8" to 9" d., ruffled, ice blue 375
Bowl, 8" to 9" d., ruffled, ice green 800
Bowl, 8" to 9" d., ruffled, marigold 350-400
Bowl, 8" to 9" d., ruffled, purple 400
Bowl, 8" to 9" d., ruffled, white 200
Compote, 6 3/4" h., aqua opalescent 450-500
Compote, 6 3/4" h., blue 400
Compote, 6 3/4" h., blue opalescent 1,500
Compote, 6 3/4" h., blue w/electric iridescence 1,050
Compote, 6 3/4" h., green 1,450
Compote, 6 3/4" h., ice blue 825-900
Compote, 6 3/4" h., ice green 500
Compote, 6 3/4" h., lime green 1,500-2,000
Compote, 6 3/4" h., marigold 325-350
Compote, 6 3/4" h., moonstone 5,000
Compote, 6 3/4" h., pastel marigold 185
Compote, 6 3/4" h., purple 450-500
Compote, 6 3/4" h., Renniger blue 1,750
Compote, 6 3/4" h., white 175-200
Plate, green 2,500
Plate, ice blue 3,500-4,000
Plate, lime ice green, ribbed exterior 5,750
Plate, marigold 800-1,000

Hearts & Flowers Plate

Plate, purple (ILLUS.) 1,000-1,200
Plate, white 2,475

HEAVY GRAPE (Imperial)
Bowl, 4" d., purple 45
Bowl, 5" d., green 19
Bowl, 5" d., purple 150
Bowl, 5" d., 2" h., marigold 30
Bowl, 5" d., 2" h., purple 26
Bowl, 6" d., green 25-35
Bowl, 7" d., green, fluted 40
Bowl, 7" d., purple 60-70
Bowl, 8" to 9" d., amber 175
Bowl, 8" to 9" d., green 54

Bowl, 8" to 9" d., light blue w/marigold
overlay.. 125
Bowl, 8" to 9" d., marigold................................... 45
Bowl, 8" to 9" d., purple................................. 75-85
Bowl, 9" d., aqua... 150
Bowl, 9" d., ruffled, smoky.............................. 225
Bowl, 10" d., purple... 335
Bowl, 12" d., marigold..................................... 135
Nut bowl, six-footed, purple............................. 75
Plate, 7" to 8" d., amber 175-200
Plate, 7" to 8" d., green 50-75
Plate, 7" to 8" d., marigold............................. 50-60
Plate, 7" to 8" d., purple.................................. 145
Plate, 9 1/2" d., stippled, marigold..................... 50

Heavy Grape Chop Plate

Plate, chop, 11" d., amber (ILLUS.).................. 255
Plate, chop, 11" d., green.......................... 240-250
Plate, chop, 11" d., lavender 410
Plate, chop, 11" d., marigold 195
Plate, chop, 11" d., purple 295
Plate, chop, 11" d., smoky............................... 500
Punch bowl, marigold....................................... 140
Punch bowl & base, marigold, 2 pcs. 400
Punch cup, amber 50
Punch cup, green 55
Punch cup, marigold.. 20
Punch cup, purple 45

HOBNAIL (Millersburg)

Hobnail Butter Dish

Butter dish, cov., purple (ILLUS.).................... 625
Cuspidor, green.. 1,250
Cuspidor, marigold 725-775
Cuspidor, purple 825-875
Rose bowl, marigold 275
Rose bowl, purple.. 325
Sugar bowl, cov., marigold 300

Vase, 15 1/2" h., marigold, variant................... 195
Vase, 16" h., purple, variant 245
Vase, 16 3/4" h., marigold, variant................... 250
Vase, 17" h., green, variant 253

HOBNAIL SWIRL - See Swirl Hobnail Pattern

HOBSTAR BAND
Pitcher, marigold... 175

Hobstar Band Tumbler

Tumbler, marigold (ILLUS.)................................ 55

HOLLY, HOLLY BERRIES & CARNIVAL HOLLY (Fenton)
Bonbon, green, two-handled.............................. 55
Bonbon, marigold, two-handled...................... 110
Bonbon, purple, two-handled............................ 65
Bowl, 5" d., marigold 28
Bowl, 6 1/2" d., crimped edge, red.................. 425
Bowl, 8" d., black amethyst............................. 225
Bowl, 8" to 9" d., amber................................... 150
Bowl, 8" to 9" d., aqua.................................... 550
Bowl, 8" to 9" d., blue.................................. 75-100
Bowl, 8" to 9" d., green.................................... 70
Bowl, 8" to 9" d., light blue w/marigold
overlay.. 180
Bowl, 8" to 9" d., marigold............................. 70-80

Holly Bowl

Bowl, 8" to 9" d., purple (ILLUS) 130
Bowl, 8" to 9" d., red.......................... 1,500-1,550
Bowl, 8" to 9" d., white 100-125
Bowl, 8" to 9" d., candy ribbon edge, blue 50-55

Bowl, 8" to 9" d., candy ribbon edge, green 150-175
Bowl, 8" to 9" d., candy ribbon edge, marigold 65
Bowl, 8" to 9" d., candy ribbon edge, pastel green 550
Bowl, 8" to 9" d., candy ribbon edge, purple 100-125
Bowl, 8" to 9" d., ice cream shape, blue   75-100,00
Bowl, 8" to 9" d., ice cream shape, celeste blue 1,500-2,000
Bowl, 8" to 9" d., ice cream shape, green 122
Bowl, 8" to 9" d., ice cream shape, ice green 2,700
Bowl, 8" to 9" d., ice cream shape, marigold 55-75
Bowl, 8" to 9" d., ice cream shape, purple 80
Bowl, 8" to 9" d., ice cream shape, red 2,000-2,500
Bowl, 8" to 9" d., ice cream shape, white .. 135-140
Bowl, 8" to 9" d., ruffled, blue 113
Bowl, 8" to 9" d., ruffled, blue opalescent 1,350
Bowl, 8" to 9" d., ruffled, emerald green 300
Bowl, 8" to 9" d., ruffled, green 160
Bowl, 8" to 9" d., ruffled, lime green 225
Bowl, 8" to 9" d., ruffled, marigold 63
Bowl, 8" to 9" d., ruffled, peach opalescent 48
Bowl, 8" to 9" d., ruffled, purple 165
Bowl, 8" to 9" d., ruffled, red 1,300-1,475
Bowl, 8" to 9" d., ruffled, vaseline 165
Bowl, 8" to 9" d., ruffled, white 100-150
Bowl, three-in-one edge, blue 50
Compote, lime green w/marigold overlay 85
Compote, small, Amberina 650
Compote, small, aqua w/marigold overlay 138
Compote, small, blue 105
Compote, small, green............................. 125-150
Compote, small, purple 75
Compote, small, red............................. 800-1,000
Compote, small, vaseline................................. 95
Dish, hat-shaped, Amberina...................... 400-425
Dish, hat-shaped, aqua, 5 3/4"..................... 75-85
Dish, hat-shaped, blue, 5 3/4" 35-45
Dish, hat-shaped, marigold, 5 3/4" 35-40
Dish, hat-shaped, purple, 5 3/4".................... 40-45
Dish, hat-shaped, red, 5 3/4"..................... 450-500
Dish, hat-shaped, vaseline, 5 3/4"................. 80-90
Goblet, blue... 45
Goblet, marigold....................................... 39
Plate, 9" to 10" d., blue 375
Plate, 9" to 10" d., green 1,025
Plate, 9" to 10" d., marigold...................... 175-200
Plate, 9" to 10" d., pastel marigold 175
Plate, 9" to 10" d., purple...................... 700-1,000
Plate, 9" to 10" d., white 200
Sauceboat, peach opalescent, handled............. 85
Sherbet, green 28
Sherbet, marigold....................................... 26
Violet bowl, marigold.................................... 17

HOLLY SPRIG - See Holly Whirl Pattern

HOLLY WHIRL or HOLLY SPRIG (Millersburg, Fenton & Dugan)
Bowl, 6" w., green, tricornered........................... 85
Bowl, 6" w., marigold, tricornered 295
Bowl, 6" w., purple, tricornered 125
Bowl, 7" d., green..................................... 60
Bowl, 7" d., marigold 55
Bowl, 7" d., purple, ruffled............................ 60-70
Bowl, 7" w., tricornered, marigold 180
Bowl, 7 1/2" w., tricornered, purple 98

Bowl, 8" d., ice cream shape, marigold, variant 125-150
Bowl, 8" d., ice cream shape, purple................ 325
Bowl, 8" to 9" d., green.................................... 80
Bowl, 8" to 9" d., marigold 75-80
Bowl, 8" w., tricornered, green 97
Bowl, 10" d., ruffled, marigold 55
Bowl, 10" d., ruffled, purple (Millersburg) .. 150-200
Bowl, ruffled, green (Millersburg) 250
Card tray, two-handled, green 50-85
Card tray, two-handled, marigold............... 75-100
Nappy, single handle, peach opalescent, (Dugan) 65
Nappy, single handle, purple (Dugan)......... 75-100
Nappy, tricornered, green (Dugan)..................... 98
Nappy, tricornered, marigold (Millersburg)......... 95
Nappy, tricornered, purple (Dugan)........... 100-125
Nappy, tricornered, purple (Millersburg).... 175-200
Nappy, two-handled, green (Dugan) 85
Nut dish, two-handled, green 100-125
Nut dish, two-handled, marigold 66
Nut dish, two-handled, purple 84
Rose bowl, blue 275-300
Sauce dish, green, 6 1/2" d. (Millersburg)... 100-125
Sauceboat, peach opalescent (Dugan)........... 135

HONEYCOMB
Bonbon, marigold.. 29

Honeycomb Rose Bowl

Rose bowl, peach opalescent (ILLUS) 143

HORSE HEADS or HORSE MEDALLION (Fenton)
Bowl, 5" d., footed, marigold 57
Bowl, 7" d., ice cream shape, marigold........... 155
Bowl, 7" to 8" d., blue 220
Bowl, 7" to 8" d., green............................. 250-300
Bowl, 7" to 8" d., marigold (ILLUS)........... 100-150

Horse Head Medallions Bowl

Bowl, 7" to 8" d., red 1,250-1,500
Bowl, footed, green 395
Bowl, footed, purple 325
Bowl, footed, ruffled, marigold 175
Bowl, jack-in-the-pulpit shaped, blue 225-300
Bowl, jack-in-the-pulpit shaped, lime green 300
Bowl, jack-in-the-pulpit shaped, marigold 75
Nut bowl, three-footed, amethyst.................... 225
Nut bowl, three-footed, aqua 1,800
Nut bowl, three-footed, blue 195
Nut bowl, three-footed, green 145
Nut bowl, three-footed, marigold 68
Nut bowl, three-footed, red........................... 1,200
Nut bowl, three-footed, smoky................. 500-525
Nut bowl, three-footed, vaseline 475
Plate, 7" to 8" d., blue......................... 1,050-1,075
Plate, 7" to 8" d., marigold.............................. 220
Rose bowl, blue 315
Rose bowl, marigold 150-200
Rose bowl, marigold, giant 500
Rose bowl, vaseline... 650

ILLINOIS SOLDIER'S & SAILOR'S PLATE
Blue 2,300
Marigold 1,850

IMPERIAL GRAPE (Imperial)
Basket, marigold 75
Basket, purple 60
Berry set: master bowl & 4 sauce dishes;
  green, 5 pcs. 125-150
Berry set: master bowl & 4 sauce dishes;
  purple, 5 pcs.. 285
Berry set: master bowl & 6 sauce dishes;
  marigold, 7 pcs. 150-200
Bowl, 6" d., marigold 35
Bowl, 6" d., ruffled, purple 75
Bowl, 8" to 9" d., aqua...................................... 75
Bowl, 8" to 9" d., marigold........................... 35-45
Bowl, 8" to 9" d., purple.................................. 140
Bowl, 9" d., low, amber 400
Bowl, 9" d., ruffled, amber............................... 150
Bowl, 10" d., green...................................... 60-70
Bowl, 10" d., marigold 40
Bowl, 10" d., purple 185
Bowl, 10" d., smoky.. 45
Bowl, 11" d., ruffled, purple 145-165
Compote, marigold 38
Compote, smoky, made from goblet............... 350
Cup & saucer, marigold............................... 75-80
Decanter w/stopper, green 125-150
Decanter w/stopper, marigold.................. 95-100
Decanter w/stopper, purple 200-250
Goblet, amber 45
Goblet, marigold.. 36
Goblet, purple 125
Goblet, smoky 75-100
Pitcher, water, amber....................................... 650
Pitcher, water, marigold 77
Pitcher, water, purple............................... 350-400
Pitcher, water, smoky 300-400
Plate, 6" d., amber................................... 140-150
Plate, 6" d., green... 74
Plate, 6" d., marigold 55
Plate, 6" d., purple 150
Plate, 7" d., green 75
Plate, 7" d., marigold 50-75
Plate, 8" d., clambroth, stippled...................... 75
Plate, 8" d., green.. 63
Plate, 9" d., green, flat..................................... 75

Plate, 9" d., green, ruffled................................ 156
Plate, 9" d., marigold, flat 85-100
Plate, 9" d., marigold, ruffled 65-75
Plate, 9" d., purple, ruffled........................... 1,500
Plate, 9" d., white, ruffled................................. 55
Rose bowl, purple 68
Sauce dish, amber....................................... 40-45
Sauce dish, marigold, ruffled 20
Sauce dish, purple.. 35
Tray, center handle, amber 30
Tray, center handle, clambroth.......................... 45
Tray, center handle, marigold........................... 63
Tray, center handle, smoky 65
Tumbler, emerald green 210
Tumbler, green 29
Tumbler, marigold....................................... 15-20
Tumbler, purple.. 40-50
Tumbler, smoky 90-100
Water bottle, green 100-125
Water bottle, marigold 135-175

Imperial Grape Water Bottle

Water bottle, purple (ILLUS.)................... 200-225
Water bottle, smoky 525
Water set: pitcher & 6 tumblers; marigold,
  7 pcs.. 195-225
Water set: pitcher & 6 tumblers; purple, 7
  pcs... 625-675
Wine, green (ILLUS.)................................... 25-30
Wine, lime green 40
Wine, marigold 30-40
Wine, purple 35-45
Wine, smoky 50

INVERTED FEATHER (Cambridge)
Compote, jelly, marigold 80

Inverted Feather Cracker Jar

Cracker jar, cov., green (ILLUS.) 200-250
Creamer, purple 160
Parfait, marigold 60

INVERTED THISTLE (Cambridge)
Plate, chop, purple 1,750
Tumbler, purple 210

JEWELED HEART (Dugan or Diamond Glass)
Bowl, 10" d., purple 100

Jeweled Heart Pitcher

Pitcher, marigold (ILLUS.) 650-850
Plate, 7" d., ruffled, peach opalescent 100
Sauce dish, peach opalescent 40-45
Sauce dish, purple 41
Spooner, green 35
Tumbler, marigold 85

KITTENS (Fenton)
Bowl, cereal, aqua 725
Bowl, cereal, blue 425-475
Bowl, cereal, marigold 200
Bowl, four-sided, marigold, ruffled 185-200
Bowl, ruffled, marigold 125
Bowl, ruffled, purple 200
Bowl, six-sided, marigold, ruffled 250-300
Cup, blue 550
Cup, marigold 125
Cup & saucer, marigold 200-250

Kittens Dish

Dish, turned-up sides, marigold (ILLUS.) .. 145-165
Dish, turned-up sides, purple 450-500
Plate, 4 1/2" d., marigold 150-200
Saucer, marigold 140

Toothpick holder, blue 450-500
Toothpick holder, marigold 150
Vase, marigold 179
Vase, marigold, child's, ruffled 143

LATTICE & GRAPE (Fenton)
Pitcher, marigold 95
Pitcher, tankard, blue 350-400
Pitcher, tankard, marigold 200
Tumbler, blue 45-55
Tumbler, marigold 30
Tumbler, purple 40
Water set: tankard pitcher & 5 tumblers;
    marigold, 6 pcs. 225-250
Water set: tankard pitcher & 6 tumblers;
    blue, 7 pcs. 675-700

LEAF & BEADS (Northwood)
Candy bowl, footed, aqua opalescent 500
Nut bowl, green, handled, w/interior pat-
    tern 175

Leaf & Beads Rose Bowl

Rose bowl, aqua opalescent (ILLUS) 400
Rose bowl, blue 225
Rose bowl, blue w/electric iridescence 300-500
Rose bowl, green 130-150
Rose bowl, ice blue 1,400
Rose bowl, ice green opalescent 3,000
Rose bowl, marigold 95-100
Rose bowl, marigold, souvenir 125

LEAF CHAIN (Fenton)
Bowl, 6" d., ruffled, red 613
Bowl, 7" d., aqua 115-125
Bowl, 7" d., blue 70
Bowl, 7" d., green, ruffled 150
Bowl, 7" d., ice green, ruffled 950
Bowl, 7" d., marigold 60
Bowl, 7" d., white 66
Bowl, 8" d., ice cream shape, blue 120
Bowl, 8" d., ice cream shape, clambroth 160
Bowl, 8" d., ice cream shape, green 145-150
Bowl, 8" d., ice cream shape, white 150
Bowl, 8" to 9" d., blue 100-125
Bowl, 8" to 9" d., clambroth 63
Bowl, 8" to 9" d., green 80
Bowl, 8" to 9" d., light blue 125
Bowl, 8" to 9" d., marigold 95-100
Bowl, 8" to 9" d., purple 84
Bowl, 8" to 9" d., vaseline 95
Bowl, 8" to 9" d., white 95-125
Bowl, 8 1/2" d., ice cream shape, marigold 45
Bowl, ruffled, purple 213

Plate, 7" to 8" d., blue **130-150**
Plate, 7" to 8" d., marigold **125-150**
Plate, 9" d., clambroth **125-150**
Plate, 9" d., green **195**

Leaf Chain Plate

Plate, 9" d., marigold (ILLUS.) **375-400**
Plate, 9" d., pastel marigold **293**
Plate, 9" d., purple **240**
Plate, 9" d., white **225-300**

LEAF & FLOWERS or LEAF & LITTLE FLOWERS (Millersburg)
Compote, miniature, green **475**
Compote, miniature, marigold **350-375**
Compote, miniature, purple **400**

LEAF TIERS
Bowl, 8" d., footed, marigold **35**
Pitcher, footed, marigold **450**
Shade, milk white w/marigold overlay **60**
Spooner, marigold **90**
Tumbler, blue **270**
Tumbler, marigold **115**
Water set: pitcher & 6 tumblers; marigold,
    7 pcs. **900**

LION (Fenton)
Bowl, 6" d., blue **250-350**
Bowl, 6" d., marigold **100-125**
Bowl, 7" d., blue **335**
Bowl, 7" d., ice cream shape, blue **300-315**

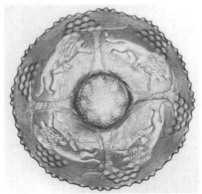

Lion Bowl

Bowl, 7" d., ice cream shape, marigold
    (ILLUS.) **175**
Bowl, 7" d., ruffled, blue **275-300**
Bowl, 7" d., ruffled, marigold **130**

LITTLE BARREL PERFUME

Little Barrel Perfume

Green (ILLUS.) **325**
Marigold **100-150**

LITTLE FISHES (Fenton)
Bowl, 6" d., three-footed, marigold **60-65**
Bowl, 6" d., three-footed, purple **175**
Bowl, 8" to 9" d., three-footed, blue **310**
Bowl, 8" to 9" d., three-footed, marigold **88**

Little Fishes Bowl

Bowl, 10" d., three-footed, blue (ILLUS.) **375**
Bowl, 10" d., three-footed, marigold **130**
Sauce dish, three-footed, blue, 5" d. **120-125**
Sauce dish, three-footed, marigold, 5" d. **50**
Sauce dish, three-footed, purple, 5" d. **138**

LITTLE STARS BOWL (Millersburg)
Bowl, 7" d., green **185**
Bowl, 7" d., marigold **135-140**
Bowl, 7" d., purple **164**
Bowl, 7 1/2" d., marigold, three-in-one
    edge **425**
Bowl, 7 1/2" d., purple, ruffled **200**
Bowl, 8" d., ice cream, green **600**
Bowl, 8" d., ruffled, green **265**
Bowl, 8" d., ruffled, marigold **90**
Bowl, 8" d., ruffled, purple **200**

LOTUS & GRAPE (Fenton)

Bonbon, two-handled, blue 363

Lotus & Grape Bonbon

Bonbon, two-handled, celeste blue (ILLUS.) 90
Bonbon, two-handled, green 85
Bonbon, two-handled, lime green 95
Bonbon, two-handled, marigold 40
Bonbon, two-handled, purple 88
Bonbon, two-handled, red 1,450-1,500
Bonbon, two-handled, teal green 225-250
Bowl, 5" d., celeste blue 1,600
Bowl, 5" d., footed, blue 125
Bowl, 5" d., footed, purple 75
Bowl, 6" d., footed, blue 65
Bowl, 6" d., footed, green 75
Bowl, 7" d., footed, marigold 41
Bowl, 8" d., ruffled, blue 93
Bowl, 8" to 9" d., blue 93
Bowl, 8" to 9" d., green 115
Bowl, 8" to 9" d., marigold 125
Bowl, 8" to 9" d., purple 105
Bowl, 9" d., ruffled, blue 80
Bowl, ruffled, blue 150
Plate, 9" d., blue 1,400

LOUISA (Westmoreland)

Bowl, 7" d., footed, green 43
Bowl, 7" d., ice cream shape, blue 250
Bowl, 8" to 9" d., three-footed, green 50
Bowl, 8" to 9" d., three-footed, marigold 46
Bowl, 8" to 9" d., three-footed, purple 51
Nut bowl, footed, green 60
Nut bowl, footed, purple 55
Plate, 9 1/2" d., footed, aqua 140-150
Plate, 9 1/2" d., footed, marigold 105
Plate, 9 1/2" d., footed, purple 110
Rose bowl, footed, amber.................................. 95
Rose bowl, footed, aqua 79
Rose bowl, footed, blue 80

Louisa Rose Bowl

Rose bowl, footed, green (ILLUS.) 57
Rose bowl, footed, lavender 110
Rose bowl, footed, marigold 40
Rose bowl, footed, purple 69

LOVING CUP (FENTON) - See Orange Tree Pattern

LUSTRE ROSE (Imperial)

Bowl, 6 1/2" d., amber..................................... 100
Bowl, 6 1/2" d., stippled, marigold 65
Bowl, 7" d., three-footed, amber 35
Bowl, 7" d., three-footed, green 40
Bowl, 7" d., three-footed, marigold 40-45
Bowl, 8" to 9" d., three-footed, amber 83
Bowl, 8" to 9" d., three-footed, clambroth........... 56
Bowl, 8" to 9" d., three-footed, green 45
Bowl, 8" to 9" d., three-footed, marigold............. 38
Bowl, 8" to 9" d., three-footed, olive green 75
Bowl, 8" to 9" d., three-footed, purple 110
Bowl, fruit, 10" d., amber................................. 275
Bowl, 10 1/2" d., three-footed, marigold............. 35
Bowl, 10 1/2 d ., three-footed, purple 350
Bowl, 10 1/2" d., three-footed, smoky 67
Bowl, 11" d., ruffled, collared base, green 75
Bowl, 11" d., ruffled, footed, marigold 43
Bowl, 11" d., ruffled, footed, smoky................... 95
Bowl, fruit, red 2,500-3,000
Bowl, ruffled, amber 60
Bowl, whimsey, centerpiece, amber.......... 150-175
Butter dish, cov., marigold.......................... 75-100
Butter dish, cov., purple 250
Creamer, marigold 37
Creamer, purple 125
Fernery, amber 115
Fernery, blue... 110
Fernery, green, 7 1/2" d., 4" h. 60
Fernery, marigold... 35
Fernery, olive 85

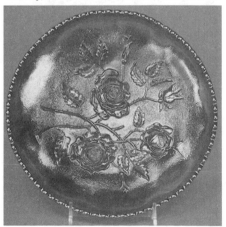

Lustre Rose Fernery

Fernery, purple (ILLUS.) 93
Fernery, smoky 110
Pitcher, water, amber...................................... 200
Pitcher, water, clambroth 105
Pitcher, water, marigold 65
Plate, 9" d., marigold 55
Rose bowl, amber....................................... 75-80

Rose bowl, clambroth 50
Rose bowl, green.. 45
Rose bowl, marigold 43
Sauce dish, clambroth 30
Sauce dish, green.. 24
Sauce dish, smoky 50
Spooner, amber... 50
Spooner, green 40
Spooner, marigold 35
Spooner, purple 150
Sugar bowl, cov., marigold 40
Tumbler, green 25
Tumbler, marigold 25
Tumbler, pastel marigold variant 100
Tumbler, purple.. 69
Water set: pitcher & 6 tumblers; marigold,
    7 pcs... 200-225

MANY FRUITS (Dugan)
Punch bowl, 9 3/4" d., purple 375-450

Maple Leaf Butter Dish & Spooner

Butter dish, cov., purple (ILLUS.).................... 145
Creamer, blue 60
Creamer, marigold 48
Creamer, purple 58
Pitcher, water, marigold 250
Pitcher, water, purple 245
Spooner, blue 70
Spooner, marigold 40
Spooner, purple (ILLUS. w/butter dish)............. 60
Sugar bowl, cov., marigold 48
Sugar bowl, cov., purple................................... 95
Table set: cov. sugar bowl, creamer &
    spooner; purple, 3 pcs......................... 200-225
Table set, blue, 4 pcs. 300-350
Tumbler, blue 65
Tumbler, marigold.. 29
Tumbler, purple... 45
Water set: pitcher & 4 tumblers; purple, 5
    pcs... 425-475

MARILYN (Millersburg)
Pitcher, water, purple 375-475
Tumbler, green 225
Tumbler, marigold.. 138
Tumbler, purple.. 150-200
Water set: pitcher & 1 tumbler; marigold, 2
    pcs.. 600

MEMPHIS (Northwood)
Berry set: master bowl & 5 sauce dishes;
    purple, 6 pcs... 750
Bowl, master berry, marigold 175
Fruit bowl & base, purple, 2 pcs. 400
Punch bowl & base, ice green,
    2 pcs... 5,000-7,000

Memphis Punch Bowl & Base

Many Fruits Punch Bowl & Base

Punch bowl & base, purple, 2 pcs.
    (ILLUS.)... 775-800
Punch bowl & base, white, 2 pcs.................... 765
Punch cup, blue.. 30-40
Punch cup, marigold... 35
Punch cup, purple 30-40
Punch cup, white 70
Punch set: bowl, base & 4 cups; marigold,
    6 pcs.. 550-600
Punch set: bowl, base & 6 cups; purple, 8
    pcs... 900-1,000

MANY STARS (Millersburg)
Bowl, 7 5/8" d., straight-sided, deep, purple.. 1,400
Bowl, 8" to 9" d., ruffled, green 413
Bowl, 8" to 9" d., ruffled, marigold.................. 418
Bowl, 10" d., ruffled, purple............................ 450
Bowl, ice cream, 10" d., green 775-800
Bowl, ice cream, 10" d., purple 850-900
Bowl, square, crimped edge, purple 3,300
Bowl, three-in-one edge, marigold 700

MAPLE LEAF (Dugan)
Bowl, 6" d., small berry, purple 35
Bowl, ice cream, footed, purple, large............. 110
Bowl, master berry or fruit, purple................... 135
Butter dish, cov., marigold 120

Punch bowl & base, purple, 2 pcs.
(ILLUS.).. **625**
Punch cup, green **35-55**
Punch cup, ice green...................................... **135**
Punch cup, marigold... **20**
Punch cup, purple **36**
Punch cup, smoky **60**
Punch cup, white **45**
Punch set: bowl, base & 10 cups; purple,
12 pcs.. **950-1,000**
Sauce dish, marigold **75**

MILLERSBURG COURTHOUSE BOWL -
See Advertising & Souvenir Items

MILLERSBURG PEACOCK -
See Peacock & Urn Pattern

MILLERSBURG PIPE HUMIDOR -
See Pipe Humidor Pattern

MILLERSBURG TROUT & FLY -
See Trout & Fly Pattern

MORNING GLORY
(Millersburg & Imperial)

Morning Glory Pitcher

Pitcher, tankard, purple (ILLUS.) **10,000**
Tumbler, purple... **1,200**
Vase, 4" to 10" h., green..................................... **79**
Vase, 4" to 10" h., marigold **50-75**
Vase, 4" to 10" h., purple............................ **125-150**
Vase, 4" to 10" h., smoky **110**
Vase, 4" to 10" h., white **150**
Vase, 10 x 12", funeral, marigold...................... **275**
Vase 12 1/2" h., funeral, purple **575-650**
Vase, 9 1/2 x 13", purple **345**
Vase, 16" h., funeral, green **210**
Vase, 18" h., marigold **200**
Vase, miniature, smoky **55**

MULTI-FRUITS -
See Many Fruits Pattern

NESTING SWAN (Millersburg)
Bowl, 9" d., green... **524**
Bowl, 9" d., marigold **450**

Bowl, 10" d., green................................... **325-375**
Bowl, 10" d., marigold **250**
Bowl, 10" d., purple... **360**

NIGHT STARS (Millersburg)
Bonbon, green... **475-500**
Bonbon, marigold... **975**

NIPPON (Northwood)
Bowl, ruffled, Basketweave exterior, purple..... **225**
Bowl, 8" d., piecrust rim, ice blue **185**
Bowl, 8" d., piecrust rim, ice green............ **600-900**
Bowl, 8" d., piecrust rim, marigold................... **250**
Bowl, 8" d., piecrust rim, pastel lime green
w/opal tips **2,950**
Bowl, 8" d., piecrust rim, purple **850**
Bowl, 8" d., piecrust rim, white........................ **270**

Nippon Bowl

Bowl, 8" to 9" d., 2 1/4" h., ice blue
(ILLUS.).. **450**
Bowl, 8" to 9" d., 3" h., green **275-325**
Bowl, ruffled, purple **500**
Plate, 9" d., green............................... **1,500-2,000**
Plate, 9" d., marigold **750**
Plate, 9" d., purple **1,700-2,000**

NU-ART HOMESTEAD PLATE (Imperial)
Amber **1,950**
Green **675-750**
Purple **975-1,050**

OCTAGON (Imperial)
Bowl, 8" to 9" d., marigold............................ **30-35**
Bowl, 8" to 9" d., pastel marigold **50**
Butter dish, cov., marigold................................. **85**
Compote, jelly, marigold **85**
Creamer, marigold **60**
Creamer, purple **180-200**
Creamer & sugar bowl, marigold variant,
pr. **110**
Decanter w/stopper, green **500**
Decanter w/stopper, marigold (ILLUS. top
of next page) **100-125**
Goblet, water, marigold...................................... **45**
Pitcher, milk, marigold....................................... **85**
Pitcher, milk, purple **250-275**
Pitcher, water, 8" h., light blue w/marigold
overlay... **125**
Pitcher, water, 8" h., marigold........................... **75**
Pitcher, water, 8" h., purple...................... **550-600**
Spooner, marigold **45**
Sugar bowl, cov., marigold **50**
Toothpick holder, marigold.............................. **130**

Octagon Wine Decanter

Tumbler, marigold... 23
Tumbler, purple.. 125
Tumblers, marigold, set of 6 95
Vase, 8" h., marigold 80-90
Wine, marigold 28
Wine set: decanter & 1 wine; marigold, 2 pcs... 150
Wine set: decanter & 4 wines; marigold, 5 pcs... 160
Wine set: decanter & 5 wines; marigold, 6 pcs... 160
Wine set: decanter & 6 wines; marigold, 7 pcs... 260-270
Wine set: decanter & 7 wines; marigold, 8 pcs... 220

OPEN ROSE (Imperial)
Berry set: master bowl & 6 sauce dishes, marigold, 7 pcs... 125
Bowl, ruffled, stippled, green........................... 60
Bowl, 5" d., blue 125
Bowl, 5" d., marigold 17
Bowl, 5" d., purple... 40-45
Bowl, 5" d., smoky... 45-50
Bowl, 6" d., ice cream shape, amber 125
Bowl, 7" d., footed, blue 55
Bowl, 7" d., footed, purple 75
Bowl, 8" to 9" d., amber 70-85
Bowl, 8" to 9" d., green 40
Bowl, 8" to 9" d., marigold............................... 37
Bowl, 8" to 9" d., purple........................... 100-125
Bowl, 8" to 9" d., vaseline, footed 150
Bowl, 10" d., amber................................. 175-200
Bowl, 10" d., marigold 85
Bowl, 11" d., marigold 60
Bowl, fruit, 11" d., collar base, smoky 225
Butter dish, cov., marigold 50
Creamer, marigold 30
Fernery, three-footed, blue 90
Plate, 9" d., amber.. 145
Plate, 9" d., green... 150
Plate, 9" d., marigold 75
Plate, 9" d., purple.. 1,325
Rose bowl, amber....................................... 75-100
Rose bowl, green.. 70-90
Rose bowl, marigold 45-55
Spooner, marigold 30
Sugar bowl, cov., marigold 40
Table set, 4 pcs., purple.............................. 1,500

Tumbler, marigold... 25
Tumbler, purple.. 115

ORANGE TREE (Fenton)
Berry set: master bowl & 6 sauce dishes; blue, 7 pcs... 300-375
Bowl, 8" to 9" d., blue 90-100
Bowl, 8" to 9" d., green............................. 225-275
Bowl, 8" to 9" d., marigold............................. 55-60
Bowl, 8" to 9" d., purple.................................. 195
Bowl, 8" to 9" d., white 100-125
Bowl, 10" d., three-footed, blue................. 250-325
Bowl, 10" d., three-footed, green 235

Large Orange Tree Bowl

Bowl, 10" d., three-footed, marigold (ILLUS.)... 175
Bowl, 10" d., three-footed, purple.................... 325
Bowl, 10" d., three-footed, white 200
Bowl, ice cream shape, blue 100
Bowl, ice cream shape, blue, w/trunk center.. 230
Bowl, ice cream shape, green......................... 300
Bowl, ice cream shape, marigold 85
Bowl, ice cream shape, purple 250-300
Bowl, ice cream shape, red 2,100
Bowl, ice cream shape, white.......................... 125
Bowl, milk white w/marigold overlay.... 1,150-1,250
Bowl, peach opalescent 1,900
Bowl, ruffled, amber 275-300
Bowl, three-in-one edge, marigold 85-90
Breakfast set: individual size creamer & cov. sugar bowl; marigold, pr. 195
Breakfast set: individual size creamer & cov. sugar bowl; purple, pr. 239
Breakfast set: individual size creamer & cov. sugar bowl; white, pr..................... 150-200
Butter dish, cov., blue 375
Butter dish, cov., marigold.............................. 350
Centerpiece bowl, footed, purple, 12" d., 4" h.. 1,000-1,500
Compote, 5" d., blue 50
Compote, 5" d., green.. 85
Compote, 5" d., marigold 35-45
Creamer, footed, blue 80
Creamer, footed, marigold 47
Creamer, footed, purple 50
Creamer, footed, white 125-175
Creamer, marigold, individual size 37
Creamer, purple, individual size 45
Creamer & sugar bowl, blue, footed, pr.......... 100
Dish, blue, ice cream, footed............................. 38
Dish, marigold, ice cream, footed.................. 30-40
Goblet, aqua 110
Goblet, blue... 55
Goblet, marigold... 57
Hatpin holder, blue.................................. 300-350
Hatpin holder, marigold 300-325

Loving cup, aqua opalescent 15,000
Loving cup, blue... 225
Loving cup, green 400-475
Loving cup, marigold...................................... 325
Loving cup, purple.. 400
Loving cup, white 150
Mug, amber 89
Mug, Amberina 385
Mug, blue... 65-75
Mug, green 875-900
Mug, lavender.. 180
Mug, lime green... 500
Mug, marigold... 45
Mug, purple 80-100
Mug, red 500
Mug, vaseline 100-150
Mug, white 948
Pitcher, water, blue 325
Pitcher, water, marigold 275
Plate, 9" d., flat, blue 400
Plate, 9" d., flat, clambroth 300-350
Plate, 9" d., flat, green 3,000
Plate, 9" d., flat, marigold 250-350
Plate, 9" d., flat, pastel marigold............... 175-200
Plate, 9" d., flat, purple 600
Plate, 9" d., flat, teal blue.................... 1,000-1,500
Plate, 9" d., flat, white.................................. 180
Plate, 9 1/2" d., trunk center, Beaded Berry
  exterior, clambroth 250
Plate, 9" d., flat, Beaded Berry exterior,
  blue 550
Plate, 9" d., trunk center, flat, Beaded Berry
  exterior, marigold 200
Plate, 9" d., trunk center, white........................ 275
Plate, 9" d., Blackberry exterior, "Souvenir
  of Hershey," blue... 335
Powder jar, cov., blue 150-175
Powder jar, cov., green 400-500
Powder jar, cov., marigold 75-100
Punch bowl & base, blue, 2 pcs. 275-300
Punch bowl & base, marigold, 2 pcs. 185-195
Punch bowl & base, white, 2 pcs. 595
Punch cup, blue.. 32
Punch cup, white 50
Punch cups, marigold, set of 6 125-150
Punch set: bowl, base & 6 cups; marigold,
  8 pcs.. 330
Punch set: bowl, base & 6 cups; white, 8
  pcs.. 900
Punch set: bowl, base & 10 cups; blue, 12
  pcs.. 650
Rose bowl, blue 85
Rose bowl, clambroth 90
Rose bowl, green..................................... 100-125
Rose bowl, purple 100-125
Rose bowl, white 200-225
Sauce dish, footed, white 100-125
Shaving mug, blue 50
Shaving mug, green 875
Shaving mug, marigold 50
Shaving mug, marigold, large 100-125
Shaving mug, olive green............................... 975
Shaving mug, purple 195
Shaving mug, red 600-650
Spooner, blue 60-70
Spooner, marigold 50
Sugar bowl, cov., blue 60
Sugar bowl, cov., marigold 98
Sugar bowl, cov., white 100

Tumbler, blue.. 60
Tumbler, marigold.. 40
Tumbler, white 100
Wine, green 225
Wine, marigold 25

ORANGE TREE ORCHARD (Fenton)
Pitcher, marigold.. 365
Pitcher, white 475
Tumbler, blue.. 50-55
Tumbler, marigold.. 60
Water set: pitcher & 3 tumblers; blue, 4
  pcs.. 500
Water set: pitcher & 4 tumblers; blue, 5
  pcs.. 600
Water set: pitcher & 6 tumblers; blue, 7
  pcs.. 675
Water set: pitcher & 6 tumblers; marigold,
  7 pcs... 850-900
Water set: pitcher & 6 tumblers; white, 7
  pcs.. 1,500

ORIENTAL POPPY (Northwood)
Pitcher, tankard, marigold.............................. 265
Pitcher, water, green.................................. 1,250
Pitcher, water, marigold 415-425
Pitcher, water, purple 750-850
Pitcher, water, white 1,500-2,000
Tumbler, ice green... 275
Tumbler, marigold.. 35
Tumbler, purple... 50-60
Tumbler, white 155-165
Water set: pitcher & 4 tumblers, white, 5
  pcs.. 2,000
Water set: pitcher & 5 tumblers, marigold,
  6 pcs... 500-600
Water set: pitcher & 6 tumblers, green, 7
  pcs... 1,800-2,500

Oriental Poppy Water Set

Water set: pitcher & 6 tumblers, purple, 7
  pcs. (ILLUS.) 1,338

PANTHER (Fenton)
Berry set: master bowl & 5 sauce dishes;
  marigold, 6 pcs. 200-375
Berry set: master bowl & 6 sauce dishes;
  marigold, 7 pcs. 350-375
Bowl, 5" d., footed, aqua 275

Bowl, 5" d., footed, blue 175
Bowl, 5" d., footed, clambroth 35
Bowl, 5" d., footed, green................. 90-100
Bowl, 5" d., footed, marigold 45-55

Panther Bowl

Bowl, 5" d., footed, red (ILLUS.) 675-750
Bowl, 5" d., footed, white................................. 475
Bowl, 9" d., claw-footed, green 625-675
Bowl, 9" d., claw-footed, marigold............ 195-225
Bowl, 9" d., claw-footed, purple............. 395-500
Bowl, 9" d., claw-footed, white 750-1,000
Bowl, low, marigold 100-125
Centerpiece bowl, marigold 575-600

PEACH (Northwood)
Bowl, 9" d., white... 225
Butter dish, cov., white................................... 225

Peach Pitcher

Pitcher, water, blue (ILLUS.)........................ 1,250
Sauce dish, white 45
Spooner, white 135-150
Sugar bowl, cov., white 125-150
Tumbler, blue.. 85-100
Tumbler, blue w/electric iridescence......... 140-150
Tumbler, marigold....................................... 2,100
Tumbler, white 95
Water set: pitcher & 5 tumblers; blue
    w/electric iridescence, 6 pcs. 1,600

PEACOCK AT FOUNTAIN (Northwood)
Berry set: master bowl & 4 sauce dishes;
    purple, 5 pcs.. 450
Bowl, berry, green... 375
Bowl, fruit, blue 1,450

Peacock at Fountain Fruit Bowl

Bowl, fruit, blue w/electric iridescence
    (ILLUS.)... 2,000
Bowl, master berry, green........................ 600-650
Bowl, master berry, marigold 200
Bowl, master berry, purple 225-250
Bowl, master berry, white........................ 400-450
Bowl, orange, three-footed, blue.................. 1,080
Bowl, orange, three-footed, marigold........ 275-300
Bowl, orange, three-footed, purple.................. 800
Butter dish, cov., marigold..................... 175-225
Butter dish, cov., purple 250-300
Compote, blue 2,500
Compote, ice blue.. 1,325
Compote, ice green 1,750-1,850
Compote, purple 750
Compote, white.. 305
Creamer, purple 100-125
Pitcher, water, blue 400-450
Pitcher, water, marigold 375
Pitcher, water, purple 400
Pitcher, water, white 1,000-1,025
Punch bowl & base, blue, 2 pcs.................. 3,000
Punch bowl & base, ice green, 2 pcs.......... 9,500
Punch bowl & base, marigold, 2 pcs............. 500
Punch bowl & base, purple, 2 pcs. 1,400-1,425
Punch cup, ice green....................................... 525
Punch cup, marigold... 40
Punch cup, purple 40-45
Punch cup, white 90
Punch set: bowl, base & 5 cups; purple,
    7 pcs... 1,900
Punch set: bowl, base & 6 cups; ice blue,
    8 pcs... 8,000
Punch set: bowl, base & 6 cups; marigold,
    8 pcs.. 750
Punch set: bowl, base & 8 cups; purple,
    10 pcs... 1,825
Sauce dish, green... 25
Sauce dish, ice blue 100-110
Sauce dish, marigold.. 30
Sauce dish, purple 45
Sauce dish, teal blue 75
Sauce dish, white 70-80
Spooner, blue 150
Spooner, blue w/electric iridescence 250
Spooner, green 185
Spooner, ice blue.. 280
Spooner, purple 100-120
Spooner, white... 183
Sugar bowl, cov., ice blue 375-400
Sugar bowl, cov., purple 115
Tumbler, blue.. 60-70
Tumbler, green 325
Tumbler, ice blue 325
Tumbler, marigold... 45

Tumbler, purple... **65-70**
Tumbler, teal blue **139**
Tumbler, white **225-250**
Water set: pitcher & 3 tumblers; purple, 4
    pcs... **600-625**

PEACOCK, FLUFFY (Fenton)
Pitcher, water, blue.. **650**
Pitcher, water, green............................... **650-700**
Pitcher, water, marigold **450-500**

Peacock, Fluffy Pitcher

Pitcher, water, purple (ILLUS) **575-600**
Tumbler, purple... **45-50**
Water set: pitcher & 4 tumblers; marigold,
    5 pcs.. **500**
Water set: pitcher & 5 tumblers; purple, 6
    pcs.. **750-800**

PEACOCK & GRAPE (Fenton)
Bowl, 8" d., collared base, amber **120**
Bowl, 8" d., collared base, blue..................... **70-90**
Bowl, 8" d., collared base, ice green, ruf-
    fled **225**
Bowl, 8" d., collared base, marigold................... **40**
Bowl, 8" d., collared base, peach opales-
    cent **575-600**
Bowl, 8" d., collared base, purple...................... **90**
Bowl, 8" d., ice cream shape, green **100-125**
Bowl, 8" d., ice cream shape, marigold..... **100-125**
Bowl, 8" d., ice cream shape, red **1,000-1,125**
Bowl, 8" d., spatula-footed, green **125-150**
Bowl, 8" d., spatula-footed, ice green opal-
    escent.. **450-500**
Bowl, 8" d., spatula-footed, marigold **55**
Bowl, 8" d., spatula-footed, purple **95-125**
Bowl, 8 3/4" d., amber................................... **160**
Bowl, 9" d., ruffled, collared base, blue..... **125-150**
Bowl, 9" d., ruffled, green............................... **100**
Bowl, 9" d., ruffled, marigold **50**
Bowl, 9" d., ruffled, purple **110**
Bowl, 9" d., ruffled, red.................................. **300**
Bowl, Bearded Berry exterior, blue **165**
Bowl, ruffled, spatula-footed, lime green
    opalescent **245**
Bowl, footed, ice cream shape, purple............. **175**
Bowl, ice cream shape, blue **125**

Bowl, three-in-one edge, collared base,
    purple **175**
Plate, 9" d., collared base, green **250**
Plate, 9" d., collared base, marigold................ **275**
Plate, 9" d., collared base, pastel marigold **750**
Plate, 9" d., dark marigold, berry exterior **950**
Plate, 9" d., flat base, marigold....................... **500**
Plate, 9" d., spatula-footed, emerald
    green **1,000-1,500**
Plate, 9" d., spatula-footed, green **175-200**
Plate, 9" d., spatula-footed, marigold **300-325**
Plate, 9" d., spatula-footed, purple **375-400**
Plate, footed, green **850**

PEACOCK TAIL (Fenton)
Berry set: 9" d. bowl & four 5" d. bowls;
    green, 5 pcs. **150**
Bonbon, two-handled, green............................. **80**

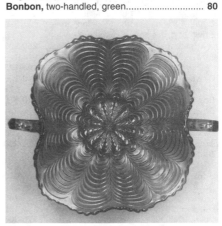

Peacock Tail Bonbon

Bonbon, two-handled, marigold (ILLUS.)........... **37**
Bonbon, tricornered, marigold **22**
Bonbon, tricornered, purple **35-40**
Bowl, 4" d., marigold **40**
Bowl, 5" d., ruffled, green............................ **20-25**
Bowl, 5" d., ruffled, marigold **24**
Bowl, 6" d., ruffled, marigold **30-35**
Bowl, 6" d., ruffled, purple **40**
Bowl, 7" d., blue, ruffled **55**
Bowl, 9" d., blue, candy ribbon edge................. **65**
Bowl, 9" d., green.. **49**
Bowl, 9" d., green, candy ribbon edge **175-200**
Bowl, 9" d., marigold, crimped **50**
Bowl, 9" d., purple, candy ribbon edge **55-65**
Bowl, 9" sq., purple, candy ribbon edge **475**
Bowl, 10" d., green, candy ribbon edge **225**
Compote, blue, 6" d., 5" h. **60**
Compote, green, 6" d., 5" h. **65**
Compote, marigold, 6" d., 5" h. **80-90**
Compote, marigold, variant, 6" d., 5" h. **90**
Compote, purple, 6" d., 5" h....................... **50-60**
Compote, purple, variant, 6" d., 5" h. **165-175**
Plate, 6" d., blue **195-225**
Plate, 6" d., purple, tricornered, Panels
    exterior **125-150**
Plate, 9" d., marigold **1,250**
Whimsey green, hat-shaped........................ **60-65**

PEACOCK & URN (Millersburg, Fenton & Northwood)

Berry set: master bowl & 6 sauce dishes; marigold, 7 pcs. (Northwood) 700
Bowl, 5" d., ice cream shape, blue, stippled..... 125
Bowl, 5 1/2" d., ruffled, blue (Millersburg) 1,700
Bowl, 6" d., ice cream, blue w/electric iridescence 375
Bowl, 6" d., ice cream shape, green (Millersburg) 200-250
Bowl, 6" d., ice cream shape, marigold (Millersburg) 85
Bowl, 6" d., ice cream shape, purple (Millersburg) 250
Bowl, 6" d., ice cream shape, purple satin 150
Bowl, 6" d., ice cream shape, white 120-150
Bowl, 7" d., ruffled, green (Millersburg)............ 250
Bowl, 7" d., ruffled, marigold (Millersburg) 395
Bowl, 7" d., ruffled, purple (Millersburg)........... 350
Bowl, 7 1/2" d., "shotgun," ruffled, green.......... 550
Bowl, 8" d., ice cream shape, green (Fenton)... 250-300
Bowl, 8" d., ice cream shape, marigold (Fenton)... 100-125
Bowl, 8" to 9" d., blue (Fenton) 240-250
Bowl, 8" to 9" d., green (Millersburg)............... 375
Bowl, 8" to 9" d., marigold (Fenton) 140-160
Bowl, 8" to 9" d., marigold, ruffled (Millersburg) 225
Bowl, 8" to 9" d., purple (Fenton) 155
Bowl, 8" to 9" d., white (Fenton)................ 225-250
Bowl, 8 3/4" d., ice cream shape, purple (Millersburg) 1,000
Bowl, 9" d., ice cream shape, blue (Fenton)..... 250
Bowl, 9" d., ice cream shape, marigold (Fenton)... 185
Bowl, 9" d., ruffled, blue (Fenton).................... 135
Bowl, 9" d., ruffled, purple (Fenton) 275-300
Bowl, 9" d., ruffled, white.............................. 295
Bowl, 9 1/2" d., berry, purple (Millersburg) 550-600
Bowl, 10" d., ice cream shape, aqua opalescent (Northwood)................................. 25,000
Bowl, 10" d, ice cream shape, blue (Northwood) 1,000
Bowl, 10" d., ice cream shape, cobalt blue, stippled (Northwood) 1,100
Bowl, 10" d., ice cream shape, green (Northwood) 1,500
Bowl, 10" d., ice cream shape, green w/bee (Millersburg)................................ 900-950
Bowl, 10" d., ice cream shape, honey amber, stippled (Northwood).................... 1,400
Bowl, 10" d., ice cream shape, ice blue (Northwood) 825
Bowl, 10" d., ice cream shape, ice green (Northwood) 1,000-1,100
Bowl, 10" d., ice cream shape, marigold (Millersburg) 375-425
Bowl, 10" d., ice cream shape, marigold (Northwood) 305
Bowl, 10" d., ice cream shape, marigold, stippled (Northwood) 700
Bowl, 10" d., ice cream shape, pastel marigold (Northwood)................................ 550-600
Bowl, 10" d., ice cream shape, pastel marigold, stippled (Northwood) 550-600
Bowl, 10" d., ice cream shape, purple (Millersburg) 1,100

Bowl, 10" d., ice cream shape, purple Northwood.. 625
Bowl, 10" d., ice cream shape, white (Northwood) 550
Bowl, 10" d., ruffled, marigold 145
Bowl, 10" d., ruffled, purple 350-400
Bowl, 10" d., three-in-one edge, purple (Millersburg) 650-700
Bowl, 10 1/2" d., ruffled, green (Millersburg) 325-350
Bowl, 10 1/2" d., ruffled, marigold (Millersburg) 225-250
Bowl, 10 1/2" d., ruffled, purple (Fenton) .. 275-300
Bowl, 10 1/2" d., ruffled, purple (Millersburg) 300
Bowl, ruffled, Bearded Berry exterior, marigold 198
Bowl, ruffled, marigold (Northwood)................. 245
Bowl, ruffled, white (Fenton) 150-175
Bowl, three-in-one edge, green....................... 375
Compote, 5 1/2" d., 5" h., aqua (Fenton) 165
Compote, 5 1/2" d., 5" h., blue (Fenton) ... 125-150
Compote, 5 1/2" d., 5" h., marigold (Fenton)... 50-60
Compote, 5 1/2" d., 5" h., white (Fenton)......... 245
Compote, green (Millersburg Giant).... 1,500-1,550
Compote, marigold (Millersburg Giant)......... 1,700
Compote, purple (Millersburg Giant)............. 2,000
Goblet, blue (Fenton) 90
Goblet, marigold (Fenton) 65
Ice cream dish, purple, 5 3/4" d. (Millersburg) 350-400
Ice cream dish, blue w/electric iridescence..... 180
Ice cream dish, green, small (Northwood)....... 950
Ice cream dish, purple, small 95
Plate, 6 1/2" d., green (Millersburg).............. 1,500

Peacock & Urn Plate

Plate, 6 1/2" d., marigold, Millersburg (ILLUS.)... 1,000
Plate, 6 1/2" d., purple (Millersburg) 1,000-1,200
Plate, 9" d., blue (Fenton)................................ 400
Plate, 9" d., marigold (Fenton)......................... 375
Plate, 9" d., purple (Fenton) 150
Plate, 9" d., white (Fenton) 400-500
Plate, chop, 11" d., marigold (Millersburg) 2,200
Plate, chop, 11" d., purple (Millersburg) 2,250
Plate, chop, 11" d., purple, (Northwood) 1,400
Sauce dish, blue (Millersburg) 1,000-1,200
Sauce dish, blue, stippled (Northwood) 150-160

Sauce dish, ice green, 6" d.
(Northwood) 375-400
Sauce dish, lavender (Millersburg) 100
Sauce dish, marigold (Northwood) 85
Sauce dish, purple (Millersburg) 100
Whimsey sauce dish, purple, 5 1/4" d. 275-300

PEACOCKS ON FENCE (Northwood Peacocks)

Bowl, 8" to 9" d., piecrust rim, aqua opalescent (ILLUS.) 3,500
Bowl, 8" to 9" d., piecrust rim, blue 760
Bowl, 8" to 9" d., piecrust rim, blue, stippled, w/ribbed back 600
Bowl, 8" to 9" d., piecrust rim, green 1,100
Bowl, 8" to 9" d., piecrust rim,
ice blue 1,400-1,450
Bowl, 8" to 9" d., piecrust rim, marigold
(ILLUS.) 375
Bowl, 8" to 9" d., piecrust rim, pastel marigold 320-350
Bowl, 8" to 9" d., piecrust rim, purple 438
Bowl, 8" to 9" d., piecrust rim, Renniger
blue, stippled 1,000
Bowl, 8" to 9" d., piecrust rim, white 1,025
Bowl, 8" to 9" d., ruffled rim, blue 700
Bowl, 8" to 9" d., ruffled rim, green 700
Bowl, 8" to 9" d., ruffled rim, purple 450
Bowl, 8" to 9" d., ruffled rim, smoky 1,750
Bowl, 8" to 9" d., ruffled rim, white 900-975
Plate, Renniger blue, stippled 2,500
Plate, w/ribbed exterior, white 488
Plate, 9" d., blue w/electric iridescence 1,200
Plate, 9" d., cobalt blue, stippled 1,725
Plate, 9" d., green 1,150
Plate, 9" d., ice blue 1,500
Plate, 9" d., ice green 350
Plate, 9" d., lavender 700-1,000
Plate, 9" d., marigold, dark 550

Peacocks on Fence Plate

Plate, 9" d., marigold (ILLUS) 475
Plate, 9" d., marigold, stippled 1,200-1,225
Plate, 9" d., pastel marigold 2,100
Plate, 9" d., purple 688
Plate, 9" d., white 650-750

PERFECTION (Millersburg)

Pitcher, water, green 3,900-4,225

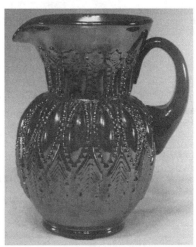

Perfection Pitcher

Pitcher, water, purple (ILLUS.) 3,200
Tumbler, purple 420-475

PERSIAN GARDEN (Dugan)

Bowl, 5" d., peach opalescent 40
Bowl, 5" d., purple 75
Bowl, 5" d., white 70-80
Bowl, 6" d., ice cream shape, white 75-80
Bowl, 10" d., marigold 50
Bowl, 10" d., ruffled, purple 400-425
Bowl, 11" d., ice cream shape, peach opalescent 750-850
Bowl, 11" d., ice cream shape, white 275-325
Fruit bowl & base, marigold, 2 pcs 225
Fruit bowl & base, peach opalescent,
2 pcs 650
Fruit bowl & base, purple, 2 pcs. 1,000
Fruit bowl & base, white, 2 pcs. 725
Fruit bowl (no base), marigold 125-130
Fruit bowl (no base), purple 250
Plate, 6" to 7" d., marigold 100-125

Persian Garden Plate

Plate, 6" to 7" d., peach opalescent
(ILLUS.) 165-200
Plate, 6" to 7" d., purple 488
Plate, 6" to 7" d., white 150-175
Plate, chop, 11" d., white 700-800

PERSIAN MEDALLION (Fenton)

Bonbon, two-handled, aqua...................... 250-300
Bonbon, two-handled, blue............................... 75
Bonbon, two-handled, green 80
Bonbon, two-handled, marigold................... 50-60
Bonbon, two-handled, purple....................... 60-70
Bonbon, two-handled, red 860
Bonbon, two-handled, vaseline 130
Bowl, 5" d., aqua..................................... 125-150
Bowl, 5" d., blue 55
Bowl, 5" d., marigold 30-35
Bowl, 5" d., purple 67
Bowl, 6" d., ruffled, marigold 30-40
Bowl, 7" d., purple, candy ribbon edge 85-95
Bowl, 8" to 9" d., blue, fluted 100-125
Bowl, 8" to 9" d., green, ice cream shape 155
Bowl, 8" to 9" d., marigold............................ 55-65
Bowl, 8" to 9" d., purple, candy
    ribbon edge 100-125
Bowl, 9" d., green, ruffled............................... 75
Bowl, 9 1/2" d., blue, footed, Grape &
    Cable exterior..................................... 325-375
Bowl, 10" d., purple 295
Bowl, fruit, purple, Grape & Cable exterior 275
Bowl, ice cream shape, blue 65
Bowl, salad shape, large, blue 400-425
Bowl, three-in-one edge, blue 100
Compote, blue, 6 1/2" d., 6 1/2" h. 110
Compote, green, 6 1/2" d., 6 1/2" h. 225-300
Compote, marigold, 6 1/2" d., 6 1/2" h. 115
Compote, purple, 6 1/2" d., 6 1/2" h. 140
Compote, candy ribbon edge, cobalt blue 200-250
Compote, three-in-one rim, purple.................. 575
Hair receiver, blue 165-195
Hair receiver, marigold 70
Hair receiver, white....................................... 125
Plate, 6 1/2" d., blue 125-150
Plate, 6 1/2" d., green.................................. 160
Plate, 6 1/2" d., marigold 75-100
Plate, 7" d., marigold 110-125
Plate, 7 3/4" d., blue 300
Plate, 9" d., blue 275

Persian Medallion Chop Plate

Plate, chop, 10 1/2" d., blue (ILLUS.) 650
Rose bowl, blue 185
Rose bowl, marigold 75-100
Rose bowl, purple.. 350
Rose bowl, white 125-135

PETER RABBIT (Fenton)

Bowl, 8" d., blue 1,000-1,100
Bowl, 8" d., green................................. 950-1,000
Bowl, 8" d., marigold 1,500

Peter Rabbit Plate

Plate, green (ILLUS.).......................... 3,500-4,000

PINE CONE (Fenton)

Bowl, 5" d., aqua..................................... 100-150

Pine Cone Bowl

Bowl, 5" d., blue (ILLUS.).................................... 45
Bowl, 5" d., marigold 60-70
Bowl, 5" d., purple 45
Bowl, 6" d., blue, ruffled 135
Bowl, 6" d., marigold 40-50
Bowl, 6" d., marigold, ruffled 58
Bowl, 6" d., purple, ruffled 175
Bowl, 7" d., blue, ruffled 85
Bowl, 7" d., purple, ruffled 85
Plate, 6 1/2" d., blue 165
Plate, 6 1/2" d., green............................... 150-175
Plate, 6 1/2" d., marigold 85
Plate, 6 1/2" d., purple 195
Plate, 7 1/2" d., amber............................. 650-700
Plate, 7 1/2" d., marigold 125

PIPE HUMIDOR (Millersburg)

Pipe Humidor

Green (ILLUS.) 6,500
Marigold 5,000

PLAID (Fenton)
Bowl, 8" d., green, deep.................................. 350
Bowl, 8" d., marigold, ice cream shape........... 155
Bowl, 9" d., ruffled, blue 240-275
Bowl, 9" d., ruffled, marigold 155
Bowl, 9" d., ruffled, red....................... 3,250-3,500
Bowl, ice cream, 10" d., blue........................... 300
Bowl, ice cream, 10" d., green 800-900
Bowl, ice cream, 10" d., purple 400-450
Bowl, ice cream, red 2,450

PLUME PANELS VASE (Fenton)
Blue 60
Green 80
Marigold 46
Red 1,150-1,175

POINSETTIA (Imperial)
Pitcher, milk, blue opalescent 260
Pitcher, milk, green 220-225

Poinsettia Milk Pitcher

Pitcher, milk, marigold (ILLUS.) 90-100
Pitcher, milk, purple 2,100
Pitcher, milk, smoky 200-250

POND LILY
Bonbon, blue 70
Bonbon, green 68
Bonbon, marigold.. 45
Bonbon, purple 75
Bonbon, white... 95

PONY
Bowl, 8" to 9" d., aqua............................ 450-500
Bowl, 8" to 9" d., ice green 850-875

Pony Bowl

Bowl, 8" to 9" d., marigold (ILLUS.)............. 85-100
Bowl, 8" to 9" d., purple.................................. 250

POPPY (Millersburg)
Compote, green 550-650
Compote, green, flared-out salver shape...... 2,800
Compote, purple 1,000-1,150

POPPY (Northwood)
Pickle dish, aqua opalescent................... 900-950

Poppy Pickle Dish

Pickle dish, blue (ILLUS.) 295
Pickle dish, green.................................... 200-250
Pickle dish, marigold 100
Pickle dish, purple 200-225
Pickle dish, white...................................... 350-400

POPPY SHOW (Northwood)
Bowl, 7" d., purple 65
Bowl, 7 1/2" d., marigold, ruffled 30
Bowl, 8" to 9" d., blue w/electric irides-
cence.. 1,125
Bowl, 8" to 9" d., clambroth 190
Bowl, 8" to 9" d., ice blue 1,425
Bowl, 8" to 9" d., ice green 2,013
Bowl, 8" to 9" d., marigold 535

Bowl, 8" to 9" d., pastel marigold 760
Bowl, 8" to 9" d., purple................................ 1,100
Bowl, 8" to 9" d., white 450
Plate, blue 3,600
Plate, blue w/electric iridescence 2,650

Poppy Show Plate

Plate, green (ILLUS.)..................................... 4,050
Plate, ice blue... 2,700
Plate, ice green 3,900-4,000
Plate, marigold 1,400
Plate, pastel marigold.................................... 2,700
Plate, purple 1,000
Plate, white... 500

POPPY SHOW VASE (Imperial)
Marigold 425

Poppy Show Vase

Purple (ILLUS) 3,600

PRIMROSE BOWL (Millersburg)
Green 130-150
Marigold 105
Purple 175-200

RAINDROPS (Dugan)
Bowl, 7" d., turned-up, fluted, peach opal-
  escent... 96
Bowl, 9" d., dome-footed, marigold.................... 90
Bowl, 9" d., dome-footed, peach opales-
  cent 90-100

Raindrops Bowl

Bowl, 9" d., dome-footed, peach opalescent, candy ribbon edge (ILLUS.) 150
Bowl, 9" d., dome-footed, purple...................... 140

RASPBERRY (Northwood)
Pitcher, milk, green 350-400
Pitcher, milk, marigold..................................... 300
Pitcher, milk, purple 350
Pitcher, milk, white....................................... 1,000
Pitcher, water, green....................................... 350
Pitcher, water, ice blue 2,100
Pitcher, water, ice green 2,000-2,150
Pitcher, water, marigold 160-175
Pitcher, water, white 650-700

Raspberry Sauceboat

Sauceboat, purple (ILLUS.) 100-125
Tumbler, green 75
Tumbler, green w/marigold overlay................. 125
Tumbler, ice blue 275-300
Tumbler, ice green................................... 550-650
Tumbler, marigold... 45
Tumbler, purple... 75
Water set: pitcher & 4 tumblers; marigold,
  5 pcs.. 350-400

RAYS & RIBBONS (Millersburg)
Bowl, 8" to 9" d., marigold............................... 85
Bowl, 8" to 9" d., purple.................................... 85
Bowl, 8" to 9" d., purple, ice cream shape 250
Bowl, 9" d., marigold, ruffled, three-in-one
  edge 150-175
Bowl, 10" d., green.................................... 100-120
Bowl, 10" d., marigold 70-75
Bowl, 10" d., purple 80-90
Bowl, 10" sq., green 200-250
Plate, chop, purple 2,100

RIPPLE VASE

Amber, 6" h. 95
Amber, 7 1/2" h. 77
Amber, 9" h. 175
Amber, 10" h. 95-100
Amber, 11 1/2" h. 125
Aqua, 10" h. 125
Aqua, 11" h. 300
Aqua, ... 145-150
Blue, 9" h. 350
Clambroth, 10" h. 75
Clambroth, funeral, 15 1/2" h. 225
Green, 8 1/4" h. 55
Green, 9 1/2" h. 85
Green, 10" h. 40-50
Green, 11" h. 38
Green, 12 1/2" h. 95
Green, 13" h. 93
Green, 15 1/2" h. 100-125
Green, funeral, mid-size 175
Ice green, 14 1/2" h. 200-245
Lavender, 7 1/2" h. 115
Lavender, 14" h. 135
Marigold, 5" h. 210
Marigold, 6" h. 100-150
Marigold, 6 1/2" h. 45-55
Marigold, 8" h. 30
Marigold, 9 1/2" h. 25-30
Marigold, 10 1/2" h. 40
Marigold, 12" h. 78
Marigold, 16 1/2" h., funeral 58
Marigold, 17" h. 65
Marigold, funeral, 17 1/2" h. 248
Marigold, funeral, 19" h. 175

Ripple Vase

Marigold, 20" h. (ILLUS.) 150-200
Purple, 8" h. 85
Purple, 10" h. 143
Purple, 11" h. 250
Purple, 11 1/2" h. 175
Purple, 12" h. 100-125
Purple, 13" h. 208
Smoky, 12" h. 86
Smoky, 15 1/2" h. 250
Teal blue, 11 1/2" h. 350
White, 9" h. 100-125
White, 9 1/2" h. 175-200

ROBIN (Imperial)

Robin Mug

Mug, marigold (ILLUS.) 75-80
Pitcher, water, marigold 310
Tumbler, marigold 75
Tumbler, smoky 500

ROSALIND (Millersburg)

Bowl, 9" d., ruffled, green 350
Bowl, 10" d., marigold 250-275
Bowl, 10" d., purple 215
Bowl, 10" d., ruffled, aqua 575
Bowl, 10" d., ruffled, green 200
Compote, tall, ruffled, purple, 6" d. 4,250
Compote, jelly, tall, flared, green 4,250
Plate, 9" d., green 1,775
Plate, 9" d., purple 1,700

ROSE SHOW

Bowl, 9" d., aqua 750-850
Bowl, 9" d., aqua opalescent 1,255
Bowl, 9" d., blue 900
Bowl, 9" d., blue opalescent 1,450-1,500
Bowl, 9" d., green 2,775-2,875
Bowl, 9" d., ice blue 900
Bowl, 9" d., ice green 1,500-2,000
Bowl, 9" d., marigold 500
Bowl, 9" d., purple 900
Bowl, 9" d., sapphire blue 3,150
Bowl, 9" d., white 400
Bowl, Renniger blue, variant 1,750
Bowl, ruffled, pastel marigold, variant 1,400
Plate, 9" d., blue 1,300-1,400
Plate, 9" d., blue, variant 2,700

Rose Show Plate

Plate, 9" d., cobalt blue (ILLUS.) **2,100**
Plate, 9" d., dark marigold **2,000**
Plate, 9" d., green... **3,200**
Plate, 9" d., ice blue...................................... **2,000**
Plate, 9" d., ice green **2,500**
Plate, 9" d., lime green **3,500-3,700**
Plate, 9" d., marigold **850**
Plate, 9" d., pastel marigold................ **1,000-1,500**
Plate, 9" d., purple **1,800-2,000**
Plate, 9" d., white.. **450-500**

ROUND UP (Dugan)
Bowl, ice cream shape, marigold **85**
Bowl, ice cream shape, peach opalescent....... **275**
Bowl, ice cream shape, white **178**
Bowl, three-in-one edge, peach opalescent..... **150**
Plate, 9" d., blue, flat **475**

Round Up Plate

Plate, 9" d., blue (ILLUS.)......................... **350-400**
Plate, 9" d., marigold, ruffled **100-125**
Plate, 9" d., peach opalescent, flat............ **700-750**
Plate, 9" d., peach opalescent, ruffled....... **200-275**
Plate, 9" d., purple, flat **350-400**
Plate, 9" d., purple, ruffled **325-350**

RUSTIC VASE
Blue, 7" to 12" h. **35-55**
Blue, 15" h.. **105**
Blue, 16" h.. **100-125**
Blue, funeral, 18" h., 5" base.................. **900-1,000**
Blue, 19" h.. **165**
Blue, funeral, 19 1/2" h.......................... **900-1,000**
Blue, funeral, 23 1/2" h., w/plunger base,
     blue **1,300**
Green 6" h. to 10 1/2" h. **75**
Green 16" h... **100-125**
Green funeral, 19" h. **1,400-2,000**
Marigold, 6" to 10 1/2" h. (ILLUS. top of
     next column).. **35**
Marigold, 11" h... **35**
Marigold, 15" h.. **100-125**
Marigold, 16" to 21 1/2" h., 5 1/2" base **100-125**
Marigold, funeral, 16" h.................................. **385**
Marigold, funeral, 19" h., marigold............ **650-675**
Purple, 6" to 10 1/2" h. **50**
Purple, 11" h. **44**
Purple, funeral, 12" h. **175**
Purple, 15" h. **160**
Purple, 16" h. **255**
Purple, 16 3/4" h. **88**

Rustic Vase

Purple, 18 1/2" h. **750-1,000**
Purple, funeral, 19" h. **1,050**
Purple, funeral, 20" h. **1,250**
Purple, funeral, 5" base.............................. **1,350**
Red, 6" to 10 1/2" h., crimped top................. **2,900**
Vaseline, funeral **3,500**
White, 6" to 12 1/2" h..................................... **175**
White, funeral, 15" h...................................... **250**
White funeral, 18" h....................................... **850**

SAILBOATS (Fenton)
Bowl, 5" d., aqua **90-100**
Bowl, 5" d., blue, ruffled **44**
Bowl, 5" d., marigold **40**
Bowl, 5" d., marigold, ice cream shape............. **40**
Bowl, 5" d., purple **95**
Bowl, 5" d., red, ruffled.................................. **525**
Bowl, 5" d., vaseline................................. **200-225**
Bowl, 6" d., blue **75**

Sailboats Bowl

Bowl, 6" d., marigold, Orange Tree exterior
     (ILLUS.)... **60**
Bowl, 6" d., marigold, ruffled **30-40**

Bowl, vaseline, ice cream shape...................... 475
Compote, marigold 85-90
Goblet, water, green 260-275
Goblet, water, marigold........................... 100-125
Goblet, water, purple............................... 225-275
Plate, 6" d., blue 548
Plate, 6" d., marigold 400-425
Wine, blue 85
Wine, marigold 30-35

SEACOAST PIN TRAY (Millersburg)
Green 575-600
Marigold 450-500
Purple 525-550

SHELL & SAND
Bowl, purple 225-275
Bowl, 7" d., teal, ruffled 175
Bowl, 8" to 9" d., purple, ruffled....................... 88
Bowl, teal 275
Mug, marigold.. 110

Shell & Sand Plate

Plate, marigold (ILLUS.) 650

SINGING BIRDS (Northwood)
Berry set: master bowl & 6 sauce dishes;
    green, 7 pcs. 400-450
Bowl, master berry, green......................... 250-275
Bowl, master berry, marigold 75
Bowl, master berry, purple 90
Butter dish, cov., marigold 295
Butter dish, cov., purple 400
Creamer, green... 150
Creamer, marigold 65-75
Creamer, purple 125-150
Mug, aqua opalescent 1,150
Mug, blue... 180
Mug, blue, stippled 675
Mug, blue w/electric iridescence 200-250
Mug, green 250-275
Mug, green, stippled................................ 400-450
Mug, ice blue.. 700-750
Mug, lavender... 250-300
Mug, marigold... 60-70
Mug, marigold, stippled 140-150
Mug, purple 95-125
Mug, purple, w/advertising, "Amazon
    Hotel".. 175-200
Mug, Renniger blue, stippled....................... 1,500
Mug, white 600-625
Pitcher, green 625
Pitcher, marigold... 350
Pitcher, purple.. 450
Sauce dish, blue w/electric iridescence.... 200-250

Sauce dish, green............................... 30-45
Sauce dish, marigold 55
Sauce dish, purple 45
Spooner, green 150
Spooner, marigold 56
Spooner, purple 100-125
Sugar bowl, cov., marigold 90-110
Table set: cov. sugar bowl, creamer &
    spooner; marigold, 3 pcs............. 225
Table set, purple, 4 pcs................... 750
Tumbler, purple............................. 55-65
Tumblers, marigold, set of 6 300
Water set: pitcher & 4 tumblers; green, 5
    pcs.. 850

Singing Birds Water Set

Water set: pitcher & 4 tumblers; purple, 5
    pcs. (ILLUS. of part) 575-675

SIX PETALS (Dugan)
Bowl, 7" d., purple 90-100

Six Petals Bowl

Bowl, 7" w., peach opalescent, tricornered
    (ILLUS.).. 70-80
Bowl, 8" d., peach opalescent....................... 85-95
Bowl, 8" d., purple 80-90
Bowl, 8" d., white....................................... 100-125
Bowl, 8 1/2" d., ruffled, peach opalescent.......... 50
Bowl, 9" d., dome-footed, peach opales-
    cent 55-60
Bowl, black amethyst, ruffled 80

SKI STAR (Dugan)
Banana bowl, peach opalescent 170
Basket, peach opalescent.............................. 520
Bowl, 5" d., ruffled, peach opalescent............... 45
Bowl, 5" d., ruffled, purple 75-95

Bowl, 6" d., ruffled, peach opalescent............... 60
Bowl, 10" d., marigold 62
Bowl, 10" d., peach opalescent....................... 125
Bowl, 10" d., purple 300-375
Bowl, 11" d., peach opalescent................ 125-150
Bowl, 11" d., purple 225-275

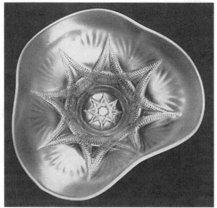

Ski Star Bowl

Bowl, tricornered, dome-footed, peach
opalescent (ILLUS.) 100-125
Plate, 6" d., crimped rim, peach opalescent..... 175
Plate, 7" d., deep, candy ribbon edge,
peach opalescent 65
Plate, 8 1/2" d., dome-footed, w/handgrip,
peach opalescent 185

SOUTACHE (Dugan)

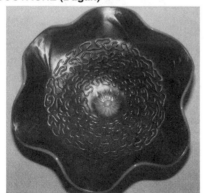

Soutache Bowl

Bowl, 8" d., dome-footed, ruffled, peach
opalescent (ILLUS.) 93
Bowl, 8" to 9" d., dome-footed, piecrust
rim, peach opalescent 159

SPRINGTIME (Northwood)

Bowl, master berry, marigold 125
Butter dish, cov., green 400
Butter dish, cov., marigold (ILLUS. top of
next column)... 250-275
Butter dish, cov., purple 300
Creamer, marigold 125
Pitcher, green 950-1,000
Pitcher, marigold... 300

Springtime Butter Dish

Sauce dish, 5" d., green 53
Sauce dish, 5" d., purple................................. 55
Spooner, green 255-275
Spooner, marigold 125
Spooner, purple 300
Sugar bowl, cov., marigold 235
Sugar bowl, open, green 165
Tumbler, green 170-175
Tumbler, marigold.. 65
Tumbler, purple.. 70-75

STAG & HOLLY (Fenton)

Bowl, 7" d., spatula-footed, blue 200-275
Bowl, 8" d., footed, ice cream shape, blue....... 184
Bowl, 8" d., footed, ice cream shape, green..... 200
Bowl, 8" d., footed, ice cream shape, mari-
gold 100-125
Bowl, 8" d., footed, ice cream shape, pur-
ple 250-275
Bowl, 8" to 9" d., footed, ice cream shape,
lavender 185
Bowl, 8" to 9" d., spatula-footed, green........... 228
Bowl, 8" to 9" d., spatula-footed, marigold 105
Bowl, 8" to 9" d., spatula-footed, purple.... 175-200
Bowl, 10" to 11" d., three-footed, blue 450
Bowl, 10" to 11" d., three-footed, green 1,050
Bowl, 10" to 11" d., three-footed,
marigold 150-200

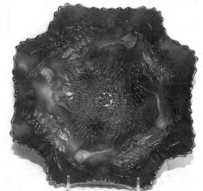

Stag & Holly Bowl

Bowl, 10" to 11" d., three-footed, purple (ILLUS.).. **425**
Bowl, 10" to 11" d., three-footed, vaseline... **300-400**
Bowl, 10 3/4" d., footed, ice cream shape, marigold... **150**
Bowl, 11" d., flat, amber.................................... **750**
Bowl, 11" d., ruffled, blue **250**
Bowl, 12" d., ice cream shape, blue.......... **300-325**
Bowl, 12" d., ice cream shape, green **900**
Bowl, 12" d., ice cream shape, marigold... **125-150**
Bowl, spatula-footed, red **1,750**
Plate, 9" d., spatula-footed, marigold **800-825**
Plate, chop, 12" d., three-footed, marigold **700-800**
Plate, chop, 13" d., three-footed, marigold.... **1,400**
Rose bowl, blue, large **1,665**
Rose bowl, marigold, large **150**
Rose bowl, marigold, giant **375-400**

STAR OF DAVID & BOWS (Northwood)

Star of David & Bows Bowl

Bowl, 7" d., dome-footed, marigold (ILLUS.)... **46**
Bowl, 7" d., dome-footed, purple................... **60-65**
Bowl, 8" to 9" d., dome-footed, fluted, green **95**
Bowl, 8" to 9" d., dome-footed, fluted, purple **90-100**
Bowl, Embossed Scroll exterior, purple **98**

STAR OF DAVID (Imperial)
Bowl, 7" d., ruffled, purple............................... **270**

Star of David Bowl

Bowl, 8" to 9" d., collared base, green (ILLUS.)... **100-125**
Bowl, 8" to 9" d., collared base, marigold......... **160**
Bowl, 9" d., flat, ruffled, purple **125-150**

STARFISH
Bonbon, peach opalescent **140**
Bonbon, purple **79**

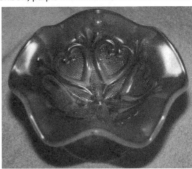

Starfish Compote

Compote, peach opalescent (ILLUS.)......... **90-100**

STIPPLED RAYS
Bonbon, two-handled, celeste blue........... **275-300**
Bonbon, two-handled, green........................ **35-45**
Bonbon, two-handled, ice green...................... **250**
Bonbon, two-handled, marigold........................ **38**
Bonbon, two-handled, purple........................ **40-50**
Bowl, 5" d., Amberina............................... **300-400**
Bowl, 5" d., blue **50**
Bowl, 5" d., green... **20-30**
Bowl, 5" d., marigold **25**
Bowl, 5" d., red.. **400-450**
Bowl, 6 1/2" d., blue, stippled, Scale Band exterior **75-100**
Bowl, 6 1/2" d., red, ruffled.............................. **395**
Bowl, 6 3/4" d., dome-footed, aqua........... **100-150**
Bowl, 7" d., red.. **250-450**
Bowl, 8" to 9" d., purple................................. **40-45**
Bowl, 8" to 9" d., teal blue **50**
Bowl, 10" d., amber... **42**
Bowl, 10" d., lavender, ruffled **75**
Bowl, 10" d., marigold, ruffled **80**

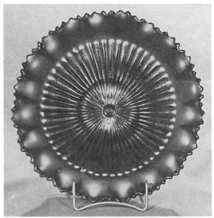

Stippled Rays Bowl

Bowl, 10" d., purple, piecrust rim (ILLUS.) **75-85**
Bowl, 10" d., white... **175**
Creamer & sugar bowl, blue, pr................ **75-100**
Creamer & sugar bowl, individual size,
   blue, pr. **55**
Creamer & sugar bowl, marigold, pr................ **50**
Plate, 6" to 7" d., marigold.................................. **50**
Rose bowl, purple... **70**
Sugar bowl, open, green **35**
Sugar bowl, open, marigold.............................. **24**

STRAWBERRY (Millersburg)
Bowl, 8" to 9" d., green **158**
Bowl, 8" to 9" d., green, three-in-one edge **300**
Bowl, 8" to 9" d., purple.................................... **250**
Bowl, 8" to 9" d., vaseline **1,375**
Bowl, 9 1/2" d., Basketweave exterior, pur-
   ple **90**
Bowl, 9 1/2" w., square, green **600**
Bowl, 10" w., tricornered, green **410**
Bowl, 10" w., tricornered, purple, candy rib-
   bon edge **425**
Compote, green **300**
Compote, marigold **375**

STRAWBERRY (Northwood)
Bowl, 5" d., purple, fluted **40**
Bowl, 6" d., green.. **65**
Bowl, 7" d., marigold... **45**
Bowl, 8" to 9" d., blue, stippled **1,000**
Bowl, 8" to 9" d., blue, stippled, piecrust rim..... **425**
Bowl, 8" to 9" d., blue, stippled, ruffled,
   Basketweave exterior............................ **500-525**
Bowl, 8" to 9" d., green, ruffled, Bas-
   ketweave exterior **145**
Bowl, 8" to 9" d., green, stippled, piecrust
   rim **700**
Bowl, 8" to 9" d., marigold................................. **55**
Bowl, 8" to 9" d., marigold, ruffled, Bas-
   ketweave exterior **55-60**
Bowl, 8" to 9" d., marigold, stippled,
   piecrust rim **450**
Bowl, 8" to 9" d., purple.................................... **145**
Bowl, 8" to 9" d., purple, ruffled, Bas-
   ketweave exterior **100-125**
Bowl, 8" to 9" d., smoky, piecrust rim............... **900**
Bowl, 8" to 9" d., stippled, ruffled, purple **425**
Bowl, 8 1/2" d., green, three-in-one edge **350**
Bowl, 9" d., marigold, piecrust rim **80**
Bowl, 9" d., marigold, stippled, ribbed exte-
   rior.. **150**
Bowl, 9" d., ruffled, Basketweave exterior,
   piecrust rim, purple.. **275**
Bowl, 10" d., green, Basketweave
   exterior **125-150**
Bowl, 10" d., ice green **1,900**
Bowl, 10" d., marigold, Basketweave exte-
   rior.. **110**
Bowl, 10" d., purple, Basketweave exterior...... **173**
Bowl, horehound, stippled, ruffled.................... **800**
Plate, 6" to 7" d., w/handgrip, green................. **205**
Plate, 9" d., Basketweave exterior, mari-
   gold **265**

Northwood Strawberry Plate

Plate, 9" d., Basketweave exterior, purple
   (ILLUS.)... **250-375**
Plate, 9" d., marigold **140**
Plate, 9" d., purple **185**
Plate, Basketweave exterior, green........... **200-275**
Plate, stippled, marigold **800-1,000**

STRAWBERRY SCROLL (Fenton)
Pitcher, water, marigold **1,850-2,000**
Tumbler, blue... **190**
Tumbler, marigold.................................... **200-225**

SUNFLOWER BOWL (Northwood)

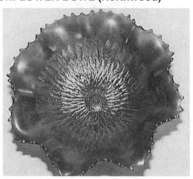

Sunflower Bowl

Bowl, 8" d., footed, blue (ILLUS.)................. **1,200**
Bowl, 8" d., footed, blue w/electric irides-
   cence.. **650-700**
Bowl, 8" d., footed, green................................. **127**
Bowl, 8" d., footed, ice blue.......................... **1,275**
Bowl, 8" d., footed, lavender **90**
Bowl, 8" d., footed, marigold **75**
Bowl, 8" d., footed, pastel marigold................. **300**
Bowl, 8" d., footed, purple **165**
Bowl, 8" d., footed, purple, Meander exte-
   rior **150-160**
Bowl 8", footed, emerald green........................ **363**

SUNFLOWER PIN TRAY (Millersburg)
Green **350**
Marigold **450**
Purple **500-550**

SWAN PASTEL NOVELTIES (Dugan)
Salt dip, amber.. 250
Salt dip, celeste blue.................................... 40-45
Salt dip, ice blue 33
Salt dip, ice green 45-50
Salt dip, marigold 100-125
Salt dip, peach opalescent........................ 375-450
Salt dip, purple.. 250-275
Salt dip, teal 350

SWIRL HOBNAIL (Millersburg)
Cuspidor, green.. 3,000
Cuspidor, marigold 1,000

Swirl Hobnail Cuspidor

Cuspidor, purple (ILLUS.)................................. 895
Rose bowl, marigold 175
Rose bowl, purple...................................... 350-400
Vase, green 700
Vase, marigold.. 350
Vase, purple 250
Vase, 10" h., green... 395
Vase, 16" h., marigold, variant.......................... 450

TEN MUMS (Fenton)
Bowl, footed, three-in-one edge, green..... 500-575
Bowl, 8" to 9" d., ribbon candy rim, blue ... 140-250
Bowl, 8" to 9" d., ribbon candy rim,
  green 325-350
Bowl, 8" to 9" d., ribbon candy rim,
  purple 200-250

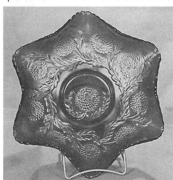

Ten Mums Plate

Bowl, 10" d., green, footed (ILLUS.) 200
Bowl, 10" d., green, ribbon candy rim 185
Bowl, 10" d., marigold, ruffled 200
Bowl, 10" d., purple, ribbon candy rim 250-300
Bowl, 10" d., purple, ruffled 250-300
Pitcher, water, marigold 750-1,000
Pitcher, water, white 1,200

Tumbler, blue... 75
Tumbler, marigold 65
Water set: pitcher & 1 tumbler; marigold,
  2 pcs.. 1,000-1,200
Water set: pitcher & 5 tumblers; blue,
  6 pcs.. 1,263
Water set: pitcher & 6 tumblers; marigold,
  7 pcs... 1,200-1,500

THIN RIB VASE
Blue, 6 1/2" h., squatty 95
Blue, 10" h. 40
Blue, 10 1/2" h. (Northwood) 85
Blue, 13" h., funeral... 150
Emerald green, 10 1/2" h................................... 60
Green, 6 1/2" h., jack-in-the-pulpit shape 130
Green, 8" h. 38
Green, 9" h. 35
Green, 10" h. (Northwood) 40-50
Green, 12" h. 93
Green, 13" h. 100-125
Green, 13 3/4" h. 225-250
Ice blue, 7" h. (Northwood) 375
Ice blue, 10 1/4" h. 318
Ice green, 7 1/2" h. (Northwood) 80
Pastel olive, 11" h... 70
Purple, 6 1/2" h., squatty.................................. 95
Purple, 13" h., funeral 275
Purple, 14" h., funeral 100-150
Purple, 14 1/2" h. 95
White, 11" h.. 110
White, 12" h.. 120
White, 13" h., funeral...................................... 257

THISTLE (Fenton)
Banana boat, amber 170

Thistle Banana Boat

Banana boat, blue (ILLUS.) 275-300
Banana boat, blue w/electric iridescence 500
Banana boat, marigold.............................. 165-175
Banana boat, purple 400-450
Bowl, 7" d., marigold 47
Bowl, 7 1/2" d., purple, ice cream shape............ 95
Bowl, 8" d., purple, three-in-one edge............. 100
Bowl, 8" to 9" d., blue, ribbon candy rim 75-80
Bowl, 8" to 9" d., blue, ruffled............................ 83
Bowl, 8" to 9" d., green, flared.................. 125-150
Bowl, 8" to 9" d., green, ribbon candy rim 165
Bowl, 8" to 9" d., green, ruffled.......................... 65
Bowl, 8" to 9" d., marigold, ribbon candy
  rim 70
Bowl, 8" to 9" d., marigold, ruffled..................... 45
Bowl, 8" to 9" d., purple, ribbon candy rim 80
Bowl, 8" to 9" d., purple, ruffled.................. 100-110
Bowl, 8 3/4" d., three-in-one edge, green 60
Bowl, 9" d., fluted, green 95-100
Bowl, 9" d., ice cream shape, marigold.............. 45
Bowl, 9" d., ice cream shape, purple.................. 65
Plate, 9" d., green... 3,375
Plate, green 350

THREE FRUITS (Northwood)

Bowl, 5" d., marigold 30
Bowl, 6" d., marigold 30
Bowl, 7" d., dome-footed, Basketweave &
   Grapevine exterior, purple........................... 150
Bowl, 8" d., dome footed 115
Bowl, 8" d., dome-footed, Basketweave &
   Grapevine exterior, white 250-275
Bowl, 8" d., ruffled, green................................. 95
Bowl, 8" d., ruffled, marigold 75-100
Bowl, 8" d., ruffled, purple 100
Bowl, 8 1/2" d., collared base, Bas-
   ketweave & Grapevine exterior, green........... 90
Bowl, 8 1/2" d., dome-footed, green......... 170-190
Bowl, 8 1/2" d., dome-footed, ruffled, Bas-
   ketweave & Grapevine exterior,
   marigold 95-125
Bowl, 8 1/2" d., piecrust rim, green 155
Bowl, 8 1/2" d., piecrust rim, marigold........... 65-75
Bowl, 8 1/2" d., piecrust rim, purple 68
Bowl, 8 1/2" d., piecrust rim, purple, Bas-
   ketweave exterior 105
Bowl, 8 1/2" d., ruffled, blue 95
Bowl, 9" d., dome-footed, Basketweave &
   Grapevine exterior, green 135
Bowl, 9" d., dome-footed, Basketweave &
   Grapevine exterior, purple........................... 145
Bowl, 9" d., piecrust rim, green, stippled,
   ribbed exterior 725-750
Bowl, 9" d., piecrust rim, smoky 500
Bowl, 9" d., purple 100-125
Bowl, 9" d., ruffled, blue 175
Bowl, 9" d., ruffled, green 190
Bowl, 9" d., ruffled, marigold 110
Bowl, 9" d., spatula-footed, aqua opales-
   cent 600-725
Bowl, 9" d., spatula-footed, emerald green...... 425
Bowl, 9" d., spatula-footed, ice
   green.. 1,045-1,075
Bowl, 9" d., spatula-footed, marigold 95
Bowl, 9" d., spatula-footed, marigold,
   Meander exterior 145
Bowl, 9" d., spatula-footed, purple 200-225
Bowl, 9" d., stippled, marigold................... 100-125
Bowl, 9" d., stippled, purple............................. 275
Bowl, 9" d., stippled, white 487
Bowl, ruffled, stippled, green........................... 300
Bowl, aqua opalescent, collared
   base 1,100-1,200
Bowl, aqua opalescent, ruffled, spatula-
   footed w/Meander exterior 1,150
Bowl, blue, stippled, footed 450
Bowl, ice blue, ruffled, stippled, footed .. 800-1,000
Bowl, ice green, dome-footed, ruffled, Vin-
   tage exterior 300
Bowl, marigold, stippled, piecrust rim 205
Bowl, marigold, stippled, ruffled, ribbed
   exterior 165-175
Bowl, purple, spatula-footed, stippled............. 165
Bowl, white, dome-footed, Basketweave &
   Meander exterior 325
Plate, 9" d., blue 825
Plate, 9" d., blue, stippled, ribbed exterior..... 1,300
Plate, 9" d., green... 255
Plate, 9" d., marigold 150-200
Plate, 9" d., purple, stippled, ribbed exterior..... 650
Plate, 9" d., stippled, aqua opalescent 2,900
Plate, 9" d., stippled, aqua opalescent,
   w/ribbed exterior............................. 3,650-4,000
Plate, 9" d., stippled, blue w/electric irides-
   cence.. 1,013

Plate, 9" d., stippled, honey amber,
   w/ribbed exterior...................................... 2,400
Plate, 9" d., stippled, lavender............. 1,250-1,400
Plate, 9" d., stippled, marigold......................... 225
Plate, 9" d., stippled, pastel marigold 750
Plate, 9 1/2" w., 12-sided, blue (Fenton) ... 250-300
Plate, 9 1/2" w., 12-sided, green (Fenton). 250-300
Plate, 9 1/2" w., 12-sided, marigold
   (Fenton)... 145
Plate, 9 1/2" w., 12-sided, purple (Fenton) 165
Plate, plain back, stretch "electric" finish,
   purple 350-400

TIGER LILY (Imperial)

Pitcher, water, green 200-250
Pitcher, water, marigold 100-125
Tumbler, aqua.. 165-175
Tumbler, blue.. 250
Tumbler, green 55-65
Tumbler, marigold.. 30-40

Tiger Lily Tumbler

Tumbler, purple (ILLUS.) 140-150
Tumblers, green, set of 6................................ 350
Water set: pitcher & 2 tumblers; green, 3
   pcs.. 390
Water set: pitcher & 6 tumblers; marigold,
   7 pcs... 394

TORNADO VASE (Northwood)

Marigold 375
Marigold, small, ribbed................................... 700

Tornado Vase

Purple, ribbed (ILLUS.) 475

TOWN PUMP NOVELTY (Northwood)

Town Pump Novelty

Green (ILLUS.) 3,450
Marigold 2,000-2,500
Purple 1,900

TREE TRUNK VASE (Northwood)

Aqua opalescent, 9" to 12" h. 500-600
Blue, 8" to 10" h. 225
Blue, 12" h. 160
Blue, 13 1/2" h. 450-525
Blue w/electric iridescence, 10 1/2" h. 126
Blue w/electric iridescence, 14" h.,
   funeral 1,375-1,500
Green, 7" h. 45-75
Green, 7 1/2" h., squatty 145
Green, 8" to 11" h. 95
Green, 10" h. 125-150
Green, 13" h. 238
Ice blue, 7" h. 500
Ice green, 7" to 11" h. 225
Ice green, 11" h. 285
Marigold, 9" to 10" h. 43
Marigold, 11" h. 70
Marigold, 12" h. 175
Marigold, 13" h. 145
Marigold, 14" h. 125
Purple, 6" h., squatty 50-75
Purple, 7" h. 215

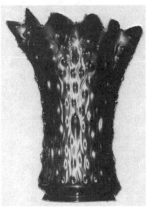

Tree Trunk Vase

Purple, 8" to 11" h. (ILLUS.) 110-120
Purple, 9" to 10" h. 80
Purple, 11" h. 90
Purple, 12" h., w/elephant foot,
   funeral 2,900-2,975
Purple, 13" h. 275
Purple, 14" h., funeral 1,700
Purple, 22" h., funeral 2,100
White, 9" h. 165

TROUT & FLY (Millersburg)

Bowl, ice cream shape, green 710
Bowl, ice cream shape, marigold 450-500
Bowl, ice cream shape, purple 575-600
Bowl, ribbon candy rim, lavender 1,050
Bowl, ribbon candy rim, marigold 350
Bowl, ribbon candy rim, purple 575
Bowl, ruffled, green 425
Bowl, ruffled, marigold 350
Bowl, square, green 1,140

Trout & Fly Square Bowl

Bowl, square, marigold (ILLUS.) 675
Bowl, square, purple 950-975
Bowl, 8 1/2" d., marigold 325

TULIP & CANE

Bowl, Three-In-One Edge, Green 600
Goblet, marigold 50
Goblet, marigold, 4 oz. 53

Tulip & Cane Wine

Wine marigold (ILLUS.) 45

TWO FLOWERS (Fenton)

Bowl, 6" d., footed, aqua 175
Bowl, 6" d., footed, blue 75
Bowl, 6" d., footed, lime green 175
Bowl, 6" d., footed, marigold 38
Bowl, 6" d., footed, vaseline 100-125
Bowl, 7" to 8" d., footed, blue 85-100
Bowl, 7" to 8" d., footed, green 90
Bowl, 7" to 8" d., footed, marigold 60-65
Bowl, 7" to 8" d., footed, purple, fluted 50-60
Bowl, 8" d., marigold, collared base 100-125
Bowl, 8" d., marigold, collared base, ice
   cream shape 133
Bowl, 8 1/2" d., blue, footed 275-300
Bowl, 9" d., footed, black amethyst, ice
   cream shape 375
Bowl, 9" d., footed, blue, ice cream shape 195
Bowl, 9" d., footed, purple, ice cream
   shape 65
Bowl, 10" d., footed, aqua 350-375
Bowl, 10" d., footed, blue 125
Bowl, 10" d., footed, blue, scalloped rim 95-100
Bowl, 10" d., footed, green, scalloped rim 95
Bowl, 10" d., footed, marigold 85

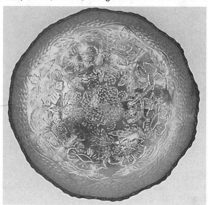

Two Flowers Fruit Bowl

Bowl, 10" d., footed, marigold, scalloped
   rim (ILLUS.) 60
Bowl, 10" d., footed, purple 525
Bowl, 10 1/2" d., blue, ruffled 125-150
Bowl, 10 1/2" d., marigold, footed, ruffled 90
Bowl, 11" d., blue 225-250
Bowl, 11" d., blue, ice cream shape 140-150
Bowl, 11" d., lime green/marigold, ice
   cream shape 175
Bowl, 11" d., marigold 115
Bowl, 11" d., purple, footed, ruffled 750
Bowl, 13" d., footed, marigold 75
Plate, 9" d., footed, marigold 600-650
Plate, chop, 11 1/2" d., three-foot, marigold .. 1,600
Rose bowl, three-footed, blue 180
Rose bowl, three-footed, giant, marigold .. 250-300
Rose bowl, three-footed, marigold 70
Rose bowl, three-footed, vaseline 150

TWO FRUITS

Banana boat, marigold 90-100
Bonbon, divided, blue 195
Bonbon, divided, green 175
Bonbon, divided, marigold 85
Bowl, large, in metal holder, marigold 125-150

VENETIAN GIANT ROSE BOWL (Cambridge)

Venetian Giant Rose Bowl

Green (ILLUS.) 1,100
Marigold 1,300

VINEYARD

Pitcher, water, marigold 100
Pitcher, water, purple 320-350
Tumbler, marigold 26
Tumbler, purple 60-70
Water set: pitcher & 1 tumbler; marigold,
   2 pcs. 125-175
Water set: pitcher & 4 tumblers; marigold,
   5 pcs. 150-200
Water set: pitcher & 5 tumblers; marigold,
   6 pcs. 155
Water set: pitcher & 6 tumblers; marigold,
   7 pcs. 173

VINTAGE or VINTAGE GRAPE

Bonbon, two-handled, blue (Fenton) 45-55
Bonbon, two-handled, purple (Fenton) 35
Bowl, 5" d., purple 28
Bowl, 6" d., blue (Fenton) 40
Bowl, 6" d., celeste blue, ruffled 1,100
Bowl, 6" d., green (Fenton) 38
Bowl, 6" d., purple (Fenton) 25-35
Bowl, 6" d., red (small flake) 2,000
Bowl, 6" d., vaseline, ruffled 120
Bowl, 6 1/2" d., ice cream shape, green 43
Bowl, 7" d., fluted, blue 42
Bowl, 7" d., fluted, green (Fenton) 33
Bowl, 7" d., green 70-75
Bowl, 7" d., purple (Millersburg) 75
Bowl, 7" d., ruffled, vaseline 115-125
Bowl, 7 1/2" d., ice cream shape, blue 55
Bowl, 8" d., piecrust rim, blue 110
Bowl, 8" d., ribbon candy rim, aqua opales-
   cent 1,700-1,900
Bowl, 8" d., ribbon candy rim, blue 95-100
Bowl, 8" d., ribbon candy rim, blue, Wide
   Panel exterior 55
Bowl, 8" d., ribbon candy rim, green 100
Bowl, 8" to 9" d., aqua opalescent 1,000-1,200
Bowl, 8" to 9" d., blue, footed (Fenton) 40-45
Bowl, 8" to 9" d., blue, ruffled 70
Bowl, 8" to 9" d., green (Fenton) 49
Bowl, 8" to 9" d., green (Millersburg) 39
Bowl, 8" to 9" d., marigold (Fenton) 35

Bowl, 8" to 9" d., purple, footed (Fenton) 38
Bowl, 8" to 9" d., purple, ruffled, footed 40-45
Bowl, 8" to 9" d., red, ruffled 2,800-3,000
Bowl, 8" to 9" d., teal blue, fluted 75
Bowl, 8" to 9" d., vaseline 200
Bowl, 9" d., green, three-in-one edge 65
Bowl, 9" d., purple 100
Bowl, 9" d., purple, ruffled (Fenton) 90
Bowl, 9 1/2" d., green..................................... 85
Bowl, 9 1/2" d., marigold, ruffled, dome-
    footed 70
Bowl, 10" d., blue 55-75
Bowl, 10" d., Hobnail exterior, green
    (Millersburg) 1,175
Bowl, 10" d., ice cream shape, blue............... 200
Bowl, 10" d., ice cream shape, red
    (Fenton)... 2,500-3,500
Bowl, 10" d., ice cream shape, vaseline
    (Fenton) 225
Bowl, 10" d., ruffled, green............................. 65
Bowl, 10" d., ruffled, purple 50
Bowl, 10" d., ruffled, vaseline w/marigold
    overlay.. 110
Bowl, 11" d., ice cream shape, marigold......... 200
Bowl, dome-footed, marigold 48
Bowl, three-in-one edge, red...................... 4,500
Compote, 7" d., blue (Fenton)......................... 90
Compote, 7" d., green, fluted (Fenton) 75
Compote, 7" d., marigold (Fenton)................... 67
Compote, 7" d., purple (Fenton) 75
Epergne, blue (Fenton) 165
Epergne, green (Fenton)................................ 150
Epergne, green, large 225-250
Epergne, marigold (Fenton) 250-300
Epergne, purple, small 95
Fernery, footed, blue (Fenton) 75-100
Fernery, footed, green (Fenton).................. 60-70
Fernery, footed, marigold (Fenton) 35-45
Fernery, footed, purple (Fenton) 57
Ice cream set: master ice cream bowl &
    four 6" d. bowls; cobalt blue, 5 pcs.............. 575
Nut dish, footed, blue, 6" d. (Fenton)........... 80-90
Nut dish, footed, green, 6" d. (Fenton) 100
Nut dish, footed, red 450-500

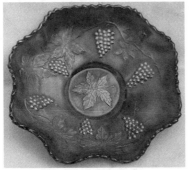

Vintage Plate

Plate, 7" d., blue, Millersburg
    (ILLUS.)... 1,000-1,500
Plate, 7" d., green (Fenton) 225-250
Plate, 7" d., marigold (Fenton)....................... 150
Plate, 7" d., purple (Fenton) 250-350
Plate, 8" d., blue 128
Plate, 8" d., green.................................. 150-175
Plate, 9" d., flat, purple 4,500

Plate, lavender 900
Powder jar, cov., marigold 85
Powder jar, cov., marigold (Fenton)............. 80-85
Powder jar, cov., purple (Fenton) 150-175
Sandwich tray, handled, aqua opalescent 90
Sandwich tray, handled, clambroth 30-35
Sandwich tray, handled, marigold................... 35
Sauce dish, blue 30
Sauce dish, blue, ice cream shape................... 32
Sauce dish, green 27
Sauce dish, marigold (Fenton)......................... 20
Wine, marigold (Fenton)................................. 28
Wine, purple (Fenton).............................. 35-45

WATER LILY & CATTAILS
Bowl, 5" d., marigold 39
Bowl, 9" d., marigold 65
Butter dish, cov., marigold...................... 150-175
Pitcher, water, marigold 450
Plate, 6" d., marigold 50
Rose bowl, marigold 30
Sauce dish, marigold, footed 125
Sauce dish, red opalescent 800
Table set: cov. sugar bowl, creamer,
    spooner & cov. butter dish; marigold,
    4 pcs.. 535
Toothpick holder, marigold 75
Tumbler, marigold................................... 45-55
Tumblers, marigold, set of 6 240
Water set: pitcher & 4 tumblers; marigold,
    5 pcs.. 625
Water set: pitcher & 6 tumblers; marigold,
    7 pcs.. 765
Whimsey, marigold 38

WATER LILY (Fenton)
Bonbon, marigold, 7 1/2" d. 25
Bowl, 5" d., aqua... 95
Bowl, 5" d., blue 70
Bowl, 6" d., aqua... 145
Bowl, 6" d., blue 83
Bowl, 6" d., green, footed 150-175
Bowl, 6" d., ice green opalescent................. 1,200
Bowl, 6" d., marigold, footed 44
Bowl, 6" d., red, footed............................. 1,133
Bowl, 6" d., red opalescent, footed 1,025-1,050
Bowl, 6" d., vaseline, footed......................... 100
Bowl, 9" d., footed, lavender, ice cream
    shape 175-200
Bowl, 9" d., footed, marigold 75
Bowl, 10" d., footed, blue, fluted 95-100
Bowl, 10" d., footed, marigold 100

WHIRLING LEAVES BOWL (Millersburg)
Green, tricornered, 9 1/2" w. 350-400
Green, 10" d. 50-75
Marigold, 9" d.. 70-80
Marigold, tricornered, 9 1/2" w. 400
Marigold, 10" d. 100
Purple, 9" d. 350-400
Purple, 9 1/2" w., tricornered.......................... 235
Purple, 10" d. 120

WIDE PANEL
Bowl, 8" to 9" d., aqua.................................... 85
Bowl, 8" to 9" d., purple 60
Bowl, 10" d., console, smoky 55
Compote, miniature, green 60
Compote, miniature, marigold.......................... 35
Compote, purple, 7" h. 400
Creamer & open sugar bowl, marigold, pr........ 50

Wide Panel Epergne

Epergne, four-lily, green (ILLUS.) **1,063**
Epergne, four-lily, ice blue **5,000-6,000**
Epergne, four-lily, marigold **900-1,000**
Epergne, four-lily, purple **2,000-2,500**
Epergne, four-lily, white **1,600-2,000**
Goblet, marigold.. **25-35**
Plate, 8" d., red... **500**
Plate, 11" d., white... **65**
Plate, chop, 14" d., marigold **80-100**
Plate, chop, 14" d., red............................. **500-750**
Plate, chop, 14" d., smoky........................... **200**
Plate, chop, 14" d., white......................... **200-300**
Rose bowl, clambroth **40**
Tumbler, marigold.. **20**
Vase, 9" h., aqua **85**
Vase, 9" h., marigold overlay.......................... **205**
Vase, 11" h., marigold **20**
Vase, 13" h., white, funeral............................ **220**
Vase, 16" h., marigold, funeral **180**

WILD ROSE

Wild Rose Bowl

Bowl, 7" d., three-footed, open heart rim,
  green, Northwood (ILLUS.) **75-85**
Bowl, 7" d., three-footed, open heart rim,
  marigold (Northwood).................................... **44**
Bowl, 7" d., three-footed, open heart rim,
  purple (Northwood) **65-75**
Candy dish, open edge, green **68**
Candy dish, open edge, purple **75**
Lamp, green, w/original burner & etched
  chimney shade, medium
  (Millersburg) **1,250-1,450**
Lamp, marigold, w/original burner & etched
  chimney shade, medium (Millersburg) **1,200**
Lamp, purple, kerosene-type w/intaglio
  Wild Rose on underside of base,
  8 1/2" h., 5 1/2" base (Millersburg)............ **5,700**

Lamp, green, kerosene-type, 9" h., 5 5/8"
  base (Millersburg) **1,500**
Lamp, marigold, sewing-type, 9" h., 6 3/4"
  base (Millersburg) **3,000**
Lamp, purple, kerosene-type, 9 1/2" h., 6"
  base (Millersburg) **2,100**
Lamp, dark marigold, kerosene-type,
  10" h., 6 1/8" base (Millersburg)............... **1,000**
Lamp, purple, Ladies Head medallions on
  interior of base, 11" h., 6 3/8" base (Mill-
  ersburg)... **4,250**
Syrup pitcher, marigold........................... **700-800**

WILD STRAWBERRY (Northwood)
Bowl, 6" d., purple **50**
Bowl, 6" d., purple, ruffled................................ **100**
Bowl, 7" d., marigold **35**
Bowl, 9" d., green... **85**
Bowl, 10" d., green.................................... **200-225**
Bowl, 10" d., ice green **2,500**
Bowl, 10" d., lime green, ruffled **1,400**
Bowl, 10" d., marigold **110**
Bowl, 10" d., purple **160-175**
Bowl, 10" d., white... **195**
Bowl, 10" d., white, ruffled............................... **650**
Plate, 6" to 7" d., w/handgrip, green **225-275**
Plate, 6" to 7" d., w/handgrip, marigold **155**
Plate, 6" to 7" d., w/handgrip, purple **265**

WINDMILL or WINDMILL MEDALLION (Imperial)
Bowl, 7" d., marigold **38**
Bowl, 8" to 9" d., ruffled, purple................. **90-100**
Bowl, 8" to 9" d., ruffled, smoky **127**
Bowl, 9" d., purple, footed **95-100**
Bowl, 10" d., purple **150**
Dresser tray, oval, purple **370**
Pickle dish, green **125**
Pickle dish, marigold (ILLUS.)........................... **37**
Pickle dish, purple **58**
Pitcher, milk, ice green **95-100**
Pitcher, milk, marigold....................................... **80**
Pitcher, milk, purple **675-750**
Pitcher, milk, smoky **200-225**
Pitcher, water, purple....................................... **900**

Windmill Tumbler

Tumbler, marigold (ILLUS.)................................ **36**
Tumbler, purple.. **150**
Water set: pitcher & 4 tumblers; marigold,
  5 pcs... **180**

WINE & ROSES
Goblet, blue.. 68
Goblet, marigold... 27
Goblet, powder blue... 30
Pitcher, cider, marigold................................... 665
Wine, aqua 150
Wine, marigold 75
Wine, vaseline.. 275

WISHBONE (Northwood)
Bowl, 7" d., three-footed, ruffled rim, marigold **65-75**
Bowl, 7 1/2" d., three-footed, ruffled rim, purple **120-130**
Bowl, 8" to 9" d., footed, blue........................... 450
Bowl, 8" to 9" d., footed, green 375
Bowl, 8" to 9" d., footed, ice blue 1,700
Bowl, 8" to 9" d., footed, ice green...... 1,600-1,675
Bowl, 8" to 9" d., footed, marigold............. 125-150
Bowl, 8" to 9" d., footed, pastel marigold 125
Bowl, 8" to 9" d., footed, purple....................... 122
Bowl, 8" to 9" d., footed, white 450-500
Bowl, 10" d., footed, blue 600
Bowl, 10" d., footed, ruffled, purple 165
Bowl, 10" d., footed, ruffled, stippled, purple 850
Bowl, 10" d., piecrust rim, blue w/electric iridescence 2,000
Bowl, 10" d., piecrust rim, green 275-300
Bowl, 10" d., piecrust rim, green, Basketweave exterior 900-975
Bowl, 10" d., piecrust rim, lavender w/marigold overlay...................................... 500
Bowl, 10" d., piecrust rim, marigold.......... 150-200
Bowl, 10" d., piecrust rim, marigold, Basketweave exterior 183
Bowl, 10" d., piecrust rim, pastel marigold 425
Bowl, 10" d., ruffled, green....................... 250-350
Bowl, 10" d., ruffled, marigold 145-150
Bowl, footed, ruffled, horehound 650
Bowl, footed, ruffled, ice blue............. 1,800-1,900
Bowl, footed, ruffled, lime green 1,200
Bowl, footed, ruffled, marigold 200
Bowl, footed, ruffled, white 800
Bowl, footed, tri-cornered, purple 1,400
Bowl, large, Basketweave exterior, emerald green 325
Bowl, Rings & Roses exterior, purple 210
Bowl, 10" d., piecrust rim, footed, white 475-500
Epergne, green 975-1,200
Epergne, marigold..................................... 500-525
Epergne, purple 750
Epergne, white 1,725-1,850
Pitcher, water, green.................................... 1,800
Pitcher, water, marigold 1,500
Pitcher, water, purple 900
Plate, 8 1/2" d., footed, marigold 475-500
Plate, 8 1/2" d., footed, purple (ILLUS. top of next column)... 325
Plate, 8 1/2" w., footed, tricornered, green.... 1,200
Plate, 8 1/2" w., footed, tricornered, purple 400
Plate, chop, 11" d., green............................. 3,000
Plate, chop, 11" d., marigold 1,200
Plate, chop, 11" d., purple 1,500-2,000
Tumbler, green 180
Tumbler, marigold..................................... 95-100
Tumbler, purple... 135-145

Wishbone Plate

WISHBONE & SPADES
Banana bowl, ruffled, peach opalescent, 10" l. 145
Bowl, footed, tri-cornered, green................. 1,000
Bowl, footed, tri-cornered, marigold 800
Bowl, 8" d., peach opalescent........................... 68
Bowl, 9" d., ice cream shape, peach opalescent.. 160
Bowl, 9 5/8" d., ruffled, purple 450
Plate, 6" d., purple 650
Plate, 6 1/2" d., peach opalescent.................. 350
Plate, 6 1/2" d., purple 650
Plate, 9" d., footed, purple 750
Plate, chop, 11" d., purple 950-1,000

WREATH OF ROSES
Bonbon, stemmed, purple (Fenton) 95
Bonbon, two-handled, blue, 8" d...................... 60
Bonbon, two-handled, green, 8" d. 75
Bonbon, two-handled, marigold, 8" d........... 35-45
Bonbon, two-handled, purple, 8" d. 60
Compote, blue, 6" d. 75
Compote, green, fluted, 6" d. 50
Compote, purple, fluted, 6" d. 35-45
Punch bowl & base, blue, 2 pcs.............. 600-700
Punch bowl & base, blue w/electric iridescence, Persian Medallion interior, 2 pcs. .. 1,100
Punch bowl & base, green, Vintage interior, 2 pcs. 475
Punch bowl & base, marigold, Persian Medallion interior, 2 pcs. 425
Punch bowl & base, marigold, Vintage interior, 2 pcs... 400
Punch bowl & base, purple, 2 pcs. 400-500
Punch cup, blue... 31
Punch cup, blue, Persian Medallion interior (Fenton) 50
Punch cup, blue, Vintage interior...................... 40
Punch cup, green 45
Punch cup, green, Persian Medallion interior... 30
Punch cup, green, Vintage interior 30-35
Punch cup, marigold , Persian Medallion interior 25-35
Punch cup, marigold, Vintage interior............... 30
Punch cup, purple 25-30
Punch cup, purple, Persian Medallion interior... 20-25
Punch cup, purple, Vintage interior 34
Punch set: bowl, base & 4 cups; purple, 6 pcs. 525
Rose bowl, marigold (Dugan) 30
Whimsey, tricornered, marigold (Dugan) 55-75

WREATHED CHERRY (Dugan)

Berry set: master bowl & 4 sauce dishes; marigold, 5 pcs. 230
Berry set: master bowl & 4 sauce dishes; purple, 5 pcs. 315
Berry set: master bowl & 4 sauce dishes; white, 5 pcs. 400-450
Bowl, berry, 9 x 12" oval, blue 290
Bowl, berry, 9 x 12" oval, marigold 90
Bowl, berry, 9 x 12" oval, pastel marigold 150
Bowl, berry, 9 x 12" oval, peach opalescent 200-250
Bowl, berry, 9 x 12" oval, purple 175
Bowl, berry, 9 x 12" oval, white 250-300
Butter dish, cov., purple 175-225
Creamer, marigold 55
Pitcher, water, white w/gold cherries 700-750
Sauce dish, 5" to 6" l., oval, marigold 32
Sauce dish, 5" to 6" l., oval, purple 35
Sauce dish, 5" to 6" l., oval, white 50-60
Spooner, marigold 55
Spooner, white 95
Tumbler, marigold 45-50
Tumbler, purple 60-70

ZIG ZAG (MILLERSBURG)

Bowl, 9 1/2" d., marigold 142
Bowl, 9 1/2" d., purple 500
Bowl, 10" d., green 250
Bowl, 10" d., purple 230-240
Bowl, 10" d., three-in-one rim, purple.............. 325
Bowl, 10" w., tricornered, purple 700
Bowl, ribbon candy rim, marigold.................... 220
Bowl, ribbon candy rim, purple................. 250-300
Bowl, square, crimped edge, purple 625

ZIPPERED LOOP LAMP (Imperial)

Finger, marigold, large 688
Finger, smoky, 5" h., 4 1/8" d. base 1,800
Hand, marigold, 4 1/2" h. 1,220-1,2500
Hand, marigold, medium 600
Sewing, marigold, small 325
Sewing, marigold, medium 600-675
Sewing, smoky, medium 895

Zippered Loop Lamp

Sewing, marigold, large (ILLUS.) 500

CENTRAL GLASS WORKS

From the 1890s until its closing in 1939, the Central Glass Works of Wheeling, West Virginia produced colorless and colored handmade glass in all the styles then popular. Decorations from etchings with acid to hand-painted enamels were used.

The popular "Depression" era colors of black, pink, green, light blue, ruby red and others were all produced. Two of their 1920s etchings are still familiar today, one named for the then President of the United States and the other for the Governor of West Virginia - these are the Harding and Morgan patterns.

From high end Art glass to mass-produced plain barware tumblers, Central was a major glass producer throughout the period.

Bonbon, two-handled, green, Morgan etching $89
Bowl, fruit, 11 3/4" w., triangular, three-toed, Frances patt., green 48
Bowl, fruit, 11 3/4" w., triangular, three-toed, Frances patt., pink 52
Box, cov., round, Frances patt., light blue 78
Candlestick, single light, Frances patt., green 42
Candlestick, single light, Old Central Spiral patt., green, 8" h. 42
Candlestick, single light, Old Central Spiral patt., pink, 4" h. 38
Candlestick, single light, two-handled, clear, Chippendale patt., "Krystol" mark 38
Champagne, beaded stem, Morgan etching, pink 38
Claret, Fuchsia etching, clear, 5 3/4" h. 32
Console set: bowl, base & a pair of single-light candlesticks; amethyst, the set 110
Cordial, Moderne patt., clear bowl w/black stem & foot 42
Cordial, No. 1236, Scott etching No. 7, clear, 1 oz. 42
Cordial, No. 1900, clear bowl w/cobalt blue twist stem & foot 44
Cordial, No. 1900, clear bowl w/green twist stem & foot 32
Creamer & sugar bowl, Frances patt., green, pr. 54

Frances Creamer & Sugar Bowl

Creamer & sugar bowl, Frances patt., pink, pr. (ILLUS.) 64
Creamer & sugar bowl, Hester etching, topaz, pr. 80
Cup & saucer, Morgan etching, colorless 42
Cup & saucer, Morgan etching, pink 150
Finger bowl, clear, Harding etching, 4 3/4" d. 46
Goblet, Balda etching, lavender, 7 1/4" h. 64
Goblet, Fuchsia etching No. 5, clear, 9 oz. 28
Goblet, Harding etching, clear, 7 1/2" h. 42

Goblet, Hester etching, topaz bowl, clear
  stem & foot 45
Goblet, Moderne patt., clear bowl, black
  stem & foot 28
Goblet, Morgan etching, twist stem, pink 58
Goblet, Scott etching No. 7, clear, 10 oz. 28
Goblet, Veninga etching, twist stem, clear 24
Pitcher, 8 1/2" h., footed, Frances patt.,
  green 160
Plate, 6 1/2" d., Balda etching, lavender 42
Plate, 7 1/2" d., Morgan etching, light blue 46
Plate, 8 1/2" d., Morgan etching, pink 48
Pousse cafe, Scott etching No. 7,
  clear, 3/4" oz. 42
Sherbet, Balda etching, lavender, 4 3/4" d. 48
Sherbet, Morgan etching, clear 45
Teapot, cov., No. 733, Thistle etching No.
  310, clear 220
Tumbler, Frances patt., green, 4" h. 28
Tumbler, Harding etching, clear 28
Tumbler, Morgan etching, clear 34
Vase, bud, black amethyst w/enameled
  Peacock design 95
Vase, straight sides, crimped rim, Frances
  patt., green, large 74
Vase, two-handled loving cup-style,
  Frances patt., green 68
Wine, Moderne patt., clear bowl, black
  stem & foot 34

CONSOLIDATED

*The Consolidated Lamp and Glass Company of
Coraopolis, Pennsylvania was founded in 1894 and
for a number of years was noted for its lighting
wares but also produced popular lines of pressed
and blown tablewares. Highly collectible glass patterns of this early era include the Cone, Cosmos,
Florette and Guttate lines.*

*Lamps and shades continued to be good sellers
but in 1926 a new "art" line of molded decorative
wares was introduced. This "Martelé" line was developed as a direct imitation of the fine glasswares
being produced by René Lalique of France and
many Consolidated patterns resembled their French
counterparts. Other popular lines produced during
the 1920s and 1930s were "Dancing Nymph," the
delightfully Art Deco "Ruba Rombic," introduced in
1928, and the "Catalonian" line, imitating 17th century Spanish glass, which debuted in 1927.*

*Although the factory closed in 1933, it was
reopened under new management in 1936 and
prospered through the 1940s. It finally closed in
1967. Collectors should note that many later Consolidated patterns closely resemble wares of other
competing firms, especially the Phoenix Glass
Company. Careful study is needed to determine the
maker of pieces from the 1920-40 era.*

*A book which will be of help to collectors is
Phoenix & Consolidated Art Glass, 1926-1980, by
Jack D. Wilson (Antique Publications, 1989).*

Consolidated Martelé Label

CONE

Cone Pattern Caster Set

Caster set, four Cone patt. shakers w/origi-
  nal metal lids, in green, light blue, darker
  blue & pink, fitted in a silver plate holder
  w/rings centered by a figural donkey
  below an upright loop handle, on a
  square footed base, 4 1/2" w., 7" h.
  (ILLUS.) **$325**
Cruet w/original stopper, yellow satin 250
Sugar shaker w/original lid, green
  opaque 165

Cone Syrup Pitcher

Syrup pitcher w/original top, cased pink
  (ILLUS.) 375

COSMOS

Cosmos Butter Dish

Butter dish, cov., blue band decoration
  (ILLUS.) **225-250**

Pitcher, water, h.p. molded flowers on
white ground.. **220**
Syrup pitcher w/original top, pink band
decoration **248**
Tumbler, pink band decoration **65**

FLORETTE
Pitcher, 6 3/4" h., bulbous w/applied clear
handle, cased pink satin............................. **144**
Syrup pitcher w/original top, pink satin **450**
Toothpick holder, blue opaque satin **110**

GUTTATE

Guttate Cased Pink Pitcher

Pitcher, 9 1/2" h., cased pink, glossy finish
(ILLUS.)... **325**
Salt & pepper shakers, green & blue, pr. **40**
Syrup pitcher w/original lid, pink cased,
glossy finish, applied clear handle, tall.. **250-275**
Toothpick holder, white **44**

LATER LINES

Ruba Rombic Bowl

Bowl, 8 x 9", 3 1/2" h., Ruba Rombic patt.,
oblong w/closed rim, jade green w/slight
opalescence, minor rim nick, ca. 1928
(ILLUS.).. **800-900**
Candlesticks, Ruba Rombic patt., smoky
topaz, pr. **595**
Creamer & open sugar bowl, Ruba Rom-
bic patt., topaz, 2 1/8" & 3 1/2" h., pr.
(minor neck on both rims) **1,265**
Dinner set: six each of goblets, sherbets,
8 1/2" d. plates & one 12" d. plate; Five
Fruits patt., each w/molded fruit design &
overall purple wash, ca. 1930, the set
(mold imperfections, slight wear to
wash).. **230**

Ruba Rombic Dresser Set

Dresser set: multifaceted oblong tray, a
large toilet bottle w/stopper & smaller
perfume bottle w/stopper; Ruba Rombic
patt., lavender finish cased over colorless, tray 10 1/2 x 11 1/2", toilet bottle
7 3/4" h., the set (ILLUS.)......................... **5,750**
Lamp, table model, Dogwood patt., Martelé
line, brass fittings, baluster-form, tan **125**
Vase, 6" h., Screech Owls patt., Martelé
line, brown decoration on a milk white
ground **90**
Vase, 6" h., Screech Owls patt., Martelé
line, brown owls on green reeds against
a custard satin ground................................. **115**
Vase, 6" h., 4" d., Dragonfly patt., Martelé
line, ovoid w/wide mouth, blue on white
satin ground **115**
Vase, 6" h., 4" d., Dragonfly patt., Martelé
line, ovoid w/wide mouth, green & brown
on white satin ground **80**
Vase, 6 1/4" h., Peonies patt., Martelé line,
pink, green & brown on milk white
ground **80**
Vase, 6 1/2" h., Chickadee patt., wide flat-
tened ovoid form w/rectangular mouth,
stained red birds on ruby leafy branches
against a clear ground................................. **110**
Vase, 6 1/2" h., Chickadee patt., wide flattened ovoid form w/rectangular mouth,
brick red birds on green leafy branches
against a custard ground............................. **144**

Consolidated "Jonquil" Vase

Vase, 6 1/2" h., Jonquil patt., slender ovoid body w/flaring mouth, deep rose peach blossoms w/green stems on a creamy custard satin ground (ILLUS.) **115**

Rare Ruba Rombic Pattern Vase

Vase, 6 1/2" h., Ruba Rombic patt., angular tapering cylindrical form, silvery grey, minor nicks (ILLUS.).................................... **633**

Vase, 10" h., Love Bird patt., bulbous ovoid body w/a small short rolled neck, pairs of salmon-colored birds on a creamy white ground **238**

Vase, 10" h., Poppy patt., wide ovoid body w/wide low flared rim, decorated w/red poppies on custard ground............................ **275**

Vase, 10 1/2" h., Dogwood patt., dark rosy peach petals on greenish tan stems on a creamy custard ground **403**

Vase, 11" h., pillow-type, Sea Gulls patt., blue ground **595**

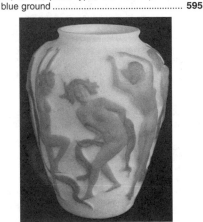

Consolidated "Dancing Girls" Vase

Vase, 11 1/2" h., Dancing Girls patt., tall ovoid body, girls & Pan relief-molded & colored in deep rose & tan on a creamy custard ground (ILLUS.).............................. **518**

CUP PLATES

Produced in numerous patterns beginning over 170 years ago, these little plates were designed to hold a cup while the tea or coffee was allowed to cool in a saucer. Cup plates were also made of ceramics. Where numbers are listed below, they refer to numbers assigned to these plates in the book, American Glass Cup Plates, *by Ruth Webb Lee and James H. Rose. Plates are of clear glass unless otherwise noted. A number of cup plates have been reproduced.*

L & R-128, round, central large eight-point star w/bull's-eyes alternating w/diamonds, band of half-round shells within rope border, clear, 3 5/16" d. (three scallops missing) **$55**

L & R-130, round, four pointed leaf cluster in center on diamond point ground, small pointed leaves rayed around the border within small knob rim band, clear, 3 7/16" d. (mold roughness, two scallops tipped) **121**

L & R-167B, round, plain concentric rings, smooth rim, clear, 3" d. (light mold roughness) **132**

L & R-197C, round, central blossomhead surrounded by delicate band of blossoms & leaves, looped arch border band, violet blue (very shallow large rim chip & underfill) **132**

L & R-250A, round, central six-point diamond point star surrounded by panels of criss-cross design, outer border of rounded pod-like devices (three tipped scallops) **33**

L & R-253, round. Roman Rosette patt., bluish green, 3 1/2" d. **77**

L & R-253, round, Roman Rosette patt., light bluish green (few scallops missing or tipped) **138**

L & R-262, round, four-point central cross alternating w/four heart-form double scrolls, outer border of alternating quatrefoils & fleur-de-lis, dark blue, 3 1/4" d. (tiny rim spall, few tipped scallops) **330**

Scrolls & Quatrefoils Cup Plates

L & R-262, round, four-point central star alternating w/heart-form double scrolls, border of alternating quatrefoils & fleur-de-lis, dark cobalt blue, eight scallops tipped (ILLUS. right) **143**

L & R-262, round, four-point central star alternating w/heart-form double scrolls, border of alternating quatrefoils & fleur-de-lis, greyish blue, few scallops tipped (ILLUS. left) **715**

L & R-277, round, large central three-arm cross alternating w/diamonds, leaf sprig & scroll border, peacock blue (small refracting line, light mold roughness) **770**

L & R-279, round, large multi-petaled central blossomhead, narrow border bands, lavender (usual mold roughness) **413**

L & R-279, round w/scalloped rim, a large multi-petaled central blossom, simple outer band decor, light green, 2 7/8" d. (light mold roughness) **176**

L & R-311, round, simple six-petal star surrounded by bull's-eyes in the center, band of diamonds in the border, deep opal opaque (mold roughness, few tipped scallops) **176**

L & R-37, round, large eight pointed-petal central blossom alternating w/tiny blossoms in center, diamond point inner band & palmette scalloped outer border, opaque white (mold roughness) **990**

L & R-37, round w/scalloped rim, center eight-petal large blossom alternating w/tiny blossoms, inner diamond point band & palmette outer border, fiery opalescent, 3 1/4" d. (moderately heavy mold roughness, chip on back rim) **154**

L & R-388, round, simple eight-petal central blossom, diamond point outer border, opaque white w/amber flashing (mold roughness) **418**

L & R-390 variant, round, smooth rim, Sunburst patt. center, diamond point border band, medium blue (light mold roughness) **165**

L & R-412, ten-sided, open five-point star in center, plain rim, peacock green (several chips & flakes on rim) **715**

L & R-440B, round, Valentine patt., lyre border, deep blue, 3 1/2" d. (two scalloped tipped, mold roughness) **165**

L & R-440B, round, Valentine patt., lyre border, greyish blue, 3 1/2" d. (small rim spall, few scallops tipped) **110**

L & R-440B, round, Valentine patt., lyre border, medium blue, few scallops tipped, mold roughness (ILLUS. w/L&R-522) **176**

Heart Pattern Cup Plate

L & R-459D, round, Heart patt., loop & dart center, brilliant emerald green, one & one-half scallops chipped, some others tipped (ILLUS.) **605**

L & R-502, round, Sunburst center patt., plain border, light green **138**

L & R-508, round, starburst center, plain border, peacock blue, 3" d. (mold roughness, one scallop tipped) **176**

Two Scarce Colored Cup Plates

L & R-522, round, Sunburst patt., plain border, deep reddish amber, two scallops tipped (ILLUS. left) **275**

L & R-523, round, Sunburst center patt., plain rim, light olive green (one scallop missing, six tipped) **121**

L & R-524, round, Sunburst center design, plain border, blue (light mold roughness) **198**

L & R-530, round, Sunburst patt., amethyst (four scallops missing, few tipped) **154**

L & R-531, round, bull's-eye & sunburst center design, plain border, knobby rim, light green (few tipped scallops) **132**

L & R-571, round, Queen Victoria design, central small bust of queen w/"Victoria" above, outer border w/a crown at the top & flowering vines around the sides (mold roughness) **44**

L & R-610A, round, sailing ship center scene framed by rope band within lacy scrolls, looping scroll outer border, deep blue, 3 1/2" d. (three scallops tipped, mold roughness) **198**

L & R-612A, octagonal, steamship center design, scroll & shield border, clear, 3 1/2" d. (mold roughness, few scallops chipped) **110**

L & R-686, round, Harp patt., harp, long leafy branches & a star in center, delicate meandering vine outer border, clear (mold roughness) **66**

L & R-80, round, tight ring of hearts in center, leafy undulating vine band & other swirled leaf sprig band, plain rim, light opal, 3 3/4" d. **358**

L & R-88, round, small florals around border band, concentric rings in center, opal, 3 3/4" d. (area of underfill, few minor rim flakes) **385**

L & R 10, round, small finely ribbed rim & ray center, 3 3/8" d. (ends of five rays tipped) **40**

L & R 15, round, ringed center surrounded w/ribbed rays, zigzag border w/smooth edge, 3 7/16" d. (small rim flake) **45**

L & R 36, round w/large scallops around rim, 3 1/4" d. **90**

L & R 36, round w/large scallops around rim, opal opaque, 3 1/4" d. **350**

L & R 38, round w/large scallops around rim w/a blossomhead in each scallop, plain center, opal, 3 1/4" d. (two tiny spalls) **340**

L & R 77, round, smooth rim, leafy vine border enclosing a ring of spiral legs around a central wheel **176**

L & R 80, round, smooth rim, leaf sprig border enclosing a leafy rope band & central cluster of hearts, 3 3/4" d. (areas of
cloudiness) 60

L & R 81, round, smooth rim, leaf sprig border enclosing a leafy rope band & central cluster of hearts, rope table ring,
opal w/lavender overtones, 3 3/4" d.
(tiny flake on rope edge) 900

L & R 109, octagonal w/incurved edges, a
central cluster of four pineapple-like
devices enclosed in a geometric border
band, opal, 3 7/16" w. (edge flakes,
roughness) 320

L & R 145b, round, checkerboard center
design w/a small cross & stippling in
each square, leaf band border, tiny scallops around rim, 2 3/4" d. (one scallop
chipped, others w/slight tipping) 525

L & R 324, round, central starburst forming
four panels each w/a starburst, rayed rim
band, finely scalloped rim, amethyst
(light mold roughness) 132

L & R 500, round, Sunburst center, finely
scalloped rim, light blue (light mold
roughnes) 231

L & R 612-A, octagonal w/finely scalloped
rim, central design of a sidewheeler
within shield & scroll border, silver nitrate
inner rim, probably Pittsburgh area, ca.
1830s (two scallops missing, five tipped) 770

DEPRESSION

*The phrase "Depression Glass" is used by col-
lectors to denote a specific kind of transparent
glass produced primarily as tablewares, in crystal,
amber, blue, green, pink, milky-white, etc., during
the late 1920s and 1930s when this country was in
the midst of a financial depression. Made to sell
inexpensively, it was turned out by such producers
as Jeannette, Hocking, Westmoreland, Indiana and
other glass companies. We compile prices on all
the major Depression Glass patterns. Collectors
should consult Depression Glass references for
information on those patterns and pieces which
have been reproduced.*

ADAM, Jeanette Glass Co., 1932-34 (Process-etched)

Bowl, 4 3/4" sq., dessert, green $21
Bowl, 4 3/4" sq., dessert, pink 23
Bowl, 5 3/4" sq., cereal, green 52
Bowl, 5 3/4" sq., cereal, pink 56
Bowl, 7 3/4" sq., dessert, green 26
Bowl, 7 3/4" sq., nappy, pink 29
Bowl, cov., 9" sq., green 85
Bowl, cov., 9" sq., pink 72
Bowl, 10" oval, vegetable, green 32
Bowl, 10" oval, vegetable, pink 34
Butter dish, cov., green 378
Butter dish, cov., pink. 86
Cake plate, footed, green, 10" sq..................... 31
Cake plate, footed, pink, 10" sq. 28
Candlestick, green, 4" h. 42
Candlestick, pink, 4" h. 51
Candlesticks, green, 4" h., pr........................... 91
Candlesticks, pink, 4" h., pr.............................. 92
Candy jar, cov., green.................................... 111

Adam Candy Jar

Candy jar, cov., pink (ILLUS.)........................... 108
Coaster, clear, 3 1/4" sq.................................. 17
Coaster, green, 3 1/4" sq. 22
Creamer, green 23
Creamer, pink 23
Cup, green 24
Cup, pink 30
Cup & saucer, green 31
Cup & saucer, pink 38
Pitcher, 8" h., 32 oz., cone-shaped, clear 35
Pitcher, 8" h., 32 oz., cone-shaped, green........ 43
Pitcher, 8" h., 32 oz., cone-shaped, pink 43
Pitcher, 32 oz., round base, pink 53
Plate, 6" sq., sherbet, green 9
Plate, 6" sq., sherbet, pink............................... 11
Plate, 7 3/4" sq., salad, green 18
Plate, 7 3/4" sq., salad, pink 18
Plate, 9" sq., dinner, green 30
Plate, 9" sq., dinner, pink................................. 37
Plate, 9" sq., grill, green 23
Plate, 9" sq., grill, pink 28
Plate, salad, round, pink.................................. 60
Plate, salad, round, yellow 110
Platter, 11 3/4" l., green 34
Platter, 11 3/4" l., pink 31
Relish dish, two-part, green, 8" sq. 25
Relish dish, two-part, pink, 8" sq. 21
Salt & pepper shakers, footed, green,
4" h., pr... 99
Salt & pepper shakers, footed, pink, 4" h.,
pr.. 86
Saucer, green, 6" sq.. 6
Saucer, pink, 6" sq. 8
Sherbet, green, 3" h.. 37
Sherbet, pink, 3" h.. 31
Sugar bowl, cov., green................................. 48
Tumbler, cone-shaped, green, 4 1/2" h., 7
oz.. 32
Tumbler, cone-shaped, pink, 4 1/2" h., 7
oz.. 35
Tumbler, iced tea, green, 5 1/2" h., 9 oz........... 59
Tumbler, iced tea, pink 5 1/2" h., 9 oz. 77
Vase, 7 1/2" h., green..................................... 91
Vase, 7 1/2" h., pink...................................... 488

AMERICAN SWEETHEART, MacBeth - Evans Glass Co., 1930-38 (Process-etched)

Bowl, 3 3/4" d., berry, pink 85
Bowl, 4 1/2" d., cream soup, Monax 125
Bowl, 4 1/2" d., cream soup, pink...................... 89
Bowl, 6" d., cereal, Monax 18
Bowl, 6" d., cereal, pink 18
Bowl, 9" d., berry, Monax 65
Bowl, 9" d., berry, pink 62

Bowl, 9 1/2" d., soup w/flanged rim, Monax....... 92
Bowl, 9 1/2" d., soup w/flanged rim, pink 75
Bowl, 11" oval vegetable, Monax 91
Bowl, 11" oval vegetable, pink 76
Console bowl, blue, 18" d. 1,688
Console bowl, Monax, 18" d. 574
Console bowl, ruby red, 18" d. 1,863
Creamer, footed, Monax 13
Creamer, footed, pink..................................... 15
Creamer, footed, ruby red 106
Cup, Monax 10
Cup, pink 20
Cup, ruby red.. 90
Cup & saucer, blue...................................... 151
Cup & saucer, Monax..................................... 13
Cup & saucer, pink 23
Cup & saucer, ruby red 131
Lamp shade, Monax 767
Pitcher, 7 1/2" h., 60 oz., jug-type, pink 1,005
Pitcher, 8" h., 80 oz., pink 764
Plate, 6" d., bread & butter, Monax 7
Plate, 6" d., bread & butter, pink......................... 7
Plate, 8" d., salad, blue................................. 130
Plate, 8" d., salad, Monax................................ 10
Plate, 8" d., salad, pink................................... 13
Plate, 8" d., salad, ruby red 102
Plate, 9" d., luncheon, Monax........................... 14
Plate, 9 3/4" d., dinner, Monax 26
Plate, 9 3/4" d., dinner, pink 39
Plate, 10 1/4" d., dinner, Monax 30
Plate, 10 1/4" d., dinner, pink 43
Plate, 11" d., chop, Monax 21
Plate, 12" d., salver, blue............................... 235
Plate, 12" d., salver, Monax............................. 27
Plate, 12" d., salver, pink................................ 23
Plate, 12" d., salver, ruby red 210
Plate, 15 1/2" d., w/center handle, blue........... 725
Plate, 15 1/2" d., w/center handle, Monax....... 235
Plate, 15 1/2" d., w/center handle, ruby red 396
Platter, 13" oval, Monax 97
Platter, 13" oval, pink 61
Salt & pepper shakers, footed, Monax, pr. 458
Salt & pepper shakers, footed, pink, pr. 563
Saucer, blue 31
Saucer, Monax 3
Saucer, pink 5
Saucer, ruby red.. 25
Sherbet, footed, pink, 3 3/4" h.......................... 25
Sherbet, footed, Monax, 4 1/4" h. 22
Sherbet, footed, pink, 4 1/4" h........................... 21
Sugar bowl, cov., Monax (only) 445
Sugar bowl, open, Monax.................................... 8
Sugar bowl, open, pink...................................... 15
Sugar bowl, open, ruby red 120
Tidbit server, three-tier, Monax 324
Tidbit server, two-tier, Monax.......................... 89
Tidbit server, two-tier, pink.............................. 56
Tidbit server, two-tier, ruby red 322
Tumbler, pink, 3 1/2" h., 5 oz. 103
Tumbler, pink, 4 1/4" h., 9 oz. 90

American Sweetheart Tumbler

Tumbler, pink, 4 3/4" h., 10 oz. (ILLUS.).......... 171

BUBBLE, BULLSEYE or PROVINCIAL, Anchor-Hocking Glass Co., 1940-65 (Press-mold)

Berry set: master bowl & 4 sauce dishes:
    clear, 5 pcs.. 7
Berry set: master bowl & 6 sauce dishes:
    blue, 7 pcs... 33
Berry set: master bowl & 6 sauce dishes:
    milk white, 7 pcs.. 13
Berry set: master bowl & 8 sauce dishes;
    clear, 9 pcs... 18
Bowl, 4" d., berry, blue 21
Bowl, 4" d., berry, clear 6
Bowl, 4" d., berry, green.................................. 10
Bowl, 4" d., berry, milk white 4
Bowl, 4" d., berry, pink 15
Bowl, 4 1/2" d., fruit, blue 12
Bowl, 4 1/2" d., fruit, clear 6
Bowl, 4 1/2" d., fruit, green................................ 9
Bowl, 4 1/2" d., fruit, milk white 4
Bowl, 4 1/2" d., fruit, ruby red 11
Bowl, 5 1/4" d., cereal, blue 14
Bowl, 5 1/4" d., cereal, clear 6
Bowl, 5 1/4" d., cereal, green 18
Bowl, 7 3/4" d., soup, blue 15
Bowl, 7 3/4" d., soup, clear 6
Bowl, 7 3/4" d., soup, pink................................. 9
Bowl, 8 3/8" d., blue 17
Bowl, 8 3/8" d., clear 14
Bowl, 8 3/8" d., green 26
Bowl, 8 3/8" d., milk white 5
Bowl, 8 3/8" d., pink 11
Bowl, 8 3/8" d., ruby red 20
Bowl, 9" d., flanged, blue 18
Candlesticks, clear, pr.................................... 17
Creamer, blue 36
Creamer, clear 6
Creamer, green 15
Creamer, milk white 4
Cup, blue 5
Cup, clear 4
Cup, green... 9
Cup, ruby red... 8

Cup & saucer, blue 6
Cup & saucer, clear 6
Cup & saucer, green 15
Cup & saucer, milk white 3
Cup & saucer, ruby red 15
Lamp, clear 34
Lamps, clear (electric), pr. 56
Pitcher w/ice lip, 64 oz., clear 65

Bubble Pitcher w/Ice Lip

Pitcher w/ice lip, 64 oz., ruby red (ILLUS.) 63
Plate, 6 3/4" d., bread & butter, blue 4
Plate, 6 3/4" d., bread & butter, green 9
Plate, 9 3/8" d., dinner, blue 8
Plate, 9 3/8" d., dinner, clear 7
Plate, 9 3/8" d., dinner, green 28
Plate, 9 3/8" d., dinner, ruby red 26
Plate, 9 3/8" d., grill, blue 20
Platter, 12" oval, blue 16
Saucer, blue 3
Saucer, ruby red 5
Sugar bowl, open, blue 25
Sugar bowl, open, clear 9
Sugar bowl, open, green 13
Sugar bowl, open, milk white 5
Tumbler, juice, green, 6 oz. 13
Tumbler, juice, ruby red, 6 oz. 10
Tumbler, old fashioned, ruby red, 3 1/4" h.,
   8 oz. 17
Tumbler, water, ruby red, 9 oz. 12
Tumbler, iced tea, clear, 4 1/2" h., 12 oz. 15
Tumbler, iced tea, ruby red, 4 1/2" h.,
   12 oz. 14
Tumbler, lemonade, ruby red, 5 7/8" h.,
   16 oz. 18

CAMEO or BALLERINA or DANCING GIRL, Hocking Glass Co., 1930-34 (Process-etched)

Bowl, 4 1/4" d., sauce, clear 5
Bowl, 4 3/4" d., cream soup, green 190
Bowl, 5 1/2" d., cereal, clear 6
Bowl, 5 1/2" d., cereal, green 38
Bowl, 5 1/2" d., cereal, yellow 44
Bowl, 7 1/4" d., salad, green 59
Bowl, 8 1/4" d., large berry, green 39
Bowl, 8 1/4" d., large berry, pink 125

Bowl, 9" d., soup w/flange rim, green 87
Bowl, 10" oval vegetable, green 33
Bowl, 10" oval vegetable, yellow 44
Butter dish, cov., green 265
Cake plate, three-footed, green, 10" d. 28
Candlesticks, green, 4" h., pr. 123
Candy jar, cov., green, 4" h. 100
Candy jar, cov., yellow, 4" h. 98
Candy jar, cov., green, 6 1/2" h. 215
Compote, mayonnaise, 5" d., 4" h., cone-
   shaped, green 40
Console bowl, three-footed, green, 11" d. 85
Console bowl, three-footed, pink, 11" d. 65
Console bowl, three-footed, yellow, 11" d. 95
Cookie jar, cov., green 60
Creamer, green, 3 1/4" h. 22
Creamer, yellow, 3 1/4" h. 22
Creamer, green, 4 1/4" h. 28
Cup, clear 5
Cup, green 15
Cup, yellow 8
Cup & saucer, green 24
Cup & saucer, yellow 11
Decanter w/stopper, green, 10" h. 200
Decanter w/stopper, green frosted, 10" h. 36
Goblet, wine, green, 4" h. 81
Goblet, water, green, 6" h. 67
Goblet, water, pink, 6" h. 164
Ice bowl, tab handles, green, 5 1/2" d.,
   3 1/2" h. 223
Jam jar, cov., closed handles, green, 2" 196
Juice set: pitcher & four 3 oz. footed tum-
   blers; green, 5 pcs. 200
Pitcher, syrup or milk, 5 3/4" h., 20 oz.,
   green 207
Pitcher, juice, 6" h., 36 oz., green 56
Pitcher, water, 8 1/2" h., 56 oz., jug-type,
   green 65
Plate, 6" d., sherbet (or ringless saucer),
   clear 2
Plate, 6" d., sherbet (or ringless saucer),
   green 7
Plate, 6" d., sherbet (or ringless saucer),
   yellow 3
Plate, 8" d., luncheon, green 13
Plate, 8" d., luncheon, yellow 10
Plate, 8 1/2" sq., green 53
Plate, 8 1/2" sq., yellow 310
Plate, 9 1/2" d., dinner, green 22
Plate, 9 1/2" d., dinner, yellow 11
Plate, 10" d., sandwich, green 20
Plate, 10" d., sandwich, pink 61
Plate, 10 1/2" d., dinner, rimmed, green 111
Plate, 10 1/2" d., grill, green 15
Plate, 10 1/2" d., grill, yellow 8
Plate, 10 1/2" d., grill, closed handles,
   green 77
Plate, 10 1/2" d., grill, closed handles, yel-
   low 7
Platter, 12", closed handles, green 27
Platter, 12", closed handles, yellow 41
Relish, footed, three-part, green, 7 1/2" 36
Salt & pepper shakers, green, pr. 73
Salt & pepper shakers, pink, pr. 1,325
Sherbet, green, 3 1/8" h. 17
Sherbet, pink, 3 1/8" h. 83
Sherbet, yellow, 3 1/8" h. 41
Sherbet, thin, high stem, green, 4 7/8" h. 38
Sherbet, thin, high stem, yellow, 4 7/8" h. 42

Sugar bowl, open, green, 3 1/4" h. 22
Sugar bowl, open, yellow, 3 1/4" h. 18
Sugar bowl, open, green, 4 1/4" h. 28
Tumbler, juice, green, 3 3/4" h., 5 oz. 33
Tumbler, water, clear, 4" h., 9 oz. 10
Tumbler, water, green, 4" h., 9 oz. 33
Tumbler, water, pink, 4" h., 9 oz. 95
Tumbler, footed, green, 5" h., 9 oz. 33
Tumbler, footed, yellow, 5" h., 9 oz. 16
Tumbler, green, 4 3/4" h., 10 oz. 28
Tumbler, green, 5" h., 11 oz. 35
Tumbler, yellow, 5" h., 11 oz. 58
Tumbler, footed, green, 5 3/4" h., 11 oz. 82
Tumbler, green, 5 1/4" h., 15 oz. 74

Cameo Vase

Vase, 5 3/4" h., green (ILLUS.) 275
Vase, 8" h., green 50
Water set: pitcher & 6 tumblers; green,
 7 pcs. 250

CHERRY BLOSSOM, Jeannette Glass Co., 1930-38 (Process-etched)

Bowl, 4 3/4" d., berry, Delphite 16
Bowl, 4 3/4" d., berry, green 20
Bowl, 4 3/4" d., berry, pink 21
Bowl, 5 3/4" d., cereal, green 53
Bowl, 5 3/4" d., cereal, pink 46
Bowl, 7 3/4" d., soup, green 108
Bowl, 7 3/4" d., soup, pink 95
Bowl, 8 1/2" d., berry, Delphite 50
Bowl, 8 1/2" d., berry, green 48
Bowl, 8 1/2" d., berry, pink 53
Bowl, 9" d., two-handled, Delphite 34
Bowl, 9" d., two-handled, green 65
Bowl, 9" d., two-handled, pink 57
Bowl, 9" oval vegetable, green 45
Bowl, 9" oval vegetable, pink 55
Bowl, 10 1/2" d., fruit, three-footed, green 100
Bowl, 10 1/2" d., fruit, three-footed, pink 107
Butter dish, cov., green 113
Butter dish, cov., pink 112
Cake plate, three-footed, green, 10 1/4" d. 31
Cake plate, three-footed, pink, 10 1/4" d. 42
Coaster, green 13

Coaster, pink 17
Creamer, Delphite 23
Creamer, green 19
Creamer, pink 22
Cup, Delphite 19
Cup, green 20
Cup, pink 22
Cup & saucer, Delphite 24
Cup & saucer, green 26

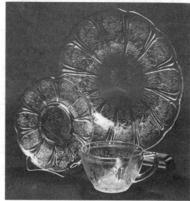

Cherry Blossom Cup & Saucer & Plate

Cup & saucer, pink (ILLUS.) 28
Mug, green, 7 oz. 363
Mug, pink, 7 oz. 180
Pitcher, 6 3/4" h., 36 oz., overall patt., Del-
 phite 92
Pitcher, 6 3/4" h., 36 oz., overall patt.,
 green 59
Pitcher, 6 3/4" h., 36 oz., overall patt., pink 78
Pitcher, 8" h., 36 oz., footed, cone-shaped,
 patt. top, green 77
Pitcher, 8" h., 36 oz., footed, cone-shaped,
 patt. top, pink 67
Pitcher, 8" h., 42 oz., patt. top, green 74
Pitcher, 8" h., 42 oz., patt. top, pink 56
Plate, 6" d., sherbet, Delphite 8
Plate, 6" d., sherbet, green 9
Plate, 6" d., sherbet, pink 9
Plate, 7" d., salad, green 21
Plate, 7" d., salad, pink 28
Plate, 9" d., dinner, Delphite 23
Plate, 9" d., dinner, green 24
Plate, 9" d., dinner, pink (ILLUS. w/cup &
 saucer) 27
Plate, 9" d., grill, green 30
Plate, 9" d., grill, pink 35
Platter, 11" oval, Delphite 42
Platter, 11" oval, green 49
Platter, 11" oval, pink 55
Platter, 13" oval, green 77
Platter, 13" oval, divided, green 90
Platter, 13" oval, divided, pink 78
Salt & pepper shakers, green, pr. 1,085
Sandwich tray, handled, Delphite,
 10 1/2" d. 24
Sandwich tray, handled, green, 10 1/2" d. 32
Sandwich tray, handled, pink, 10 1/2" d. 36
Saucer, Delphite 5
Saucer, green 5
Saucer, pink 6
Sherbet, Delphite 12

Sherbet, green 20
Sherbet, pink 19
Sugar bowl, cov., clear 18
Sugar bowl, cov., Delphite.............................. 35
Sugar bowl, cov., green 39
Sugar bowl, cov., pink 38
Sugar bowl, open, Delphite 18
Sugar bowl, open, pink................................... 14
Tumbler, patt. top, green, 3 1/2" h., 4 oz. 32
Tumbler, patt. top, pink, 3 1/2" h., 4 oz. 22
Tumbler, juice, footed, overall patt., Del-
    phite, 3 3/4" h., 4 oz. 20
Tumbler, juice, footed, overall patt., green,
    3 3/4" h., 4 oz. 22
Tumbler, juice, footed, overall patt., pink,
    3 3/4" h., 4 oz. 23
Tumbler, footed, overall patt., Delphite,
    4 1/2" h., 8 oz. 21
Tumbler, footed, overall patt., green,
    4 1/2" h., 8 oz. 41
Tumbler, footed, overall patt., pink,
    4 1/2" h., 8 oz. 39
Tumbler, patt. top, green, 4 1/4" h., 9 oz.
    (ILLUS.)... 26
Tumbler, patt. top, pink, 4 1/4" h., 9 oz. 24
Tumbler, footed, overall patt., Delphite,
    4 1/2" h., 9 oz. 22
Tumbler, footed, overall patt., green,
    4 1/2" h., 9 oz. 32
Tumbler, footed, overall patt., pink,
    4 1/2" h., 9 oz. 39
Tumbler, patt. top, pink, 5" h., 12 oz. 78

JUNIOR SET:
Creamer, Delphite.. 51
Creamer, pink.. 48
Cup, pink 38
Cup & saucer, Delphite 47
Cup & saucer, pink 45
Plate, 6" d., Delphite 14
Plate, 6" d., pink 11
Saucer, Delphite.. 7
Saucer, pink 8
Set, Delphite, 14 pcs. 345
Set, pink, 14 pcs. 410
Sugar bowl, Delphite 46
Sugar bowl, pink.. 45

COLONIAL or KNIFE & FORK (Press-mold)
Bowl, 3 3/4" d., berry, pink 53
Bowl, 4 1/2" d., berry, green............................ 18
Bowl, 4 1/2" d., berry, pink 15
Bowl, 4 1/2" d., cream soup, green 71
Bowl, 5 1/2" d., cereal, clear 33
Bowl, 7" d., soup, green 69
Bowl, 7" d., soup, pink.................................... 72
Bowl, 9" d., green 34
Bowl, 9" d., pink 38
Butter dish, cov., clear 44
Butter dish, cov., pink................................... 700
Celery or spooner, clear 75
Creamer or milk pitcher, clear, 5" h., 16
    oz. 22
Cup & saucer, pink 18
Goblet, cordial, green, 3 3/4" h., 1 oz.............. 31
Goblet, wine, clear, 4 1/2" h., 2 1/2 oz. 15
Goblet, wine, green, 4 1/2" h., 2 1/2 oz............ 26
Goblet, cocktail, green, 4" h., 3 oz. 27
Goblet, claret, green, 5 1/4" h., 4 oz. 25

Goblet, water, clear, 5 3/4" h., 8 1/2 oz............. 21
Goblet, water, green, 5 3/4" h., 8 1/2 oz. 33
Pitcher, ice lip or plain, 7" h., 54 oz., clear........ 33
Pitcher, ice lip or plain, 7" h., 54 oz., green 54
Pitcher, ice lip or plain, 7" h., 54 oz., pink 56
Plate, 6" d., sherbet, clear 4
Plate, 6" d., sherbet, green................................ 8
Plate, 6" d., sherbet, pink 7
Plate, 10" d., dinner, green.............................. 63
Plate, 10" d., dinner, pink 62
Plate, 10" d., grill, clear.................................. 19
Plate, 10" d., grill, green 25
Plate, 10" d., grill, pink................................... 26
Platter, 12" oval, clear 14
Platter, 12" oval, green.................................... 26
Platter, 12" oval, pink 33
Salt & pepper shakers, clear, pr. 72
Salt & pepper shakers, green, pr................... 145
Sherbet, clear, 3 3/8" h. 7
Sherbet, green, 3 3/8" h................................. 15
Sherbet, pink, 3 3/8" h.................................... 11
Sugar bowl, cov., clear 23
Sugar bowl, cov., green 26
Sugar bowl, cov., pink 60
Tumbler, whiskey, clear, 2 1/2" h., 1 1/2
    oz. 12
Tumbler, whiskey, green, 2 1/2" h., 1 1/2
    oz. 16
Tumbler, whiskey, pink, 2 1/2" h., 1 1/2 oz. 14
Tumbler, footed, pink, 3 1/4" h., 3 oz. 17
Tumbler, juice, green, 3" h., 5 oz. 24
Tumbler, juice, pink, 3" h., 5 oz. 20
Tumbler, footed, green, 4" h., 5 oz. 43
Tumbler, footed, pink, 4" h., 5 oz. 31
Tumbler, water, clear, 4" h., 9 oz. 14
Tumbler, water, green, 4" h., 9 oz. 21
Tumbler, water, pink, 4" h., 9 oz. 21

CUBE or CUBIST, Jeannette Glass Co., 1929-33 (Press-mold)
Bowl, 4 1/2" d., deep, pink 7
Bowl, 4 1/2" d., dessert, green 9
Bowl, 4 1/2" d., dessert, pink............................. 5
Butter dish, cov., green 68
Butter dish, cov., pink..................................... 68
Candy jar, cov., green, 6 1/2" h. 33
Candy jar, cov., pink, 6 1/2" h. 33
Creamer, clear, 2 5/8" h. 2

Cube Creamer

Creamer, pink, 2 5/8" h. (ILLUS.) 6
Creamer, clear, 3 1/2" h. 1
Creamer, green, 3 1/2" h................................... 8

Creamer, pink, 3 1/2" h. 7
Cup & saucer, green 11
Cup & saucer, pink... 11
Pitcher, 8 3/4" h., 45 oz., green 273
Pitcher, 8 3/4" h., 45 oz., pink 228
Plate, 6" d., sherbet, clear 1
Plate, 6" d., sherbet, green............................... 5
Plate, 6" d., sherbet, pink 4
Plate, 8" d., luncheon, green 8
Plate, 8" d., luncheon, pink................................. 7
Powder jar, cov., three-footed, green 34
Powder jar, cov., three-footed, pink.................. 37
Salt & pepper shakers, green, pr..................... 32
Salt & pepper shakers, pink, pr. 34
Sherbet, footed, green 8
Sherbet, footed, pink... 8
Sugar bowl, cov., green, 3" h. 23
Sugar bowl, cov., pink, 3" h. 22
Sugar bowl, open, clear, 2 3/8" h. 2
Sugar bowl, open, pink, 2 3/8" h.......................... 4
Tumbler, green, 4" h., 9 oz. 73
Tumbler, pink, 4" h., 9 oz. 68

DAISY or NUMBER 620, Indiana Glass Company, 1933-40 (Press-mold)
Bowl, 4 1/2" d., cream soup, amber.................. 10

Daisy Bowl

Bowl, 6" d., cereal, amber (ILLUS.)................... 25
Bowl, 6" d., cereal, clear 9
Bowl, 7 3/8" d., berry, amber............................. 14
Bowl, 7 3/8" d., berry, clear................................. 6
Bowl, 9 3/8" d., berry, amber............................. 31
Bowl, 9 3/8" d., berry, clear................................ 13
Bowl, 10" oval vegetable, amber........................ 18
Creamer, footed, amber 8
Cup & saucer, amber 7
Cup & saucer, clear.. 6
Plate, 6" d., sherbet, amber................................. 4
Plate, 6" d., sherbet, clear 2
Plate, 7 3/8" d., salad, amber 10
Plate, 7 3/8" d., salad, clear................................. 5
Plate, 8 3/8" d., luncheon, amber 6
Plate, 8 3/8" d., luncheon, clear.......................... 3
Plate, 9 3/8" d., dinner, amber............................. 8
Plate, 9 3/8" d., dinner, clear 4
Plate, 11 1/2" d., amber (cake or sandwich)....... 16
Plate, 11 1/2" d., clear (cake or sandwich) 7
Platter, 10 3/4" l., amber 15
Relish dish, three-part, amber, 8 3/8"............... 30
Relish dish, three-part, clear, 8 3/8" 10

Sugar bowl, open, footed, amber 7
Sugar bowl, open, footed, clear........................... 4
Tumbler, footed, amber, 9 oz............................. 23
Tumbler, footed, amber, 12 oz............................ 42
Tumbler, footed, clear, 12 oz. 20

DIANA, Federal Glass Co., 1937-41 (Press-mold)
Bowl, 5" d., cereal, amber 11
Bowl, 5" d., cereal, pink.................................... 10
Bowl, 5 1/2" d., cream soup, amber 16
Bowl, 5 1/2" d., cream soup, clear 7
Bowl, 5 1/2" d., cream soup, pink....................... 32
Bowl, 9" d., salad, pink 19
Candy jar, cov., round, clear 19
Candy jar, cov., round, pink 45
Coaster, amber, 3 1/2" d. 11
Coaster, clear, 3 1/2" d. 3
Coaster, pink, 3 1/2" d.. 7
Console bowl, pink, 11" d................................... 40
Creamer, oval, amber 9
Plate, 9 1/2" d., dinner, amber............................. 9
Plate, 9 1/2" d., dinner, clear 6
Plate, 9 1/2" d., dinner, pink 16
Platter, 12" oval, amber...................................... 13
Salt & pepper shakers, amber, pr.................... 101
Salt & pepper shakers, clear, pr. 21
Salt & pepper shakers, pink, pr. 82
Sherbet, amber 10
Sherbet, pink.. 15
Sugar bowl, open, oval, amber............................ 9
Sugar bowl, open, oval, clear 4
Sugar bowl, open, oval, pink 14
Tumbler, amber, 4 1/8" h., 9 oz. 26
Tumbler, clear, 4 1/8" h., 9 oz............................. 26
Tumbler, pink, 4 1/8" h., 9 oz. 53

JUNIOR SET
Junior set: 6 cups, saucers & plates
    w/round rack; clear, set 100
Junior set: 6 cups, saucers & plates
    w/round rack; pink, set 400

DOGWOOD or APPLE BLOSSOM or WILD ROSE, MacBeth-Evans, 1929-32 (Process-etched)
Bowl, 5 1/2" d., cereal, green 37
Bowl, 5 1/2" d., cereal, pink............................... 33
Bowl, 8 1/2" d., berry, Monax 44
Bowl, 8 1/2" d., berry, pink 62
Bowl, 10 1/4" d., fruit, green............................ 350
Bowl, 10 1/4" d., fruit, pink 630
Cake plate, heavy solid foot, green, 13" d. 125
Cake plate, heavy solid foot, pink, 13" d. 140
Creamer, thin, green, 2 1/2" h. 46
Creamer, thin, pink, 2 1/2" h............................. 19
Creamer, thick, footed, pink, 3 1/4" h. 19
Cup, Monax 36

Dogwood Cup & Saucer

Cup & saucer, green (ILLUS.) 47
Cup & saucer, Monax 39
Cup & saucer, pink 22
Pitcher, 8" h., 80 oz., American Sweetheart
   style, pink 560
Pitcher, 8" h., 80 oz., decorated, pink 253
Plate, 6" d., bread & butter, green 9
Plate, 6" d., bread & butter, pink 9
Plate, 8" d., luncheon, clear 4
Plate, 8" d., luncheon, green 12
Plate, 8" d., luncheon, pink 10
Plate, 9 1/4" d., dinner, pink 36
Plate, 10 1/2" d., grill, border design, pink 26
Plate, 10 1/2" d., grill, overall patt., pink 25
Platter, 12" oval, pink 738
Sherbet, low foot, pink 37
Sugar bowl, open, thin, green, 2 1/2" h. 31
Sugar bowl, open, thin, pink, 2 1/2" h. 18
Sugar bowl, open, thick, footed, pink,
   3 1/4" h. 19
Tumbler, decorated, pink, 3 1/2" h., 5 oz. 299
Tumbler, decorated, green, 4" h., 10 oz. 83
Tumbler, decorated, pink, 4" h., 10 oz. 42
Tumbler, decorated, green, 4 3/4" h., 11
   oz. 116
Tumbler, decorated, pink, 4 3/4" h., 11 oz. 50
Tumbler, decorated, pink, 5" h., 12 oz. 72
Tumbler, molded band, pink 22

DORIC, Jeannette Glass Co., 1935-48 (Press-mold)
Bowl, 4 1/2" d., berry, green 11
Bowl, 4 1/2" d., berry, pink 10
Bowl, 5 1/2" d., cereal, green 68
Bowl, 5 1/2" d., cereal, pink 85
Bowl, 8 1/4" d., large berry, green 32
Bowl, 8 1/4" d., large berry, pink 24
Bowl, 9" d., two-handled, pink 16
Bowl, 9" oval vegetable, green 36
Bowl, 9" oval vegetable, pink 40
Butter dish, cov., green 85
Butter dish, cov., pink 70
Cake plate, three-footed, green, 10" d. 24
Cake plate, three-footed, pink, 10" d. 30
Candy dish, three-section, Delphite, 6" 8
Candy dish, three-section, green, 6" 11
Candy dish, three-section, pink, 6" 9
Candy jar, cov., green, 8" h. 43
Candy jar, cov., pink, 8" h. 49
Coaster, green, 3" d. 19
Coaster, pink, 3" d. 19
Creamer, green, 4" h. 13
Creamer, pink, 4" h. 15

Cup, green 12
Cup, pink 11
Cup & saucer, green 17
Cup & saucer, pink 14
Pitcher, 5 1/2" h., 32 oz., green 44
Pitcher, 5 1/2" h., 32 oz., pink 45
Pitcher, 7 1/2" h., 48 oz., footed, pink 425
Plate, 6" d., sherbet, green 6
Plate, 6" d., sherbet, pink 6
Plate, 7" d., salad, green 21
Plate, 7" d., salad, pink 17
Plate, 9" d., dinner, green 20
Plate, 9" d., dinner, pink 19
Plate, 9", grill, pink 24
Platter, 12" oval, green 36
Platter, 12" oval, pink 32
Relish, square inserts in metal holder, pink 48
Relish or serving tray, green, 8" x 8" 21
Relish or serving tray, pink, 8" x 8" 24
Relish tray, green, 4" x 4" 12
Relish tray, pink, 4" x 4" 12
Relish tray, green, 4" x 8" 20
Relish tray, pink, 4" x 8" 21
Salt & pepper shakers, green, pr. 38
Sandwich tray, handled, green, 10" d. 18

Doric Sandwich Tray

Sandwich tray, handled, pink, 10" d.
   (ILLUS.) 17
Saucer, green 5
Saucer, pink 5
Sherbet, footed, Delphite 7
Sherbet, footed, green 18
Sherbet, footed, pink 16
Sugar bowl, cov., green 40
Sugar bowl, cov., pink 28
Tumbler, pink, 4 1/2" h., 9 oz. 72
Tumbler, footed, pink, 4" h., 10 oz. 67
Tumbler, footed, pink, 5" h., 12 oz. 82

FLORAL or POINSETTIA, Jeannette Glass Co., 1931-35 (Process-etched)
Bowl, 4" d., berry, green 21
Bowl, 4" d., berry, pink 27
Bowl, 7 1/2" d., salad, green 26
Bowl, 7 1/2" d., salad, pink 28
Bowl, 8" d., cov. vegetable, green 54
Bowl, 9" oval vegetable, green 27
Bowl, 9" oval vegetable, pink 24
Butter dish, cov., green 110
Butter dish, cov., pink 113
Candlesticks, green, 4" h., pr. 100
Candy jar, cov., green 44
Candy jar, cov., pink 46
Coaster, green, 3 1/4" d. 14

Coaster, pink, 3 1/4" d....................................... 15
Creamer, green 20
Creamer, pink.................................... 15
Cup, green....................................... 14
Cup, pink 13
Cup & saucer, green 25
Cup & saucer, pink............................. 26
Lamp, green 502
Pitcher, 5 1/2" h., 24 oz., green 675
Pitcher, 8" h., 32 oz., cone-shaped, pink 40
Pitcher, 8" h., 32 oz., cone-shaped, green........ 38
Pitcher, lemonade, 10 1/4" h., 48 oz.,
    green...................................... 270
Pitcher, lemonade, 10 1/4" h., 48 oz., pink 347
Plate, 6" d., sherbet, green...................... 10
Plate, 6" d., sherbet, pink 8
Plate, 8" d., salad, green 13
Plate, 8" d., salad, pink...................... 13
Plate, 9" d., dinner, green...................... 22
Plate, 9" d., dinner, pink 25
Platter, 10 3/4" oval, green...................... 22
Platter, 10 3/4" oval, pink 23
Platter, 11" oval, scalloped edge, pink 140
Relish, two-part, oval, green 20
Relish, two-part, oval, pink...................... 21
Salt & pepper shakers, footed, green,
    4" h., pr. 55
Salt & pepper shakers, flat, pink, 6" h., pr. 49
Saucer, pink 12
Sherbet, green 19
Sherbet, pink 19
Sugar bowl, cov., green 35
Sugar bowl, cov., pink 30
Sugar bowl, open, green 11
Sugar bowl, open, pink 12
Tray, closed handles, pink, 6" sq...................... 25
Tumbler, juice, footed, green, 4" h., 5 oz. 27
Tumbler, juice, footed, pink, 4" h., 5 oz............. 20
Tumbler, water, footed, green, 4 3/4" h.,
    7 oz. 25
Tumbler, water, footed, pink, 4 3/4" h.,
    7 oz. 23
Tumbler, green, 4 1/2" h., 9 oz. 230
Tumbler, lemonade, footed, green,
    5 1/4" h., 9 oz. 93
Vase, 6 7/8" h., octagonal, clear...................... 298

FLORENTINE or POPPY NO. 2, Hazel Atlas Glass Co., 1932-35 (Process-etched)
Bowl, 4 1/2" d., berry, clear...................... 11
Bowl, 4 1/2" d., berry, green.................... 13
Bowl, 4 1/2" d., berry, pink...................... 17
Bowl, 4 1/2" d., berry, yellow.................... 22
Bowl, 4 3/4" d., cream soup, plain rim,
    clear 13
Bowl, 4 3/4" d., cream soup, plain rim,
    green 15
Bowl, 4 3/4" d., cream soup, plain rim, pink....... 17
Bowl, 4 3/4" d., cream soup, plain rim, yel-
    low................................... 22
Bowl, 8" d., clear................................... 19
Bowl, 8" d., green................................... 29
Bowl, 8" d., pink................................... 31
Bowl, 8" d., yellow................................... 38

Florentine Vegetable Bowl

Bowl, 9" oval, cov., vegetable, yellow
    (ILLUS.)................................... 83
Butter dish, cov., clear.................................... 110
Butter dish, cov., green 99
Butter dish, cov., yellow 155
Candlesticks, green, 2 3/4" h., pr. 53
Candlesticks, yellow, 2 3/4" h., pr. 70
Candy dish, cov., clear 117
Candy dish, cov., green 105
Candy dish, cov., pink 155
Candy dish, cov., yellow 165
Coaster-ashtray, clear, 3 3/4" d. 18
Coaster-ashtray, green, 3 3/4" d. 19
Coaster-ashtray, yellow, 3 3/4" d. 30
Coaster-ashtray, green, 5 1/2" d. 30
Coaster-ashtray, yellow, 5 1/2" d. 39
Compote, 3 1/2", ruffled, cobalt blue.................. 50
Compote, 3 1/2", ruffled, pink 35
Creamer, clear 8
Creamer, green 10
Creamer, yellow 12
Cup & saucer, clear 10
Cup & saucer, green 14
Cup & saucer, yellow.................................... 14
Gravy boat w/platter, yellow, 11 1/2" oval 115
Pitcher, 6 1/4" h., 24 oz., cone-shaped,
    yellow................................... 170
Pitcher, 7 1/2" h., 28 oz., cone-shaped,
    clear 30
Pitcher, 7 1/2" h., 28 oz., cone-shaped,
    green................................... 42
Pitcher, 7 1/2" h., 28 oz., cone-shaped,
    yellow................................... 36
Pitcher, 7 1/2" h., 48 oz., straight sides,
    green................................... 93
Pitcher, 7 1/2" h., 48 oz., straight sides,
    pink................................... 147
Plate, 6" d., sherbet, clear 4
Plate, 6" d., sherbet, green 5
Plate, 6" d., sherbet, yellow 6
Plate, 8 1/2" d., salad, clear 8
Plate, 8 1/2" d., salad, green 10
Plate, 8 1/2" d., salad, pink 6
Plate, 8 1/2" d., salad, yellow 13
Plate, 10" d., dinner, clear 13
Plate, 10" d., dinner, green 20
Plate, 10" d., dinner, yellow 20
Plate, 10 1/4" d., grill, clear 12
Plate, 10 1/4" d., grill, green 14
Plate, 10 1/4" d., grill, yellow 15
Platter, 11" oval, clear.................................... 8
Platter, 11" oval, green.................................... 19
Platter, 11" oval, yellow.................................... 22
Platter, 11 1/2", for gravy boat, yellow 45
Relish dish, three-part or plain, clear, 10" 14
Relish dish, three-part or plain, green, 10"....... 30
Relish dish, three-part or plain, pink, 10" 24
Relish dish, three-part or plain, yellow, 10" 32

Salt & pepper shakers, clear, pr. 40
Salt & pepper shakers, green, pr. 44
Salt & pepper shakers, yellow, pr. 53
Sherbet, clear.. 9
Sherbet, green 11
Sherbet, yellow 12
Sugar bowl, cov., clear 25
Sugar bowl, cov., yellow 38
Sugar bowl, open, clear... 9
Sugar bowl, open, green 9
Sugar bowl, open, yellow 12
Tumbler, footed, clear, 3 1/4" h., 5 oz................. 15
Tumbler, footed, green, 3 1/4" h., 5 oz. 14
Tumbler, footed, yellow, 3 1/4" h., 5 oz.............. 20
Tumbler, juice, yellow, 3 1/2" h., 5 oz................. 20
Tumbler, footed, clear, 4" h., 5 oz...................... 14
Tumbler, footed, green, 4" h., 5 oz. 15
Tumbler, footed, yellow, 4" h., 5 oz.................... 18
Tumbler, water, clear, 4" h., 9 oz. 10
Tumbler, water, green, 4" h., 9 oz...................... 14
Tumbler, water, pink, 4" h., 9 oz. 16
Tumbler, water, yellow, 4" h., 9 oz. 24
Tumbler, footed, green, 4 1/2" h., 9 oz. 30
Tumbler, footed, yellow, 4 1/2" h., 9 oz.............. 37
Tumbler, blown, clear, 5" h., 12 oz. 20
Tumbler, blown, green, 5" h., 12 oz. 16
Tumbler, iced tea, clear, 5" h., 12 oz. 24
Tumbler, iced tea, green, 5" h., 12 oz. 33
Tumbler, iced tea, yellow, 5" h., 12 oz. 55
Vase (or parfait), 6" h., clear 29
Vase (or parfait), 6" h., green 33
Vase (or parfait), 6" h., yellow 63

HOLIDAY or BUTTONS AND BOWS, Jeannette Glass Co., 1947-mid '50s (Press-mold)*All items in pink unless otherwise noted.*

Bowl, 5 1/8" d., berry.. 15
Bowl, 7 3/4" d., flat soup 56
Bowl, berry, 8 1/2" d.. 32
Bowl, 9 1/2" oval vegetable................................. 27
Butter dish, cov. 44
Cake plate, three-footed, 10 1/2" d. 110
Candlesticks, 3" h., pr. 112
Console bowl, 10 3/4" d. 116
Creamer, footed 11
Cup & saucer, plain or rayed base 13
Pitcher, milk, 4 3/4" h., 16 oz., iridescent........... 27

Holiday Milk Pitcher

Pitcher, milk, 4 3/4" h., 16 oz. (ILLUS.).............. 71
Pitcher, 6 3/4" h., 52 oz...................................... 38
Plate, 9" d., dinner.. 24

Plate, 13 3/4" d., chop 99
Platter, 8 x 11 3/8" oval 21
Platter, 8 x 11 3/4" oval, iridescent.................... 12
Sandwich tray, 10 1/2" d. 22
Saucer 5
Sugar bowl, cov. 33
Sugar bowl, open 10
Tumbler, footed, 4" h., 5 oz................................. 51
Tumbler, footed, 6" h., 9 oz............................... 172
Tumbler, 4" h., 10 oz... 23

IRIS or IRIS & HERRINGBONE, Jeannette Glass Co., 1928-32 (Press-mold)

Bowl, 4 1/2" d., berry, beaded rim, amber
  iridescent.. 11
Bowl, 4 1/2" d., berry, beaded rim, clear 49
Bowl, 5" d., cereal, clear 149
Bowl, 5" d., sauce, ruffled rim, amber iri-
  descent... 27
Bowl, 5" d., sauce, ruffled rim, clear..................... 8
Bowl, 7 1/2" d., soup, amber iridescent............. 70
Bowl, 7 1/2" d., soup, clear 172
Bowl, 8" d., berry, beaded rim, amber iri-
  descent... 23
Bowl, 8" d., berry, beaded rim, clear 117
Bowl, 9 1/2" d., salad, amber iridescent............. 16
Bowl, 9 1/2" d., salad, clear............................... 15
Bowl, 11 1/2" d., fruit, ruffled rim, amber iri-
  descent... 19
Bowl, 11" d., fruit, straight rim, clear 72
Bowl, 11 1/2" d., fruit, ruffled rim, clear 14
Butter dish, cov., amber iridescent.................... 49
Butter dish, cov., clear.. 49
Candlesticks, two-branch, amber irides-
  cent, pr. 44
Candlesticks, two-branch, clear, pr.................... 42
Candy jar, cov., clear 190
Coaster, clear.. 116
Creamer, footed, amber, iridescent.................... 12
Creamer, footed, clear 12
Cup, demitasse, clear... 36
Cup, clear 15
Cup & saucer, amber iridescent 24
Cup & saucer, clear.. 28
Goblet, wine, amber iridescent, 4" h., 3 oz. 30
Goblet, wine, clear, 4 1/4" h., 3 oz. 17
Goblet, clear, 5 1/2" h., 4 oz.............................. 28
Goblet, clear, 5 1/2" h., 8 oz.............................. 28
Lamp shade, blue 88
Lamp shade, clear 93
Lamp shade, pink 77
Pitcher, 9 1/2" h., footed, amber iridescent........ 45
Pitcher, 9 1/2" h., footed, clear.......................... 39
Plate, 5 1/2" d., sherbet, amber iridescent 14
Plate, 5 1/2" d., sherbet, clear........................... 16
Plate, 8" d., luncheon, clear............................. 138
Plate, 9" d., dinner, amber iridescent 46
Plate, 9" d., dinner, clear 62
Plate, 11 3/4" d., sandwich, amber irides-
  cent 32
Plate, 11 3/4" d., sandwich, clear 44
Saucer, demitasse, clear................................... 140
Saucer, amber iridescent 11
Saucer, clear 13
Sherbet, footed, amber iridescent, 2 1/2" h........ 18
Sherbet, footed, clear, 2 1/2" h. 27
Sherbet, footed, clear, 4" h. 25
Sugar bowl, cov., footed, amber iridescent 27
Sugar bowl, cov., footed, clear 26

Sugar bowl, open, footed, amber irides-
cent 10
Sugar bowl, open, footed, clear 12
Tumbler, clear, 4" h. 158
Tumbler, footed, amber iridescent, 6" h. 23
Tumbler, footed, clear, 6" h. 19

Iris Tumbler

Tumbler, footed, clear, 6 1/2" h. (ILLUS.) 36
Vase, 9" h., amber iridescent 26
Vase, 9" h., clear 24

LACE EDGE or OPEN LACE, Hocking Glass Co., 1935-38 (Press-mold)
Bowl, 6 1/2" d., cereal, pink 30
Bowl, 7 3/4" d., salad or butter dish bottom,
pink 30
Bowl, 9 1/2" d., plain or ribbed, pink 29

Lace Edge Butter Dish

Butter dish or bonbon, cov., pink (ILLUS.) 69
Candy jar, cov., ribbed, pink, 4" h. 55
Compote, cov., 7" d., footed, pink 60
Compote, open, 7" d., footed, pink 25
Console bowl, three-footed, pink,
10 1/2" d. 245
Cookie jar, cov., pink, 5" h. 80
Creamer, pink 24
Cup, pink 25
Cup & saucer, pink 39
Flower bowl w/crystal block, pink 35
Plate, 7 1/4" d., salad, pink 22
Plate, 8 1/4" d., luncheon, clear 4

Plate, 8 1/4" d., luncheon, pink 24
Plate, 10 1/2" d., dinner, pink 34
Plate, 10 1/2" d., grill, pink 26
Plate, 13" d., solid lace, pink 58
Platter, 12 3/4" oval, clear 10
Platter, 12 3/4" oval, pink 51
Platter, 12 3/4" oval, five-part, clear 17
Platter, 12 3/4" oval, five-part, pink 40
Relish dish, three-part, deep, pink,
7 1/2" d. 66
Relish plate, three-part, pink, 10 1/2" d. 25
Relish plate, four-part, solid lace, pink,
13" d. 66
Sherbet, footed, clear 10
Sherbet, footed, pink 126
Sugar bowl, open, pink 21
Tumbler, pink, 4 1/2" h., 9 oz. 23
Tumbler, footed, pink, 5" h., 10 1/2 oz. 76

MADRID, Federal Glass Co., 1932-39 (Process-etched)
Ashtray, amber, 6" sq. 264
Ashtray, green, 6" sq. 195
Bowl, 4 3/4" d., cream soup, amber 20
Bowl, 5" d., sauce, amber 6
Bowl, 5" d., sauce, blue 35
Bowl, 5" d., sauce, green 10
Bowl, 7" d., soup, amber 17
Bowl, 7" d., soup, green 18
Bowl, 8" d., salad, amber 14
Bowl, 8" d., salad, green 16
Bowl, 9 3/8" d., large berry, amber 22
Bowl, 9 3/8" d., large berry, pink 24
Bowl, 9 1/2" d., salad, deep, amber 33
Bowl, 10" oval vegetable, amber 21
Bowl, 10" oval vegetable, green 21
Butter dish, cov., amber 76
Butter dish, cov., green 95
Cake plate, amber, 11 1/4" d. 16
Cake plate, clear, 11 1/4" d. 15
Cake plate, pink, 11 1/4" d. 14
Candlesticks, amber, 2 1/4" h., pr. 24
Candlesticks, pink, 2 1/4" h., pr. 25
Console bowl, flared, amber, 11" d. 15
Console bowl, flared, iridescent, 11" d. 16
Console bowl, flared, pink, 11" d. 17
Cookie jar, cov., amber 47
Cookie jar, cov., pink 37
Creamer, amber 8
Creamer, green 11
Cup, amber 6
Cup, blue 18
Cup, clear 5
Cup, green 10
Cup, pink 8
Cup & saucer, amber 10
Cup & saucer, green 15
Cup & saucer, pink 15
Gelatin mold, amber, 2 1/8" h. 14
Hot dish coaster, amber, 5" d. 40
Jam dish, amber, 7" d. 25
Jam dish, green, 7" d. 25
Lazy susan, walnut base w/seven clear hot
dish coasters 871

Madrid Juice Pitcher

Pitcher, juice, 5 1/2" h., 36 oz. amber
(ILLUS.)... 40
Pitcher, 8" h., 60 oz., square, amber 47
Pitcher, 8" h., 60 oz., square, blue.................. 167
Pitcher, 8" h., 60 oz., square, clear 22
Pitcher, 8" h., 60 oz., square, green 145
Pitcher, 8 1/2" h., 80 oz., jug-type, amber......... 65
Pitcher w/ice lip, 8 1/2" h., 80 oz., amber 65
Plate, 6" d., sherbet, amber.................................. 4
Plate, 6" d., sherbet, blue.................................. 15
Plate, 6" d., sherbet, clear 4
Plate, 6" d., sherbet, green.................................. 7
Plate, 6" d., sherbet, pink.................................... 4
Plate, 7 1/2" d., salad, amber 10
Plate, 7 1/2" d., salad, green 9
Plate, 7 1/2" d., salad, pink.................................. 9
Plate, 8 7/8" d., luncheon, amber 8
Plate, 8 7/8" d., luncheon, blue.......................... 25
Plate, 8 7/8" d., luncheon, clear 6
Plate, 8 7/8" d., luncheon, green 11
Plate, 10 1/2" d., dinner, clear 20
Plate, 10 1/2" d., grill, amber 9
Plate, 10 1/2" d., grill, green 19
Platter, 11 1/2" oval, amber................................ 21
Platter, 11 1/2" oval, blue................................... 35
Platter, 11 1/2" oval, green................................. 19
Relish plate, amber, 10 1/2" d. 15
Relish plate, clear, 10 1/2" d................................ 7
Salt & pepper shakers, amber, 3 1/2" h.,
flat, pr. 47
Salt & pepper shakers, green, 3 1/2" h.,
flat, pr. 63
Salt & pepper shakers, footed, amber,
3 1/2" h., pr. 148
Saucer, amber.. 4
Saucer, blue... 12
Saucer, green... 5
Saucer, pink... 7
Sherbet, amber 8
Sherbet, blue.. 18
Sherbet, clear... 7
Sherbet, green.. 12
Sugar bowl, cov., amber.................................... 69
Sugar bowl, cov., clear....................................... 33
Sugar bowl, cov., green...................................... 58
Sugar bowl, open, amber 8
Sugar bowl, open, blue....................................... 19
Sugar bowl, open, green 11
Tumbler, juice, amber, 3 7/8" h., 5 oz. 15
Tumbler, juice, clear, 3 7/8" h., 5 oz. 14
Tumbler, footed, amber, 4" h., 5 oz. 27
Tumbler, footed, green, 4" h., 5 oz. 38

Tumbler, amber, 4 1/2" h., 9 oz. 15
Tumbler, clear, 4 1/2" h., 9 oz............................ 10
Tumbler, green, 4 1/2" h., 9 oz. 25
Tumbler, pink, 4 1/2" h., 9 oz............................. 22
Tumbler, footed, amber, 5 1/4" h., 10 oz. 29
Tumbler, footed, clear, 5 1/4" h., 10 oz.............. 11
Tumbler, amber, 5 1/2" h., 12 oz. 24
Tumbler, clear, 5 1/2" h., 12 oz.......................... 18
Tumbler, green, 5 1/2" h., 12 oz. 33

MANHATTAN or HORIZONTAL RIBBED, Anchor Hocking Glass Co., 1938-43 (Press-mold)

Ashtray, clear, 4" d. 13
Ashtray, clear, 4 1/2" sq..................................... 22
Bowl, 4 1/2" d., sauce, two-handled, clear........... 9
Bowl, 5 3/8" d., berry, two-handled, clear 18
Bowl, 5 3/8" d., berry, two-handled, pink............ 16
Bowl, 5 1/2" d., cereal, clear 91
Bowl, 7 1/2" d., large berry, clear 16
Bowl, 8" d., two-handled, clear........................... 23
Bowl, 9" d., salad, clear..................................... 20
Bowl, 9 1/2" d., fruit, clear 36
Candleholders, clear, 4 1/2" sq., pr.................... 20
Candy dish, open, three-footed, pink 12
Coaster, clear, 3 1/2" d. 13
Compote, 5 3/4" h., clear.................................... 37
Compote, 5 3/4" h., pink..................................... 34
Creamer, oval, clear... 9
Creamer, oval, pink.. 15
Cup & saucer, clear.. 25
Pitcher, juice, 24 oz., ball tilt-type, clear............. 31
Pitcher w/ice lip, 80 oz., ball tilt-type, clear....... 43
Pitcher w/ice lip, 80 oz., ball tilt-type, pink 85
Plate, 6" d., sherbet or saucer, clear 7
Plate, 8 1/2" d., salad, clear.............................. 16
Plate, 10 1/4" d., dinner, clear........................... 23
Plate, 14" d., sandwich, clear 23

Manhattan Relish Tray

Relish tray, four-part, clear, 14" d. (ILLUS.)....... 18
Relish tray, five-part, clear w/clear inserts,
14" d. 48
Relish tray, five-part, pink w/pink inserts,
14" d. 47
Relish tray insert, pink 6
Relish tray insert, ruby... 5
Salt & pepper shakers, square, clear,
2" h., pr. 31
Salt & pepper shakers, square, pink, 2" h.,
pr. 55
Sherbet, clear.. 11
Sherbet, pink.. 20
Sugar bowl, open, oval, clear 11

Sugar bowl, open, oval, pink 11
Tumbler, footed, clear, 10 oz. 18
Tumbler, footed, green, 10 oz. 17
Vase, 8" h., clear 19
Wine, clear, 3 1/2" h. 6

MAYFAIR or OPEN ROSE, Hocking Glass Co., 1931-37 (Process-etched)

Bowl, 5", cream soup, pink 55
Bowl, 5 1/2", cereal, blue 52
Bowl, 5 1/2", cereal, pink 32
Bowl, 7", vegetable, blue 66
Bowl, 7", vegetable, pink 31
Bowl, 9 1/2" oval vegetable, blue 75
Bowl, 9 1/2" oval vegetable, pink 36
Bowl, 10", cov. vegetable, blue 140

Mayfair Covered Vegetable Bowl

Bowl, 10", cov. vegetable, pink (ILLUS.) 169
Bowl, 10", open vegetable, blue 73
Bowl, 10", open vegetable, pink 39
Bowl, 11 3/4" d., low, blue 74
Bowl, 11 3/4" d., low, pink 76
Bowl, 12" d., fruit, deep, scalloped, blue 110
Bowl, 12" d., fruit, deep, scalloped, green 39
Bowl, 12" d., fruit, deep, scalloped, pink 68
Butter dish, cov., blue 328
Butter dish, cov., pink 76
Cake plate, footed, blue, 10" 80
Cake plate, footed, pink, 10" 33
Cake plate, handled, blue, 12" 73
Cake plate, handled, pink, 12" 45
Candy jar, cov., blue 334
Candy jar, cov., pink 63
Celery dish, pink, 10" l. 43
Celery dish, two-part, blue, 10" l. 69
Celery dish, two-part, pink, 10" l. 285
Cookie jar, cov., blue 298
Cookie jar, cov., pink 54
Creamer, footed, blue 97
Creamer, footed, pink 31
Cup, blue 56
Cup, pink 20
Cup & 5 3/4" underplate, blue 77
Cup & 5 3/4" underplate, pink 34
Cup & saucer w/cup ring pink 44
Decanter w/stopper, pink, 10" h., 32 oz. 236
Goblet, cocktail, pink, 4" h., 3 oz. 120
Goblet, water, pink, 5 3/4" h., 9 oz. 80
Pitcher, juice, 6" h., 37 oz., blue 202
Pitcher, juice, 6" h., 37 oz., clear 19
Pitcher, juice, 6" h., 37 oz., pink 63
Pitcher, 8" h., 60 oz., jug-type, blue 203
Pitcher, 8" h., 60 oz., jug-type, pink 72
Pitcher, 8 1/2" h., 80 oz., jug-type, pink 124
Plate (or saucer), 5 3/4", blue 25
Plate (or saucer), 5 3/4", pink 14
Plate, 6 1/2" d., sherbet, off-center indenta-
tion, blue 35

Plate, 6 1/2" d., sherbet, pink 14
Plate, 8 1/2", luncheon, blue 57
Plate, 8 1/2", luncheon, pink 30
Plate, 9 1/2", dinner, pink 58
Plate, 9 1/2", grill, blue 56
Plate, 9 1/2", grill, pink 46
Platter, 12" oval, open handles, blue 75
Platter, 12" oval, open handles, pink 36
Relish, four-part, blue, 8 3/8" 83
Relish, four-part, pink, 8 3/8" 37
Salt & pepper shakers, flat, blue, pr. 319
Sandwich server w/center handle, green,
12" 42
Sandwich server w/center handle, pink,
12" 44
Saucer w/cup ring, pink 35
Sherbet, flat, blue, 2 1/4" h. 129
Sherbet, footed, pink, 3" h. 17
Sugar bowl, open, footed, blue 95
Sugar bowl, open, footed, pink 30
Tumbler, whiskey, pink, 2 1/4" h., 1 1/2 oz. 83
Tumbler, juice, footed, pink, 3 1/4" h., 3 oz. 103
Tumbler, juice, blue, 3 1/2" h., 5 oz. 177
Tumbler, water, blue, 4 1/4" h., 9 oz. 127
Tumbler, water, pink, 4 1/4" h., 9 oz. 39
Tumbler, footed, blue, 5 1/4" h., 10 oz. 130
Tumbler, footed, pink, 5 1/4" h., 10 oz. 45
Tumbler, iced tea, pink, 5 1/4" h., 13 1/2
oz. 64
Tumbler, iced tea, footed, pink, 6 1/2" h.,
15 oz. 49
Vase, 5 1/2" x 8 1/2", sweetpea, hat-
shaped, blue 119

MISS AMERICA, Hocking Glass Co., 1935-38 (Press-mold)

Bowl, 4 1/2" d., berry, green 13
Bowl, 6 1/4" d., berry, clear 10
Bowl, 6 1/4" d., berry, pink 29
Bowl, 8" d., fruit, curved in at top, pink 90
Bowl, 8 3/4" d., fruit, deep, pink 86
Bowl, 10" oval vegetable, pink 35
Butter dish, cov., pink 598
Cake plate, footed, clear, 12" d. 30
Cake plate, footed, pink, 12" d. 58
Candy jar, cov., clear, 11 1/2" h. 62
Candy jar, cov., pink, 11 1/2" h. 183
Celery tray, clear, 10 1/2" oblong 15
Celery tray, pink, 10 1/2" oblong 37
Coaster, clear, 5 3/4" d. 16
Coaster, pink, 5 3/4" d. 35
Compote, 5" d., clear 15
Compote 5" d., pink 31
Creamer, footed, clear 12
Creamer, footed, pink 23
Cup, clear 11
Cup, green 14
Cup, pink 27
Cup & saucer, clear 14
Cup & saucer, pink 35
Goblet, wine, clear, 3 3/4" h., 3 oz. 24
Goblet, wine, pink, 3 3/4" h., 3 oz. 113
Goblet, juice, clear, 4 3/4" h., 5 oz. 24
Goblet, juice, pink, 4 3/4" h., 5 oz. 109
Goblet, water, clear, 5 1/2" h., 10 oz. 20
Goblet, water, pink, 5 1/2" h., 10 oz. 60
Pitcher, 8" h., 65 oz., clear 60
Pitcher, 8" h., 65 oz., pink 158

Pitcher w/ice lip, 8 1/2" h., 65 oz., pink 188
Plate, 5 3/4" d., sherbet, clear 6
Plate, 5 3/4" sherbet, pink 12
Plate, 6 3/4" d., green.. 9
Plate, 8 1/2" d., salad, clear.............................. 15
Plate, 8 1/2" d., salad, pink................................ 25
Plate, 10 1/4" d., dinner, clear 17
Plate, 10 1/4" d., dinner, pink 41
Plate, 10 1/4" d., grill, clear.............................. 11
Plate, 10 1/4" d., grill, pink................................ 26
Platter, 12 1/4" oval, clear 15
Platter, 12 1/4" oval, pink 38
Relish, four-part, clear, 8 3/4" d. 11

Miss America Relish

Relish, four-part, pink, 8 3/4" d. (ILLUS.) 26
Relish, divided, clear, 11 3/4" d.......................... 21
Salt & pepper shakers, pink, pr. 70
Saucer, clear 5
Saucer, pink 7
Sherbet, clear.. 9
Sherbet, pink.. 17
Sugar bowl, open, footed, clear........................ 8
Sugar bowl, open, footed, pink......................... 21
Tumbler, juice, clear, 4" h., 5 oz. 18
Tumbler, juice, pink, 4" h., 5 oz......................... 60
Tumbler, water, clear, 4 1/2" h., 10 oz. 18
Tumbler, water, green, 4 1/2" h., 10 oz............. 18
Tumbler, water, pink, 4 1/2" h., 10 oz. 39
Tumbler, iced tea, pink, 6 3/4" h., 14 oz. 93

MODERNTONE, Hazel Atlas Glass Co., 1934-42, late 1940s & early 1950s (Press-mold)

Ashtray w/match holder, cobalt blue, 7 3/4" d.. 209
Ashtray w/match holder, pink, 7 3/4" d. 62
Bowl, 4 3/4" d., cream soup, amethyst.............. 17
Bowl, 4 3/4" d., cream soup, cobalt blue........... 24
Bowl, 4 3/4" d., cream soup, platonite............... 12
Bowl, 5" d., berry, amethyst 25
Bowl, 5" d., berry, cobalt blue 30
Bowl, 5" d., cream soup w/ruffled rim, cobalt blue... 55
Bowl, 5" d., cream soup w/ruffled rim, platonite 7
Bowl, 6 1/2" d., cereal, cobalt blue................... 117
Bowl, 7 1/2" d., soup, cobalt blue...................... 187
Bowl, 8 3/4" d., large berry, amethyst 46
Bowl, 8 3/4" d., large berry, cobalt blue 55
Butter dish w/metal lid, cobalt blue 111

Cheese dish w/metal lid, cobalt blue, 7" d...... 433
Creamer, amethyst... 11

Moderntone Pieces

Creamer, cobalt blue (ILLUS.) 11
Cup, amethyst 11
Cup, cobalt blue 11
Custard cup, amethyst 14
Custard cup, cobalt blue 21
Plate, 5 7/8" d., sherbet, amethyst 5
Plate, 5 7/8" d., sherbet, cobalt blue.................... 7
Plate, 6 3/4" d., salad, cobalt blue 12
Plate, 7 3/4" d., luncheon, amethyst................... 9
Plate, 7 3/4" d., luncheon, cobalt blue 12
Plate, 8 7/8" d., dinner, amethyst 12
Plate, 8 7/8" d., dinner, cobalt blue.................... 22
Plate, 10 1/2" d., sandwich, amethyst 39
Plate, 10 1/2" d., sandwich, platonite 20
Platter, 11" oval, cobalt blue 48
Platter, 12" oval, amethyst................................. 51
Platter, 12" oval, cobalt blue 128
Salt & pepper shakers, amethyst, pr. 43
Salt & pepper shakers, cobalt blue, pr. (ILLUS. w/creamer) 44
Salt & pepper shakers, platonite, pr. 25
Saucer, amethyst 4
Saucer, cobalt blue 5
Saucer, platonite 5
Sherbet, amethyst.. 12
Sherbet, cobalt blue... 13
Sugar bowl, open, amethyst.............................. 12
Sugar bowl, open, cobalt blue (ILLUS. w/creamer) 11
Tumbler, whiskey, cobalt blue, 1 1/2 oz............ 46
Tumbler, water, cobalt blue, 4" h., 9 oz. 40

LITTLE HOSTESS PARTY SET

Creamer, 1 3/4" h., dark.................................... 14
Creamer, 1 3/4" h., pastel 17
Cup, 1 3/4" h., dark.. 12
Cup & saucer, dark.. 17
Plate, 5 1/4" d., dark... 13
Plate, 5 1/4" d., pastel 10
Saucer, 3 7/8" d., dark... 9
Saucer, 3 7/8" d., pastel 8
Sugar bowl, 1 3/4" h., dark 14
Sugar bowl, 1 3/4" h., pastel............................. 15
Tea set, dark, 16 pcs... 295
Tea set, pastel, 16 pcs....................................... 257
Teapot, cov., 3 1/2" h., dark 110

MOROCCAN AMETHYST, Hazel Ware, Division of Continental Can, 1960s (Early 1960s -not true Depression)

Ashtray, 3 3/4" triangle 7
Ashtray, 6 7/8" triangle 12
Bowl, 4 3/4" w. octagonal, fruit............................ 9
Bowl, 5 3/4" sq., cereal, deep 11

Bowl, 6" d. 11
Bowl, 7 3/4" oval 17
Bowl, 7 3/4" rectangle 15
Bowl, 10 3/4" 31
Candy jar, cov., short 33
Candy jar, cov., tall 37
Chip & dip set, w/metal holder (5 3/4" &
10 3/4" bowls) 41

Moroccan Amethyst Cup & Saucer

Cup & saucer (ILLUS.) 9
Goblet, wine, 4" h., 4 1/2 oz. 11
Goblet, juice, 4 3/8" h., 5 1/2 oz. 10
Goblet, water, 5 1/2" h., 10 oz. 13
Plate, 5 3/4" w. octagonal 5
Plate, 7 1/4" w., salad 8
Plate, 9 3/4" w., dinner 9
Sandwich server, w/metal center handle,
12" 19
Tumbler, juice, 2 1/2" h., 4 oz. 9
Tumbler, Old Fashioned, 3 1/4" h., 8 oz. 13
Tumbler, water, crinkled bottom, 4 1/4" h.,
11 oz. 11
Tumbler, water, 4 5/8" h., 11 oz. 11
Tumbler, iced tea, 6 1/2" h., 16 oz. 15
Vase, 8 1/2" h., ruffled 38

NORMANDIE or BOUQUET & LATTICE, Federal Glass Co., 1933-40 (Process-etched)

Bowl, 5" d., berry, Sunburst iridescent 5
Bowl, 6 1/2" d., cereal, Sunburst iridescent 7
Bowl, 10" oval vegetable, amber 15
Bowl, 10" oval vegetable, Sunburst irides-
cent 17
Creamer, footed, pink 9
Cup & saucer, amber 10
Cup & saucer, pink 12

Normandie Cup & Saucer

Cup & saucer, Sunburst iridescent
(ILLUS.) 8
Pitcher, 8" h., 80 oz., pink 168
Plate, 6" d., sherbet, pink 7
Plate, 8" d., salad, amber 9
Plate, 8" d., salad, pink 12
Plate, 11" d., dinner, amber 41
Plate, 11" d., dinner, pink 111
Plate, 11" d., grill, pink 20
Plate, 11" d., grill, Sunburst iridescent 11
Platter, 11 3/4" oval, Sunburst iridescent 14
Salt & pepper shakers, amber, pr. 49
Salt & pepper shakers, pink, pr. 75
Sherbet, pink 10
Sherbet, Sunburst iridescent 6
Sugar bowl, open, Sunburst iridescent 7
Tumbler, juice, amber, 4" h., 5 oz. 30
Tumbler, water, amber, 4 1/2" h., 9 oz. 21
Tumbler, iced tea, pink, 5" h., 12 oz. 142

(OLD) FLORENTINE or POPPY NO. 1, Hazel Atlas Glass Co., 1932-35 (Process-etched)

Ashtray, clear, 5 1/2" 18
Ashtray, green, 5 1/2" 21
Ashtray, pink, 5 1/2" 27
Ashtray, yellow, 5 1/2" 28
Bowl, 5" d., berry, clear 11
Bowl, 5" d., berry, cobalt blue 27
Bowl, 5" d., berry, green 11
Bowl, 5" d., berry, pink 19
Bowl, 5" d., berry, yellow 13
Bowl, 6" d., cereal, clear 20
Bowl, 6" d., cereal, pink 20
Bowl, 6" d., cereal, yellow 38
Bowl, 8 1/2" d., clear 22
Bowl, 8 1/2" d., green 36
Bowl, 8 1/2" d., pink 36
Bowl, 9 1/2" oval, cov., vegetable, clear 47
Bowl, 9 1/2" oval, cov., vegetable, pink 54
Bowl, 9 1/2" oval, cov., vegetable, yellow 85
Butter dish, cov., clear 134
Butter dish, cov., green 138
Butter dish, cov., yellow 169
Coaster-ashtray, clear, 3 3/4" d. 14
Coaster-ashtray, green, 3 3/4" d. 20
Coaster-ashtray, pink, 3 3/4" d. 32
Coaster-ashtray, yellow, 3 3/4" d. 26
Creamer, plain rim, clear 7
Creamer, plain rim, green 13
Creamer, plain rim, pink 18
Creamer, ruffled rim, cobalt blue 71
Cup, clear 8
Cup, green 9
Cup, pink 9
Cup, yellow 10
Nut dish, handled, ruffled rim, clear 25
Nut dish, handled, ruffled rim, cobalt blue 72
Nut dish, handled, ruffled rim, green 24
Nut dish, handled, ruffled rim, pink 20
Pitcher, 6 1/2" h., 36 oz., footed, clear 42
Pitcher, 6 1/2" h., 36 oz., footed, green 41
Pitcher, 6 1/2" h., 36 oz., footed, pink 45
Pitcher, 6 1/2" h., 36 oz., footed, yellow 37

(Old) Florentine Pitcher & Tumbler

Pitcher, 7 1/2" h., 48 oz., clear (ILLUS.) 66
Pitcher, 7 1/2" h., 48 oz., green 77
Pitcher, 7 1/2" h., 48 oz., pink 135
Plate, 6" d., sherbet, clear 5
Plate, 6" d., sherbet, green 12
Plate, 6" d., sherbet, pink 7
Plate, 8 1/2" d., salad, clear............................... 8
Plate, 8 1/2" d., salad, green 10
Plate, 8 1/2" d., salad, pink 12
Plate, 8 1/2" d., salad, yellow 14
Plate, 10" d., dinner, clear................................ 14
Plate, 10" d., dinner, green 25
Plate, 10" d., dinner, pink 30
Plate, 10" d., grill, clear...................................... 11
Platter, 11 1/2" oval, yellow 26
Salt & pepper shakers, footed, clear, pr. 39
Salt & pepper shakers, footed, green, pr......... 36
Salt & pepper shakers, footed, pink, pr. 57
Salt & pepper shakers, footed, yellow, pr........ 57
Saucer, clear 4
Saucer, green 3
Saucer, pink 5
Sherbet, footed, clear, 3 oz............................... 10
Sherbet, footed, green, 3 oz. 14
Sherbet, footed, pink, 3 oz................................ 12
Sherbet, footed, yellow, 3 oz............................. 11
Sugar bowl, cov., green...................................... 27
Sugar bowl, cov., pink 45
Sugar bowl, open, clear...................................... 9
Sugar bowl, open, green 9
Sugar bowl, open, pink 14
Sugar bowl, open, ruffled rim, cobalt blue 48
Sugar bowl, open, ruffled rim, green 30
Sugar bowl, open, ruffled rim, pink.................... 38
Tumbler, juice, footed, clear, 3 3/4" h., 5
   oz. (ILLUS. w/pitcher)..................................... 10
Tumbler, juice, footed, green, 3 3/4" h., 5
   oz. 16
Tumbler, juice, footed, yellow, 3 3/4" h., 5
   oz. 20
Tumbler, ribbed, clear, 4" h., 9 oz..................... 14
Tumbler, water, footed, green, 4 3/4" h., 10
   oz. 24

Tumbler, water, footed, pink, 4 3/4" h., 10
   oz. 25
Tumbler, water, footed, yellow, 4 3/4" h.,
   10 oz. 23

OYSTER & PEARL, Anchor Hocking Glass Corp., 1938-40 (Press-mold)
Bowl, 5 1/4" heart-shaped, w/handle, pink......... 13
Bowl, 5 1/4" heart-shaped, w/handle, white
   w/pink 9
Bowl, 5 1/2" d., w/handle, clear........................... 9
Bowl, 5 1/2" d., w/handle, ruby........................... 13
Bowl, 6 1/2" d., handled, pink............................. 18
Bowl, 6 1/2" d., handled, ruby 23
Bowl, 10 1/2" d., fruit, clear 20
Bowl, 10 1/2" d., fruit, pink 31
Bowl, 10 1/2" d., fruit, ruby 55
Bowl, 10 1/2" d., fruit, white w/green................. 14
Bowl, 10 1/2" d., fruit, white w/pink 14
Candleholders, pink, 3 1/2" h., pr...................... 31
Candleholders, ruby, 3 1/2" h., pr. 55
Candleholders, white w/green, 3 1/2" h.,
   pr. 14
Plate, 13 1/2" d., sandwich, pink 33
Plate, 13 1/2" d., sandwich, ruby 49
Relish, divided, pink, 10 1/4" oval 15

PATRICIAN or SPOKE, Federal Glass Co., 1933-37 (Process-etched)
Bowl, 4 3/4" d., cream soup, amber 17
Bowl, 4 3/4" d., cream soup, clear 13
Bowl, 4 3/4" d., cream soup, green 23
Bowl, 4 3/4" d., cream soup, pink...................... 19
Bowl, 5" d., berry, amber................................... 12
Bowl, 5" d., berry, clear..................................... 12
Bowl, 5" d., berry, green.................................... 14
Bowl, 5" d., berry, pink...................................... 14
Bowl, 8 1/2" d., large berry, amber.................... 45
Bowl, 8 1/2" d., large berry, green..................... 39
Bowl, 8 1/2" d., large berry, pink 28
Bowl, 10" oval vegetable, amber........................ 32
Bowl, 10" oval vegetable, clear.......................... 30
Bowl, 10" oval vegetable, green......................... 32
Bowl, 10" oval vegetable, pink 19
Butter dish, cov., amber..................................... 96
Butter dish, cov., clear....................................... 91
Butter dish, cov., green 126
Butter dish, cov., pink.. 282
Cookie jar, cov., amber....................................... 89
Cookie jar, cov., green.. 478
Creamer, footed, amber 10
Creamer, footed, green 14
Cup & saucer, amber.. 17
Cup & saucer, clear.. 16
Cup & saucer, green 20
Jam dish, amber, 6".. 32
Pitcher, 8" h., 75 oz., molded handle,
   amber 118
Pitcher, 8" h., 75 oz., molded handle, clear 107
Pitcher, 8" h., 75 oz., molded handle,
   green 148
Pitcher, 8" h., 75 oz., molded handle, pink 119
Pitcher, 8 1/4" h., 75 oz., applied handle,
   clear 128
Pitcher, 8 1/4" h., 75 oz., applied handle,
   green 110

Plate, 6" d., sherbet, amber............................... 10
Plate, 6" d., sherbet, green................................... 9
Plate, 6" d., sherbet, pink 8
Plate, 7 1/2" d., salad, amber 17
Plate, 7 1/2" d., salad, green 15
Plate, 7 1/2" d., salad, pink............................... 12
Plate, 9" d., luncheon, amber 11
Plate, 9" d., luncheon, green 14
Plate, 10 1/2" d., dinner, amber.......................... 9
Plate, 10 1/2" d., dinner, pink 52
Plate, 10 1/2" d., grill, amber 14

Patrician Grill Plate

Plate, 10 1/2" d., grill, green (ILLUS.)................ 19
Platter, 11 1/2" oval, amber................................ 30
Salt & pepper shakers, amber, pr.................... 61
Salt & pepper shakers, green, pr..................... 62
Sherbet, amber 12
Sherbet, green 14
Sugar bowl, cov., amber.................................. 63
Sugar bowl, cov., clear 54
Sugar bowl, cov., pink 70
Sugar bowl, open, amber 8
Sugar bowl, open, green 12
Tumbler, amber, 4" h., 5 oz. 34
Tumbler, clear, 4" h., 5 oz................................ 20
Tumbler, green, 4" h., 5 oz. 26
Tumbler, pink, 4" h., 5 oz................................. 33
Tumbler, footed, amber, 5 1/4" h., 8 oz. 55
Tumbler, amber, 4 1/2" h., 9 oz. 29
Tumbler, iced tea, amber, 5 1/2" h., 14 oz........ 46
Tumbler, iced tea, green, 5 1/2" h., 14 oz......... 60

PETALWARE, MacBeth-Evans Glass Co., 1930-40 (Press-mold)

Bowl, 4 1/2" d., cream soup, clear 6
Bowl, 4 1/2" d., cream soup, decorated
  Cremax or Monax.. 12
Bowl, 4 1/2" d., cream soup, pink..................... 18
Bowl, 4 1/2" d., cream soup, plain Cremax
  or Monax 14
Bowl, 5 3/4" d., cereal, clear 5
Bowl, 5 3/4" d., cereal, Florette 13
Bowl, 5 3/4" d., cereal, pink............................. 11
Bowl, 5 3/4" d., cereal, plain Cremax or
  Monax 9
Bowl, 5 3/4" d., cereal, Red Trim Floral 42

Bowl, 7" d., soup, plain Cremax or Monax 70
Bowl, 9" d., large berry, clear 11
Bowl, 9" d., large berry, decorated Cremax
  or Monax 32
Bowl, 9" d., large berry, pink 23
Bowl, 9" d., large berry, plain Cremax or
  Monax 21
Creamer, footed, clear 4
Creamer, footed, decorated Cremax or
  Monax 14
Creamer, footed, plain Cremax or Monax 6
Creamer, footed, Red Trim Floral...................... 33
Cup & saucer, clear... 4
Cup & saucer, decorated Cremax or
  Monax 13
Cup & saucer, Florette 13
Cup & saucer, pink 10
Cup & saucer, plain Cremax or Monax............... 8
Lamp shade, Monax, 6" h. 15
Lamp shade, Cremax, 9" h. 17
Lamp shade, Monax, 11" h............................... 18
Lamp shade, pink, 12" h................................... 21
Mustard jar, w/metal cover, cobalt blue............. 15
Plate, 6" d., sherbet, clear 2
Plate, 6" d., sherbet, Florette............................. 6
Plate, 6" d., sherbet, pink 4
Plate, 6" d., sherbet, plain Cremax or
  Monax 4
Plate, 6" d., sherbet, Red Trim Floral 22
Plate, 8" d., salad, clear..................................... 2
Plate, 8" d., salad, decorated Cremax or
  Monax 10
Plate, 8" d., salad, Florette 9
Plate, 8" d., salad, pink...................................... 6
Plate, 8" d., salad, plain Cremax or Monax 4
Plate, 9" d., dinner, clear 6
Plate, 9" d., dinner, decorated Cremax or
  Monax 12
Plate, 9" d., dinner, Florette 15
Plate, 9" d., dinner, pink 18
Plate, 11" d., salver, decorated Cremax or
  Monax 18
Plate, 11" d., salver, Florette 17
Plate, 11" d., salver, pink.................................. 17
Plate, 11" d., salver, plain Cremax or
  Monax 11
Plate, 12" d., salver, Florette 18
Plate, 12" d., salver, Red Trim Floral................ 44
Platter, 13" oval, pink 22
Platter, 13" oval, plain Cremax or Monax........... 13
Sugar bowl, open, footed, clear.......................... 5
Sugar bowl, open, footed, decorated Cre-
  max or Monax 11
Sugar bowl, open, footed, Florette 12
Sugar bowl, open, footed, plain Cremax or
  Monax 7

PRINCESS, Hocking Glass Co., 1931-35 (Process-etched)

Bowl, 4 1/2", berry, green................................. 31
Bowl, 4 1/2", berry, pink 33
Bowl, 5", cereal, green 42
Bowl, 5", cereal, pink....................................... 39
Bowl, 9" octagon, salad, green 46
Bowl, 9" octagon, salad, pink 46
Bowl, 9 1/2" hat shape, green 53
Bowl, 10" oval vegetable, green........................ 33

Bowl, 10" oval vegetable, pink 47
Butter dish, cov., green 112
Butter dish, cov., pink..................................... 113
Cake stand, green, 10" 34
Cake stand, pink, 10" 37
Candy jar, cov., green.. 68
Candy jar, cov., pink 74
Coaster, green, 4"... 46

Princess Cookie Jar

Cookie jar, cov., green (ILLUS.) 62
Creamer, oval, amber 14
Cup & saucer, green 22
Cup & saucer, pink.. 23
Cup & saucer, yellow... 12
Pitcher, 6" h., 37 oz., jug-type, green................ 64
Pitcher, 6" h., 37 oz., jug-type, pink 73
Pitcher, 8" h., 60 oz., jug-type, green................ 58
Pitcher, 8" h., 60 oz., jug-type, pink 79
Plate, 5 1/2", sherbet, amber............................... 4
Plate, 5 1/2", sherbet, green............................... 10
Plate, 5 1/2", sherbet, pink 11
Plate, 8" d., salad, green 16
Plate, 8", salad, amber 15
Plate, 8", salad, pink... 18
Plate, 9 1/2", dinner, amber............................... 12
Plate, 9 1/2", dinner, green................................ 31
Plate, 9 1/2", dinner, pink 27
Plate, 9 1/2", dinner, yellow 15
Plate, 9 1/2", grill, amber 7
Plate, 9 1/2", grill, green 10
Plate, 9 1/2", grill, pink...................................... 15
Plate, 9 1/2", grill, yellow 8
Platter, 12" oval, closed handles, green............. 30
Relish, divided, pink, 7 1/2"................................ 34
Salt & pepper (or spice) shakers, green,
    5 1/2" h., pr.. 55
Salt & pepper shakers, yellow, 4 1/2" h.,
    pr.. 78
Sherbet, footed, green 26
Sherbet, footed, pink... 25
Sugar bowl, cov., yellow.................................... 27
Tumbler, juice, pink, 3" h., 5 oz.......................... 32
Tumbler, water, green, 4" h., 9 oz...................... 31
Tumbler, water, pink, 4" h., 9 oz. 29
Tumbler, water, yellow, 4" h., 9 oz..................... 24
Tumbler, footed, green, 5 1/4" h., 10 oz. 32
Tumbler, footed, pink, 5 1/4" h. 10 oz. 29
Tumbler, footed, yellow, 5 1/4" h., 10 oz........... 22
Tumbler, footed, green, 6 1/2" h., 12 1/2
    oz. 98
Tumbler, footed, pink, 6 1/2" h., 12 1/2 oz. 94

Tumbler, iced tea, pink, 5 1/4" h., 13 oz. 31
Tumbler, iced tea, yellow, 5 1/4" h., 13 oz. 28
Vase, 8" h., green 38
Vase, 8" h., pink.. 58

QUEEN MARY or VERTICAL RIBBED, Hocking Glass Co., 1936-49 (Press-mold)

Ashtray, clear, 3 1/2" d. 5
Ashtray, ruby, 3 1/2" d. 8
Bowl, 4" d., nappy, clear 4
Bowl, 4" d., nappy, pink.. 7
Bowl, 4" d., nappy, single handle, clear 4
Bowl, 4" d., nappy, single handle, pink 6
Bowl, 5" d., berry, clear....................................... 7
Bowl, 5 1/2" d., two-handled, pink...................... 16
Bowl, 6" d., cereal, clear 7
Bowl, 6" d., cereal, pink...................................... 27
Bowl, 7" d., nappy, clear 8
Bowl, 7" d., nappy, pink...................................... 12
Bowl, 8 3/4" d., large berry, clear 9
Butter (or jam) dish, cov., clear 26
Butter (or jam) dish, cov., pink........................ 160
Candlesticks, two-light, clear, 4 1/2" h., pr. 16
Candy dish, cov., pink 60
Cigarette jar, clear, 2 x 3" oval 6
Coaster, clear, 3 1/2" d. 3
Coaster, pink, 3 1/2" d... 4
Coaster-ashtray, clear, 4 1/4" sq....................... 4
Coaster-ashtray, pink, 4 1/4" sq......................... 9
Compote, 5 3/4" d., clear 7
Creamer, oval, clear 5
Creamer, oval, pink 13

Queen Mary Cup & Saucer

Cup & saucer, clear (ILLUS.)............................... 8
Cup & saucer, pink 18
Plate, 6" d., sherbet, clear 4
Plate, 6" d., sherbet, pink 6
Plate, 8 1/2" d., salad, clear................................. 7
Plate, 9 3/4" d., dinner, clear 14
Plate, 9 3/4" d., dinner, pink 61
Plate, 12" d., sandwich, clear 12
Plate, 12" d., sandwich, pink 28
Plate, 14" d., serving, clear............................... 11
Relish, three-part, clear, 12" d. 11
Relish, four-part, clear, 14" d. 9
Salt & pepper shakers, clear, pr. 21
Sherbet, footed, clear.. 5
Sherbet, footed, pink... 10
Sugar bowl, open, oval, clear 5
Sugar bowl, open, oval, pink 10
Tumbler, juice, pink, 3 1/2" h., 5 oz.................... 16
Tumbler, water, clear, 4" h., 9 oz. 7

Tumbler, water, pink, 4" h., 9 oz. 17
Tumbler, footed, clear, 5" h., 10 oz. 29
Tumbler, footed, pink, 5" h., 10 oz. 72

RING or BANDED RINGS, Hocking Glass Co., 1927-33 (Press-mold)

Bowl, 5" d., berry, clear 4
Bowl, 5" d., berry, green 6
Bowl, 7" d., soup, clear 12
Bowl, 8" d., large berry, green 12
Cocktail shaker, clear w/multicolored bands 27
Creamer, footed, clear 5
Cup & saucer, clear 6
Cup & saucer, green 8
Goblet, green, 7 1/4" h., 9 oz. 15
Pitcher, 8 1/2" h., 80 oz., clear w/multicolored bands 33
Pitcher, 8 1/2" h., 80 oz., green 40
Plate, 6 1/4" d., sherbet, clear 2
Plate, 6 1/4" d., sherbet, clear w/multicolored bands 3
Plate, 6 1/2" d., off-center ring, clear 5
Plate, 6 1/2" d., off-center ring, clear w/multicolored bands 7
Plate, 6 1/2" d., off-center ring, green 6
Plate, 8" d., luncheon, clear 4
Plate, 8" d., luncheon, clear w/multicolored bands 6
Salt & pepper shakers, clear, 3" h., pr. 18
Sherbet, low, clear w/multicolored bands 16
Sherbet, footed, clear, 4 3/4" h. 5
Sherbet, footed, clear w/multicolored bands, 4 3/4" h. 9
Sugar bowl, open, footed, clear 5
Sugar bowl, open, footed, clear w/multicolored bands 7
Tumbler, whiskey, clear w/multicolored bands, 2" h., 1 1/2 oz. 10
Tumbler, clear, 3 1/2" h., 5 oz. 5
Tumbler, clear w/multicolored bands, 3 1/2" h., 5 oz. 7
Tumbler, green, 3 1/2" h., 5 oz. 7
Tumbler, clear, 4 1/4" h., 9 oz. 5
Tumbler, green, 4 1/4" h., 9 oz. 10
Tumbler, clear, 5 1/8" h., 12 oz. 6
Tumbler, green, 5 1/8" h., 12 oz. 10
Tumbler, cocktail, footed, green, 3 1/2" h. 12
Tumbler, water, footed, clear w/multicolored bands, 5 1/2" h. 10
Tumbler, iced tea, footed, clear, 6 1/2" h. 7

ROYAL LACE, Hazel Atlas Glass Co., 1934-41 (Process-etched)

Bowl, 4 3/4" d., cream soup, blue 47
Bowl, 4 3/4" d., cream soup, clear 17
Bowl, 4 3/4" d., cream soup, green 34
Bowl, 4 3/4" d., cream soup, pink 34
Bowl, 5" d., berry, clear 18
Bowl, 5" d., berry, pink 45
Bowl, 10" d., berry, blue 90
Bowl, 10" d., berry, green................................... 34
Bowl, 10" d., three-footed, ruffled edge, clear 47
Bowl, 10" d., three-footed, ruffled edge, pink 88

Bowl, 10" d., three-footed, straight edge, blue 92
Bowl, 10" d., three-footed, straight edge, green 58
Bowl, 10" d., three-footed, straight edge, pink 72
Bowl, 11" oval vegetable, blue 72
Bowl, 11" oval vegetable, clear 21
Bowl, 11" oval vegetable, pink 43

Royal Lace Butter Dish

Butter dish, cov., clear (ILLUS.) 75
Butter dish, cov., green 287
Butter dish, cov., pink 200
Candlesticks, rolled edge, pink, pr. 114
Candlesticks, ruffled edge, blue, pr. 356
Candlesticks, straight edge, blue, pr. 143
Candlesticks, straight edge, clear, pr. 32
Cookie jar, cov., blue 434
Cookie jar, cov., clear 41
Cookie jar, cov., green...................................... 117
Cookie jar, cov., pink 70
Creamer, footed, blue 61
Creamer, footed, clear 14
Creamer, footed, green 30
Cup, blue 38
Cup, clear 9
Cup, green 21
Cup, pink 22
Cup & saucer, blue 54
Cup & saucer, clear 14
Cup & saucer, green 33
Cup & saucer, pink 30
Pitcher, 48 oz., straight sides, blue................. 197
Pitcher, 48 oz., straight sides, clear................. 39
Pitcher, 48 oz., straight sides, green 120
Pitcher, 48 oz., straight sides, pink 111
Pitcher, 8" h., 68 oz., w/ice lip, clear 58
Pitcher, 8" h., 68 oz., w/ice lip, pink 124
Pitcher, 8 1/2" h., 96 oz., w/ice lip, clear 58
Pitcher, 8 1/2" h., 96 oz., w/ice lip, green......... 153
Plate, 6" d., sherbet, blue 17
Plate, 6" d., sherbet, clear 8
Plate, 6" d., sherbet, green 14
Plate, 6" d., sherbet, pink 10
Plate, 8 1/2" d., luncheon, green 21
Plate, 8 1/2" d., luncheon, pink......................... 25
Plate, 9 7/8" d., dinner, blue 53
Plate, 9 7/8" d., dinner, clear 21
Plate, 9 7/8" d., dinner, green............................ 36
Plate, 9 7/8" d., dinner, pink 33
Plate, 9 7/8" d., grill, blue.................................. 37
Plate, 9 7/8" d., grill, clear 9
Plate, 9 7/8" d., grill, green 29
Plate, 9 7/8" d., grill, pink.................................. 21

Platter, 13" oval, blue 73
Platter, 13" oval, clear 15
Platter, 13" oval, green.. 43
Platter, 13" oval, pink 46
Salt & pepper shakers, blue, pr. 335
Salt & pepper shakers, clear, pr. 42
Salt & pepper shakers, green, pr. 162
Salt & pepper shakers, pink, pr. 97
Sherbet, footed, blue.. 51
Sherbet, footed, clear.. 17
Sherbet, footed, green 29
Sherbet, footed, pink... 24
Sherbet in metal holder, blue 40
Sherbet in metal holder, clear 6
Sugar bowl, cov., blue 215
Sugar bowl, cov., clear...................................... 28
Sugar bowl, cov., green..................................... 85
Sugar bowl, cov., pink 74
Sugar bowl, open, blue 25
Sugar bowl, open, clear...................................... 9
Sugar bowl, open, green 25
Sugar bowl, open, pink 19
Tumbler, blue, 3 1/2" h., 5 oz. 64
Tumbler, green, 3 1/2" h., 5 oz. 32
Tumbler, pink, 3 1/2" h., 5 oz. 29
Tumbler, blue, 4 1/8" h., 9 oz............................ 53
Tumbler, clear, 4 1/8" h., 9 oz........................... 16
Tumbler, green, 4 1/8" h., 9 oz. 39
Tumbler, pink, 4 1/8" h., 9 oz. 30
Tumbler, clear, 4 7/8" h., 10 oz......................... 27
Tumbler, clear, 5 3/8" h., 12 oz......................... 33
Tumbler, pink, 5 3/8" h., 12 oz. 59

ROYAL RUBY, Anchor Hocking Glass Co., 1939-60s (Press-mold)
Ashtray, 4 1/2" sq. 8
Bowl, 4 1/4" d., berry.. 8
Bowl, 7 1/2" d., soup 15
Bowl, 8" oval vegetable................................... 38
Bowl, 8 1/2" d., berry.. 24
Bowl, 10" d., popcorn, deep 43
Bowl, 11 1/2" d., salad 38
Creamer, flat 8
Creamer, footed 8
Cup, round 6
Cup & saucer, round 9
Goblet, ball stem 13
Lamp 46
Pitcher, 3 qt., tilted or upright........................... 47
Plate, 6 1/2" d., sherbet...................................... 4
Plate, 7" d., salad 8
Plate, 7 3/4" d., luncheon 6
Plate, 9" d., dinner... 12
Playing card or cigarette box, divided,
    clear base.. 64
Popcorn set, 10" d. serving bowl & six
    5 1/4" d. bowls, 7 pcs. 125
Punch bowl 38
Punch cup 3
Punch set, punch bowl, base & 8 cups,
    10 pcs.. 110
Sherbet, footed 7
Sugar bowl, flat 7
Sugar bowl w/slotted lid, footed...................... 17
Tumbler, juice, 5 oz. 8
Tumbler, water, 9 oz. 7
Tumbler, water, 10 oz. 9

Vase, various styles, large................................. 18
Vase, 4" h., ball-shaped...................................... 5

SANDWICH, Anchor Hocking Glass Co., 1939-64 (Press-mold)
Bowl, 4 5/16" d., clear 5
Bowl, 4 5/16" d., green.. 5
Bowl, 4 7/8" d., berry, amber.............................. 4
Bowl, 4 7/8" d., berry, clear 8
Bowl, 5 1/4" d., scalloped, amber....................... 6
Bowl, 6 1/2" d., smooth or scalloped,
    amber 7
Bowl, 6 1/2" d., smooth or scalloped, clear 8
Bowl, 6 1/2" d., smooth or scalloped, ruby 25
Bowl, 6 3/4" d., cereal, amber 15
Bowl, 6 3/4" d., cereal, clear 36
Bowl, 8" d., scalloped, clear 9
Bowl, 8" d., scalloped, green............................. 61
Bowl, 8" d., scalloped, pink 19
Bowl, 8" d., scalloped, ruby 47
Bowl, 8 1/2" oval vegetable, clear 8
Butter dish, cov., clear...................................... 42
Cookie jar, cov., amber...................................... 37
Cookie jar, green (no cover made) 17
Creamer, clear 6

Sandwich Cup & Saucer

Cup & saucer, amber (ILLUS.) 7
Cup & saucer, clear... 4
Cup & saucer, green 45
Custard cup, clear 4
Custard cup, green 3
Custard cup, ruffled, clear 13
Custard cup liner, green 2
Pitcher, juice, 6" h., clear 63
Pitcher, juice, 6" h., green................................ 195
Pitcher w/ice lip, 2 qt., clear............................. 79
Pitcher w/ice lip, 2 qt., green 450
Plate, 7" d., dessert, clear 11
Plate, 8" d., clear 5
Plate, 9" d., dinner, amber 9
Plate, 9" d., dinner, clear 17
Plate, 9" d., dinner, green 125
Plate, 9" d., snack, clear..................................... 7
Plate, 12" d., sandwich, amber.......................... 21

Punch bowl & base, clear 47
Punch cup, clear... 3
Punch cup, opaque white 2
Sherbet, footed, clear....................................... 8
Sugar bowl, open, clear..................................... 7
Sugar bowl, open, green 26
Tumbler, juice, green, 3 oz. 4
Tumbler, clear, 5 oz. 6
Tumbler, green, 5 oz.. 4
Tumbler, footed, clear, 9 oz. 28
Tumbler, water, clear, 9 oz. 8
Tumbler, water, green, 9 oz............................... 5

SHARON or CABBAGE ROSE, Federal Glass Co., 1935-39 (Chip-mold)

Bowl, 5" d., berry, amber................................... 8
Bowl, 5" d., berry, green.................................. 17
Bowl, 5" d., berry, pink 14
Bowl, 5" d., cream soup, amber........................ 25
Bowl, 5" d., cream soup, green......................... 60
Bowl, 5" d., cream soup, pink........................... 51
Bowl, 6" d., cereal, amber................................ 17
Bowl, 6" d., cereal, green 27
Bowl, 6" d., cereal, pink................................... 28
Bowl, 7 1/2" d., soup, amber............................ 48
Bowl, 7 1/2" d., soup, pink............................... 56
Bowl, 8 1/2" d., berry, amber............................. 7
Bowl, 8 1/2" d., berry, green............................ 33
Bowl, 8 1/2" d., berry, pink.............................. 36
Bowl, 9 1/2" oval vegetable, amber.................... 18
Bowl, 9 1/2" oval vegetable, green..................... 36
Bowl, 9 1/2" oval vegetable, pink 36
Bowl, 10 1/2" d., fruit, amber............................ 21
Bowl, 10 1/2" d., fruit, pink 46
Butter dish, cov., green 101
Butter dish, cov., pink...................................... 60
Cake plate, footed, amber, 11 1/2" d. 23
Cake plate, footed, clear, 11 1/2" d. 12
Cake plate, footed, green, 11 1/2" d. 66
Cake plate, footed, pink, 11 1/2" d. 42
Candy jar, cov., amber..................................... 44
Candy jar, cov., green.................................... 174
Candy jar, cov., pink 61
Creamer, amber.. 14
Creamer, green 25
Creamer, pink... 18
Cup, amber.. 9
Cup, green... 19
Cup, pink 14
Cup & saucer, green 32
Cup & saucer, pink.. 25
Jam dish, green, 7 1/2" d., 1 1/2" h. 43
Pitcher, 9" h., 80 oz., green........................... 448
Pitcher, 9" h., 80 oz., pink............................. 139
Pitcher w/ice lip, 9" h., 80 oz., amber 140
Pitcher w/ice lip, 9" h., 80 oz., pink................ 192
Plate, 6" d., bread & butter, amber...................... 5
Plate, 6" d., bread & butter, green 9
Plate, 6" d., bread & butter, pink........................ 9
Plate, 7 1/2" d., salad, amber 14
Plate, 7 1/2" d., salad, pink............................. 33
Plate, 9 1/2" d., dinner, amber......................... 10
Plate, 9 1/2" d., dinner, green.......................... 25
Plate, 9 1/2" d., dinner, pink............................ 22
Platter, 12 1/2" oval, amber............................. 17
Platter, 12 1/2" oval, green.............................. 32
Platter, 12 1/2" oval, pink................................ 32

Salt & pepper shakers, green, pr...................... 73
Salt & pepper shakers, pink, pr. 52
Saucer, amber... 7
Saucer, green.. 9
Saucer, pink 11
Sherbet, footed, amber 12
Sherbet, footed, green 37
Sherbet, footed, pink 15
Sugar bowl, cov., amber.................................. 31
Sugar bowl, cov., pink..................................... 44
Sugar bowl, open, amber 7
Sugar bowl, open, pink.................................... 14
Tumbler, amber, 4" h., 9 oz. 24
Tumbler, pink, 4" h., 9 oz................................ 45

Sharon Tumblers

Tumbler, amber, 5 1/4" h., 12 oz. (ILLUS. left) 59
Tumbler, green, 5 1/4" h., 12 oz. 130
Tumbler, pink, 5 1/4" h., 12 oz. 54
Tumbler, footed, amber, 6 1/2" h., 15 oz. (ILLUS. right) 136
Tumbler, footed, pink, 6 1/2" h., 15 oz. 59

SWIRL or PETAL SWIRL, Jeannette Glass Co., 1937-38 (Press-mold)

Bowl, 5 1/4" d., cereal, Delphite 14
Bowl, 5 1/4" d., cereal, pink............................. 11
Bowl, 5 1/4" d., cereal, ultramarine 17
Bowl, 9" d., salad, Delphite 30
Bowl, 9" d., salad, pink 21
Bowl, 9" d., salad, ultramarine 29
Bowl, 10" d., fruit, closed handles, footed, ultramarine 34
Bowl, 9" d., rimmed, pink 18
Butter dish, cov., pink.................................... 223
Butter dish, cov., ultramarine 363
Candleholders, double, ultramarine, pr............. 56
Candy dish, cov., pink 120
Candy dish, cov., ultramarine.......................... 173
Candy dish, open, three-footed, pink, 5 1/2" d. 14
Candy dish, open, three-footed, ultramarine, 5 1/2" d. 20
Coaster, pink, 3 1/4" d., 1" h. 12
Coaster, ultramarine, 3 1/4" d., 1" h. 13

Console bowl, footed, ultramarine,
10 1/2" d. 33
Creamer, Delphite 11
Creamer, pink.. 9
Creamer, ultramarine 16
Cup, ultramarine.. 15
Cup & saucer, Delphite 16
Cup & saucer, ultramarine................................ 20
Plate, 6 1/2" d., sherbet, Delphite....................... 8
Plate, 6 1/2" d., sherbet, pink 7
Plate, 6 1/2" d., sherbet, ultramarine 7
Plate, 7 1/4" d., ultramarine.............................. 14
Plate, 8" d., salad, ultramarine 19
Plate, 9 1/4" d., dinner, Delphite....................... 16
Plate, 9 1/4" d., dinner, pink 16
Plate, 9 1/4" d., dinner, ultramarine 22
Plate, 12 1/2" d., sandwich, pink 17
Plate, 12 1/2" d., sandwich, ultramarine 30
Platter, 12" oval, Delphite................................. 35
Salt & pepper shakers, ultramarine, pr............ 48
Sherbet, pink.. 16
Sherbet, ultramarine 24
Soup bowl w/lug handles, ultramarine............. 53
Sugar bowl, open, pink...................................... 10
Sugar bowl, open, ultramarine 15
Tumbler, footed, ultramarine, 9 oz.................... 45
Tumbler, ultramarine, 4" h., 9 oz....................... 38
Tumbler, ultramarine, 5 1/8" h., 13 oz.............. 153
Vase, 6 1/2" h., pink... 17

Swirl Vase

Vase, 8 1/2" h., ultramarine (ILLUS.)................. 32

TEA ROOM, Indiana Glass Co., 1926-31 (Press-mold)

Banana split dish, flat, green, 7 1/2"............... 99
Banana split dish, footed, green, 7 1/2"........... 78
Bowl, 8 3/4" d., salad, green 150
Bowl, 8 3/4" d., salad, pink.............................. 130
Bowl, 9 1/2" oval vegetable, green.................... 69
Bowl, 9 1/2" oval vegetable, pink 76
Candlesticks, green, pr..................................... 66
Candlesticks, pink, pr....................................... 64
Celery or pickle dish, green, 8 1/2" 35
Celery or pickle dish, pink, 8 1/2" 35
Creamer, pink, 3 1/4" h. 26
Creamer, footed, green, 4 1/2" h....................... 20
Creamer, footed, pink, 4 1/2" h. 20
Creamer & open sugar bowl on center-
handled tray, pink 93
Creamer & open sugar bowl on rectan-
gular tray, green... 90

Creamer & open sugar bowl on rectan-
gular tray, pink 60
Cup, green... 59
Finger bowl, green 115
Finger bowl, pink 90
Goblet, green, 9 oz. 78
Goblet, pink, 9 oz. 70
Ice bucket, green 85
Ice bucket, pink.. 67
Lamp, electric, green, 9" 152
Lamp, electric, pink, 9" 127
Mustard, cov., pink... 210
Parfait, pink 135
Pitcher, 64 oz., green....................................... 140
Pitcher, 64 oz., pink 175
Plate, 8 1/4" d., luncheon, green 32
Plate, 8 1/4" d., luncheon, pink......................... 31
Plate, 10 1/2" d., two-handled, green 50
Plate, sandwich, w/center handle, green.......... 203
Plate, sandwich, w/center handle, pink 155
Relish, divided, green 25
Salt & pepper shakers, green, pr...................... 70
Salt & pepper shakers, pink, pr. 63
Saucer, green.. 25
Sherbet, low, flared edge, green 30
Sherbet, low, flared edge, pink 26
Sherbet, low footed, green................................. 30
Sherbet, low footed, pink 26
Sugar bowl, cov., green, 3" h. 100
Sugar bowl, cov., pink, 3" h. 130
Sugar bowl, open, footed, green, 4 1/2" h. 22
Sugar bowl, open, footed, pink, 4 1/2" h........... 17
Sugar bowl, open, rectangular, green 23
Sundae, footed, ruffled, green......................... 115
Tray, rectangular, for creamer & sugar
bowl, green... 48
Tray, rectangular, for creamer & sugar
bowl, pink 59
Tray w/center handle, for creamer & sugar
bowl, green... 225
Tray w/center handle, for creamer & sugar
bowl, pink 225
Tumbler, footed, green, 6 oz............................. 42
Tumbler, footed, pink, 6 oz. 32
Tumbler, green, 4 3/16" h., 8 oz. 105
Tumbler, footed, green, 5 1/4" h., 8 oz. 35
Tumbler, footed, pink, 5 1/4" h., 8 oz............... 31
Tumbler, footed, pink, 11 oz. 51
Tumbler, footed, green, 12 oz........................... 70
Vase, 6 1/2" h., ruffled rim, green 110
Vase, 6 1/2" h., ruffled rim, pink...................... 113
Vase, 9 1/2" h., ruffled rim, green 156
Vase, 11" h., straight, green 151
Vase, 11" h., straight, pink.............................. 165

WINDSOR DIAMOND or WINDSOR, Jeannette Glass Co., 1936-46 (Press-mold)

Ashtray, Delphite, 5 3/4" d. 48
Ashtray, green, 5 3/4" d..................................... 45
Ashtray, pink, 5 3/4" d....................................... 42
Bowl, 4 3/4" d., berry, clear 6
Bowl, 4 3/4" d., berry, green 11
Bowl, 4 3/4" d., berry, pink 10
Bowl, 5" d., cream soup, green 30
Bowl, 5" d., cream soup, pink............................ 21
Bowl, 5" d., pointed edge, clear 7
Bowl, 5" d., pointed edge, pink.......................... 29
Bowl, 5 1/8" or 5 3/8" d., cereal, clear................. 7
Bowl, 5 1/8" or 5 3/8" d., cereal, green............... 25
Bowl, 5 1/8" or 5 3/8" d., cereal, pink 26

Bowl, 7" d., three-footed, clear 7
Bowl, 7" d., three-footed, pink 33
Bowl, 8" d., pointed edge, clear 13
Bowl, 8" d., pointed edge, pink 65
Bowl, 8" d., two-handled, clear 6
Bowl, 8" d., two-handled, green 21
Bowl, 8" d., two-handled, pink 19
Bowl, 8 1/2" d., berry, clear 11
Bowl, 8 1/2" d., berry, pink 24
Bowl, 9 1/2" oval vegetable, clear 9
Bowl, 9 1/2" oval vegetable, green..................... 32
Bowl, 9 1/2" oval vegetable, pink 28
Bowl, 10 1/2" d., pointed edge, clear 25
Bowl, 10 1/2" d., pointed edge, pink................ 154
Bowl, 10 1/2" d., salad, clear............................ 19
Bowl, 7 x 11 3/4" boat shape, clear.................... 20
Bowl, 7 x 11 3/4" boat shape, green 37
Bowl, 7 x 11 3/4" boat shape, pink 38
Bowl, 12 1/2" d., fruit, clear 28
Bowl, 12 1/2" d., fruit, pink 128
Butter dish, cov., clear 27
Butter dish, cov., green 91
Butter dish, cov., pink.................................... 54
Cake plate, footed, clear, 10 3/4" d..................... 8
Cake plate, footed, pink, 10 3/4" d. 23
Candlestick, clear, 3" h.................................... 14
Candlestick, pink, 3" h.................................... 47
Candlesticks, clear, 3" h., pr. 24
Candlesticks, pink, 3" h., pr........................... 95
Coaster, green, 3 1/4" d 16
Coaster, pink, 3 1/4" d.................................... 13
Creamer, flat, clear.. 5
Creamer, flat, green 17
Creamer, flat, pink... 12
Creamer, footed, clear 7
Cup & saucer, clear.. 7
Cup & saucer, green 19
Cup & saucer, pink 15

Windsor Diamond Pitcher

Pitcher, 4 1/2" h., 16 oz., clear (ILLUS.) 23
Pitcher, 4 1/2" h., 16 oz., pink.......................... 209
Pitcher, 6 3/4" h., 52 oz., clear 12
Pitcher, 6 3/4" h., 52 oz., green 62
Pitcher, 6 3/4" h., 52 oz., pink.......................... 30
Plate, 6" d., sherbet, clear 3
Plate, 6" d., sherbet, green 7
Plate, 6" d., sherbet, pink 6
Plate, 7" d., salad, green 25
Plate, 7" d., salad, pink..................................... 23
Plate, 9" d., dinner, clear 7
Plate, 9" d., dinner, green.................................. 23
Plate, 9" d., dinner, pink 26
Plate, 10 1/4", sandwich, handled, clear 9

Plate, 10 1/4", sandwich, handled, green 24
Plate, 10 1/4", sandwich, handled, pink.............. 18
Plate, 13 5/8" d., chop, clear 10
Plate, 13 5/8" d., chop, green 41
Plate, 13 5/8" d., chop, pink.............................. 43
Platter, 11 1/2" oval, clear................................. 8
Platter, 11 1/2" oval, green................................ 22
Platter, 11 1/2" oval, pink 23
Powder jar, cov., clear 14
Relish, divided, pink, 11 1/2"........................... 276
Salt & pepper shakers, green, pr. 52
Salt & pepper shakers, pink, pr. 37
Sherbet, footed, clear....................................... 5
Sherbet, footed, green 15
Sherbet, footed, pink 13
Sugar bowl, cov., flat, clear 9
Sugar bowl, cov., flat, green 33
Sugar bowl, cov., flat, pink 33
Tray, pink, 4" sq., w/handles 10
Tray, pink, 4" sq., without handles..................... 61
Tray, green, 4 1/8 x 9", w/handles 15
Tray, pink, 4 1/8 x 9", w/handles 17
Tray, clear, 8 1/2 x 9 3/4", w/handles 5
Tray, clear, 8 1/2 x 9 3/4", without handles 13
Tray, green, 8 1/2 x 9 3/4", w/handles.............. 29
Tray, pink, 8 1/2 x 9 3/4", w/handles 23
Tray, pink, 8 1/2 x 9 3/4", without handles........ 145
Tumbler, clear, 3 1/4" h., 5 oz........................... 10
Tumbler, green, 3 1/4" h., 5 oz. 33
Tumbler, pink, 3 1/4" h., 5 oz. 25
Tumbler, clear, 4" h., 9 oz................................. 6
Tumbler, green, 4" h., 9 oz. 35
Tumbler, pink, 4" h., 9 oz. 20
Tumbler, clear, 5" h., 12 oz............................... 9
Tumbler, green, 5" h., 12 oz. 47
Tumbler, pink, 5" h., 12 oz. 32
Tumbler, footed, clear, 4" h., 9 oz....................... 7
Tumbler, footed, clear, 5" h., 11 oz..................... 9
Tumbler, footed, clear, 7 1/4" h.......................... 17

DUGAN-DIAMOND

The Dugan and Diamond Glass factories operated in Indiana, Pennsylvania between 1904 and
1931. Thomas E.A. Dugan and Alfred Dugan, cous-
ins of Harry Northwood, reopened the former Northwood factory in that city in 1904 and operated as
the Dugan Glass Company until 1913. After 1913
and until the factory's destruction by fire in 1931, it
was known as the Diamond Glass Company.

Both companies produced decorative pressed
glasswares similar to lines being produced by the
Northwood factory during those years including
opalescent glass, colored and decorated wares and
Carnival and Stretch glass. The Dugan's "Diamond-
D" trademark was introduced in late 1906.

*Dugan's Diamond-D" trademark, introduced
in late 1906.*

DUGAN PATTERNS

EARLY COLORED AND OPALESCENT LINES

Beaded Ovals in Sand (Erie) pitcher, water, green $175

Beaded Ovals in Sand spooner, light green 100

Beaded Ovals in Sand toothpick holder,, light green 250

Clubs & Spades Tumbler

Clubs & Spades tumbler, green w/gold trim (ILLUS.) 50

Cornflower Pitcher & Tumbler

Cornflower pitcher, emerald green & gold (ILLUS. left) 275

Cornflower tumbler, emerald green & gold (ILLUS. right) 45

Fan bowl, master berry, custard 125

Fan butter dish, cov., green 185

Fan Creamer

Fan creamer, dark blue w/gold, "Diamond-D" mark, ca. 1907 (ILLUS.) 175

Fan creamer, green 100

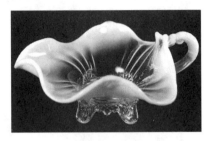

Fan Gravy Boat

Fan gravy boat, clear opalescent, "Diamond-D" mark (ILLUS.) 90

Fan pitcher, water, custard.............................. 250

Fan sugar bowl, cov., blue w/gold.................. 175

Fan sugar bowl, cov., green............................ 135

Inverted Fan & Feather butter dish, cov., blue opalescent 450

Inverted Fan & Feather Creamer

Inverted Fan & Feather creamer, blue opalescent w/gold trim (ILLUS.).................. 145

Inverted Fan & Feather Creamer

Inverted Fan & Feather creamer, green
w/gold (ILLUS.) **125**

Inverted Fan & Feather pitcher, water,
green w/gold... **175**

Inverted Fan & Feather sauce dish, green
w/gold... **50**

Inverted Fan & Feather Sauce Dish

Inverted Fan & Feather sauce dish, pink
slag (ILLUS.) **225**

Inverted Fan & Feather spooner, blue
opalescent w/gold **200**

Inverted Fan & Feather spooner, green
w/gold.. **100**

Maple Leaf butter dish, cov., custard **350**

Maple Leaf creamer, blue w/gold **150**

Maple Leaf Creamer

Maple Leaf creamer, dark cobalt blue
w/gold trim, D-in-diamond mark (ILLUS.)..... **275**

Maple Leaf Salt Shaker

Maple Leaf salt shaker, custard (ILLUS.) **375**
Maple Leaf sugar bowl, cov., blue w/gold....... **175**

Maple Leaf Sugar Bowl

Maple Leaf sugar bowl, cov., dark cobalt
blue w/gold trim, D-in-diamond mark
(ILLUS.)... **250**

Nestor compote, open, jelly, blue..................... **75**

Nestor cruet w/original stopper, ame-
thyst... **250**

Nestor pitcher, water, amethyst **175**

Nestor Salt Shaker

Nestor salt shaker w/original lid, amethyst w/gold & white trim, ca. 1905 (ILLUS.).. 110

New York (Beaded Shell) bowl, master berry, blue opalescent................................. 160

New York butter dish, cov., light green 400

New York Creamer

New York creamer, green w/gold trim (ILLUS.).. 100

New York creamer, light green........................ 125

New York pitcher, water, light green.............. 450

New York sugar bowl, cov., light green 250

New York tumbler, light green 65

Quill Tumbler

Quill tumbler, ruby w/gold trim (ILLUS.).......... 125

S-Repeat goblet, blue.. 75

S-Repeat (National) cruet w/original stopper, blue 250

S-Repeat pitcher, water, purple 175

S-Repeat punch cup, purple 50

S-Repeat syrup jug w/original metal lid, light green 450

S-Repeat tumbler, blue 50

S-Repeat wine, purple w/gold (ILLUS. left)........ 75

S-Repeat Decanter & Wine

S-Repeat wine decanter w/original stopper, purple w/gold trim, top of photo cropped (ILLUS. right)................................. 175

Venetian or Japanese Striped Vase

Venetian or Japanese vase, light blue green w/amber stripes (ILLUS.) 95

Venetian or Japanese Vase

Venetian or Japanese Vase, twisted, light blue green w/amber stripes (ILLUS.) **110**

Victor Salt Shaker

Victor (Jewelled Heart) salt shaker w/original top, blue (ILLUS.)...................... **110**
Victor pitcher, water, light green **150**
Victor spooner, clear opalescent **75**
Victor sugar shaker w/original metal lid, blue **300**
Victor syrup jug w/original metal lid, blue, ca. 1905.. **450**
Victor tumbler, green opalescent...................... **60**
Victor tumbler, light green................................. **30**

"GOOFUS" LINES

Cherry Compote

Cherry compote, open, ruffled sides, hexagonal base (ILLUS.) **55**

Holly Bowl

Holly bowl, smooth rim (ILLUS.)........................ **50**

CARNIVAL GLASS LINES

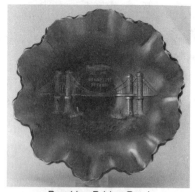

Brooklyn Bridge Bowl

Brooklyn Bridge bowl, marigold (ILLUS.)......... **60**

Butterfly & Tulip Bowl

Butterfly & Tulip bowl, Feather Scroll exterior, marigold (ILLUS.) **200**

Grape & Cable Perfume Bottle

Grape & Cable perfume bottle w/stopper, purple (ILLUS.) **650**

Grape Delight Bowl

Grape Delight bowl, purple (ILLUS.).......... **80-100**

Lattice & Daisy Pitcher

Lattice & Daisy pitcher, tankard-type, marigold (ILLUS.)... **225**

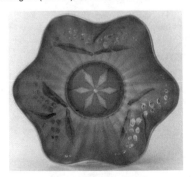

Stippled Petals Bowl

Stippled Petals bowl, peach opal w/h.p. lily of the valley decoration inside (ILLUS.).. **195 +**

DIAMOND GLASS-WARE COMPANY PATTERNS

BLACK GLASS

Candleholder

Candleholder, hexagonal socket & round foot, "Jack and the Bean Stalk" decoration, ca. 1928 (ILLUS.) **25**

Console Bowl & Base

Console bowl & base, gold band decoration, ca. 1924-28 (ILLUS.).................. **45**

Tall Vase

Vase, tall ovoid body w/short cylindrical neck, "hammered gold" band decoration (ILLUS.).. **145**

CLEAR DECORATED ITEMS

Decorated Tankard Pitcher

Pitcher, tall footed tankard-style w/ruffled rim, applied angled handle h.p. decorated bands around the middle, ca. 1920 (ILLUS.) **75**

Blue Bird Tumblers

Tumblers, Blue Bird decoration, ca. 1916, each (ILLUS.) **25**

Wine Decanter

Wine decanter w/bulbous stopper, h.p. w/large daisy-like blossoms, leaves & bands (ILLUS.) **65**

CUT PIECES

Basket

Basket, shallow upturned sides, applied center handle, cut flowers around the sides (ILLUS.) **65**

Vase with Swags & Berries

Vase, wide slightly flaring cylindrical iridescent blue body w/swelled, closed mouth, cut w/stylized swags & berries (ILLUS.) **100**

STRETCH GLASS

Console Bowl

Console bowl, shallow widely flaring sides, blue stretch, on a separate black glass base, ca. 1924 (ILLUS.) **60**

OTHER LINES

"Adam's Rib" Pattern Pitcher

Pitcher, tankard-type, "Adam's Rib" patt.,
blue stretch (ILLUS.) **600**

Sandwich Server

Sandwich server w/central handle, green
stretch, ca. 1927 (ILLUS.) **75**

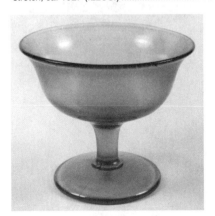

Sherbet

Sherbet, footed, blue stretch (ILLUS.) **25**

Candleholder w/Leaf-decorated Base

Candleholder, amber w/gold leafy decorative base band, ca. 1927 (ILLUS.).................. **20**

Candleholder with Flared Base

Candleholder, green w/fluted base, ca.
1928 (ILLUS.).. **20**

Green Candlestick

Candlestick, iridescent green w/white trim
(ILLUS.)... **50**

Candlestick w/Geometric Decoration

Candlestick, satin-finished blue w/h.p. geometric decoration (ILLUS.) **60**

Candy Jar w/Geometric Decoration

Candy jar, cov., satin-finished blue w/h.p. geometric decoration (ILLUS.) **100**

Cobalt Blue Candlestick/Vase

Candlestick/vase, blown, cobalt blue w/gold trim (ILLUS.) **55**

Vanity Set

Vanity set: a pair of tall bottles, cov. powder dish & oblong tray; rose-pink, gold band trim, the set (ILLUS.) **125**

Covered Candy Jar

Candy jar, cov., iridescent blue (ILLUS.) **85**

"Barcelona" Line Vase

Vase, "Barcelona" line, black glass w/twisted body & flared rim (ILLUS.) **125**

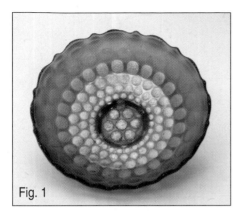

Fig. 1

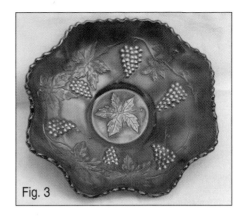

Fig. 3

Fig. 2

Fig. 4

Fig. 1: Green Coin Spot pattern bowl, $30-50. Courtesy of Yesterday's Treasures, Galena, IL

Fig. 2: Strawberry pattern purple plate, 9" d., $300-375. Courtesy of Temples Antiques, Eden Prairie, MN

Fig. 3: Fenton Vintage pattern red bowl, $1,000-1,500. Courtesy of Ruth Eaves, Marmora, NJ

Fig. 4: Persian Garden 6" d. plate in peach opalescent, $150-200. Photo courtesy of Ruth Eaves, Marmora, NJ

Fig. 5: Peacocks on the Fence shallow bowl in marigold, $375. Photo courtesy of Temples Antiques, Eden Prairie, MN

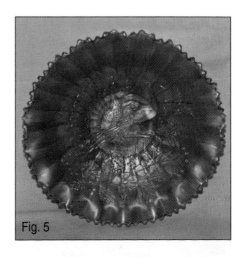

Fig. 5

Carnival Glass

Fig. 6

Fig. 10

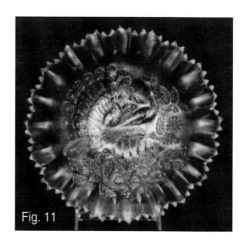

Fig. 11

Fig. 7

Fig. 8

Fig. 9

Fig. 6: Broken Arches punch set in marigold, 7 pcs., $425-450

Fig. 7: Imperial Grape pattern green wine, $35. Courtesy of Johanna Billings, Danielsville, PA

Fig. 8: Venetian Giant green rose bowl, $1,100-1,200. Photo courtesy of Woody Auctions, Douglass, KS

Fig. 9: Red Dragon & Lotus pattern bowl, $1,500-1,700. Photo courtesy of Woody Auctions, Douglass, KS

Fig. 10: Windmill pattern oval relish dish in marigold, $37. Courtesy of Yesterday's Treasures, Galena, IL

Fig. 11: Peacocks on the Fence aqua bowl, $3,500. Photo courtesy of Wood Auctions, Douglass, KS

Depression Glass

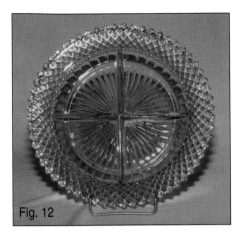
Fig. 12

Fig. 14

Fig. 13

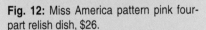

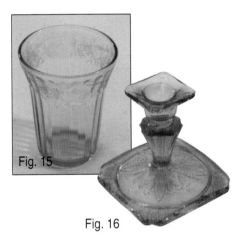
Fig. 15

Fig. 16

Fig. 17

Fig. 12: Miss America pattern pink four-part relish dish, $26.

Fig. 13: Royal Lace green dinner plate, $36. Photo courtesy of Yesterday's Treasures, Galena, IL

Fig. 14: Florentine #2 yellow creamer, $12, open sugar bowl, $12 and vase or parfait, $63. Photo courtesy of Yesterday's Treasures, Galena, IL

Fig. 15: Green Cherry Blossom tumbler, $26. Photo courtesy of Yesterday's Treasures, Galena, IL

Fig. 16: Adam pattern pink 4" h. candlestick, $50. Photo courtesy of Yesterday's Treasures, Galena, IL

Fig. 17: Lace Edge pink footed covered compote, 7" d., $50. Photo courtesy of Johanna Billings, Danielsville, PA

Fig. 18: Parrot pattern green footed creamer, $50, open sugar, $38, and cup and saucer, $60. Photo courtesy of Yesterday's Treasures, Galena, IL

Fig. 18

Fig. 19

Fig. 23

Fig. 20

Fig. 24

Fig. 21

Fig. 22

Fig. 19: Beaded Shell (New York) green creamer with gold trim, $100. Photo courtesy of Dr. James Measell

Fig. 20: Victor (Jewelled Heart) salt shaker in blue, $110. Photo courtesy of Dr. James Measell

Fig. 21: Venetian or Japanese twisted vase, light bluish green with amber stripes, $100. Photo courtesy of Dr. James Measell

Fig. 22: Blue opalescent Inverted Fan & Feather spooner with gold trim, $125-150. Courtesy of Dr. James Measell

Fig. 23: Pink slag Inverted Fan & Feather sauce dish, $225. Photo courtesy of Dr. James Measell

Fig. 24: Nautilus (Argonaut Shell) blue opalescent creamer, $195. Courtesy of Dr. James Measell

Dugan-Diamond Glass

Fig. 27

Fig. 25

Fig. 2

Fig. 28

Fig. 29

Fig. 30

Fig. 25: Satin-finished blue candlestick with hand-painted geometric decoration, $60. Courtesy of Dr. James Measell

Fig. 26: Nestor pattern salt shaker in purple with gold trim, ca. 1904, $80. Courtesy of Dr. James Measell

Fig. 27: Fan pattern clear opalescent gravy boat, made from the creamer mold, $95. Courtesy of Dr. James Measell

Fig. 28: 'Barcelona' line black glass vase with twisted body and flared rim, $125. Photo courtesy of Dr. James Measell

Fig. 29: Black tall ovoid vase with 'hammered gold' band decoration, $145. Photo courtesy of Dr. James Measell

Fig. 30: Blue Iridescent urn-form candy jar, $85. Photo courtesy of Dr. James Measell

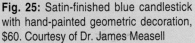

Fig. 31

Fig. 37

Fig. 33

Fig. 32

Fig. 38

Fig. 34

Fig. 35

Fig. 36

Fig. 31: Hen on Nest covered dish in amber, $125. Photo courtesy of Dr. James Measell

Fig. 32: Dewey pattern blue mug, $325. Photo courtesy of Dr. James Measell

Fig. 33: Nile Green Buffalo paperweight, $1,250. Photo courtesy of Dr. James Measell

Fig. 34: Cord Drapery sugar bowl in milk glass, $500. Photo courtesy of Dr. James Measell.

Fig. 35: Holly Amber tumbler with beaded rim, $700. Photo courtesy of Dr. James Measell

Fig. 36: Fighting Cocks green covered dish, $1,750. Photo courtesy of Dr. James Measell

Fig. 37: Austrian canary water pitcher, $650. Photo courtesy of Dr. James Measell

Fig. 38: Herringbone Buttress green cruet, $550. Photo courtesy of Dr. James Measell

Fig. 39

Fig. 41

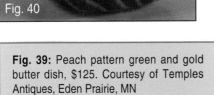

Fig. 40

Fig. 42

Fig. 43

Fig. 39: Peach pattern green and gold butter dish, $125. Courtesy of Temples Antiques, Eden Prairie, MN

Fig. 40: Royal Ivy cranberry opalescent Swirl pitcher, $1,200. Photo courtesy of Dr. James Measell

Fig. 41: Holly clear opalescent creamer with color decoration, $145. Courtesy of Dr. James Measell

Fig. 42: Spanish Lace rose bowl in clear opalescent, $90. Courtesy of Dr. James Measell

Fig. 43: 'Granite Ware' Paneled Sprig sugar bowl with gold trim, $175. Photo courtesy of Dr. James Measell

Fig. 44: Green pitcher with gold trim and hand-painted grapevine decoration, with original Northwood label on the base, $475. Photo courtesy of Dr. James Measell

Fig. 45: Sunburst on Shield blue opalescent cruet, $450. Courtesy of Dr. James Measell

Fig. 44

Fig. 45

Fig. 46

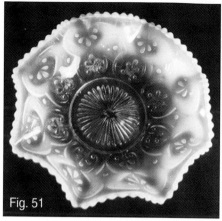

Fig. 51

Fig 47

Fig. 52

Fig. 48

Fig. 49

Fig. 50

Fig. 46: Apple Blossom opaque white fairy lamp with painted decoration, $500. Photo courtesy of Dr. James Measell

Fig. 47: Flat Flower opaque green syrup jug, $400. Photo courtesy of Dr. James Measell

Fig. 48: Carnelian (Everglades) blue opalescent cruet with original stopper, $500. Courtesy of Dr. James Measell

Fig. 49: Cactus opaque pink salt shaker, $90. Photo courtesy of Dr. James Measell

Fig. 50: Vaseline opalescent Alaska pattern butter dish with enameled decoration, $550. Courtesy of Dr. James Measell

Fig. 51: Northwood Cashews pattern clear opalescent bowl, $65. Courtesy of Dr. James Measell

Fig. 52: Klondyke (Fluted Scrolls) topaz opalescent spooner, $110. Photo courtesy of Dr. James Measell

Fig. 54

Fig 53

Fig. 55

Fig. 56

Fig. 57

Fig. 58

Fig. 59

Fig. 60

Fig. 53: Pump novelty vase in blue opalescent, $125. Courtesy of Dr. James Measell

Fig. 54: Leaf Umbrella pattern salt shaker in Rose DuBarry, $100-125. Courtesy of Harold Coalmer

Fig. 55: Frosted Leaf and Basketweave blue opalescent spooner, $100. Courtesy of Dr. James Measell

Fig. 56: Blue opalescent Holly creamer with gold trim, $200. Courtesy of Dr. James Measell

Fig. 57: Blue iridescent glass covered pitcher, $600. Photo courtesy of Dr. James Measell

Fig. 58: Grape and Leaf opaque blue syrup jug, $350. Photo courtesy of Dr. James Measell

Fig. 59: Cactus pattern cranberry salt shaker with white opalescent vertical stripes, $150. Courtesy of Harold Coalmer

Fig. 60: Jewel pattern rubina water pitcher, $350. Photo courtesy of Dr. James Measell

Fig. 61

Fig. 65

Fig. 62

Fig. 63

Fig. 66

Fig. 64

Fig. 61: Majestic pattern ruby-stained rose bowl, $65-75. Photo courtesy of Johanna Billings, Danielsville, PA

Fig. 62: Klondike clear frosted and amber-stained tumbler, $125-135. Photo courtesy of Temples Antiques, Eden Prairie, MN

Fig. 63: Delaware creamer with rose stain and gold trim, $55-60. Photo courtesy of Temples Antiques, Eden Prairie, MN

Fig. 64: Green S-Repeat condiment set on tray, the set $250-275. Photo courtesy of Temples Antiques, Eden Prairie, MN

Fig. 65: Skilton (Early Oregon) pattern ruby-stained milk pitcher, 6 1/2" h., $125-150. Photo courtesy of Temples Antiques, Eden Prairie, MN

Fig. 66: Alaska pattern blue opalescent sugar bowl, $150-175. Photo courtesy of Temples Antiques, Eden Prairie, MN

Car Vases

Fig. 67

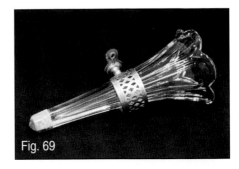

Fig. 69

Fig. 68

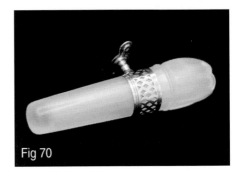

Fig 70

Fig. 67: Frosted green vase with Model T fitting, 8" l. $135. Photo courtesy of Robert G. Jason-Ickes, Olympia, WA

Fig. 68: Pair of Blossom and Band pattern vases in marigold carnival glass, 7 1/2" l. $185 pr. Photo courtesy of Robert G. Jason-Ickes, Olympia, WA

Fig. 69: Clear paneled flaring vase with silver tip and metal Model T fitting, 8 1/2" l. $85. Photo courtesy of Robert G. Jason-Ickes, Olympia, WA

Fig. 70: Frosted yellow tulip-form vase with a Model T fitting, 8 1/4" l. $135. Photo courtesy of Robert G. Jason-Ickes, Olympia, WA

Fig. 71: Pair of crackle design marigold carnival glass vases, 7 1/4" l. $155 pr. Photo courtesy of Robert G. Jason-Ickes, Olympia, WA

Fig. 72: Clear vases with incurved mouth and floral and fern etching, 7 1/2" l. $175 pr. Photo courtesy of Robert G. Jason-Ickes, Olympia, WA

Fig. 71

Fig. 72

Fig. 73

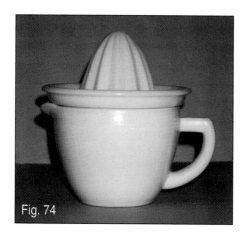

Fig. 74

Fig. 76

Fig. 75

Fig. 73: Two sapphire blue Fire King mugs. Heavy thick one (left) reportedly a shaving mug, thin one (right) a coffee mug. Each $30-50. Photo courtesy of Kate Trabue, Eureka, CA

Fig. 74: Jeannette Glass Jade-ite reamer on pitcher base, 6 1/4" h. $20-25. Photo courtesy of Bobbie Zucker Bryson, Tuckahoe, NY

Fig. 75: Royal Ruby ball-shaped Swirl pattern 80 oz. pitcher by Anchor Hocking. $40-45. Photo courtesy of Kate Trabue, Eureka, CA

Fig. 76: Jeannette Glass ultramarine reamer, 5 1/4" d. $120. Photo courtesy of Bobbie Zucker Bryson, Tuckahoe, NY

Fig. 77

Fig. 78

Fig. 79

Fig. 77: Blue Circle pattern covered canisters by the Hocking Glass Company. Each $27-30. Photo courtesy of Kate Trabue, Eureka, CA

Fig. 78: Cobalt blue Chevron pattern open sugar bowl, 4" h. $12-15. Photo courtesy of Kate Trabue, Eureka, CA

Fig. 79: McKee butterscotch "Sunkist" reamer, 6" d. $850. Photo courtesy of Bobbie Zucker Bryson, Tuckahoe, NY

Fig. 80: Beads & Bars pattern Jadeite Fire King milk pitcher by Anchor Hocking. $175-250. Courtesy of Kate Trabue, Eureka, CA

Fig. 81: Fenton glass French Blue reamer on pitcher base, 6 3/8" h. $3,500. Photo courtesy of Bobbie Zucker Bryson, Tuckahoe, NY

Fig. 80

Fig. 81

Fig. 82

Fig. 83

Fig. 84

Fig. 86

Fig. 87

Fig. 85

Fig. 88

Fig. 89

Fig. 82: Cambridge glass cocktail with rounded purple glass insert in Farber Brothers chrome stem, 5 3/8" h. $12-15. Photo courtesy of George and Judy Swan, Dubuque, IA

Fig. 83: Consolidated Guttate pattern cased pink water pitcher, 9 1/2" h. $325. Photo courtesy of Temples Antiques, Eden Prairie, MN

Fig. 84: Duncan & Miller amber Hobnail pattern cologne bottle and stopper. $40-50. Photo courtesy of Tom and Neila Bredehoft, St. Louisville, OH

Fig. 85: Duncan & Miller dark blue Terrace pattern covered urn. $200-250. Photo courtesy of Tom and Neila Bredehoft, St. Louisville, OH

Fig. 86: Fenton glass cranberry opalescent Hobnail pattern cruet with original stopper. $75-125. Photo courtesy of The Galena Shoppe, Galena, IL

Fig. 87: Fenton glass green opalescent ruffled Hobnail pattern bowl. $30-40. Photo courtesy of The Galena Shoppe, Galena, IL

Fig. 88: Fostoria blue Baroque pattern rose bowl. $75-100. Photo courtesy of Johanna Billings, Danielsville, PA

Fig. 89: Heisey Yeoman pattern 2 oz. oil cruet with original stopper in Moongleam. $100-125. Photo courtesy of Tom and Neila Bredehoft, St. Louisville, OH

Miscellaneous Companies & Lines

Fig. 91

Fig. 92

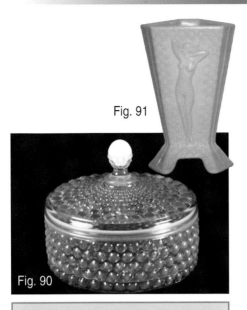

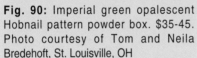

Fig. 90

Fig. 93

Fig. 94

Fig. 95

Fig. 96

Fig. 90: Imperial green opalescent Hobnail pattern powder box. $35-45. Photo courtesy of Tom and Neila Bredehoft, St. Louisville, OH

Fig. 91: McKee glass triangular Art Deco style 'Art Nude' 8" vase in Skokie Green. $1,000-1,500.

Fig. 92: Milk glass Cat on Lacy Base covered dish by Atterbury, ca. 1880s. $125. Photo courtesy of Frank Chiarenza, Newington, CT

Fig. 93: Milk glass Steer's Head covered dish by Challinor, Taylor, ca. 1880s. $5,500. Photo courtesy of Frank Chiarenza, Newington, CT

Fig. 94: New Martinsville Muranese square crimped sauce dish. $145. Photo courtesy of Dr. James Measell

Fig. 95: New Martinsville Modernistic No. 33 creamer and open sugar in opaque jade green with silver overlay. $200 pr. Photo courtesy of Dr. James Measell

Fig. 96: New Martinsville No. 37 (Moondrops) pattern 2 oz. amber handled tumbler with simulated cut decoration, $18, and 2 oz. green handled tumbler, $15. Photo courtesy of Dr. James Measell

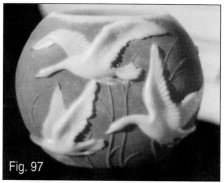

Fig. 97

Fig. 102

Fig. 103

Fig. 98

Fig. 99

Fig. 100

Fig. 101

Fig. 97: Phoenix glass Wild Geese pattern vase with reddish brown stain, 9 1/2" h. $225-250. Photo courtesy of Robert Gordon, San Antonio, TX

Fig. 98: Sandwich glass Loop pattern 11" vases in medium electric blue. Pair $3,500-4,500. Photo courtesy of Collector's Sales & Services, Pomfret Center, CT

Fig. 99: Tiffin glass No. 17578 goblet with Wisteria bowl. $30-40. Photo courtesy of Tom and Neila Bredehoft, St. Louisville, OH

Fig. 100: L.G. Wright Moon and Star pattern amber cruet with original stopper. $135. Photo courtesy of Dr. James Measell

Fig. 101: L.G. Wright cranberry opalescent Drapery pattern milk pitcher. $300. Photo courtesy of Dr. James Measell

Fig. 102: L.G. Wright Argonaut pattern Chocolate glass butter dish. $125. Photo courtesy of Dr. James Measell

Fig. 103: L.G. Wright purple slag Turkey covered dish. $55. Photo courtesy of Dr. James Measell

DUNCAN & MILLER

Duncan & Miller Glass Company, a successor firm to George A. Duncan & Sons Company, produced a wide range of pressed wares and novelty pieces during the late 19th century and into the early 20th century. During the Depression era and after, they continued making a wide variety of more modern patterns, including mold-blown types and also introduced a number of etched and engraved patterns. Many colors, including opalescent hues, were produced during this era and especially popular today are the graceful swan dishes they produced in the Pall Mall and Sylvan patterns.

The numbers after the pattern name indicate the original factory pattern number. The Duncan factory was closed in 1955. Also see ANIMALS and PAT-TERN GLASS.

Almond dish, Early American Sandwich patt., clear $12
Ashtray, Canterbury patt. (No. 115), clear, 3"... 12
Ashtray, Early American Sandwich patt. (No. 41), clear, 3" sq. 8
Basket, handled, etched First Love patt., 10" oval 175
Basket, Early American Sandwich patt., clear, 12" 100
Basket w/loop handle, Early American Sandwich patt., amber, 6" h. 150
Basket w/loop handle, Early American Sandwich patt., clear, 12"............................. 295
Bonbon, heart-shaped, handled, Early American Sandwich patt., clear, 5" 15
Bowl, bouillon, Spiral Flutes patt., pink 15
Bowl, cream soup, Spiral Flutes patt., amber 25
Bowl, fruit, Canterbury patt. (No. 115), clear 8
Bowl, 5" d., Early American Sandwich patt., clear 10
Bowl, 8" d., Spiral Flutes patt., clear 18
Bowl, 9" d., Canterbury patt. (No. 115), clear 30
Bowl, 9" d., tab-handled, Caribbean patt., clear 35
Bowl, 9" d., tab-handled, Caribbean patt., clear 35
Bowl, 10" d., flared, etched First Love patt., clear 50
Bowl, 10 1/2" d., 5" h., crimped rim, etched First Love patt., clear....................... 60
Bowl, 11 1/2" d., fluted, Early American Sandwich patt.. 50
Bowl, Canterbury patt., oval, clear 35
Butter dish, w/metal cover, Teardrop patt. (No. 301), clear, 1 lb....................... 20
Cake salver, pedestal foot, Early American Sandwich patt., clear, 13" d., 5" h. 80
Candlestick, three-light, Canterbury patt. (No. 115), clear, 6" h. 35
Candlesticks, Canterbury patt. (No. 115), pink opalescent, 3" h., pr.......................... 65
Candlesticks, two-light, Canterbury patt., clear, 6" h., pr. 50
Candy dish, cov., Early American Sandwich patt., clear, 6" sq. 425
Candy dish, cov., Canterbury patt. (No. 115), clear, 7" h. 33

Candy dish, cov., footed, Early American Sandwich patt., green, 8" h. 75
Celery dish, etched Beverly patt., amber, 11" l. 15
Champagne, Early American Sandwich patt., clear, 5 1/4" h. 17
Champagne, Teardrop patt. (No. 301), clear, 5" h., 5 oz. (ILLUS. top of next column) 10
Claret, Canterbury patt., clear, 5" h. 20
Coaster, Early American Sandwich patt., clear, 5" d. 11
Cocktail, Early American Sandwich patt., clear, 3 oz... 13
Cocktail, Teardrop patt., clear, 4 1/2" h., 3 1/2 oz. 14
Cocktail, Caribbean patt., blue, 4 3/4" h., 3 oz. 45
Cocktail shaker, etched First Love patt., clear, 16 oz.. 135
Cologne bottle w/original stopper, Hob-nail patt., amber, 6 1/2" h., 8 oz. (ILLUS.)... 40-50
Compote 5" h., 7" w., Puritan patt., green.......... 40
Cordial, etched First Love patt., clear, 3 3/4" h., 1 oz. 60

Teardrop Champagne

Cordial, Teardrop patt., clear, 4" h., 1 oz. 30
Cornucopia vase, footed, Three Feathers patt. (No. 117), clear, 8" h. 21
Creamer, Early American Sandwich patt., clear 8
Creamer, Festive patt. (No. 155), aqua.............. 25
Creamer, Teardrop patt., (No. 301), clear 5
Creamer & cov. sugar bowl on tray, Festive patt. (No. 155), aqua, 3 pcs. 85
Creamer & sugar bowl, individual-size, Early American Sandwich patt., clear, pr........ 18
Cup, Canterbury patt., clear 10
Cup, Puritan patt., footed, clear........................... 7
Cup & saucer, Canterbury patt. (No. 115), clear 14
Cup & saucer, Early American Sandwich patt., clear 14
Cup & saucer, demitasse, Puritan patt., pink 21
Deviled egg plate, Early American Sandwich patt., clear, 12" d. 71

Epergne, Early American Sandwich patt.,
clear 250

Finger bowl & liner, Spiral Flutes patt.,
amber, 2 pcs. 25

Goblet, Caribbean patt., clear, 4" h., 3 oz. 25

Goblet, etched Buttercup patt., low 20

Goblet, water, Early American Sandwich
patt., clear 18

Goblet, water, Spiral Flutes patt., green 15

Goblet, Caribbean patt., clear, 3 oz., 4" h. 25

Goblet, Teardrop patt., clear, 4 oz., 5" h. 12

Goblet, juice, footed, etched First Love
patt., clear, 4 1/2" h., 5 oz. 24

Goblet, Teardrop patt., clear, 5 3/4" h., 9
oz. 14

Goblet, water, Canterbury patt., clear,
7 1/4" h. 17

Goblet, etched First Love patt., clear,
6 3/4" h. 28

Ice tub, handled, Spiral Flutes patt., pink 52

Lamp, oil-type, Mardi Gras patt. (No. 42),
clear 195

Lamp shade, Mardi Gras patt. (No. 42),
clear 39

Model of a swan, Pall Mall patt. (No. 30),
clear, 5" l 15

Model of a swan, Sylvan patt. (No. 122),
pink opalescent, 5 1/2" l. 95

Model of a swan, Pall Mall patt. (No.
30 1/2), clear, 7" l. 15

Model of a swan, Pall Mall patt. (No. 30),
cranberry stained, 8" l. 29

Model of a swan, Pall Mall patt. (No.
30 1/2), clear, 10" l. 40

Nut bowl, Early American Sandwich patt.,
clear 11

Nut cup, Spiral Flutes patt., amber 12

Oyster cocktail, Early American Sandwich patt., clear 18

Parfait, Spiral Flutes patt., amber 25

Pitcher, Caribbean patt., blue, 16 oz.,
4 3/4" h. 275

Pitcher, Iris patt., clear 35

Pitcher w/ice lip, 8" h., Early American
Sandwich patt., clear, 80 oz. 120

Pitcher w/ice lip, Early American Sandwich patt., clear, 1/2 gal., 8" h. 110

Plate, 7" d., Early American Sandwich
patt., clear 5

Plate, 7" d., Puritan patt., green 7

Plate, 7" d., Spiral Flutes patt., amber 4

Plate, 7" d., Spiral Flutes patt., pink 4

Plate, 7 1/2" d., Canterbury patt., (No. 115),
clear 10

Plate, salad, 7 1/2" sq., etched First Love
patt., clear 20

Plate, salad, 8" d., Early American Sandwich patt., clear 10

Plate, salad, 8" d., Early American Sandwich patt., green 10

Plate, salad, 8 1/2" d., etched First Love
patt., clear 20

Plate, dinner, 9 1/2" d., Early American
Sandwich patt., clear 39

Plate, dinner, 10 1/2" d., Puritan patt., clear....... 25

Plate, sandwich, 11" d., two-handled, Canterbury patt. (No. 115), clear 22

Plate, cracker, 13" d., Early American
Sandwich patt., clear 40

Plate, 14" d., Teardrop patt., clear..................... 35

Plate, chop, 14" d., etched Beverly patt.,
amber 28

Plate, torte, 14" d., Canterbury patt. (No.
115), clear 25

Plate, torte, 14" d., Teardrop patt. (No.
301), clear 22

Plate, 16" d., Early American Sandwich
patt., clear 105

Plate, Lazy Susan, 18" d., Teardrop patt.,
w/leaf cutting, clear 125

Plateau for cheese plate, Teardrop patt.,
(No. 301), clear 15

Punch bowl & ladle, Festive patt. (No.
155), clear, 2 pcs........................ 50

Relish dish, two-part, Teardrop patt., (No.
301), round, clear........................ 8

Relish dish, three-part, Canterbury patt.,
chartreuse, 8"........................ 25

Relish dish, three-part, Canterbury patt.,
handled, clear, 9" d. 18

Relish dish, three-part, etched First Love
patt., clear, 6 x 10 1/2"........................ 45

Relish dish, five-part, Caribbean patt.,
clear........................ 40

Relish dish, six-part, Teardrop patt., clear......... 30

Canterbury Rose Bowl

Rose bowl, Canterbury patt., Jasmine, yellow opalescent (ILLUS.) 90-110

Salt dip, Early American Sandwich patt.,
clear........................ 8

Salt & pepper shakers, etched First Love
patt., clear, pr........................ 35

Sauce ladle, Festive patt. aqua 40

Saucer, Early American Sandwich patt.,
clear........................ 4

Sherbet, Early American Sandwich patt.,
clear, 5 oz........................ 10

Sherbet, Early American Sandwich patt.,
green........................ 10

Soup plate w/flanged rim, Puritan patt.,
pink, 8" d........................ 35

Sugar bowl, Early American Sandwich
patt., clear, 5 oz........................ 8

Sugar bowl, etched First Love patt., clear......... 18

Tumbler, Spiral Flutes patt., green, 2 1/2
oz........................ 10

Tumbler, juice, Canterbury patt., clear,
4 1/4" h........................ 8

Tumbler, juice, Early American Sandwich
patt., clear, 5 oz........................ 10

Tumbler, etched Buttercup patt., footed, 12
oz........................ 25

Tumbler, iced tea, Early American Sandwich patt., clear, 12 oz........................ 18

Tumbler, iced tea, flat, Spiral Flutes patt.,
green........................ 65

Tumbler, juice, for ice dish, etched Shirley patt, pink.......... 10
Urn, cov., Terrace patt., No. 111, 5111 1/2, Royal Blue (ILLUS. in color section) **200-250**
Vase, 4" h., Canterbury patt. (No. 115), clear 17
Vase, 5" h., Canterbury patt., amber 25
Vase, 5" h., 6" d., Hobnail patt., pink opalescent.......... 65
Vase, 6" h., Canterbury patt. (No. 115), clear 25
Vase, 8 3/4" h., Spiral Flutes patt., green 25
Vase, 9 1/2" h., ruffled rim, Caribbean patt., blue 175
Vase/flower arranger, 7" h., Canterbury patt. (No. 115), clear 40
Vase/flower arranger, 8" h., Canterbury patt. (No. 115), clear 35
Violet vase, 3" h., Canterbury patt. (No. 115), clear 15
Wine, Caribbean patt., blue, 3 oz. 35
Wine, Caribbean patt., clear, 3 oz. 15
Wine, etched First Love patt., clear, 5 1/4" h., 3 oz. 26
Wine, Early American Sandwich patt., clear....... 19

FENTON

Fenton Art Glass Company began producing glass at Williamstown, West Virginia, in January 1907. Organized by Frank L. and John W. Fenton, the company began operations in a newly built glass factory with an experienced master glass craftsman, Jacob Rosenthal, as their factory manager. Fenton has produced a wide variety of collectible glassware through the years, including Carnival. Still in production today, their current productions may be found at finer gift shops across the country.

William Heacock's three-volume set on Fenton, published by Antique Publications, is the standard reference in this field.

Fenton Mark

Basket, Rose Burmese, No. 7731.......... **$80**
Basket, Hobnail patt., French Opalescent, 7 1/2".......... 35
Bowl, 7" d., Hobnail patt., green opalescent (ILLUS. in color section).......... **30-40**
Bowl, 9 3/4" d., fruit, Mandarin Red on black glass stand, No. 846, 2 pcs. 85
Bowl, 10" d., low sides, Wisteria, stretch finish.......... 80
Bowl, 10" d., Silver Crest, No. 7221, yellow jonquil decoration w/gold trim on crest edge 46
Bowl, 12" d., Silver Crest 28
Bowl, 14" d., Peach Crest 60
Cocktail glass, Historic America patt., clear 22
Cookie jar, cov., Big Cookies patt., black, handled 125

Cruet w/original stopper, Coin Dot patt., No. 418, pink opalescent.......... 75
Cruet w/original stopper, Dot Optic patt., cobalt blue opalescent 75
Cruet w/original stopper, Drape patt., cranberry opalescent.......... 75
Cruet w/original stopper, Drape patt., mulberry opalescent.......... 75
Cruet w/original stopper, Fern patt., No. 815, Persian blue opalescent.......... 75

Cranberry Opalescent Fenton Cruet

Cruet w/original stopper, Hobnail patt., cranberry opalescent (ILLUS.) 80
Cruet w/original stopper, Rose Burmese....... 100
Cruet w/original stopper, Swirl patt., French Opalescent.......... 75
Epergne, one-lily, Rose Burmese, No. 7202 125
Epergne, three-lily, Diamond Lace patt., white opalescent 115
Goblet, Historic America patt., clear.......... 30
Lamp, Gone-with-the-Wind type, Poppy patt., custard, 24" h. 250

Cranberry Opalescent Hobnail Pitcher

Pitcher, footed spherical form, cranberry opalescent Hobnail patt., applied clear handle (ILLUS.).......... 35
Plates, 8" d., Silver Crest, set of 8.......... 155
Rose bowl, No. 857, Periwinkle blue 48

Small Hobnail Vase

Vase, 6" h., footed, trumpet-form w/flaring ruffled rim, Hobnail patt. (ILLUS.).................. 15
Vase, 8" h., double crimped rim, Hobnail patt., No. 3958, milk glass............................. 25
Vase, fan-type, dolphin base, Jade green.......... 35

FOSTORIA

One of the most recognized names in American glass is Fostoria. Opening in Fostoria, Ohio in the late 1880s, it relocated to Moundsville, West Virginia in 1892. Although the original Fostoria factory closed in the 1980s, the company name is still in use today to mark glass produced around the world for the concern which acquired the company's assets.

In the 1940s and 1950s Fostoria glassware was a favorite choice for new brides and these patterns retain great popularity with collectors today. Fostoria's American pattern is one of longest lived lines in American glass. First introduced in 1915 it is still being produced in a limited range of pieces but other factories.

Fostoria Label

Appetizer or ice cream set: 10 1/2" oblong tray w/six individual 1 3/4" h. inserts, American patt., amber, the set .. **$1,100**
Ashtray, individual, Century patt., clear, 2 3/4".. 12
Ashtray, American patt., clear, 2 7/8" sq. 6
Ashtray, American patt., clear, 5" sq. 100
Ashtray, Coin patt., ruby, 5 1/2"........................ 34
Banana split dish, American patt., clear, 3 1/2" w., 9" l.. 1,200
Basket, w/reeded handle, American patt., clear, 7 x 9".. 148
Beer mug, American patt., clear, 12 oz., 4 1/2" h... 88
Bell, American patt., clear................................ 290

Bonbon, three-footed, American patt., clear, 7" d.. 15
Bonbon, three-footed, American patt., red, 7" d... 125
Bonbon, three-footed, Colony patt., clear, 7" d.. 12
Bottle w/original stopper, cordial, American patt., clear, 9 oz., 7 1/4" h........................ 75
Bowl, cream soup, Colony patt., clear.............. 77
Bowl, almond, 2 1/4" d., footed, Colony patt., clear 17
Bowl, 4 1/2" d., three-handled, American patt., clear 98
Bowl, 8 1/2" d., three-handled, American patt., clear 300
Bowl, 8 1/2" d., two-handled, Chintz etching, clear.. 45
Bowl, 9" d., Century patt., clear........................ 30
Bowl, 9" oval, Coin patt., ruby.......................... 46
Bowl, 9 3/8" w., 4" h., Colony patt., clear 85
Bowl, salad, 9 3/4" d., Colony patt., clear 40

Colony High-footed Bowl

Bowl, 10 1/2" d., high-footed, Colony patt., clear (ILLUS.) 112
Bowl, fruit, 10 1/2" d., three-footed, American patt., clear... **40-45**
Bowl, 11" d., footed, rolled edge, Century patt., clear 43
Bowl, 11" tri-cornered, three footed, American patt., clear... 40
Bowl, 12 1/2" oval, 2 7/8" h., No. 2545, Flame patt., Navarre etching, clear 113
Bowl, fruit, low, 14" d., Colony patt., clear.......... 70
Bowl, toddler's, American patt., No. 150, clear 25
Butter dish, cov., Colony patt., No. 2412, clear, 1/4 lb.. 38
Butter dish, cov., oblong, American patt., clear, 1/4 lb., 3 1/4 x 7 1/2", 2 1/8" h. 14
Cake plate, handled, Chintz etching, No. 2496, clear, 10" d. 40
Cake plate, handled, Colony patt., clear, 10" d. 22
Cake plate, three-footed, American patt., clear, 12" d. 25
Cake salver, American patt., clear, 10" sq. 250
Cake salver, Colony patt., clear, 12" d.............. 75
Cake stand, Coin patt., amber 140
Cake stand, Coin patt., clear, 10" d. 78
Candlestick, Coin patt., ruby, 4 1/2" h. 46

Candlestick, Colony patt., No. 2412, clear,
7" h. 30
Candlestick, two-light, Flame patt., clear 80
Candlestick, Baroque patt., clear w/Lido
etching, 4" h. 32
Candlestick, Coronet patt., clear, 4 1/2" h. 20
Candlestick, Chintz etching, clear 5 1/2" h. 30
Candlestick, Romance etching, clear,
5 1/2" h. 38
Candlestick, Colony patt., No. 2412, clear,
7" h. 30
Candlestick, two-light, American patt.,
clear, 4 3/8" h. 35

Baroque Two-light Candlestick

Candlestick, two-light, Baroque patt., clear
(ILLUS.) 24
Candlestick, two-light, Chintz etching,
clear 38
Candlestick, three-light, Romance etching,
clear 55
Candlesticks, Chintz etching, No. 2490,
clear, 4" h., pr. 50
Candlesticks, Navarre patt., No. 2496,
clear, 4" h., pr. 45
Candlesticks, Century patt., clear,
4 1/2" h., pr. 34
Candlesticks, triple-light, Navarre etching,
clear, 6 3/4" h., pr. 150
Candlesticks, Colony patt., w/eight prisms,
clear, 7 1/2" h., pr. 195
Candlesticks, cone-footed, American patt.,
clear, 15 points, small, pr. 400
Candlesticks, cone-footed, American patt.,
clear, 16 points, large, pr. 300
Candlesticks, two-light, Romance etching,
No. 6023, clear, pr. 38
Candy dish, cov., three-part, Chintz etch-
ing, clear 165
Candy dish, cov., three-part, Royal etch-
ing, amber 60
Candy dish, cov., Coin patt., ruby, 4 1/4" 42
Candy dish, cov., Coin patt., ruby, 6" 58
Candy dish, cov., American patt., "wed-
ding bowl," milk glass, 8" h. 125
Celery dish, Chintz etching, clear 40
Celery tray, American patt., clear, 10" l. 17
Centerpiece, American patt., clear, shal-
low, 17" 550
Chamber candles, American patt., clear,
pr. 95
Champagne, Romance etching, clear,
7" h. 18
Champagne, Chintz etching, clear 20
Champagne, Holly cutting, clear 12
Cheese compote, American patt., clear 24

Chintz Cheese & Cracker Set

Cheese & cracker set, Chintz etching,
clear, 2 pcs. (ILLUS.) 70
Cigarette box, cov., American patt., clear 30
Cigarette box, cov., Baroque patt.,
No. 2496, clear 38
Claret, American Lady patt., clear, 3 1/2
oz., 4 5/8" h. 18
Claret, American patt., clear, 4 7/8" h.,
7 oz. 63
Cocktail, American Lady patt., cobalt blue,
3 1/2 oz., 4" h. 75
Cocktail, footed, American patt., clear,
3 oz. 12
Cocktail, American Lady patt., clear, 3 1/2
oz., 4" h. 14
Cocktail, Holly cutting, clear, 3 1/2 oz.,
5 1/4" h. 14
Cocktail, Romance etching, clear, 3 1/2 oz. 18
Cocktail, Chintz etching., clear, 5" h. 20
Cologne bottle w/original stopper, Amer-
ican patt., clear 100
Compote, 8", Lucere No. 1515, blue milk
glass 75
Compote, cov., jelly, Colony patt., clear 35
Compote, cov., 6 1/2" h., Colony patt.,
clear 30
Compote, open, 4 3/8" h., Century patt.,
clear 20
Compote, open, 4 1/2" h., Navarre etching,
clear 35
Condiment tray, cloverleaf-shaped, Ameri-
can patt., clear 250
Console set: bowl & pr. of double candle-
sticks; Chintz etching, clear, the set 125
Console set: No. 2402 Art Deco-style bowl
& pair of candleholders, Ebony, the set 70
Cordial, Colonial Dame patt., clear,
3 1/2" h. 42
Cordial, Colonial Dame patt., green bowl,
clear foot & stem, 3 1/2" h. 46
Cordial, Mayflower etching, clear, 3 3/4" h. 44
Cordial, June etching, Topaz, 3 7/8" h. 98
Cordial, Navarre etching, clear, 1 oz.,
3 7/8" h. 65
Cordial, Lido etching, clear, 4" h. 34

Fostoria American Cracker Jar

Cracker jar, cov., American patt., clear
(ILLUS.) 800
Creamer, American patt., clear, medium 9
Creamer, American patt., hexagonal foot,
clear 800
Creamer, Chintz etching, clear........................... 20
Creamer, American patt., clear, 4 1/4" h.,
9 1/2 oz. 12
Creamer, individual, Century patt., clear,
4 oz. 9
Creamer, individual, Colony patt., clear,
3 1/4" h., 4 oz. 6
Creamer & cov. sugar bowl, American
patt., clear, large, pr. 45
Creamer & open sugar bowl, Colony
patt., clear, pr. 12
Creamer & open sugar bowl, Jamestown
patt., pink, pr. 50
Creamer, open sugar bowl & undertray,
individual, American patt., clear, the set 38
Creamer, open sugar bowl & undertray,
individual size, Century patt., clear, the
set 33
Creamer & sugar bowl, Coronet patt.,
clear, pr. 12
Creamer & sugar bowl, footed, Navarre
etching, clear, 4 1/4" h., pr. 45
Creamer & sugar bowl, Romance etching,
clear, pr. 30
Cruet w/original stopper, American patt.,
clear, 5 oz. 28
Cruet w/original stopper, Coin patt., clear,
6" h. 42
Crushed fruit jar, cov., American patt.,
clear, 10" h. (chip on lid)............................ 1,600
Cup, footed, Colony patt., clear, 6 oz. 7
Cup, American patt., clear, 7 oz. 8
Cup, Century patt., clear 17
Cup & saucer, American patt., flared, clear....... 12
Cup & saucer, Century patt., clear 14
Cup & saucer, Colony patt., clear 10
Cup & saucer, Fairfax patt., orchid................... 14
Cup & saucer, Kashmir etching, blue 56
Decanter w/original stopper, Coin patt.,
clear 94
Decanter w/original stopper, American
patt., clear, 24 oz., 9 1/4" h. 90

Dresser bowl, oblong, American patt.,
clear, 1 3/4 x 5" 600
Figure of Madonna, clear, 10" h........................ 45
Figure of Madonna & Child, clear,
13 1/2" h. 95
Finger bowl, Colony patt., clear........................ 75
Finger bowl, American patt., clear,
4 1/2" d. 90
Glove box, cov., American patt., clear
(some stretch marks) 600
Goblet, American Lady patt., clear, 10 oz.,
6 1/8" h.. 17
Goblet, American Lady patt., cobalt blue,
10 oz., 6 1/8" h. 80
Goblet, American patt., clear, 5 1/2" h. 14
Goblet, American patt., clear, 5 1/2" h.,
9 oz. 13
Goblet, American patt., clear, 6 7/8" h. 26
Goblet, American patt., hexagonal foot,
clear, 10 oz... 15
Goblet, Century patt., clear, 10 1/2 oz.,
5 3/4" h. 19
Goblet, Chintz etching, clear, 9 oz..................... 34
Goblet, Colonial Dame patt., clear,
6 1/2" h. 22
Goblet, Colonial Dame patt., green bowl,
clear stem & foot, 6 1/2" h. 26
Goblet, Colony patt., clear, 5 1/4" h. 14
Goblet, Holly cutting, clear, 10 oz, 8 3/8" h. 18
Goblet, Jamestown patt., blue, 6" h. 14
Goblet, Jamestown patt., blue, 9 oz.,
4 1/4" h. 20
Goblet, Jamestown patt., clear......................... 12
Goblet, Jamestown patt., green, 6" h. 14
Goblet, Jamestown patt., pink, 6" h. 22

June Etched Goblet

Goblet, June etching, clear, 8 1/4" h.
(ILLUS.).. 46
Goblet, June etching, pink, 8 1/4" h. 94
Goblet, Lido etching, clear, 7 1/2" h. 21
Goblet, Navarre etching, blue, 10 oz. 45
Goblet, Navarre etching, clear, 7 5/8" oz. 52
Goblet, Navarre etching, pink, 7 5/8" oz. 72
Goblet, Romance etching, clear, 9 oz. 28
Goblet, Sunray patt., clear, 5 3/4" h. 22
Gravy boat w/undertray, Chintz etching,
clear, 2 pcs. 75

Hair receiver, cov., American patt., clear,
3" sq. 725
Hairpin box, cov., American patt., clear,
1 1/2 x 1 2/4", 3 1/2" l. 2,000
Honey jar, cover & spoon, American patt.,
clear 500
Hurricane lamp, American patt., clear,
8 1/2" h. 325
Ice bowl, Colony patt., footed, clear 200
Ice bucket, Century patt., clear (no handle) 50
Ice bucket, Chintz etching, clear 140
Ice bucket, Colony patt., clear 200
Ice dish, American patt., clear 35
Ice dish w/juice tumbler, Hermitage patt.,
Topaz 22
Ice tub, American patt., clear, 5 5/8" d.,
3 3/4" h. 98
Ice tub, American patt., clear, 6 1/2" d.,
4 1/2" h. 55
Ice tub liner, American patt., clear, large 95
Jewel box, cov., American patt., clear,
2 1/4 x 5 1/4", 2" h. 400
Marmalade, cover & spoon, American
patt., clear, the set 118
Mayonnaise bowl, divided, American patt.,
clear, 3 1/4" d., 6 1/4" h. 15
Mayonnaise bowl, Century patt., clear 18
Mayonnaise bowl, Colony patt., clear 15
Mayonnaise bowl & liner, Colony patt.,
clear, 2 pcs. 25
Mayonnaise bowl, underplate & spoon,
Century patt., clear, 3 pcs. 40
Mayonnaise bowl w/underplate, Colony
patt., clear, 2 pcs. 35
Mayonnaise bowl w/underplate,
Romance etching, clear, 2 pcs. 36
Muffin tray, American patt., clear, 10" 36
Mug, Bicentennial, No. 2493/705, clear,
15 oz. 24
Mustard jar, cov., American patt., clear 30
Mustard jar, cover & spoon, round, Amer-
ican patt., clear (inkwell), the set 1,200
Nappy, American patt., flared, green, 4 1/2" 150
Nappy, handled, American patt., clear,
4 1/2" d. 10
Nappy, handled, Century patt., clear,
4 1/2" d. 10
Nappy, tri-cornered, handled, American
patt., clear, 5" 10
Nappy, American patt., deep, clear, 8" d. 90
Novelty, model of a top hat, American
patt., clear, 2 1/2" h. 25
Olive dish, American patt., clear, 6" l. 12
Oyster cocktail, American Lady patt.,
clear, 4 oz., 3 1/2" h. 14
Oyster cocktail, Colony patt., clear,
3 3/8" h., 4 oz. 12
Oyster cocktail, American patt., clear,
4 1/2 oz. 13
Parfait, June etching, blue, 5 1/2" h. 94
Party plate, Century patt., clear, 8" 24
Pickle dish, Colony patt., clear 25
Pickle dish, American patt., clear, 8" l. 13
Pickle dish, Century patt., clear, 8 3/4" 15
Pickle jar, cov., American patt., clear, 6" h. 550
Pin tray, oval, American patt., clear,
4 1/2 x 5 1/2" 138
Pitcher, 6 1/2" h., American patt., clear,
3 pt. 75

Pitcher, American patt., clear, 1 pt. 40
Pitcher, milk, Century patt., clear 60
Pitcher, 5 3/8" h., Coin patt., ruby 140
Pitcher, 6 1/2" h., Coin patt., clear 89

Colony Pattern Pitcher

Pitcher, 7 3/4" h., Colony patt., No. 2412,
clear (ILLUS.) 80
Pitcher, 7 1/2" h., Jamestown patt., pink 120
Pitcher, Jenny Lind patt., milk glass 95
Pitcher, Sunray patt., frosted clear, 2 qt. 58
Pitcher, Vesper etching, No. 5100, footed,
amber 310
Pitcher w/ice lip, American patt., clear 45
Pitcher w/ice lip, 8 1/2" h., Colony patt.,
clear, 3 pt. 260
Plate, bread & butter, 6" d., American patt.,
clear 8
Plate, salad, 7" d., Baroque patt., clear 4
Plate, 7 3/8" d., Kashmir etching, blue 38
Plate, 7 1/2" d., Chintz etching, clear 17
Plate, 7 1/2" d., Navarre patt., clear 18
Plate, salad, 7 1/2" d., American patt., clear 11
Plate, salad, 7 1/2" l., crescent-shaped,
Century patt., clear 30
Plate, 8 1/4" d., Jamestown patt., pink 21
Plate, 9" d., Colony patt., clear 18
Plate, 9 1/2" d., Colony patt., clear 34
Plate, dinner, 9 1/2" d., American patt.,
clear 24
Plate, dinner, 9 1/2" d., Trojan etching,
topaz 20
Plate, 12" d., footed, Colony patt., clear 125
Plate, torte, 13" d., Colony patt., clear 28
Plate, torte, 13 1/2" oval, American patt.,
clear 45
Plate, torte, 14" d., American patt., clear 55
Plate, torte, 14" d., Century patt., clear 30
Plate, torte, 14" d., Holly cutting, clear 38
Plate, torte, 15" d., Colony patt., clear 60
Plate, dinner, Chintz etching, clear 75
Plate, Holly cutting, clear 8
Plate, Meadow Rose etching, clear 12
Plate, salad, American Lady patt., cobalt
blue 15
Plate, sandwich, center handle, Colony
patt., clear 35
Platter, 10 1/2" l., American patt., clear 43
Platter, 12" l., American patt., clear 35
Pomade or rouge box, cov., American
patt., clear, 2" sq. 395

Puff box, cov., American patt., clear,
1 1/2" d. 725

Puff box, cov., American patt., clear,
2 1/2" d. 700

Puff box, cov., American patt., clear, 3" sq. 225

Puff box, cov., American patt., clear, 4 1/2"
sq. 1,400

Punch bowl, Tom & Jerry-type, pedestal
footed, American patt., clear, 12" d. 235

Punch cup, American patt., clear 8

Relish dish, boat-shaped, handled,
divided, American patt., clear, 12" l. 20

Relish dish, two-part, Chintz etching, clear 38

Relish dish, two-part, Colony patt., clear,
7 1/4" 16

Relish dish, two-part, Century patt., clear,
7 3/8" l. 16

Relish dish, three-part, American patt.,
clear, 9 1/2" l. 45

Relish dish, three-part, two-handled, Col-
ony patt., clear, 13" 24

Relish dish, three-part, Romance etching,
clear 35

Relish dish, four-part, rectangular, Ameri-
can patt., clear, 9" l.. 38

Relish dish, four-part, American patt.,
clear, 10" sq. 190

Ring holder, American patt., clear............. 650-700

Rose bowl, Baroque patt., topaz 50

Victoria Pattern Rose Bowl

Rose bowl, Victoria patt., clear w/satin fin-
ish (ILLUS.) **100-150**

Rose bowl, American patt., clear, 5" d.............. 35

Baroque Rose Bowl

Rose bowl, Baroque patt., blue (ILLUS.) **75-100**

Rose bowl Colony patt., footed, clear.............. 125

Salt dip w/spoon, American patt., clear, 2
pcs.. 20

Salt & pepper shakers Century patt.,
clear, pr. 20

Salt & pepper shakers Coin patt., ruby, pr........ 52

Salt & pepper shakers, Colony patt., clear,
3 5/8" h., pr... 15-20

Salt & pepper shakers, Coronet patt.,
footed, clear, pr. 15

Salt & pepper shakers, Mesa patt., No.
4186, ruby, pr. 28

Salt & pepper shakers, Navarre etching,
clear, 3 1/4" h., pr. 65

Salt shakers, individual, American patt.,
clear, 3" h., set of 3 37

Salver, Century patt., clear, 12 1/4" 36

Sauce boat & underplate, American patt.,
clear, 2 pcs... 55

Sherbet, American Lady patt., clear, 5 1/2
oz., 4 1/8" h. 12

Sherbet, American Lady patt., cobalt blue,
5 1/2 oz., 4 1/8" h. 60

Sherbet, American patt., footed, handled,
clear, 4 1/2 oz... 145

Sherbet, American patt., low, flared, clear,
5 oz., 3 1/4" h. 9

Sherbet, Century patt., clear, 5 1/2 oz.,
4 1/4" h. 13

Sherbet, Chintz etching, clear 21

Sherbet, Coin patt., clear, 5 1/8" h. 26

Sherbet, Jamestown patt., amber 9

Sherbet, Jamestown patt., blue, 6 1/2 oz.,
4 1/4" h. 17

Sherbet, Navarre patt., clear, 6 oz. 24

Shrimp bowl, American patt., clear,
12 1/4" 395

Spice box, cov., American patt., clear 900

Spooner, American patt., clear, 3 3/4" h. 62

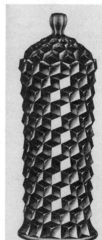

American Pattern Straw Jar

Straw jar, cov., American patt., clear
(ILLUS.).. 323

Sugar bowl, cov., American patt., clear,
5 1/4" h. 60

Sugar bowl, individual, Baroque patt.,
Topaz 16

Sugar bowl, individual, Colony patt., clear.......... 6

Sugar bowl, individual, Century patt.,
clear, 3 3/8" h. 9

Sugar bowl, American patt., clear, medium......... 9

Sugar bowl, American patt., hexagonal
foot, clear 800

Sugar bowl, Chintz etching, clear...................... 20

Sugar shaker, American patt., clear, tall 235

Sundae, American patt., clear, 6 oz.,
3 1/8" h. 9

Syrup pitcher, cov., American patt., clear,
5 1/4" h. 120

Toothpick holder, American patt., clear............ 24

Toothpick holder, Priscilla patt., No. 676,
clear 23

Tray, tidbit, Colony patt., clear w/patterned
top 85

Tray, tidbit, Colony patt., three-toed, clear,
7 1/2" 18

Tray, muffin, handled, Colony patt., clear,
8 3/8" 45

Tray, snack, Colony patt., clear, 10 1/2"............. 40

Tray, center-handled, Chintz etching, clear,
11" d. 40

Tray for creamer & sugar bowl, Colony
patt., clear 15

Trifle bowl, American patt., deep, clear.......... 395

Tumbler, Coin patt., ruby, 9 oz., 4 1/4" h. 105

Tumbler, Colony patt., clear, 4" h. 22

Tumbler, footed, American patt., clear, 9
oz., 4 3/8" h. 12

Tumbler, footed, Kashmir etching, green,
5" h. 42

Tumbler, footed, Line 4020, black foot,
clear bowl.. 32

American Pattern Iced Tea Tumbler

Tumbler, iced tea, American patt., clear, 12
oz., 5 3/4" h. (ILLUS.).................................... 22

Tumbler, iced tea, Coin patt., ruby,
5 1/2" h. 95

Tumbler, iced tea, footed, Colony patt.,
clear, 12 oz., 5 1/2" h. 22

Tumbler, iced tea, footed, Holly cutting,
clear, 12 oz., 6" h. 18

Tumbler, iced tea, footed, Jamestown
patt., blue 21

Tumbler, iced tea, June etching, Topaz 58

Tumbler, Jamestown patt., amber, 12 oz.,
5 1/8" 16

Tumbler, Jamestown patt., amber, 9 oz.,
4 1/4" h. 6

Tumbler, Jamestown patt., green, 5 1/4" h. 28

Tumbler, juice, footed, American Lady
patt., clear, 5 oz., 4 1/8" h. 14

Tumbler, juice, footed, American Lady
patt., cobalt blue, 5 oz., 4 1/8" h.................... 65

Tumbler, juice, footed, Jamestown patt.,
blue 20

Tumbler, juice, footed, Jamestown patt.,
smoke, 5 oz., 4 3/4" h.................................... 10

Tumbler, juice, Jamestown patt., ruby,
4 3/4" h. 22

Tumbler, juice, Mayflower etching, clear,
4 7/8" h. 19

Tumbler, whiskey, American patt., clear, 2
oz., 2 1/2" h. 10

Urn, cov., Colony patt., clear w/patterned
base 85

Vase, sweet pea, 4 1/2" h., American patt.,
clear 75

Navarre Etched Vase

Vase, 5" h., Navarre etching, No. 4128,
clear (ILLUS.) 125

Vase, 6" h., American patt., aqua 150

Vase, 6" h., American patt., peach 150

Vase, 6" h., handled, Coronet patt., clear.......... 45

Vase, bud, 6" d., Colony patt., clear 12

Vase, 6 1/2" h., footed, American patt.,
amber 80

Vase, 7" h., footed, cupped, Colony patt.,
clear 45

Vase, 7 1/2" h., handled, Century patt.,
clear 75

Vase, 9 1/2" h., flared rim, American patt.,
clear 175

Vase, 10" h., cupped-in top, American patt.,
clear 250

Vase, 10" h., straight sides, American patt.,
clear 80
Vase, 12" h., Colony patt., clear 275
Vase, 12" h., straight sides, American patt.,
clear 150
Vase, 13" h., Lotus patt., amber 220
Vase, 14" h., Colony patt., clear 550
Vase, 18" h., Heirloom patt. No. 5056, blue
opalescent 74
Vase, bud, Coin patt., clear 32
Vase, bud, Coin patt., ruby 38
Vase, Coin patt., clear 34
Vegetable bowl, Century patt., clear,
9 1/2" oval 25
Water bottle, American patt., clear,
9 1/4" h., 44 oz. 800
Water carafe, Carmen patt., ca. 1900,
clear 95
Water set: pitcher w/ice lip & six flared tum-
blers; American patt., clear, 7 pcs. 100
Wedding bowl, American patt., clear, large.. 1,000
Wine, American Lady patt., clear, 2 1/2 oz........ 28
Wine, American patt., clear, 2 1/2 oz.,
4 3/8" h. 12
Wine, Century patt., clear................................... 27
Wine, Century patt., clear, 3 1/2 oz.,
4 1/2" h. 24
Wine, Chintz etching, clear................................ 44
Wine, Colonial Dame patt., green bowl,
clear foot & stem, 4 3/4" h. 36
Wine, Jamestown patt., amber, 4 oz., 4
5/16" h. 8
Wine, Jamestown patt., green, 4 5/16" h., 4
oz. 20
Wine, Jamestown patt., pink, 4 5/16", 4 oz. 20
Wine, June etching, pink, 5 3/8" h. 112
Wine, Navarre etching, clear, 6 1/2" h. 90
Wine, Navarre etching, clear, 7 1/4" h. 150
Wine, Navarre etching, pink, 6 1/2" h. 82
Wine, Romance etching, clear, 3 oz.................. 35
Wine, Sunray patt., clear, 4 7/8" h. 32

FRY

Numerous types of glass were made by the H.C. Fry Company, Rochester, Pennsylvania. One of its art lines was called Foval and was blown in 1926-27. Cheaper was its milky-opalescent ovenware (Pearl Oven Ware) made for utilitarian purposes but also now being collected. The company also made fine cut glass.

Collectors of Fry Glass will be interested in the recent publication of a good reference book, The Collector's Encyclopedia of Fry Glassware, by The H.C. Fry Glass Society (Collector Books, 1990).

Fry Foval Beverage Set

Beverage set: 10 1/2" h. jug-form pitcher,
6 1/2" h. spherical cov. teapot & six

4 1/2" h. conical tumblers; Foval, each in
a white body decorated around the body
w/a slender silver overlay scroll & vine
design, applied jade green handle on
pitcher & teapot, also teapot spout &
feet, one tumbler w/overlay loss, nicks to
teapot cover, the set (ILLUS.) **$1,380**
Cruet w/original stopper, Foval, milky
white w/a Delft blue stopper & applied
handle, 9 3/4" h. 110
Pitcher, cov., 11" h., water, Foval, milky
white w/Delft blue finial & applied han-
dle, early 20th c.. 187
Vase, 12" h., cylindrical, Pearl art line,
pulled loopings, pink..................................... 375

GREENTOWN

Greentown glass was made in Greentown, Indiana, by the Indiana Tumbler & Goblet Co. from 1894 until 1903. In addition to its famed Chocolate and Holly Amber glass, it produced other types of clear and colored glass. Miscellaneous pieces are listed here. Also see PATTERN GLASS.

Animal covered dish, Cat on Hamper,
amber **$465**
Animal covered dish, Cat on Hamper,
blue 465

Rare Fighting Cocks Animal Dish

Animal covered dish, Fighting Cocks,
green (ILLUS.).. 1,750

Greentown Amber Hen on Nest Dish

Animal covered dish, Hen on Nest, amber
(ILLUS.)... 200
Animal covered dish, Hen on Nest, blue........ 265

Herringbone Buttress Berry Bowl

Bowl, master berry, Herringbone Buttress patt., amber (ILLUS.).................................... **400**

Butter dish, cov., Leaf Bracket patt., clear **145**

Cord Drapery Amber Compote

Compote, open, ruffled rim, Cord Drapery patt., amber (ILLUS.).................................... **450**

Green Austrian Pattern Creamer

Creamer, Austrian patt., dark emerald green, 4" h. (ILLUS.) **225**

Herringbone Buttress Creamer

Creamer, Herringbone Buttress patt., green w/gold trim (ILLUS.) **275**

Herringbone Buttress Green Cruet

Cruet w/original stopper, Herringbone Buttress patt., green (ILLUS.) **550**

Cruet w/original stopper, Leaf Bracket patt., clear **285**

Blue Dewey Pattern Mug

Mug, Dewey patt., blue (ILLUS.) **325**

Greentown Amber Corn Vase

Novelty, Corn vase, amber (ILLUS.)............... **125**

Greentown Buffalo Paperweight

Paperweight, figural, Buffalo, opaque Nile
Green (ILLUS.).. **1,250**
Pitcher, Squirrel patt., clear **170**

Austrian Pitcher in Canary

Pitcher, water, Austrian patt., canary
(ILLUS.).. **650**

Brazen Shield Pitcher & Tumbler

Pitcher, water, Brazen Shield patt., blue
(ILLUS. right).. **250**

Dewey Green Pitcher with Gold Trim

Pitcher, water, Dewey patt., emerald green
w/gold decoration (ILLUS.)........................... **275**

Dewey Pattern Green Salt Shaker

Salt shaker w/metal lid, Dewey patt.,
emerald green (ILLUS.).................................. **85**

Cord Drapery Salt Shaker

Salt shaker w/metal top, Cord Drapery
patt., amber (ILLUS.)..................................... **275**

Herringbone Buttress Green Spooner

Spooner, Herringbone Buttress patt.,
green w/gold trim (ILLUS.) **250**

Opaque White Cord Drapery Sugar

Sugar bowl, cov., Cord Drapery patt.,
opaque white (ILLUS.) **500**

Toothpick holder, figural Sheaf of Wheat
patt., Nile Green **605**
Tumbler, Brazen Shield patt., blue (ILLUS.
left w/pitcher).. **45**

Herringbone Buttress Green Tumbler

Tumbler, Herringbone Buttress patt., green
(ILLUS.).. **240**

Cord Drapery Handled Tumbler

Tumbler w/applied handle, Cord Drapery
patt., blue (ILLUS.) **650**

Herringbone Buttress Amber Wine

Wine, Herringbone Buttress patt., amber
(ILLUS.).. **450**

HEISEY

Numerous types of fine glass were made by A.H. Heisey & Co., Newark, Ohio, from 1895. The company's trademark, an H enclosed within a diamond, has become known to most glass collectors. The company's name and molds were acquired by Imperial Glass Co., Bellaire, Ohio, in 1958, and some pieces have been reissued. The glass listed below consists of miscellaneous pieces and types. Also see ANIMALS and PATTERN GLASS.

Heisey Diamond "H" Mark

Ashtray, Mahabar patt., clear, 3" sq. $12
Basket, Lariat patt., footed, clear, 10" 225
Bowl, cream soup, two-handled, Yeoman patt., Sahara (yellow) 25
Bowl, 6" d., Empress patt., Sahara 35
Bowl, jelly, 6 1/2" d., footed, Orchid etching, clear... 62
Bowl, 8" d., Rococo patt., clear.......................... 85
Bowl, 8" d., Twist patt., nasturtium-type, Moongleam (light green) 109
Bowl, 9" d., Twist patt., floral-type, Moongleam (green).................................... 69
Bowl, gardenia, 9" d., Queen Ann patt., Orchid etching, clear 60
Bowl, 10" d., Orchid etching, crimped rim, Queen Anne blank, clear............................. 68
Bowl, 11" d., Minuet etching, floral-type, clear 95
Bowl, 11" d., New Era patt., floral-style, clear 85

Ridgeleigh Floral Bowl

Bowl, 11 1/2" d., Ridgeleigh patt., floral-type, clear (ILLUS.) 30-40
Bowl, 13" d., Rose etching, shallow floral-type, clear.. 88
Bowl, 13" l., Ipswich patt., oval, floral-type, clear 36
Butter dish, cov., Orchid etching, clear 145
Butter dish, cov., Rose etching, clear 145
Butter dish, cov., square, Orchid etching, clear 235
Butter dish, cov., Rose etching, clear, cabachon, 1/4 lb... 375
Cake plate, Rose etching, footed, clear, 15" d... 325
Candleholder, Queen Ann patt., No. 1509, dolphin-footed, clear..................................... 45

Candlesticks, one-light, Orchid etching, clear, 3" h., pr.. 50
Candlesticks, Pluto patt., No. 114, Moongleam, 3 1/2" h., pr........................... 60
Candlesticks, two-light, Empress patt., No. 301, amber arms, pr..................................... 485
Candlesticks two-light, Lariat patt., clear, pr. 70
Candlesticks two-light, Lariat patt. w/Moonglo cutting clear, pr. 80
Candlesticks, two-light, Waverly patt., Orchid etching, clear, pr. 120
Candlesticks, three-light, Empress patt., No. 301, Sahara w/clear bobeches, pr. 950
Candlesticks, three-light, Rose etching, clear, pr. 300
Candy box, cov., Stanhope patt., round, clear w/black knob stem on round foot........ 350
Candy dish, cov., Lariat patt., caramel 75
Candy dish, cov., Orchid etching, clear, tall w/seahorse stem 250
Candy dish, cov., Plantation patt., footed, tall, clear, 8" h. 185
Candy dish, cov., Rose etching, clear, tall, seahorse stem.. 250
Candy dish, cov., Plantation patt., clear, 5" h. 195
Catsup bottle w/stopper, Old Sandwich patt., clear 70
Celery dish, Plantation patt., clear, 13" l........... 50
Celery tray, Empress patt., Sahara 35
Celery tray, Rose etching, Waverly blank, clear, 12" l.. 48
Celery tray, New Era patt., clear, 13" l............. 35
Celery vase, Fandango patt., clear.................... 85
Champagne, Lariat patt., clear........................... 12
Champagne, saucer-type, Albermarle patt., clear 25
Champagne, saucer-type, Carcassone patt., clear stem w/Sahara bowl, 6 oz. 35
Champagne, saucer-type, Minuet etching, No. 5010, clear, 6 oz................................. 30
Champagne, saucer-type, Old Dominion patt., Empress etching, clear stem w/Marigold bowl 20
Champagne, saucer-type, Orchid etching, clear, 6 oz...................................... 31
Champagne, saucer-type, Pied Piper etching, clear... 28
Cheese dish, cov., Lariat patt., footed, clear, 5" d. 45
Cigarette box, cov., Lariat patt., clear............... 48
Cigarette holder, square, footed, Orchid etching, clear... 132
Claret, New Era patt., clear, 4 oz. 22
Coaster, Lariat patt., clear 12
Coaster, Plantation patt., clear, 4" d. 50
Cocktail, Carcassone patt., clear stem w/Sahara bowl, 3 oz.................................. 35
Cocktail, figural rooster stem, clear 40
Cocktail, figural sea horse stem, clear............. 148
Cocktail, Lariat patt. w/Moonglo cutting, clear 25
Cocktail, Minuet etching, No. 5010, clear, 3 1/2 oz. 35
Cocktail, New Era patt., high stem, clear, 3 1/2 oz. 18
Cocktail, Orchid etching, clear, 4 oz. 44

Cocktail, Orchid etching, No. 5025, clear, 4 oz. 36

Cocktail, Rosalie etching, Kenilworth (No. 4092) blank, clear, 3 oz. 10

Cocktail, saucer-type, Old Dominion patt., Empress etching, clear stem w/Marigold bowl 20

Cocktail, Stanhope patt., clear, 3 1/2 oz. 35

Cocktail icer w/insert, Orchid etching, clear 275

Cocktail shaker, cov., Orchid etching, No. 4225, clear, 1 pt. 295

Compote, 6" h., Waverly patt., Orchid etching, clear 50

Compote, 6 1/2" d., Rose etching, Waverly blank, low footed, clear 53

Compote, 7" h., Empress patt., oval, Sahara 110

Compote, 7" h., oval, Rose etching, clear 158

Compote, 7" h., Twist patt., Flamingo (pink) 65

Compote, Charter Oak etching, pink 65

Compote, Orchid etching, low, footed, clear 50

Cordial, New Era patt., clear, 1 oz. 45

Cordial, Rose etching, clear, 1 oz. 138

Cordial, Chintz patt., No. 3389, clear, 1 oz. 120

Cornucopia-vase, Warwick patt., cobalt blue, signed, 5 1/2" h 125

Creamer, Empress patt., dolphin-footed, Sahara 40

Creamer, Empress patt., pink 50

Creamer, miniature, Sawtooth Band patt., floral etching, ca. 1900 55

Creamer, Ridgeleigh patt., clear 30

Creamer, individual size, Ridgeleigh patt., clear 20

Creamer & open sugar bowl, Plantation patt., footed, clear, pr. 72

Creamer & open sugar bowl, individual size, Rose etching, clear, pr. 90

Creamer & sugar bowl, individual, Empress patt., oval, Sahara, pr. 70

Cruet, Lariat patt., oil, clear, 6 oz. 75

Heisey Twist Pattern Cruet

Cruet w/original stopper, Twist patt., Moongleam (ILLUS.) 79

Cruet w/stopper, Orchid etching, footed, 3 oz. 200

Cruet w/stopper, Rose etching, clear 225

Cup, Old Sandwich patt., pink 60

Cup, Waverly patt., clear 12

Cup & saucer, Crystolite patt., clear 24

Cup & saucer, Empress patt., Sahara 32

Cup & saucer, New Era patt., clear 65

Cup & saucer, Orchid etching, footed, clear 40

Cup & saucer, Rose etching, clear 90

Cup & saucer, Waverly patt., clear 20

Decanter w/sterling stopper, sherry, Orchid etching, clear 270

Decanter w/stopper, Old Sandwich patt., cobalt blue, No. 98, 1 pt. 550

Decanter w/stopper, sherry, oval, Orchid etching, clear 360

Decanters w/stoppers, Ridgeleigh patt., clear, 1 pt., pr. 325

Goblet, Albemarle patt., clear 30

Goblet, Carcassone patt., clear stem w/Sahara bowl, 11 oz. 50

Goblet, Carcassone patt., clear stem w/Sahara bowl, 11 oz., short 45

Goblet, Empress patt., Sahara, 9 oz. 65

Goblet, Graceful patt., No. 5022, clear 40

Goblet, Lariat patt., blown, clear, 10 oz. 22

Goblet, Lariat patt. w/Moonglo cutting, clear, 10 oz. 27

Goblet, Minuet etching, clear 45

Goblet, Old Dominion patt., Marigold (dark yellow), 8 3/4" h. 55

Goblet, Orchid etching, clear, tall, 10 oz. 50

Goblet, Orchid etching, low stem, No. 5025, clear, 10 oz. 44

Goblet, Rose etching, clear, 9 oz. 42

Goblet, Twist patt., Flamingo, 9 oz. 39

Goblet, Victorian patt., two-ball stem, clear 26

Goblets, Victorian patt., clear, 9 oz., set of 8 110

Ice tub, Twist patt., Moongleam 95

Jelly dish, Plantation patt., Ivy etching, two-handled, 6 1/2" h. 63

Lemon dish, cov., Yeoman patt., round, Moongleam, 5" d. 45

Mayonnaise set, Rose etching, clear, 3 pcs. 135

Mustard jar, cover & spoon, Empress patt., Sahara 90

Nut dish, Empress patt., footed, Sahara 30

Nut dish or ashtray, New Era patt., individual size, clear 60

Oil cruet w/original stopper, Victorian patt., clear, 3 oz. 68

Oyster cocktail, Ipswich patt., footed, clear 22

Parfait, Yeoman patt., clear 9

Pilsner glass, New Era patt., clear, 12 oz. 60

Pitcher, Orchid etching, Donna blank (No. 3484), clear, 1/2 gal. 625

Pitcher, Plantation patt., blown, w/ice lip, clear, 1/2 gal. 450

Pitcher, Rose etching, clear, 76 oz. 660

Heisey Puritan Pitcher

Pitcher, water, Puritan patt., clear, 3 qt.
(ILLUS.).. **125-150**
Pitcher, Orchid etching, clear.......................... **535**
Plate, 4 3/4" d., Colonial patt., clear **5**
Plate, 6" d., Empress patt., round, Sahara **14**
Plate, 6" w., New Era patt., clear...................... **35**
Plate, 7" d., Crystolite patt., two-handled,
clear **20**
Plate, 7" d.., Empress patt., Moongleam **175**
Plate, 7" d.., Empress patt., Sahara **15**
Plate, 7" d.., Empress patt., Tangerine.............. **165**
Plate, salad, 7" d., Crystolite patt., clear............. **15**
Plate, salad, 7" d., Orchid etching, clear **21**
Plate, 7 1/2" d., Empress patt., Alexandrite........ **90**
Plate, 8" d., Fandango patt., clear...................... **45**
Plate, 8" d., Minuet etching, luncheon, clear....... **21**
Plate, 8" sq.., Empress patt., Sahara **22**
Plate, salad, 8" d., Empress patt., Sahara.......... **18**
Plate, torte, 14" d., Waverly patt., Rose
etching, clear **79**
Plate, Acorn patt., dinner, clear **59**
Plate, dinner, Lariat patt., clear **115**
Plate, dinner, Rose etching, clear **395**
Plate, Orchid etching, center-handled, clear..... **135**
Platter, dinner, Orchid etching, clear................ **235**
Punch bowl, Ridgeleigh patt., clear, 11" d....... **169**
Punch cup, Lariat patt., clear **8**
Punch cup, Locket & Chain patt., ca. 1900,
clear **35**
Punch set: 9 qt. Dr. Johnson punch bowl,
six cups & ladle; Plantation patt., clear, 8
pcs.. **1,100**
Punch set: 14" d. punch bowl, 21" d.
underplate, six punch cups & ladle; Lar-
iat patt., clear, 9 pcs. **190**
Punch set: 14" d. punch bowl, 21" d.
underplate & eight punch cups; Lariat
patt., original hooks, clear, 10 pcs............... **225**
Relish dish, three-part, New Era patt.,
clear, 13" l.. **40**
Relish dish, three-part, Orchid etching,
Waverly blank, clear, 11" l............................. **65**
Relish dish, three-part, Plantation patt.,
clear, 11" l.. **67**
Relish dish, three-part, Rose etching, oval,
clear, 11" l. **80**
Relish dish, three-part, Lariat patt., clear,
12".. **28**
Relish dish, three-part, Crystolite patt.,
clear, 9 1/2" **29**

Relish dish, four-part, Rose etching,
Waverly blank, round, clear, 9" d. **70**
Relish dish, four-part, Plantation patt.,
clear, 8" l. **70**
Relish tray, three-part, Crystolite patt.,
clear, 12" l. **32**
Rose bowl, Mermaid etching, clear, 5" d. **500**

Heisey Pillows Rose Bowl

Rose bowl, pedestal foot, Pillows patt.
(No. 325), clear (ILLUS.) **225-250**
Salt dip, Fandango patt., No. 1201, clear **22**
Salt & pepper shakers, Orchid etching,
clear, pr. **85**
Salt & pepper shakers, Rose etching,
clear, pr. **120**
Sandwich server, Rose etching, Waverly
blank, center-handled, clear, 14" d. **175**
Sherbet, Carcassone patt., clear stem
w/Sahara bowl, 6 oz. **40**
Sherbet, Colonial patt., clear............................. **10**
Sherbet, Lariat patt., blown, clear, 5 oz............. **14**
Sherbet, Lariat patt. w/Moonglo cutting,
clear **20**
Sherbet Old Dominion patt., Empress etch-
ing, clear stem w/Marigold bowl, low............. **18**
Sherbet, Orchid etching, No. 5025, clear.......... **22**
Sherbet, Pied Piper etching, clear..................... **25**
Sherbet, Rose etching, clear, 6 oz. **22**
Sherbet, Victorian patt., two-ball stem,
clear **15**
Spooner, Greek Key patt., clear, large.............. **89**
Stem, Saturn patt., Zircon (blue green), 10
oz. **125**
Sugar bowl, Empress patt., dolphin-footed,
Sahara.. **40**
Sugar bowl, Lariat patt., clear........................... **20**
Syrup bottle w/top, Plantation patt., clear....... **150**
Toothpick holder, Continental patt., clear....... **125**
Toothpick holder, Pineapple & Fan patt.,
green **185**
Tray, Ridgeleigh patt., oval, clear, 10 1/2" l........ **39**
Tumbler, iced tea, Lariat patt., Moonglo
cutting, footed, clear, 12 oz. **32**
Tumbler, iced tea, Minuet etching, No.
5010, 12 oz. **60**

Tumbler, iced tea, Orchid etching, clear, 12 oz. 64

Tumbler, iced tea, Orchid etching, No. 5025, clear, 9 1/2 oz. 60

Tumbler, iced tea, Twentieth Century patt., Dawn 60

Tumbler, juice, Carcassone patt., clear stem w/Sahara bowl, 5 oz. 40

Tumbler, juice, Ipswich patt., Sahara 42

Tumbler, juice, Plantation patt., footed pressed, clear, 5 oz. 50

Tumbler, juice, Provincial patt., footed, clear, 5 oz. 11

Tumbler, juice, Twist patt., footed, Fla-mingo, 5 oz. 29

Tumbler, soda, Ipswich patt., clear, 5 oz. 30

Tumbler, soda, Ipswich patt., clear, 8 oz. 30

Tumbler, toddy, Old Sandwich patt., clear, 6 1/2 oz. 9

Tumbler, water, Ipswich patt., Sahara 52

Tumbler, Arch patt., cobalt blue 100

Tumbler, Duquesne patt., Tangerine, 5 1/4" h. 155

Tumbler, Greek Key patt., flat, clear, 10 oz. 99

Tumbler, Provincial patt., footed, clear, 8 oz. 15

Tumbler, Saturn patt., flat bottom, Zircon, 10 oz. 75

Tumblers, iced tea, Lariat patt., Moonglo etching, blown, footed, 12 oz., set of six 195

Vase, 4" h., Ivy etching, No. 4224, clear.......... 275

Vase, 7" h., Lariat patt., footed, clear 45

Vase, 7" h., Warwick patt., Sahara 95

Violet vase, Orchid etching, clear, 4" h............ 145

Wine, Albermarle patt., clear, 2 1/2 oz. 20

Wine, Orchid etching, No. 5025, clear, 3 oz. 70

Wine, pressed Lariat patt., clear, 3 1/2 oz. 20

HISTORICAL & COMMEMORATIVE

Reference numbers are to Bessie M. Lindsey's book, American Historical Glass.

Barry plate, center scene of St. Bernard dog, frosted center, No. 523, 10" d. $125

Admiral Dewey Pitcher

Dewey (Admiral) pitcher, bust portrait of Dewey & flagship Olympia reverse, w/mounted cannons, crossed rifles, U.S. & Cuban flags & stacks of cannon balls toward base, clear, 9 1/2" h., No. 400 (ILLUS.) 75

Dewey (Admiral) plate, bust portrait of Dewey, clear, 5 1/2" d., No. 392 15

Egyptian pattern bread tray, Cleopatra center, inscribed w/daily bread motto, clear, 8 1/2 x 13 1/4", No. 504 80

Garfield Drape pitcher, clear w/applied handle, three swags around the body of floral & foliage festoons against a lightly stippled ground, clear, 8 3/4" h., No. 305 135

Garfield Drape plate, 11 1/4" d., center portrait bust of Garfield surrounded by a circle of stars & inscribed "We Mourn our Nation's Loss....," Garfield Drape border, scalloped rim, clear 75

Liberty Bell Signer's platter, clear, 9 1/2 x 13", No. 42 125

Lincoln Drape with Tassel Pattern gob-let, clear, 6" h., No. 280 135

Lincoln - Garfield Martyr's Mug

Martyr's mug, Lincoln & Garfield bust por-traits & inscription, clear, 2 5/8" h., No. 272 (ILLUS.) 295

McCormick Reaper platter, clear, 8 x 13", No. 119 145

Old Statehouse tray, shows Indepen-dence Hall above "Old Statehouse, Phil-adelphia, Erected 1735," clear, round, No. 32 55

Pluck series bread tray, Dog Cart Over-turned, Gillinder, clear 110

Pluck series bread tray, Dog Chasing Rabbit scene, Gillinder, clear 110

Pluck series bread tray, Dog Chasing Rabbit scene, Gillinder, frosted center 110

Rock of Ages bread tray, clear w/milk white center, No. 236 350

Three Graces plate, "Faith, Hope & Char-ity," clear, 10" d., No. 230 135

IMPERIAL

From 1902 until 1984 Imperial Glass of Bellaire, Ohio produced hand made glass. Early pressed glass production often imitated cut glass and may bear the raised "NUCUT" mark in the interior cen-ter. In the second decade of the 1900s Imperial was one of the dominate manufacturers of iridescent or Carnival glass. When glass collecting gained popu-larity in the 1970s, Imperial again produced Carni-val and a line of multicolored slag glass. Imperial purchased molds from closing glass houses and continued many lines popularized by others includ-ing Central, Heisey and Cambridge. These reis-

sues may cause confusion but they were often marked.

Imperial Nucut Mark   Later Imperial Marks

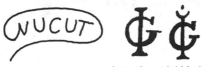

Early Imperial Cross Mark

CANDLEWICK

Ashtray, heart-shaped, clear, 4" $10
Ashtray, clear, No. 400/133, 5" d.........................8
Ashtray, No. 400/60, clear, 6"............................ 150
Ashtray, w/embossed eagle center, No. 1776/1, clear, 6 1/2" 70
Ashtray, No. 400/118, clear.............................. 12
Ashtray set, nested, round, No. 400/450, clear, 3 pcs...................................... 50
Baked apple dish, No. 400/53X, blue, 6 1/2"...................................... 85
Baked apple dish, No. 400/53X, clear, 6 1/2"...................................... 25
Basket, No. 400/40/0, clear, 6 1/2" h. 36
Basket, No. 400/40/0, clear w/gold beads, 6 1/2" h. 60
Basket, No. 400/73/0, clear, 11" 255

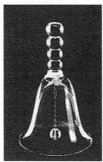

Candlewick Bell

Bell, No. 400/108, clear, 5" h. (ILLUS.) 59
Bonbon, heart-shaped, handled, clear, 5" 24
Bonbon bowl, handled, No. 400/40H, clear, 5"...................................... 25
Bonbon bowl, handled, No. 400/51H, clear, 6"...................................... 36
Bonbon bowl, heart-shaped, No. 400/174, clear, 6 1/2"...................................... 22
Bowl, 5", heart-shaped, clear............................ 18
Bowl, 5", heart-shaped, No. 400/49H, clear..... 175
Bowl, 5" sq., No. 400/231, clear....................... 150
Bowl, 5 1/2", heart-shaped, No. 500/53H, clear 45
Bowl, cream soup, 5 1/2" d., No. 400/50, clear 50
Bowl, 6" d., clear, No. 400/3F 12
Bowl, 6" h., No. 400/182, three-toed, clear 73

Bowl, 7" sq., No. 400/233, clear...................... 160
Bowl, 8-8 1/2" d., No. 400/74B, clear.............. 110
Bowl, 8-8 1/2" d., No. 400/74B, ruby............... 450
Bowl, 8 1/2" d., handled, No. 400/72B, clear 39
Bowl, 8 1/2" d., No. 400/69, clear w/cutting 55
Bowl, 9" sq., No. 400/74SC, four-toed, crimped, ribbed, black w/flower.................... 550
Bowl, 9-10", heart-shaped, No. 400/73H, clear 55
Bowl, 10" d., fruit, footed, No. 400/103C, clear 229
Bowl, 10-11", No. 400/75F, float-type, clear....... 45
Bowl, salad, 10" d., No. 400/75B, clear............. 50
Bowl, 10 1/2" d., bell-shaped, No. 400/63B, clear 55
Bowl, 10 1/2" d., No. 400/63B, clear 55
Bowl, 11" l, oval, divided, No. 400/125A, clear 550
Bowl w/underplate, 8" d., two-handled w/10" underplate, bowl No. 400/4272B, underplate No. 400/4272D, clear, the set....... 55
Butter dish, cov., No. 400/144, clear, 5 1/2" d. 30
Butter dish, cov., No. 400/276, clear.............. 140
Butter dish, cov., round, clear 64

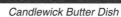

Candlewick Butter Dish

Butter dish, cov., w/beaded top, No. 400/161, clear, 1/4 lb. (ILLUS.) 33
Butter & jam dish, No. 400/262, three-part, clear, 10 1/2"...................................... 193
Cake plate, 71 birthday candle holes, clear, 13"...................................... 340
Cake plate, No. 400/160, clear w/swirl center, 72 candle holes in rim, 13-14" d............ 390
Cake plate, two-handled, clear, 13" d. 75
Cake stand, No. 400/67D, low-footed, clear, 10" d. 68
Canape set, plate No. 400/36 & 3 1/2 oz. tumbler, No. 400/142, clear, 2 pcs. 60
Candle/flower holder, No. 400/40C, clear, 5" h. 47
Candleholders, No. 400/100, clear, pr. 55
Candleholders, No. 400/147, clear, pr. 72
Candleholders, No. 400/207, 4 1/2" h., clear, pr. 260
Candleholders, No. 400/79R, clear, pr.............. 27
Candleholders, No. 400/81, 3 1/2" h., clear, pr. 112
Candleholders, No. 400/86, clear, pr. 84
Candlestick, single light chamberstick w/handle, clear 52
Candlestick, single light, Eagle, clear............... 85
Candlestick, single light, mushroom form, clear 28
Candlestick, three-light, clear........................... 78
Candy box, cov., No. 400/59, clear, 5 1/2-6 1/2"...................................... 55
Candy box, cov., No. 400/260, clear, 7" 225

Candy box, cov., three-part, No. 400/110,
clear, 7" d. **172**
Candy dish, No. 400/51C, clear, 6" d. **65**
Celery tray, oval, handled, No. 400/105,
clear, 13 1/2" l. **42**
Center bowl, No. 100/13B, Viennese Blue,
11" d. **150**
Center bowl, No. 400/131B, oval, flat,
clear, 14" **450**
Champagne/sherbet, No. 3400, saucer-
type, clear, 6 oz. **17**
Cheese & cracker set, No. 400/88, clear,
10" d., 2 pc. **65**
Cigarette box, cov., clear, 3" **28**
Coaster, No. 400/78, clear, 4" d. **6**
Cocktail, No. 3400, clear, 4 oz. **16**
Compote, 4 1/2", clear **26**
Compote, 4 1/2" h., No. 400/63B, no bead
stem, clear. **32**
Compote, 5" h., No. 400/220, clear.................. **145**
Compote, 5 1/2" h., No. 400/66B, two-
bead stem, clear... **30**

Imperial Compote with Rose Decoration

Compote, 10" h., crimped, three-bead
stem, No. 400/103F, clear w/h.p. pink
roses & blue ribbons (ILLUS.) **260-400**
Compote, 10" h., fruit, No. 400/103C, clear **275**
Compote, 10" h., No. 400/103F, clear
w/sterling silver base.................................... **325**
Compote, 10 1/2" h., No. 400/63B, clear **33**
Console bowl, three-toed, No. 400/205,
clear, 10" l. **33**
Cordial, No. 3400, clear, 1 oz. **48**
Cordial, ruby, 4 1/2" h. **95**
Cordial decanter, applied handle, No.
400/82, clear etched (top chip).................... **495**
Creamer, clear **16**
Creamer, individual, No. 400/96, clear............... **7**
Creamer & sugar bowl, beaded handle,
No. 400/30, clear, pr...................................... **15**
Creamer & sugar bowl, individual, No.
400/122, clear, pr.. **21**
Creamer, sugar bowl & undertray, clear,
the set **42**
Cruet w/original stopper, handled, clear......... **48**
Cruet w/original stopper, No. 400/119,
clear **25**
Cruet w/original stopper, No. 400/275,
clear, 6 oz.. **75**

Cruet w/original stopper, No. 400/278,
handled, clear, 4 oz...................................... **95**
Cruet w/original stopper, No. 500/121/O,
clear **75**
Cup, coffee, No. 400/37, clear............................ **8**
Cup, tea, No. 400/35, clear **8**
Cup & saucer, demitasse, No. 400/77AD,
clear **30**
Cup & saucer, No. 400/35, clear **13**
Cup & saucer, No. 400/37, clear **14**
Decanter   w/original   stopper,   No.
400/163, clear, 26 oz.................................... **875**
Epergne set, No. 400/196, clear, 2 pc. **295**
Goblet, cocktail, No. 400/190, clear, 3 1/2-
4 oz. **19**
Goblet, No. 3400, water, black, 7 1/2" h. **200**
Goblet, No. 3400, water, clear, 7 1/2" h. **22**
Goblet, No. 3400, water, ruby, 7 1/2" h.. .... **118**
Goblet, No. 3400, wine, clear, 4 oz. **28**
Goblet, No. 400/19, clear, 4 3/4 h. **14**
Goblet, No. 400/190, water, clear, 10 oz........... **25**
Gravy boat, No. 100/169, clear....................... **185**
Honey dish, clear, 4 3/4" **119**
Hurricane candle lamp, No. 400/79, clear,
2 pcs... **165**
Ice tub, No. 400/168, tab-handled, clear, 7"..... **173**
Icer, No. 400/53C, clear, 6" **75**
Icer & liner, No. 400/53, clear......................... **135**
Jelly/ashtray, No. 400/33, clear, 4" **14**
Knife, No. 4000, clear **550**
Marmalade set, No. 400/8918, clear, 3
pcs... **110**
Mayonnaise bowl & underplate, No.
400/23, clear, 2 pcs. **34**
Mayonnaise set: divided bowl & under-
plate; No. 400/84, clear, 2 pcs. **80**
Mint bowl, ring-handled, No. 400/51F,
clear, 6" **28**
Mustard jar, cov., footed, No. 400/156,
clear **26**
Mustard jar, cover & spoon, clear, 3 pcs. **58**
Nappy, fruit, No. 400/1F, blue, 5" **45**
Nappy, handled, No. 400/51, clear, 6" **16**
Pastry tray, No. 400/68D, clear, 11 1/2" d. **60-70**
Pickle/celery dish, No. 400/57, clear,
7 1/2".. **32**
Pitcher, juice/cocktail, No. 400/19, clear,
40 oz. **325**
Plate, 4 1/2" d., No. 400/34, clear...................... **9**
Plate, bread & butter, 6" d., two-handled,
No. 400/1D, clear **6**
Plate, canapé, 6" d., w/off-center indenta-
tion, No. 400/36, clear................................... **16**
Plate, 7" d., No. 400/52E, two-handled,
black... **375**
Plate, salad, 7" d., No. 400/3D, clear **9**
Plate, luncheon, 9" d., No. 400/7D, clear **15**
Plate, dinner, 10 1/2" d., No. 400/10D,
clear **44**
Plate, 11" d., No. 400/145D, two-handled,
clear **30**
Plate, torte, 12 1/2" d., cupped edge, No.
400/75V, clear **33**
Plate torte, 13", No. 400/75V, rolled edge,
clear **58**
Plate, 14" d., No. 400/92D, clear **35**
Plate, torte, 17" d., clear **34**
Plate, torte, 17" d., cupped edge, No.
400/20V, clear **72**

Platter, 16" l., oval, two-handled, No. 400/131D, clear 234

Punch set: 13" d. punch bowl, 17" d. cupped-edge underplate, 12 cups & ladle; No. 400/20, clear, 15 pcs 260

Punch set: punch bowl, ladle, underplate & 12 punch cups; clear, 15 pcs. 190

Relish dish No. 400/54, clear, 6 1/2" 20

Relish dish, two-part, handled, clear, 6 1/2" 12

Relish dish, two-part, No. 400/84, clear, 6 1/2" 22

Relish dish, two-part, No. 400/234, clear, 7" sq. 140

Relish dish, two-part, oval, No.400/268, clear, 8" l. 31

Relish dish, two-part, No. 400/52, clear 25

Relish dish, cov., three-part, rectangular, No. 400/216, clear, 10" l............................ 1,250

Relish dish, three-part, three-toed, No. 400/208, clear 127

Relish dish, four-part, No.400/112, clear, 10 1/2" l. 33

Relish tray, three-part, handled, No. 400/213, clear, 10" l. 74

Relish tray, five-part, No. 400/104, clear 65

Relish tray, five-part, five-handled, No. 400/56, clear, 10 1/2" l. 55

Relish tray, five-part, No. 3900/120, clear, 13" 65

Salad fork, No. 400/75, clear 15

Salad serving set, fork & spoon, No. 475, clear, 9 1/2" l., the set.............................. 46

Salt dip, No. 400/61, clear, 2" 12

Salt & pepper shakers, amethyst, pr. 110

Salt & pepper shakers, individual, No. 400/109, clear, pr. 20

Salt & pepper shakers w/chrome tops, No. 400/190, footed, clear, pr...................... 100

Candlewick No. 400/247 Shakers

Salt & pepper shakers w/chrome tops, No. 400/247, clear, pr. (ILLUS.) 45

Salt shaker w/chrome top, No. 400/96, clear 8

Seafood cocktail, No. 400/190, clear, 3 1/2-4 oz. 89

Sherbet, tall, No. 400/190, clear, 5 oz. 18

Sugar bowl, clear... 12

Tray, lemon, center-handled, No. 400/221, clear, 5 3/4" 42

Tray, mint, center-handled, No. 400/149D, clear, 9" d. 36

Tray, No. 400/159, clear, 9" l............................. 29

Tray, No. 400/72C, two-handled, crimped, clear, 10" 30

Tumbler, juice, No. 400/19, clear, 4" h., 5 oz. 6

Tumbler, flat, No. 400/19, clear, 5 1/2" h. 14

Tumbler, iced tea, footed, No. 400/19, clear, 6" h., 12 oz. 26

Tumbler, iced tea, No. 3400, clear, 6 1/2" h. 28

Tumbler, water, No. 400/19, clear, 10 oz.......... 15

Tumblers, iced tea, footed, No. 400/19, clear, 12 oz., set of 6.................................... 77

Vase, bud, 7" h., domed foot, No. 400/186, clear 450

Vase, 8" h., fan-shaped w/beaded handles, No. 400/87F, blue... 121

Vase, 8" h., fluted rim w/beaded handles, No. 400/87C, clear 44

Vase, 8 1/2" h., No. 400/21, flared rim, clear 413

Vase, Peachblow, cased heat sensitive red over white... 180

Vase, two open beaded arms, crimped top, clear 38

Vegetable bowl, No. 400/69B, clear w/cutting, 8 1/2" d. 55

Wine, No. 3400, clear, 4 oz. 16

CAPE COD

Ashtray, clear.. 10

Baked apple dish, clear, 5 3/4" 12

Bar bottle, clear 150

Basket, clear, 11" h. 195

Basket, No. 160/73/0, clear............................... 350

Book end, Lu-tung/Mandarin, No. 5030, jade 85

Bowl, spider, 4 1/2" d., handled, No. 160/180, clear 25

Bowl, 5" w., heart-shaped, No. 160/49H, clear 20

Bowl, spider, 6 1/2" d., divided, handled, No. 160/187, clear 32

Bowl, 8 1/2" d., low, clear.................................... 34

Bowl, 11" oval, clear.. 90

Butter dish, cov., clear, 1/4 lb............................ 42

Butter dish, cov., round, clear 52

Cake stand, No. 160/103D, clear, 11" d. 115

Cake stand, footed, clear, 12" d........................ 94

Candlestick, single light, clear, 3" h.................. 22

Candlestick, single light, clear, 5" h.................. 24

Candy jar, cov., bamboo handle, clear 74

Center bowl, No. 160/75L, ruffled edge, clear 65

Cigarette box, cov., clear.................................... 38

Cigarette lighter, stemmed, purple slag........... 40

Coaster, clear, 3" sq.. 10

Coaster, No. 160/78, clear 10

Cape Cod Cocktail

Cocktail, No. 1602, clear, 3 1/2 oz.
(ILLUS.) 10
Compote, 7" d., No. 160/48B, clear 28
Cookie jar, cov., clear 110
Cordial, clear, 3 3/4" h. 12
Cordial, No. 1602, milk white, 1 1/2 oz. 15
Creamer, clear, 3" sq. 38
Creamer, clear, 4 1/2" h. 10
Creamer & open sugar bowl, No. 160/30,
clear, pr. 24
Cruet w/original stopper, No. 160/119,
amber, 4 oz. 28
Cruet w/original stopper, No. 160/119,
Verde green, 4 oz. 45
Cruet w/original stopper, blown, No.
160/70, clear, 5 oz. 60
Cruet w/original stopper, No. 160/70,
clear, 5 oz. 27
Cruet w/original stopper, No. 160/241,
clear, 6 oz. 55
Cup & saucer, clear 12
Decanter w/original stopper, clear,
8 1/2" h. 124
Decanter w/original stopper, clear,
9 3/4" h. 89
Decanter w/original stopper, ruby-
stained, 9 3/4" h. 119
Decanter w/original stopper, clear, 13" h. 142
Decanter w/original stopper, No.
160/163, clear, 30 oz. 75
Decanter w/original stopper, square-
shaped, No. 160/212, clear, 24 oz. 80
Decanters w/original stoppers, square-
shaped, clear, in chrome rack w/lock, the
set 225
Egg cup, No. 160/225, clear 32
Epergne, bowl w/trumpet, clear 78
Goblet, water, clear, 5 1/2" h. 10
Goblet, water, pink, 6 1/4" h. 28
Goblet, water, amber, 6 1/2" h. 10
Goblet, water, clear, 6 1/2" h. 14
Goblet, magnum, No. 160, clear, 14 oz. 28
Goblet, water, No. 1600, clear, 10 oz. 15
Goblet, water, No. 1602, Verde green, 9
oz. 8
Lamp, hurricane-type, clear, 12" h. 96
Mayonnaise bowl, lader & underplate,
clear, 3 pcs. 36
Mug, clear, 4 3/4" h. 42
Mug, clear, 12 oz. 58
Mustard jar, cover & spoon, clear, 3 pcs. 22
Oyster cocktail, No. 1602, clear 9

Perfume bottle w/original stopper, round,
clear 48
Pitcher, 8 1/2" h., clear 94
Pitcher, 10" h., clear 240
Pitcher, milk, No. 160/240, clear, 16 oz. 50
Plate, 8 1/2" d., amber 8
Plate, 8 1/2" d., pink 19
Plate, 9" d., clear 26

Cape Cod Dinner Plate

Plate, dinner, 10" d., No. 160/10D, clear
(ILLUS.) 58
Plate, torte, 13 1/2" d., clear 32
Punch bowl & base, clear, 2 pcs. 125
Relish dish, three-part, oval, No. 160/55,
clear, 9 1/2" l. 18
Relish dish, three-part, No. 160/1602,
clear 150
Salad serving set, fork & spoon, clear,
9 1/2" l., the set 28
Salt dip, clear, 2 1/4" d. 16
Salt & pepper mill, amber, pr. 55
Salt & pepper shakers w/original tops,
individual, No. 160/251, clear, pr. 18
Salt & pepper shakers w/original tops,
individual, original factory label, No.
160/251, clear, pr. 25
Salt & pepper shakers w/original tops,
Verde green, pr. 40
**Salt & pepper shakers w/original tops &
undertray,** clear, the set 42
Sherbet, No. 1600, clear, 6 oz. 7
Sherbet, tall, No. 1602, Verde green, 6 oz. 15
Sugar bowl, clear, 4 1/4" h. 10
Tray, for creamer & sugar, No. 160/29,
clear, 7" l. 15
Tumbler, flat, clear, 3 3/4" h., 6 oz. 20
Tumbler, flat, clear, 6 1/2" h., 14 oz. 22
Tumbler, iced tea, flat, clear, 5 1/2" h. 18
Tumbler, iced tea, amber, 6" h. 12
Tumbler, iced tea, clear, 6" h. 16
Tumbler, iced tea, pink, 6" h. 34
Tumbler, juice, footed, No. 1602, clear, 6
oz. 12
Tumbler, juice, footed, No. 1602, Verde
green, 6 oz. 15
Tumbler, juice, No. 1600, clear, 5 1/4" h., 6
oz. 12
Tumbler, water, footed, No. 1602, clear, 10
oz. 9

Tumbler, water, No. 160, clear, 10 oz. 12
Vegetable bowl, divided, oval, clear, 11" l. 79
Whiskey set w/metal rack, No. 160/260, clear bottles w/raised letters "Bourbon," "Rye" & "Scotch," the set 650
Wine, clear, 4" h. 6

FREE-HAND WARE

Candlestick, slender baluster-form stem w/cushion foot in clear w/white heart & vine decoration, a tall cylindrical irides-cent dark blue socket, original paper label, 10" h. 440
Vase, 6 1/2" h., Mosaic design, deep cobalt blue body shaded & swirled w/opal & lined in iridescent orange 489
Vase, 8" h., small swelled base below the tall slightly flaring cylindrical body w/a widely flaring flattened & deeply ruffled rim, iridescent metallic hues of purple, green & blue in a wavy random design 121
Vase, 8 1/2" h., cylindrical, iridescent green heart & vine design on a white ground, marigold lining w/some wear 385
Vase, 8 1/2" h., decorated w/a dark blue drapery design on a marigold iridescent ground 275
Vase, 8 1/2" h., simple cylindrical form, orange iridescent ground decorated w/blue hanging heart design, cased over white, rim possibly ground 575
Vase, 8 3/4" h., green heart & vine decora-tion on opaque white body w/iridescent lustre overall 690
Vase, 9 1/2" h., bulbous base w/a wide flared neck, white cased to a cobalt blue exterior, interior of rim flashed in brilliant iridescent orange, polished pontil, early 20th c. 575
Vase, 10" h., bulbous ovoid bottom below a tall trumpet neck, exterior in a mottled taffeta w/amber shoulder band, slate blue interior 220
Vase, 10" h., tall slender form, iridescent orange exterior w/deep orange throat 193
Vase, 10 1/2" h., jack-in-the-pulpit-form, wide flared mouth of opaque white w/orange stretch iridescence, raised on an elongated stem w/blue pulled loops, on a blue disk foot w/overall orange & gold iridescence on exterior, polished pontil w/gold foil label, ca. 1925 1,610
Vase, 10 1/2" h., tall body w/flared rim, a white swagged design on an iridescent ground, stretched multi-hued design at the rim 523
Vase, 10 3/4" h., very slender baluster-form body w/flaring short neck, overall orange iridescence w/a blue pulled drapery design cased on milk glass 748
Vase, 11" h., slender swelled cylindrical body w/short rolled neck, overall orange lustre over a milk glass body, ground pontil 98

MISCELLANEOUS PATTERNS & LINES

Animal covered dish, Atterbury lion, pur-ple slag 90

Basket, Daisy patt., marigold carnival, marked "IG" 42
Basket, Daisy patt., marigold carnival, unmarked 48
Basket w/arched overhead handle, Mon-ticello patt., No. 698, clear, 10" h. 42
Bowl, pearl amethyst iridescent stretch glass, Iron Cross mark 100
Box, cov., model of duck on nest, jade green slag 46
Candlestick, single light, No. 3130, spiral, green, 3 1/2" h. 24
Candlestick, single light, Packard patt. No. 320, vaseline, 8 1/2" h. 54
Candy box, cov., Zodiac patt., No. 619, azure blue, carnival 54
Compote, No. 3297, shell bowl w/dolphin stem, black w/gold decoration 140
Creamer & sugar bowl, owl form, red slag, pr. 60
Cup & saucer, Grape patt., No. 473, rubig-old & marigold carnival 62
Decanter w/original stopper, Grape patt., marigold carnival, marked "IG" 64
Decanter w/original stopper, Grape patt., marigold carnival, unmarked 95
Ivy ball, Hobnail patt., No. 742, black 68
Lamp, Zipper Loop patt., marigold carnival, 8" h. 400
Paperweight, model of a tiger, Heisey mold, amber & caramel slag 100
Pitcher, crackle Tree of Life, marigold car-nival 40
Pitcher, No. 701, green w/clear reeded applied handle 80
Pitcher, Windmill patt., marigold carnival, unmarked 70
Plate, 8" d., Spun patt., reeded, clear 8
Plate, 8" d., Spun patt., reeded, red 38
Powder box, cov., Hobnail patt., green opalescent (ILLUS. in color section) 35-45

Molly Rose Bowl w/Silver Deposit

Rose bowl, Molly line, black w/silver deposit floral decoration, 5" h. (ILLUS.) 40-50
Tumbler, crackle Tree of Life, marigold car-nival 8
Tumbler, Hobnail patt., No. 742, clear 14
Tumbler, Windmill patt., carnival, unmarked 18
Vase, Hobnail patt., No. 742, flip, amber 38
Vase, Loganberry patt., ball top, purple car-nival 2,200

Vase, bud, 5" h., Spun patt., reeded, amber....... 28
Vase, 10" h., Hanging Vine & Heart, white
cased w/orange.. 450
Vase, 10" h., Loganberry patt., marigold
carnival.. 240
Vase, 12" h., Poppy Show patt., Helios
green carnival.. 1,050
Vase, 12" h., Poppy Show patt., marigold
carnival.. 600
Vase, fan-shaped, clear...................................... 84
Vase, three looped feet, orange w/blue
Hanging Vine & Heart 650
Wine, Old Williamsburg patt., amber.................. 18
Wine, Old Williamsburg patt., Azalea 18

KITCHEN GLASSWARE

ANCHOR HOCKING
Bowl, 6 1/2" d., splash proof, Turquoise
Blue, "Fire-King" logo $20
Bowl, 6 1/2" d., splash proof, white w/red
or black polka dots, "Fire-King" logo 20-25
Bowl, 6 1/2" d., teardrop shape, Turquoise
Blue, "Fire-King" logo 20-25
Bowl, 7 1/2" d., splash proof, Turquoise
Blue, "Fire-King" logo 20-24
Bowl, 7 1/2" d., splash proof, white w/red
or black polka dots, "Fire-King" logo 25-30
Bowl, 8" d., teardrop shape, Turquoise
Blue, "Fire-King" logo 30-35
Bowl, 8 1/2" d., splash proof, Turquoise
Blue, "Fire-King" logo 20-24
Bowl, 8 1/2" d., splash proof, white w/red
or black polka dots, "Fire-King" logo 30-35

Bowl w/Polka Dots

Bowl, 9 1/2" d., splash proof, white w/red
or black polka dots, "Fire-King" logo
(ILLUS.).. 35-40
Bowl, 9 1/2" d., teardrop shape, Turquoise
Blue, "Fire-King" logo 35
Bowl, 11" d., teardrop shape, Turquoise
Blue, "Fire-King" logo 45

Butter Dish

Butter dish, clear cover, Jad-ite Green
base, "Fire-King" logo, 1/4 lb. (ILLUS.) ... 75-100

Mug, Jad-ite Green, "Fire-King" logo,
3 1/2" h... 10
Mug, Turquoise Blue, "Fire-King" logo,
3 1/2" h... 8-10
Refrigerator dish, clear cover, Jad-ite
Green base, "Fire-King" logo, 4 x 8".............. 15
Refrigerator drippings dish, cov., white
w/tulips, "Fire-King" logo 25-30
Shakers, white w/red or black polka dots,
"Fire-King" logo, each................................ 10-20
Shakers, white w/tulips, "Fire-King" logo,
each 15-25

FEDERAL
Bowl, 6 1/2" d., vertical rib, flanged rim,
transparent green....................................... 8-15
Bowl, 6 1/2" d., vertical rib, flanged rim,
transparent pink 80-12
Bowl, 7 1/2" d., vertical rib, flanged rim,
transparent green....................................... 9-15
Bowl, 7 1/2" d., vertical rib, flanged rim,
transparent pink 10-15
Bowl, 8 1/2" d., vertical rib, flanged rim,
transparent green...................................... 11-16
Bowl, 8 1/2" d., vertical rib, flanged rim,
transparent pink 20
Bowl, 9 1/2" d., vertical rib, flanged rim,
transparent green...................................... 14-22
Bowl, 9 1/2" d., vertical rib, flanged rim,
transparent pink 25
Butter dish, tab-handled, vertical rib, transparent amber, 1 lb. 35-45
Butter dish, tab-handled, vertical rib, transparent amber, 1/4 lb. 18-25
Butter dish, tab-handled, vertical rib, transparent pink, 1 lb....................................... 42-48
Butter dish, tab-handled, vertical rib, transparent pink, 1/4 lb..................................... 25-35

Measuring Cup

Measuring cup, three-spout, w/handle,
crystal (ILLUS.) 15-18
Measuring cup, three-spout, w/handle,
transparent amber..................................... 35-38
Measuring cup, three-spout, w/handle,
transparent pink 35-38
Measuring cup, three-spout, without han-
dle, crystal 15-20
Measuring cup, three-spout, without han-
dle, transparent amber 38-42
Measuring cup, three-spout, without han-
dle, transparent green 25-30
Reamer, vertical panels, transparent amber.. 22-25

Reamer, vertical panels, transparent green .. **30-35**
Reamer, vertical ribs, transparent amber **25-30**
Reamer, vertical ribs, transparent pink......... **30-35**
Refrigerator dish, cov., transparent amber, 4 x 4"... **10-12**
Refrigerator dish, cov., transparent amber, 4 x 8"... **15-20**
Refrigerator dish, cov., transparent amber, 8 x 8"... **30-40**
Refrigerator dish, cov., transparent pink, 4 x 4"... **10-15**
Refrigerator dish, cov., transparent pink, 4 x 8"... **22-26**
Refrigerator dish, cov., transparent pink, 8 x 8"... **35-40**

HAZEL-ATLAS

Bowl, 7 5/8" d., Crisscross patt., transparent cobalt blue.............................. **55**
Bowl, 8 3/8" d., Crisscross patt., transparent cobalt blue.............................. **65**
Bowl, 9 5/8" d., Crisscross patt., transparent green.................................... **35**
Bowl, 9 5/8" d., Crisscross patt., transparent pink...................................... **45**
Butter dish, cov., Crisscross patt., transparent cobalt blue, 1 lb.................. **125**
Butter dish, cov., Crisscross patt., transparent cobalt blue, 1/4 lb............. **115**
Butter dish, cov., Crisscross patt., transparent green or pink, 1 lb. **55**
Butter dish, cov., Crisscross patt., transparent green or pink, 1/4 lb. **45**
Measuring cup, three-spout, embossed "Kelloggs," transparent green.................. **20-25**

Measuring Cups: Left: w/"H.A." logo, Right: embossed "Kelloggs"

Measuring cup, three-spout, embossed "Kelloggs," transparent pink (ILLUS. right).. **23-28**
Measuring cup, three-spout, transparent green, "H.A." logo (ILLUS. left)................. **22-28**
Measuring cup, transparent green, 2 cup **23-28**
Reamer, Crisscross patt., transparent cobalt blue, large........................ **300**
Reamer, Crisscross patt., transparent green, large.................................. **25**
Reamer, Crisscross patt., transparent pink, large.. **250**
Reamer, tab-handle, Crisscross patt., transparent green..................................... **25-30**
Reamer, tab-handle, Crisscross patt., transparent pink **300**
Refrigerator dish, cov., Crisscross patt., clear, 3 1/2 x 5 3/4" **25**
Refrigerator dish, cov., Crisscross patt., transparent cobalt blue, 4 x 4".................. **45-50**
Refrigerator dish, cov., Crisscross patt., transparent cobalt blue, 8 x 8"..................... **130**

Crisscross Refrigerator Dish

Refrigerator dish, cov., Crisscross patt., transparent green, 3 1/2 x 5 3/4" (ILLUS.).. **50**
Refrigerator dish, cov., w/flat knob handle, transparent cobalt blue, 5 1/4" d. **65-75**
Refrigerator dish, cov., w/flat knob handle, transparent green, 5 1/4" d....................... **25-30**
Shakers, square, embossed "Salt" or "Pepper," transparent green, each................... **30-35**
Shakers, square, embossed "Salt" or "Pepper," transparent pink, each **50-60**
Shakers, square, enameled lettering "Salt" or "Pepper," Platonite White, each............. **9-12**

HOCKING

Bowl, 6 3/4" d., vertical rib, rolled rim, Vitrock White.................................... **7-10**
Bowl, 7 1/2" d., vertical rib, rolled rim, Vitrock White.................................... **9-12**
Bowl, 8 1/2" d., vertical rib, rolled rim, Vitrock White.................................... **11-15**
Bowl, 9 1/2" d., vertical rib, rolled rim, Vitrock White.................................... **13-16**
Bowl, 10 1/4" d., vertical rib, rolled rim, Vitrock White.................................... **15-20**
Bowl, 11 1/4" d., vertical rib, rolled rim, Vitrock White.................................... **20-25**

Block Optic Butter Dish

Butter dish, cov., top embossed "Butter," Block Optic patt., transparent green (ILLUS.).. **55-60**
Measuring cup, cov., Vitrock White, 2 cup ... **45-55**
Measuring cup, single spout, transparent green.. **25-30**
Measuring cup, single spout, transparent green, 2 cup.. **20-25**
Measuring cup, single spout, vertical rib, transparent green, 2 cup **40-50**

Measuring cup, single spout, vertical rib, transparent pink, 2 cup **35-45**
Reamer, tab-handle, Vitrock White, small . **100-110**
Reamer, Vitrock White, large **20-30**
Refrigerator dish, cov., Vitrock White, 4 x 4" **12-15**
Refrigerator dish, cov., Vitrock White, 8 x 8" **25-35**
Shaker, square, transparent green **30-45**
Shaker, square, Vitrock White........................ **8-15**
Shakers, round, "Salt," "Pepper," "Flour," & "Sugar," white w/black circle, the set..... **110-125**
Shakers, round, "Salt," "Pepper," "Flour," & "Sugar," white w/blue or red circle, the set **100**

JEANNETTE
Bowl, 5 1/2" d., horizontal rib, Delphite Blue **30-40**

Horizontal Ribbed Bowls

Bowl, 5 1/2" d., horizontal rib, Jeannette Green (ILLUS. bottom front)...................... **15-25**
Bowl, 6" d., vertical rib, Delphite Blue **35-50**
Bowl, 6" d., vertical rib, Jeannette Green **10-15**
Bowl, 7" d., vertical rib, Delphite Blue **25-35**
Bowl, 7" d., vertical rib, Jeannette Green **12-18**
Bowl, 7 1/2" d., horizontal rib, Delphite Blue **40-50**
Bowl, 7 1/2" d., horizontal rib, Jeannette Green (ILLUS. top left) **18-28**
Bowl, 8" d., vertical rib, Delphite Blue **30-40**
Bowl, 8" d., vertical rib, Jeannette Green **25-30**
Bowl, 9" d., vertical rib, Delphite Blue **40-55**
Bowl, 9" d., vertical rib, Jeannette Green **25-30**
Bowl, 9 3/4" d., horizontal rib, Delphite Blue **75-85**
Bowl, 9 3/4" d., horizontal rib, Jeannette Green (ILLUS. top right)........................... **25-35**
Butter dish, "Jennyware," Ultramarine, 1 lb. **160-185**
Butter dish, top embossed "Butter," Delphite Blue, 1 lb. **300-325**
Butter dish, top embossed "Butter," Jeannette Green, 1 lb. **55-60**
Butter dish, top embossed "Butter," transparent green, 1 lb. **40-50**
Butter dish, top embossed "Butter," transparent pink, 1 lb.. **60-70**
Canister, "Cereal," w/glass lid, Delphite Blue, 29 oz. **135-140**
Canister, "Cereal," w/glass lid, Jeannette Green, 29 oz. **40-50**
Canister, "Cereal," w/glass lid, Jeannette Green, 48 oz. **120-130**
Canister, "Coffee," w/glass lid, Delphite Blue, 29 oz. **135-140**

Tea, Coffee & Sugar Canisters

Canister, "Coffee," w/glass lid, Jeannette Green, 48 oz. (ILLUS. center) **120-130**
Canister, "Coffee," w/screw-on lid, horizontal rib, Delphite Blue, 40 oz. **350-375**

Tea & Coffee Canisters

Canister, "Coffee," w/screw-on lid, horizontal rib, Jeannette Green, 40 oz. (ILLUS. right) **175-225**
Canister, "Sugar," w/glass lid, Delphite Blue, 29 oz. **130-135**
Canister, "Sugar," w/glass lid, Jadite Green, 48 oz. (ILLUS. right w/coffee & tea canisters)..................................... **130-140**
Canister, "Sugar," w/glass lid, Jeannette Green, 29 oz. **40-50**
Canister, "Sugar," w/screw-on lid, horizontal rib, Delphite Blue, 40 oz. **350-400**
Canister, "Sugar," w/screw-on lid, horizontal rib, Jeannette Green, 40 oz............. **150-160**
Canister, "Tea," w/glass lid, Delphite Blue, 29 oz. **135-140**
Canister, "Tea," w/glass lid, Jeannette Green, 29 oz. **40-50**
Canister, "Tea," w/glass lid, Jeannette Green, 48 oz. (ILLUS. left w/coffee & sugar canisters)..................................... **160-170**
Canister, "Tea," w/screw-on lid, horizontal rib, Delphite Blue, 20 oz. **150-175**
Canister, "Tea," w/screw-on lid, horizontal rib, Jeannette Green, 20 oz. (ILLUS. left)..... **120**
Canister, w/glass lid, no lettering, Jeannette Green, 48 oz. **60-75**
Measuring cup, tab handle, Delphite Blue, 1 cup **65-80**
Measuring cup, tab handle, Delphite Blue, 1/2 cup **35-45**
Measuring cup, tab handle, Delphite Blue, 1/3 cup **25-35**
Measuring cup, tab handle, Delphite Blue, 1/4 cup **25-35**

Graduated Measuring Cups

Measuring cup, tab handle, Jeannette Green, 1 cup (ILLUS. right) **40**

Measuring cup, tab handle, Jeannette Green, 1/2 cup (ILLUS. right center) **35**

Measuring cup, tab handle, Jeannette Green, 1/3 cup (ILLUS. left center) **30**

Measuring cup, tab handle, Jeannette Green, 1/4 cup (ILLUS. left) **30**

Measuring pitcher, Delphite Blue, embossed sunflower bottom, 2 cup **75-85**

Measuring pitcher, Jadite Green, embossed cunflower bottom, 2 cup **50-65**

Measuring pitcher, Jeannette Green, embossed sunflower bottom, 2 cup **42-50**

Measuring pitcher, transparent green, embossed sunflower bottom, 2 cup **35-40**

Measuring Pitcher w/Reamer Top

Measuring pitcher, reamer top, Jeannette Green, embossed sunflower bottom, 2 cup (ILLUS.) **55-65**

Milk Pitcher

Pitcher, milk, Jeannette Green, 36 oz. (ILLUS.) **65-75**

Reamer, Delphite Blue, small **70-90**

Reamer, Jeannette Green, large **40-50**

Small Jeannette Green Reamer

Reamer, Jeannette Green, small (ILLUS.) **35-40**

Refrigerator dish, cov., Delphite Blue, 4 x 4" **60**

Refrigerator dish, cov., Delphite Blue, 4 x 8" **75**

Refrigerator dish, cov., Delphite Blue, 5 1/2" d. **50-75**

Refrigerator dish, cov., Jeannette Green, 4 x 4" **15-25**

Refrigerator dish, cov., Jeannette Green, 4 x 8" **20-30**

Round Refrigerator Dish

Refrigerator dish, cov., Jeannette Green, 5 1/2" d. (ILLUS.) **30-40**

Refrigerator Dish w/Embossed Floral Cover

Refrigerator dish, w/embossed floral cover, Jeannette Green, 5" sq. (ILLUS.) ... **35-45**

Refrigerator dish, w/embossed floral cover, Jeannette Green, 5 x 10" **75**

Refrigerator drippings dish, cov., w/lettering, Jadite Green **180**

Refrigerator drippings dish, cov., w/lettering, Jeannette Green **60**

Horizontal Ribbed Refrigerator Drippings Dish

Refrigerator drippings dish, cov., without lettering, horizontal rib, Jeannette Green (ILLUS.).. **30-40**

Salt box, wood top, Jeannette Green **250-300**

Shakers, round, horizontal rib, "Flour" or "Sugar," Delphite Blue, 4 1/2" h., each......... **100**

Shakers, round, horizontal rib, "Flour" or "Sugar," Jadite Green, 4 1/2" h., each...... **35-45**

Shakers, round, horizontal rib, "Flour" or "Sugar," Jeannette Green, 4 1/2" h., each **30-40**

Shakers, round, horizontal rib, "Salt & Pepper," Delphite Blue, 4 1/2" h., each **45-65**

Shakers, round, horizontal rib, "Salt & Pepper," Jadite Green, 4 1/2" h., pr..................... **35**

Horizontal Rib Salt & Pepper Shakers

Shakers, round, horizontal rib, "Salt & Pepper," Jeannette Green, 4 1/2" h., each (ILLUS.).. **25-35**

Shakers, square, "Flour" or "Sugar," Delphite Blue, 4 1/2" h., each **125-150**

Shakers, square, "Flour" or "Sugar," Jadite Green, 4 1/2" h., each **45-60**

Jeannette Shakers

Shakers, square, "Flour" or "Sugar," Jeannette Green, 4 1/2" h., each (ILLUS. right) **50-75**

Shakers, square, "Salt & Pepper," Delphite Blue, 4 1/2" h., each **125**

Shakers, square, "Salt & Pepper," Jadite Green, 4 1/2" h., pr.................................... **65-80**

Shakers, square, "Salt & Pepper," Jeannette Green, 4 1/2" h., each (ILLUS. left).. **60-75**

MCKEE

Bowl, 6" d., Skokie Green, McKee logo **15-18**

Bowl, 7" d., Skokie Green, McKee logo **15-20**

Bowl, 8" d., Skokie Green, McKee logo **18-28**

Bowl, 8" d., white w/red polka dots, McKee logo **20-25**

Bowl, 8" d., white w/red ships, McKee logo **40**

Bowl, 9" d., Poudre Blue, McKee logo **80-90**

Bowl, 9" d., Skokie Green, McKee logo **25-30**

Butter dish, Chalaine Blue, tab-handled, vertical rib, McKee logo, 1 1/2 lb. **350-400**

Butter dish, French Ivory, tab-handled, vertical ribbed, McKee logo, 1 1/2 lb. **75-85**

Butter dish, French Ivory w/green stripe, McKee logo, 1 lb. **45-65**

Butter dish, French Ivory w/polka dots, McKee logo, 1 lb. **125**

Poudre Blue Butter Dish

Butter dish, Poudre Blue, McKee logo, 1 lb. (ILLUS.) **175-250**

Butter dish, Skokie Green, tab-handled, vertical ribbed, McKee logo, 1 1/2 lb. **60-80**

M\cKee Butter Dish with Ships

Butter dish, white w/ships, McKee logo, 1 lb. (ILLUS.) **75-80**

Canister, "Coffee," w/screw-on lid, French Ivory w/red polka dots, 28 oz. **75-100**

Canister, "Coffee," w/screw-on lid, French Ivory w/red polka dots, 48 oz. **50-100**

Canister, "Coffee," w/screw-on lid, Skokie Green, 28 oz. **200**

Canister, "Coffee," w/screw-on lid, Skokie Green, McKee logo, 48 oz. **125-175**

Canister, "Flour," w/screw-on lid, French Ivory w/red polka dots, 28 oz. **75-100**

Canister, "Flour," w/screw-on lid, French Ivory w/red polka dots, 48 oz. **50-100**

Canister, "Flour," w/screw-on lid, Skokie
Green, 28 oz. **150-200**

Canister, "Flour," w/screw-on lid, Skokie
Green, McKee logo, 48 oz. **575**

Canister, "Sugar," w/screw-on lid, French
Ivory w/red polka dots, 28 oz. **75-100**

Canister, "Sugar," w/screw-on lid, French
Ivory w/red polka dots, 48 oz. **50-100**

Canister, "Sugar," w/screw-on lid, Skokie
Green, 28 oz. **150-200**

Canister, "Sugar," w/screw-on lid, Skokie
Green, McKee logo, 48 oz. **125-175**

Canister, "Tea," w/screw-on lid, French
Ivory w/red polka dots, 28 oz. **75-100**

Canister, "Tea," w/screw-on lid, French
Ivory w/red polka dots, McKee logo, 48
oz. **100-150**

Canister, "Tea," w/screw-on lid, Skokie
Green, 28 oz. **65-75**

Canister, "Tea," w/screw-on lid, Skokie
Green, McKee logo, 48 oz. **125-175**

Canister, w/glass lid, "Cereal," round, white
w/red ships, 48 oz. **75**

Canister, w/glass lid, "Coffee," round,
Skokie Green, 24 oz. **80-90**

Canister, w/glass lid, round, French Ivory
w/red polka dots, 10 oz. **30-40**

Canister, w/glass lid, round, French Ivory
w/red polka dots, 24 oz. **35-45**

Canister, w/glass lid, round, French Ivory
w/red polka dots, 40 oz. **35-45**

Canister, w/glass lid, round, French Ivory
w/red polka dots, 48 oz. **30-50**

Canister, w/glass lid, round, Skokie Green,
10 oz. **18-25**

Canister, w/glass lid, round, Skokie Green,
40 oz. **75**

Canister, w/glass lid, round, Skokie Green,
48 oz. **85**

Canister, w/glass lid, round, white w/red
ships, 10 oz. **20-30**

Canister, w/glass lid, round, white w/red
ships, 24 oz. **25-35**

Canister, w/glass lid, round, white w/red
ships, 48 oz. **40-60**

Measuring cup, two-spout, Chalaine Blue,
McKee logo **575-650**

Measuring cup, two-spout, Seville Yellow,
McKee logo **200-300**

Measuring cup, two-spout, Skokie Green,
McKee logo **160-225**

Measuring pitcher, Chalaine Blue, McKee
logo, 4 cup.. **450-500**

Measuring pitcher, French Ivory, McKee
logo, 4 cup... **35-45**

Measuring pitcher, French Ivory w/green
or red dots, McKee logo, 2 cup **75-85**

Measuring pitcher, Poudre Blue, McKee
logo, 2 cup... **80-90**

Measuring pitcher, Poudre Blue, McKee
logo, 4 cup.. **550-600**

Measuring pitcher, Seville Yellow, McKee
logo, 4 cup.. **115-125**

Measuring Pitcher, Skokie Green, McKee
logo, 2 cup.. **45**

McKee Measuring Pitcher

Measuring pitcher, Skokie Green, McKee
logo, 4 cup (ILLUS.) **145-155**

Reamer, "Sunkist," Chalaine Blue **175**

Reamer, "Sunkist," Skokie Green...................... **65**

McKee "Sunkist" Reamer

Reamer, "Sunkist," white (ILLUS.)...................... **65**

Refrigerator dish, cov., French Ivory w/red
polka dots, McKee logo, 4 x 5".................. **30-40**

Refrigerator dish, cov., French Ivory w/red
polka dots, McKee logo, 5 x 8".................. **35-45**

Refrigerator dish, cov., Skokie Green,
McKee logo, 4 x 5" **40**

Refrigerator dish, cov., Skokie Green,
McKee logo, 5 x 8" **50**

Refrigerator dish, cov., white w/red ships,
McKee logo, 4 x 5".................................. **15-16**

Refrigerator dish, cov., white w/red ships,
McKee logo, 5 x 8".................................. **20-25**

Refrigerator Drippings Dish

Refrigerator drippings dish, cov., white
w/red ships, "Drippings," McKee logo,
4 x 5" (ILLUS.).. **35-40**

Rolling pin, French Ivory, 13 1/2" **200-300**

Rolling pin, Poudre Blue, 13 1/2" **400-500**

Rolling pin, Seville Yellow, 13 1/2" **250-350**

Rolling pin, Skokie Green, 13 1/2" **1,200-1,800**

Shakers, Roman Arch style, "Flour" or
"Sugar," black, 4 1/4" h., each.................. **20-30**

Shakers, Roman Arch style, "Flour" or "Sugar," French Ivory, 4 1/4" h., each **20-35**

Shakers, Roman Arch style, "Flour" or "Sugar," French Ivory w/blue or red polka dots, 4 1/4" h., each........................ **50-60**

Shakers, Roman Arch style, "Flour" or "Sugar," French Ivory w/green polka dots, 4 1/4" h., pr... **350**

Shakers, Roman Arch style, "Flour" or "Sugar," red letters, 4 1/4" h., each **35-45**

Salt, Pepper & Sugar Shakers

Shakers, Roman Arch style, "Flour" or "Sugar," Skokie Green, 4 1/4" h., each (ILLUS. right)... **45-65**

Shakers, Roman Arch style, "Flour" or "Sugar," white, 4 1/4" h., each................... **40-65**

Shakers, Roman Arch style, "Flour" or "Sugar," white w/red ships, 3 3/4" h., each **20-25**

Roman Arch Salt & Pepper Shakers

Shakers, Roman Arch style, "Salt & Pepper," black, 4 1/4" h., pr. (ILLUS.).................. **50**

Shakers, Roman Arch style, "Salt & Pepper," French Ivory w/blue or red polka dots, 4 1/4" h., pr....................................... **65-75**

Shakers, Roman Arch style, "Salt & Pepper," Skokie Green, 4 1/4" h., pr. (ILLUS. left w/sugar)... **35-45**

Shakers, Roman Arch style, "Salt & Pepper," white, 4 1/4" h., pr. **35-45**

Red Ships Salt & Pepper Shakers

Shakers, Roman Arch style, "Salt & Pepper," white w/red ships, 3 3/4" h., pr. (ILLUS.).. **35-45**

Water dispenser, w/glass top, French Ivory, 4 1/2 x 5 x 11"............................. **150-175**

Water Dispenser

Water dispenser, w/glass top, Skokie Green, 4 1/2 x 5 x 11" (ILLUS.)............. **300-325**

Water jug, ovoid shape w/depressed handles, w/stopper, Skokie Green **125-150**

Water jug, ovoid shape w/depressed handles, without stopper, Skokie Green **100**

MISCELLANEOUS

Fry Glass Co., measuring cup, single spout, Pearl White opalescent **55**

Fry Glass Co., measuring cup, three-spout, Pearl White opalescent **75**

Fry Glass Co., reamer, ring handle, ribbed, transparent canary yellow **325-350**

Fry Glass Co., reamer, tab handle, indented ribbing, transparent amber **350-400**

Fry Reamer w/Indented Ribbing

Fry Glass Co., reamer, tab handle, indented ribbing, transparent green (ILLUS.).. **25-35**

Owens-Illinois Glass Co., canister w/screw-on top, diagonal rib pattern, transparent forest green, 20 oz. **30-40**

Owens-Illinois Glass Co., canister w/screw-on top, diagonal rib pattern, transparent forest green, 40 oz. **35-45**

Owens-Illinois Glass Co., shaker, square, transparent forest green, 4 1/2" h., each... **10-12**

Owens-Illinois Sugar & Flour Shakers

Owens-Illinois Glass Co., shakers, ovoid shape "Flour" or "Sugar," transparent forest green, 4 1/2" h., each (ILLUS.)............. **35**

Tipp City Glass Co., "Salt" & "Pepper" shakers w/metal stand & covers, white w/small floral decoration, 3" h. shakers, 3 pcs. **40-50**

Tipp City Spice Set

Tipp City Glass Co., spice set: eight shakers w/metal stand; white w/cherries, 3" h. shakers, 9 pcs. (ILLUS.) **135-140**

Tipp City Glass Co., spice set: eight shakers w/metal stand; white w/poppies, 3" h shakers, 9 pcs. **75-80**

LACY

Lacy Glass is a general term developed by collectors many years ago to cover the earliest type of pressed glass produced in this country. "Lacy" refers to the fact that most of these early patterns consisted of scrolls and geometric designs against a finely stippled background which gives the glass the look of fine lace. Formerly this glass was often referred to as "Sandwich" for the Boston & Sandwich Glass Company of Sandwich, Massachusetts which produced a great deal of this ware. Today, however, collectors realize that many other factories on the East Coast and in the Pittsburgh, Pennsylvania and Wheeling, West Virginia areas also made lacy glass from the 1820s into the 1840s. All pieces listed are clear unless otherwise noted. Numbers after salt dips refer to listings in Pressed Glass Salt Dishes of the Lacy Period, 1825-1850, *by Logan W. and Dorothy B. Neal. Also see CUP PLATES and SANDWICH GLASS.*

Bowl, toy-size, footed oval form w/scalloped rim & lacy sides, very light aqua, 3/4" h. (two small chips on base) **$165**

Bowl, 6 1/4" w., hexagonal, the center w/six long diamond point diamonds alternating w/small scrolls, the wide border composed of leafy scrolls alternating w/scroll cartouches, New England (mold roughness) **55**

Compote, open, 4 3/4" d., 3 1/2" h., round Heart patt. bowl, on an double-knob applied pedestal & round foot w/pontil, two chips, mold roughness **440**

Compote, open, 5 3/4" d., 3 3/4" h., Roman Rosette patt., wide shallow flared bowl joined by a wafer to the unrecorded ribbed pedestal base (few chips, mold roughness) **198**

Compote, open, 6" d., 4" h., deep curved Roman Rosette patt. bowl on an applied baluster stem resting on a cup plate foot (mold roughness on cup plate base) **2,475**

Large Roman Rosette Lacy Compote

Compote, open, 6 1/4" d., 10 1/2" h., Roman Rosette patt., deep widely flaring bowl attached w/a wafer to the short stem & round patterned base, one inch line & several small rim chips (ILLUS.) **825**

Compote, open, 6 3/4" d., 2 3/4" h., wide shallow Peacock Eye patt. w/Bull's-eye scalloped rim raised on a short Hairpin patt. pedestal foot, Midwestern (two scallops missing at rim, mold roughness) .. **1,430**

Creamer, Heart & Scale patt., clambroth, 4 1/2" h. **385**

Creamer, toy-size, footed ovoid body w/flared rim & integral handle, lacy scroll design, light fiery opalescent, 1 3/4" h. (mold roughness, base chips) **385**

Creamer, toy-size, footed ovoid body w/flared rim & integral handle, lacy scroll design, rare smokey amethyst, 1 3/4" h. (crack next to handle, chip w/short crack on base) **495**

Dish, cov., oblong w/undulating flanged rim, base w/central pointed cartouche reserve framed by a border in the Princess Feather patt., matching stepped & domed cover w/arched loop handle, very rare, 5 1/2 x 10 1/2" (few base scallops chipped) **8,250**

Dish, rectangular w/cut corners, the bottom w/a central star framed by C- and S-scrolls, the border w/cartouche panels, Midwestern, 7 1/4" l. (mold roughness, two scallops chipped, two tipped) **209**

Dish, round, a leaf & blossom cluster in the center, the wide border band composed of blossoms, swirled leaves & scrolls, unlisted, 5 1/2" d. (several scalloped tipped, mold roughness) **143**

Dish, round, Roman Rosette patt., fiery opalescent, probably Boston & Sandwich, 5 1/2" d. (light mold roughness) **198**

Dish, toy-size, shallow oval form w/scrolled lacy border design, clear, 3" l. (light mold roughness) **66**

Lamp, miniature, blown spherical font on an applied knopped stem on an inverted lacy cup plate foot, 4" h. (chips on base) **385**

Plate, 5 5/8" d., the wide outer border w/wide arched fern-like leaves alternating w/narrowing diamond point arches, undocumented (two scallops chipped, two tipped)... **308**

Plate, 6" d., central four-point star framed by leaves & scrolls, wide border band of leaf sprigs & small buttons, rope border, Midwestern (light mold roughness) **77**

Plate, 6 1/4" d., round w/the center composed of a wide rayed strawberry diamond design, a border of cross-hatched strawberry diamond panels & small fan scallops, pre-lacy (few chips & mold roughness) **330**

Plate, 7 1/4" w., paneled edges, the round center w/large pairs of acanthus leaves alternating w/small palmettes within a ring of scrolled small acanthus leaves & an outer border of palmettes & fans, very rare, New England (few minor chips, three scallops tipped) **303**

Large Heart & Lyre Lacy Plate

Plate, 9 1/4" d., Heart & Lyre (Harp) patt., wide border band of alternating hearts & lyres, bands of strawberry diamond design around the central eight-point star, attributed to the Boston & Sandwich Glass Co., mold roughness, three scallops damaged (ILLUS.) **330**

Plate, 9 1/2" d., flanged rim, large four-point star in bottom framed by a band w/small swirled panels, outer wide zig-zag border band & scalloped rim, probably Boston & Sandwich (few scallops tipped, light mold roughness) **55**

Salt dip, Classical sofa-form, Eagle patt., the outscrolled corners formed by perched American eagles looking back over their shoulders, looped rope border above a shield on each side, probably Boston & Sandwich Glass Co., opaque white (EE-3b) **1,430**

Salt dip, Classical sofa-form w/S-scroll ends & scalloped rim, lyre design on each side, medium blue, probably Boston & Sandwich Glass Co., LE-2 (some mold roughness on one foot) **935**

Salt dip, Classical sofa-shaped, high outscrolled legs supporting the S-scrolled

sides decorated w/lacy scrolls below the scrolled serpentine rim, very rare, PE1 (light mold roughness)................................. **523**

Salt dip, cov., Classical sofa-form w/high scrolled ends & legs, the high domed cover w/a berry finial, rare (CD-2A).......... **2,090**

Salt dip, footed oval form, deep upright sides w/heavily pressed swags alternating w/crosshatched rondels around the rim, light opalescent, OL-16a (rim chip, interior flaking)... **550**

Salt dip, footed rectangular form w/slightly flaring patterned sides, central divider on interior, attributed to Pittsburgh area, cobalt blue, DI-12 variant (several small chips, mold roughness) **550**

Salt dip, footed round & flared bowl w/a design of panels w/fine diamond point below a bull's-eye each separated by a thin rim, purplish blue, PR-1b (mold roughness, slight rim underfill) **248**

Rare Lafayet Boat Salt Dip

Salt dip, model of a sidewheeler, "Lafayet" on side of wheel, silvery opaque light blue, BT-8 (ILLUS.) **2,750**

Salt dip, model of a wagon, deep rectangular sides w/stars & diamonds on each side, molded round wheels, rare, WN1A (heavy mold roughness & spalls) **385**

Salt dip, oval, Peacock Eye patt., scalloped rim of round "eyes," PO2A (light mold roughness) **121**

Salt dip, paddle side-wheeler boat shape, "Lafayet" molded on sides, company marking on stern, opalescent purplish blue, Boston & Sandwich Glass Co. (BT-3) **1,650**

Salt dip, rectangular, corner posts & overall strawberry diamond design sides, Boston & Sandwich Glass Co., deep purplish blue, SD-12 (mold roughness, few small chips) **413**

Salt dip, rectangular, post corners on peg feet, overall strawberry diamond design on sides, deep purplish blue, Boston & Sandwich Glass Co., SD-15 (mold roughness, few small chips)........................ **413**

Salt dip, rectangular w/corner posts & tiny knob feet, the sides w/embossed baskets of fruit, medium green, JY2b, 3" l. (rim chips) **193**

Salt dip, rectangular w/paneled sides, corner posts & peg feet, long sides molded w/baskets of flowers, blossoms In end panels, heavy scalloped rim, opaque white, NE1A (light mold roughness, bottom corner lightly tipped)............................. **220**

Salt dip, rectangular w/scrolled ends & flat rectangular base, the sides w/branched sprigs below a rim band of roundels, clear (OG-1) **523**

Salt dip, rectangular w/slightly flaring sides, each side w/a top row of hearts above a band of Gothic arches, on small peg feet, GA4 (light mold roughness) **143**

Salt dip, rounded footed form, the curved sides composed of pointed Gothic arches, octagonal foot, cobalt blue, unlisted, 3" d. **248**

Salt dip, sleigh-form, inwardly scrolled ends & outscrolled legs, scrolled rim & scroll designs on the sides, cobalt blue, CN-1A (chip on one corner) **413**

Strainer, round, a border of circles & swags around a plain interior pierced w/five small holes, 4 1/8" d. (mold roughness) **132**

Sugar bowl, cov., Gothic Arch patt., round foot & octagonal finely detailed Gothic arch side panels w/flaring, flanged rim, matching domed cover w/button finial, fiery opalescent, 5" h. (in-the-making line on foot) **550**

Sugar bowl, cov., Gothic Arch patt., round foot & octagonal finely detailed Gothic arch side panels w/flaring, flanged rim, matching domed cover w/button finial, light bluish fiery opalescent, 5 1/4" h. (in-the-making line on foot) **935**

Sugar bowl, cov., Gothic Arch patt., round foot & octagonal finely detailed Gothic arch side panels w/flaring, flanged rim, matching domed cover w/button finial, electric blue, 5 1/4" h. **1,320**

Tea plate, octagonal, beaded outer border, inner border of leafy scrolls around a central scene of a tall-masted sailing ship above "Union," 6 5/8" w. (small rim chips) **963**

Tea plate, octagonal, shells & scrolls around central oval reserve showing a sidewheel steamboat & "Pittsburgh," 6 1/2" w. (edge chips) **880**

Midwestern Lacy Tea Plate

Tea plate, round w/finely scalloped rim, border of bull's-eyes & shells around a band of roundels & a central pinwheel, probably Midwestern, blue, ca. 1830-45, light mold roundness, 5 7/8" d. (ILLUS.) **220**

Toddy plate, round, Lyre patt., leafy scroll border band & scalloped rim, probably Boston & Sandwich Glass Co., medium blue, 4 3/4" d. **468**

Toddy plate, round, multi-paneled sides each panel w/graduated rows of facing C-scrolls, scalloped rim, bright light amethyst, unlisted, 5" d. (light mold roughness) **550**

LOTUS

The Lotus Glass Company was a glass decorating firm located in Barnesville, Ohio from 1912 until their closing circa 1994. Lotus at one time or another utilized every know glass decorating technique: metallic banding, needle etching, deep plate acid-etching, hand-cutting, hand-painting and more. Lotus-decorated stemware and tableware lines were often made to compliment existing china patterns. In 1960 Lotus acquired the Chicago-based Glastonburry Company, another glass decorating firm specializing in cutting. The glass blanks used by Lotus came from many of America's finest glasshouses. Some of the etching and decorations are unique such as the very modern La Furiste motif. Others, such as Rambler Rose, are so similar to designs by other frims that they are nearly indistinguishable.

Basket, footed, No. 459, applied clear handle & crest, milk glass w/gold encrusted floral design No. 975 .... **$120**

Candlestick, single light, black w/Morning Glory color enameled decoration, 8" h. **42**

Candlestick, single light, low form, green w/La Furiste etching No. 0907, 3 1/2" h. **38**

Candlestick, single light, tall form, pink w/La Furiste etching No. 0907, 5 1/2" h. **68**

Candy box, cov., three-part, milk glass in Crows Foot patt., the cover w/Springtime silver deposit decoration **125**

Chocolate box, cov., clear w/Poppy decoration, 6" d. **95**

Compote, open, 5" d., Crows Foot patt., milk glass w/Springtime silver deposit decoration **86**

Compote, open, 7" d., Crows Foot patt., milk glass w/Springtime silver deposit decoration **94**

Console bowl, cupped rim, multicolored enameled floral decoration, 12" d. **48**

Console bowl, flared rim, clear crest, milk glass w/gold encrusted floral design No. 975, 14" d. **84**

Console bowl, footed, cupped rim, black w/Morning Glory enameled decoration, 10" d. **54**

Black Console with Lola Decoration

Console bowl, rolled rim, black w/silver
Lola decoration (ILLUS.) 80

Cordial, clear, Butterfly etching No.
1014, 3/4 oz. 58

Cordial, clear, La Furiste etching No. 0907,
1 1/2 oz. 62

Cup & saucer, clear, Butterfly etching No.
1014 28

Goblet, clear, Butterfly etching No. 1014, 9
oz. 32

Goblet, footed, clear bowl, black foot,
McGuire etching No. 1001, 9 oz. 42

Goblet, water, No. 18, clear w/gold bands,
La Furiste etching No. 0907, 9 oz. 32

Goblet, water, No. 18, green w/gold bands,
La Furiste etching No. 0907, 9 oz. 42

Goblet, water, No. 18, rose pink w/gold
bands, La Furiste etching No. 0907, 9
oz. 48

Flanders Etched Pitcher

Pitcher, jug-form, clear, Flanders etching,
4 pt. (ILLUS.) 108

Pitcher, jug-form, rose pink, La Furiste
etching No. 0907, 2 qt. 138

Plate, salad , 7" w., square, black, McGuire
etching No. 1001 22

Plate, salad , 8" w., square, black, McGuire
etching No. 1001 24

Plate, dinner, 9" d., clear, Butterfly etching
No. 1014 32

Plate, dinner, 9" w., square, black, McGuire
etching No. 1001 34

Rose bowl, rose pink, La Furiste etching
No. 0907, 5 1/2" h. 90

Salt & pepper shakers w/original tops,
clear, Butterfly etching No. 1014, pr. 65

Server, center-handled, green w/La Furiste
etching No. 0907, 10 1/2" d. 58

Server, center-handled, milk glass
w/Springtime silver deposit decoration 95

Vase, rectangular, milk glass, Springtime
silver deposit decoration 115

Call of the Wild Decorated Black Vase

Vase, three-toed, black, Call of the Wild silver deposit decoration (ILLUS.) 160

Vase, three-toed, black, Lola silver deposit
decoration 95

Vase, triangular, milk glass, crimped clear
crest w/gold encrusted floral No. 975
decoration, 4 1/2" h. 38

MCKEE

*The McKee name has been associated with
glass production since 1834, first producing window
glass and later bottles. In the 1850s a new factory
was established in Pittsburgh, Pennsylvania, for
production of flint and pressed glass. The plant was
relocated in Jeanette, Pennsylvania in 1888 and
operated there as an independent company almost
continuously until 1951 when it sold out to Thatcher
Glass Manufacturing Company. Many types of collectible glass were produced by McKee through the
years including Depression, Pattern, Milk Glass
and a variety of utility kitchenwares. See these categories for additional listings.*

KITCHENWARES

Batter pitcher, Red Polka Dots patt.............. $175

Bowl, 8" d., Red Polka Dots patt. 18

Bowl, 9" d., 5" h., flared, Red Ships patt. on
white opal 37

Bowl, 9 1/2" d., Tulips patt. on white opal 40

Canister, cov., French Ivory, 40 oz. 90

Canister, cov., Green Polka Dots patt. on
French Ivory, 48 oz. 75

Canister, cov., round, "Flour," Skokie
Green, 5" h. 145

Canister, cov., round, Skokie Green, no
lettering, 5" h. 90

Custard cup, marked "Sunkist," Skokie
Green 75

Custard cup, Skokie Green 28

Egg beater bowl w/spout, French Ivory........... 60

Egg beater bowl w/spout, Skokie Green......... 18

Egg cup, Chalaine Blue 25

Flour shaker w/original metal top, large
box, French Ivory 45

Flour shaker w/original metal top, Roman Arch style, Chalaine blue 140

Flour shaker w/original metal top, Roman Arch style, French Ivory, 4 1/4" h. 35

Flour shaker w/original metal top, Roman Arch style, Red Polka Dot patt. on French Ivory, 4 1/4" h. 45

Flour shaker w/original metal top, small box, French Ivory 40

Measuring cup, two pour spouts, Seville Yellow... 275

Pepper shaker w/original metal top, Roman Arch patt., Chalaine blue 22

Pepper shaker w/original metal top, Roman Arch patt., white opal 25

Roman Arch Pepper Shaker

Pepper shaker w/original metal top, Roman Arch style, French Ivory, 4 1/4" h. (ILLUS.)... 30

Pepper shaker w/original metal top, small box, French Ivory 30

Reamer, marked "Sunkist," Skokie Green 60

Refrigerator dish, cov., triangular, French Ivory 75

Refrigerator dish, cov., French Ivory, 4 x 5" 40

Refrigerator dish, cov., rectangular, Red Ship patt. on white opal, 4 x 5"...................... 35

Refrigerator dish, cov., Skokie Green, 4 x 5" 52

Refrigerator dish, cov., rectangular, Red Ships patt. on white opal, 4 x 8" 38

Sugar shaker, Roman Arch style, French Ivory, 4 1/4" h. 35

Sugar shaker w/original metal top, black w/white lettering 35

Sugar shaker w/original metal top, Chalaine Blue 190

Sugar shaker w/original metal top, large box, French Ivory 45

Sugar shaker w/original metal top, small box, French Ivory 35

Tom & Jerry cup, Skokie Green....................... 28

PRES-CUT LINES

Compote, open, 9 1/8" h., Puritan patt., wide shallow bowl w/a scalloped rim, slender swelled pedestal on a round foot, Skokie Green, early 20th c. 110

Compote, 11 1/2" d, Rock Crystal patt., footed, amber 65

Pitcher, "Eclipse," line, Yutec patt., clear 45

Pitcher, water, cov., Rock Crystal patt., pink.. 350

Pitcher, tankard, 8 1/2" h., Toltec patt., clear 100

Sundae, Rock Crystal patt., ruby....................... 35

Tumbler, Rock Crystal patt., footed, pink, 7 oz. 25

MISCELLANEOUS PATTERNS & PIECES

Bowl, berry, French Ivory 10

Bowl, w/pour spout, French Ivory...................... 26

Bowl, 8" d., Laurel patt., Skokie Green 45

Bowl, berry, 9" d., Laurel patt., French Ivory 25

Tumbler, French Ivory....................................... 12

Vase, 8" h., Sarah patt., Skokie Green.............. 48

Bottoms-Up Whiskey Tumbler & Base

Whiskey tumbler & base, Buttoms-Up patt., Seville Yellow, 2 pcs. (ILLUS.) 275

Whiskey tumbler & base, Buttoms-Up patt., Skokie Green, satin finish, 2 pcs. 138

MILK GLASS

Opaque white glass, or "opal," has been called "milk-white glass" perhaps to distinguish it from transparent or "clear-white glass." Resembling fine white porcelain, it was viewed as an inexpensive substitute. Opacity is obtained by adding bone ash or oxide of tin to clear molten glass. By the addition of various coloring agents, the opaque mixture can be turned into blue milk glass, or pink, yellow, green, caramel, even black milk glass. Collectors of milk glass now accept not only the white variety but virtually any opaque color and color mixtures, including slag or marbled glass. It has been made in numerous forms and shapes in this country and abroad from about the first quarter of the 19th century. Many of the items listed here were also made in colored opaque glass which collectors call blue or green or black 'milk glass.' It is still being produced, and there are many reproductions of earlier pieces. Pieces are all-white unless otherwise noted. Also see HISTORICAL, PATTERN GLASS and WESTMORELAND.

Animal covered dish, "American Hen," eagle w/eggs inscribed "Porto Rico," "Cuba," & "Philippines," 6" l., 4" h. $55

Animal covered dish, Bull's Head mustard jar, w/separate tongue spoon, original paint, Atterbury.. 250

Animal covered dish, Cat on Drum, Porteaux, France, 4 5/8" d. 110

Animal covered dish, Cat on lattice base, blue glass eyes, Westmoreland Specialty Company, early 20th c. 110

Animal covered dish, Cat on lattice base, original red glass eyes, Atterbury, 1880s (ILLUS. in color section)............................. 125

Setter Dog on Square Base Dish

Animal covered dish, Dog, Setter on square base, Vallerysthal (ILLUS.) 200-250

Animal covered dish, Dolphin with fish finial, Kemple, excellent, 7 1/2" l. 65

Animal covered dish, Dominecker Duck w/wavy base, glass eyes, fired-on paint, Challinor, Taylor & Co., 8" l. (top rim chip under tail, tiny open bubble on base) 310

Animal covered dish, Dove on split-ribbed base, signed "McKee" 275

Animal covered dish, Duck, Atterbury, very good, 11" l. 200

Animal covered dish, Duck, blue & white slag, L. G. Wright, Atterbury type, good, 6" l. 50

Animal covered dish, Duck on Basket, caramel slag satin, original factory sticker Jan. 1946 manufacturing date, Imperial, excellent 50

Animal covered dish, Duck on Rush Base, very good, 5 1/2" l. 60

Animal covered dish, Duck Swimming, blue, Vallerysthal, 5" l. (mite bite on edge) 80

Animal covered dish, Duck Swimming, traces of paint, Vallerysthal, 5 3/4" l. (crack on top edge of base) 270

Animal covered dish, Duck w/amethyst head, Atterbury, 11" l., 5" h. 350-400

Animal covered dish, Duck w/wavy base, glass eyes, Challinor, Taylor & Co., 5 1/4" h. 125-150

Animal covered dish, Elephant w/rider, blue, signed "Vallerystahl," 7" l. (broken bubble on ear) 600

Animal covered dish, Fish, blue, some original paint, signed "Vallerysthal," 7" l. (small chip inside nose of fish) 450

Cat on Split-Ribbed Base Dish

Animal covered dish, Cat on split-ribbed base, signed "McKee," 5 1/2" l. (ILLUS.)...... 375

Chicks on Round Basket Dish

Animal covered dish, Chicks on Round Basket, Westmoreland Specialty Company, old paint, early 20th c., 4 1/2" w., 3" h. (ILLUS.)... 90-110

Animal covered dish, Cow on oval paneled base, maker unknown, 6 1/4" l. 400-450

Animal covered dish, Crawfish on two-handled oblong base, overall 7 1/2" l. 160

Animal covered dish, Crouching Rabbit, Portieux, 7" l.. 275

Animal covered dish, Deer on fallen tree base, Flaccus, 6 3/4" l. 250-275

Animal covered dish, Dog on oval wide rib base, blue head, Westmoreland Specialty Company, early 20th c., 5 1/2" l. 55-60

Animal covered dish, Dog on Steamer Rug w/floral base, blue, Vallerysthal, excellent, 5" h... 130

Animal covered dish, Dog on Steamer Rug w/floral base, opaque yellow, Vallerysthal, round paper label "P.V. France," excellent, 5" h. 260

Animal covered dish, Dog, Pomeranian on diamond & stippled base, fair paint, Sandwich Glass Co., excellent, 4 3/4" l........ 450

Entwined Fish Covered Dish

Animal covered dish, Fish, Entwined Fish on lacy-edge base, shell finial, Atterbury, 7 1/2" d. (ILLUS.).................................... **200-225**

Animal covered dish, Fish, Vallerysthal, 7" l. **225-250**

Animal covered dish, Fox on ribbed top & lacy-edge base, Atterbury, 7 3/4" l. **143**

Animal covered dish, Frog sitting, mouth slightly open, signed "Vallerysthal"........ **225-250**

Animal covered dish, Hen on Basketweave base, blue body w/white head, Westmoreland Specialty Company excellent, 5 1/2" l. **35**

Animal covered dish, Hen on Basketweave base, blue, Vallerysthal, excellent, 6" l. **140**

Animal covered dish, Hen on Basketweave base, Challinor, Taylor & Co., 7" l. **70**

Animal covered dish, Hen on Basketweave base, signed "Vallerysthal," good, 7 1/2" l. **200-250**

Animal covered dish, Hen on Flared Basketweave Base, orange slag, Kanawha, excellent, 7 1/4" h. **100**

Animal covered dish, Hen on lacy base, blue, Atterbury, excellent, 7" l. **210**

Animal covered dish, Hen on lacy base, blue marble top, white base, red eyes, Atterbury, excellent, 7 1/2" l. **310**

Animal covered dish, Hen on Ribbed Base, red eyes, Atterbury, excellent, 7 1/4" l. **160**

Animal covered dish, Hen on rush base, excellent, 5 1/2" l. **40**

Animal covered dish, Hen on Scalloped Basket base, blue, Vallerysthal, top excellent, 5" l. (small flake on base rim)........ **60**

Animal covered dish, Hen w/amethyst head, lacy base, Atterbury **200-225**

Horse on Split-Ribbed Base Dish

Animal covered dish, Horse on split-ribbed base, 1989 convention commemorative, Summit Art Glass Co., excellent, 5 1/2" l. (ILLUS.).. **160**

Animal covered dish, Horse on split-ribbed base, McKee **275-300**

Animal covered dish, Hummingbird, ca. 1930s, Consolidated, excellent, 7" **200**

Lamb on Split-Ribbed Base Dish

Animal covered dish, Lamb on split-ribbed base, 1991 convention commemorative, Boyd's Crystal Art Glass Co., excellent, 5 1/2" l. (ILLUS.)............................ **70**

Animal covered dish, Lion, Majestic Lion, molded bird & foliage base, 6 3/4" h. **3,400**

Animal covered dish, Lion on Lacy Base, caramel slag, Imperial, excellent, 8 1/2" l. **160**

Lion on Scroll Base Dish

Animal covered dish, Lion on scroll base, 5 3/4" l. (ILLUS.).. **75**

Animal covered dish, Lion on split-ribbed base, McKee, top signed, mint, 5 1/2" l. (base not McKee).. **240**

Animal covered dish, Lion, Ribbed Lion on lacy-edged base, patent-dated, Atterbury, very good, 7 1/4" l. **145**

Animal covered dish, Love Birds, Westmoreland, marked entwined "WG" in base, good, 5 x 6" **40**

Animal covered dish, Mother Eagle, Challinor, Taylor, near perfect, 7" l. **650**

Animal covered dish, Owl Head on split-ribbed base, McKee **800-1,000**

Animal covered dish, Peep Emerging from Egg on Basket, top sits down on flange, not on top, traces of paint, very good, 3 1/2" h. **260**

Animal covered dish, Peep on Basket, Gillinder, much paint, excellent, 3 1/2" h. **170**

Animal covered dish, Pig on split-ribbed base, McKee, 5 1/2" l. (chip on tail)........... **4,100**

Animal covered dish, Quail on Scroll Base, excellent, 6 1/2" l................................. **65**

Animal covered dish, Rabbit, Flat-Eared Rabbit on split-ribbed base, McKee, 5 1/2" l. 300

Animal covered dish, Rabbit, green slag, 1988 convention commemorative, Summit, excellent, 5 1/2" l. 400

Animal covered dish, Rabbit, Lop-eared, some paint, signed "Vallerysthal," excellent, 6 1/2" l. 725

Animal covered dish, Rabbit on Diamond Basket with Eggs, blue, Westmoreland Specialty Co. drilled eyes, very good, 7 1/2" l. 60

Animal covered dish, Rabbit on split-ribbed base, green w/white head, green base, excellent, 5 1/2" l. 300

Atterbury Rabbit Dish

Animal covered dish, Rabbit, original red glass eyes, patent date stamped on bottom, Atterbury, 9" l. (ILLUS.) 250-275

Animal covered dish, Rabbits Cuddling, green, maker unknown, 6 1/4" l., 5 1/4" h. (lid repaired) 1,750

Animal covered dish, Robin on pedestal Nest, signed "Vallerysthal" 275

Animal covered dish, Rooster, base & top w/stippled interior, Kemple, "K" in circle on bottom, most of paint on comb, 7 1/4" l. (slight roughness base & top rims) 70

Animal covered dish, Rooster on Basketweave Base, Challinor, Taylor, 7 1/2" l. 90

Animal covered dish, Rooster on wide rib base, Westmoreland Specialty Company, 5 1/2" l. 45

Animal covered dish, Rooster Standing, blue, signed "Portieux," 9" h. (two no-show flea bites on top) 100

Animal covered dish, Snail on Strawberry, Vallerysthal, 5" h. (chip on inside flange of top) 90

Animal covered dish, Snapping Turtle, excellent, 9 3/4" l. 350

Animal covered dish, Squirrel, McKee, excellent, 5 1/2" l. (probably not old base) 225

Animal covered dish, Squirrel on acorn-shaped base, signed "Vallerysthal," 7 1/4" l. 215

Animal covered dish, Squirrel on fancy base, Vallerysthal, excellent, 5" l. 90

Animal covered dish, Steer's Head, old eyes, Challinor Taylor, small chips inside bottom rim, 7 7/8" l. (ILLUS. in color section) 5,500

Animal covered dish, Swan on Water, basketweave bottom, moulded eye, Challinor, Taylor, mismatch ?, 7" l. (small chips & roughness top & bottom rims) 160

Animal covered dish, Swan, open neck, signed in raised letters inside base, Vallerysthal, 5 1/2" l. (minor roughness top & bottom edges) 80

Animal covered dish, Swan, purple slag, L.G. Wright, good, 5 1/2" l. 80

Animal covered dish, Swan w/raised wings & glass eyes on lacy-edged base, Atterbury, 9 1/2" l. 150-175

Animal covered dish, Swan with Raised Wing, flat place for glass eyes, Atterbury, excellent, 10 1/4" l. 170

Imperial Turkey Covered Dish

Animal covered dish, Turkey, entwined "IG" on base, Imperial, ca. 1952-60 (ILLUS.) 60

Animal covered dish, Turkey on ribbed base, McKee, 5 1/2" l. 85

Animal covered dish, Turkey on split-ribbed base, McKee 250-275

Animal covered dish, Turkey Standing, L.E. Smith ?, excellent, 7 1/8" h. 90

Animal covered dish, Turtle on two-handled oblong base, Westmoreland Specialty Co., overall 7 1./2" l. 225-250

Animal covered dish, Turtle with Snail, Portieux, excellent, 8" l. 475

Ashtray, figural clown, excellent, some paint, maker unknown, 3 3/4 x 6 1/4" 105

Banana boat, open lace top w/basket base, blue, Atterbury, excellent, 11" w. 130

Basket, cov., w/metal tray insert to hold three perfume bottles, clear top w/embossed painted flowers, excellent, good paint, 4 1/4" d., the set (few small rust spots on tray) 70

Basket, two-handled, chick emerging from egg on cover 75

Bonbon container, La Tsarine, figural bust of Alexandra of Russia w/"LA Tsarine" & "Bonbons - John Tavernler" embossed above metal base closure, 13" h. (rusty metal closure) 200

Bone dish, Sardines & Salmon embossed inside bottom, Flaccus, excellent, 6 1/2" l., 2 pcs. 70

Book ends, Fighting Cock, Kemple Glass, very good, 8 1/4" h., pr. 90

Bottle, Baby Emerging from Egg, ground neck w/cork, black paint on baby, gold paint in cracks of shells, half of crescent-shaped label - "Rose," 2 1/2" h. 204

Bottle, Eagle patt., plastic silver lid, good, 5 3/4" h. 25

Bottle, Spanish Lady, red shawl, tambourine under arm, good, 12 1/4" h. 120

Bottle, Spanish Parrot, 8" h. (slight age lines) 75

Bottle w/original stopper, Pinch Bottle, yellow, very good, rare, 9 1/2" h. 55

Bottles, Billiken, shaker caps, base impressed "The God Of Things As They Ought To Be" & "Billiken," one w/label marked "Black Pepper Union Spice Co. Chicago, Ill.," 4 1/8" h., pr. 130

Bowl, cov., 6 1/2" d., Rib & Scroll patt., four-footed, Vallerysthal, excellent 45

Bowl, 7" d., 5" h., Chain & Petal Edge patt. 35

Bowl, 8" d., footed Wide Weave Basket design, Atterbury, open 60

Bowl, 8 3/4" d., 3 1/2" h., Crinkled Lacy Edge patt. 38

Rectangular Open Edge Bowl

Bowl, 8 3/4 x 9 1/4", rectangular w/open edge loop border (ILLUS.) **55-60**

Bowl, 10" d., 4 1/2" h., Acanthus Leaf patt., all-white 75

Bowl, 10" l., 5 3/4" h., oblong, Shell patt., two ribbed & two petal feet 55

Box, cov., heart-shaped, embossed floral design highlighted w/touches of blue & gold, McKee 35

Bread tray, Basketweave patt., Atterbury, patent-dated 1874, 9 3/4 x 12" 65

Butter dish, cov., Blackberry patt. 75

Butter dish, cov., Cow, top & bottom signed "Vallerysthal," some paint, 7" l. (few cooling lines) 450

Butter dish, cov., Daisy & Tree of Life patt. 175

Butter dish, cov., Dolphin & Shell, blue, Vallerysthal, excellent, 5" d. 80

Cake salver, Open Hand, 6 1/4" h. (nick on top edge) 70

Cake stand, Lacy Edge patt., Atterbury, 12" d., 2 3/4" h. 55

Candlestick, Sirene, Portieux, mint, 9 1/2" h. 250

Candlesticks, dolphin-footed, snake wrapped around column, blue, Portieux, excellent, 9 3/4" h., pr. **206**

Candy container, model of opera glasses, 2 7/8" h. **150**

Candy container, model of trunk, domed, very good **70**

Candy container, Oaken Bucket, good brown paint, tin closure, small **60**

Candy container, Oaken Bucket, good green paint, tin closure, large **60**

Candy container, Trumpet, closure, good paint **140**

Celery vase, fluted, Challinor Taylor, blue, good, 8 1/4" h. **85**

Celery vase, 9" h., The Hunt ("Trophee,") blue, Portieux, excellent **175**

Christmas bulb, Boy with Hat, "Little Chubby Man," good paint, excellent, 3 3/4" h. **35**

Cigarette box, cov., Turtle, Thousand Eye patt., Westmoreland, excellent, 7 1/2" l. **100**

Compote, cov., Melon with Leaf & Net patt., small size **75-90**

Compote, open, 6 1/4" h., square, Portieux, excellent **20**

Compote, open, 6 7/8" h., Chimeres design, blue, Portieux, excellent **70**

Compote, open, 7 1/2" h., Jenny Lind figural bust pedestal, ribbed bowl **110**

Goddess of Liberty Compote

Compote, open, 7 5/8" h., Goddess of Liberty patt., figural stem (ILLUS.) **125-150**

Compote, open, 8 1/4" d., 8 1/4" h., Atlas stem, scalloped rim, Atterbury **45**

Atterbury Lacy Edge Compote

Compote, open, 10" h., lacy-edge, ribbed
base, Atterbury, excellent (ILLUS.) 65
Compote, open, basin top w/dolphin base,
excellent, Westmoreland?............................ 195
Condiment or salt set: carousel-type
w/removable revolving tray of three cups
supported by a center column w/blunt,
knob-like top; swirl design, Portieux,
6 1/2" h., 2 pcs. 90
Covered dish, Admiral Dewey on round
basket base, "Dewey" on cover,
5 1/2" h. 300-350
Covered dish, Automobile, signed
"Portieux," France 175
Covered dish, Battleship "Maine," 7 1/2" l.,
3 1/2" h. 53
Covered dish, Boy with Dog (Puppy Love),
divided inside, excellent, 4 1/4" 410
Covered dish, Cinderella's Coach, L.E.
Smith, excellent, 6 3/4" l. 210
Covered dish, Fainting Couch, good paint,
very good, 5" l. 220
Covered dish, Hand & Dove on lacy-edged
base, Atterbury, 8 3/4" l., 4 3/4" h. 125-150
Covered dish, heart-shaped w/"Love
Laughs at Locks," good paint, excellent,
4 1/2" w. 50
Covered dish, Little Red Schoolhouse, all
original labels, excellent brown paint,
Westmoreland Specialty Co., excellent,
3 3/4" h. 150
Covered dish, Log Cabin, excellent brown
paint, all original labels, Westmoreland
Specialty Company, excellent, 4" h. 130
Covered dish, Moses in Bulrushes, excel-
lent, 5 1/2" l. 250
Covered dish, Pineapple, blue, Valleryst-
hal, excellent, 7 1/2" h. 25

Robed Santa Claus on Sleigh Dish

Covered dish, Robed Santa Claus on
Sleigh, some gold, Dobson & Co., very
good, 8" l. (ILLUS.)...................................... 300
Covered dish, Santa Claus, Santa on
Sleigh base, large head, Westmoreland
Specialty Company, early 20th c.,
5 1/2" l. 90-125

Covered dish, Snare Drum w/Cannon fin-
ial, 4 1/2" d., 4" h. 70-90
Covered dish, Stagecoach, Fostoria, 7" l
(small nick on running board)...................... 200
Covered dish, Trunk with Straps, France,
5 1/2" l. (small chip on base) 30
Creamer, Apple Blossom patt., decorated
& w/yellow band 25
Creamer, Louis XV patt., blue, excellent,
4 1/2" h. 20
Creamer, Paneled Flower patt. 85
Creamer, Swan patt., 5" h. 50-60
Creamer, miniature, Owl w/glass eyes,
3 1/2" h. 40
Cuspidor, lady's, fluted, blue, excellent,
8" d. 140
Dresser bottles w/stoppers, Leaf patt.,
green & gold decoration, 10" h., pr................ 50
Dresser jar, cov., Versailles patt.,
3 x 3 1/2" 65
Dresser tray, Actress patt., Fostoria Glass
Co. 55-65
Figure, American Indian Chief, no paint
shows "C or G" on back of right leg,
excellent, 6 1/2" h. 150
Figure, Dewey bust, Gillinder ?, good, 5" h...... 130
Flask, Klondike, "Woodley House" label,
closure, excellent 70
Flask, "Night Cap," imprinted w/face of man
wearing night cap, metal closure, good
paint, excellent, 4" h. 80
Flowerpot, Neptune patt., Portieux, excel-
lent, 6" h. 200
Fruit jar, Owl, threaded metal closure
w/embossed eagle on insert, original
eyes, excellent, 6 1/4" h., 1 pt. 140

Westmoreland Covered Gravy Boat

Gravy boat, cov., figural dolphin lid, Westmoreland, excellent, 7 1/4" l. (ILLUS.)............ 50
Holy water font, crucifix form, frosted,
6 1/2" h. (small chip on center under top
rim) 55
Inkwell, model of a Minstrel boy............... 125-135
Jar, cov., embossed British royal arms on
sides, figural bust portrait of Queen Vic-
toria on cover 95
Jardiniere, Mermaid patt., blue, Portieux,
6 1/2" w., 12" l., 5" h. 375
Lamp, Chubby Dog, Consolidated, excel-
lent & excellent paint, new wiring,
6 1/2" h. 350
Lamp, Skull, battery lit type, good, 3" to
5" h. 40
Lamp globe, "Fels Point," ovoid, vase-form
w/embossed sailboat, very good,
16 1/2" h. 100

Marmalade jar, Monkey patt., smooth top & rays on bottom, good paint, excellent, Duncan, 4 3/4" h... 303

Match holder, figural Indian Head, Challinor, Taylor, 4 3/4" h................................. 75

Match holder, model of an Easter basket w/chicken head on one side, & rabbit on reverse, gold & yellow paint, excellent, McKee, 4 1/4" l... 65

Match holder, model of bulldog head w/striker on back of head, possibly McKee, 2 1/4" h..................................... **125-150**

Match holder, model of pickle, green paint, excellent.. 35

Match holder, Old Man with Basket, blue, Portieux, excellent, 4" h.............................. 190

Match holder, pierced for hanging, basket-shaped w/scrolls & relief-molded painted rabbit & chick, attributed to Eagle Glass Co.. 125

Match holder, pierced for hanging, figural butterfly, Alpha, good, 4 1/8" w., 3 1/2" h.. 50

Match holder, pierced for hanging, Jolly Jester, 4 1/4" h... 90

Match holder, pierced for hanging, figural cluster of grapes, Challinor, Taylor, good, 4 1/4" h... 100

Model of car, Model T Convertible, 4" l. (age cracks inside bottom).......................... 105

Model of egg, Easter Egg with Emerging Chick, flat base, Gillinder, good paint, excellent, 2 1/2" l.. 45

Model of egg, Easter Egg with Emerging Chick, flat base, Gillinder, good paint, excellent, 3 1/4" l.. 55

Model of egg, Ugly Chick Emerging from Egg, excellent, 5" l.................................... 260

Model of egg, w/recessed portrait panel, gold paint, 4 1/4" l. (rim chip).................... 70

Model of rolling pin, blown, small amount of paint, ca. 1860s, England.......................... 50

Mug, Bird & Wheat, Atterbury, Eastlake, excellent, some paint, 2 1/4" h........................ 40

Mug, Bleeding Heart patt., U.S. Glass, 3 1/4" h. (small chip on bottom edge, not visible from side view).................................. 50

Mug, Cupids in Arches patt., good, 3 3/8" h.. 25

Mug, elephant handle, panels w/relief-molded nursery characters, signed "IG," Imperial, excellent, 3" h............................... 40

Mug, Grumpy Old Man & Woman, double-faced, opalescent, 2" h. (minor interior roughness)....................................... 90

Mug, Swan & Cattails patt. 45

Mustard jar, cov., hexagonal, Dutch scene decoration, Westmoreland, some paint, 4 1/4" h. (age marks).................................. 45

Mustard jar, cov., square, Oriental design, gold & blue paint, Westmoreland Specialty Company, 3 1/2" h. 35

Paperweight, Queen Victoria Bust, black, Thomas Kidd & Co., 3 1/2" l. (small flake on left side of headdress)............................ 850

Paperweight, St Bernard Dog, signed "Valerysthal," excellent paint, 5 1/2" l. (line across bottom, small flake underside).......... 300

Paperweight, Turtle, PL mark by front leg, 5" l. (two stress lines on bottom rim)............. 40

Pickle dish, model of a fish, Atterbury, 5 1/4 x 8".. 32

Challinor, Taylor Fish Pickle Dish

Pickle dish, model of a fish on base, waffle pattern on sides, glass or molded eyes, Challinor, Taylor & Company, 9" l., 3" h. (ILLUS.).. 140

Pin, oval black glass cameo w/profile of woman smelling flowers, gold wire wrap around edge, excellent, 1 1/4"........................ 50

Pitcher, tankard-type, Opaque Scroll patt........ 125

Pitcher, water, Wild Iris patt. 75

Pitcher, 7" h., bulbous body w/wide cylindrical neck, pinched spout & large C-form handle, embossed decoration of three little birds perched on branches on each side w/leaf decoration around neck, traces of paint (age marks)................. 100

Pitcher, 7" h., milk, Block Daisy patt. 70

Pitcher, 8" h., figural owl, white eyes not original, Challinor, Taylor, near perfect 150

Plaque, "Easter," Horseshoe with Rabbit, embossed rabbit, basket, chick, signed "P.L. Co." on back, fair paint, excellent, 6 1/4" l. 70

Lincoln Plaque

Plaque, Lincoln, Kemple, excellent, 8 1/4" h. (ILLUS.).. 210

Plaque, Lincoln, Westmoreland, rare original, excellent, 8 1/4" l. 305

Plaque, Madonna, relief-molded three dimensional design, 5 1/4" l. (small chip on back edge) **50**

Plaque, Sunken Rabbit with Clover, some paint, very good, 5 1/2" l............................. **370**

Plate, 4 3/8" d., Rising Sun patt......................... **50**

Plate, 6" d., Three Puppies patt., open leaf border, Westmoreland Specialty Company, early 20th c....................................... **155**

Plate, 6 1/4" d., Mother Goose patt., w/bunnies in relief... **183**

Plate, 6 3/8" d., "Easter Lay," chicks w/floral banner w/musical note, White, excellent **90**

Plate, 6 3/4" d., Easter Rabbits, in cabbage patch, old paint..................................... **45**

Plate, 7" d., Challinor's Forget-Me-Not patt........ **40**

Plate, 7" d., Roger Williams Memorial, flag, fleur-de-lis & eagles border **150-160**

Three Bears Plate

Plate, 7" d., Three Bears patt., traces of original brown, green & gilt paint (ILLUS.)... **45-55**

Plate, 7 1/4" d., "Easter," chick & basket of eggs, excellent paint, very good.................... **50**

Plate, 7 1/4" d., "Easter," Chicks, leaf & loop border, gold, yellow & green paint, Westmoreland, excellent............................... **25**

Plate, 7 1/4" d., "Easter," rabbits & eggs, scroll border **38**

Plate, 7 1/4" d., "Easter," Setting Hen and Chicks, slight gold paint **45**

Plate, 7 1/4" d., Lacy-Edge Indian patt., good paint **50-75**

Plate, 7 1/4" d., Pansy patt., molded openwork border **50-75**

Plate, 7 1/4" d., Pussy Cat, good paint, excellent... **470**

Plate, 7 1/4" d., Queen Victoria profile w/some gilding, club & fan border (age cracks in bowl of plate) **210**

Plate, 7 1/4" d., Spring Meets Winter, excellent... **45**

Plate, 7 1/4" d., Taft Campaign **60**

Plate, 7 1/4" d., Wm. McKinley & Wife & their home in Canton, Ohio w/"IT IS GOD'S WAY HIS WILL BE DONE," **125**

Plate, 7 1/2" d., Crown Border patt..................... **30**

Plate, 7 1/2" d., "Easter Opening," two chicks emerging from eggs & lily-of-the-valley, excellent paint, very good **70-95**

Plate, 7 1/2" d., Easter Sermon, no paint, very good **160**

Plate, 7 1/2" d., Hare & Cloverleaf patt., scalloped & beaded border **70-90**

Plate, 7 1/2" d., Maid of the Mist, boat & waterways on bottom, two flags on top, no paint, very good... **75**

Plate, 7 1/2" d., Owl Lovers, excellent................ **35**

Plate, 7 1/2" d., Sunken Rabbit w/"Easter Greetings," excellent **55**

Plate, 7 1/2" d., U.S. Battleship Maine, variant, Gothic border, white w/color decal (minor age cracks on border & minor flea bites on back rim)... **55**

Plate, 7 1/2" d., Yoked Slatted Border patt.... **30-40**

Plate, 6 1/2 x 7 3/4", Horseshoe & Anchor patt., patent-dated on back "December 10, 1901" **45**

Plate, 8" d., Fan & Circle Border patt., Atterbury... **30**

Plate, 8" d., Single Forget-Me-Not patt., openwork border **20**

Plate, 8" sq., Backward-C Border patt.............. **45**

Plate, 8 1/4" d., Three Puppies patt., open leaf border, Westmoreland Specialty Company, early-20th c. **125-150**

Lattice Edge Plate with Decoration

Plate, 9" d., Lattice Edge Border patt., painted trumpet vine center decoration (ILLUS.)... **45-65**

Plate, 9 1/4" d., Lincoln on Backward C border, L. E. Smith, excellent **40**

Plate, 9 3/4" d., Columbus, center bust of Columbus w/"1492 - 1892" on shoulders, club & shell border, mounted in footed silver plate holder w/handles, very good, good paint **55**

Plate, 11" d., Pinwheel Border patt., shallow pedestal, h.p. center **50**

Platter, 11 1/2" oval, Rock of Ages, white & clear, dated, excellent **105**

Platter, 10 1/2 x 13 3/4", model of a fish, flattened form w/scale details, Atterbury, patent-dated "June 4, 1872".................. **125-150**

Pomade jar, cov., Black Face, face forms lid, 2 7/8" h. (roughness around inside of base, several age cracks around rim) **155**

Punch set: 4 5/8" d. punch bowl & six 1 5/8" d. cups; Little Red Riding Hood patt., Nursery Rhyme series, decorated w/scenes from the fairy tale, 7 pcs. (flake on edge of two cups) **130**

Relish dish, model of a bird, flattened form w/oval dished center, attributed to Hemingray Glass Company, ca. 1876, 5 x 10 3/4", 2" h. **75**

Salt dip, footed, Strawberry patt. **40**

Salt dip, model of a basket w/handle, Atterbury, patent-dated, excellent, 3 3/4" l. **40-50**

Salt dip, model of sleigh w/eagle head between front runners, old gold paint on rim, 4 3/4" l. (mold roughness & glass overruns on runners, tiny peck on upper rim) **80**

Salt dip, open, master, double, Fighting Roosters, marked "SV" on base, 6 1/4 l. (stress mark on base & rim) **130**

Salt dip, open, master, Flying Fish, blue & yellow paint, excellent, 4 1/2" l. **180**

Salt dip, open, master, Swan, Gillinder, excellent, 5 1/2" l. (no chariot) **55**

Salt & pepper shaker (dredge) w/original top, Twin, figural stein, dispenses salt from one side & pepper from the other, Atterbury, 3 3/8" h. (1/8" chip to base rim) **75**

Salt & pepper shakers w/original tops, Heron & Lighthouse patt., pr. **95**

Salt & pepper shakers w/original tops, Scroll patt., pr. **50**

Shaker w/original top, Hen & Rabbit, egg-shaped, M. T. Thomas, patent applied for 1900, excellent, 3" h. **25**

Shaving mug, Centennial patt., decorated w/helmeted head of Viking, base marked "Patent Shaving Mug July 16," Brooks & McGrady, 3 1/4" h. (mold mark, small crack on side) **85**

Smoke bell, cranberry trim on fluted rim, w/original brass chain, 7" h. **55**

Smoking set, match holder & tray, some gold, 5 1/2" l., 2 pcs. (small chip under edge of tray) **20**

Spooner, Acanthus Leaf patt., base marked "Pat'd Apr. 23, '78," 4 5/8" h. **55**

Spooner, Blackberry patt. **50**

Spooner, Flower & Panel patt. **40**

Spooner, Strawberry patt., Bryce Brothers, good, 6" h. **40**

Sugar bowl, cov., figural pear, blue, gold painted leaves & stem, Vallerysthal, 5 1/2" h. **370**

Sugar bowl, cov., Melon with Leaf patt., patent-dated 1878 .... **90-110**

Sugar bowl, cov., model of a beehive, Vallerysthal **85**

Sugar bowl, cov., Renaissance patt., blue, Portieux, 6 1/2" d. (mold marks inside bowl, two shades of blue) **50**

Sugar bowl, cov., Roman Cross patt. (ILLUS. top of next column) **65**

Sugar bowl, cov., Versailles patt., pink decoration, 6" h. **45**

Sugar shaker w/original top, Challinor's Forget-Me-Not patt. **110**

Roman Cross Sugar Bowl

Sugar shaker w/original top, Little Shrimp patt. **75**

Syrup pitcher w/original top, Challinor's Banded Shells patt., h.p. apple blossoms & green shells **95**

Fishnet & Poppies Syrup Pitcher

Syrup pitcher w/original top, Fishnet & Poppies patt. (ILLUS.) **175**

Syrup pitcher w/original top, Heavy Scroll patt. **75**

Syrup pitcher w/original top, Torquay patt., h.p. yellow stripes **150**

Table set, The Family, figural heads, Little Boy creamer, excellent, Little Girl spooner, very good, Mother cov. sugar, very good, Father cov. butter, the set (sugar cover (hat) missing, butter w/tiny nicks) **1,500**

Toothpick holder, Horseshoe & Clover patt. **40-50**

Tray, Indian Chief's Head, lightly etched "Youghiocheny Opalescent Glass," Youghiocheny, excellent, 7 1/4" l. **75**

Tray, Old Man Smoking Pipe, excellent,
7 1/2" l. 65
Tray, Dahlia (in corners) patt., 8 x 10 1/4" 50
Tray, fish-shaped, excellent, Sweden,
10 1/2" l. 50
Tray, Diamond Grill patt. center, "Give Us
This Day" border, 10 x 12" 25
Trinket box, cov., Three Kittens patt., great
paint, Westmoreland, 2 1/2" sq. (chip
underside lid) 60
Trivets/ashtrays, marked w/entwined "IG,"
Imperial, good, in original box, 5 1/2" h.,
set of 4 28
Vase, 9 1/4" h., Three Figures with Satyr,
Portieux, very good 80
Water set: pitcher & six tumblers; Floral
Band patt., reddish floral trim, 7 pcs.
(one tumbler w/tiny nick) 90

Scroll Pattern Water Set

Water set: tankard pitcher & four tumblers;
Scroll patt., Challinor, Taylor & Com-
pany, 1880s, 5 pcs. (ILLUS.) 245
Whimsey, model of a canoe, enameled
flowers & gold trim, 6" l. 15
Whimsey, model of a Straw Hat (College
Hat), w/old paint, McKee, 4" d. 55
Whimsey, model of Uncle Sam's Hat, color
decoration, w/coin bank closure inside
brim 75
Whimsey vase, model of a hand holding a
cornucopia, ruffled rim, 8 1/2" h. 90

MONONGAH GLASS

*When fire destroyed the Rochester Tumbler
Company in Pennsylvania, some of the managers
and expert glassmen relocated to Fairmont, West
Virginia and opened their own company, Monongah
Glass. From 1904 until 1930 this company grew
until it had three factories and nearly one thousand
employees.*

*It was a highly regarded manufacturer of elegant
glass from the 1910s through the 1920s and produced popular colored patterns such as Bo-Peep*

*and Springtime. This latter pattern was a hand-
crafted design later reintroduced as the machine-
pressed Depression era Ballerina (Cameo) pattern
by Hocking Glass which had purchased Monongah.*

Almond dish, individual, footed, clear,
Grape etching No. 806, 1 1/2 oz. $12
Almond dish, individual, footed, clear,
Roseland etching No. 800, 1 1/2 oz. 24
Bowl, finger-type, clear bowl w/green foot,
Bo-Peep etching No. 854 42
Bowl, grapefruit, clear, Roseland etching
No. 800, 20 oz. 38
Compote, open, 6" d., tall footed, Roseland
etching No. 800, clear optic design 68
Compote, open, 6" d., tall footed, Spring-
time etching No. 270, clear 86
Compote, open, 7" d., low footed, Rose-
land etching No. 800, clear optic design 58
Creamer & sugar bowl, Secretary's Primrose etching No. 850, applied handles,
clear, pr. 58
Creamer & sugar bowl, Springtime etch-
ing No. 270, applied handles, clear
w/gold band decoration, pr. 78
Decanter w/original stopper, No. 41, No.
803 etching, clear 85

Springtime Etched Decanter

Decanter w/original stopper, No. 41,
Springtime etching No. 270, clear
(ILLUS.) 168
Goblet, Key Block Optic No. 13, pink, 10
oz. 28
Goblet, water, Bo-Peep etching No. 854,
rose pink 68
Goblet, water, clear bowl w/green twist
stem & foot, Arlene No. 655 cutting 35
Goblet, water, No. 6101, clear optic bowl
on double-melon green stem & green
foot 28
Goblet, water, No. 6102, herringbone optic
clear bowl, green twist stem & foot 32
Goblet, water, No. 6120, clear bowl
w/amber stem & foot, No. 660 cutting 28
Goblet, water, Roseland etching No. 800,
clear 34

Mug, toy, pressed Hobnail patt., clear 12
Parfait, Springtime etching No. 270, clear,
5 1/2 oz. 48

Arlene Cut Covered Pitcher

Pitcher, cov., jug-form, Arlene cutting No.
655, clear body w/green cover, handle &
foot, 58 oz. (ILLUS.) 108
Pitcher, cov., jug-form, Bo-Peep etching
No. 854, clear body w/green cover, han-
dle & foot 160
Pitcher, cov., jug-form, No. 20, Maxwell
cutting No. 660, clear body w/amber
cover, handle & foot, 58 oz. 87
Pitcher, jug-form, clear icicle & pinwheel
design body, No. 73 panel cutting, 31 oz. 42
Pitcher, jug-form, No. 20, Vida etching No.
808, clear body w/amber handle & foot 94
Pitcher, jug-form, Secretary's Primrose
etching No. 850, clear 95
Pitcher, jug-form, spiral optic design, rose
pink w/applied handle & foot 48
Pitcher, jug-form, Springtime etching No.
270, clear w/gold trim on the sheared
angled lip, 60 oz. 148
Pitcher, jug-form, Springtime etching No.
3270, clear w/gold trim, flat rim w/lip, 50
oz. 110
Plate, 6 1/2" d., salad, No. 10340, Spring-
time etching No. 270, clear 28
Plate, 7" d., Roseland etching No. 800,
star-cut bottom, clear 22
Plate, 7 1/2" d., salad, No. 10340, Bo-Peep
etching No. 854, green 40
Plate, 7 1/2" d., salad, No. 10340, Maxwell
cutting No. 600, amber 22
Plate, 8 1/2" d., Springtime etching No.
270, clear 34
Punch bowl, Bo-Peep etching No. 854,
rose pink 360
Salt dip, individual, footed, Grape etching
No. 805, clear, 3/4 oz. 14
Salt dip, individual, footed, Roseland etch-
ing No. 800, clear, 3/4 oz. 26
Sherbet, Roseland etching No. 800, pink 40
Tumbler, iced tea, footed, Bo-Peep etching
No. 854, rose pink 46
Tumbler, iced tea, handled, Roseland
etching No. 800, clear 36

Tumbler, iced tea, handled, Springtime
etching No. 270, clear 42
Tumbler, Secretary's Primrose etching No.
850, clear, 13 oz. 28

Bo-Peep Etched Vase

Vase, 9" h., No. 0713 barrel-shaped
w/crimped rim, Bo-Peep etching No.
854, rose pink (ILLUS) 168
Whiskey shot glass, Key Block Optic
design No. 13, pink, 1 3/4 oz. 18
Whiskey shot glass, Springtime etching
No. 270, clear, 2 1/2 oz. 40
Wine, Vida etching No. 808,clear bowl on
amber twist stem 36

MORGANTOWN
(OLD MORGANTOWN)

*Morgantown, West Virginia was the site where a
glass firm named the Morgantown glass Works
began in the late 19th century but the company
reorganized in 1903 to become the Economy Tumbler Company, a name it retained until 1929. By the
1920s the firm was producing a wider range of better quality and colorful glass tablewares and to
reflect this fact, they resumed their earlier name,
Morgantown Glass Works, in 1929. Today their
many quality wares of the Depression era are grow-
ing in collector demand.*

Bowl, dessert, Krinkle patt., yellow $30
Bowl, finger, footed Sunrise Medallion
(Dancing Girl) etching, clear 45
Bowl, individual salad, Krinkle patt., moss
green 22
Bowl, 5" d., Krinkle patt., moss green 25
Candlestick, Decor line, pineapple 38
Champagne, American Beauty etching,
No. 7668 25
Champagne, Art Moderne patt., green 50
Champagne, Art Moderne patt., transpar-
ent green 50
Champagne, Georgian patt., No. 7667,
Alexandrite 50
Champagne, Golf Ball patt., cobalt bowl
w/clear golf ball stem 44
Champagne, Golf Ball patt., ruby bowl
w/clear golf ball stem, large 25

Champagne, Monroe patt., No. 7690, red
& crystal 35
Champagne, Plantation patt., No 8445,
cobalt blue 120
Champagne, Plantation patt., ruby 40
Champagne, saucer type, No. 7692 50
Champagne, Sunrise Medallion (Dancing
Girl) etching, No. 7664, clear 95
Champagne, Yale patt., No. 7684, ruby red 50
Champagne-sherbet, Button patt., ruby
red 18
Champagnes, Hampton No. 7614, green
Palm Optic bowl, crystal stem, set of 4 100
Claret, Button patt., ruby red 24
Claret, Golf Ball patt., ruby bowl w/clear
golf ball stem 22
Claret, Old English patt., Stiegel green, 5
oz. 30
Cocktail, Carlton No. 7606-1/2 stem, 3 1/2
oz. 20
Cocktail, flat, Krinkle patt., ruby red 10
Cocktail, Golf Ball patt., cobalt bowl
w/clear golf ball stem 34
Cocktail, Golf Ball patt., ruby bowl w/clear
golf ball stem 31
Cocktail, Golf Ball patt., Steigel green bowl
w/clear golf ball stem 35
Cocktail, Old Fashion, Krinkle patt., ame-
thyst 13
Cocktail, Plantation patt., No. 8445, cobalt
blue 110
Cocktail, Polynesian Bis (aka Mai Tai),
amber stem 25
Cocktail, Superba etching, Legacy patt.,
No. 7654-1/2, clear 30
Cocktail, American Beauty etching, pink,
3 1/4 oz. 60
Cocktail, Carlton etching, platinum Marco
decoration, No. 7653, 3 1/2 oz. 45
Cocktail, twist, Elizabeth etching, blue,
5 1/2" 55
Cordial, Golf Ball patt., cobalt blue bowl
w/clear golf ball stem 50
Cordial, Golf Ball patt., ruby bowl w/clear
golf ball stem 50
Cordial, Golf Ball patt., smoke bowl w/clear
golf ball stem 39
Cordial, Golf Ball patt., Stiegel green bowl
w/clear golf ball stem 39
Cordial, Plantation patt., No.8445, cobalt
blue 175
Cordial, Sunrise Medallion patt., crystal 110
Dinner service: ten 8" plates, 5 water gob-
lets, 4 champagnes, 3 footed water tum-
blers; Mikado patt., 22 pcs. 120
Goblet, American Beauty etching, No.
7668 32
Goblet, Fontinelle patt., ebony filament
stem, 7 1/2", 9 oz. 160
Goblet, Golf Ball patt., emerald green bowl
w/clear golf ball stem 53
Goblet, Majesty patt., Spanish Red 30
Goblet, Sunrise Medallion (Dancing Girl)
etching, No. 7630, Azure blue 50
Goblet, water, Art Moderne patt., green 65
Goblet, water, Button patt., Cobalt blue 35
Goblet, water, Button patt., ruby red 22
Goblet, water, Carlton etching, ebony fila-
ment stem 120
Goblet, water, Churchill, No. 7692, cobalt 90
Goblet, water, Golf Ball patt., cobalt blue
bowl w/clear golf ball stem 44

Goblet, water, Golf Ball patt., ruby bowl
w/clear golf ball stem 30
Goblet, water, Golf Ball patt., smoke bowl
w/clear golf ball stem 26
Goblet, water, Old English patt., No. 7678,
ruby red 35
Goblet, water, Plantation patt., No. 8445,
cobalt blue 135
Goblet, water, tulip-shaped, Golf Ball patt.,
ruby bowl w/clear golf ball stem 56
Goblet, juice, Golf Ball patt., Ritz Blue bowl
w/clear golf ball stem, 5" h. 50
Goblet, iced tea, Golf Ball patt., Ritz Blue
bowl w/clear golf ball stem, 6 3/4" h. 60
Goblet, Golf Ball patt., cobalt blue bowl
w/clear golf ball stem, 9 oz. 60
Goblet, water, Golf Ball patt., Crystal
w/clear golf ball stem, No. 7643, 9 oz. 30
Goblet, water, Krinkle patt., pink, 10 oz. 14
Goblet in pierced metal stem holder,
cupped, amber 4
Goblet in pierced metal stem holder,
cupped, amethyst 8
Goblet in pierced metal stem holder,
cupped, emerald 4
Goblet in pierced metal stem holder,
cupped, heliotrope 7
Goblet in pierced metal stem holder,
flared, amethyst 7
Highball, Krinkle patt., Amethyst, 12 oz. 14
Ivy ball vase, Golf Ball patt., ruby w/clear
golf ball stem 225
Ivy ball vase, Peacock Optic patt., No.
7643, meadow green w/golf ball stem,
4" d. 89
Parfait, etched Fuchsia patt., clear, 5
15/16" 35
Pitcher, juice, Krinkle patt., amethyst 45
Pitcher, Krinkle patt., ruby w/crystal han-
dle, 50 oz. 150
Plate, 7 1/2" d., Sunrise Medallion (Danc-
ing Girl) etching, clear 18
Plate, 7 1/2" sq., Bridge Set, ebony 12
Sherbet, Fontinelle patt., ebony filament
stem, tall 120
Sherbet, footed, Krinkle patt., emerald
green 16
Sherbet, footed, Krinkle patt., moss green 14
Sherbet, Golf Ball patt., amber bowl
w/clear golf ball stem 20
Sherbet, Golf Ball patt., amethyst bowl
w/clear golf ball stem 20
Sherbet, Golf Ball patt., cobalt blue bowl
w/clear golf ball stem 29
Sherbet, Golf Ball patt., smoke bowl
w/clear golf ball stem 22
Sherbet, Golf Ball patt., topaz bowl w/clear
golf ball stem 22
Sherbet, low, Golf Ball patt., ruby bowl
w/clear golf ball stem 19
Sherbet, Sunrise Medallion patt., crystal 25
Sherbet, footed, Krinkle patt, amethyst,
6 oz. 14
Sherbet, Golf Ball patt., No. 7643, teal bowl
w/clear golf ball stem, 7 oz. 20
Tumbler, iced tea, footed, Krinkle patt.,
emerald green, 5 1/2" h. 20
Tumbler, iced tea, footed, Krinkle patt.,
moss green 21
Tumbler, iced tea, footed, Krinkle patt.,
pink 25

Tumbler, iced tea, Golf Ball patt., green
bowl w/clear golf ball stem 28
Tumbler, juice, flat, Krinkle patt., amber 8
Tumbler, juice, flat, Krinkle patt., pastel............. 10
Tumbler, juice, footed, Golf Ball patt., ruby
bowl w/clear golf ball stem 25
Tumbler, Sunrise Medallion patt., blue,
3 1/4" h., 3 oz. 150
Tumbler, water, footed, Mayfair (Sears Flo-
rentine) patt. 14
Tumbler, water, Mayfair patt. 30
Tumbler, water, Sunrise Medallion patt.,
crystal.. 35
Tumbler, American Beauty etching, clear,
10 oz., 3 3/4" h. 45
Tumbler, Queen Mary patt., pink, 5" h. 65
Tumbler, juice, Krinkle patt., amethyst,
6 oz. 8
Tumbler, Sunrise Medallion, crystal,
footed, 6 1/8" h. 40
Tumbler, Palm Optic patt., No. 9715, 9 oz. 10
Tumbler, footed, Krinkle patt., amethyst,
10 oz. 10
Tumbler, American Beauty patt., clear,
10 oz., 3 3/4" h. 45
Tumbler, Golf Ball patt., Cobalt blue
w/clear golf ball stem, 12 oz......................... 50
Tumbler, Golf Ball patt., Stiegel green
w/clear golf ball stem, 12 oz......................... 48
Tumbler, footed, Krinkle patt., amethyst,
13 oz. 20
Tumbler, Krinkle patt., amethyst, 14 oz. 13
Vase, 4" w., Kimble Ivy Ball, No. 7643, ruby
w/clear base & golf ball stem 95
Vase, 6" h., squat, Palm Optic patt., No. 59,
aquamarine 135
Vase, bud, 6" h., petite, Palm Optic patt.,
No. 46, Venetian green w/clear foot 35
Whiskey, footed, Art Moderne patt., clear &
black 85
Whiskey, footed, Krinkle patt., yellow 30
Wine, Button patt., ruby red 22
Wine, Golf Ball patt., cobalt blue bowl
w/clear golf ball stem.................................... 48
Wine, Golf Club patt., ruby bowl w/clear
golf ball stem... 32
Wine, low, Golf Club patt., ruby bowl
w'clear golf ball stem 50
Wine, Majesty patt., Spanish red...................... 35
Wine, Old English patt., No. 7678, cobalt
blue 65
Wine, Old English patt., ruby bowl w/clear
gold ball stem 55
Wine, Plantation patt., No.8445, cobalt blue..... 165
Wine, American Beauty etching, No. 7565,
clear, 2 oz. 65
Wine, American Beauty patt., No. 7565,
clear, 2 oz.. 65
Wine, Sunrise Medallion patt., crystal, 2 1/2
oz. 45
Wine, Golf Ball patt., No. 7643, crystal
w/clear golf ball stem, 3 oz. 20
Wine, Russel Wright, smoke, 4 oz. 20

NEW MARTINSVILLE

The New Martinsville Glass Manufacturing Company operated from 1900 to 1944, when it was
taken over by new investors and operated as the
Viking Glass Company. In its time, the New Martinsville firm made an iridescent art glass line called

Muranese along with crystal pattern glass (included
ruby-stained items) and, later, the transparent and
opaque colors which were popular during the 1920s
and 1930s. Measell's New Martinsville Glass 1900-
1944 covers this company's products in detail.

Covered Batter Jug

Batter jug, cov., dark green (ILLUS.)............... $95
Bonbon, Janice patt., clear............................... 20
Book end, "Nautilus," clear, 6" h...................... 22
Book ends, Clipper Ship patt., No. 499,
clear, 5 3/4" h., pr... 60
Bowl, cream soup, Moondrops patt., amber....... 70
Bowl, 8" d., three-footed, Moondrops patt.,
amber.. 22
Bowl, 11" oval, Janice patt., No. 4551-2SJ,
two swan handles, red 225

No. 18 Bowl

Bowl, 15" oval, No. 18, amber (ILLUS.) 90
Bride's basket, Muranese, vivid gold iri-
descence in ornate silver-plated holder,
9".. 400
Butter dish, cov., Carnation patt. (No. 88
Line), clear w/ruby-stain & gold decora-
tion 275
Butter dish, cov., Old Glory patt. (No. 719
Line), clear w/gold decoration 100

No. 10/4 Candleholders

Candleholder, No. 10/4, blue (ILLUS. left) 35
Candleholder, No. 10/4, jade green
(ILLUS. right)... 45
Candleholder, No. 10/4, light green
(ILLUS. center)... 35

Modernistic Candleholders

Candleholders, Modernistic patt. (No. 33 Line), light green w/cut decoration, pr. (ILLUS.) **125**
Candy box, cov., Janice patt. (No. 45 Line), light blue **125**
Candy box, cov., Modernistic patt. (No. 33 Line), black w/traces of silver overlay **90**

Modernistic Candy Box

Candy box, cov., Modernistic patt. (No. 33 Line), blue, satin finish (ILLUS.) **125**

Covered Candy Jar

Candy jar, cov., clear w/h.p. orange decoration & gold trim (ILLUS.) **52**
Celery dish, Janice patt., No. 4521-1SJ, oval, swan handle, red, 11" l. **125**
Celery dish, Janice patt., No. 4521-2SJ, oval, two swan handles, red, 11" l. **225**
Celery vase, Rock Crystal patt. (No. 49 Line), overall gold decorated **160**

Moondrops Comport & Sherbet

Comport, 4" d., stemmed, Moondrops patt. (No. 37 Line), cobalt blue (ILLUS. left) **40**
Comport, No. 35 (Statesman), jade green, small **45-50**

New Martinsville Console Bowl

Console bowl, blue w/black base (ILLUS.) **65**
Creamer, Carnation patt. (No. 88 Line), clear w/ruby-stain & gold decoration **125**

Rock Crystal Child's Creamer

Creamer, child's, Rock Crystal patt. (No. 49 Line), overall gold decorated (ILLUS.) **125**
Creamer, Klear-Kut (No. 705 Line), clear w/ruby-stain **185**
Creamer, Old Glory patt. (No. 719 Line), clear w/gold decoration **75**
Creamer & sugar bowl, Modernistic patt. (No. 33 Line), green satin finish, pr. **110**

Silver Overlay Creamer & Sugar Bowl

Creamer & sugar bowl, Modernistic patt. (No. 33 Line), opaque jade green w/Call of the Wild silver overlay, pr (ILLUS.)........... **200**
Creamer & sugar bowl, Moondrops patt. (No. 37 Line), amber, pr. **45**

No. 35 Creamer & Sugar Bowl

Creamer & sugar bowl, No. 35 (Statesman), jade green, pr. (ILLUS.) **60**
Creamer & sugar bowl w/tray, individual, Janice patt. (No. 45 Line), light blue, the set **60**
Creamer & sugar bowl w/tray, Janice patt. (No. 45 Line), light blue, the set **75**
Cruet set: oil & vinegar cruets w/original tops & tray; Janice patt (No. 45 Line), light blue, the set........................... **75**
Cruet w/original stopper, Celtic patt. (No. 100 Line), clear w/gold decoration **175**
Cruet w/original stopper, Prelude patt., clear **50**
Cup & saucer, Janice patt., blue **22**
Cup & saucer, Moondrops patt., amber **10**
Cup & saucer, Moondrops patt., red **20**

No. 34 Cup & Saucer

Cup & saucer, No. 34 (Addie), jade green & black, pr. (ILLUS.)...................................... **20**
Cup & saucer, No. 34 (Addie), ruby, pr. **20**

No. 35 Cup & Saucer

Cup & saucer, No. 35 (Statesman), jade green, pr. (ILLUS.) **25**

Satin-finished Dresser Set

Dresser set: two perfume bottles w/original stoppers & powder box on rectangular tray; blue, satin finish, the set (ILLUS.) **250**

Hand-painted Dresser Set

Dresser set: two perfume bottles w/original stoppers & powder box on rectangular tray; green w/h.p. floral decoration, the set (ILLUS.) **325**
Finger bowl, Rock Crystal patt. (No. 49 Line), overall gold decorated........................ **100**
Flower bowl, Janice patt. (No. 45 Line), crimped rim, light blue **95**
Goblet, luncheon, Janice patt. (No. 45 Line), light blue.. **35**
Ivy vase, Janice patt. (No. 45 Line), light blue **65**
Mayonnaise dish, Janice patt., clear, 6" **18**

Moondrops Mug

Mug, handled, Moondrops patt. (No. 37 Line), amber, large (ILLUS.)........................... **60**
Night lamp, miniature, By-the-Sea patt., opaque pink.. **425**

Flowering Vine Miniature Night Lamp

Night lamp, miniature, Flowering Vine patt., opaque green (ILLUS.)........................ 300

Night lamp, miniature, Iris patt., opaque pink.. 400

Pitcher, Celtic patt. (No. 100 Line), clear w/gold decoration 85

Pitcher, Klear-Kut (No. 705 Line), clear w/ruby-stain... 325

Pitcher, Rock Crystal patt. (No. 49 Line), overall gold decorated................................. 225

Plate, 6 1/8" d., Moondrops patt., amber.............. 4

Plate, 8" d., Janice patt., blue............................ 12

Plate, 8 1/2" d., Moondrops patt., amber.............. 8

Platter, Janice patt., blue 50

Powder box, cov., Martha Washington patt., pink satin finish 145

Punch bowl w/underplate & ladle, Radiance patt. (No. 42 Line), ruby, the set.......... 450

Relish dish, two-part, Radiance patt. (No. 42 Line), w/metal handle, red (light wear on handle) 38

Moondrops Relish Tray

Relish tray, three-part, handled, Moondrops patt. (No. 37 Line), cobalt blue (ILLUS.).. 75

Salt & pepper shakers w/original tops, Janice patt. (No. 45 Line), light blue, pr. 110

Salt & Pepper shakers w/original tops, Radiance patt. (No. 42 Line), ruby, pr......... 100

Sandwich tray, No. 34 (Addie), black........... 75-80

Sandwich tray, No. 34 (Addie), jade green 90

Sandwich tray, No. 35 (Statesman), jade green... 80

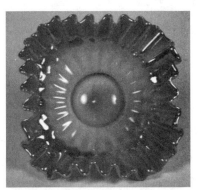

Muranese Sauce Dish

Sauce dish, Muranese, square, crimped rim (ILLUS.).. 145

Shade, gas, Muranese 125

Sherbet, Janice patt., blue 18

Sherbet, stemmed, Moondrops patt. (No. 37 Line), cobalt blue (ILLUS. right w/comport) 50

Sherbet, Moondrops patt., red, 4 1/2" h............. 27

New Martinsville Smoking Set

Smoking set, two ashtrays & cigarette pack holder on rectangular tray, amethyst, the set (ILLUS.) 275

Soup bowl, Moondrops patt., red.................... 115

Spooner, Carnation patt. (No. 88 Line), clear w/ruby-stain & gold decoration 125

Spooner, Old Glory patt. (No. 719 Line), clear w/gold decoration 80

Sugar bowl, cov., Carnation patt. (No. 88 Line), clear w/ruby-stain & gold decoration 200

Klear-Kut Sugar Bowl

Sugar bowl, cov., Klear-Kut (No. 705 Line), clear w/ruby-stain (ILLUS.) **225**

Sugar bowl, cov., Old Glory patt. (No. 719 Line), clear w/gold decoration **90**

Sugar bowl, individual, Moondrops patt., red **13**

Sugar bowl, Moondrops patt., amber **10**

Swan dish, Sweetheart shape, emerald green, 5" l. **20**

Swan dish, Janice patt., crystal body, cobalt blue head, 12" l. **76**

Sweetmeat w/holder, Muranese (Sun Glow Peach Blow) **250**

Tumbler, Celtic patt. (No. 100 Line), clear w/gold decoration **20**

Moondrops Handled Tumblers

Tumbler, handled, Moondrops patt. (No. 37 Line), amber w/simulated cut decoration, 2 oz. (ILLUS. left) **18**

Tumbler, handled, Moondrops patt. (No. 37 Line), green, 2 oz. (ILLUS. right) **15**

Tumbler, Janice patt., footed, blue **20**

Tumbler, Klear-Kut (No. 705 Line), clear w/ruby-stain **85**

Moondrops Tumbler

Tumbler, Moondrops patt. (No. 37 Line), amethyst, 12 oz. (ILLUS.) **22**

Tumbler, Muranese (Peach Blow) **250**

Tumbler, water, Rock Crystal patt. (No. 49 Line), overall gold decorated **45**

Tumbler, whiskey, Moondrops patt., red, 1 3/4" h. **14**

Tumbler, Moondrops patt., red, 3 1/4" h., 3 oz. **14**

Tumbler, Moondrops patt., pink, 4 7/8" h., 9 oz. **13**

Tumbler, Moondrops patt., handled, green, 9 oz. **27**

Vase, 8" h., Janice patt. (No. 45 Line), flared rim, light blue **200**

Vase, Janice patt., cupped rim, red **165**

Vase, Janice patt., flared, black **150**

Modernistic Vase

Vase, Modernistic patt. (No. 33 Line), black (ILLUS.) **100**

Vase, Modernistic patt. (No. 33 Line), blue satin finish **80**

Satin-finished Vase

Vase, Modernistic patt. (No. 33 Line), pink, satin finish (ILLUS.) **85**

Vase, 3 1/2" h., Janice patt., blue **25**

Wine, Moondrops patt., red, 4" h. **20**

NORTHWOOD

Harry Northwood (1860-1919) was born in England, the son of noted glass artist John North-wood. Brought up in the glass business, Harry immigrated to the United States in 1881 and shortly thereafter became manager of the La Belle Glass Company, Bridgeport, Ohio. Here he was responsible for many innovations in colored and blown glass. After leaving La Belle in 1887 he opened The Northwood Glass Company in Martins Ferry, Ohio in 1888. The company moved to Ellwood City, Pennsylvania in 1892 and Northwood moved again to take over a glass plant in Indiana, Pennsylvania in 1896. One of his major lines made at the Indiana, Pennsylvania plant was Custard glass (which he called "ivory"). It was made in several patterns and some pieces were marked on the base with "Northwood" in script.

Harry and his family moved back to England in 1899 but returned to the U.S. in 1902 at which time he opened another glass factory in Wheeling, West Virginia. Here he was able to put his full talents to work and under his guidance the firm manufactured many notable glass lines including opalescent wares, colored and clear pressed tablewares, various novelties and probably best known of all, Carnival glass. Around 1906 Harry introduced his famous "N" in circle trade-mark which can be found on the base of many, but not all, pieces made at his factory. The factory closed in 1925.

In this listing we are including only the clear and colored tablewares produced at Northwood factories. Specialized lines such as Custard glass, Carnival and Opalescent wares are listed under their own headings in our Glass category.

Northwood Signature
Mark, ca. 1898

Northwood "N" in
Circle Mark, ca. 1906

Almond Dish

Almond dish, cov., low-sided round ribbed dish w/low domed cover w/knob finial, Chinese Coral, Wheeling, West Virginia factory (ILLUS.) **$90**

Berry set: master bowl & six sauce dishes; Regal patt., clear opalescent, Wheeling, West Virginia factory, 7 pcs. **225**

Berry set: master bowl & 6 sauce dishes; Leaf Umbrella patt., cranberry, Martins Ferry, Ohio factory, 7 pcs. **600**

No. 643 Covered Bonbon

Bonbon, cov., footed, No. 643, Rosita Amber, Wheeling, West Virginia factory (ILLUS.) **60**

Grape Frieze Bonbon

Bonbon, low round dish w/applied loop handle on one side, Grape Frieze patt., "Verre D'or" decoration on dark amethyst, Wheeling, West Virginia factory (ILLUS.) **90**

Stretch Bowl

Bowl, deep lobed sides, on square flaring foot, pearl Stretch glass, Wheeling, West Virginia factory (ILLUS.) **60**

Bowl, master berry, Chrysanthemum Swirl patt., clear opalescent, Martins Ferry, Ohio factory **70**

Posies & Pods Master Berry Bowl

Bowl, master berry, Posies and Pods patt., green w/gold trim, Wheeling, West Virginia factory (ILLUS.) **85**

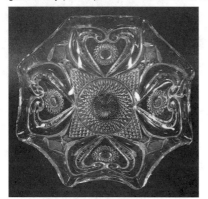

Valentine (No. 14) Bowl

Bowl, octagonal lobed sides, Valentine (No. 14) patt., Wheeling, West Virginia factory (ILLUS.) **30**

Cashews Bowl

Bowl, 8" d., Cashews patt., crimped rim, clear opalescent, Wheeling, West Virginia factory (ILLUS.) **35**

Butter dish, cov., Alaska patt., blue opalescent w/h.p. decoration, Indiana, Pennsylvania factory **300**

Butter dish, cov., Apple Blossom patt., decorated milk glass, Indiana, Pennsylvania factory **60**

Butter dish, cov., Peach patt., clear, Wheeling West Virginia factory **75**

Celery tray, Alaska patt., blue opalescent, Indiana, Pennsylvania factory **375**

Celery vase, Cherry Thumbprint patt., clear, Wheeling West Virginia factory **95**

Celery vase, Chrysanthemum Swirl patt., cranberry opalescent, satin finish, Martins Ferry, Ohio factory **165**

Cologne bottle w/original stopper, Leaf Mold patt., vaseline w/cranberry spatter, Martins Ferry, Ohio factory **450**

Brecciated Marble Compote

Compote, open, Brecciated Marble glass, Wheeling, West Virginia factory (ILLUS.) **400**

Northwood Stretch Compote

Compote, open, deep flaring bowl on a tall stem w/double knobs, round foot, blue, Wheeling West Virginia factory (ILLUS.) **75**

Iceland Poppy Compote

Compote, open, Iceland Poppy patt., "Verre D'or" decoration on dark blue, Wheeling, West Virginia factory (ILLUS.) **125**

Console set: footed compote & pair of
9 1/2" h. candlesticks; Chinese Coral, 3
pcs., Wheeling West Virginia factory.............. **85**

Belladonna Blue Creamer

Creamer, Belladonna (No.31) patt., blue
w/h.p. decoration, Wheeling, West Vir-
ginia factory (ILLUS.) **90**

Cherry & Cable Color-stained Creamer

Creamer, Cherry & Cable patt., color-
stained trim, Wheeling, West Virginia
factory (ILLUS.) **40**
Creamer, Cherry Thumbprint patt., clear,
Wheeling, West Virginia factory **35**
Creamer, child's size, Belladonna (No. 31)
patt., clear, Wheeling, West Virginia fac-
tory **45**

Grape & Leaf Decorated Creamer

Creamer, Grape and Leaf patt., opaque
white w/h.p. decoration, Indiana, Penn-
sylvania factory (ILLUS.) **125**

Four-footed Square Hobnail Creamer

Creamer, Hobnail, four-footed, amber, La
Belle Co., Bridgport, Ohio (ILLUS.) **100**
Creamer, Intaglio patt., blue opalescent,
Indiana, Pennsylvania factory **95**
Creamer, Klondyke (Fluted Scrolls) patt.,
blue opalescent, Indiana, Pennsylvania
fáctory **95**

Leaf Medallion Green Creamer

Creamer, Leaf Medallion (Regent) patt.,
green w/gold, Wheeling, West Virginia
factory (ILLUS.) **145**

Leaf Umbrella Creamer and Pitcher

Creamer, Leaf Umbrella patt., Rose du
Barry, Martins Ferry, Ohio factory
(ILLUS. left) **375**

Lustre Flute Creamer

Creamer, Lustre Flute, green, Wheeling, West Virginia factory (ILLUS.) **50**

Creamer, Lustre Flute patt., blue opalescent, Wheeling, West Virginia factory **90**

Creamer, Memphis patt., clear w/gold trim, Wheeling, West Virginia factory **40**

Mikado (Flower & Bud) Creamer

Creamer, Mikado (Flower & Bud) patt., clear w/gold & enameled trim, Wheeling, West Virginia factory (ILLUS.) **125**

Creamer, Netted Oak patt., decorated milk glass, Indiana, Pennsylvania factory **60**

Panelled Holly Opalescent Creamer

Creamer, Paneled Holly patt., white opalescent w/enameled decoration, Wheeling, West Virginia factory (ILLUS.) **60-70**

Panelled Holly Creamer

Creamer, Panelled Holly patt., blue opalescent w/gold trim (ILLUS.) **200**

Creamer, Peach patt., clear w/gold & red trim, Wheeling, West Virginia factory **72**

Creamer, Scroll with Acanthus patt., blue opalescent, Wheeling, West Virginia factory **125**

Scroll with Acanthus Creamer

Creamer, Scroll with Acanthus patt., "Mosaic," (slag) glass, Wheeling, West Virginia factory (ILLUS.) **100**

Creamer & cov. sugar bowl, Netted Oak patt., decorated milk glass, Indiana, Pennsylvania factory, pr. **195**

Chrysanthemum Swirl Cruets

Cruet w/original faceted stopper, Chrysanthemum Swirl patt., cranberry opalescent, note difference in stripe widths, Martins Ferry, Ohio factory, each (ILLUS.) **200-250**

Carnelian (Everglades) Cruet

Cruet w/original stopper, Carnelian (Everglades) patt., canary opalescent, Wheeling, West Virginia factory (ILLUS.) **700**

Cruet w/original stopper, Diadem (Sunburst on Shield) patt., blue opalescent, Wheeling, West Virginia factory **850**

Encore (Jewel & Flower) Cruet

Cruet w/original stopper, Encore (Jewel & Flower) patt., blue opalescent, Wheeling, West Virginia factory (ILLUS.) **750**

Cruet w/original stopper, Leaf Umbrella patt., cased blue w/clear facet-cut stopper, Martins Ferry, Ohio factory, 7" h. **275**

Paneled Sprig Cruet & Shakers

Cruet w/original stopper, Paneled Sprig patt., milk white w/color trim, Ellwood City, Pennsylvania factory (ILLUS. center) **300**

Cruet w/original stopper, Regal patt., blue opalescent, Wheeling, West Virginia factory **750**

Teardrop Flower Cruet

Cruet w/original stopper, Teardrop Flower patt., amethyst, Wheeling, West Virginia factory (ILLUS.) **750**

Grape & Leaf Cruet

Cruet w/replaced stopper, Grape & leaf patt., cased opaque green, Ellwood City, Pennsylvania factory (ILLUS.)..................... **100**

Leaf Umbrella Pattern Cruet

Cruet w/replaced stopper, Leaf Umbrella patt., crystal w/a frosted smoky finish, Martins Ferry, Ohio factory (ILLUS.) **100**

Fluted Scrolls Dish

Dish, Fluted Scrolls patt., tricornered, ruffled edge, three-footed, canary opalescent, 7" w., Ellwood City, Pennsylvania factory (ILLUS.) **42**

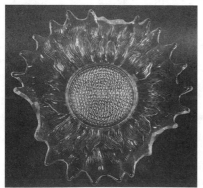

Sunflower Dish

Dish, Sunflower patt., rolled rim, clear, Wheeling West Virginia factory (ILLUS.)........ **30**

Grape & Cable Blue Dresser Tray

Dresser tray, oval, Grape & Cable patt., cobalt blue, Wheeling, West Virginia factory (ILLUS.).. **250**

Decorated Apple Blossom Fairy Lamp

Fairy lamp, Apple Blossom patt., opaque white w/h.p. decoration, Indiana, Pennsylvania factory (ILLUS.) **500**

Southern Gardens Fruit Dish

Fruit dish, Southern Gardens patt., Verre d'Or treatment, blue w/gold decoration, Wheeling, West Virginia factory, 10" d. (ILLUS.)... **325**

Kerosene Lamp w/Grape Decoration

Lamp, hand-type, kerosene, globular font w/molded ribs on a flaring foot w/finger grip handle & interior grape pattern, clear, Wheeling, West Virginia factory (ILLUS.).. **175**

Singing Birds Mug

Mug, Singing Birds patt., blue opalescent, Wheeling, West Virginia factory (ILLUS.)........ **60**
Mug, Singing Birds patt., blue opalescent, Wheeling, West Virginia factory **90**

Decorated Northwood Pitcher w/Label

Pitcher, bulbous panelled shape, green w/h.p. grapevine decoration & gold trim, original Northwood label on the base, Wheeling, West Virginia factory (ILLUS.)..... **475**

Blue Covered Pitcher w/Iridescence

Pitcher, cov., footed ovoid body, blue w/light iridescence, Wheeling, West Virginia factory (ILLUS.) **600**
Pitcher, milk, Leaf Umbrella patt., blue w/milk glass lining, Martins Ferry, Ohio factory (ILLUS. right w/creamer) **500**

Rare Opalescent Royal Oak Pitcher

Pitcher, Royal Oak patt., cranberry opalescent Swirl design, Martins Ferry, Ohio factory (ILLUS.) **1,200**

Clear Decorated Northwood Pitcher

Pitcher, tankard, panelled, clear w/h.p. floral decoration & gold trim, Wheeling, West Virginia factory (ILLUS.) **160**

Decorated Green Tankard Pitcher

Pitcher, tankard, panelled, dark green w/h.p. floral decoration & gold trim, Wheeling, West Virginia factory (ILLUS.) **175**

Green Intaglio Water Pitcher

Pitcher, water, Intaglio patt., green w/gold decoration, Indiana, Pennsylvania factory (ILLUS.) **165**

Rubina Jewel Pattern Pitcher

Pitcher, water, Jewel patt., rubina, Martins Ferry, Ohio factory (ILLUS.) **350**
Pitcher, water, Netted Oak patt., decorated milk glass, Indiana, Pennsylvania factory **175-200**

Pump Novelty

Pump & Trough, white opalescent, 2 pcs., Ellwood City, Pennsylvania factory (ILLUS.) **100**
Salt & pepper shakers w/original metal tops, Apple Blossom patt., opaque white w/h.p. decoration, Indiana, Pennsylvania factory the pair **325**
Salt & pepper shakers w/original tops, Apple Blossom patt., decorated milk glass, Indiana, Pennsylvania factory, pr......... **60**
Salt & pepper shakers w/original tops, Paneled Sprig patt., milk white w/color trim, Indiana, Pennsylvania factory, pr. (ILLUS. left & right w/cruet) **150**
Salt & pepper shakers w/original tops, Paneled Sprig patt., white opalescent w/lattice design, Indiana, Pennsylvania factory, 3 1/4" h., pr. **85**

Bow and Tassel Blue Salt Shaker

Salt shaker w/original top, Bow and Tassel patt., opaque blue, Ellwood City, Pennsylvania factory (ILLUS.) **50**

Salt shaker w/original top Cactus patt., cranberry opalescent, Ellwood City, Pennsylvania factory **325**

Opaque Green Cactus Salt Shaker

Salt shaker w/original top Cactus patt., opaque green, Ellwood City, Pennsylvania factory (ILLUS.) **85**

Opaque Pink Cactus Salt Shaker

Salt shaker w/original top Cactus patt., opaque pink, Ellwood City, Pennsylvania factory (ILLUS.) **90**

Salt shaker w/original top, Leaf Mold patt., pink & white cased spatter, Martins Ferry, Ohio factory **143**

Salt shaker w/original top, Leaf Umbrella patt., cased blue, Martins Ferry, Ohio factory **75**

Salt shaker w/original top, Parian Swirl patt., milk glass w/floral decoration, Martins Ferry, Ohio factory **125**

Parian Swirl Salt Shaker

Salt shaker w/original top, Parian Swirl patt., opaque blue w/h.p. decoration, Martins Ferry, Ohio factory (ILLUS.) **145**

Ribbed Opal Lattice Salt Shaker

Salt shaker w/original top, Ribbed Opal Lattice patt., cranberry, Martins Ferry, Ohio factory (ILLUS.) **60-75**

Sauce dish, Leaf Medallion (Regent) patt., purple w/gold trim, Wheeling, West Virginia factory **40**

Decorated Singing Birds Sauce Dish

Sauce dish, Singing Birds patt., clear w/blue decoration, Wheeling, West Virginia factory (ILLUS.) **40**

Northwood Luna Ivory Shade

Shade, domed Luna Ivory glass w/embossed scroll design trimmed w/nutmeg brown stain, Wheeling, West Virginia factory (ILLUS.) **100**

Trumpet-shaped Shades

Shades, trumpet-shaped w/molded ribs, marigold Carnival finish, Wheeling, West Virginia factory, each (ILLUS.) **60-75**

Northwood Sherbet & Underplate

Sherbet & underplate, No. 685 sherbet & No. 729 underplate, jade green, Wheeling, West Virginia factory, 2 pcs. (ILLUS.) **100**

Northwood No. 722 Snack Set

Snack set: cup & underplate; No. 722, Chinese Coral, Wheeling, West Virginia factory, 2 pcs. (ILLUS.) **95**

Spooner, Cherry Thumbprint patt., clear, Wheeling, West Virginia factory **55**

Klondyke Opalescent Spooner

Spooner, Klondyke (Fluted Scrolls) patt., topaz opalescent, Indiana, Pennsylvania factory (ILLUS.) **110**

Spooner, Netted Oak patt., decorated milk glass, Indiana, Pennsylvania factory **45**

Spooner, Plums & Cherries patt., clear w/ruby & gold trim, Wheeling, West Virginia factory **75**

Belladonna Sugar Bowl

Sugar bowl, cov., Belladonna patt., clear w/enameled trim, Wheeling, West Virginia factory (ILLUS.) **50**

Sugar bowl, cov., Cherry thumbprint patt., clear, Wheeling, West Virginia factory **100**

Sugar bowl, cov., Panelled Sprig patt., Granite Ware (rough speckled white surface) w/gold decoration, Ellwood City, Pennsylvania factory (ILLUS.) **175**

Panelled Sprig Granite Ware Sugar

Sugar bowl, cov., Peach patt., clear w/gold & red trim, Wheeling, West Virginia factory **75**

Regal Sugar Bowl

Sugar bowl, cov., Regal patt., emerald green w/gold trim, Wheeling, West Virginia factory (ILLUS.) **95**

Decorated Venetian Sugar Bowl

Sugar bowl, cov., Venetian patt. opaque white w/h.p. scenic decoration, Indiana, Pennsylvania factory (ILLUS.)..................... **175**

Aurora Pattern Rubina Sugar Shaker

Sugar shaker w/original top, Aurora patt., rubina, Martins Ferry, Ohio factory (ILLUS.).. **250**

Sugar shaker w/original top, Chrysanthemum Swirl patt., blue opalescent, Martins Ferry, Ohio factory **225**

Daisy & Fern Sugar Shaker

Sugar shaker w/original top, Daisy & Fern patt., Parian Swirl mold, clear opalescent, Ellwood City, Pennsylvania factory (ILLUS.).. **100**

Sugar shaker w/original top, Leaf Mold patt., pink & white cased spangle, Martins Ferry, Ohio factory **358**

Sugar shaker w/original top, Leaf Umbrella patt., cased crystal, Martins Ferry, Ohio factory **295**

Sugar shaker w/original top, Netted Oak patt., decorated milk glass, Indiana, Pennsylvania factory 130

Netted Oak Green Sugar Shaker

Sugar shaker w/original top, Netted Oak patt., light green, Indiana, Pennsylvania factory (ILLUS.) 165

Sugar shaker w/original top, Paneled Sprig patt., decorated milk glass, Indiana, Pennsylvania factory 50-100

Sugar shaker w/original top, Parian Swirl, grey satin, Martins Ferry, Ohio factory 325

Sugar shaker w/original top, Parian Swirl patt., decorated milk glass, Martins Ferry, Ohio factory 130

Sugar shaker w/original top, Quilted Phlox patt., cased pink, Indiana, Pennsylvania factory, 4 3/4" h. 160

Sugar shaker w/original top, Quilted Phlox patt., milk glass decorated w/blue flowers, Indiana, Pennsylvania factory 195

Sugar shaker w/original top, Quilted Phlox patt., undecorated milk glass, Indiana, Pennsylvania factory 140

Beaded Star & Mums Sweets Dish

Sweets dish, Beaded Star and Mums patt., Verre d'Or treatment, green w/gold decoration, Wheeling, West Virginia factory, 6" d. (ILLUS.).. 210

Garden Mums Sweets Dish

Sweets dish, Garden Mums patt., Verre D'or decoration on green, 6" d., Wheeling, West Virginia factory (ILLUS.) 185

Ribbons & Overlapping Squares Sweets Dish

Sugar shaker w/original top, Spanish Lace patt., cranberry opalescent, Ellwood City, Pennsylvania factory (ILLUS.).. 435

Spanish Lace Sugar Shaker

Sweets dish, Ribbons & Overlapping Squares patt., "Verre d'or" decoration on blue, 6" d., Wheeling, West Virginia factory (ILLUS.) **175**

Syrup jug w/original top, Apple Blossom patt., undecorated milk glass, Indiana, Pennsylvania factory **80**

Flat Flower Syrup Jug

Syrup jug w/original top, Flat Flower patt., opaque green, Ellwood City, Pennsylvania factory (ILLUS.) **400**

Grape & Leaf Blue Syrup Jug

Syrup jug w/original top, Grape and Leaf patt., opaque blue, Indiana, Pennsylvania factory (ILLUS.) **350**

Syrup jug w/original top, Grape and Leaf patt., opaque pink w/crystal handle, Indiana, Pennsylvania factory (ILLUS. top of next column) **400**

Syrup jug w/original top, Leaf Mold patt., opal-cased red spatter w/silver mica flakes, Martins Ferry, Ohio factory **695**

Pink Grape & Leaf Syrup Jug

Syrup jug w/original top, Netted Oak patt., milk glass w/green & gold decoration, Indiana, Pennsylvania factory **90**

Quilted Phlox Syrup Pitcher

Syrup jug w/original top, Quilted Phlox patt., opaque green, Ellwood City, Pennsylvania factory (ILLUS.) **275-300**

Opalescent Stripe Syrup Jug

Syrup jug w/original top, Stripe patt., cranberry opalescent , Martins Ferry, Ohio factory (ILLUS.) **250**

Swirl & Leaf Toothpick Holder

Toothpick holder, Swirl & Leaf patt., opaque pink, Ellwood City, Pennsylvania factory (ILLUS.) **60-75**

Tumbler, Apple Blossom patt., decorated milk glass, Indiana, Pennsylvania factory **45**

Tumbler, Crystal Queen patt., Indiana, Pennsylvania factory **45**

Tumbler, Daffodil patt., cranberry opalescent, Wheeling, West Virginia factory **500**

Gold Rose Tumbler

Tumbler, Gold Rose patt., green, Wheeling, West Virginia factory (ILLUS.) **50**

Tumbler, Memphis patt., green w/gold rim, Wheeling, West Virginia factory (ILLUS. top of next column) **38**

Tumbler, Netted Oak patt., decorated milk glass, Indiana, Pennsylvania factory **40**

Tumbler, Oriental Poppy patt., green w/gold trim, Wheeling, West Virginia factory **30**

Tumbler, Paneled Cherry patt., clear, Wheeling, West Virginia factory **30**

Memphis Tumbler

Tumbler, Paneled Holly patt., blue opalescent, Wheeling, West Virginia factory **100**

Northwood Enameled Floral Tumblers

Tumbler, plain design, blue Carnival finish w/enameled florals, Wheeling, West Virginia factory (ILLUS. left) **30-35**

Tumbler, plain design, green w/enameled flower, Wheeling, West Virginia factory (ILLUS. right) **25-30**

Beads & Bark Vase

Vase, Beads & Bark patt., "Mosaic" (slag) glass, Wheeling, West Virginia factory (ILLUS.) **60-70**

Rosita Amber Twisted Vase

Vase, No. 727, twisted, Rosita Amber, Wheeling, West Virginia factory (ILLUS.) **65**

Northwood Etruscan Vase

Vase, ovoid w/short flared neck, Etruscan line (note brown streaked decoration), Wheeling, West Virginia factory (ILLUS.) **450**

Water set: pitcher & three tumblers; Intaglio patt., green w/gold trim, Wheeling, West Virginia factory, 4 pcs. **300**

Water set: pitcher & four tumblers; Apple Blossom patt., decorated milk glass, Indiana, Pennsylvania factory, 5 pcs. **350-400**

Peach Pattern Water Set

Water set: pitcher & four tumblers; Peach patt., green w/gold trim, Wheeling, West Virginia factory, 5 pcs. (ILLUS. of part) **300**

Water set: pitcher & six tumblers; Barbella patt., cobalt blue w/gold trim, Wheeling, West Virginia factory, 7 pcs. **350**

Water set: pitcher & six tumblers; Cherry Thumbprint patt., clear, Wheeling, West Virginia factory, 7 pcs. **225**

Water set: pitcher & six tumblers; Plums & Cherries patt., clear w/ruby & gold trim, Wheeling, West Virginia factory, 7 pcs. **350**

PADEN CITY

The Paden City Glass Manufacturing Company began operations in Paden City, West Virginia in 1916, primarily as a supplier of blanks to other companies. All wares were hand-made, that is, either hand-pressed or mold-blown. The early products were not particularly noteworthy but by the early 1930s the quality had improved considerably. The firm continued to turn out high quality glassware in a variety of beautiful colors until financial difficulties nessitated its closing in 1951. Over the years the firm produced, in addition to tablewares, items for hotel and restaurant use, light shades, shaving mugs, perfume bottles and lamps.

Bowl, two-handled, Orchid etching, red **$250**
Bowl, 9" d., footed, Peacock & Rose etching, pink **175**
Bowl, 11" d., footed, Ardith etching, Mrs. "B" line No. 411, yellow **55**
Bowl, 11" d., footed, Mrs. "B" line, yellow **57**
Bowl, 11" d., rolled edge, Cupid etching, pink.. **400**
Bowl, 11 3/4" d., rolled edge, Black Forest etching, pink **250**
Bowl, 13 1/4" d., rolled edge, Black Forest etching, green **300**
Cake plate, Cupid etching, footed, pink (scratches) **180**
Cake plate, footed, Peacock & Rose etching, pink.. **155**
Cake plate, Ardith etching, No. 300, footed, topaz, 11" d. **145**
Cake salver, Regina etching, No. 555 line, clear **125**
Candlesticks, Black Forest etching, green, pr. **110**
Candy dish, cov., square, Ardith etching, green **150**

Cheese plate, Lela Bird etching, green.............. 64
Compote, Cupid etching, pink.......................... 325
Compote, 6 1/2" h., Black Forest etching,
    pink.. 100
Console bowl, rolled edge, Peacock &
    Rose etching, green, 14" l. 180
Creamer & sugar bowl, Black Forest etch-
    ing, green, pr. 90
Cup, Ardith etching, yellow............................... 35
Cup, Black Forest etching, red 120
Cup, Futura etching, No. 836 line, cobalt
    blue 9
Cup & saucer, Crow's Foot (No. 412) line,
    red 15
Cup & saucer, Cupid etching, pink.................. 165
Cup & saucer, Nora Bird etching, pink 210
Gravy boat, Ardith etching, green..................... 80
Gravy boat, Ardith etching, green..................... 80
Ice tub, Black Forest etching, pink 155
Ice tub, Cupid etching, green 325
Ice tub, Cupid etching, pink............................. 325
Ice tub, Peacock & Wildrose etching, green..... 215
Mayonnaise dish & ladle, Nora Bird etch-
    ing, green, 2 pcs. 120
Mayonnaise dish, liner & ladle, Orchid
    etching, yellow, 3 pcs. 160
Mayonnaise dish & underplate, Cupid
    etching, green 230
Plate, two-handled, Ardith etching, pink 125
Plate, 10" sq., Orchid etching, red.................... 85
Plate, 11" d., Gazebo etching, clear.................. 50
Punch set: punch bowl & seven punch
    cups; No. 555 line, clear, the set................... 75
Server, center-handled, Black Forest etch-
    ing, green 80
Server, swan-necked center handle,
    Gazebo etching, Line 1504, clear, 10" l. 100
Tray, center-handled, No. 1504 line, clear 35
Tray, Cupid etching, oval, pink 380
Tray, center-handled, Lela Bird etching,
    pink, 10 1/2" l. 125
Tumbler, Crow's Foot (No. 412) line, flat,
    blue 100
Tumbler, Regina (No. 210) line, clear, 5 oz......... 3
Vase, elliptical, Peacock & Rose etching,
    green.. 375
Vase, 10" h., Lela Bird etching, black.............. 165
Vase, 10" h., Peacock & Rose etching,
    black.. 325
Water set: pitcher & six tumblers; Ardith
    etching, green, 7 pcs.................................... 550
Water set: pitcher & six tumblers; Ardith
    etching, green, 7 pcs.................................... 575

PATTERN

Though it has never been ascertained whether glass was first pressed in the United States or abroad, the development of the glass pressing machine revolutionized the glass industry in the United States and this country receives the credit for improving the method to make this process feasible. The first wares pressed were probably small flat plates of the type now referred to as "lacy," the intricacy of the design concealing flaws.

In 1827, both the New England Glass Co., Cambridge, Mass. and Bakewell & Co., Pittsburgh, took out patents for pressing glass furniture knobs and soon other pieces followed. This early pressed

glass contained red lead which made it clear and resonant when tapped (flint.) Made primarily in clear, it is rarer in blue, amethyst, olive green and yellow.

By the 1840s, early simple patterns such as Ashburton, Argus and Excelsior appeared. Ribbed Bellflower seems to have been one of the earliest patterns to have had complete sets. By the 1860s, a wide range of patterns was available.

In 1864, William Leighton of Hobbs, Brockunier & Co., Wheeling, West Virginia, developed a formula for "soda lime" glass which did not require the expensive red lead for clarity. Although "soda lime" glass did not have the brilliance of the earlier flint glass, the formula came into widespread use because glass could be produced cheaply.

An asterisk (*) indicates a piece which has been reproduced.

ACTRESS
Bowl, 8" d., Adelaide Neilson $65
Bread tray, Miss Neilson, 12 1/2" l., frosted..... 110
Cake stand, frosted stem......................... 150-165
Celery vase, Pinafore scene........................... 160
Celery vase, frosted rim, stem & foot, 9" h. 220
Cheese dish, cov., "Lone Fisherman" on
    cover, "The Two Dromios" on
    underplate 225-250
Cologne bottle w/original stopper, 11" h. 90
Compote, cov., 6" d., 10" h. 95

Actress Compote

Compote, cov., 10" d., 14 1/2" h., Fanny
    Davenport & Maggie Mitchell (ILLUS.)......... 200
Compote, open, 6" d., 3" h................................ 55
Compote, open, 8" d., 5" h........................... 65-70
Creamer, clear 75
Creamer, frosted 100
Creamer, Miss Neilson & Fanny Davenport..... 110
Dresser box, cov. 3 1/2" d. 60
Dresser box, cov., footed, 2 1/2 x 6" oval.......... 75
Egg cup 70
Goblet, clear bowl, frosted stem 135
Goblet, frosted bowl 125
Mug, Pinafore scene 50

Pitcher, water, 9" h., Miss Neilson & Maggie Mitchell 350
Platter, 7 x 11 1/2", Pinafore scene................. 125
Relish, Maude Granger, 5 x 9"........................... 63
Salt & pepper shakers w/original tops, pr....... 100
Salt shaker w/original pewter top...................... 85
Sauce dish, Maggie Mitchell & Fanny Davenport, 4 1/2" d., 2 1/4" h. 20
Sauce dish, clear, footed.................................. 16
Spooner, frosted 68
Sugar bowl, cov., Lotta Crabtree & Kate Claxton.. 130
Table set, creamer, cov. sugar bowl, cov. butter dish, spooner, 4 pcs........................... 275

ALASKA (Lion's Leg)
Banana boat, blue opalescent................. 200-250
Banana boat, emerald green.................... 165-185
Bowl, 8" sq., blue opalescent.......................... 295
Bowl, 8" sq., canary opalescent...................... 130
Bowl, 8" sq., canary opalescent w/enameled florals.. 200
Bowl, 8" sq., clear opalescent w/enameled florals.. 65
Bowl, 8" sq., emerald green w/enameled florals.. 100-125

Alaska Butter Dish

Butter dish, cov., canary opalescent (ILLUS.).. 288
Butter dish, cov., clear opalescent.................. 102
Butter dish, cov., emerald green 93
Card tray, blue opalescent............................... 29
Celery tray, blue opalescent w/enameled florals.. 250
Celery tray, emerald green w/gold............ 100-115
Creamer, blue opalescent................................. 85

Alaska Creamer

Creamer, canary opalescent (ILLUS.)................ 85
Creamer, clear opalescent................................ 50
Creamer, emerald green 75-85
Creamer & cov. sugar bowl, blue opalescent, pr. 225

Creamer & cov. sugar bowl, blue, pr. 110
Cruet w/original stopper, blue opalescent 276
Cruet w/original stopper, blue opalescent w/enameled florals 300
Cruet w/original stopper, canary opalescent w/enameled florals 275-325
Cruet w/original stopper, emerald green w/enameled florals 225
Pitcher, water, blue opalescent............... 300-350
Pitcher, water, blue opalescent w/enameled florals... 500-525
Pitcher, water, clear opalescent w/enameled florals & gold trim.................................... 125
Salt & pepper shakers w/original tops, emerald green, pr.. 95
Salt shaker w/original top, blue opalescent 75-85
Sauce dish, blue opalescent....................... 55-60
Sauce dish, blue opalescent w/enameled florals.. 65
Sauce dish, canary opalescent................... 35-40
Sauce dish, canary opalescent w/enameled florals.. 45
Sauce dish, clear opalescent.......................... 30
Sauce dish, clear opalescent w/enameled florals.. 30
Sauce dish, white opalescent..................... 55-60
Spooner, blue opalescent 65-75
Spooner, canary opalescent 60-70
Spooner, canary opalescent w/enameled florals.. 113
Sugar bowl, cov., blue opalescent........... 175-200
Sugar bowl, cov., canary opalescent....... 250-300
Sugar bowl, cov., canary opalescent w/enameled florals 248
Table set: canary opalescent, 4 pcs. 650-700
Tumbler, blue opalescent 78
Tumbler, blue opalescent w/enameled florals 150
Tumbler, canary opalescent 75-85
Water set: pitcher & 6 tumblers; canary opalescent, 7 pcs. 775-800

ALEXIS - See Priscilla Patter**I**

AMAZON (Sawtooth Band)
Bowl, 5" d. 12
Butter dish, cov. 78
Butter dish, cov., child's miniature.................... 60
Cake stand, 8" to 9 1/2" d. 40
Champagne 30-35
Compote, cov., 6" d. 35
Compote, cov., 7" d., 11 1/2" h. 75
Compote, open, jelly, 4 1/2" d. 35
Compote, open, 8 3/4" d., 7 1/4" h. 45-55
Compote, open, 9 1/2" d., 8" h. 50
Cordial, clear.. 30-40
Creamer 49
Creamer, child's miniature (ILLUS. top of next page) 30
Cruet w/bar in hand stopper, clear 80
Goblet, engraved 30
Goblet, plain 25
Salt dip, master size 15
Salt shaker w/original top 30
Sauce dish, flat or footed, each 11
Spooner 35
Spooner, child's miniature............................... 28
Sugar bowl, cov. 65
Syrup pitcher w/original top 85

Amazon Child's Creamer

Table set: cov. butter dish, creamer, cov.
sugar bowl & spooner; child's miniature,
4 pcs.. 160
Tumbler, plain 23
Vase, double-bud 40
Wine 35-40

ANIMALS & BIRDS ON GOBLETS & PITCHERS

GOBLETS
Alligator, acid-etched....................... 130
Bear climber, acid-etched 95
Bird in Swamp 75-85
Bird & roses, acid-etched............... 55-75
Birds at Fountain, pressed 50-55
Deer & Castle, acid-etched............ 25-35
Deer & Doe, acid-etched................... 25
Deer & Doe w/lily-of-the-valley, pressed 133
Dog w/rabbit in mouth, acid-etched 65-75
Dragon, pressed 1,900
Elephant, acid-etched 26
Elk & Doe, pressed 140-150
Falcon Strawberry, pressed............. 35
Flamingo Habitat, acid-etched 35
Flying Birds, pressed 103
Flying Storks, pressed, pr. 95

Frog & Spider Goblet

Frog & Spider, pressed (ILLUS.).............. 350
Giraffe, acid-etched........................... 72
Horse, acid-etched 76

Horse, Cat & Rabbit, pressed 950-1,000
Hummingbirds w/Frog, acid-etched 70
Ibex, acid-etched 51
Leopard, acid-etched 150
Lion in the Jungle, acid-etched.............. 140
Monkey Climber, acid-etched.............. 125
Monkey Swinging, acid-etched.............. 70
Nestlings, acid-etched 45-50
Ostrich Looking at Moon, pressed.............. 120
Owl in Horseshoe, pressed............... 110
Owl & Possum, pressed............... 100-125
Pigs in Corn, pressed....................... 463
Pigs in Corn, tassel at right 600
Reversed Elephant, acid-etched............ 98
Rooster, acid-etched......................... 225
Rooster & Hen, acid-etched 135-155
Scarab 93
Snake Stalking Monkey, acid-etched 50
Squirrel, pressed, non-Greentown................. 725
Stag, acid-etched............................. 70
Stork Eating, acid-etched 96
Stork & Flowers, acid-etched............. 65
Stork Walking, acid-etched 18
Three Deer 225
Tiger, acid-etched 60
Two camels, acid-etched................... 130
Two Giraffes, acid-etched 130
Two Herons, acid-etched............... 90-100
Whippet, acid-etched 15

PITCHERS
Bird & Castle, acid-etched.................. 60
Bringing Home Cows, pressed............ 600
Crane, tankard, acid-etched............... 45
Deer & Oak Tree, pressed 160-170
Deer Racing, pressed...................... 110
Dog & Cat, pressed..................... 275-300
Dog w/Rabbit in Hole 155
Flamingo Habitat, acid-etched 120-125
Fox & Crow, pressed 375-400
Heron, pressed.......................... 175-200
Heron w/Fish, acid-etched................. 75
Heron w/Snake, tankard, acid-etched........ 65
Heron wading, pressed 375
Kingfisher, tankard, acid-etched.............. 60
Oasis Camel Caravan, acid-etched 100
Pointer, pressed............................. 200
Racing Deer, pressed...................... 150

Squirrel Pitcher

Squirrel, pressed, non-Greentown
(ILLUS.)................................ 275-325

Stag in Brambles, 11" h., tankard, acid-
etched **55-65**
Two Swans in Rushes, acid-etched **55**

APOLLO
Butter dish, cov., flanged rim **70**
Cake stand, engraved, 9" d. **45-50**
Celery vase **45-55**
Compote, cov., 6" d. **60**
Compote, open, 5" d. **25**
Creamer, engraved **50**
Creamer, plain... **45**
Cruet w/original stopper, frosted **90**
Cruet w/original stopper, plain......................... **75**
Goblet, engraved **35**
Goblet, frosted **40**
Goblet, plain.. **30**
Lamp, kerosene-type, amber, 7" h. **150**
Lamp, kerosene-type, blue, 9" h. **265**
Lamp, kerosene-type, clear, 10" h. **60**
Lamp, kerosene-type, blue base w/canary
yellow font **255**
Pitcher, water, bulbous **75-85**
Salt dip, master size **20**
Sauce dish, flat or footed................................. **11**
Sugar bowl, cov... **50**
Sugar bowl, cov., etched.................................. **75**
Sugar shaker w/original top **60-65**
Syrup pitcher w/original top **125**
Tumbler, frosted.. **25-30**

ART (Job's Tears)
Banana stand **85-95**
Bowl, 7" d., flared rim, footed............................ **25**
Bowl, 8" sq., shallow **33**
Butter dish, cov., clear **60**
Butter dish, cov., ruby-stained **100**
Cake stand, 9" to 10 1/2" d. **68**
Celery vase **55**
Compote, cov., 7" d. **80**
Compote, cov., 9" d. **60**
Compote, open, 7" d. **57**
Compote, open, 9" d., 7 1/4" h........................... **48**
Cracker jar, cov., 7" d., 8" h. to top of finial **150**
Creamer **49**
Cruet w/original stopper, ruby-stained........... **175**

Art Goblet

Goblet (ILLUS.) **55-65**
Mug **50**
Pitcher, milk, clear **100**

Pitcher, water, bulbous **83**
Punch cup **20**
Salt shaker w/original top **25**
Sauce dish, flat or footed, each........................ **15**
Sugar bowl, cov., engraved.............................. **44**
Sugar bowl, cov., plain **45**
Sugar bowl, open **28**
Toothpick holder **30**
Vinegar jug **45**
Wine **110**

ASHBURTON
Ale glass, flint, 6 1/2" h. **130**
Celery vase, plain rim, flint............................. **140**
Celery vase, scalloped rim, canary yellow,
flint... **775**
Celery vase, scalloped rim, clear, flint **108**
Champagne, flint... **65-75**
Claret, flint, 5 1/4" h... **65**
Cordial, flint, 4 1/4" h.. **65**
Cordial, non-flint.. **85**
Creamer, applied handle, flint **175**
Decanter, bar lip & facet-cut neck, clear,
flint, qt... **75**
Egg cup, clear, flint **25-30**
Egg cup, double... **95**
Goblet, barrel-shaped, flint............................. **105**
Goblet, flared, flint, clear **40-45**
Goblet, short, flint.. **45**
Honey dish, 3 1/2" d. **8**
Mug, applied handle, 4 3/4" h............................ **88**
Pitcher, water, applied hollow handle, flint....... **425**
Sauce dish, flint **8**
Sugar bowl, cov., fiery opalescent, flint **1,650**

Ashburton Sugar Bowl

Sugar bowl, cov., flint (ILLUS.)....................... **102**
Tumbler, bar, flint.. **65-70**
Tumbler, water, footed...................................... **93**
Tumbler, whiskey, applied handle, flint............ **135**
Vase, 10 1/2" h., scallop rim **140-150**
Wine, clear, flint... **40**
Wine, non-flint **35**

ATLANTA (Lion or Square Lion's Head)

Butter dish, cov. 105
Cake stand 110
Cake stand, frosted, 9" w., 5 3/4" h. 320
Celery vase 88
Compote, cov., 5" sq., 6" h. 123
Compote, cov., 7" sq., high stand 188
Compote, cov., 7" sq., low stand 110-150
Compote, cov., 9" sq., 13" h. 175
Compote, open, 6" sq., 7 1/2" h. 80
Creamer 60
Cruet w/original stopper 125
Cruet w/original stopper engraved 290
*Goblet (ILLUS. top of next column) 60-70
Mustard jar 750
Relish, boat-shaped 28
Salt dip, master size 117
Sauce dish 25-35
Spooner 60
Spooner, ruby-stained 75
Sugar bowl, cov., engraved 160
Sugar bowl, cov., plain 90-95
Toothpick holder, clear & frosted satin
  milk glass 35-75
Tumbler, engraved 60
Tumbler, plain 45
Tumbler, ruby-stained 80
Wine 85-110

Atlanta Goblet

ATLAS (Crystal Ball or Cannon Ball)

Bowl, open, 6" d. 37
Butter dish, cov. 41
Cake stand, clear, 8" to 10" d. 48
Champagne, 5 1/2" h. 33
Claret, 4 3/4" h. 38
Compote, cov., 8" d., 8" h. 48
Compote, open, 5" d., 4" h. 80
Compote, open, 7" d. 80
Creamer, flat or pedestal base 25-30
Creamer, ruby-stained, w/gold trim 40
Goblet, engraved 45

Goblet, plain 27
Goblet, ruby-stained 65
Salt dip, master size 21
Sauce dish, flat or footed, clear 11
Spooner, clear 40

Atlas Toothpick Holder

Toothpick holder (ILLUS.) 26
Toothpick holder ruby-stained 65
Tumbler 25
Wine 28

AZTEC

Bonbon, footed, 7" d., 4 1/2" h. 14
Bowl, 8 1/2" d., open, sapphire blue 45
Bowl, 9" w., triangular 14
Butter dish, cov. 40
Carafe, water 50-60
Champagne 35
Cordial 20
Cracker jar, cov. 40

Aztec Creamer

Creamer (ILLUS.) 30
Pitcher, lemonade, 1/2 gal. 50
Pitcher, water, jug-type w/applied handle 50
Pitcher, water, tankard-type, pressed
  handle, 1/2 gal. 50
Punch cup 5
Relish 15
Salt shaker w/original top 25
Sauce dish 10
Sugar bowl, cov. 35
Syrup pitcher w/original nickeled silver
  tin top 75
Tray, flat 15

Tumbler, ice tea 20
Tumbler, water 20
Tumbler, whiskey 20
Wine 25

BABY FACE
Butter dish, cov., 5 1/4" d. 150
Celery vase 100
Champagne 140
Compote, cov., 5 1/4" d., 6 1/2" h. 140
Compote, cov., 5 1/4" d., 8 1/2" h. 150
Compote, cov., 6" d., 9 1/2" h. 160
Compote, cov., 7" d., high stand 180
Compote, cov., 8" d., high stand, scalloped
    rim 350-425

Baby Face Compote

Compote, open, 8" d., 4 3/4" h. (ILLUS.) 85
Cordial 275
Creamer 100-200
Goblet 100-135
Goblet, etched 325
Knife rest 95-100
Pitcher, water 300
Salt dip 50
Spooner 75
Sugar bowl, cov. 150-175
Table set, cov. butter dish, cov. sugar
    bowl, creamer & spooner, 4 pcs. 600

BALDER - See Pennsylvania Pattern

BAMBOO - See U.S. Glass Co. Broken Column Pattern

BANDED PORTLAND (Portland w/Diamond Point Band, Virginia (States series), Portland Maiden Blush (when pink-stained)
Berry set: master bowl & 4 sauce dishes;
    pink-stained, 5 pcs. 175
Bowl, 6" d., open, deep, straight-sided,
    clear 25
Bowl, 6" d., open, deep, straight-sided,
    pink-stained 40
Butter dish, cov., pink-stained 173
Celery tray, pink-stained, 10" oval 75
Celery tray, clear, 5 x 12" 28
Celery vase, clear 33
Cologne bottle w/original stopper, clear,
    large 49
Cologne bottle w/original stopper, clear,
    small 35

Cologne bottle w/original stopper, pink-
    stained, small 65
Compote, cov., 8" d., high stand 105
Compote, open, jelly 25
Compote, open, 7" d. 30
Compote, open, 8 1/4" d., 8" h., scalloped
    rim 38
Creamer, pink-stained 50
Creamer, individual size, clear 35
Creamer, individual size, pink-stained 45
Cruet w/original stopper, clear 60
Cruet w/original stopper, pink-stained 175
Dresser jar, cov., clear, 3 1/2" d. 36
Goblet, clear 45
Goblet, pink-stained 55
Goblet, yellow-stained 85
Pickle dish, 4 x 6" 20
Pin tray, souvenir, pink-stained 25
Pitcher, water, 9 1/2" h., clear 95
Pitcher, water, 9 1/2" h., pink-stained 135
Pitcher, tankard, 11" h., pink-stained 238
Pomade jar, cov. 28
Punch cup, clear 11
Punch cup, pink-stained 35
Ring tree, gold-stained 75
Ring tree, pink-stained 125
Salt & pepper shakers w/original tops,
    clear, pr. 45
Salt & pepper shakers w/original tops,
    pink-stained, pr. 84
Salt shaker w/original top, clear 20
Salt shaker w/original top, pink-stained 50
Sauce dish, clear, 4 1/2" d. 15

Banded Portland Sauce Dish

Sauce dish, pink-stained, 4 1/2" d.
    (ILLUS.) 21
Sauce dish, boat-shaped, clear, 4 3/4" l. 10
Sugar bowl, cov., clear 45
Sugar bowl, cov., gold-stained 80
Sugar bowl, individual size, clear 24
Sugar bowl, individual size, pink-stained 35
Sugar shaker w/original top, clear 50
Sugar shaker w/original top, pink-stained 135
Sugar shaker w/original top, vaseline-
    stained 60
Syrup jug w/original top, pink-stained 250
Toothpick holder, clear 41
Toothpick holder, pink-stained 45-60
Tumbler, clear 20-25
Tumbler, pink-stained 44
Vase, 6" h., flared, clear 32
Vase, 6" h., flared, pink-stained 35
Vase, 9" h., clear 42
Wine, blue-stained 45
Wine, clear 20
Wine, clear w/gold trim 42
Wine, pink-stained 60

BARBERRY
Bowl, cov., 8" d. 45
Butter dish, cov., pattern on base rim 93
Cake stand, 11" d. 125
Celery vase 40
Compote, cov., 8" d., high stand, shell fin-
ial.. 99
Creamer 45
Egg cup 30
Goblet 25
Pitcher, milk 75

Barberry Water Pitcher

Pitcher, water, 9 1/2" h., applied handle
(ILLUS.).. 125
Plate, 6" d., amber... 38
Salt dip, master size 25
Sauce dish, flat or footed................................ 25
Spooner, footed 32
Sugar bowl, cov., shell finial 46
Sugar bowl, open 28
Syrup jug w/original top 125
Tumbler, footed.. 32
Wine 35-40

BASKETWEAVE
Bread plate, amber 30
Bread plate, blue 40
Creamer, amber 35
Cup, blue 30
Cup & saucer, amber 28
Cup & saucer, canary yellow............................ 45
*Goblet, amber.. 20-25
*Goblet, blue 35
*Goblet, canary yellow 30-35
*Goblet, clear 20
Pitcher, milk, blue 80
*Pitcher, water, amber 50
*Pitcher, water, blue... 90
*Pitcher, water, canary yellow........................... 85
Pitcher, water, clear 55
Plate, 8 3/4" d., handled, amber........................ 24
Plate, 8 3/4" d., handled, blue 20
Plate, 8 3/4" d., handled, clear 11
Sauce dish 10
*Tray, water, scenic center, amber, 12" 41
*Tray, water, scenic center, blue, 12".......... 90-100

*Tray, water, scenic center, canary yellow,
12"... 70
*Tray, water, scenic center, clear, 12" 50
*Tray, water, scenic center & six goblets,
amber, 7 pcs. 125
Tray, water, 12" d., w/scenic center, pitcher
& 6 stemmed goblets, amber, 8 pcs............. 125
Vase, 8 1/2" h. 20
Wine 35

BEADED DEWDROP - See Wisconsin Pattern

BEADED GRAPE (California)
Bowl, 5 1/2" sq., clear 15
Bowl, 5 1/2" sq., green 20-25
Bowl, 6 1/2 sq., clear....................................... 12
Bowl, 6 1/2" sq., green 21
Bowl, 7 1/2" sq., green 32

Beaded Grape Bowl

Bowl, 8" sq., clear (ILLUS.) 24
Bowl, 6 1/4 x 8 1/2" rectangle, green 28
Butter dish, cov., square, clear......................... 55
Butter dish, cov., square, green 75
Cake stand, green, 9" sq., 6" h. 145
Celery tray, clear 28
Celery tray, green 35
*Compote, cov., 8 1/2" sq., high stand,
clear 125
Compote, open, jelly, 4" sq., green.................... 75
Compote, open, 8 1/2" sq., high stand,
clear 60
Compote, open, 8 1/2" sq., high stand,
green 85
Cordial 40
Creamer, clear 60
Creamer, green 90
Cruet w/original stopper, clear......................... 70
Cruet w/original stopper, green 100
Egg cup 30
*Goblet, clear 35
*Goblet, green 50
Pitcher, milk, green 150
Pitcher, water, square, green.......................... 125
Pitcher, water, tankard, clear 60
Pitcher, water, tankard, green w/gold 135
Platter, 7 1/4 x 10 1/4", clear........................... 55
Platter, 7 1/4 x 10 1/4", green 85
Salt & pepper shakers w/original tops,
green, pr... 75
*Sauce dish, clear... 10
*Sauce dish, green 20
Sauce dish, handled, clear 20

Sauce dish, handled, green 30
Spooner, clear 40
Sugar bowl, cov., green.................................... 60
Toothpick holder, clear.................................... 30
Toothpick holder, green w/gold trim 70
*Tumbler, clear 28
*Tumbler, green 45
*Wine, clear.. 35
*Wine, green... 66

BEADED LOOP (Oregon, U.S. Glass Co.)

Bowl, berry, 7" d.. 17
Bowl, 8 1/4" d. 20
Bowl, berry, 9 1/2" l., 6 3/4" w. oval, clear.......... 25
Bowl, berry, 9 1/2" l., 6 3/4" w. oval, ruby-
    stained.. 35
Bread platter 35
Bread tray 35
Butter dish, cov., clear 70
Butter dish, cov., ruby-stained 125
Cake stand, 8" d., 5" h. 50
Cake stand, 9" to 10 1/2" d. 56
Carafe, individual size 30
Celery vase, clear, 7" h. 30
Compote, cov., 6" d., 10" h. 95
Compote, cov., 7" d. 80
Compote, cov., 11" 125
Compote, open, jelly, clear 31
Compote, open, 5 1/4" d., 4 1/2" h., clear.......... 20
Compote, open, 6 1/2" d., clear 20
Compote, open, 7" d., clear 27
Compote, open, 7 1/2" d., low stand, clear 38
Creamer, clear 40
Creamer, ruby-stained 70
Cruet w/faceted stopper, clear 35
Cruet w/faceted stopper, ruby-stained 75
Goblet, clear w/gold trim 50

Beaded Loop Goblet

*Goblet (ILLUS.)... 49
Mug, footed, clear... 40
Mug, ruby-stained... 55
Pitcher, pint, 7" h. 44
Pitcher, milk, 8 1/2" h. 55
Pitcher, water, tankard.................................... 60

Salt & pepper shakers w/original tops,
    pr.. 43
Sauce dish, flat or footed, each 13
Spooner, clear 28
Spooner, ruby-stained 55
*Sugar bowl, cov., clear.................................... 39
Sugar bowl, cov., ruby-stained 55
Toothpick holder 48
Tumbler, clear.. 49
Tumbler, ruby-stained..................................... 35
Vase, small 43
Wine 65-70

BEARDED HEAD - See Viking Pattern

BELLFLOWER

Bowl, 6" d., 1 3/4" h., single vine...................... 150
Bowl, 8" d., 2" h., round, single vine, scal-
    lop & point rim, plain polished base 180
Butter dish, cov. 200
Castor set, 4-bottle, w/pewter stand 400
Castor set, 5-bottle, single vine, w/pewter
    stand 675
Celery vase, w/cut bellflowers 313
Champagne, barrel-shaped, fine rib, single
    vine, knob stem, rayed base 85
Champagne, fine rib, double vine, w/cut
    bellflowers, 5" h. 450
Cologne bottle w/stopper, clambroth............ 500
Compote, open, 7" d., 5" h., fine rib, double
    vine.. 90-100
Compote, open, 8" d. 85
Compote, open, 8" d., high stand 190
Compote, open, coarse rib, single vine, low
    foot w/scallop rim, 8" d., 5" h. 250
Cordial, barrel-shaped, knob stem, rayed
    base 165
Cordial, fine rib, single vine, knob stem 150
Cordial, fine rib, single vine, plain stem 120-125
Creamer, fine rib, single vine, applied han-
    dle 275

Bellflower Decanter

Decanter, double vine, flint, qt., no stopper
    (ILLUS.)... 110
Decanter w/bar lip, cut shoulder, single
    vine, w/stopper.. 550

Decanter w/bar lip, double vine, qt. 140
Decanter w/bar lip, single vine, qt. 188
Egg cup, coarse rib 28
Egg cup, double vine, w/cut bellflowers 75
Egg cup, fine rib, single vine 44
Goblet, barrel-shaped, fine rib, single vine,
knob stem, rayed base 75
*Goblet, barrel-shaped, fine rib, single
vine, plain stem 35
Goblet, coarse rib, flared top 90
Goblet, fine rib, double vine, w/cut bellflow-
ers 425
Goblet, fine rib, single vine, w/cut bellflow-
ers, 5 1/2" h. 2,050
Goblet, single vine w/cut bellflowers,
6 1/4" h. 400
Honey dish, scalloped rim, star base, 3" d. 100
Lamp, whale oil, pattern on inside of font,
top of ribs scalloped, scalloped base,
9" h. (replaced collar, hard to see inter-
nal line under collar, probably factory
flaw) 650
Lamp, whale oil, brass stem, marble base 300
Pitcher, double vine, straight sides, 1 pt.,
6 1/4" h. 1,800
Pitcher, milk, double vine, 7" h. 550-575
Pitcher, milk, single vine, 7 1/2" h. 1,800
Pitcher, water, 8 3/4" h., coarse rib, double
vine 488
Sauce dish, single vine 16
Spooner, low foot, double vine 90
Spooner, scalloped rim, single vine 65
Sugar bowl, cov., double vine 150-200
Sugar bowl, cov., single vine 80-100
Sugar bowl, cov., octagonal, domed lid,
8" h. 1,325
Syrup pitcher w/original top, applied han-
dle, fine rib, single vine, clear 625
Syrup pitcher w/original top, applied han-
dle, milk white 1,100
Tumbler, bar, fine rib, single vine 113
Tumbler, whiskey, single vine, 2 7/8" h. 230
Tumbler, double vine, w/cut bellflowers,
3 1/2" h. 400
Tumbler, fine rib, double vine, 4 7/8" h. 275
Wine, barrel-shaped, knob stem, fine rib,
single vine 50
Wine, barrel-shaped, knob stem, fine rib,
single vine, rayed base 115
Wine, fine-rib, single vine, straight sides 40
Wine, double vine w/cut bellflowers, 4" h. 250

BIRD & FERN - See Hummingbird Pattern

BIRD & STRAWBERRY (Bluebird)
Bowl, 7 1/2" d., footed, clear 62
Bowl, 7 1/2" d., footed, w/color 70
Bowl, 9" d., flat, clear 55
Bowl, 9" d., flat, w/color 75
Bowl, 10" d., flat, clear 60-70
Butter dish, cov., clear 165
Butter dish, cov., w/color 200-225
Cake stand, 9" to 9 1/2" d. 98
*Celery tray, 10" l. 50-60
Celery vase, pedestal base, 7 1/2" h. 65
Compote, cov., jelly, 4 1/2" d., 7 1/2" h.,
clear 165
Compote, cov., jelly, 4 1/2" d., 7 1/2" h.,
w/color 250
Compote, cov., 6" d., low stand, clear 85
Compote, cov., 6" d., low stand, w/color 125
Creamer, clear 60-70

Creamer, w/color 115
Dish, heart-shaped 65
Goblet, flared bowl, w/color 725
Pitcher, water, clear 300-350
Pitcher, water, w/color 450-500
Punch cup 25
Spooner, clear 60
Spooner, w/color 100-125
Sugar bowl, cov., clear 65
Tumbler, clear 43

Bird & Strawberry Tumbler

Tumbler, w/color (ILLUS.) 95
Wine 55-65

BLEEDING HEART
Bowl, cov., flat, 8" d. 175
Cake stand, 9 1/2" to 11" d. 90
Compote, cov., 8" d., high stand w/Bleed-
ing Heart finial 150
Compote, cov., 9" d., 12" h., w/Bleeding
Heart finial 100-125
Creamer 55
Egg cup 40
Goblet, knob stem 55-65
Honey dish 15
Mug, 3" h. 50
Pitcher, water 148
Relish, 3 5/8" x 5 1/8" oval 56
Sauce dish, flat 12

Bleeding Heart Spooner

Spooner (ILLUS.)... 36
Sugar bowl, cov... 85
Sugar bowl, open 30
Tumbler, footed.. 95-100
Wine, knob stem.. 195
Wine, plain stem.. 70

BOW TIE
Bowl, 6" d... 20-25
Bowl, berry, 8" d.. 32
Compote, cov., 7" d. 165
Compote, open, 6 1/2" d., low stand................. 40
Compote, open, 8 1/4" d., high stand 53
Goblet 54
Pitcher, milk 58
Pitcher, water.. 85-90
Punch bowl 125
Salt dip, master size 95
Salt & pepper shakers w/original tops,
   pr.. 70
Salt shaker w/original top 45
Spooner 35

BROKEN COLUMN (Irish Column, Notched Rib or Bamboo)
Banana stand 195
Bowl, 7" d.. 40
Bowl, 9" d.. 32
Bowl, cov., vegetable 95
Butter dish, cov. 115
Celery tray, 5 x 10", w/red notches................... 65
Celery vase, clear... 73
Celery vase, ruby-stained 155
Compote, cov., 5" d., high stand, clear............. 70
Compote, cov., 5" d., high stand w/red
   notches.. 225
Compote, cov., 7" d., high stand............... 175-200
Compote, cov., 8" d., high stand................... 175
Compote, cov., 8" d., high stand w/red
   notches.. 525
Compote, open, 6" d., high stand 35
Compote, open, 7" d., low stand 50
Compote, open, 8" d., high stand, ruby-
   stained... 350
Compote, open, 8" d., low stand........................ 63
Compote, open, 9" d., 7 1/2" h., clear............... 75
Compote, open, 9" d., 7 1/2" h. w/red
   notches.. 175
*Creamer, clear.. 35-40
Creamer, w/red notches................................. 250
Cruet w/original stopper, w/red notches 525
Decanter w/original stopper, 10 1/2" h. 85
*Goblet, clear (ILLUS. top of next column) 60
Pickle castor, cov., clear, original ornate
   frame... 238
Pickle castor, ruby-stained, w/frame &
   tongs 413
*Pitcher, water, clear...................................... 123
Pitcher, water, w/red notches 450
Relish, 3 3/4 x 5"... 13
Relish, 6 1/2" l.. 18
Relish, clear, 9" l., 5" w. 25-30
Relish, w/red notches, 9" l., 5" w....................... 78
Salt & pepper shakers w/original tops,
   pr.. 85
Salt shaker w/original top, w/red notches........ 75
Sauce dish, w/red notches 32
*Spooner, clear.. 32
Spooner, w/red notches................................. 125
*Sugar bowl, cov., clear.................................... 72

Broken Column Goblet

Sugar bowl, cov., w/red notches..................... 150
Sugar bowl open, clear.................................... 30
Sugar bowl, open, w/red notches 73
Sugar shaker w/metal top 110
Sugar shaker w/metal top, w/red
   notches.. 450-500
Syrup pitcher w/metal top, clear 175-200
Syrup pitcher w/metal top, w/red notches...... 405
Tumbler, clear.. 48
Tumbler, w/red notches 75-100
*Wine 85

BRYCE - See Ribbon Candy Pattern

BULL'S EYE
Ale glass 65
Bitters bottle 100
Bowl, 8" d.. 45
Carafe, flint, qt. 123
Celery vase, flint 85
Champagne 154
Claret, flint... 75
Compote, open, 8 1/4" d., low stand................ 125
Cordial, flint... 138
Creamer, applied handle, flint 155
Decanter, w/bar lip, qt. 188
Decanter, w/original stopper, pt. 175-200
Decanter w/bar lip, flint, qt. 190
Egg cup, cov. 200-225
Egg cup, clear, flint, 3 3/4" h. 60
Egg cup, opalescent milk glass...................... 500
Goblet, flint.. 80-90
Lamp, miniature, flint....................................... 60
Lamp, whale oil, complete............................. 138
Pitcher, water, non-flint 85
Salt dip, master size, footed, flint..................... 63
Sugar bowl, cov., flint.................................... 135
Tumbler, bar, flint.. 100
Tumbler, footed, flint.. 95
Tumbler, footed, non-flint................................. 65
Tumbler, whiskey, flint................................... 125
Wine, knob stem, flint....................................... 50

BUTTON ARCHES

Banana dish, green 35

Button Arches Souvenir Bowl

Bowl, 8" d., ruby-stained, souvenir
(ILLUS.)... 60
Butter dish, cov., clear 52
***Butter dish,** cov., ruby-stained 95
Celery vase, ruby-stained, souvenir 75-85
Compote, open, jelly, 4 1/2" h., ruby-
stained................. 40
***Creamer,** ruby-stained 38
Creamer, ruby-stained, souvenir, 3 1/2" h.......... 30
Cruet w/original stopper, ruby-stained.... 180-185
***Goblet,** ruby-stained 50
Mug, child's, ruby-stained, souvenir 23
Mug, clear... 25
Mug, ruby-stained.. 30-35
Pitcher, water, tankard, 12" h., ruby-
stained.. 145
Pitcher, water, tankard, ruby-stained, sou-
venir of Pan American Exposition 150
Punch cup, clear.. 9
Punch cup, ruby-stained...................................... 19
Salt dip 19
Salt & pepper shakers w/original tops,
clear, small, pr....................................... 35
Salt shaker w/original top, ruby-stained 27
Sauce dish, clear 17
Sauce dish., ruby-stained 30
Spooner, ruby-stained w/clear band................. 63
Sugar bowl, cov., clear 45
***Sugar bowl,** cov., ruby-stained......................... 85
Syrup pitcher w/original top, clear 133
Syrup pitcher w/original top, ruby-stained..... 175
Toothpick holder, clear...................................... 15
Toothpick holder, ruby-stained.......................... 28
Tumbler, clear... 16
Tumbler, ruby-stained.. 47
Whiskey shot glass, ruby-stained..................... 47
Wine, clear 31
Wine, ruby-stained 38

CABLE

Bowl, 8" d., footed... 75
Butter dish, cov. 90
Cake stand, 9" d. 95
Castor set w/stand, 3-bottle.................... 250-300
Celery vase 150
Compote, cov., 12" h. 120
Compote, open, 7" d., 5" h............................... 52
Compote, open, 8" d., 4 3/4" h................. 75-100
Compote, open, 9" d., 4 1/2" h.......................... 70
Creamer, clear 100-150

Decanter w/bar lip, qt............................... 95-125
Decanter w/stopper, pt. 225-275
Decanter w/stopper, qt. 313

Cable Egg Cup

Egg cup, clear (ILLUS.)....................................... 65
Egg Cup, cov., blue opaque, 5 1/4" h. 2,200
Goblet 90-100
Goblet, lady's 210
Lamp, whale oil, all glass, 8 3/4" h. 188
Lamp, whale oil, brass & marble base,
8 3/4" 175-200
Lamp, whale oil, all glass, 11" h. 200-225
Pitcher, water, 9 1/2" h., applied handle 425
Salt dip, individual size 37
Salt dip, master size 63
Spooner, clear 30
Sugar bowl, cov.. 175
Sugar bowl, open 65-75
Tumbler, footed.. 135
Tumbler, whiskey 150-175
Wine 200-225

CANADIAN

Bowl, 6" d., handled 28
Bowl, berry, 7" d., 4 1/2" h., footed.................... 69
Bowl, 8" d., handled 45
Bowl, 9 1/2" d. 55
Bread plate, handled, 10" d. 40-50
Butter dish, cov. 63
Cake stand, 9 3/4" d., 5" h. 35-50
Celery vase 70
Compote, cov., 6" d., 9" h. 124
Compote, cov., 7" d., low stand 133
Compote, cov., 7" d., 11" h. 113
Compote, cov., 8" d., low stand 92
Compote, cov., 8" d., 11" h. 150
Compote, open, 6" d., footed 40
Compote, open, 7" d., 6" h. 35
Compote, open, 8" d., 5" h. 48
Cordial 37
Creamer 67

Canadian Goblet

Goblet (ILLUS.) 70-75
Honey dish, flat, 3 1/2" d. 15
Marmalade jar, cov. 210
Pitcher, milk, 8" h. 113
Pitcher, water 95
Plate, 6" d., handled 32
Plate, 7" d., handled 45
Plate, 8" d., handled 44
Plate, 8 1/2" d., handled 35
Plate, 9" d. 36
Sauce dish, flat or footed, each 19
Spooner 45
Sugar bowl, cov. 70
Sugar bowl, open 21
Wine 40

CARDINAL BIRD
Butter dish, cov. 95
Butter dish, cov., three unidentified birds 98
Creamer 35-45

Cardinal Bird Goblet

*Goblet (ILLUS.) 40-45
Honey dish, cov., 3 1/2" h. 35

Honey dish, open 19
Sauce dish, flat or footed, each 14
Spooner 25-35
Sugar bowl, cov. 55

CATHEDRAL
Bowl, 6" d., clear 16
Bowl, 7" d., clear 20
Bowl, berry, 8" d., amber 48
Bowl, berry, 8" d., blue 40
Bowl, berry, 8" d., canary 28
Cake stand, amber 55
Cake stand, canary 60
Cake stand, clear, 10" d., 4 1/2" h. 38
Compote, cov., 8" d., high stand, blue 185
Compote, open, 7 1/2" d., high stand, ame-
    thyst, fluted rim 145
Compote, open, 10 1/2" d., 8" h., clear,
    shaped rim 55
Compote, open, 10 1/2" d., 8" h., ruby-
    stained 125
Creamer, clear 35
Creamer, ruby-stained 50
Cruet w/original stopper, amber 118
Goblet, amber 39
Goblet, canary 42
Goblet, clear 26
Goblet, ruby-stained 65
Lamp, kerosene-type, blue font, amber
    base, 12 3/4" h. 310
Pitcher, water, clear 125
Pitcher, water, ruby-stained 178
Relish, fish-shaped, clear 32
Relish, fish-shaped, ruby-stained 55
Salt dip, canoe-shaped, blue 33
Salt dip, master size, amber 25
Sauce dish, flat or footed, blue 25
Sauce dish, flat or footed, ruby-stained 22
Spooner, amber 43
Spooner, clear 28
Spooner, ruby-stained 40
Sugar bowl, cov., clear 45
Sugar bowl, cov., ruby-stained 70
Sugar bowl, open, clear 23
Sugar bowl, open, ruby-stained 29
Tumbler, amber 31
Tumbler, ruby-stained 43
Wine, amber 50
Wine, canary 65
Wine, clear 28
Wine, ruby-stained 45

CHANDELIER (Crown Jewel)
Butter dish, cov. 95
Cake stand, 10" d. 100-125

Chandelier Celery Vase

Celery vase (ILLUS.) **55-65**
Compote, open, 6 1/2" d. **40-45**
Creamer **50-60**
Goblet **45-50**
Goblet, engraved **68**
Inkwell **80-90**
Pitcher, water, tankard, 1/2 gal. **115-120**
Pitcher, water, tankard, 1/2 pt. **50-60**
Spooner **40-45**
Sugar bowl, cov. **55-65**
Sugar shaker w/original top **65**
Tumbler **43**

CLASSIC

Berry set, master bowl & 8 sauce dishes, 9
pcs. **475**
Butter dish, cov., open log feet **200-225**
Celery vase, collared base **140**
Celery vase, open log feet **165-185**
Compote, cov., 6 1/2" d., collared base **175-200**
Compote, cov., 7 1/2" d., 8" h., open log
feet **300**
Compote, cov., 9" d., open log feet. **350**
Creamer, open log feet **135-145**

Classic Goblet

Goblet (ILLUS.) **200-225**
Marmalade jar, cov., open log feet **550-650**
Pitcher, milk, 8 1/2" h., open log feet **400-500**
Pitcher, water, 9 1/2" h., collared base **250-275**
Pitcher, water, 9 1/2" h., open log feet. **340**
Plate, 10" d., "Blaine" or "Hendricks,"
signed Jacobus **210**
Plate, 10" d., "Cleveland" **185-200**
Plate, 10" d., "Logan" **230**
Plate, 10" d., "Warrior" **120-125**
Plate, 10" d., "Warrior," signed Jacobus. **225**
Sauce dish, open log feet **35-40**
Spooner, collared base **95**
Spooner, open log feet **125-150**
Sugar bowl, cov., open log feet. **200**
Sugar bowl, open, collared base **75-85**
Sugar bowl, open, open log feet. **150**

COLLINS - See Crystal Wedding Pattern

COLORADO (Lacy Medallion)

Berry set: master bowl & 6 sauce dishes;
clear w/gold, 7 pcs. **125**
Bowl, 4" d., blue **39**
Bowl, 4" d., green w/gold **20**
Bowl, 5" d., blue, ruffled rim **35**

Bowl, 5" d., clear, flared edge **20**
Bowl, 5" d., green w/gold **45**
Bowl, 7" d., blue, footed, scalloped rim **25**
Bowl, 7" d., clear, footed **25**
Bowl, 7" d., green, flat **23**
Bowl, 8" d., blue, turned-up sides **65**
Bowl, 8" d., green w/gold, turned-up sides. **63**
Bowl, 9" d., clear, footed, three turned-up
sides **32**
Bowl, 9" d., green, footed, crimped edge **40**
Bowl, 9" d., green w/gold **43**
Butter dish, cov., blue w/gold **260**
Butter dish, cov., clear. **63**
Butter dish, cov., green **125**
Cake plate, handled, blue, 12" d. **180**
Cake stand, clear **65**
Card tray, blue **40**
Card tray, blue w/gold **120**
Card tray, clear **20**
Card tray, green **33**
Celery vase, clear **35**
Celery vase, green **48**
Celery vase, green w/gold **70**
Cheese dish, cov., blue w/gold **70**
Compote, open, 8" d., 7" h., beaded rim,
green **100-125**
Compote, open, 10 1/2" d., high stand,
blue **215**
Compote, open, 10 1/2" d., 7" h., green
w/gold **135**
Creamer, blue **80**
Creamer, clear **34**
Creamer, green **55**
Creamer, green, souvenir **65**
Cup & saucer, green **45**
Match holder, green **35**

Colorado Mug

Mug, clear, 2 1/2" h. (ILLUS.) **25**
Mug, green **30**
Mug, ruby-stained. **55**
Nappy, tricornered, blue w/gold. **48**
Nappy, tricornered, clear. **20**
Nappy, tricornered, green w/gold **30**
Pitcher, 6" d., blue w/gold **115**
Pitcher, 6" d., green w/gold. **42**
Pitcher, water, blue w/gold. **400**
Pitcher, water, clear w/gold. **116**
Pitcher, water, green w/gold **275-300**
Salt shaker w/original top, green w/gold. **45**
Sauce dish, clear **13**
Sauce dish, green w/gold **25**
Spooner, blue w/gold **55**

Spooner, clear 40
Spooner, green w/gold................................. **60-70**
Sugar bowl, cov., clear, large 42
Sugar bowl, cov., green, large................... **85-100**
Sugar bowl, cov., green w/gold, large 110
*Toothpick holder, clear w/gold 40
Tumbler, clear.. 35
Tumbler, green w/gold 40
Tumbler, green w/gold, souvenir 30
Tumbler, ruby-stained, souvenir 40
Vase, 12" h., trumpet-shaped, green.............. 275
Vase, 14" h., trumpet-shaped, clear 60
Water set: pitcher & 6 tumblers; green
   w/gold, 7 pcs. 450
Wine, clear 30
Wine, green w/gold.. 35
Wine, ruby-stained w/gold 40

COLUMBIAN COIN
Butter dish, cov., frosted coins........................ 150
Cake stand, frosted coins, 10" 495
Claret, gilded coins.. 125
Compote, open, 8" d., clear coins...................... 68
Creamer, gilded coins 125
Cruet w/original stopper, frosted coins 195
Goblet, frosted coins 120
*Goblet, gilded coins 90
Lamp, kerosene-type, milk white, 8" h. 400
Mug, frosted coins 120
Pitcher, water, 10" h., gilded coins................... 135
Relish, frosted coins, 5 x 8"............................... 58
Sauce dish, flat or footed, frosted coins,
   each 47
Sauce dish, flat, clear coins, 4 1/2" d.............. 55
Spooner, frosted coins 80
Spooner, gilded coins 78
Sugar bowl, open 100
Syrup pitcher w/original top, frosted
   coins 325
*Toothpick holder, frosted coins...................... 163
*Tumbler, clear coins 30
*Tumbler, gilded coins 55
Water set, pitcher & 6 tumblers, gilded
   coins, 7 pcs. **400-450**
Wine, clear coins 95
Wine, frosted coins.. 113

COMPACT - See Snail Pattern

CORD DRAPERY
Bowl, 6 1/4" d., green, footed........................... 115
Bowl, 7" d., flat 23
Bowl, 8 1/4" d., amber, footed, fluted rim 180
Butter dish, cov., clear 53
Cake stand, clear 43
Cake stand, green, 10" d. 55
Creamer, clear (ILLUS. top of next column)....... 65
Cruet w/original stopper, blue........................ 375
Cruet w/original stopper, clear........................ 85
Pickle dish, amber, 5 1/4 x 9 1/4" oval 70
Pickle dish, clear, 5 1/4 x 9 1/4" oval............ 30-35
Pickle dish, cobalt blue, 5 1/4 x 9 1/4" oval 75
Punch cup 12
Sauce dish, blue, flat or footed, each 35
Sauce dish, clear, flat or footed, each 12
Spooner 43
Sugar bowl, cov., clear..................................... 55
Sugar bowl, open, clear..................................... 20
Toothpick holder 90
Tray, amber.. 160

Cord Drapery Creamer

Tumbler, clear.. 75
Wine, emerald green 300

CORD & TASSEL
Butter dish, cov. 48
Castor bottle 32
Celery vase 48
Compote, cov., 10" d. 103
Compote, open, 8" d., low stand...................... 27
Cordial 53
Creamer 30

Cord & Tassel Goblet

Goblet (ILLUS.) **35-45**
Lamp, kerosene-type, applied handle **100-125**
Salt shaker w/original top, blue........................ 50
Sugar bowl, open 26
Table set, creamer, open sugar bowl &
   spooner, 3 pcs. **75-80**
Wine **25-35**

CORONA - See Sunk Honeycomb Pattern

COTTAGE (Dinner Bell or Finecut Band)

Banana bowl, flat base 55
Bowl, oval, blue 95
Butter dish, cov., clear 47
Cake stand, amber 75
Cake stand, clear 37
Celery vase, clear 32
Compote, cov., 8" d., high stand, amber 180
Compote, open, jelly, 4 1/2" d., 4" h., clear 22
Compote, open, jelly, 4 1/2" d., 4" h., green .. 45-50
Compote, open, 8 1/4" d., 7 1/2" h. 58
Creamer, clear 30

Cottage Cruet with Original Stopper

Cruet w/original stopper (ILLUS.) 65
Cup & saucer 39
*Goblet, amber 53
*Goblet, blue 68
*Goblet, clear 20-25
Honey dish 22
Pitcher, water, 2 qt. 60
Plate, 6" d. 14
Plate, 7" d. 20
Relish 40-45
Sauce dish, amber 25
Sauce dish, clear 15
Sauce dish, green 50
Tray, water, clear 40-45
Tray, water, green 65
Waste bowl, amber 55-60

CROESUS

Bowl, 6 3/4" d., green, footed 150
Bowl, 7" d., 4" h., green w/gold, footed 65
Bowl, 7" d., 4" h., purple, footed 67
Bowl, 7" d., 4" h., purple w/gold, footed 210
Bowl, 8" d., green 88
Bowl, 8" d., green w/gold 113
Bowl, 8" d., purple 158
Bowl, berry or fruit, 9" d., green 135
Bowl, 10" d., purple, footed 155
*Butter dish, cov., green 140-150
Butter dish, cov., green w/gold 185
*Butter dish, cov., purple 275
Cake stand, high stand, 10" d 495
Celery vase, green w/gold 150-170
Celery vase, purple w/gold 425

Compote, open, jelly, green 245
Compote, open, jelly, purple 275
Condiment tray, green 125
Condiment tray, purple 109
Cracker jar, green w/gold 145
*Creamer, clear 60
*Creamer, green 139
*Creamer, purple 148
Creamer, individual size, green, 3" h. 138
Creamer, individual size, purple, 3" h. 145-155
Creamer, individual size, purple w/gold,
   3" h. 185
Cruet w/original stopper, green w/gold,
   6 1/2" h. 200-250
Cruet w/original stopper, miniature,
   green, 4" h. 325
Cruet w/original stopper, green 325-375
Cruet w/original stopper, purple 365
Pitcher, child size, green 58
Pitcher, milk, green 90
Pitcher, water, green 235-285
Salt & pepper shakers w/original tops,
   green, pr. 250
Salt & pepper shakers w/original tops,
   purple, pr. 210
Salt & pepper shakers w/original tops,
   purple w/gold, pr. 265
Salt shaker w/original top, green w/gold 115
Salt shaker w/original top, purple 98
Sauce dish, green w/gold 45
Sauce dish, purple w/gold 38
*Spooner, clear 99
*Spooner, green 105
*Spooner, green w/gold 90
*Spooner, purple 115
*Sugar bowl, cov., clear 130
*Sugar bowl, cov., green 169
Sugar bowl, cov., green w/gold 175
*Sugar bowl, cov., purple 110-120
*Sugar bowl, cov., purple w/gold 200-215
Sugar bowl, open, green 75-85
Toothpick holder, clear w/gold 85
*Toothpick holder, green 85-90
*Toothpick holder, purple 165
*Tumbler, clear 25-30
*Tumbler, green 55-65
*Tumbler, green w/gold 75
*Tumbler, purple 85

Croesus Water Set

Water set: pitcher & 6 tumblers; green, 7
   pcs. (ILLUS.) 575-675

CROWN JEWEL - See Chandelier Pattern

CRYSTAL WEDDING (Collins)

Banana stand, 10" h. 123
Bowl, cov., 7" sq. 95
Bowl, 7" d., scalloped edge 65
Butter dish, cov., amber-stained 100
Butter dish, cov., clear 75
Butter dish, cov., ruby-stained 130
Cake stand, 10" sq. 98
Celery vase 50
Compote, cov., 6" sq., high stand 65
Compote, open, 5" sq., low stand 45
Compote, open, 6" sq. 47
Compote, open, 6" sq., high stand, scal-
   loped rim 50
Compote, open, 7" sq., high stand 50
Compote, open, 8" sq., low stand 55
Creamer, clear 65
Creamer, ruby-stained 125
Creamer & cov. sugar bowl, amber-
   stained, pr. 180-195
Cruet w/original stopper, amber-stained 225
Cruet w/original stopper, canary 225
Cruet w/original stopper, clear 175
*Goblet, clear 40
*Goblet, ruby-stained 65
Goblet w/fern etching 73
Honey dish, cov., 6" sq. 80
Honey dish, cov., 7". 90
Humidor, w/resilvered top, 5" h. 125
Lamp, kerosene-type, 8" h. 145
Lamp, kerosene-type, banquet-style, blue
   base, clear font. 280
Lamp base, kerosene-type, square font,
   10" h. 225
Pitcher, 12" h., tankard, water 165-185
Pitcher, milk, square 150
Plate, 10" sq., engraved 45
Plate, 10" sq., plain 35
Relish 20
Salt dip, individual 30
Salt dip, master size 55
Spooner, canary 45
Spooner, clear 40
Sugar bowl, cov., amber-stained 135
Sugar bowl, cov., clear 60

Crystal Wedding Sugar Bowl

Sugar bowl, cov., ruby-stained (ILLUS.) 125
Syrup pitcher w/original top 185

Syrup pitcher w/original top, ruby-stained 250
Table set: creamer, cov. sugar bowl &
   spooner; clear, 3 pcs. 175
Table set: creamer, cov. sugar bowl, cov.
   butter dish & spooner; ruby-stained, 4
   pcs. 450-475
Tumbler, clear 45
Tumbler, ruby-stained 65
Wine 75
Wine, ruby-stained 39

CURRIER & IVES

Bread plate, clear, handled 45-50
Bread plate, children sawing felled log,
   frosted center 75
Cake stand, blue 118
Cake stand, clear 65
Celery 50
Cordial, 3 1/2" h. 50
Cup & saucer, clear 40
*Goblet, blue 65-70
*Goblet, canary 85
*Goblet, clear 23
Lamp, kerosene-type, 8" h. 80
Mug, clear 25
Pitcher, milk 65
Pitcher, water, amber 135
Pitcher, water, blue 155

Currier & Ives Pitcher

Pitcher, water, clear (ILLUS.) 85
Salt & pepper shakers w/original tops,
   amber, pr. 165
Salt & pepper shakers w/original tops,
   blue, pr. 190
Sugar bowl, cov. 35-45
Syrup jug w/original top, amber 210
Syrup jug w/original top, blue 162
Syrup jug w/original top, clear 125
Tray, water, amber, Balky Mule on Railroad
   Tracks, 9 1/2" d. 103
Tray, water, blue, Balky Mule on Railroad
   Tracks, 9 1/2" d. 165
Tray, water, clear, Balky Mule on Railroad
   Tracks, 9 1/2" d. 65
Tray, water, canary, Balky Mule on Rail-
   road Tracks, 10 1/2" d. 175
Tray, water, clear, Balky Mule on Railroad
   Tracks, 10 1/2" d. 88
Tumbler, amber 57

Tumbler, clear.. 40
Wine, blue 55
Wine, clear 19
Wine, ruby-stained 85
Wine set, decanter w/original stopper & 6
    wines, 7 pcs. 150

CURTAIN TIEBACK
Bowl, 7 1/2" sq., flat 18
Bread plate 37
Butter dish, cov. 37
Cake stand, 11 1/4" d., 7 1/4" h. 130

Curtain Tieback Celery Vase

Celery vase (ILLUS.) 30
Compote, cov., 7 1/2" d., low stand 28
Goblet, ... 20
Relish 10
Sauce dish, flat or footed................................. 11
Spooner 28
Sugar bowl, cov.. 30
Sugar bowl, open 20

CUT LOG
Cake stand, 9 1/4" d., high stand...................... 74
Cake stand, 10 1/2" d., high stand................ 65-75
Celery vase 20-30
Compote, cov., 7 1/4" d., high stand................. 90
Compote, cov., 8" d., high stand........................ 70
Compote, open, jelly, 5" d................................. 40
*Compote, open, 6" d., flared rim, high
    stand 40
Compote, open, 7 1/2" d., high stand 50
Compote, open, 8" d., high stand 60
*Compote, open, 9" d., high stand..................... 75
Creamer 50-60
Creamer, individual size.................................... 15
Creamer & cov. sugar bowl, pr. 125
Creamer & cov. sugar bowl, individual
    size, pr.. 50
Cruet w/original stopper, small, 3 3/4" h......... 45
Cruet w/original stopper, 4" h. 65
Cruet w/original stopper, large, 5" h. 75

Cut Log Goblet

Goblet (ILLUS.).. 50-55
Honey dish, cov... 95
Mug, 3 1/4" h. 15-25
Mustard jar w/cover 58
Olive dish, handled, 5" d. 30
Pitcher, helmet shaped w/design on han-
    dle 125
Pitcher, water, tankard, clear 85-95
Salt & pepper shakers w/original tops,
    pr. 140
Sauce dish, flat or footed, each 20-30
Spooner 40-45
Sugar bowl, cov... 45-50
Sugar bowl, open, individual size 30
Tumbler, juice 40-45
Tumbler, water... 55
Vase, 15" h. 48
Vase, 16" h. 56
Vase, 18" h., pulled-up 60
Wine 20-25
Wines, set of 6 150

DAHLIA
Banana bowl, 12 1/2", green 125-160
Bread platter, 8 x 12"..................................... 40
Butter dish, cov., canary................................ 65
Butter dish, cov., clear.................................... 54
Cake stand, canary, 9 1/2" d........................... 75
Cake stand, clear, 9 1/2" d.......................... 30-35
Cake stand, amber, 10" d. 75
Cake stand, clear, 10" d.................................. 25
Champagne, amber 75
Champagne, clear 35
Compote, cov., 7" d., high stand, clear 85
Cordial, clear 40
Creamer, amber 55
Creamer, clear 25
Cruet w/original stopper, clear........................ 45
Egg cup, clear... 25
Egg cup, double 45-50
Goblet, blue.. 60
Goblet, clear... 33
Mug, amber 45
Mug, blue.. 60
Mug, child's, blue... 45

Mug, child's, clear... 30
Pickle dish, amber... 40
Pickle dish, shell handles.................................. 55
Pitcher, milk, clear, applied handle.................. 51
Pitcher, water, amber....................................... 105

Dahlia Water Pitcher

Pitcher, water, clear (ILLUS.)............................ 45
Plate, 7" d., amber.. 43
Plate, 7" d., clear.. 18
Plate, 9" d., amber, w/handles......................... 25
Plate, 9" d., blue, w/handles............................ 50
Plate, 9" d., clear, w/handles........................... 18
Relish, amber, 5 x 9 1/2"................................... 20
Sauce dish, amber, flat..................................... 22
Sauce dish, canary, flat.................................... 35
Spooner, amber... 48
Spooner, apple green.. 65
Spooner, canary.. 55
Spooner, clear... 35
Sugar bowl, cov., clear................................ 45-55
Wine, amber.. 70
Wine, clear.. 45

DAISY & BUTTON
Banana boat, amber.. 90
Banana boat, blue... 110
Banana boat, clear, 14" l................................... 50
Banana boat, green... 100
Basket, branch handles, amber, small oval....... 50
Boot, high-top, ruby-stained buttons.............. 125
Bowl, 6" d., blue... 45
Bowl, 8" sq., amber... 50
Bowl, 8" w., clear, tricornered.......................... 45
Bowl, 8 1/2" sq., blue.. 50
Bowl, 9" sq., amber...................................... 30-35
Bowl, 9" sq., Amberina................................... 183
Bowl, 9 1/2" d., canary..................................... 43
Bowl, 10" d., amber, deep................................ 67
Bowl, 10 x 11" oval, 7 3/4" h., canary,
  flared.. 95
Bowl, fruit, rectangular, ornate silver plate
  frame... 250
Butter chip, square, Amberina.......................... 75
*Butter dish, cov., model of Victorian
  stove, green.. 215
Butter dish, cov., scalloped base, clear........... 65
Butter dish, cov., square, amber...................... 59
Canoe, amber, 8" l.. 115

Canoe, Amberina, 8" l..................................... 495
Canoe, amber, 12" l... 63
Canoe, clear, 14" l... 26
Castor set, 3-bottle,amber, clear & blue, in
  clear glass frame... 120
Celery tray, flat, boat-shaped, 14" l.,
  canary... 125
Celery tray, flat, boat-shaped, 4 1/2 x 14",
  clear... 90
Celery vase, square.. 45
Cheese dish, cov., amber................................ 160
*Cruet w/original stopper, amber.................... 100
Cup & saucer, blue.. 65

Daisy & Button Finger Bowl

Finger bowl, blue, 4 3/8" d., 2 7/8" h.
  (ILLUS.).. 32
Goblet, ruby-stained rim & buttons................... 50
*Hat shape, amber, 2 1/2" h............................. 28
Hat shape, clear, 8 x 8", 6" h............................ 60
Humidor, cov., amber...................................... 185
Inkwell, amber... 145
Inkwell, blue.. 175
Inkwell w/original insert, cat seated on
  cover... 210
Match holder, wall-hanging scuff, clear............ 65
*Pickle castor, sapphire blue insert, w/sil-
  ver plate frame & tongs.............................. 238
Pitcher, water, canary, bulbous, applied
  handle, scalloped top.................................. 135
Pitcher, water, clear, bulbous, applied han-
  dle.. 125-150
Pitcher, water, ruby-stained buttons, bul-
  bous, applied handle................................... 325
Powder jar, cov., amber 3 3/4" d., 2" h............. 30
Relish, "Sitz bathtub," amber.......................... 125
*Salt & pepper shakers w/original tops,
  blue, pr... 48
Sauce dish, amber, rectangular........................ 36
Sauce dish, clear, cloverleaf-shaped............... 24
*Slipper, canary, "1886 patent"........................ 55
*Slipper, clear, "1886 patent"..................... 50-55
Slipper, ruby-stained buttons........................... 80
Sugar bowl, cov., barrel-shaped, blue.............. 50
Sugar bowl, cov., clear..................................... 35
Syrup pitcher w/original pewter top, blue..... 175
Toothpick holder, amber, w/brass rim &
  base... 15
Toothpick holder, coal hod form, amber........... 35
Toothpick holder, three-footed, Amberina...... 275
Tray, water, amber, 11" d.................................. 90
Tray, ice cream, blue, handled,
  9 1/4 x 16 1/2"... 60-80
Tumbler, water, amber....................................... 26
Tumbler, water, canary................................ 25-30

Tumbler, water, canary, pattern half way
up 30
Waste bowl, clear 30
Whimsey, "canoe," wall hanging-type,
ruby-stained buttons, 11" l........................... 110
Whimsey, "umbrella," original metal han-
dle, canary.. 425

DAISY & BUTTON WITH CROSSBARS (Mikado)

Bread or water tray, amber, 9 x 12"............. 40-45
Bread or water tray, canary yellow, 9 x 12"....... 52
Bread or water tray, clear, 9 x 12" 32
Butter dish, cov., clear 45
Cake stand, amber 60
Cake stand, blue.. 85
Cake stand, clear... 45
Castor set, three-bottle, w/tray 65
Compote, cov., clear, 7" d., low stand 25
Compote, cov., clear, 7" d., high stand............. 50
Compote, open, canary yellow, 7" d., high
stand 45-50
Compote, open, blue, 9 1/2" d. 78
Creamer, canary yellow 50
Creamer & open. sugar bowl, clear, pr. 30
Cruet w/original stopper, amber 75
Cruet w/original stopper, blue....................... 110
Finger bowl, canary yellow............................... 35

Daisy & Button with Crossbars Goblet

Goblet, clear (ILLUS.) 32
Mug, canary yellow, 3" h. 40
Pitcher, milk, canary yellow 75
Pitcher, water, canary yellow........................... 135
Relish, amber, 4 1/2 x 8"................................... 30
Salt shaker w/original top, amber................... 25
Salt shaker w/original top, blue...................... 30
Salt shaker w/original top, clear 15
Sugar bowl, open, individual size, blue 35
Sugar bowl, open, individual size, canary
yellow 30
Sugar bowl, open, individual size, clear 25
Syrup pitcher w/original top, clear 70
Toothpick holder, blue...................................... 40
*Toothpick holder, ruby-stained 45
Tumbler, amber 40
Tumbler, blue.. 45

Tumbler, canary yellow...................................... 40
Tumbler, clear... 25
Water set: pitcher & 6 tumblers; canary
yellow, 7 pcs... 300-375
Wine, amber 35
Wine, canary yellow 35

DAISY & BUTTON WITH NARCISSUS

*Bowl, 6 x 9 1/2" oval, footed 46
Decanter w/original stopper 52
Goblet 20
Pitcher, water, clear.. 60

D&B with Narcissus Decorated Pitcher

Pitcher, water, cranberry-stained color
(ILLUS.).. 75-100
Punch cup 11
Sauce dish, flat or three-footed, each............... 18
Sugar bowl, cov... 35
Tray, 10 1/2" d.. 40-50
Tumbler 17
Water set: pitcher & 6 tumblers; cranberry-
stained, gold trim, 7 pcs. 125
Water set: pitcher & 8 tumblers; amber, 9
pcs... 125
*Wine, clear 15-20

DAISY & BUTTON WITH THUMBPRINT PANELS

Berry set: master bowl & 4 sauce dishes;
amber panels, 5 pcs............................. 100-125
Berry set: 10" d. cloverleaf-shaped bowl &
eight 5" d. sauce dishes; canary, 9 pcs........ 110
Bowl, 8" sq., clear 25
Bowl, berry, cov., 8" d., 8" h., amber panels....... 55
Butter dish, cov., amber panels.............. 150-200
Butter pat, amber panels 20
Compote, cov., 7" d., high stand 45
Compote, cov., 7" d., low stand 60
Compote, open, 6" d., low stand....................... 35
Cruet w/swirled stopper, amber...................... 78
Cruet w/swirled stopper, clear 50
Pitcher, water, canary 133
Sauce dish, 4 1/2" w., amber panels, clo-
verleaf-shaped 15
Sauce dish, blue panels, flat or footed, 5"
sq., each... 20
Sauce dish, amber, cloverleaf-shaped 15
Sauce dish, blue, cloverleaf-shaped................. 19
Sauce dish, clear, cloverleaf-shaped................ 15
Spooner, amber panels 65
Sugar bowl, cov., amber panels 60
Sugar bowl, open, clear..................................... 25

Syrup jug w/original top, amber panels 175
Tumbler, amber panels 65-70

DAISY IN PANEL - See Two Panel Pattern

DAKOTA (Baby Thumbprint)
Butter dish, cov., ruby-stained w/flared
  edge on base 250
Cake stand, 8" d., engraved 50
Cake stand, 8" d., plain................................... 175
Cake stand, 9" d., engraved 250
Cake stand, 9 1/2" d. 180
Cake stand, 10 1/2" d., engraved 213
Cake stand, 10 1/2" d., plain.......................... 250
Cake stand, w/high domed cover 375
Castor set: salt shaker, oil & vinegar cruets
  w/originat stoppers & tray, 4 pcs. 300
Celery vase, flat base, clear, engraved 50
Celery vase, pedestal base, engraved 48
Celery vase, pedestal base, plain..................... 42
Celery vase, pedestal base, ruby-stained........ 110
Compote, open, jelly, 5" d., 5 1/2" h., plain........ 45
Compote, open, 9" d., high stand,
  engraved 45
Compote, open, 10" d., high stand 45
Creamer, hotel 65
Cruet w/original stopper, engraved 170
Cruet w/original stopper, plain...................... 95
Doughnut stand, cov....................................... 300
Goblet, clear, engraved.................................... 42
Goblet, clear, plain 60
Goblet, ruby-stained, engraved 95
Goblet, ruby-stained, plain 85
Honey dish 25
Mug, clear... 45
Mug, ruby-stained, 3 1/2" h. 65
Pitcher, milk, jug-type, engraved, pt. 120-130
Pitcher, milk, tankard, engraved, pt. 120
Pitcher, milk, tankard, engraved, qt. 125
Pitcher, milk, tankard, ruby-stained, pt. 135
*Pitcher, water, tankard, engraved
  leaves, 1/2 gal. 140-150
Pitcher, tankard, 12" h., souvenir engrav-
  ing 115
Plate or water tray, 10" d. 93
Plate or water tray, 10 1/2" d., ruffled 135
Salt & pepper shakers w/original tops,
  ruby-stained, pr. 165
Salt shaker w/original top, ruby-stained 85
Sauce dish, flat or footed, clear, engraved,
  each 18
Sauce dish, flat or footed, clear, plain,
  each 15
Sauce dish, flat or footed, cobalt blue,
  each 95
Sugar bowl, cov., engraved.............................. 75
Sugar bowl, cov., plain.................................... 50
Waste bowl, engraved...................................... 75
Waste bowl, plain 58
Wine, clear, engraved 30-40
Wine, clear, plain 25
Wine, ruby-stained 55

DEER & PINE TREE
Bowl, 5 1/2 x 8", clear 40-45
Bread tray, amber, 8 x 13"............................... 95
Bread tray, apple green, 8 x 13" 165
Bread tray, blue, 8 x 13" 125
Bread tray, canary yellow, 8 x 13" 185
Bread tray, clear, 8 x 13" 75

Deer & Pine Tree Butter Dish

Butter dish, cov. (ILLUS.)................................ 110
Cake stand 90-165
Celery vase 110
Compote, cov., 8" sq., high stand............. 150-225
Compote, open, 7 x 9", high stand................... 68
*Goblet 45
Honey dish 25
Marmalade jar, cov. 188
Mug, child's, amber 50
Mug, child's, apple green................................ 43
Mug, child's, canary yellow............................. 55
Mug, child's, clear.. 39
Mug, large, clear.. 47
Pickle castor w/metal frame 275
Pickle dish 35
Pitcher, milk 165-175
Pitcher, water.. 130-150
Sauce dish, clear, flat or footed, each 15-20
Spooner 85
Sugar bowl, cov... 90
Tray, water, amber, 11 x 15" 120
Tray, water, apple green, 11 x 15" 160
Tray, water, canary yellow, 11 x 15"................ 150
Tray, water, clear, 11 x 15"............................. 95

DELAWARE (Four Petal Flower)
Banana boat, amethyst w/gold, 11 3/4" l. ... 75-125
Banana boat, green w/gold, 11 3/4" l................ 70
Banana boat, rose w/gold, 11 3/4" l................ 118
Berry set: boat-shaped master bowl & 4
  boat-shaped sauce dishes; clear w/rose
  flowers & gold, 5 pcs. 150-200
Berry set: boat-shaped master bowl in sil-
  ver plate holder & 4 boat-shaped sauce
  dishes; rose w/gold, 5 pcs. 125-150
Berry set: round master bowl & 5 sauce
  dishes; rose w/gold, 6 pcs. 200-250
Berry set: round master bowl & 6 sauce
  dishes; green w/gold, 7 pcs. 175
Bowl, 8" d., amethyst w/gold 90-125
Bowl, 8" d., clear 50
Bowl, 8" d., green w/gold 40-50
Bowl, 8" d., rose w/gold.................................. 50
Bowl, 9" d., rose w/gold, scalloped rim 75
Bride's basket, boat-shaped open bowl,
  rose w/gold, in silver plate frame, 11 1/2"
  oval.. 395
Bride's basket, boat-shaped open bowl,
  green w/gold, miniature............................... 175
Butter dish, cov., clear............................... 95-110
*Butter dish, cov., green w/gold 113
Butter dish, cov., rose w/gold 145

Claret jug, green w/gold.................................. 150
Claret jug, rose w/gold................................. 75-95
Compote, 9 1/2" d., 6 1/2" h., green, pewter base 85-110
Creamer, clear w/gold...................................... 45
*Creamer, green w/gold 54
Creamer, individual size, clear w/gold............... 25
Creamer & cov. sugar bowl, green w/gold, pr.. 132
Cruet w/original stopper, clear...................... 100
Cruet w/original stopper, green w/gold......... 310
Cruet w/original stopper, rose w/gold 460
Custard cup, green w/gold 35
Custard cup, rose w/gold 42
Pin tray, rose w/gold 75-85
Pitcher, tankard, green w/gold 150
Pitcher, water, clear w/gold......................... 50-75
Pomade jar w/jeweled cover, rose w/gold...... 335
Salt & pepper shakers w/original tops, green w/gold, pr. 495
Salt shaker w/original top, clear 75-150
Sauce dish, boat-shaped, green w/gold 20
Sauce dish, boat-shaped, rose w/gold 38
Sauce dish, round, green w/gold...................... 23
Spooner, clear w/gold 50
Spooner, green 35
Spooner, green w/gold...................................... 75

Delaware Spooner

Spooner, rose w/gold (ILLUS.) 55-60
Sugar bowl, cov., clear 63
*Sugar bowl, cov., green w/gold....................... 78
Sugar bowl, cov., rose w/gold 90
Sugar bowl, open, clear.................................... 34
Sugar bowl, open, green w/gold........................ 45
Sugar bowl, open, rose w/gold 40
Sugar bowl, individual size, green.................... 55
Sugar bowl, individual size, green w/gold 30
Sugar bowl, individual size, rose w/gold............ 95
Table set: cov. butter dish, cov. sugar bowl & spooner; rose w/gold, 3 pcs. 300-350
Toothpick holder, clear..................................... 38
Toothpick holder, clear w/rose-stained florals & gold 145
Toothpick holder, green w/gold 100
Toothpick holder, rose w/gold 120

Tumbler, clear 12
Tumbler, clear w/gold 40
Tumbler, green w/gold 35
Tumbler, rose w/gold 53
Water set: water pitcher & 3 tumblers; rose w/gold, 4 pcs. 295

DEWEY (Flower Flange)

Bowl, 8" d., amber... 45
Bowl, 8" d., clear 35
Bowl, 8" d., green 63
*Butter dish, cov., amber 80
Butter dish, cov., canary yellow...................... 175
*Butter dish, cov., clear 50
*Butter dish, cov., green............................... 70-75
Butter dish, cov., amber, miniature 60-75
Butter dish, cov., green, miniature 75-80
Condiment set: cruet, tray, salt & pepper shakers; amber, 4 pcs. 250-300
Creamer, amber 50-60
Creamer, clear 30
Creamer, green 50
Creamer, cov., amber, individual size 75
Creamer & cov. sugar bowl, amber, pr. 125
Creamer & cov. sugar bowl, green 150
Cruet w/original stopper, amber 130

Dewey Cruet

Cruet w/original stopper, canary yellow (ILLUS.)... 185
Finger bowl, amber 35
Mug, amber 85
Mug, canary yellow.. 55
Mug, clear.. 30-35
Mug, green 55-60
Pitcher, water, amber..................................... 100
Pitcher, water, canary yellow 295
Pitcher, water, clear 55-65
Pitcher, water, green...................................... 145
Plate, footed, canary yellow 80
Salt & pepper shakers w/original tops, green pr. 125
Sauce dish, canary yellow 42
Sauce dish, clear 10
Sugar bowl, cov., amber.................................. 85
Sugar bowl, cov., canary yellow 80
Sugar bowl, cov., green................................... 80

Tray, serpentine shape, amber, small 45
Tumbler, amber 60
Tumbler, canary yellow..................................... 60
Tumbler, green 45

DIAMOND & BULL'S EYE BAND - See Reverse Torpedo Pattern

DIAMOND MEDALLION - See Grand Pattern

DIAMOND POINT

Bowl, 7" d., blue, flint.. 110
Bowl, 8 1/2" d., clear, flint.................................. 95
Butter dish, cov., clear, flint.............................. 83
Cake stand, clear, non-flint, 9" d. 75
Cake stand, clear, flint, 10" d. to 12" d...... 175-275
Candlesticks, clear, flint, pr..................... 145-175
Castor set, 4-bottle, clear, flint, in silver
    plate frame 350
Celery vase, pedestal base w/knob stem,
    clear, flint... 80-90
Champagne, clear, flint............................. 125-150
Claret, clear, flint 80-90
Compote, open, clear, 6" d., high stand,
    flint... 75
Compote, open, clear, 7" d., low stand, flint.. 70-75
Compote, open, milk white, 7" d., high
    stand, flint... 175
Compote, open, clear, 7 1/2" d., high
    stand, flint... 125-150
Compote, open, clear, 8" d., shallow bowl,
    high stand, non-flint...................................... 95
Compote, open, milk white, 10 1/4" d., high
    stand,flint.. 350
Cordial, clear, flint 195
Decanter, w/bar lip, clear, flint, pt. 150
Decanter w/bar lip, clear, flint, qt. 130
Decanter w/original stopper, clear, flint,
    pt. 150
Decanter w/original stopper, clear, flint,
    qt. 175
Egg cup, clambroth, flint 133
Egg cup, clear, flint 45-50
Egg cup, powder blue opaque, flint 300

Diamond Point Egg Cup

Egg cup, cov., powder blue opaque, flint
    (ILLUS. 700-900
Goblet, clear, flint 50-65
Goblet, clear, non-flint...................................... 38
Honey dish, milk white, flint 60
Lamp, whale oil, w/wafer connector, clear,
    flint, 10 1/8" h. 295
Mug, clear, flint 45
Pickle castor, blue non-flint insert, original
    silver plate frame & lid................................. 160
Pitcher, milk, applied handle, clear, flint.... 140-150
Pitcher, tankard, applied handle, clear,
    flint, qt... 158
Pitcher, water, clear, non-flint 75
Plate, 8" d., milk white, flint............................. 125
Sauce dish, clear, flint, 4 1/4" d. 13
Spillholder, clear, flint................................... 35-45
Spillholder, clear w/gold rim, flint.................... 165
Sugar bowl, cov., flat base, clear, flint........ 95-125
Sugar bowl, cov., footed, clear, flint.......... 175-200
Sugar shaker w/original top, bulbous,
    clear, non-flint....................................... 200-250
Syrup pitcher w/original top, clear, non-
    flint.. 75
Toothpick holder, clear, non-flint 35
Tumbler, whiskey, clear, flint........................... 125
Wine, clear, flint 95

DIAMOND QUILTED

Butter dish, cov., canary................................... 75
Celery vase, blue 50
Celery vase, deep amethyst 68
Champagne, clear 22
Claret, clear... 40
Compote, cov., 7" d., low stand, blue 65
Compote, cov., 8" d., 13" h., amber.................. 95
Compote, cov., 8" d., 13" h., clear 75
Compote, open, 8" d., low stand, canary 52
Compote, open, 9" d., low stand, blue 40
Compote, open, 9" d., low stand, canary 37
Cordial, amber 33
Creamer, amber 38
Creamer, amethyst... 40
Creamer, turquoise blue................................... 68
*Goblet, amber 48
*Goblet, amethyst 30-35
*Goblet, blue 37
*Goblet, canary 33
*Goblet, clear 28
Mug, amber 20
Mug, amethyst.. 30
Mug, clear... 15
Pickle castor, w/silver plate frame, cover &
    tongs 225
Pitcher, water, amber.. 54
Pitcher, water, blue 80
Pitcher, water, canary 75
*Salt dip, amber, master size, rectangular 32
Sauce dish, amber, flat or footed, each............. 12
Sauce dish, amethyst, flat or footed, each 18
Sauce dish, canary, flat or footed, each 10
Sauce dish, turquoise blue, flat or footed,
    each 11
Spooner, amethyst.. 38
Spooner, canary 37
Sugar bowl, cov., amber................................... 68
Sugar bowl, cov., amethyst 85
Sugar bowl, cov., blue 35-40
Sugar bowl, cov., canary 55

Tray, water, cloverleaf-shaped, amber,
10 x 12" **30-40**
Tray, water, cloverleaf-shaped, canary,
10 x 12" **30-35**
*Tumbler, amethyst... **40**
*Tumbler, canary **25-30**
*Tumbler, clear **25**
Waste bowl, blue, 4 1/2" d. **38**
*Wine, amethyst **42**
Wine, clear **17**

DIAMOND THUMBPRINT
Bitters bottle, pt... **350-400**
Bowl, 7" d., footed, scalloped rim..................... **150**
Bowl, 8" d., footed, scalloped rim..................... **150**
Bowl, 9" d., 4 1/2" h., applied pedestal **150**
Cake stand, 9" to 11" **350-400**
Cake stand, 12" d. **400**
Celery vase **175**
Champagne, knob stem............................. **200-250**
Champagne, plain stem............................ **325-375**
Compote, open, 7" d., low stand................... **70-75**
Compote, open, 8" d., high stand **125**
Compote, open, 8" d., low stand...................... **125**
Cordial, 4" h. **200-225**
Cup plate **50**
Decanter w/bar lip, pt...................................... **205**
Decanter w/original stopper, pt. **240**
Decanter w/original stopper, qt. **330**
*Goblet **475-525**
Honey dish **23**
Lamp, whale oil, original burner, brass
stem, marble base................................. **265-300**
Relish **65**
Salt dip, master size **45**
Sauce dish, flat **16**
Spillholder, clear **45**
*Sugar bowl, cov. **150**
*Tumbler **100-125**
Tumbler, whiskey **126**
Tumbler, bar, 3 3/4" h. **143**
Wine **220**

DINNER BELL - See Cottage Pattern

DORIC - See Feather Pattern

DOUBLE LEAF & DART - See Leaf & Dart Pattern

DOUBLE LOOP - See Ribbon Candy Pattern

DRAGON
Butter dish, cov. **450**
Compote cov., 8 1/4" d., 8" h. **825**
Compote cov., 8 1/4" d., 9 3/4" h. **825**
Goblet **1,775-1,800**
Spooner **300**
Sugar bowl, open **325**

DRAPERY
Butter dish, cov. **60**
Cake plate, square, footed........................... **40-45**
Celery vase **40**
Creamer, applied handle.............................. **35-40**
Egg cup **28**
Goblet **40**
Pitcher, water, applied handle **75**
Plate, 6" d.. **35**
Sauce dish, flat **17**

Sugar bowl, cov... **40-45**
Tumbler **35**
Water set, pitcher & 6 tumblers, 7 pcs. **275-325**

EARLY OREGON - See Skilton Pattern

EGG IN SAND
Bread tray, clear, handled **30-35**
Butter dish, cov. **48**
Creamer, clear **32**

Egg in Sand Goblet

Goblet, clear (ILLUS.) **28**
Pitcher, water, amber... **70**
Pitcher, water, blue **98**
Pitcher, water, clear **38**
Sauce dish **12**
Spooner, blue **60**
Spooner, clear **35**
Sugar bowl, cov., blue **85-95**
Tray, water, flat.. **45**
Tumbler, amber **35**
Tumbler, blue... **65**
Tumbler, clear.. **30**
Water set, pitcher & four goblets, amber, 5
pcs.. **250**
Water set, pitcher & four goblets, blue, 5
pcs.. **350**
Water set, pitcher, tray & five goblets,
clear, 7 pcs..................................... **225-240**

EGYPTIAN
Bowl, 8 1/2" d.. **65**
Bread platter, Cleopatra center, 9 x 12" **50**
*Bread platter, Salt Lake Temple center .. **220-225**
Compote, cov., 8" d., high stand, sphinx
base **280**
Creamer **55**
Goblet **45**
Honey dish **20**
Pitcher, water.. **275**
Plate, 12" d., handled **80**
Relish, 5 1/2 x 8 1/2" **25**
Sauce dish, flat **21**

Egyptian Spooner

Spooner (ILLUS.)... 35-45
Sugar bowl, cov.. 68
Sugar bowl, open 32
Table set, 4 pcs...................................... 250-275

EMERALD GREEN HERRINGBONE -
See Paneled Herringbone Pattern

ESTHER
Berry set: master bowl & 6 sauce dishes;
  green, 7 pcs. 245-255
Bowl, 8" d., clear 35
Bowl, 9" d., green, footed.................................. 25
Butter dish, cov., amber-stained 125-150
Butter dish, cov., clear 63
Butter dish, cov., green.......................... 125-150
Cake stand, 10 1/2" d., 6" h., amber-
  stained.. 95
Cake stand, 10 1/2" d., 6" h., clear 75
Cake stand, 10 1/2" d., 6" h., green 140
Cake stand, 10 1/2" d., 6" h., ruby-stained 110
Celery vase, amber-stained....................... 95-100
Celery vase, green w/gold 95
Cheese dish, cov., amber-stained, high
  dome 140
Cheese dish, cov., clear, high dome 90
Cheese dish, cov., green, high dome 175-200
Cheese dish, cov., ruby-stained, high
  dome 140
Compote, cov., 8" d., high stand.................... 100
Compote, open, 4" d., amber-stained.............. 78
Compote, open, jelly, 5" d., amber-stained
  w/enamel decoration........................... 125-135
Compote, open, jelly, 5" d., clear 60
Compote, open, jelly, 5" d., green 70-75
Compote, open, 8" d., high stand 40-50
Cracker jar, cov., amber-stained 225
Cracker jar, cov., clear............................. 100-120
Cracker jar, cov., green 250-275
Cracker jar, cov., ruby-stained........................ 250
Creamer, amber-stained 70
Creamer, clear 60
Creamer, ruby-stained 75
Creamer & cov. sugar bowl, amber-
  stained, pr. 175

Cruet w/original stopper, green,
  miniature 225-250
Cruet w/original stopper, green, small 85
Doughnut stand w/turned edge 60-75
Goblet, amber-stained w/enamel decora-
  tion 95-100
Goblet, clear... 80
Goblet, green 100
Marmalade jar, cov. 95
Pickle dish, clear 25
Pickle dish, ruby-stained 45
Pitcher, water, clear.................................. 75-100
Pitcher, water, green.............................. 275-300
Plate, 5 1/2" d., green, footed.......................... 75
Plate, large, amber-stained w/enamel dec-
  oration 150-175
Plate, small, amber-stained w/enamel dec-
  oration 50
Relish, clear, 4 1/2 x 8 1/2" 20
Sauce dish, clear.. 25

Esther Sauce Dish

Sauce dish, clear, engraved (ILLUS.)............... 25
Sauce dish, green... 35
Sauce dish, green w/gold 35-40
Spooner, clear 34
Spooner, green w/gold...................................... 85
Sugar bowl, cov., amber-stained................ 75-80
Sugar bowl, cov., clear 40
Sugar bowl, cov., green 135
Syrup jug w/original spring lid, amber-
  stained.. 360
Toothpick holder, amber-stained............. 145-155
Toothpick holder, green.......................... 100-125
Toothpick holder, green w/gold 140-160
Tray, ice cream, green 145
Tumbler, amber-stained............................. 50-55
Tumbler, clear.. 32
Wine, clear 33
Wine, ruby-stained, souvenir........................... 75

EXCELSIOR
Bar bottle, flint, pt. 75-90
Bar bottle, flint, qt. 100-115
Bowl, 4 1/2" h., footed, scalloped rim............... 45
Butter dish, cov. 100
Candlestick, flint, 8 1/4" h........................ 150-165
Candlesticks, flint, 9 1/2" h., pr...................... 275
Carafe, rayed base, 6 1/4" h., 1 1/2 pt....... 125-150
Castor set, 4-bottle, non-flint, in pewter
  frame 225-250
Celery vase, flint 75-80
Champagne 98
Claret, flint... 45
Cologne bottle w/faceted stopper 145
Cordial 110

Creamer, applied handle........................... 100-125
Decanter, flared lip, pt... 95
Egg cup 35-45
Egg cup, double, clear 75

Excelsior Flip Glass

Flip glass, 8" h. (ILLUS.).................................. 200
Goblet, "barrel," flint 75
Goblet, flint.. 70-80
Lamp, kerosene, flint font, brass collar,
    black iron stem & base............................. 195
Lamps, whale oil, 9 3/4" h. to collar,
    11 1/4" h. to burner, pr. 295-300
Mug 45
Pickle jar, cov. 60
Pitcher, milk, flint... 250
Pitcher, water, flint 325
Salt dip, master size 40
Shaving mug, dated Sept. 20, 1870, gold
    trim 170
Spooner 65
Sugar bowl, cov... 125-160
Sweetmeat compote, cov., flint, 9 3/4" h.. 125-150
Syrup pitcher, applied handle 125
Syrup pitcher w/original top, green............. 750+
Tray, wine.. 60
Tumbler, bar, flint, 3 1/2" h............................ 75-85
Tumbler, footed, flat.................................... 75-100
Tumbler, footed, flint 75-90
Wine, flint... 60-65

EYEWINKER

Berry set, master bowl & five sauce
    dishes, 6 pcs. 125-135
*Butter dish, cov... 80-85
Cake stand, 9 1/2" d. 200
Compote, open, 4" d., 5" h., scalloped rim.... 30-35
Compote, open, 6 1/2" sq., high stand............. 70
Compote, open, 9 1/2" d., high stand 125-150
Compote, open, 10" d., high stand 140-160
Cracker jar, cov. 125
Cruet w/original stopper 110
Doughnut stand 75-85
*Goblet 40
*Honey dish, cov. 90
Lamp, kerosene-type, w/original burner,
    9 1/2" h... 180

Plate, 10" sq., 2" h., turned-up sides 65

Eyewinker Salt Shaker

Salt & pepper shakers w/original tops,
    pr. (ILLUS. of one)... 43
Spooner 45-50

FEATHER (Doric, Indiana Swirl or Finecut & Feather)

Banana boat, footed, clear 120
Banana boat, footed, green 200
Bowl, 6 1/2" d... 20
Bowl, 7" oval 25
Cake stand, 8 1/2" d. 45-55
Cake stand, clear, 9 1/2" h............................ 55-65
Cake stand, clear, 11" d................................. 110
Compote, cov., 6 1/4" d., low stand 50-55
Compote, cov., 7" d., high stand.............. 100-110
Compote, cov., 8 1/2" d., high stand........ 100-125
Compote, open, jelly, 4 1/2" d., 4 3/4" h.,
    amber-stained 150
Cordial 100-120
Creamer, amber-stained 175
Cruet w/original stopper, clear..................... 55
Doughnut stand, 8" w., 4 1/2" h. 60-65
Honey dish, 3 1/2" d. 15
Marmalade jar, cov. 90-100
Pickle dish 25
Pitcher, water, clear 60-65
Pitcher, water, green 125-150
Plate, 10" d., clear.. 35-40
Plate, 10" d., green.. 45-55
Relish, 8 1/4" oval, green 40
Salt & pepper shakers w/original tops,
    clear, pr. 65-75
Salt & pepper shakers w/original tops,
    green, pr... 150-180
Salt shaker w/original top, clear...................... 35
Salt shaker w/original top, green 75-85
Sauce dish, amber-stained, flat or footed,
    each 25
Sauce dish, clear, flat or footed, each 10
Spooner, amber... 195
Spooner, amber-stained 60
Spooner, clear 25-30

Feather Sugar Bowl

Sugar bowl, cov., clear (ILLUS.).................. **50-55**
Sugar bowl, cov., green........................... **110-130**
Sugar bowl, cov., child's..................................... **25**
Syrup pitcher w/original top, clear **100-125**
Syrup pitcher w/original top, green **200-250**
Table set, cov. butter dish, cov. sugar
    bowl, creamer & spooner, 4 pcs.................. **155**
Toothpick holder, clear............................... **75-85**
Tumbler, green **95**
Vase, 10" h., green... **25**
Wine, amber-stained **95**

FESTOON
Bowl, berry, 5 1/2 x 9" rectangle **20-25**
Cake stand, high pedestal, 9" d. **45-50**
Cake stand, high pedestal, 10" d. **60**
Compote, open, jelly **35-40**
Compote, open, 9" d., high stand **55-65**

Festoon Creamer

Creamer (ILLUS.)... **25**
Egg cup **25-30**
Finger bowl, 4 1/2" d., 2" h. **20-25**
Marmalade jar, cov. **40-45**
Mug, handled.. **30-35**
Pitcher, water... **64**

Plate, 9" d. **46**
Spooner **35**
Sugar bowl, cov. **50-55**
Table set, 4 pcs.. **150-175**
Tray, water, 10" d. **50**
Tumbler **26**
Waste bowl **46**
Water set, pitcher, tray & 4 tumblers,
    6 pcs.. **215-225**

FINECUT BAND - See Cottage Pattern

FINECUT & FEATHER -
See Feather Pattern

FISHSCALE
Bone dish, 4 x 5 1/2" **25**
Bowl, 12" d. **25**
Bowl, cov., 7" d. **55**
Bowl, cov., 12" d. **40-45**
Cake stand, 8" d. **33**
Celery vase **35**
Compote, open, jelly **20-25**
Compote, open, 7" d., high stand **31**
Condiment tray **35**
Goblet **30-35**
Lamp base, kerosene-type, pedestal base,
    original burner **75-85**
Mug **40-45**
Pitcher, milk **30-35**
Plate, 7" d. **21**
Plate, 8" d. **31**

Fishscale Plate

Plate, 9" sq. (ILLUS.)..................................... **30-35**
Relish, 5 x 8 1/2" **20**
Salt & pepper shakers w/original tops,
    pr. **45**
Shoe w/attached sq. underplate, amber........ **150**
Shoe w/attached sq. underplate, blue **150**
Shoe w/attached sq. underplate, clear **125**
Shoe w/attached sq. underplate, vaseline..... **160**
Spooner **26**
Tray, water, round **75**

FLORIDA - See Paneled Herringbone Pattern

FLOWER FLANGE - See Dewey Pattern

FLUTE
Ale glass 50
Bar bottle, clear, flint, pt. 75
Bar bottle, blue, flint, qt. 250
Bowl, 7 1/4" d., footed 30
Butter dish, cov. 60
Candlesticks, miniature, 4" h., pr. 45
Celery vase 80
Cordial 30
Creamer & sugar bowl, miniature, pr. 60
Egg cup, single 27
Egg cup, single, handled 50
Goblet 38
Lamp, whale oil 75
Mug, applied handle 75
Pitcher, milk 85
Salt dip, hexagonal, blue 40-45
Salt dip, master size, footed 35-40
Sauce dish, 4 1/2" d. 10
Sugar bowl, open 15
Tumbler, whiskey, clear, handled 43
Tumbler, whiskey, vaseline , handled........... 90-95
Wine 33

FLYING ROBIN - See Hummingbird Pattern

FROSTED CIRCLE
Butter dish, cov. 55-60
Celery tray 20
Compote, cov., 7" d. 110
Compote, open, 5 3/4" d., 5 1/8" h. 24
Compote, open, 9" d., 8 1/2" h. 60-65
Cruet w/original stopper 65

Frosted Circle Goblet

*Goblet (ILLUS.) 45
Pitcher, water, tankard 150
Salt & pepper shakers w/original tops,
   pr. 80
Sugar bowl, cov. 75
Sugar shaker w/original top 48

Syrup pitcher w/original top 115-125
Tumbler 41
Wine 40

FROSTED LION (Rampant Lion)
Bread tray, oval, lion handles, frosted or
   non-frosted, 10" l. 110
Bread tray, amber, rope edge, closed handles, 10 1/2" d. 85
Bread tray, canary, rope edge, closed handles, 10 1/2" d. 150-200
Butter dish, cov., collared base, rampant
   lion finial 165-170
Cheese dish, cov., rampant lion finial 625
Cologne bottle w/stopper 1,000-1,200
Compote, cov., 5" d., 8 1/2" h. 175
Compote, cov., 5 1/2 x 8 3/4" oval,
   8 1/4" h., rampant lion finial 170-180
*Compote, cov., 6 3/4" oval, 7" h., collared
   base, rampant lion finial 150-175
Compote, cov., 8" d., high stand, overall
   floral etching.. 545
Compote, open, 7" oval, 7 1/2" h. 140
Compote, open, 8" d. 175
Creamer 85-95
Creamer child's, clear & frosted 90-110
Cup & saucer, child's, clear frosted or blue
   opaque 80-225
*Egg cup 83

Frosted Lion Goblet

*Goblet (ILLUS.)... 135
Inkwell 750-900
Marmalade jar, cov., lion's head finial............. 155
Paperweight, embossed "Gillinder & Sons,
   Centennial".. 238
*Pitcher, water 550-750
Relish 50
*Sauce dish, 4" & 6" d. 20-25
*Spooner 100
Spooner, child's, clear & frosted 110-125
Sugar bowl, cov., crouched lion finial 100-125
Syrup pitcher w/original dated top 463
Wine, 4 1/8" h. 750-1,000

FROSTED WAFFLE -
See Hidalgo Pattern

GALLOWAY (Mirror)

Basket, twisted handle, 5 x 8 1/2 x 10" 70
Bowl, 9 1/2" d., flat 25-30
Butter dish, cov., clear 65-70
Butter dish, cov., rose-stained 140-150
Celery vase, clear 30
Celery vase, rose-stained 75
Compote, open, 10" d., 8" h., scalloped rim....... 75
Cracker jar, cov. 175
Creamer, clear 20-25
Creamer, rose-stained 75
Cruet w/stopper 55-60
Mint dish, footed 30-35
Nappy, handled, gold rim, 5" d. 30
Nappy, handled, tricornered, 5 3/4" w. 30-35
Pickle castor w/silver plate lid, no frame.... 75-85
Relish, 8 1/4" l. 17
Salt & pepper shakers w/original tops,
    gold trim, 3" h., pr. 48
Spooner, clear 23
Spooner, rose-stained 80
Sugar bowl, cov., clear 85
Syrup pitcher w/metal spring top, clear 73
Tray, flat, 8" d. 195
Tumbler, clear 30
Waste bowl 38
Wine, clear 40-45

GARFIELD DRAPE

Garfield Drape Bread Plate

Bread plate, "We Mourn Our Nation's
    Loss," 11 1/2" d. (ILLUS.) 54
Butter dish, cov. 75-80
Creamer 50-55
Goblet 66
Goblet, lady's 50-100
Pitcher, milk 120-140
Pitcher, water 160
Spooner 30-40
Sugar bowl, cov. 80
Tumbler, flat 35-40
Tumbler, footed 55-65

GEORGIA - See Peacock Feather Pattern

GONTERMAN

Bowl, cov., 7" d., high stand, frosted clear
    w/amber stain 90
Bowl, cov., 8" d., high stand, frosted clear
    w/amber stain 95

Bowl, 7" d., low stand, frosted clear
    w/amber stain 80
Bowl, 8" d., low stand, frosted clear
    w/amber stain 85
Butter dish, cov., frosted clear w/amber
    stain 135-150
Cake stand, high stand, frosted clear
    w/amber stain, 10" d 125-135
Celery vase, pedestaled, smooth rim,
    frosted clear w/amber stain 100-110
Compote, cov., 5" d., high stand, frosted
    clear w/amber stain 110-120
Compote, cov., 7" d., high stand, frosted
    clear w/amber stain 115-125
Compote, cov., 8" d., high stand, frosted
    clear w/amber stain 125-140
Compote, open, 5" d., high stand, frosted
    clear w/amber stain 65-75

Gonterman Compote

Compote, open, 7" d., high stand, frosted
    clear w/amber stain (ILLUS.) 75-85
Compote, open, 8" d., high stand, frosted
    clear w/amber stain 80-90
Creamer, frosted clear w/amber stain 185
Goblet, frosted clear w/amber stain 550
Honey, flat, frosted clear w/amber stain,
    3 1/2" d. 30
Honey, footed, frosted clear w/amber stain,
    3 1/2" d. 30
Pitcher, milk, frosted clear w/amber stain, 1
    qt. 165-175
Pitcher, water, frosted clear w/amber
    stain, 1/2 gal. 180-195
Salt shaker w/original top, frosted clear
    w/amber stain 75-80
Sauce dish, footed, frosted clear w/amber
    stain, 4" d. 30-35
Sauce dish, frosted clear w/amber stain,
    4" d. 30-35
Sauce dish, footed, frosted clear w/amber
    stain, 4 1/2" d. 30-35
Sauce dish, frosted clear w/amber stain,
    4 1/2" d. 30-35
Spooner, frosted clear w/amber stain 175-200
Sugar bowl, cov., frosted clear w/amber
    stain 120-130

GOOD LUCK - See Horse Shoe Pattern

GOOSEBERRY

Butter dish, cov. 50

Gooseberry Compote

Compote, cov., 7" d. (ILLUS.) 95-100
Creamer 50
*Goblet 35
*Mug 35-45
Mug, child's, blue opaque............................. 40-50
Sugar bowl, cov., milk white 50
Sugar bowl, open, clear.................................... 40
Syrup pitcher w/dated top, applied han-
dle, milk white... 105
Tumbler, bar 38
Tumbler, water.. 32

GRAND (Diamond Medallion)

Bowl, 6 1/4 x 9" oval....................................... 25
Bread plate, 10" d. 19
Butter dish, cov. 35-45
Cake stand, 8" d. 30-35
Cake stand, 8 1/2" d. 35
Cake stand, 10" d. 35-40
Compote, cov., 6" d., 9" h. 65
Compote, cov., 8" d., low stand 80
Cordial 50

Grand Creamer

Creamer, footed (ILLUS.).................................. 25
Goblet 25-35
Pitcher, water.. 39
Pitcher, water, pink-stained diamonds.............. 65
Spooner 23
Sugar bowl, cov... 32
Wine 25-30

GRAPE & FESTOON

Butter dish, cov., stippled leaf 65
Celery vase, stippled leaf................................. 50
Compote, cov., 8" d., high stand, acorn fin-
ial, stippled leaf 110
Compote, cov., 8" d., low stand, acorn fin-
ial, stippled leaf 85
Compote, open, 8" d., low stand.................. 40-50
Creamer & sugar bowl, stippled leaf, pr. 75-85
Goblet, stippled leaf 45-50
Goblet, veined leaf 45-50
Lamp, kerosene-type, stippled leaf,
7 1/2" h. 95-100
Mug 35-40
Pitcher, milk, 7" h. 75-90
Pitcher, water, stippled leaf...................... 95-100
Pitcher, water, veined leaf 90-95
Plate, 6" d., stippled leaf................................. 25
Relish, stippled leaf 20
Salt dip, stippled leaf, footed...................... 35-40
Sauce dish, stippled leaf, flat, 4" d.................. 10
Sauce dish, veined leaf, flat............................. 10

Grape & Festoon Spooner

Spooner, stippled leaf (ILLUS.)..................... 40-50
Spooner, veined leaf.................................... 40-50
Sugar bowl, cov., stippled leaf.................... 55-60
Sugar bowl, open, stippled leaf 25-30
Syrup pitcher w/original dated top, stip-
pled leaf... 90-100
Wine, stippled leaf 50

GRASSHOPPER (Locust, Long Spear)

Butter dish, clear, no insect........................ 50-55
Butter dish, cov., canary................................. 95
Celery vase, w/insect................................... 65-70
Compote, cov., 7" d., 7 3/4" h. 50-55
Compote, cov., w/insect, 8 1/4" d. 70
Creamer, no insect 35
Creamer, w/insect 50
Marmalade jar, cov., w/insect 115
Pitcher, water, w/insect........................... 100-125
Sauce dish, footed, w/insect....................... 20-25
Spooner, amber 80
Spooner, clear, no insect 55-60
Spooner, clear, w/insect.............................. 60-70
Sugar bowl, cov., no insect 70
Sugar bowl, cov., w/insect 90
Sugar bowl, open 20
Sugar bowl, open, w/insect 30

GREEK KEY (Heisey's Greek Key)

Bowl, 8 1/2" d. 65
Butter dish, cov. 125
Celery tray, 9" l. 38
Champagne 90-100
Compote, open, jelly, 5" d., low stand.............. 28
Compote, open, 6" d., 7" h............................... 19
Creamer 35

Creamer & open sugar bowl, pr........................ 56
Creamer & sugar bowl, individual size, pr. 125
Goblet 70
Humidor, cov. 285
Ice tub, hotel size... 135
Ice tub, small.. 95
Lamp, kerosene-type, large 85-95
Lamp, kerosene-type, miniature...................... 100
Nappy, handled... 30
Nut dish, individual size 22
Pickle dish, 8" l.. 25
Pitcher, pt.. 125
Pitcher, tankard, clear, 1 1/2 qt....................... 225
Plate, 5 1/2" d.. 25
Plate, 6 3/4" d.. 30
Plate, 9" d.. 30
Punch bowl & pedestal base, 2 pcs.............. 250
Punch cup 15
Punch set, bowl, base & 12 cups, 14 pcs........ 430
Relish, 9" l.. 30
Salt dip, master size 20
Sauce dish 10
Sherbet 23
Soda fountain (straw-holder) jar 128
Spooner 75
Sugar bowl, open 25-30
Toothpick holder 400
Tumbler 75
Vase, 6 1/2" h., footed 65-70
Wine 75-125

HALLEY'S COMET
Celery vase 42
Goblet 40-45
Jar, cov., three-footed 49
Pitcher, water, tankard, engraved................... 135
Pitcher, water, tankard, plain 60-65
Relish, 4 1/2 x 7".. 15
Spooner 30-40
Tumbler 50-75

Halley's Comet Wine

Wine (ILLUS.).. 65

HAND (Pennsylvania, Early)
Celery vase 35-40
Cordial 85
Creamer 30-40
Cruet w/original stopper, applied handle 60-65

Hand Goblet

Goblet (ILLUS.).. 50-55
Marmalade jar, cov. 50-55
Mug 45-50
Pitcher, water.. 85-95
Salt dip, master size 35-40
Salt shaker w/original top, 4" h. (single) 25-30
Sugar bowl, cov. 55-60
Syrup pitcher w/original top, 4" h. 140-150
*Tumbler, juice.. 35
*Tumbler, water 50
*Tumbler, whiskey 25
Wine, clear 45-55

HARP
Goblet, flared sides 2,000-2,225
Lamp, kerosene, hand-type w/applied fin-
    ger grip 236
Lamp, kerosene, hexagonal font, shaped
    base, brass collar, flint, 9 1/2" h. 350-400
Salt dip, master size 55
Spillholder 90-95

Harp Spooner

Spooner (ILLUS.)...................................... 100-125

HEART WITH THUMBPRINT
Banana boat, 6 1/2 x 11"........................ 120-125
Bowl, 8" d., 2" h., flared rim............................. 41

Bowl, 9" d. 45
Carafe 100-125
Celery vase 74
Cologne bottle w/original faceted stop-
   per 45-55
Compote, open, 8 1/2" d., high stand 155
Cordial, 3" h. 215-275
Creamer & open sugar bowl, individual
   size, clear, pr. 30-40
Cruet w/original stopper 75-90
Cruet w/original stoppers, green w/gold,
   pr. 275-400
Goblet, clear............. 55-65

Heart with Thumbprint Goblet

Goblet, green (ILLUS.) 475
Ice bucket 145
Lamp, kerosene-type, finger, clear,
   4 1/2" h. 175-185
Lamp, kerosene-type, finger, green,
   4 1/2" h. 300
Lamp, kerosene-type, clear, 8" h. 185-200
Lamp, kerosene-type, green, 9" h. 250
Mustard jar w/silver plate cover, clear 95
Nappy, heart-shaped, clear............................... 37
Nappy, heart-shaped, green 40-45
Olive dish, clear... 25
Olive dish, handled, green............................... 35
Plate, 6" d., green.. 65
Powder jar w/silver plate cover 65
Punch cup, clear.. 25
Salt & pepper shakers w/original tops,
   pr. 80-95
Salt shaker w/original top 40-48
Sauce dish, clear.. 15-20
Sauce dish, green.. 32
Sugar bowl, open, individual size, green
   w/gold.. 60
Syrup jug w/original pewter top 90-100
Tray, 4 1/4 x 8 1/4" 35
Tumbler, green 115-120
Tumbler, water, clear w/gold............................ 65
Tumbler, water, ruby-stained 90
Vase, 6" h., clear, trumpet-shaped 60
Waste bowl 120
Wine, clear 46

HEARTS OF LOCH LAVEN -
See Shuttle Pattern

HIDALGO (Frosted Waffle)
Bowl, 5 1/2" sq., 2 1/2" h. 20
Bowl, 7 1/2" sq., footed 25
Bowl, 9" sq., clear & frosted 35
Bowl, 9 1/2" sq. 35
Bowl, salad, 11" sq.. 35
Bread plate 60-65
Celery vase, amber-stained............................. 60
Celery vase, clear 25-30
Creamer, ruby-stained 63
Cruet w/original stopper, amber-stained........ 195
Cruet w/original stopper, clear....................... 70
Goblet, amber-stained 40
Goblet, clear.. 30
Goblet, engraved 35
Goblet, frosted 30-35

Hidalgo Goblet

Goblet, ruby-stained (ILLUS.) 45-50
Pitcher, water.. 50
Salt dip, master, square 45
Syrup pitcher w/original top 75-85
Waste bowl 45

HOBNAIL
Cake stand, pedestal base, square 85
Celery vase, canary, footed 70-95
Celery vase, clear, footed, square 20-25
*Cruet w/original stopper, amber.................. 100
*Cruet w/original stopper, clear, 4 1/2" h. 40
Dish in silverplate holder, canary 95
Egg cup, single 29
Goblet, amber 28
Goblet, blue.. 26
*Goblet, clear 15-20
Mug, clear 10
Salt shaker w/original top, blue.................. 30-35
Spooner, amber, ruffled rim 30

Spooner, canary, ruffled rim 38
Sugar shaker w/original top, amber 55
Syrup pitcher w/original top, clear 72
Toothpick holder, canary 35-45
*Toothpick holder, clear 56
Tray, water, blue, 11 1/2" d. 48
*Tumbler, clear 20
*Tumbler, ten-row, amber 60
*Tumbler, ten-row, blue 25-30
Tumbler, ten-row, clear 25
Tumbler, ten-row, Rubina Frosted 95
Tumbler, ten-row, ruby-stained 110
Wine, blue 25

Hobnail Wine

*Wine, clear (ILLUS.)... 15

HOBNAIL WITH THUMBPRINT BASE
Butter dish, cov. 55
Butter dish, cov., child's, amber 95

Hobnail with Thumbprint Base Creamer

Creamer, amber (ILLUS.).................................. 31
Creamer, blue 45-50
Creamer, clear 40
Finger bowl, blue, scalloped rim....................... 45
Pitcher, 8" h., amber 59

Spooner, amber 25
Sugar bowl, cov... 35
Waste bowl, amber.. 29
Waste bowl, blue 30-35

HONEYCOMB
Ale glass 39
Cake stand, 10 1/2" d. 75
Carafe 90-100
Celery vase, clear, non-flint 24
Celery vase, flint 70
Celery vase New York Honeycomb, flint....... 60-70
Champagne, flint....................................... 35-45
Compote, open, 7" d., 7" h., flint 45-50
Compote, open, 8" d., 6 1/4" h., flint 95-100
Compote, open, 11" d., 8" h., flint 100-125
Finger bowl, flint 45
Goblet, Banded Vernon Honeycomb 55
Goblet, buttermilk.. 48
Goblet, flint.. 25

Honeycomb Goblet

*Goblet, non-flint (ILLUS.).................................. 18
Pitcher, 7 1/4" h., bulbous, applied handle 95
Pitcher, milk, flint..................................... 150-200
Pitcher, water, New York Honeycomb 120
Pitcher, water, 9" h., applied handle, flint.. 115-125
Pomade jar, cov., flint 48
Relish 30
Salt dip, pedestal base, flint............................. 35
Sugar bowl, cov., flint 75
Sugar bowl, open, scalloped rim 35
Syrup pitcher w/pewter top, flint 128
Tumbler, footed, flint 35-40
Tumbler, whiskey, footed, handled, flint............. 45
Tumbler, whiskey, Vernon Honeycomb 125
Wine, flint.. 32
*Wine, non-flint... 11
Wine, Barrel Honeycomb............................. 20-25
Wine, New York Honeycomb, flint.................... 28

HORN OF PLENTY (McKee's Comet)
Bar bottle w/original stopper, qt. 135-145
Bar bottle w/pewter pour spout, 12"............. 200
Bowl, 7 1/2" d. 75

Bowl, 6 1/4 x 9" oval.. 145
Butter dish, cov. 115-120
Butter dish & cover w/Washington's
head finial 675-700
Cake stand, 8 1/4" d., 4 1/4" h. 1,850
Celery vase 160-165
Champagne 150-165
Compote, cov., 8 1/4" oval, 5 3/4" h. 350
Compote, cov., 8 1/4" h. 185
Compote, open, 6" d.. 100
Compote, open, 6 3/4" d., 3 1/2" h............... 75-85
Compote, open, 7" d., clear 75
Compote, open, 7" d., 3" h. 123
Compote, open, 7" d., 7 1/2" h., waffle
base 105
Compote, open, 8" d., low stand.................... 125
Compote, open, 8" d., 6" h....................... 135-140
Compote, open, 8" d., 8" h. 180
Compote, open, 9" d., low stand.................... 105
Compote, open, 9" d., 8 1/2" h...................... 200
Cordial 140
Creamer, applied handle, 5 1/2" h........... 250-275
Creamer, applied handle, 7" h.................. 175-200
Creamer & cov. sugar bowl, pr. 325
Decanter w/original stopper, pt. 200-225
Decanter w/original stopper, qt. 180-190
Dish, low foot, 8" d. 95
Egg cup, 3 3/4" h. 45-50
*Goblet 90-110
Honey dish 15-20
Peppersauce bottle w/stopper 175-200
Pitcher, water, 9" h.................................. 600-650
Plate 20-30
Plate, 6" d., clear 85-100
Relish, 5 x 7" oval 65-85
Salt dip, master size, oval............................... 75
Sauce dish, 3 1/2" to 5" d. 15
Spillholder, clambroth 550-650
Spooner, 4 1/2" h., clear 60-70
Spooner, w/yellow-stained rim................. 175-200

Horn of Plenty Sugar Bowl

Sugar bowl, cov. (ILLUS.) 140-150
Sugar bowl, open 50
Tumbler, bar 100-125
*Tumbler, water, 3 5/8" h. 95-110
Tumbler, whiskey, 3" h............................. 100-115

Tumbler, whiskey, handled 150-175
Wine 140-150

HORSESHOE (Good Luck or Prayer Rug)

Bowl, cov., 5 x 8" oval, flat, triple horse-
shoe finial 310
Bowl, open, 6 x 9" oval.............................. 35-40
Bowl, open, 6 1/2 x 10" oval....................... 35-45
*Bread tray, single horseshoe handles........ 45-55
Bread tray, double horseshoe handles.............. 95
Butter dish, cov. 150-200
Cake stand, 8" d., 6 1/2" h. 85

Horseshoe Cake Stand

Cake stand, 9" d., 6 1/2" h. (ILLUS.)............. 80-90
Cake stand, 10" d. 85-95
Cake stand, 10 3/4" d. 100
Celery vase clear 65-85
Compote, cov., 6" d., 10 1/2" h. 250
Compote, cov., 12" d. 110-120
Compote, cov., 7" d., high stand.................. 75-85
Compote, cov., 8" d., high stand............... 85-100
Compote, cov., 7" d., low stand 55-65
Compote, cov., 8" d., low stand 65-85
Creamer 40-45
Doughnut stand, 7" d. 75-80
Finger bowl open, 6" d. 75-85
Goblet, knob stem 60-65
Goblet, plain stem 35-45
Marmalade jar, cov. 175-200
Pitcher, milk 100-125
Pitcher, water.. 90-125
Plate, 7" d... 45-50
Relish, 5 x 7" 15-20
Salt dip, individual size 30-35
Salt dip, master size, horseshoe shape........ 75-85
Sauce dish, flat or footed, each.................. 10-15
Spooner 35-40
Sugar bowl, cov... 80-90
Table set, 4 pcs.. 345
Waste bowl, 4" d., 2 1/2" h........................... 60-70
Wine 200-225

HUBER
Ale glass 55

Huber Celery Vase

Celery vase (ILLUS.) 50-60
Champagne, barrel-shaped 100-125
Champagne, straight sides 45-50
Claret 48-55
Compote, open, 11" d., 10 1/4" h................. 85-90
Cordial 40-45
Creamer 80
Egg cup, handled 30-35
Egg cup, single 19
Egg cup, double 30
Flip glass, 5" h... 75-80
Goblet, barrel-shaped, clear 40
Goblet, straight-sided, clear 25
Spooner 32
Sugar bowl, open 20-25
Tumbler, bar 45-50
Tumbler, water.. 50-55
Tumbler, whiskey, handled 50-55
Vase 25
Wine, clear 25
Wine, engraved 40

HUMMINGBIRD (Flying Robin or Bird & Fern)
Bowl, 6" d., amber... 35
Butter dish, cov., amber 95
Butter dish, cov., blue 165
Celery vase, amber....................................... 80-85
Celery vase, clear... 33
Creamer, clear 40-45
Goblet, amber 60-65
Goblet, blue.. 70-80
Goblet, clear... 60-65
Pitcher, milk, amber 65
Pitcher, milk, blue 120
Pitcher, milk, clear 80-90
Pitcher, water, amber...................................... 130
Pitcher, water, blue 145
Sauce dish 12
Spooner, blue 50
Sugar bowl, cov., clear 55
Tray, water, blue... 125
Tumbler, amber 50-60
Tumbler, blue.. 70-80
Tumbler, clear... 45-50
Waste bowl 120
Wine 75-85

ILLINOIS
Basket, applied reeded handle,
    7 x 11 1/2" 140-145
Bowl, 8" sq. 35

Illinois Butter Dish

*Butter dish, cov., 7" sq. (ILLUS.) 70-75
Candlestick 70
Celery tray 40-45
Compote, open 145
Creamer, small 29
Creamer, large 45
Cruet w/original stopper 108
Lamp shade, banquet-style 450
Pitcher, water, squatty, silver plate rim,
    clear 100-125
Pitcher, water, squatty, silver plate rim,
    green 150
Plate, 7" sq.. 45-55
Relish, 3 x 8 1/2" 20
Salt dip, individual size 15-20
Soda fountain (straw-holder) jar, clear,
    no lid, 12 1/2" h. 155
Soda fountain (straw-holder) jar, cov.,
    clear, 12 1/2" h. 300-325
Syrup pitcher w/original pewter top 95
Toothpick holder 40-45
Tumbler 55-65
Vase, 9 1/2" h., green 125

INDIANA SWIRL - See Feather Pattern

INVERTED FERN
Cake stand 475
Champagne 155
Compote, open, 8" d. 55-60
Creamer, applied handle.......................... 125-150
Egg cup 35-45

Inverted Fern Goblet

*Goblet (ILLUS.).. 35

Salt dip, master size, footed 33
Sauce dish, 4" d... 14
Spooner 50-55
Sugar bowl, cov.. 95-125
Sugar bowl, open 25-30
Tumbler 95

IVY IN SNOW
Bowl, 8" d., ruby-stained ivy sprigs 65
Bowl, 6 x 9" oval... 20
*Butter dish, cov... 50
*Cake stand, amber-stained ivy sprigs, 10"
   sq. 125
*Celery vase, 8" h. 30
Cheese dish, cov. 37

Ivy in Snow Compote

*Compote, cov., 8" d., 13" h. (ILLUS.) 60
Coridal, ruby-stained ivy sprigs......................... 80
Goblet, ruby-stained..................................... 60-65
Goblet, ruby-stained top, "Souvenir of Bal-
   timore, Maryland" 75-80
Honey dish, cov., amber-stained ivy
   sprigs.. 125-150
Pickle dish 20-25
*Spooner, clear... 25
Spooner, ruby-stained ivy sprigs 45-50
Sugar bowl, cov., clear 30-35
Tumbler, clear 20
Wine, ruby-stained, souvenir............................ 70

JACOB'S LADDER (Maltese)
Celery vase (ILLUS. top of next column) 85
Compote, cov., 9 1/2" d., high stand............... 165
Compote, open, dolphin stem, smooth rim,
   high stand.. 425
Compote, open, 9 1/2" d., high stand 45-68
Compote, open, 10" d., 5" h. 30-35
Compote, open, 13 1/2" d., high stand 75
*Creamer 32
Goblet 65
Marmalade jar, cov. 125-135
Pickle castor, complete w/stand.............. 175-200
Pitcher, milk 150-175
Pitcher, water, applied handle 185-200
Plate, 6" d., amber.. 125
Plate, 9" d. 60

Jacob's Ladder Celery Vase

Salt dip, master size, footed 30-35
Spooner 25-30
Tumbler, ... 85-90
Tumbler, bar 75
Wine 40-45

JEWEL & CRESCENT - See Tennessee Pattern

JEWEL & DEWDROP - See Kansas Pattern

JEWEL & FESTOON (Loop & Jewel)
Champagne 42
Dresser bottle w/matching stopper,
   7 1/2" h.. 50
Goblet 17
Pickle dish 18
Punch cup 18
Sauce dish 12
Spooner 29
Sugar bowl, cov. 33
Toothpick holder 30
Vase, 8 3/4" h. 40
Wine 30

JOB'S TEARS - See Art Pattern

JUMBO AND JUMBO & BARNUM

Jumbo Butter Dish

Butter dish & cover w/frosted elephant
   finial, oblong (ILLUS.)........................... 675-700

Butter dish & cover w/frosted elephant finial, round.. **375-400**
Castor set, w/four original bottles & metal tops, amber.. **450-500**
Castor set, w/four original bottles & metal tops, clear.. **275**
Celery vase, etched.................................... **175-200**
Creamer **235-250**
Creamer w/Barnum head at handle.......... **250-275**
Goblet **1,000-1,200**
Pitcher, water, w/elephant in base.................. **695**
Spoon rack, blue **700-775**
Spoon rack, clear w/frosted elephant........ **425-500**
Spoon rack, clear **300-400**
Sugar bowl, w/Barnum head handles & cover w/frosted elephant finial............... **450-475**

KANSAS (Jewel & Dewdrop)
Bowl, 5 x 7" oval... **30**
Bread tray, "Our Daily Bread," 10 1/2" oval **47**
Butter dish, cov. **70**
Cake stand, 8" to 10" d. **55-60**
Celery vase **75**
Compote, open, 7" d., high stand **88**
Compote, open, 8" d., high stand **60-65**
Creamer **50**
Goblet **49**

Small Kansas Mug

Mug, small, 3 1/2" h. (ILLUS.) **35-45**
Mug, large **55-60**
Relish, 8 1/2" oval **26**
Salt shaker w/original top **60**
Sauce dish, 4" d.. **16**
Spooner **75**
Sugar bowl, cov. **100**
Sugar bowl, open **55**
Syrup jug w/original top **175-190**
Toothpick holder **40**
Tumbler, water, footed...................................... **57**
Wine, clear **40-50**

KENTUCKY
Cake stand, 9 1/2" d. **38**
Cruet w/original stopper **35-40**
Nappy, handled, clear **10**
Nappy, handled, green....................................... **20**
Pitcher, water... **55**
Sauce dish, clear, footed **9**
Spooner **35**
Sugar bowl, cov... **30**
Toothpick holder, green **98**

Toothpick holder, green w/gold **125**
Tumbler, green **50**
Wine, clear **30**
Wine, green **45**

KING'S CROWN (Also see Ruby Thumbprint)
Banana stand **195**
Butter dish, cov. **65**
Cake stand, 10" d. **85**
Castor set, salt & pepper shakers, oil bottle w/stopper & cov. mustard jar in original frame, 4 pcs. **325**
Celery vase, plain **62**
Champagne, clear **30**
*Compote, cov., 5" d., 5 1/2" h., engraved........ **33**
Compote, cov., 6" d., 6" h. **85**
Compote, cov., 8" d., 12" h. **61**
Compote, cov., 11" d. **145**
Compote, open, jelly **38**
Compote, open, 7 1/2" d., high stand **41**
Creamer, clear **48**
Creamer, w/green thumbprints.......................... **75**
*Creamer, individual size, clear........................ **19**
*Cup & saucer **55**
Goblet, clear.. **25**
Goblet, clear w/amber thumbprints **21**
Honey dish **50**
Ice cream tray **40**
Lamp, kerosene-type, pedestal base, 8" h....... **120**
*Lamp, kerosene-type, stem base, 10" h. **195**
Lamp, kerosene-type, low hand-type w/finger hold **195**

King's Crown Mustard Jar

Mustard jar, cov. (ILLUS.)............................ **40-50**
Nappy, handled, 5" d.................................... **20-25**
Nappy, 7 1/2" d... **32**
Pitcher, tankard, 8 1/2" h. **100**
Pitcher, tankard, 11" h. **110**
Pitcher, tankard, 13" h., engraved **225**
Relish, 7 1/2 x 10 1/2" oval **24**
Salt & pepper shakers w/original tops, pr. **65-70**
Sauce dish, boat-shaped.................................. **21**
Spooner **39**
Toothpick holder, clear.................................... **20**
Toothpick holder, rose stain, souvenir......... **30-35**
Tumbler, amber **38**
Tumbler, blue **35**
*Tumbler, clear **22**

Wine, clear 21
Wine, w/amber thumbprints............................... 22
Wine, w/amethyst thumbprints 18
Wine, w/green thumbprints................................ 15

KLONDIKE (Amberette or English Hobnail Cross)

Bowl, 6" sq., frosted w/amber cross................ 188
Bowl, 7" sq., frosted w/amber cross................ 185
Bowl, master berry or fruit, 8" sq., frosted
  w/amber cross... 250
Bowl, 11" sq., frosted w/amber cross.............. 265
Butter dish, cov., frosted w/amber cross.. 450-475
Cake stand, 8" sq., clear................................. 175
Cake stand, 8" sq., clear w/amber cross 200
Cake stand, 8" sq., frosted w/amber cross 350
Celery tray, clear 60
Celery tray, clear w/amber cross 200
Celery tray, clear w/amber cross,
  5 1/2 x 12".. 245
Celery vase, clear w/amber cross............. 115-125
Champagne, clear 85-90
Champagne, clear w/amber cross 250-300
Champagne, frosted w/amber cross 500-600
Condiment set: tray, cruet, salt & pepper
  shakers, clear, 4 pcs. 200
Condiment set: tray, cruet, salt & pepper
  shakers, clear w/amber cross, 4 pcs..... 475-550
Condiment set: tray, cruet, salt & pepper
  shakers, frosted w/amber cross,
  4 pcs... 900-1,000
Condiment set: tray, cruet, salt & pepper
  shakers & toothpick holder; frosted
  w/amber cross, 5 pcs. 950-1,050
Condiment tray, scalloped rim, frosted
  w/amber cross, 5 1/4" sq.............................. 450
Creamer, clear w/amber cross 85-90
Cruet w/original stopper, clear w/amber
  cross.. 425
Cup, frosted w/amber cross 100
Dish, oval, flat, shallow, clear......................... 120

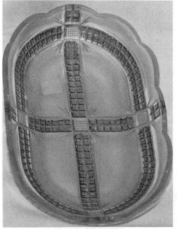

Klondyke Dish

Dish, oval, flat, shallow, frosted w/amber
  cross, 6 1/4 x 9 1/4" (ILLUS.) 248
Goblet, clear.. 70-75
Goblet, clear w/amber cross 165
Goblet, frosted w/amber cross 350

Pitcher, water, square, clear w/amber
  cross.. 225
Pitcher, water, square, frosted w/amber
  cross.. 375
Punch cup, clear w/amber cross 60
Punch cup, frosted w/amber cross 120-130
Salt & pepper shakers w/original tops,
  clear w/amber cross, pr...................... 225-250
Sauce dish, frosted w/amber cross, flat or
  footed, each 75
Spooner, clear 75
Spooner, clear w/amber cross 155
Sugar bowl, cov., frosted w/amber cross,
  4" d., 6 3/4" h... 295
Sugar bowl, open, frosted w/amber
  cross... 175-180
Toothpick holder, frosted w/amber
  cross... 350-425
Tumbler, frosted w/amber cross (ILLUS.)........ 190
Vase, 8" h., trumpet-shaped, clear 45-50
Vase, 8" h., trumpet-shaped, frosted
  w/amber cross... 340
Wine, frosted w/amber cross 495

LACY MEDALLION -See Colorado Pattern

LEAF & DART (Double Leaf & Dart)

Bowl, 7" oval, flat... 25
Celery vase, pedestal base 25-35
Creamer, applied handle............................. 35-45
Cruet w/original stopper 110
Egg cup 25-30
Goblet 40-45
Pitcher, milk 90-95
Pitcher, water, applied handle 110
Salt dip, open, master size 74
Spooner 30-35
Sugar bowl, cov.. 45-55
Sugar bowl, open.. 25-30

Leaf & Dart Tumbler

Tumbler, footed (ILLUS.) 25-30
Wine 40-45

LIBERTY BELL

Bowl, 6" d., footed...................................... 60-65
Bowl, berry or fruit, 8" d., footed................ 95-100
Bread platter, w/thirteen original states,
  twig handles, 8 1/4 x 13" 70
*Bread platter, "Signer's," twig handles.... 120-130
Butter dish, cov. 125
Butter dish, cov., miniature........................... 143
Compote, open, 6" d. 95
Creamer, applied handle 75
Creamer, miniature 88
Creamer & cov. sugar bowl, pr. 150-175

Liberty Bell Goblet

*Goblet (ILLUS.).. 30
Mug, miniature, 2" h. 175
Pitcher, water.. 750
Plate, 6" d., no states, dated 55-65
Relish, shell handles, 7 x 11 1/4" 59
Salt shaker w/original pewter top 130
Sauce dish 20-25
Spooner 50-60
Sugar bowl, cov... 110
Sugar bowl, cov., miniature 195
Sugar bowl, open 25-30
Syrup pitcher w/original top 90

LILY-OF-THE-VALLEY
Butter dish, cov. 100
Celery vase 66
Champagne 175-200
Compote, cov., 8" d., low stand 127
Compote, cov., 8 1/2" d., high stand............... 138
Compote, open, 7" d., low stand....................... 56
Creamer, plain base, applied handle 62
Creamer, three-footed, molded handle 60-65
Goblet, plain.. 80-85
Pitcher, milk, applied handle..................... 200-225

Lily-of-the-Valley Pitcher

Pitcher, water, bulbous, applied handle
(ILLUS.).. 120
Relish, 4 1/2 x 7" 23

Salt dip, cov., master size, three-footed.......... 225
Spooner, plain base..................................... 40-45
Spooner, three-footed.. 50
Sugar bowl, cov., three-footed 80
Sugar bowl, open, three-footed 55
Tumbler, footed... 55
Wine 175

LINCOLN DRAPE & LINCOLN DRAPE WITH TASSEL
Butter dish, cov. 125-150
Compote, cov., 6" d., high stand (sweet-
meat) 325-375
Compote, open, 6" d. 90
Compote, open, 6 3/4" d., 5 1/4" h.............. 65-75
Compote, open, 7 1/8" d., 5" h................. 115-125
Compote, open, 9" d. 105

Lincoln Drape Egg Cup

Egg cup (ILLUS.) 45-50
Goblet 95-100
Goblet w/tassel 375-475
Lamp, all glass, full size 175-200
Lamp, clear w/milk glass base 300-350
Plate, 6" d. 95-100
Sugar bowl, open 40-45

LION, FROSTED - See Frosted Lion Pattern

LION - See Frosted Lion Pattern (Gillinder)

LION'S LEG - See Alaska Pattern

LOG CABIN
Bowl, cov., 5 1/4 x 3 5/8"................................. 125
Butter dish, cov. 345-375
Compote, cov... 350
*Creamer, 4 1/4" h.................................. 125-175
Honey dish, cov. 190
Lamp, dated 1875 200
Marmalade jar, cov. 175-225
Pickle jar, cov., 6 3/4" h. 95-100
Pitcher, water.. 450-550
Salt dip, master size 110
Sauce dish, flat oblong 85
*Spooner, clear 145

Log Cabin Sugar Bowl

*Sugar bowl, cov., clear, 8" h. (ILLUS.) **375-450**
Sugar bowl, cov., canary **675**
Sugar bowl, open **75**

LOOP & DART
Butter dish, cov., round ornaments, flint **70-75**
Butter pat, round ornaments **29**
Celery vase, round ornaments, flint **60**
Egg cup, round ornaments **30-40**
Goblet, round ornaments **45-55**
Pitcher, water, round ornaments **125**
Salt dip, master size, diamond ornaments **28**
Salt dip, master size, round ornaments **45**
Spooner, diamond ornaments **29**
Wine, round ornaments **35-45**

LOOP & JEWEL - See Jewel & Festoon Pattern

LOOP & PILLAR -See Michigan Pattern

LOOP (Seneca Loop)
Bowl, 9" d., flint **80**
Butter dish, cov., flint **195**
Celery vase, flint **65**
Celery vase, non-flint **28**
Champagne, non-flint **30**
Creamer, clear, flint **73**
Egg cup, flint **30-35**

Loop Goblet

Goblet, flint (ILLUS.) **25**
Goblet, non-flint **18**
Pitcher, water, applied handle, flint **195**
Sugar bowl, cov., flint **75-100**
Syrup jug w/original pewter top, applied
   handle, clear, flint **95**
Wine, non-flint **15**

LOOP WITH STIPPLED PANELS - See Texas Pattern

LOOPS & DROPS - See New Jersey Pattern

LOUISIANA
Bowl, cov., round, 6" d. **40**
Bowl, cov., round, 7" d. **40**
Bowl, cov., round, 8" d. **45**
Bowl, open, round, 6" d. **45**
Bowl, open, round, 7" d. **35**
Bowl, open, round, 8" d. **40**
Bowl, open, square, 6" w. **30**
Bowl, open, square, 7" w. **30**
Bowl, open, square, 8" d. **35**
Bowl, open, square, 9" w. **40**
Butter dish, cov. **80-85**
Cake stand, high stand, 7" d. **55**
Cake stand, high stand, 10" d. **75**
Celery vase **45**
Compote, cov., high stand, 6" d. **50**
Compote, cov., high stand, 7" d. **50**
Compote, cov., high stand, 8" d. **55**
Compote, open, deep bowl, jelly, 5 1/2" d. **18**
Compote, open, deep bowl, 7" d. **22**
Compote, open, deep bowl, 8" d. **28**
Compote, open, flared bowl, 6" d. **28**
Compote, open, shallow bowl, 8" d. **30**
Compote, open, shallow bowl, 10" d. **30**
Creamer **40-45**
Dish, cov., handled, 6" d. **35**
Dish, open, handled, 6" d. **20**

Louisiana Goblet

Goblet (ILLUS.) 35
Match holder on attached saucer base 35-40
Mustard jar, cover & underplate 45-50
Pickle dish, boat-shaped 20
Pitcher, milk, pressed handle........................... 40
Relish tray 15
Salt & pepper shakers w/original tops,
    pr.. 45
Salt shaker w/original top 20
Sauce dish, round, 4" d. 10
Sauce dish, round, 4 1/2" d. 10
Sauce dish, square, 4 1/2" w. 7
Spooner 30
Sugar bowl, cov. 45-50
Tumbler, water.. 25-30
Wine 40-45

MAGNET & GRAPE
Butter dish, cov., frosted leaf, flint................. 185
Champagne, frosted leaf, flint.................. 190-200
Champagne, stippled leaf, non-flint 55-60
Compote, open, stippled leaf, 7 1/4" d.,
    high stand, non-flint...................................... 50
Egg cup, frosted leaf, flint 75-80
Goblet, clear leaf, non-flint 35-40

Magnet & Grape Goblet

*Goblet, frosted leaf, flint (ILLUS.) 90-100
Goblet, stippled leaf, non-flint 35-40
Salt dip, frosted leaf, flint 65-70
Salt dip, master size, frosted leaf, flint 80-85
Salt dip, stippled leaf, non-flint..................... 15-20
Spooner, frosted leaf, flint............................ 90-95
Sugar bowl, open, frosted leaf, flint 35-40
Sugar bowl, open, stippled leaf, non-flint 25-30
Syrup pitcher w/spring lid, stippled leaf,
    non-flint 175-200
*Tumbler, frosted leaf, flint......................... 110-120
Tumbler, stippled leaf, non-flint.................... 35-40
*Wine, frosted leaf, flint 100-110
Wine cooler, frosted leaf, flint .... 2,500+

MAINE (Stippled Flower Panels)
Bowl, master berry, 8 1/2" d., clear 40
Butter dish, cov. 68
Cake stand, 8 1/2" d., green 65
Compote, cov., green, small 65

Maine Jelly Compote

Compote, open, jelly, 4 3/4" d. (ILLUS.) 24
Creamer 28
Cruet w/original stopper 60
Mug 55
Pitcher, milk 65-70
Platter, oval 38
Salt & pepper shakers, w/original tops, pr... 80-85
Sauce dish 13
Spooner 32
Syrup pitcher w/original top, clear.................. 70
Toothpick holder, clear................................... 385
Wine, clear 40-45

MALTESE - See Jacob's Ladder Pattern

MARYLAND (Inverted Loops & Fans or Loops & Fans)
Banana bowl, flat, 5 x 11 1/4".......................... 41
Bowl, 8 1/4" d. 20
Butter dish, cov. 65-70
Cake stand, 8" d. 42
Cake stand, 9" d. 65
Compote, open, jelly 18
Goblet clear w/ruby stain.............................. 55-60

Maryland Goblet

Goblet (ILLUS.)... 30
Pitcher, milk, ruby-stained........................ 100-115
Pitcher, water, clear 55-60

Pitcher, water, ruby-stained 170-175
Salt & pepper shakers w/original tops,
   pr. 65
Toothpick holder, clear 40-45
Toothpick holder, suby-stained 85-100
Tumbler 29
Wine, clear 40-45
Wine, ruby-stained 70-75

MASCOTTE
Apothecary jar, cov. 65
Butter dish, cov., engraved 85
Butter dish, cov., plain 38
Cake basket w/handle 76
Cake stand, 12" d. 155
Cheese dish, cov. 65
Compote, cov., 8" d., 12" h. 85-90

Mascotte Creamer

Creamer, clear (ILLUS.) 45
Goblet, plain 30
Jar, cov., pyramid, flat base, three jars-
   high, bottom of jar sections embossed
   "Patented May 20, 1873" (minor rough-
   ness inside rim of lid, sold w/two extra
   lids, one w/flakes inside rim, one
   w/roughness to finial) 1,000
Marmalade jar, cov., 4 1/2" d., 8" h., clear.... 25-30
Pitcher, water 75-80
Salt dip, individual size 25
Salt & pepper shakers w/original tops,
   pr. 55-60
Salt shaker w/original top 30-35
Sauce dish, flat or footed, each 10
Spooner, clear, plain 22
Sugar bowl, cov., plain 39
Tray, water, clear, plain 59
Tumbler, clear, plain 25
Wine, clear, plain 26

MASSACHUSETTS
Bar bottle, bar lip, 11" h. 44

Basket w/applied handle, 4 1/2 x 4 1/2",
   4 3/4" h. 55
Bowl, 8" l., pointed sides 35

Massachusetts Butter dish

*Butter dish, cov., clear (ILLUS.) 75
Carafe 36
Champagne 45
Cologne bottle w/stopper 48
Cordial 55
Creamer 28
Cruet w/original stopper, miniature,
   3 1/2" h. 55
Goblet 40-45
Mug, 3 1/2" h., clear 20-25
Plate, 6" sq., w/advertising 90
Rum jug, 5" h. 80-90
Whiskey, handled 80-85
Whiskey shot glass, clear 16

MC KEE'S COMET - See Horn of Plenty Pattern

MICHIGAN (Paneled Jewel or Loop & Pillar)
Bowl, 8" d., clear 36
Bowl, 8" d., pink-stained w/gold trim 65-70
Bowl, 8 3/4" d., scalloped & flared rim 28
Bowl, 9" d. 25
Bowl, 9" d., pink-stained 45
Bowl, 10" d. 35
Butter dish, cov., clear 60
Butter dish, cov., pink-stained 185
Butter dish, cov., yellow-stained, enam-
   eled florals 185
Carafe, water, clear 55-60
Carafe, water, pink-stained 100-110
Celery vase, clear 35
Celery vase, pink-stained, gold rim 75
Compote, open, 6 1/2" d., scalloped rim 40-45
Compote, open, 8 1/2" d., high stand 65
Compote, open, 8 1/2" d., pink-stained 60-65
Compote, open, 9 1/4" d. 85
Compote, open, flared, 9 3/4" d., pink-
   stained, enameled florals 250-275
Creamer, 4" h., clear 30
Creamer, 4" h., pink-stained 95
Creamer, individual size, clear 45
Creamer & sugar bowl, pink-stained, gold
   trim, pr. 95
Cruet w/original stopper 125
Egg cup 25
Goblet, clear 35

Michigan Goblet

Goblet, clear w/gold (ILLUS.) 40
Goblet, clear w/pink stain, gold trim 75
Honey dish, 3 1/2" d. 8
Mug, clear 30-35
Mug, pink-stained, gold trim 38
Mug, yellow-stained, enameled florals **45-55**
Parfait 30
Pitcher, miniature, clear 35-40
Pitcher, miniature, pink-stained 58
Pitcher, water, 8" h. 50
Pitcher, water, tankard, 12" h., clear.................. 75
Pitcher, water, tankard, 12" h., pink-
stained... **175-185**
Platters, 8 1/2 x 12 1/2", 7 1/4 x 10 1/4",
6 1/2 x 9 1/2", nested set of 3...................... 125
Punch bowl, 8" d., 4 1/2" h. 50
Punch cup, clear 10
Punch cup, enameled decoration...................... 30
Punch cup, pink-stained 30-35
Relish, clear 18
Relish, pink-stained 24
Salt & pepper shakers w/original tops,
clear, pr. 70-75
Salt & pepper shakers w/original tops,
pink-stained, pr.. **80-85**
Salt & pepper shakers w/original tops,
individual size, pr....................................... 70-75
Salt shaker w/original top, clear 28
Salt shaker w/original top, enameled dec-
oration 32
Salt shaker w/original top, pink-stained........... 45
Salt shaker w/original top, yellow-stained,
enameled florals..................................... 35-40
Sauce dish, clear 14
Sauce dish, pink-stained 30
Spooner, pink-stained.. 71
Spooner, clear, child's 60
Sugar bowl, cov., blue-stained 150
Sugar bowl, cov., clear...................................... 75
Sugar bowl, cov., pink-stained, gold trim...... 75-80
Sugar bowl, cov., child's, 4 3/4" h................. 70-75
Sugar bowl, individual size 21
Syrup jug w/pewter top 165
Toddy mug, clear, tall 45
Toddy mug, pink-stained, gold trim, tall............. 37

Toothpick holder, blue-stained 75
***Toothpick holder,** clear.................................... 45
Toothpick holder, pink-stained, gold
trim **175-180**
Toothpick holder, yellow-stained............. 160-165
Toothpick holder, yellow-stained, enam-
eled florals.. **175-190**
Tumbler, clear 25-30
Tumbler, clear w/gold trim................................. 36
Tumbler, pink-stained, gold trim........................ 65
Tumbler, yellow-stained, enameled florals.... 35-45
Vase, 6" h., pink-stained, enameled florals ... 35-40
Vase, 8" h., pink-stained.................................... 75
Waste bowl 68
Wine, blue-stained... 50-55
Wine, clear 40
Wine, yellow-stained 55

MINERVA
Bowl, footed 40
Bread tray, 13" l. 75
Butter dish, cov. 80
Cake stand, 8" d. 100-110
Cake stand, 9" d. 90
Cake stand, 10 1/2" d. 110-115
Champagne 150-175
Compote, cov., 7" d., low stand 100
Compote, cov., 7" d., 10 3/4" h. 145
Compote, cov., 8" d., high stand............. 140-150
Compote, cov., 8" d., low stand 100-110
Compote, open, 8" d., 8 1/2" h.......................... 75
Compote, open, 10" d., 9" h.............................. 65
Creamer 70
Goblet 85-95
Marmalade jar, cov. 150
Pickle dish, "Love's Request is Pickles,"
oval... 28
Pitcher, water.. 100-110
Plate, 8" d., Bates (J.C.) portrait center,
scalloped rim 75
Plate, 9" d., handled, plain center..................... 56

Minerva "Mars" Center Plate

Plate, 10" d., Mars center (ILLUS.).................... 50
Platter, 13" oval.. 59
Relish, 5 x 8" oblong 34
Sauce dish, footed, 4" d................................... 17
Sauce dish, flat, 5" d.. 20
Spooner 40

Sugar bowl, cov. 90-95
Sugar bowl, open 20-25
Table set, creamer, cov. butter dish &
    spooner, 3 pcs. 195
Waste bowl, 6" d. 55
Wine 50

MINNESOTA
Banana bowl, flat 50-55
Basket w/applied reeded handle 75
Bowl, 6" sq. 32
Bowl, 7 1/2 x 10 1/2" 38
Bowl, 7 1/2 x 10 1/2", ruby-stained 375
Bowl, 8" sq. 32
Bowl, 8 1/2" d., clear 40
Bowl, 8 1/2" d., ruby-stained 70
Carafe 48
Celery tray, 13" l. 34
Cheese dish, cov. 58
Cracker jar, cov. 85-100
Creamer, clear w/gold 50
Creamer, clear, 3 1/2" h. 36
Cruet w/original stopper 55-65
Doughnut stand 40-45
Goblet, clear. 30

Minnesota Goblet

Goblet clear w/gold (ILLUS.) 35
Mug 25
Spooner, clear 35
Spooner, clear w/gold 53
Sugar bowl, cov. 37
Syrup pitcher w/original top 65
Toothpick holder, three-handled, clear 25-30
Toothpick holder, three-handled, green 115
Tumbler 18
Wine 15-20

MIRROR - See Galloway Pattern

MISSOURI (Palm & Scroll)
Bowl, 8" d., clear 21
Celery vase, clear 35-40
Creamer, clear 35

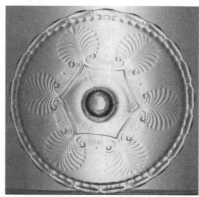

Missouri Doughnut Stand

Doughnut stand, 6" d. (ILLUS.) 55
Mug, clear. 30
Mug, green 40
Pitcher, milk, clear 45
Pitcher, milk, green 125
Pitcher, water, tankard, green 120-125
Sauce dish, clear 11
Sauce dish, green 18
Spooner, clear 24
Spooner, green 40
Sugar bowl, cov., clear 49
Syrup pitcher 68
Tumbler, clear 30
Tumbler, green 45
Tumbler, ruby-stained 45
Wine, clear 36
Wine, green 50-55

MOON & STAR
Bowl, cov., 6" d. 26
*Bowl, cov., 7" d. 34
Bowl, 7" d., footed 25
*Bowl, 9" d., flat 40
Bread tray, scalloped rim, 6 1/2 x 10 3/4" 60-65
Cake stand, 10" d. 95
Carafe, water 40
Celery vase 45
*Compote, cov., 6" d., high stand 75
Compote, cov., 8" d., 12" h. 55-65
Compote, cov., 10" d., high stand 93
Compote, cov., 10 1/2" d., 16 1/4" h. 185
Compote, open, 6" d., high stand 28
Compote, open, 8" d., 8" h. 44

Moon & Star Compote

Compote, open, 9" d., 6 1/2 h. (ILLUS.)............. 35
Compote, open, 10" d., high stand 100-125
*Egg cup 40
*Goblet 35-40
Lamp, kerosene-type, table model, clear
font, milk white base, 15" h. 100-110
*Pitcher, water, 9 1/4" h., applied rope han-
dle 155-175
Relish, oblong 20
Salt dip, individual size, footed 32
*Salt dip, master size 20-25
*Spooner 45
*Sugar bowl, cov. 65
*Syrup pitcher w/original top 125
*Tumbler, flat 40
*Wine 43

NAIL

Bowl, berry, master, ruby-stained 90
Butter dish, cov. 70-75
Celery tray, flat, 5 x 11" 75
Celery vase, engraved................................. 45-50
Celery vase, ruby-stained 65
Claret 55
Compote, jelly, clear, 5 1/4" 68
Compote, jelly, ruby-stained, 5 1/4" d. 90
Compote, 7" d., ruby-stained 100-110
Compote, 8" d., clear, engraved 85
Creamer, clear, engraved 35
Creamer, clear, plain... 40
Creamer, ruby-stained, 4 1/2" h. 95
Goblet, clear, engraved................................ 45-55
Goblet, clear, plain 40-45
Goblet, ruby-stained...................................... 70-80
Pitcher, water, engraved........................... 100-125
Pitcher, water, plain... 83
Pitcher, water, ruby-stained 150-175
Pitcher, water, ruby-stained w/engraving........ 195
Salt shaker w/original top, clear
w/engraving.. 65
Salt shaker w/original top, ruby stained
w/engraving.. 75
Sauce dish, clear, flat or footed, each 20
Sauce dish, ruby-stained, flat or footed,
each 50
Spooner, clear, plain... 45
Spooner, ruby-stained 75-85
Sugar bowl, cov., clear w/engraved cover......... 48
Sugar bowl, cov., ruby-stained 125
Syrup jug w/original top, ruby-stained 230
Tumbler, clear.. 20-25
Tumbler, ruby-stained...................................... 60
Wine, clear, engraved 45
Wine, clear, plain... 30-35
Wine, ruby-stained, souvenir............................ 50

NAILHEAD

Bowl, 7 3/4" d., 2 5/8" h.................................... 40
Cake stand, 9" to 12" d. 40
Cake stand, 12" d. 55-60
Celery vase 45

Nailhead Compote

Compote, cov., 6 1/4" d., 6 1/4" h. (ILLUS.).. 30-35
Compote, cov., 6 1/4" d., 9 1/2" h. 45
Cordial 20
Creamer, clear 27
Goblet, engraved 45-55
Goblet, plain... 29
Pitcher, water.. 65-75
Plate, 7" sq. 19
Plate, 9" sq. 22
Sauce dish, 4"... 9
Sugar bowl, cov.. 35
Tumbler, clear... 30
Wine 18

NEW ENGLAND PINEAPPLE

Bar bottle, qt.. 275
Cake stand 150-160
Castor set, 2 castor bottles & 2 mustard
jars in frame, set.................................. 175-220
Champagne 175-210
Compote, open, 8" d., 5" h........................ 150-200
Compote, open, 8" d., 7" h............................. 140
Compote, open, 9" d. 145
*Cordial, 4" h.. 119
Creamer, applied handle.......................... 150-175
Decanter w/original stopper, qt.............. 250-275

New England Pineapple Egg Cup

Egg cup (ILLUS.) 50-55
*Goblet 85

Goblet, lady's **125-130**
Goblets, set of 5.. **425-450**
Pitcher, milk, 1 qt. **650**
Pitcher, water... **400**
Spooner **65-70**
Sugar bowl, cov. **140-145**
Sugar bowl, open **25-30**
Tumbler, water.. **95-100**
Tumbler, water, extra large...................... **125-130**
Tumbler, whiskey, applied handle **180-190**
*Wine **160-170**
Wines, set of 3 .... **480-500**

NEW HAMPSHIRE (Bent Buckle)
Creamer, individual, 3 1/4" h., clear **35**
Cruet w/original stopper, clear......................... **60**
Cruet w/original stopper, rose-stained........... **250**
Goblet, clear.. **21**
Goblet, rose-stained................................... **60-65**
Mug, medium size, clear **23**
Mug, large size, rose-stained **60**
Olive dish, diamond-shaped, 6 5/8" w.,
    rose-stained... **20**
Pitcher, water, tankard, clear, 1/2 gal. **150**
Salt shaker w/original top, small &
    tapered w/fluted neck, clear **50**
Sauce dish, round, rose-stained, 4" d.............. **14**
Sugar bowl, cov., breakfast size, clear............. **14**
Sugar bowl, cov., breakfast size, rose-
    stained... **17**
Sugar bowl, open, individual, double-han-
    dled, rose-stained.. **21**
Tumbler, water, clear................................... **20-25**
Vase, 6" h., thick stem, rose-stained **25**
Wine, flared bowl, clear **19**
Wine, flared bowl, rose-stained **55**
Wine, straight-sided, rose-stained..................... **45**

NEW JERSEY (Loops & Drops)
Bowl, 7 1/2" d. **75**
Bowl, 9" d. **29**
Celery tray, flat **35**
Cruet w/original stopper **75**
Goblet, clear.. **30-35**
Goblet, ruby-stained................................... **110-120**
Goblet, w/gold trim **35**
Olive dish **18**
Pitcher, ruby-stained................................... **200-220**
Pitcher, water, bulbous **95-110**
Plate, 10 1/2" d. **36**
Sauce dish, flat **11**
Spooner, clear **40**
Sugar bowl, cov. **45-50**
Toothpick holder, clear.................................... **47**
Tumbler, clear.. **26**
Vase, 10" h., green... **40-50**

OLD MAN OF THE MOUNTAIN - See Viking Pattern

OPEN ROSE
Butter dish, cov. **65**
Compote, open, 7 1/2" d. **33**
Creamer **48**
Egg cup **23**
*Goblet **25-30**
Pitcher, water, applied handle **170**
Relish, 5 1/2 x 8" **14**
Salt dip, master size **24**
Sauce dish **15**

Open Rose Spooner

*Spooner (ILLUS.) **40**
Sugar bowl, cov. **54**
Sugar bowl, open **24**
Tumbler **43**
Tumbler, applied handle **65**
Water set, pitcher & 6 goblets, 7 pcs. **325-350**

OREGON NO. 1 - See Beaded Loop Pattern

PALM & SCROLL - See Missouri Pattern

PALMETTE
Bowl, 8" d., flat **25**
Bowl, 9" d., footed **28**
Bread tray, handled, 9" **30**
Butter dish, cov. **60-65**
Butter pat **45**
Cake stand **45**
Castor set, three-bottle, complete..................... **75**
Celery vase **53**
Champagne **68**
Compote, cov., 8" d., high stand................... **80-85**
Compote, open, 7" d., low stand........................ **30**
Creamer, applied handle.............................. **55-60**
Egg cup **30-35**

Palmette Goblet

Goblet (ILLUS.)... **40-50**

Lamp, kerosene-type, table model w/stem,
clear 110
Lamp, kerosene-type, table model w/stem,
milk white 135
Pitcher, water, applied handle 150
Sauce dish 8
Sugar bowl, cov. 70-75
Syrup pitcher w/original top, applied han-
dle 125
Wine 75-100

PANELED DEWDROP

Bowl, 8 1/2" oval 24
Bread platter, 9 1/2 x 12 1/2" 45
Butter dish, cov. 50-55
Cordial, 3 1/4" h. 30-40
Creamer 25-30
Goblet 35
Marmalade jar, cov. 43
Mug, applied handle 35
Pitcher, milk 43
Plate, 7" to 10" d. 15-30
Relish, 4 1/2 x 7" 13-16
Sauce dish, flat or footed 5-10
Spooner 32
Sugar bowl, open 30
Tumbler, applied handle 40
Wine 30

PANELED FORGET-ME-NOT

Bowl, berry, large 45
Bowl, oval, small 25

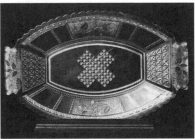

Paneled Forget-me-not Bread Platter

Bread platter, 7 x 11" oval (ILLUS.) 29
Butter dish, cov. 63
Cake stand, 8" d., amethyst 295
Cake stand 10" to 11" d. 65
Celery vase 30-35
Compote, cov., 7" d., 10" h. 81
Compote, cov., 8" d., high stand 89
Compote, open, 7" d., high stand 45
Compote, open, 8 1/2" d., high stand 35-40
Goblet, amethyst 225-250
Goblet, clear 40-45
Marmalade jar, cov. 145
Pitcher, water, blue 88
Pitcher, water, clear 65-70
Relish, handled, 4 1/2 x 7 3/4" 24
Relish, scoop-shaped, 9" l. 20-25
Salt dip 10-15
Sauce dish, flat or footed 13
Spooner 30-35
Sugar bowl, cov. 40-45
Wine 80-85

PANELED HERRINGBONE (Emerald Green Herringbone or Florida)

Banana bowl, folded-up sides, green 60-65
Berry set: 9" d. master bowl & 8 sauce
dishes; green, 9 pcs. 100
Bowl, cov., 8" d., green 35
Bowl, 6" d., clear 20
Bowl, 6" d., green 40
Bowl, 7 1/2" d., green 55
Bowl, master berry, 9" sq., green 35
Bowl, master berry, 10 3/4" sq., green 37
Bowl, oval vegetable, green, medium 30
Bowl, oval vegetable, green, large 35
Bread tray, green 40-45
Butter dish, cov., green 80-85
Cake stand, clear 45
Cake stand, green 80
Celery vase, green 55
Compote, open, jelly, 5 1/2" sq., green 30
Cordial, green 40
Creamer, clear 20
Creamer, green 45-50
Cruet w/original stopper, green 65-70
***Goblet,** clear 30

Paneled Herringbone Goblet

***Goblet,** green (ILLUS.) 38
Marmalade jar, green 45
Pickle dish, green 23
Pitcher, milk 45
Pitcher, milk, green 55-65
Pitcher, water, clear 50
***Plate,** 9" sq., clear 28
***Plate,** 9" sq., green 35
Relish, 4 1/2 x 8" oval, green 14
Spooner, green w/gold 75
Sugar bowl, cov., green 50
Sugar bowl, open, green 28
Syrup pitcher w/original top, clear 175
Tumbler, clear 20
Tumbler, green 30

PANELED JEWEL - See Michigan Pattern

PANELED THISTLE

Basket w/applied handle, 4 3/4 x 7", 2 1/2" h.	35
Bowl, 10" d., footed, deep	35
Bread plate	40
Celery vase	53
***Champagne,** flared, w/bee	38
Cheese dish, cov., footed	55
Cheese dish, cov., footed, w/bee	75
Compote, cov., 6" d., high stand	60
Compote, cov., 7" d., 11" h., w/bee	70
Compote, open, 5" d., high stand	25
Cordial	60
Cruet w/stopper	40-50
Doughnut stand, 6"	35
Egg cup	37
***Goblet**	37
Honey dish, cov., round	75-80
***Honey dish,** cov., square	90-95
Nappy, handled, 5" d.	20
Pitcher, milk	50-55
***Pitcher,** water, clear w/bee	68
Pitcher, water, ruby-stained	85-90
***Plate,** 7" sq., w/bee	34
Relish, 4 x 5"	15
Salt dip, individual size	16
***Toothpick holder**	30
Water set, pitcher & 4 tumblers, 5 pcs.	175

Paneled Thistle Wine

***Wine** (ILLUS.)	30-35
***Wine,** w/bee	40-45

PAVONIA (Pineapple Stem)

Bowl, 9" d., 3 3/4" h.	25
Butter dish, cov., clear, engraved	85
Butter dish, cov., clear, plain	72
Butter dish, cov., ruby-stained	100-115
Cake stand, 10" d.	70-75
Celery vase, engraved	75-125
Celery vase, plain	40
Compote, cov., 6" d., high stand	55
Compote, cov, 8" d., engraved	125

Compote, open, 7" d.	50
Creamer, ruby-stained	63
Creamer & open. sugar bowl, clear, engraved, hotel size, pr.	145
Cup, custard, applied handle	20-25

Pavonia Finger bowl

Finger bowl, 7" d. (ILLUS.)	36
Goblet, engraved	45
Goblet, plain	30-35
Olive dish	20-25
Pitcher, water, tall tankard, clear, engraved	110-125
Pitcher, water, tall tankard, clear, plain	65-70
Pitcher, water, tall tankard, ruby-stained	135-140
Pitcher, water, tall tankard, ruby-stained, engraved	175-190
Sauce dish, flat or footed, each	15
Spooner, clear	41
Tray, water	75
Tray, water, engraved	110-125
Tumbler, clear	25
Tumbler, clear, acid-etched	20-30
Tumbler, ruby-stained	35
Waste bowl, clear, engraved	65
Waste bowl, ruby-stained	85-90
Water set: tankard pitcher & 4 tumblers; clear, 5 pcs.	168
Wine, clear, engraved	30
Wine, clear, plain	25

PEACOCK FEATHER (Georgia)

Bonbon dish, footed	23
Bowl, 8" d.	30
Bread plate	30-35
Butter dish, cov.	40
Cake stand, 8 1/2" d., 5" h.	35-40
Celery tray, 11 3/4" l.	35

Peacock Feather Compote

Compote, open, 8" d., high stand (ILLUS.)	43
Creamer	24
Creamer & cov. sugar bowl, pr.	100

Cruet w/original stopper 70
Decanter w/original stopper 70
Goblet 25
Lamp, kerosene-type, low hand-type
w/handle, 5 1/4" h., blue........................ 160-165
Lamp, kerosene-type, low hand-type
w/handle, 5 1/2" h., clear 85-90
Lamp, kerosene-type, table model w/han-
dle, 9" h., blue 250-275
Lamp, kerosene-type, table model, 10" h.,
amber... 225-250
Mug 35-40
Pitcher, water.. 55
Salt & pepper shakers w/original tops,
pr. 85
Sauce dish 13
Spooner 30-35
Sugar bowl, cov. 37
Table set, creamer, cov. sugar bowl & cov.
butter dish, 3 pcs. 125
Tumbler 35
Water set, pitcher & six tumblers, 7 pcs.... 250-275

PENNSYLVANIA (Balder or Kamoni)
Bowl, berry or fruit, 8 1/2" d., clear w/gold
trim 30
Butter dish, cov., clear 54
Carafe 47
Celery vase 28-35
Champagne 35
Cheese dish, cov. 65-70
Compote, open, 5" h., child's 15-20
Cracker jar, cov. 42
Creamer, child's 60-65
Creamer, 3" h., clear w/gold trim, individual....... 35
Creamer, 3" h., green w/gold trim, individ-
ual 55
Creamer, 4" h., table size................................ 35
Creamer 6 1/2" h. 45
Decanter w/original stopper, handleless,
10 3/4" h. 110
Decanter w/original stopper, handled,
10 3/4" h. 90
Goblet, clear.. 24
Goblet, clear w/gold 35-38
Pitcher, water... 65
Plate, 8" d. 30
Punch bowl, 10" d., 5" h., on 6" h. pedestal
base 150-160
Salt shaker w/original top 25-30
Sauce dish, boat-shaped................................ 22
Sauce dish, round or square 12
Spooner, child's 24
Sugar bowl, cov., child's, clear w/gold trim........ 35
Sugar bowl, cov., child's, green w/gold trim..... 160
Sugar bowl, cov., clear.................................... 45
Sugar bowl, cov., ruby-stained 75-80
Sugar bowl, open, individual size, clear
w/gold trim 25-28
Syrup pitcher w/original top 70-75
Toothpick holder, clear............................... 30-40
Toothpick holder, clear w/gold 40-45
Toothpick holder, green 143
Tumbler, juice, clear 12
Tumbler, juice, green 21
Whiskey shot glass, clear............................... 13

Pennsylvania Wine

Wine, clear (ILLUS.) 10-15
Wine, green 35
Wine, ruby-stained, souvenir........................ 45-50

PENNSYLVANIA, EARLY - See Hand Pattern

PINEAPPLE STEM - See Pavonia Pattern

PLEAT & PANEL (Darby)
Bowl, 8" rectangle, footed 34
Bread tray, closed handles, 8 1/2 x 13"........ 40-45
Bread tray, pierced handles.......................... 25-30

Pleat & Panel Celery Vase

Celery vase, footed (ILLUS.) 65
Compote, cov., 8" d., high stand.................... 145
Compote, open, 7" d., high stand 31
*Goblet, clear 30
Pitcher, milk 160-180
Pitcher, water... 105
Plate, 6" sq. 20-25

Relish, open, handled, 5 x 8 1/2" 24
Spooner 28
Sugar bowl, open 19

PLUME
Butter dish, cov., clear 42
Celery vase, clear 35
Compote, cov., 6 1/2" d., 12" h. 60
Compote, open, 9" d., collared base............. 40-45
Creamer, ruby-stained 125

Plume Goblet

*Goblet, clear (ILLUS.) 35
Pitcher, water, bulbous, clear, engraved 80
Pitcher, water, bulbous, clear, plain.................. 65
Tumbler, clear.. 50
Tumbler, ruby-stained, souvenir 43

POLAR BEAR
*Goblet, clear 100-125
Goblet, clear & frosted 145-175
Goblet, flared rim, frosted 125-150
Pitcher, water, clear 525-550
Pitcher, water, frosted.................................. 1,050
Tray, water, frosted, 16" l. 225-250

Polar Bear Waste Bowl

Waste bowl, frosted (ILLUS.)............................ 115

PORTLAND
Basket w/high handle 110-120
Bowl, 9" d.. 25
Cake stand, 10 1/2" 125
*Celery tray 20
Celery vase 39
Cruet w/original stopper 60-65

Portland Goblet

Goblet, clear (ILLUS.) 42
Lamp, keosene, 9" h. 55-60
Pin tray, water, miniature 26
Pitcher, water.. 40-45
Punch cup 19
Salt shaker w/original top 23
Sauce dish, 4 1/2" d... 8
Sugar bowl, cov.. 50
Sugar shaker w/original top 58
Vase, 6" h., scalloped rim................................ 22
Wine 23
Wine, clear w/gold trim 27

PORTLAND MAIDEN BLUSH - See Banded Portland Pattern

PRIMROSE
Bowl, 8" d., flat... 35
Creamer, clear 28
Plate, 4 1/2" d., amber or blue, each............. 15-20
Plate, 4 1/2" d., clear 12
Wine, blue 48
Wine, clear 25

PRINCESS FEATHER (Rochelle)
Cake plate w/closed handles, 9" d.................. 55
Celery vase 65

Princess Feather Compote

Compote, cov., 8" d., low stand (ILLUS.)......... 125
Egg cup, clear.. 29

Goblet, buttermilk 45
Goblet, flint 40
Pitcher, water, bulbous, applied handle,
    flint.. 110
Plate, 6" d., clear, non-flint 25
Plate, 7" d., clear, non-flint 22
Plate, 9" d., clear, non-flint 38
Spooner, clear, non-flint.................................... 45
Spooner, fiery opalescent milk white, flint,
    5 1/8" h. 115-120
Sugar bowl, cov., clear, non-flint 63

PRISCILLA (Alexis)
Cake stand, 9" to 10" d., high stand 70
Compote, cov., jelly 55-60
Compote, cov., 6" d., 10" h. 55-65
Doughnut stand, 4 1/4 x 5 3/4" 41
Pitcher, water, bulbous (2 styles)................... 130
*Sauce dish, ruby-stained............................... 55
Syrup pitcher w/original pewter top,
    clear 120-125
Toothpick holder 40-50
Tumbler (ILLUS.) 44

PSYCHE & CUPID
Bread tray 60
Butter dish, cov. 95
Celery vase 51
Compote, cov., 6 1/2" d., 8" h. 100
Creamer 50

Psyche & Cupid Goblet

Goblet (ILLUS.) 45-50
Pitcher, water.. 65-70
Relish, 6 1/2 x 9 1/2".. 33
Spooner 45-50
Sugar bowl, cov.. 60

PYGMY - See Torpedo Pattern

QUEEN (Daisy & Button with Pointed Panels)
Butter dish, domed cover, blue 68
*Cake stand blue, 6 1/2" d. 45
Compote, cov., amber, round 95
Compote, open, amber, round........................... 75
Goblet, amber 38

Queen Goblet

Goblet, apple green (ILLUS.) 38
Wine, clear 17

RAMPANT LION - See Frosted Lion Pattern

REVERSE TORPEDO (Diamond & Bull's Eye Band)
Banana stand 170
Butter dish, cov. 95
Cake stand 75-85
Celery vase 70
Compote, open, jelly 50
Compote, open, 6" d., piecrust rim 40
Compote, open, 8" d., piecrust rim, high
    stand 105
Compote, open, 8 1/2 x 10" oval, 9 1/4" h.,
    ruffled rim 125
Goblet 55
Goblet w/engraved flower 85
Pitcher, water, tankard............................. 125-150
Sauce dish 19
Spooner 42
Syrup pitcher w/original top 215
Tumbler 51

RIBBED IVY
Butter dish, cov. 115-125
Champagne 200-220
Compote, open, 8 1/2" d., 7 1/2" h., high
    stand 85-95
Egg cup 36

Ribbed Ivy Goblet

Goblet (ILLUS.) 45-65
Salt dip, open, master size, beaded rim 30
Sugar bowl, cov. 100-125
Tumbler, bar 105-125
Tumbler, water.. 85-95
Tumbler, whiskey 100-125
Tumbler, whiskey, handled 190
Wine 65

RIBBED PALM
Bowl, 8" d., footed 50-60
Butter dish, cov. 125-145
Celery vase 95-100
Champagne 120-125
Egg cup 34
*Goblet 45-50
Pitcher, water, 9" h., applied handle 265-300
Plate, 6" d. 45-50
Salt dip, master size 38
Sauce dish 12
Spooner 40
Sugar bowl, cov. 225
Sugar bowl, open 40-45
Water set, pitcher & seven goblets, clear,
    the set (flakes on pitcher pontil, chips on
    goblets, one w/check in foot)....................... 440
*Wine 65-70

RIBBON CANDY (Bryce or Double Loop)
Bowl, cov., 6 1/4" d., footed 35
Butter dish, cov., flat 35-40
Butter dish, cov., footed 55-60
Cake stand, 8" to 10 1/2" d. 80
Compote, cov., 7" d. 90

Ribbon Candy Creamer

Creamer (ILLUS.)... 35
Cruet w/faceted stopper 225
Doughnut stand 150
Goblet 75-85
Pitcher, milk 30-35
Spooner 40
Sugar bowl, cov... 45
Table set, 4 pcs.. 125-150
Wine 95

RIBBON (Early Ribbon)
Bread tray 40
Butter dish, cov. 85
Celery Vase 40-45
Cheese dish, cov. 160
Compote, open, 8" d., low stand...................... 45
Compote, open, 8" d., 8" h., frosted dolphin
    stem on dome base............................ 190-225
Compote, open, 8 1/2" d., 4 1/2" h.................... 70
Creamer 35
*Goblet 30-35
Marmalade jar, cov. 125
Pitcher, water.. 125
Sauce dish, flat or footed................................ 12

Ribbon Spooner

Spooner (ILLUS.).. 30-35
Sugar bowl, cov., 4 1/4" d., 7 3/4" h. 65-70
Tray, water, 15" 115

ROMAN ROSETTE
Bowl, 6" d. 43
Bread platter, 9 x 11".................................... 43
Butter dish, cov., clear.................................... 45
Compote, cov., 7" d., high stand...................... 95

Roman Rosette Creamer

Creamer, clear (ILLUS.) 37
*Goblet 40-50

Mug, 3" h. 16
Plate, 7" d. 35
Punch cup, clear.. 14
Relish, 3 1/2 x 8 1/2" 13
Salt shaker w/original top 15
Sauce dish 40-50
Spooner, clear 26
Spooner, ruby-stained 65
Tumbler, clear... 35
Wine, clear 45-50
Wine, ruby-stained 60-65

ROMAN ROSETTE, EARLY
Honey dish, opalescent, flint, 4 1/8" d. 65
Mug, cobalt blue 60
Plate, 6" d., medium golden amber 413
Plate, 9 1/2" d., clear, flint................................ 248

ROSE IN SNOW
Berry set, 8 1/4" sq. footed bowl & 4 footed
   sauce dishes, 5 pcs. 75
Bitters bottle w/original stopper 100
Bowl, 8 1/2 x 11 1/2" oval................................... 48
Butter dish, cov., round 60
Butter dish, cov., square 77
Cake plate, handled, amber, 10" d.................... 50
Cake plate, handled, blue, 10" d. 80
Cake stand, clear, 9" d............................... 90-100
Compote, cov., 7" d., low stand 125
Compote, cov., 8" d., 10" h., clear 90-95
Compote, open, 6" d., canary 42
Compote, open, 8" d., high stand 70
Creamer, round, amber............................... 30-35
Creamer, round, clear 40-45
Creamer, square, canary 60

Rose in Snow Creamer

Creamer, square, clear (ILLUS.) 32
*Goblet, amber.. 45
*Goblet, blue 85
*Goblet, canary 35-45
*Goblet, clear 35
Marmalade jar, cov., 5 3/4" d............................ 55
Mug, clear, 3 1/2" h. 35
*Mug, applied handle, "In Fond Remem-
   brance," clear.. 50
Mug, blue, large.. 105
Pitcher, water, applied handle, blue................. 225
Pitcher, water, applied handle, canary............. 160
Pitcher, water, applied handle, clear........ 125-135
Plate, 5" d. 26
Plate, 6" d. 30

Plate, 6 1/2" d., handled, clear 19
*Plate, 9" d., amber 40
*Plate, 9" d., blue.. 63
*Plate, 9" d., clear....................................... 25-30
Relish, 6 1/4 x 9 1/4" 18
Spooner, round 25
*Sugar bowl, cov., square 47
Tumbler 41

ROSE SPRIG
Bowl, 5 x 8", canary 48
Bowl, 6 x 9" oblong, canary.............................. 51
Cake stand, clear, 9" octagon, 6 1/2" h............. 70
Celery vase, amber.................................... 45-50
Celery vase, canary 110
Celery vase, clear 45
Compote, cov., high stand, large, clear 75
*Goblet, blue 68

Rose Sprig Goblet

*Goblet, clear (ILLUS.).................................. 30-35
Pitcher, milk, clear 65
Pitcher, water, amber....................................... 60
Pitcher, water, canary 60
Plate, 6" sq., canary 48
Punch bowl, footed, clear............................... 345
*Whimsey, sleigh (salt dip), clear,
   4 x 4 x 6" 110
Whimsey, sitz bath-shaped bowl, blue,
   7 x 10" 80
Wine, canary 65
Wine, clear 45-50

ROYAL CRYSTAL
Cologne bottle w/original stopper, ruby-
   stained, 4 oz.. 50
Cruet w/original stopper, 5 oz., clear.......... 30-35
Cruet w/original stopper, 5 oz., ruby-
   stained.. 395
Pitcher, bulbous, water, 1/2 gal., clear............ 115
Pitcher, tankard, water, 9 1/2" h., 1/2 gal.,
   ruby-stained 95
Salt shaker w/original top, ruby-stained........... 65
Sauce dish, flat, 4" d., ruby-stained 25
Spoonholder, ruby-stained 56
Sugar bowl, cov., 7 1/2" h., ruby-stained........... 89

Syrup pitcher w/original metal top, 6" h.,
 ruby-stained 275
Tumbler, water, 4" h., 1/3 pt., ruby-stained... **25-35**
Wine, 4" h., clear 35
Wine, 4" h., ruby-stained **60-65**

ROYAL IVY (Northwood)
Bowl, 8" d., craquelle (cranberry & vaseline
 spatter) **150-175**
Bowl, 8" d., frosted rubina crystal.............. **150-200**
Bowl, fruit, 9" d., craquelle (cranberry &
 vaseline spatter)... 235
Bowl, fruit, 9" d., frosted rubina crystal...... **105-125**
Bowl, fruit, 9" d., rubina crystal......................... 170
Butter dish, cov., clear & frosted..................... 120
Butter dish, cov., frosted rubina crystal........... 375
Creamer, clear & frosted................................... 81
Creamer, craquelle (cranberry & vaseline
 spatter).. 220
Creamer, frosted rubina crystal................ **175-200**
Creamer, rubina crystal................................... 140
Cruet w/original stopper, craquelle (cran-
 berry & vaseline spatter) 703
Cruet w/original stopper, frosted rubina
 crystal.. 450

Royal Ivy Cruet

Cruet w/original stopper, rubina crystal
 (ILLUS.)... 310
Pickle castor, clear & frosted insert, com-
 plete w/silver plate frame **125-150**
Pitcher, water, cased spatter (cranberry &
 vaseline w/white lining) **325-350**
Pitcher, water, clear & frosted..................... **75-100**
Pitcher, water, craquelle (cranberry &
 vaseline spatter)... 375
Pitcher, water, frosted craquelle 200
Pitcher, water, frosted rubina crystal **350-400**
Pitcher, water, rubina crystal 295
Rose bowl, cased spatter (cranberry &
 vaseline w/white lining) **250-300**
Rose bowl, frosted rubina crystal 130
Rose bowl, rubina crystal 79
Salt & pepper shakers w/original tops,
 cased spatter (cranberry & vaseline
 w/white lining), pr. 225
Salt shaker w/original top, clear & frosted 60

Sauce dish, craquelle (cranberry & vase-
 line spatter) **50-65**
Sauce dish, rubina crystal 35
Spooner, clear & frosted 36
Spooner, craquelle (cranberry & vaseline
 spatter) **135-145**
Spooner, frosted rubina crystal 160
Sugar bowl, cov., clear & frosted................. **40-45**
Sugar bowl, cov., frosted rubina crystal........... 220
Sugar bowl, cov., rubina crystal....................... 124
Sugar shaker w/original top, cased spat-
 ter (cranberry & vaseline w/white lining) 300
Sugar shaker w/original top, frosted
 rubina crystal.. **325-350**
Syrup pitcher w/original top, cased spat-
 ter (cranberry & vaseline w/white lining) 895
Syrup pitcher w/original top, frosted
 rubina crystal.. **500-525**
Toothpick holder, cased spatter (cran-
 berry & vaseline w/white lining) **250-300**
Toothpick holder, clear & frosted................ **45-50**
Toothpick holder, craquelle (cranberry &
 vaseline spatter)... 250
Toothpick holder, frosted rubina crystal 105
Toothpick holder, rubina crystal 85
Tumbler, clear & frosted 36
Tumbler, craquelle (cranberry & vaseline
 spatter) 81
Tumbler, frosted craquelle 100
Water set: pitcher & 6 tumblers; cased
 spatter (cranberry & vasline w/white lin-
 ing), 7 pcs... 955
Water set: pitcher & 6 tumblers; clear &
 frosted, 7 pcs.. 295

ROYAL OAK

Royal Oak Butter Dish

Butter dish, cov., frosted crystal (ILLUS.).......... 55
Butter dish, cov., frosted rubina crystal.... **225-300**
Butter dish, cov., rubina crystal....................... 193
Creamer, frosted crystal.................................... 75
Creamer, frosted rubina crystal................ **200-225**
Pickle castor, frosted rubina crystal insert,
 w/silver plate frame & cover 390
Pitcher, 8 1/2" h., frosted crystal **100-110**
Pitcher, water, frosted rubina crystal......... **275-300**
Salt shaker w/original top, rubina crystal 108
Sauce dish, rubina crystal 45

Sugar bowl, cov., frosted rubina crystal 170
Sugar shaker w/original top, frosted
    rubina crystal.. 225-250
Table set: creamer, cov. sugar bowl & cov.
    butter dish; frosted crystal, 3 pcs. 275
Toothpick holder, frosted rubina crystal 150
Toothpick holder, rubina crystal 120
Tumbler, frosted rubina crystal 84
Water set: pitcher & 4 tumblers; rubina
    crystal, 5 pcs. 565

RUBY THUMBPRINT
Bowl, master berry or fruit, 8" l., boat-
    shaped, engraved 145
Bowl, master berry or fruit, 10" l., boat-
    shaped 145
Castor set, 4-bottle, in clear glass frame .. 365-425
Celery vase 75
*Claret 75
Compote, open, jelly, 5 1/4" h............................ 95
Compote, open, 7" d., engraved 170
Compote, open, 7" d., plain 130
Compote, open, 8 1/2" d., 7 1/2" h., scal-
    loped rim 220
*Cordial, plain 24
Creamer, engraved 68
*Creamer, plain 45-50
Creamer, individual size................................... 28
*Cup, plain... 24
Cup & saucer, engraved............................... 60-65
*Cup & saucer, plain.. 57
Goblet, engraved vintage band 70
*Goblet, plain 50
Pitcher, milk, 7 1/2" h., bulbous 100
Pitcher, milk, tankard, 8 3/8" h........................ 145

Ruby Thumbprint Pitcher

Pitcher, water, tankard, 11" d., w/engraved
    leaf band (ILLUS.) 325
Pitcher, water, bulbous, large 250
*Plate, 8 1/4" d... 20
Salt & pepper shakers w/original tops,
    pr. 90
Sauce dish, boat-shaped................................. 45

Sauce dish, round, engraved............................ 48
*Sherbet 18
Spooner 70
Sugar bowl, open, individual size, 2 1/2" h........ 31
Toothpick holder, engraved............................. 45
Toothpick holder, plain 31
Tumbler, engraved... 61
*Tumbler, plain.. 38
Water set, tankard pitcher & 6 tumblers, 7
    pcs.. 385
*Wine 38
Wine, engraved 35

S-REPEAT
Butter dish, cov., apple green 125-150
Butter dish, cov., clear.................................... 125
Butter dish, cov., sapphire blue w/gold 150
Condiment set, amethyst 430

S-Repeat Condiment Set

Condiment set, apple green (ILLUS.)....... 250-275
Condiment tray, apple green........................... 55
*Cruet, apple green 110
Decanter w/stopper, wine, amethyst.............. 155
Decanter w/stopper, wine, apple green
    w/gold.. 138
Decanter w/stopper, wine, sapphire blue
    w/gold.. 158
Salt & pepper shakers, apple green, pr......... 103
*Wine, apple green.. 45
*Wine, sapphire blue 50

SANDWICH STAR
Decanter w/bar lip, qt.............................. 120-125
Inkwell, hinged brass cover, 3 1/4" h. 1,210
Spooner, clambroth 385-400
Spooner, electric blue 1,535
Wine 300

SAWTOOTH
Celery vase, knob stem, flint............................ 50
Celery vase, knob stem, non-flint 33
Champagne, non-flint 33
Compote, cov., 8" d., high stand, flint 75

Sawtooth Compote

Compote, open, 7 1/2" d., 7 1/2" h., flint (ILLUS.).. **55**
Compote, open, 8" d., amber............................ **30**
Compote, open, 11 1/4" d., 8 3/4" h., milk white, flint **80-85**
Creamer, applied handle, clear, flint **65-70**
Decanter w/original stopper, flint, 14" h........ **140**
Egg cup, flint **44**
Goblet, knob stem, flint **40-45**
Goblet, knob stem, non-flint **20-25**
Goblet, plain stem, non-flint **19**
Pitcher, water, applied handle, clear, flint **175**
Pomade jar, cov. **75-80**
Salt dip, cov., individual size, footed, flint **35**
Salt dip, cov., master size, footed, clear, flint.. **86**
Salt dip, cov., master size, footed, clear, non-flint **35**
Salt dip, cov., master size, footed, milk white, flint **75**
Salt dip, individual size, footed, flint.................. **19**
Salt dip, master size, clear, flint **50**
Sauce dish, canary, flat **23**
Sauce dish, clear **10**
Spillholder, clear, flint.. **50**
Spooner, clear, non-flint............................... **55-65**
Spooner, child's **21**
Sugar bowl, cov., clear, non-flint **27**
Sugar bowl, cov., cobalt blue, plain stem, 1870s **83**
Wine, flint.. **39**
Wine, non-flint **13**

SAWTOOTH BAND - See Amazon Pattern

SENECA LOOP - See Loop Pattern

SHELL & JEWEL (Victor)
Bowl, 8" d... **30**
Butter dish, cov. **85**
Cake stand, 10" d., 5" h. **40**
Compote, cov., 8 1/2" d., high stand.................. **75**
Creamer **45**
Pitcher, water, amber.. **80**

Shell & Jewel Pitcher

Pitcher, water, clear (ILLUS.)............................. **55**
Pitcher, water, green..................................... **90-95**
Sugar bowl, cov. **43**
Tumbler, amber **24**
Tumbler, blue **50**
Tumbler, clear **19**
Water set: pitcher & 6 tumblers; amber, 7 pcs.. **225-250**
Water set: pitcher & 6 tumblers; clear, 7 pcs.. **190**

SHELL & TASSEL
Bowl, 10" oval, clear.. **59**
Bowl, 8" d., cov., canary, collared base **120**
Bride's basket, 8" oval blue bowl in silver plate frame **320-350**
Butter dish, cov., round, dog finial.................... **154**
Cake stand, shell corners, 9" sq. **94**
Cake stand, shell corners, 10" sq. **100-125**
Celery vase, round, handled.............................. **80**
Compote, open, 6 1/2" sq., 6 1/2" h. **50**

Shell & Tassel Compote

Compote, open, 8 1/2" sq., 8" h. (ILLUS.)..... **50-55**
Creamer, round **35-45**
Creamer, square **60**

*Goblet, round, knob stem **45-55**
Mug, miniature, blue.. **145**
Oyster plate, 9 1/2" d...................................... **250**
Pitcher, water, round.. **150**
Pitcher, water, square...................................... **110**
Platter, 8 x 11" oblong.. **54**
Platter, 9 x 13" oval... **51**
Relish, amber, 5 x 8".. **95**
Relish, blue, 5 x 8" **100-110**
Relish, canary, 5 x 8" **125**
Salt dip, shell-shaped **17**
Salt shaker w/original top **110**
Sauce dish, flat or footed, 4" to 5" d., each **15**
Spooner, round **40**
Spooner, square **52**
Sugar bowl, cov., round, dog finial **128**
Table set, 4 pcs.. **398**
Tray, ice cream... **125**
Tumbler, clear.. **40**
Vase **175**

SHOSHONE
Bowl, 8" d., ruffled, green.................................. **23**
Bowl, master berry, ruby-stained **110**
Cake stand, green **60**
Celery vase, ruby-stained **95-100**
Cruet w/original stopper, clear......................... **52**
Goblet, clear w/gold trim **80-85**
Plate, 7 1/2" d., green....................................... **19**
Plate, 9 1/4" d., clear **20**
Sugar bowl, cov., clear w/gold trim................... **42**
Toothpick holder, clear w/gold trim **30**
Wine, ruby-stained **45-50**

SHRINE
Butter dish, cov. **85**
Celery vase **70**
Compote, open, jelly **20-25**
Goblet **50-55**
Pickle dish **21**
Pitcher, water.. **70**
Salt & pepper shakers w/original tops,
pr.. **75**
Sauce dish **16**
Toothpick holder **90**
Tumbler, 4" h. **35**

SHUTTLE (Hearts of Loch Laven)
Cake stand **145-150**
Goblet **50**
Pitcher, water... **115**
Punch cup **10**
Wine **13**

SKILTON (Early Oregon)
Bowl, 7 3/4" d., 2 1/2" h.................................... **13**
Butter dish, cov., ruby-stained **90**
Compote, open, 8 1/2" d., low stand, clear **24**
Decanter, whiskey.. **29**
Goblet **32**

Skilton Ruby-stained Goblet

Goblet, ruby-stained (ILLUS.) **75**
Pitcher, milk, ruby-stained.............................. **110**
Pitcher, water, tankard, clear **40-45**
Tumbler, ruby-stained....................................... **31**
Wine **34**

SNAIL (Compact)

Snail Banana Stand

Banana stand, 10" d., 7" h. (ILLUS.) **275**
Bowl, berry, 8" d., 4" h..................................... **34**
Bowl, cov., vegetable, 5 1/2 x 8" **125**
Bowl, 9" d., 2" h... **40-50**
Butter dish, cov., clear.................................... **102**
Butter dish, cov., ruby-stained................. **135-145**
Cake stand, 10" d. **120**
Celery vase **42**
Cheese dish, cov. **150**
Compote, cov., 7" d., 8" h., engraved **160**
Compote, cov., 7" d., 11 1/2" h. **155**
Cruet w/original stopper, clear....................... **145**
Goblet **125**
Pitcher, milk, bulbous, applied handle,
large **195-215**
Pitcher, water, tankard.............................. **125-130**
Rose bowl, large **65-75**
Spooner, clear **45**
Spooner, ruby-stained **85**
Sugar bowl, cov., clear, plain **69**

Sugar bowl, cov., ruby-stained 135-145
Syrup jug w/original brass top 145-165
Table set, 4 pcs... 275
Tumbler, clear 55-65
Vase, 12 1/2" h., scalloped rim 80

SPIREA BAND
Bowl, 8" oval, flat, amber 18
Bowl, 8" oval, flat, blue...................................... 36
Celery vase, blue 60
Creamer, amber 28
Creamer, clear 26
Goblet, amber 35-45
Goblet, blue 40-45
Goblet, canary... 40
Platter, 8 1/2 x 10 1/2", blue............................. 26
Platter, 8 1/2" x 10 1/2", canary 28
Relish, blue, 5 1/2 x 8".................................... 15
Relish, amber, 5 1/2 x 9".................................. 17
Sauce dish, amber, flat or footed, each.......... 6-12
Sauce dish, blue, flat or footed, each 12
Spooner, amber 30
Wine, amber 53
Wine, blue 30-35
Wine, clear 15-20

SQUARE LION'S HEAD - See Atlanta Pattern

SUNK HONEYCOMB (Corona)
Cruet w/original stopper, clear........................ 28
Decanter w/original stopper, ruby-stained..... 110
Mug, clear.. 63
Mug, ruby-stained, 3" h. 41
Mug, ruby-stained, souvenir 25
Pitcher, water, bulbous, ruby-stained 145
Punch cup 14
Sauce dish, ruby-stained, engraved, 4" d......... 35
Syrup pitcher w/original top,
    ruby-stained 120-125
Toothpick holder, ruby-stained........................ 75
Wine, clear, engraved 19
Wine, clear, plain... 13
Wine, ruby-stained 45-50

SWAN
Compote, open, 10" d., 7 1/2" h...................... 165

Swan Creamer

Creamer, clear (ILLUS.) 50-60
*Creamer, milk white 34
Goblet, amber 60
Goblet, canary... 90
Goblet, clear... 325
Marmalade jar, cov. 130
Mug, footed, ring handle, opaque blue.............. 45

Pitcher, water... 185-200
Sauce dish, clear, flat or footed, each 21

Swan Spooner

Spooner, clear (ILLUS.) 55

TEARDROP & TASSEL

Teardrop & Tassel Butter Dish

Butter dish, cov., clear (ILLUS.) 135
Compote, cov., 5" d., 7 1/2" h., clear 85
Compote, open, 8 1/2" d., clear 50
Creamer, white opaque................................. 70-75
Creamer & cov. sugar bowl, white
    opaque, pr. 175
Goblet, clear... 175
Pitcher, water, cobalt blue 210
Tumbler, cobalt blue 65-75

TENNESSEE (Jewel & Crescent)
Bowl, master berry, flat, round 20
Bread plate 50
Butter dish, cov. 85
Cake stand, 10 1/2" d., high stand............... 60-70
Celery vase 85
Creamer 60-65
Goblet 195
Mug 90
Pitcher, milk, 1 qt. 95-100
Salt shaker w/original top 95
Sauce dish, flat, round.................................... 15
Spooner 50
Toothpick holder 75
Wine 100-125

TEXAS (Loop with Stippled Panels)

Bowl, 7" d. 15
Bowl, 8" oval 35-45
Butter dish, cov., clear 113
Butter dish, cov., ruby-stained 165
Cake stand, 9 1/2" to 10 3/4" d. 145
Compote, open, jelly 90-95
Compote, cov., 6" d., 11" h. 195
Compote, cov., 7" d., high stand 125
Creamer 51
*Creamer, individual size 30
Cruet w/original stopper, clear 95
Goblet, clear 95-100
Pitcher, water, 8 1/2" h. 225
Pitcher, water, straight-sided w/inverted
    design, 3 pt. 145-150
Plate, 8 3/4" d. 63
Relish, handled, ruby stained, 8 1/2" l. 55
Sauce dish, flat or footed, each 15
Spooner 53
Spooner, ruby-stained 115
Sugar bowl, cov. 85

Texas Toothpick Holder

Toothpick holder, clear (ILLUS.) 25-30
Toothpick holder, clear w/gold 30
Toothpick holder, ruby-stained 175
Tumbler 58
Vase, bud, 8" h. 35
Vase, 9" h. 35
*Wine, clear 80-90
Wine, ruby-stained 120-125

THISTLE, PANELED - See Paneled Thistle Pattern

THOUSAND EYE

Butter dish, cov., amber 100
Butter dish, cov., blue 135
Butter dish, cov., clear 80-85
Cake stand, amber, 8 1/2" to 10" d. 50-55
Cake stand, blue, 8 1/2" to 10" d. 125
Cake stand, clear, 8 1/2" to 10" d. 75
Celery vase, three-knob stem, clear to
    opalescent w/purple tint 110-125
Cologne bottle w/matching stopper 26
*Compote, open, 6" d., low stand, apple
    green 36
Compote, open, 8" d., 6" h., three-knob
    stem, amber 39
Compote, open, 9 1/2" d., low stand,
    amber 31
Creamer, blue 45

Cruet stand w/pr. cruets & stirrup han-
    dle, blue, set 150
Cruet w/original three-knob stopper,
    amber 105
Cruet w/original three-knob stopper,
    apple green 90-95
Cruet w/original three-knob stopper,
    blue 145
Cruet w/original three-knob stopper,
    canary 110-115
Egg cup, amber 65
*Goblet, amber 28
*Goblet, blue 45
Goblet, blue 60
*Goblet, canary 34

Thousand Eye Goblet

*Goblet, clear (ILLUS.) 30
Lamp, kerosene-type, pedestal base, blue,
    12" h. 163
*Mug, amber, 3 1/2" h. 20-25
*Mug, apple green, 3 1/2" h. 25
*Mug, blue, 3 1/2" h. 27
*Mug, clear, 3 1/2" h. 28
Pitcher, water, three-knob stem, amber.... 150-155
Pitcher, 10" h., footed, canary 99
Plate, 6" d., amber 21
Plate, 8" d., amber 30-35
Plate, 10" sq., w/folded corners, blue 40
Plate, 10" sq., w/folded corners, clear 27
Salt dip, amber, cart shape, 3 1/2" 90
Salt shaker w/original top, canary 55
Sauce dish, amber, flat or footed, each 13
Spooner, three-knob stem, clear 30
String holder, apple green 140
Syrup pitcher w/original pewter top,
    footed, apple green 184
Syrup pitcher w/original top, amber 125
Syrup pitcher w/original top, blue 225
*Toothpick holder, blue 50
*Toothpick holder, canary 40
*Toothpick holder, clear 20-25
Tray, water, blue, 12 1/2" d. 95-100
Tray, water, clear, 12 1/2" d. 40-45
Tray, blue, 14" oval 70
*Tumbler, amber 25
*Tumbler, blue 45

Waste bowl, clear 45
Whimsey, model of a four-wheeled cart,
   amber 103

THREE FACE
*Butter dish, cov., plain 190
*Cake stand, 8" to 10 1/2" d..................... 175-250
*Champagne 245
Champagne, hollow stem, 3 1/2" d., 4" h...... 4,600

Three Face Compote

*Compote, cov., 6" d., high stand
   (ILLUS.)... 150-175
Compote, cov., 7" d., high stand..................... 285
Compote, cov., 8" d., high stand..................... 295
Compote, cov., 10" d., high stand.................. 275
Compote, open, 8 1/2" d., high stand 90-100
Compote, open, 9 1/2" d., high stand,
   engraved 375
Compote, open, 9 1/2" d., high stand, plain..... 168
*Cracker jar, cov. 1,475
Creamer 85-90
*Goblet, engraved 100-125
*Goblet, plain 50
*Lamp, kerosene-type, pedestal base,
   8" h. 200-250
Marmalade jar, cov. 325
Pitcher, milk 750
Pitcher, water... 575
*Salt dip, individual 43
*Salt shaker w/original top 65
*Sauce dish, 4" d. 35
*Spooner, engraved.................................. 120-125
*Spooner, plain 70
*Sugar bowl, cov. 125-150
Table set, 4 pcs... 500
*Wine 208
*Wine etched 300

THREE PANEL
Bowl, 7" d., footed, amber............................ 25-30
Bowl, 7" d., footed, clear 20
Bowl, 9" d., footed, canary 45
Bowl, 9" d., footed, clear 23
Bowl, 10" d., amber.. 35
Bowl, 10" d., canary 40

Compote, open, 8 1/2" d., low stand,
   amber 40
Compote, open, 9" d., canary 43
Compote, open, 10" d., low stand, amber.......... 40
Creamer, amber 40
Creamer, blue 40
Creamer, canary 25-35
*Goblet, amber... 40-45
*Goblet, blue 30-35
*Goblet, canary 36
*Goblet, clear 22
Mug, blue, small 40
Sauce dish, footed, canary 15-20
Spooner, amber 30
Spooner, clear 12
Sugar bowl, cov., amber................................. 38
Sugar bowl, cov., canary 55

TONG
Compote, open, 8" d. 125
Sugar bowl, cov. 70
Tumbler 20

TORPEDO (Pygmy)
Bowl, cov., master berry................................. 80
Bowl, 7" d., clear, flat 24
Bowl, 8" d., clear 33
Bowl, 8" d., ruby-stained 75
Butter dish, cov. 110
Compote, open, 8" d., high stand, flared
   rim 110
Creamer, collared base 55
Cup & saucer 60-65
Goblet, clear... 45-55
Lamp, kerosene, hand-type w/finger grip,
   w/burner & chimney 125-150
Marmalade jar, cov. 55
Pickle castor, silver plate cover & tongs.......... 250
Pitcher, milk, 8 1/2" h., clear 85
Pitcher, milk, 8 1/2" h., ruby-stained 120
Salt & pepper shakers w/original tops,
   pr. 90-95
Sauce dish 16
Spooner 35-40
Sugar bowl, cov. 95

Torpedo Syrup Jug

Syrup jug w/original top, clear (ILLUS.).. 100-125
Syrup jug w/original top, ruby-stained 250

Tumbler, clear, plain 35-40
Waste bowl 65-70
Wine, clear 85
Wine, ruby-stained 103

TREE OF LIFE - PORTLAND
Butter dish, cov. 75
Butter pat, amber... 28
Butter pat, blue 25
Butter pat, canary 25-30
Butter pat, clear 13
Celery vase 60
Celery vase, in silver plate holder............. 100-125
Compote, open, 7 3/4" d., signed "P.G.
  Co." 75
Compote, open, 8 1/2" d., 5" h., signed
  "Davis"... 93
Compote, open, 9 1/2" d., Infant Samuel
  stand 195-200
Creamer, amber, in silver plate holder.............. 95
Epergne, Infant Samuel stand, signed
  "Davis," 2 pcs. 390-400
*Goblet 70-90
Goblet, signed "Davis" 100-125
Pitcher, water, amber, applied handle,
  signed "Davis" 225-250
Pitcher, water, clear, applied handle................. 82
Plate, 6 1/2" d., clear 32
Sauce dish, leaf-shaped, amber....................... 12
Sauce dish, leaf-shaped, clear 12
Sugar bowl, cov., clear 69
Sugar bowl, open 19
Tray, ice cream, clear, 14" rectangle................. 36
Vase, 12" h., clear 145
Waste bowl, apple green 95

Tree of Life - Portland Waste Bowl

Waste bowl, blue (ILLUS.)............................ 60-70
Waste bowl, clear 33
*Wine 55

TREE OF LIFE WITH HAND (Tree of Life-Wheeling)
Cake stand, 8 3/4" d. 80
Cake stand, frosted base, 11 1/2" d.......... 115-125
Celery vase 56
Compote, open, 8" d., clear hand & ball
  stem 50-55
Compote, open, 9" d., frosted hand & ball
  stem 83
Compote, open, 10" d., 10" h., frosted
  hand & ball stem 95

Tree of Life with Hand Creamer

Creamer, w/hand & ball handle (ILLUS.)............ 75

TRIPLE TRIANGLE
*Goblet, ruby-stained 50
Mug, clear... 30
Mug, ruby-stained.. 35
Pitcher, water, 8" h., ruby-stained, 1/2 gal. 125
Spoonholder, handled, clear 25
Spoonholder, handled, ruby-stained 33
Sugar bowl, cov., clear 40
Sugar bowl, cov., ruby-stained 50
Tumbler, water, ruby-stained 35
*Wine, clear 40
*Wine, ruby-stained 40

TWO PANEL (Daisy in Panel)
Celery vase, canary 45-50
Creamer, amber 36
Creamer, clear 23

Two Panel Goblet

*Goblet, amber (ILLUS.)...................................... 34
*Goblet, apple green 32
*Goblet, blue 41
*Goblet, canary 42
*Goblet, clear 25
Relish, amber.. 17

Salt dip, individual size, amber 14
Salt dip, individual size, apple green 24
Sauce dish, apple green, flat or footed,
  each 12
Sauce dish, canary, flat or footed, each 15-19
Spooner, amber 36
Spooner, blue 40-45
Spooner, canary 30-35
Sugar bowl, cov., apple green 55
Tray, water, apple green, 10 x 15" oval 65-70
Waste bowl, amber 35
*Wine, apple green 35
*Wine, blue 38

U.S. COIN

Bowl, berry, 6" d., clear coins, plain rim 500
*Bowl, berry, 6" d., frosted coins, plain rim 475
Bowl, berry, 7" d., clear quarters, plain rim 425
Bowl, berry, 8" d., clear half dollars, plain
  rim 450
Bowl, berry, 8" d., frosted half dollars, plain
  rim 400
Bowl, berry, 9" d., clear dollars, plain rim...... 1,100
Bowl, berry, 9" d., frosted dollars, plain rim...... 800
Bowl, berry, 6" d., clear coins, scalloped
  rim 900
Bowl, berry, 6" d., frosted coins, scalloped
  rim 1,175
Bowl, berry, 7" d., clear quarters, scalloped
  rim 900
Bowl, berry, 7" d., frosted quarters, scal-
  loped rim 1,067
Bowl, berry, 8" d., clear half dollars, scal-
  loped rim 900-1,000
Bowl, berry, 8" d., frosted half dollars, scal-
  loped rim 1,000-1,150
Bowl, berry, 9" d., clear dollars, scalloped
  rim 1,350
Bowl, berry, 9" d., frosted dollars, scal-
  loped rim 1,500-1,600
Bowl, cov., 6" d., frosted quarters 650
Bowl, cov., 7" d., frosted quarters 600
Bowl, cov., 8" d., frosted half dollars 600
Bowl, cov., 9" d., frosted dollars.................... 1,500
*Bread tray, frosted dollars & half
  dollars... 350-385
Butter dish, cov., clear dollars & half dol-
  lars 450
Butter dish, cov., frosted dollars & half dol-
  lars 350-450
Cake plate, clear dollars & quarters, 7" d......... 450
Cake plate, frosted dollars & quarters, 7" d...... 400
Cake stand, clear dollars, 10" d. 375-385
Cake stand, frosted dollars, 10" d.................... 425
Celery tray, clear quarters 300
Celery tray, frosted quarters 325
Celery vase, frosted quarters.................... 330-350
Champagne, flared rim, clear half dimes 1,000
Champagne, flared rim, frosted half
  dimes... 900-1,000
Claret, flared rim, clear half dimes 800
Claret, flared rim, frosted half dimes 700
Claret, straight rim, clear half dimes................ 800
Claret, straight rim, frosted half dimes 700
Compote, cov., 6" d., high stand, clear
  dimes & quarters 450
*Compote, cov., 6" d., high stand, frosted
  dimes & quarters 400-450

U.S. Coin Compote

Compote, cov., 7" d., high stand, frosted
  dimes & quarters (ILLUS.).................... 600-700
Compote, cov., 8" d., high stand, clear
  quarters & half dollars 550
Compote, cov., 8" d., high stand, frosted
  quarters & half dollars 550
Compote, cov., 9" d., high stand, clear dol-
  lars 3,000
Compote, cov., 9" d., high stand, frosted
  dollars & quarters 1,500-2,000
Compote, cov., 6" d., low stand, clear
  twenty cent pieces & quarters 650-700
Compote, cov., 6" d., low stand, frosted
  twenty cent pieces & quarters 600-650
Compote, open, 7" d., high stand, flared
  rim, clear dimes & quarters 450
Compote, open, 7" d., high stand, flared
  rim, frosted dimes & quarters 450
Compote, open, 7 1/4" d., high stand,
  straight rim, clear dimes & quarters 450-500
Compote, open, 7 1/4" d., high stand,
  straight rim, frosted dimes & quarters 300
Compote, open, 7 1/4" h., high stand,
  flared & scalloped rim, clear dimes &
  quarters 900
Compote, open, 7 1/4" h., high stand,
  flared & scalloped rim, frosted dimes &
  quarters 800
Compote, open, 8 1/4" d., high stand,
  flared rim, clear dimes & quarters 450-500
Compote, open, 8 1/4" d., high stand,
  flared rim, frosted dimes & quarters 500
Compote, open, 8 1/4" d., high stand, scalloped rim, clear quarters & dimes 1,000
Compote, open, 8 1/4" d., high stand, scalloped rim, frosted quarters &
  dimes... 1,000-1,200
Compote, open, 8 1/4" d., high stand,
  straight rim, clear dimes & quarters 500
Compote, open, 8 1/2" d., high stand,
  straight rim, frosted dimes & quarters 475
Compote, open, 9 1/4" d., high stand, scalloped rim, clear quarters & dimes 1,200
Compote, open, 9 1/4" d., high stand, scalloped rim, frosted quarters & half dollars .. 1,200

Compote, open, 9 1/2" d., high stand, flared rim, clear quarters & half dollars 850

Compote, open, 9 1/2" d., high stand, flared rim, frosted quarters & half dollars.. 900-1,200

Compote, open, 9 3/4" d., high stand, straight rim, clear quarters & half dollars...... 500

Compote, open, 9 3/4" d., high stand, straight rim, frosted quarters & half dollars 500

Compote, open, 10 1/4" d., high stand, scalloped rim, clear quarters & half dollars 1,500

Compote, open, 10 1/4" d., high stand, scalloped rim, frosted quarters & half dollars...................... 1,500-1,800

Compote, open, 10 1/2" d., high stand, flared rim, clear quarters & half dollars 1,000

Compote, open, 10 1/2" d., high stand, flared rim, frosted quarters & half dollars..................................... 1,200-1,500

Compote, open, 10 1/2" d., high stand, straight rim, clear quarters & half dollars...... 700

Compote, open, 10 1/2" d., high stand, straight rim, frosted quarters & half dollars 600

Compote, open, 6" d., low stand, flared & scalloped rim, frosted twenty cent pieces.. 800-900

Compote, open, 6" d., low stand, straight top w/scalloped rim, clear twenty cent pieces... 1,000

Compote, open, 7" d., low stand, flared & scalloped rim, frosted twenty cent pieces..... 900

Compote, open, 7" d., low stand, straight top w/scalloped rim, frosted twenty cent pieces.. 800

***Creamer,** frosted quarters.............................. 800

Cruet w/original stopper, frosted quarters, 5 1/2" h.. 800

Epergne, frosted quarters & dollars 900

Finger bowl, flared rim, clear coins 800

Finger bowl, flared rim, frosted coins 750

Finger bowl, straight rim, clear coins 800

Finger bowl, straight rim, frosted coins 700-750

Goblet, straight top, clear dimes, 6 1/2" h. 300

Goblet, straight top, frosted dimes, 6 1/2" h. 300

Goblet, flared top, clear half dollars, 7" h. 900

Goblet, flared top, frosted half dollars, 7" h. 500-700

Goblet, straight top, clear half dollars, 7" h. 900

Goblet, straight top, frosted half dollars, 7" h. 500

Lamp, kerosene-type, flaring font, frosted half dollars, 11" h.................................. 1,000

Lamp, kerosene-type, flaring font, frosted half dollars, 11 1/2" h............................. 1,000

Lamp, kerosene-type, flaring font, frosted quarters, 8 1/2" h................................ 800-900

Lamp, kerosene-type, flaring font, frosted quarters, 9 1/2" h................................ 900-950

Lamp, kerosene-type, flaring font, frosted quarters, 10" h.................................. 900-950

Lamp, kerosene-type, handled, clear twenty cent pieces, 5" h. 825

Lamp, kerosene-type, handled, clear quarters, 5" h... 800-900

Lamp, kerosene-type, round font, clear quarters, 8" h... 850

Lamp, kerosene-type, round font, frosted quarters, 8" h... 825

Lamp, kerosene-type, round font, frosted quarters, 8 1/2" h....................................... 750

Lamp, kerosene-type, round font, clear half dollars, 9 1/2" h. 850

Lamp, kerosene-type, round font, frosted half dollars, 9 1/2" h.................................. 800

Lamp, kerosene-type, round font, clear half dollars, 10" h. 850

Lamp, kerosene-type, round font, frosted half dollars, 10" h....................................... 800

Lamp, kerosene-type, round font, frosted half dollars, 10 1/2" h.................................. 850

Lamp, kerosene-type, round font, clear dollars, 11 1/2" h. 900

Lamp, kerosene-type, round font, frosted dollars, 11 1/2" h. 750-850

Lamp, kerosene-type, round font, frosted half dollars, 11 1/2" h.................................. 875

Lamp, kerosene-type, square font, clear quarters & half dollars, 8 1/2" h. 850

Lamp, kerosene-type, square font, frosted quarters & half dollars, 8 1/2" h. 800-900

Lamp, kerosene-type, square font, clear quarters & dollars, 9 1/2" h........................... 850

Lamp, kerosene-type, square font, frosted quarters & dollars, 9 1/2" h................... 800-850

Lamp, kerosene-type, square font, frosted half dollars & dollars, 10 1/4" h.................... 825

Lamp, kerosene-type, square font, frosted half dollars & dollars, 11" h.......................... 900

Lamp, kerosene-type, square font, clear dollars, 11 1/2" h. 925

Lamp, kerosene-type, square font, frosted half dollars & dollars, 11 1/2" h.................... 875

Mug, frosted dollars... 450

Pickle dish, clear half dollars, 3 3/4 x 7 1/2" 250

Pickle dish, frosted half dollars, 3 3/4 x 7 1/2" 250

Pitcher, milk, clear half dollars 800

Pitcher, milk, frosted half dollars 800

Pitcher, water, frosted dollars 700

Preserve dish, frosted half dollars in rim, dollars in base, 5 x 8" 350

Salt & pepper shakers w/original tops, clear coins 375

Salt & pepper shakers w/original tops, frosted coins, pr..................................... 375

Salt shaker w/original top, frosted coins........ 175

Sauce dish, flat, plain rim, clear quarters, 3 3/4" d. 300

Sauce dish, flat, plain rim, frosted quarters, 3 3/4" d. 300

Sauce dish, flat, plain rim, clear quarters, 4 1/4" d. 175

Sauce dish, flat, plain rim, frosted quarters, 4 1/4" d. 200-250

Sauce Dish, flat, scalloped rim, frosted quarters, 4" d.. 350

Sauce dish, flat, scalloped rim, clear quarters, 4 1/2" d. 125

Sauce dish, flat, scalloped rim, frosted quarters, 4 1/2" d.. 475

Sauce dish, footed, plain top, clear quarters 100

Sauce dish, footed, plain top, frosted quarters **125-135**
Sauce dish, footed, scalloped rim, frosted quarters 375
Spooner, clear quarters 225
*Spooner, frosted quarters............................. 250
Sugar bowl, cov., clear quarters & half dollars 350
*Sugar bowl, cov., frosted quarters & half dollars... **400-450**
Syrup jug w/original dated pewter top, clear coins 600
Syrup jug w/original dated pewter top, frosted coins... 630
Toothpick holder, clear dollars 176
Toothpick holder, clear w/ruby-stain, clear dollars.. 2,000
*Toothpick holder, frosted dollars.................. 150
Tumbler, clear dime on side 300
Tumbler, dollar in base, clear sides w/clear 1879 coin.. **100-125**
Tumbler, dollar in base, clear sides w/frosted 1882 coin 200
Tumbler, dollar in base, paneled sides w/clear 1878 coin 150
Water tray, frosted coins................................. 800
Wine, frosted half dimes........................... **700-800**

VICTOR - See Shell & Jewel Pattern

VIKING (Bearded Head or Old Man of the Mountain)
Apothecary jar w/original stopper **120-125**
Bowl, cov., 8" oval... 100
Bowl, 8" sq. 45
Butter dish, cov., clear 115
Celery vase 50-55
Compote, cov., 9" d., low stand 170
Compote, cov., 12" h. 135-145
Compote, open, 8" d., high stand 63
Creamer 65
Mug, applied handle 63
Pickle dish, 7" l. 45
Pitcher, water, 8 3/4" h., clear.................. 110-115
Pitcher, water, 8 3/4" h., clear & frosted ... 240-250
Salt dip, master size 40-45
Sauce dish, footed... 17

Viking Sugar Bowl

Sugar bowl, cov. (ILLUS.) 73

VIRGINIA - See Banded Portland Pattern

WAFFLE AND THUMBPRINT
Celery vase, flint 115
Champagne, flint...................................... 110-150
Claret, flint 110
Compote, open, 6" d., 6" h., flint 150-175
Decanter w/bar lip, flint, pt. 120
Decanter w/bar lip, qt. 95
Egg cup, flint 43
Goblet, flint... 75-80
Lamp, w/original two-tube burner, hand-type w/applied handle, flint, 3" h.................. 135
Salt dip, master size, flint................................... 29

Waffle and Thumbprint Spooner

Spooner, flint (ILLUS.) 79
Sweetmeat dish, cov. 100-125
Tumbler, bar, flint....................................... 95-125
Tumbler, footed, flint 95
Wine, flint.. 70

WASHINGTON CENTENNIAL
Bowl, 8 1/2" oval 21

Washington Centennial Bread Platter

Bread platter, Carpenter's Hall center (ILLUS.)... 100-115
Bread platter, George Washington center, frosted 100-115
Bread platter, Independence Hall center........... 85
Cake stand, 8 1/2" to 11 1/2" d. 55-75

Celery vase 57
Goblet 40-45
Pitcher, milk 350
Pitcher, water... 155-225
Relish, bear paw handles, dated 1876.............. 45
Sauce dish, flat or footed, each 10

WASHINGTON, EARLY

Early Washington Celery Vase

Celery vase, flint (ILLUS.)......................... 165-175
Decanter w/original stopper, flint, qt. 215
Egg cup, flint.. 55-60
Goblet, flint.. 85-100
Salt dip, master size, flat, round, flint............ 35-45

WASHINGTON (State)

Pitcher, milk, ruby-stained 145
Salt dip, individual, 1 7/8" d............................ 35
Toothpick holder, clear w/enamel decora-
tion 40

WESTWARD HO

Bread platter 115
***Butter dish,** cov...................................... 175-200
***Celery vase** 138
Compote, cov., 5" d., high stand.............. 100-110
Compote, cov., 6" d., high stand.................... 325
***Compote,** cov., 6" d., low stand..................... 120
***Compote,** cov., 4 x 6 3/4" oval, low stand 150
Compote, cov., 5 x 7 3/4" oval, high
stand 200-225
Compote, cov., 8" d., high stand.................... 295
Compote, cov., 8" d., low stand (ILLUS.
top of next column)...................................... 495
Compote, cov., 5 1/2 x 8" oval, high stand 473
Compote, cov., 8" d., 14" h. 350
Compote, cov., 6 1/2 x 10" oval,
low stand 225-250
Compote, open, 5" d. 150
Compote, open, 7" d., high stand 135-145
Compote, open, 7" d., low stand..................... 175
Compote, open, 8" d. 125
Compote, open, 9" oval, high stand................ 100
***Creamer** 175
***Goblet** 80-85
Marmalade jar, cov. 258
Mug, child's, clear, 2 1/2" h. 225
Pickle dish, oval 65
Pitcher, milk, 8" h. 598

Pitcher, water... 375-425
Platter, 9 x 13".. 175
Relish, deer handles 100

Westward Ho Compote

Sauce dish, footed... 43
Spooner 160
***Sugar bowl,** cov. 125-150
Sugar bowl, open 55
Wines, set of 6 350

WHEAT & BARLEY

Bread plate, clear 30-35
Cake stand, amber, 8" to 10" d. 44
Compote, cov., 8 1/2" d., high stand................ 48
Compote, open, jelly, amber........................ 25-35
Compote, open, jelly, blue 35

Wheat & Barley Creamer

Creamer, clear (ILLUS.) 30
***Goblet,** amber... 60
***Goblet,** blue 65
***Goblet,** clear 40-45
Mug, amber 55
Mug, clear... 22
Pitcher, milk, amber 55-60
Pitcher, milk, clear 40
Pitcher, water, amber..................................... 90
Pitcher, water, blue 83

Plate, 9" d., amber, closed handles **40-45**
Sauce dish, flat, handled, amber **12**
Sauce dish, footed, amber **12**
Spooner, amber **35-45**
Spooner, clear **28**
Sugar bowl, cov., clear **35-40**
Tumbler, amber **30**
Tumbler canary **28**

WILDFLOWER

Basket, cake, oblong w/metal handle **130**
Bowl, 5 3/4" sq., canary **33**
Bowl, 5 3/4" sq., clear **20**
Bowl, 6 1/2" sq., amber **30**
Butter dish, cov., apple green, footed **95**
Butter dish, cov., canary, collared base **75**
Celery vase, canary **80**
Celery vase, clear **31**
***Champagne,** amber **55-65**
Compote, cov., 7" d., canary **80**
Compote, cov., 8" d., blue, high stand **125**
Compote, open, 7" d., low stand, blue **39**
***Creamer,** amber.. **30**

Wildflower Creamer

***Creamer,** clear (ILLUS.) **35-45**
***Goblet,** apple green **30-40**
***Goblet,** blue **30**
***Goblet,** canary **40**
Pitcher, water, amber.. **55**
Pitcher, water, apple green **135**
Pitcher, water, clear **38**
Plate, 10" sq., amber **40**
Plate, 10" sq., apple green **33**
Plate, 10" sq., canary **27**
Relish, apple green **22**
***Salt dip,** turtle-shaped, apple green **128**
Salt & pepper shakers w/original tops,
   blue, pr. **80-90**
Salt & pepper shakers w/original tops,
   canary, pr. **130**
***Salt shaker w/orginal top,** amber.................... **35**
***Salt shaker w/orginal top,** apple green **45-55**
***Sauce dish,** blue, flat or footed, each.............. **15**
Spooner, canary **40**
***Sugar bowl,** cov., blue.................................... **50**
Syrup pitcher w/original top, canary **265-275**
Tumbler, amber **31**
Tumbler, apple green... **45**
Tumbler, blue... **40**

WILLOW OAK

Bowl, cov., 7" d., flat.. **49**
Bowl, open, 7" d., clear **32**
Bread plate, amber, 9" d................................... **40**
Bread plate, clear, 9" d. **35**
Bread plate, amber, 11" d.................................. **40**
Butter dish, cov., clear...................................... **50**
Cake stand, amber, 8" to 10" d. **70**
Compote, cov., 6" h. **95**
Compote, open, 7" d., high stand, clear.............. **26**
Compote, open, 8" d., low stand, amber....... **50-55**
Creamer, amber **27**
Creamer, clear **40**
Goblet, amber **40-45**
Goblet, blue... **65**
Goblet, clear... **30**
Pitcher, milk, amber... **85**
Pitcher, milk, clear **30-40**

Willow Oak Pitcher

Pitcher, water, amber (ILLUS.) **65-75**
Plate, 9" d. handled, amber **41**
Plate, 9" d. handled, blue **45**
Plate, 9" d. handled, clear **25-30**
Sauce dish, clear, flat or footed, each **15**
Spooner, clear **40**
Sugar bowl, cov., clear **75**
Sugar bowl, open **21**
Tray, water, amber, 10 1/2" d. **125**
Tray, water, blue, 10 1/2" d. **55-60**
Tray, water, clear, 10 1/2" d. **35-40**
Tumbler, clear.. **55**
Water set: pitcher, tray & 5 goblets; clear, 7
   pcs.. **285**

WISCONSIN (Beaded Dewdrop)

Bowl, 8" d. **36**
Bowl, 8 1/2" oblong **35**
Butter dish, cov. **79**
Cake stand, 8 1/4" d., 4 3/4" h. **36**
Cake stand, 9 3/4" d. **85**
Celery tray, flat, 5 x 10" **36**
Celery vase **35-40**
Compote, open, 6 1/2" d., 6 1/2" h...................... **45**
Compote, open, 7 1/2" d., 5 1/2" h...................... **50**
Cruet w/original stopper **45**
Cup & saucer **40**

Dish, cov., oval 36
Doughnut stand, 6" d. 45
Goblet 100-125
Marmalade jar, cov. 175
Mug, 3 1/2" h. 50-55
Mustard jar, cov., bulbous 60
Nappy, handled, 4" d. 34
Pitcher, milk 55-60
Plate, 5" sq. 20
Sauce dish 12
Spooner 33
Sugar shaker w/original top 126

Wisconsin Wine

Wine (ILLUS.) 75

X-RAY
Bowl, berry, 8" d., beaded edge, clear 85
Bowl, berry, 8" d., beaded edge, emerald
   green 65
Butter dish, cov., amethyst w/gold 250
Butter dish, cov., emerald green w/gold 95
Celery vase, clear w/gold 89
Celery vase, emerald green w/gold 95
Compote, cov., high stand, clear 55
Creamer, breakfast size, emerald green
   w/gold 60
Cruet w/original stopper, emerald green
   w/gold 175

X-Ray Pitcher

Pitcher, water, 9 1/2" h., clear, w/gold, 1/2
   gal. (ILLUS.) 50
Pitcher, water, 9 1/2" h., emerald
   green, 1/2 gal. 140
Salt & pepper shakers, emerald green
   w/gold, pr. 225
Sauce dish, emerald green, 4 1/2" d. 25
Spooner, emerald green w/gold 45
Sugar bowl, cov., amethyst w/gold 150
Sugar bowl, cov., emerald green w/gold 50-60
Sugar bowl, cov., emerald green w/gold,
   breakfast size 60
Table set, emerald green, 4 pcs. 240-250
Toothpick holder, clear 30
Toothpick holder, emerald green 50-55

PHOENIX

This ware was made by the Phoenix Glass Co. of Beaver County, Pennsylvania, which produced various types of glass from the 1880s. One special type that attracts collectors now is a molded ware with a vague resemblance to cameo in its "sculptured" decoration. Similar pieces with relief-molded designs were produced by the Consolidated Lamp & Glass Co. (which see) and care must be taken to differentiate between the two companies' wares. Some Consolidated molds were moved to the Phoenix plant in the mid 1930s but later returned and used again at Consolidated. These pieces we will list under "Consolidated."

Cake tray, Jewel & Dewdrop patt., blue on
   white ground, 11 1/2" d. $145
Candlesticks, milk glass, Early American
   line, Sawtooth patt., 6 3/4" h., pr. 38
Cigarette box, cov., Phlox patt., floral
   design on front, back & cover w/raised
   bands on sides, white on blue ground,
   4 1/2" 125
Cigarette box, cov., Phlox patt., floral
   design on front, back & cover w/raised
   bands on sides, white on brown ground,
   4 1/2" 140
Vase, 4 3/4" h., globular w/flaring rim,
   Jewel patt., white design on pearlized
   burgundy ground 75
Vase, 4 3/4" h., globular w/flaring rim,
   Jewel patt., white design on pearlized
   powder blue ground 80
Vase, 6" h., wide ovoid body w/slightly flar-
   ing rim, Figured patt., stylized florals,
   satin finish over milk glass, labeled 90
Vase, 7" h., baluster-form, Fern patt., white
   leaves on brown ground 100
Vase, 7" h., bulbous base w/trumpet-form
   sides, Bluebell patt., pearlized burgundy
   finish 95
Vase, 7" h., bulbous base w/trumpet-form
   sides, Bluebell patt., white on brown
   ground 110
Vase, 7" h., Starflower patt., spherical
   w/raised bands alternating w/panels of
   sculptured flowers, white on blue ground 140
Vase, 7" h., Starflower patt., spherical
   w/raised bands alternating w/panels of
   sculptured flowers, white on brown
   ground 140

Cosmos Vase in White on Brown

Vase, 7 1/2" h., rounded rectangular form, Cosmos patt., white blossoms & foliage centered by raised bands, brown ground (ILLUS.)...................... 125

Vase, 7 1/2" h., rounded rectangular form, Cosmos patt., white blossoms & foliage centered by raised bands, blue ground........ 150

Vase, 8 1/4" h., fan-shaped, Freesia patt., white blossoms & leaves on brown ground.......................... 125

Vase, 9 1/2" h., 11 1/2" w., pillow-shaped, Wild Geese patt., white birds on brown ground........................ 220

Vase, 9 1/2" h., 11 1/2" w., pillow-shaped, Wild Geese patt., white birds on blue ground, original paper label.......................... 230

Vase, 9 1/2" h., 11 1/2" w., pillow-shaped, Wild Geese patt., white birds on tan ground w/pearlized finish 259

Vase, 10" h., Madonna patt., relief-molded bust on brown ground 220

Vase, 10" h., Madonna patt., relief-molded pearlized bust on burgundy ground............. 177

Vase, 10 1/2" h., baluster-form, Wild Rose patt., white florals & stems on brown ground........................ 125

Vase, 10 1/2" h., baluster-form, Wild Rose patt., white florals & stems on slate blue ground........................ 489

Vase, 11 1/2" h., bulbous base tapering to wide cylindrical neck, Philodendron patt., white leaves on blue ground 160

Vase, 11 1/2" h., bulbous base tapering to wide cylindrical neck, Philodendron patt., white leaves on brown ground 160

Vase, 18" h., tall ovoid body, Thistle patt., pearlized powder blue ground...................... 520

PILLAR-MOLDED

This heavily ribbed glassware was produced by blowing glass into full-sized ribbed molds and then finishing it by hand. The technique evolved from earlier "pattern moulding" used on glass since ancient times but in pillar-molded glass the ribs are very heavy and prominent. Most examples found in this country were produced in the Pittsburgh, Pennsylvania area from around 1850 to 1870, but similar English-made wares made before and after this period are also available. Most American items were made from clear flint glass and colored exam-

ples or pieces with colored strands in the ribs are rare and highly prized. Some collectors refer to this as "steamboat" glass believing that it was made to be used on American riverboats, but most likely it was used anywhere that a sturdy, relatively inexpensive glassware was needed, such as taverns and hotels.

Bar bottle, eight-rib, tapering conical form w/a double applied collar below the small cylindrical neck fitted w/a pewter jigger cap, clear, 10" h. (small lip chips)..... **$220**

Rare Pillar-Molded Candlestick

Candlestick, eight-rib, bulbous tapering ribbed stem topped by a thick applied wafer & a ringed & tooled tall cylindrical socket w/flattened rim, on a short applied stem & wide disk foot, rough pontil, clear, 10 1/8" h. (ILLUS.) **2,200**

Pillar-Molded Swirled Celery Vase

Celery vase, eight-rib, tall inverted bell-form bowl w/ribs swirled to the right in the upper half, on an applied knop stem & heavy disc foot, probably Pittsburgh, 9" h. (ILLUS.)... 385

Celery vase, eight-rib, tall tulip-form bowl w/a widely flaring flat rim, knobbed pedestal on a thick applied disk foot, clear, ca. 1860, 9 7/8" h. 187

Celery vase, eight-rib, tall waisted tulip-shaped bowl w/ferns, grapes & leaves engraved between ribs, applied knob stem & disk foot, clear, probably Pittsburgh, 10 3/4" h.. **209**

Celery vase, eight-rib, very tall waisted tulip-form bowl w/scalloped rim, on an applied knop stem & round foot, ground pontil, clear, 10 7/8" h................................. **193**

Compote, 3 7/8" h., eight-rib, a deep rounded bowl w/folded rim & very heavy ribs on a short wafer stem & thin disk foot, cobalt blue, 19th c. **1,265**

Compote, 4 3/8" h., eight-rib, wide squatty bulbous bowl w/heavy ribs & widely flared rim w/a band of cut punties, on a short applied stem & foot, ground pontil, emerald green, attributed to Pittsburgh, mid-19th c. **1,100**

Creamer, eight-rib, bulbous body tapering to a wide arched spout, applied strap handle, bottom ground flat, 5 5/8" h. (minor wear) **275**

Creamer & open sugar bowl, eight-rib, each w/squatty thick heavy ribs forming the body, the creamer w/a high plain neck w/wide spout, applied handle w/curled end, raised on three-wafer pedestal & applied foot w/polished pontil, matching sugar w/wide plain upper sides w/folded rim, matching stem & foot, clear, 19th c., each 4" h., pr. **2,750**

Cruet w/original hollow blown stopper, eight-rib, bulbous ovoid body tapering to a tall slender neck w/arched spout, applied long strap handle w/end curl, rough pontil, clear, Pittsburgh, 9 1/2" h. **275**

Decanter w/bar lip, miniature, eight-rib, tapering conical sides below triple applied rings at the base of the tall neck w/bar lip, polished pontil, clear, 6" h. **330**

Decanter w/pewter jigger top, eight-rib, tapering conical form w/applied rim & hollow strap handle w/curled end, clear, Pittsburgh, 9 1/4" h...................................... **303**

Pillar-Molded Syrup Pitcher

Syrup pitcher w/hinged metal lid, eight-rib, sharply tapering conical form w/ringed neck fitted w/a pewter collar w/arched spout & hinged lid w/scroll finial, applied long strap handle w/end curl, clear, wear & residue under base, 11" h. (ILLUS. bottom of previous column)............ **495**

RUBY-STAINED

This name derives from the color of the glass, a deep red. The red staining was thinly painted on clear pressed glass patterns and refired at a low temperature. Many pieces were further engraved as souvenir items and were very popular from the 1890s into the 1920s. This technique should not be confused with "flashed" glass where a clear glass piece is actually dipped in molten glass of a contrasting color. Also see PATTERN GLASS.

Creamer, individual, Truncated Cube patt........ **$40**
Creamer, Prize patt. **110**
Creamer & sugar bowl, Flower & Pleat patt., pr. **138**

Heavy Gothic Ruby-stained Goblet

Goblet, Heavy Gothic patt. (ILLUS.)................... **85**
Relish dish, Box-in-Box patt. **30**

McKee's Majestic Pattern Rose Bowl

Rose bowl, Majestic patt., McKee (ILLUS.) **70**
Spooner, Prize patt. **95**
Syrup pitcher w/original top, Hexagon Block patt. **150**

SANDWICH

Numerous types of glass were produced at The Boston & Sandwich Glass Works in Sandwich, Massachusetts, on Cape Cod, from 1826 to 1888. Those listed here represent a sampling. Also see PATTERN GLASS and LACY.

All pieces are pressed glass unless otherwise noted. Numbers after salt dips refer to listings in Pressed Glass Salt Dishes of the Lacy Period, 1825-1850, by Logan W. and Dorothy B. Neal.

Candlestick, Acanthus Leaf patt., paneled waisted stem & matching flared socket on a domed paneled base, all w/leaf designs, medium translucent opaque blue, 9 1/2" h. (minor imperfections) **$3,300**

Candlestick, figural dolphin stem w/petal socket, on a stepped square base, canary, 9 3/4" h. (small chip on one petal, some light mold roughness) **660**

Candlesticks, flaring hexagonal base below the ringed stem supporting a heavy paneled tulip-form socket, deep golden amber, 7" h., pr. (one w/mold roughness & tiny base corner chip, other w/two large chips) **605**

Christmas salt & pepper shakers, barrel-shaped w/patented metal lid w/pointed finial, amethyst, 2 5/8" h., pr. **303**

Amber Christmas Salt & Peppers

Christmas salt & pepper shakers, barrel-shaped w/patented metal lid w/pointed finial, golden amber, 2 5/8" h., pr. (ILLUS.)... **154**

Christmas salt & pepper shakers, barrel-shaped w/patented metal lid w/pointed finial, rare emerald green, 2 5/8" h., pr. **1,320**

Compote, cov., Loop patt., pagoda-form cover w/knob finial, paneled base joined to flaring bowl w/a wafer, round foot, clear, 9 1/2" h. (some mold roughness) **275**

Lamp, kerosene table model, cut-overlay, inverted pear-shaped font in light emerald green cut to clear w/stars, quatrefoil, elongated ovals, punties & pointed ovals, fitted w/a brass collar & reeded standard on a square stepped marble base, mid-19th c., 12 3/4" h. (minor imperfections)... **1,150**

Lamp, kerosene table model, cut-overlay, the inverted pear-shaped cobalt blue to clear 'Washington cut' design font fitted w/a brass collar & connector on an opalescent white columnar standard & square base w/gilt trim, mid-19th c., 13 3/4" h. (mold imperfections, gilt wear)..... **748**

Fine Sandwich Cut-Overlay Lamp

Lamp, kerosene table model, cut-overlay, the inverted pear-shaped font in cranberry cut to white cut to clear w/bands of stars, quatrefoils & elongated oval, punties & pointed ovals, fitted w/a brass collar, reeded brass stem on a square stepped marble base w/brass trim, mid-19th c., minor imperfections, 11 1/2" h. (ILLUS.)..................................... **3,738**

Lamps w/hurricane shades, the clam-broth pressed three-dolphin figural base w/hexagonal rim mounted w/a round embossed brass collar holding the tall clear cylindrical shade w/flared rim, 18" h., pr. (one w/interior crack around heads of dolphins, other w/longer crack around two heads & down the base)......... **2,200**

Scent bottle w/original pointed stopper, Elongated Loop patt., lime green, polished pontil, 7" h.. **750**

Scent bottle w/original stopper, Star & Punty patt., canary yellow **550**

Vase, 7 1/4" h., Pressed Leaf patt., tall slender flared leaf-design bowl w/pointed scallops on rim, short paneled stem on flaring scalloped foot, canary.......... **825**

Vase, 9 7/8" h., tulip-form paneled bowl on a flaring octagonal pedestal foot, dark amethyst, mid-19th c. (minute base chips, rim roughness)............................... **1,035**

Vase, 10" h., tulip-form, the tall flaring octagonal bowl w/scrolled rim raised on a flaring octagonal pedestal base, amethyst (minor foot flakes)............................ **1,760**

SENECA

Seneca operated from 1891 until 1983. Starting in Ohio it soon relocated to Morgantown, West Virginia where it gained a world class reputation for high quality lead cut crystal. Seneca glass was exported as early as the late 1890s and would be commissioned by U.S. embassies, presidential palaces and dignitaries. While known for colorless crystal, the period of the 1920s through the 1940s and the 1970s and '80s saw major production in a rainbow of colors. Colored patterns by Seneca were produced in a variety of shapes and forms making it a good collectible.

Seneca "Drfitwood" Advertisement

Bell, classic, cut 1450, 3" h. $65
Bell, moss green, 3" h. 32
Bell, ruby, 4" h. 42
Bell, hanging-type, Christmas 1978 18
Bell, Liberty w/pewter & wood stand,
    etched 1976, signed "Seneca" 85
Bowl, 4 1/2" d., Cascade, cobalt blue 32
Bowl, fruit/sauce, Candlewick etching, ruby
    foot & stem, clear bowl 32
Bowl, fruit/sauce, Driftwood, plum 12
Candlestick, No. 4 clear, cut 853, 10" h. 98
Candlestick, mushroom shape No. 30,
    clear w/cut 900 48
Candlestick, mushroom shape No. 30,
    ruby w/clear foot 120
Candy jar, cov., stemmed cutting 778,
    clear 90
Compote, 7" d., clear line No. 449, cut 597 68
Compote, Driftwood, Apple green 24
Cordial, clear Majestic cut, 5 1/8" h. 58
Cordial, square clear foot, cobalt bowl 64
Creamer & sugar bowl, No. 1934,
    stemmed clear cut, pr 189
Goblet, water, Cascade, ruby w/clear foot,
    6" h. 32
Goblet, water, cut 1445 Heritage, 8 1/2" h. 54
Goblet, water, airtwist stem cut 795 125
Goblet, water, Artichoke, clear w/black foot 28
Goblet, water, Artichoke, Delphine blue 22
Goblet, water, Candlewick etching, depres-
    sion green stem & foot, clear bowl 38
Goblet, water, Candlewick etching, ruby
    foot & stem, clear bowl 45
Goblet, water, Driftwood, Apple green 19
Goblet, water, Driftwood, Avocado green 8
Goblet, water, Driftwood, clear 9
Goblet, water, Driftwood, cobalt blue 24
Goblet, water, Driftwood, ruby 28
Goblet, water, Estes etching, platinum rim
    line 499 65
Goblet, water, No. 903, Naomi platinum
    encrusted band, cobalt bowl, square foot
    line 903 48
Goblet, water, No. 903, square foot,
    opaque green/jade optic bowl 125
Parfait, Driftwood, pink, 5" 18
Pitcher, Driftwood, plum, 32 oz. 48
Pitcher, Cascade, cobalt blue, 40 oz. 74
Pitcher, Driftwood, Apple green, 66 oz. 58
Pitcher, Driftwood, ruby, 66 oz. 89
Plate, 8" d., clear cut 779 48
Plate, 8" d., Sang Blue etch, clear 42
Plate, Driftwood, Apple green 14
Plate, Driftwood, cobalt blue 21
Punch bowl & ladle, clear cut 326, 2 pcs. 480
Roly poly, Driftwood, Avocado green 44
Tree, stackable four-piece box, moss green 58
Tree, stackable four-piece box, ruby
    w/drape optic 120
Tumbler, highball, Driftood, pink, 5" h. 14
Tumbler, iced tea, Driftwood, gray 9
Tumbler, iced tea, Driftwood, yellow 12
Tumbler, juice, flat, Driftwood, cobalt blue 14
Tumbler, footed, Driftwood, Apple green 10
Vase, 1 1/2" h., Driftwood, ruby 32
Vase, 7 1/2" h., Driftwood, amber 18

DOROTHY C. THORPE DESIGNS

Largely a self-taught designer, Dorothy Thorpe (1901-1989) had a successful career that, by 1947, had led her to open her own design firm and sand-carving plant. Her glass often includes deeply incised sand-blasted designs of monumental size. Her signature appears generally sand-carved as a stylized "DTC" monogram.

Bowl, 5" d., 2 1/2" h., clear, oversize sand-
    carved single leaf design, signed
    w/monogram mark $48
Cigarette box, cov., sand-carved w/an
    oversized leaf & branch wrapping
    around, signed w/monogram mark 59
Coffee server, clear, sand-carved floral
    design, Lucite handle, signed w/mono-
    gram mark 95
Goblet, water, trumpet-shaped, wide silver
    band decoration, 7 1/2" h. 35
Tray, round, three-sectioned serving-type
    w/dip bowl, multicolored floral decal,
    Dorothy Thorpe replica signature 38
Vase, tall bulbous form w/flared top & thick
    wafer foot, sand-carved single large
    flower, signed w/monogram mark 129
Vase, 3 1/2" h., 4 1/4" d., inverted cone-
    form, sand-carved oversized violets,
    signed w/monogram mark 59
Vase, 6" h., clear, sand-carved iris design,
    signed w/monogram mark 54
Wine, trumpet-shaped, decorated w/a wide
    silver band 40

TIFFIN

A wide variety of fine glasswares were produced by the Tiffin Glass Company of Tiffin, Ohio. Beginning as a part of the large U.S. Glass Company

early in the 20th century, the Tiffin factory continued making a wide range of wares until its final
closing in 1984. One popular line is now called
"Black Satin" and included various vases with
raised floral designs. Many other acid-etched and
hand-cut patterns were also produced over the
years and are very collectible today. The three "Tiffin Glassmasters" books by Fred Bickenheuser, are
the standard references for Tiffin collectors.

Tiffin Glass Label

Basket, favor-type, No. 310, blue satin **$40**
Basket, favor-type, No. 310, canary 32
Basket, favor-type, No. 310, emerald green 25
Basket, favor-type, No. 310, rose pink 30
Basket, Black Satin, No. 9574, 6" h. 85
Basket, flower, cut Empress patt., No.
6553, green, 13" h. 400
Candlesticks, double, etched Fuchsia
patt., ball center, clear, pr. 150
Candlesticks, double, etched June Night
patt., No. 17392, clear, pr. 80
Candlesticks, etched Cadena patt., No.
5831, yellow, pr. 115
Candlesticks, model of a cat, Black Satin,
No. 69, pr. 275

Cherokee Rose Etched Candlestick

Candlesticks, two-light, etched Cherokee
Rose patt., No. 5902, clear, pr. (ILLUS.
of one) 127
Candy dish, cov., pedestal foot, Gazebo
etching, blue 145
Champagne, Classic (platinum) patt., clear 25
Champagne, cut Charlton patt., clear 22
Champagne, cut Mystic patt., clear 26
Champagne, etched Cherokee Rose patt.,
No. 15018, clear 27
Champagne, etched Cherokee Rose patt.,
No. 17399 stem, clear, 4 oz. 31
Champagne, etched Cherokee Rose patt.,
No. 17403, clear 20
Champagne, etched Cordelia patt., No.
17328, clear 12
Champagne, etched Empire patt., No.
15018, pink 21

Champagne, etched Flanders patt., clear 15
Champagne, etched Flanders patt., No.
15018, yellow 21
Champagne, etched Flanders patt., yellow 21
Champagne, etched June Night patt., clear 15
Champagne, etched Persian Pheasant
patt., No. 17358, clear 24
Claret, etched Bridal patt., No. 15073,
green 25
Claret, etched Cherokee Rose patt., No.
17399, clear 50
Claret, etched Empire patt., No. 15018,
pink, 4 oz. 45
Claret, etched Flanders patt., yellow 65
Claret, etched June Night patt., clear,
6 1/4" h. 40
Claret, etched Persian Pheasant patt., No.
17358, clear 39
Claret, gold-encrusted Minton patt., clear 20
Cocktail, cut Lausanne patt., clear 17
Cocktail, etched Byzantine patt., No.
15037, clear 20
Cocktail, etched Byzantine patt., No.
15048, yellow 15
Cocktail, etched Cherokee Rose patt., No.
15018, clear 18
Cocktail, etched Cherokee Rose patt., No.
17399, clear, 3 1/2 oz. 18
Cocktail, etched Cherokee Rose patt., No.
17403, clear, 3 1/2 oz. 25
Cocktail, etched Cordelia patt., No. 17328,
clear 12
Cocktail, etched Flanders patt., No. 15024,
pink, 4 3/4" h. 45
Cocktail, etched Flanders patt., No. 15024,
yellow, 4 3/4" h. 31
Cocktail, etched Fuchsia patt., No. 15083,
clear, 4 1/4" h. 19
Cocktail, etched June Night patt., clear,
3 1/2 oz. 16
Cocktail, etched Persian Pheasant patt.,
clear 18
Cocktail, etched Persian Pheasant patt.,
No. 17358, clear, 4 1/2 oz. 39
Cocktail, Wistaria (light pink) 35
Compote, open, 10" d., 5 3/4" h., twisted
stem, interior decorated w/two
colorful h.p. cockatoos, sprays of green
leaves & white enamel dots on Black
Satin ground 125
Compote, stemmed, etched Flanders patt.,
pink 750
Console bowl, 13" d., rolled edge, etched
Flanders patt., pink 272

Byzantine Etched Console Bowl

Console bowl, flared, etched Byzantine
patt., clear, 12 5/8" (ILLUS.) 135
Cordial, Classic (platinum) patt., clear 50
Cordial, cut Mystic patt., clear 25
Cordial, etched Cadena patt., yellow 80

Cordial, etched Cherokee Rose patt., No. 17399, clear **48**

Cordial, etched Cherokee Rose patt., No. 17403, clear, 1 oz.. **55**

Cordial, etched Classic patt., No. 14185, clear **69**

Cordial, etched Flanders patt., pink, 5 1/16" h.. **150**

Cordial, etched Fuchsia patt., clear, 1 oz. **80**

Cordial, etched Fuchsia patt., No. 15083, clear **43**

Cordial, etched June Night patt., clear, 5 1/4" h.. **48**

Cordial, etched Persian Pheasant patt., clear **46**

Cordial, etched Rambling Rose patt., clear **28**

Cordial, etched Rose patt., No. 17474, clear **25**

Cordial, Wistaria (light pink) **65**

Cornucopia, Twilight cutting, clear **125**

Creamer, etched Cherokee Rose patt, No. 17399, clear **22**

Creamer, etched Flanders patt., flat, pink **230**

Creamer & sugar bowl, etched Fuchsia patt., No. 5902, clear, pr.............................. **56**

Creamer & sugar bowl, etched Rosalind patt., No. 5831, mandarin, pr. **110**

Cup & saucer, etched Flanders patt., pink, pr.. **120**

Cup & saucer, etched Flanders patt., yellow, pr... **100**

Cup & saucer, etched Flanders patt., clear, pr.. **45**

Decanter w/original stopper, Classic (platinum) patt., clear **525**

Decanter w/original stopper, etched Byzantine patt., No. 185, yellow........................ **600**

Decanter w/original stopper, etched Cadena patt., No. 185, yellow **547**

Decanter w/original stopper, etched Cadena patt., squatty, yellow...................... **373**

Decanter w/original stopper, etched Classic patt., No. 14179, clear, 30 oz................. **375**

Decanter w/original stopper, etched Dolores patt., No. 14179, clear, 1 qt. **133**

Decanter w/original stopper, etched Flanders patt., pink w/tall clear stopper........ **500**

Decanter w/original stopper, etched Flanders patt., round, tall, pink (foot repaired).. **450**

Decanter w/original stopper, etched Flanders patt., squatty, yellow...................... **525**

Decanter w/original stopper, etched Thistle patt., No. 17179, clear............................ **160**

Dinner bell, etched June Night patt., No. 1508, clear, (clapper replaced) **75**

Flower arranger, Twilight cutting, freeform, clear (manufacturing flaw).................... **60**

Goblet, etched Cadena patt., footed, No. 15065, clear, 5 1/4" h. **21**

Goblet, etched Classic patt., No. 14185, clear **33**

Goblet, sherry, etched Cherokee Rose patt. No. 17399, clear.................................... **40**

Goblet, sherry, etched June Night patt., clear **39**

Goblet, water, cut Mystic patt., clear.................. **28**

Cherokee Rose Etched Goblet

Goblet, water, etched Cherokee Rose, No. 17399, clear, 9 oz. (ILLUS.) **32**

Goblet, water, etched Cherokee Rose, No. 17403, clear, 9 oz.. **29**

Goblet, water, etched Cordelia patt., No. 15048, clear **22**

Goblet, water, etched Cordelia patt., No. 17328, clear **18**

Goblet, water, etched Flanders patt., pink **74**

Goblet, water, etched Flanders patt., yellow... **30**

Goblet, water, etched Fuchsia patt., No. 15083, clear, 7 1/2" h. **25**

Goblet, water, etched June Night patt., No. 17392, clear **25**

Goblet, water, etched Rosalind patt., No. 15042, yellow **22**

Goblet, water, etched Thistle patt., clear........... **22**

Goblet, water, gold-encrusted Minton patt., clear **24**

Goblet, water, No. 17578 stem, Wistaria (ILLUS. in color section) **27**

Lamp, figural Santa Claus in brick chimney, ca. 1924-29 .... **2,000**

Paperweight, model of a pheasant, female, head down, No. 6042, blue, 7 1/2" h., 16" l.. **450**

Parfait, cut Mystic patt., clear............................ **27**

Parfait, etched Classic patt., No. 14185, clear **69**

Parfait, etched June Night patt., clear, 6 5/8" h. **60**

Parfait, etched June Night patt., No. 17392, clear, 4 1/2 oz... **28**

Parfait, etched Rosalind patt., No. 15042 , yellow... **32**

Pitcher, Classic (platinum) patt., flat, clear....... **225**

Pitcher, footed, Double Columbine patt., cut No. 405 design, No. 194, clear w/amber trim **170**

Pitcher, footed, etched Cadena patt., No. 194, clear (no lid) **225**

Flanders Etched Covered Pitcher

Pitcher, cov., footed, etched Flanders patt., pink, 64 oz. (ILLUS.) **573**
Pitcher, footed, etched Flanders patt., pink, 64 oz. **495**
Pitcher, footed, etched Rosalind patt., No. 128, mandarin **390**
Pitcher, milk, Twilight cutting, clear.................. **225**
Plate, 6 1/2" d., handled, etched Cordelia patt., No. 5831, yellow.................... **22**
Plate, 6 1/2" d., handled, etched Fuchsia patt., No. 5831, clear...................................... **23**
Plate, 7" d., etched Byzantine patt., yellow **15**
Plate, 7 1/2" d., Alhambra patt., No. 5831, yellow **12**

Cadena Etched Plate

Plate, 7 1/2" d., etched Cadena patt., No. 5831, clear (ILLUS.) **9**
Plate, 8" d., etched Flanders patt., pink **22**
Plate, 8" d., etched June Night patt., clear **11**

Plate, salad, 8" d., etched Cherokee Rose patt., clear **13**
Relish, three-part, etched Cherokee Rose patt., No. 5902, clear, 6 1/2" l........................ **35**
Rose bowl, footed, Twilight cutting, clear **170**
Rose bowl, footed, Wistaria (light pink) **125**
Sherbet, etched Byzantine patt., low, clear........ **12**
Sherbet, etched Cadena patt., clear **23**
Sherbet, etched Cadena patt., low, yellow......... **15**
Sherbet, etched Cordelia patt., clear, 3 3/4" h. **8**
Sherbet, etched Cordelia patt., No. 15048, clear **15**
Sherbet, etched Flanders patt., low, pink.......... **12**
Sherbet, etched Fuchsia patt., No. 15083, clear **16**
Sherbet, pressed King's Crown patt., blue......... **10**
Sherbet, Wistaria patt., Wistaria (light pink) **24**
Torchere lamp, No. 16265, clear satin w/black metal base, bright black glass lid, 13 3/4" h. **390**
Tray, center-handled, etched Flanders patt., clear **300**
Tray, center-handled, etched Flanders patt., pink.. **430**
Tumbler, etched Classic patt., flat, clear, 8 oz. **44**
Tumbler, flat, etched Rambling Rose patt., clear **13**
Tumbler, footed, etched Classic patt., clear, 2 1/2 oz., 2 3/4" h. **40**
Tumbler, footed, etched Cordelia patt., No. 17328, clear, 10 oz...................................... **15**
Tumbler, footed, etched Fuchsia patt., No. 15083, clear, 6 5/16" h., 12 oz. **32**
Tumbler, iced tea, etched Cherokee rose patt., No. 17403, clear................................. **35**
Tumbler, iced tea, etched Flanders patt., pink... **70**
Tumbler, iced tea, etched June Night patt., clear, 6 5/8" h. **34**
Tumbler, juice, footed, etched Byzantine patt., clear **17**
Tumbler, juice, footed, etched Fuchsia patt., No. 15083, clear.................................... **19**
Tumbler, juice, footed, etched June Night patt., No. 17403, clear **26**
Tumbler, juice, Twilight cutting, No. 17524, clear **34**
Tumbler, whiskey, footed, etched Classic patt., No. 14185, clear, 2 oz. **75**
Vase, 5" h., etched Poppy patt., No. 16256, pink... **55**
Vase, bud, 6" h., etched Cherokee Rose patt., No. 14185, clear................................... **38**
Vase, 6 1/2" h., bud, etched Fuchsia patt., clear **30**
Vase, 8" h., No. 17430, Wistaria (light pink) **200**
Vase, bud, 8 1/4" h., etched Fuchsia patt., clear **30**
Vase, 8 1/2" h., Poppy patt., black.................... **95**
Vase, 8 1/2" h., Twilight cutting, blue................. **65**
Vase, bud, 10 1/2" h., Classic (platinum) patt., clear **65**

Cherokee Rose Etched Bud Vase

Vase, bud, 11" h., etched Cherokee Rose patt., No. 17399, beaded, clear (ILLUS.) 46

Vase, bud, 11" h., etched Fuchsia patt., No. 15082, clear 100

Vase, bud, 11" h., etched Rosalind patt., yellow w/gold rim 78

Wine, etched Cadena patt., yellow 35

Wine, etched Classic (platinum) patt., clear, 4 15/16" h. 32

Wine, etched Flanders patt., clear 29

Wine, etched Flanders patt., yellow 39

Wine, etched Fuchsia patt., No. 15083, clear, 5 1/16" h. 37

Wine, etched Thistle patt., clear 17

Wine, Pink Rain patt., No. 17477, Wistaria (light pink) 30

Wine, Twilight cutting, No. 175247, clear 36

WESTMORELAND

In 1890 Westmoreland opened in Grapeville, Pennsylvania and as early as the 1920s was producing colorwares in great variety. Cutting and decorations were many and are generally under appreciated and undervalued. Westmoreland was a leading producer of milk glass in "the antique style." The company closed in 1984 but some of their molds continued in use by others.

Early Westmoreland Label & Mark

Animal covered dish, Camel, amber satin, Humphrey $48

Animal covered dish, Duck, rimmed base, blue milk glass 45

Animal covered dish, Duck, ruby carnival 65

Animal covered dish, Eagle, two-part, w/added eyes, milk white 85

Animal covered dish, Hen on Nest, looking left, green slag 58

Animal covered dish, Hen on Nest, looking left, milk white, red decoration 38

Animal covered dish, Mother Eagle w/chicks, milk white 85

Animal covered dish, Rabbit, ruby carnival 50

Ashtray, Beaded Grape patt., milk white 10

Ashtray, square, Paneled Grape patt., milk white, large 19

Paneled Grape Banana Bowl

Banana bowl, bell-footed, Paneled Grape patt., No. 47, milk white, 12" (ILLUS.) 125

Basket, No. 752, ruby-stained ribs w/h.p. floral medallion 52

Basket, oval, American Hobnail patt., lilac opalescent, small 32

Basket, Pansy patt., two handles meet from sides, amber 12

Basket, Paneled Grape patt., No. 118, milk white, 8" h. 55

Basket, Paneled Grape patt., footed, scalloped, milk white, 10 1/2" 90

Bell, No. 1902, blue satin w/Mary Gregory decoration 28

Bell, No. 1902, green satin w/h.p. white daisy 18

Bonbon, heart-shaped, handled, Waterford patt., No. 36, clear w/ruby stain, 8" 69

Bowl, cov., 4" sq., Beaded Grape patt., milk white 30

Bowl, cov., 5" sq., footed w/flared rim, Beaded Grape patt., milk white 20

Bowl, 6" d., footed, crimped rim, Paneled Grape patt., milk white 21

Bowl, 6" d., footed, Old Quilt patt., milk white 18

Bowl, 8 1/2" d., lipped rim, Paneled Grape patt., milk white 90

Bowl, 9" d., footed, lipped, Paneled Grape patt., milk white 88

Bowl, 9" d., 6" h., skirted base, Paneled Grape patt., milk white 45

Bowl, 9 1/2" d., 3" h., bell-shaped, Paneled Grape patt., milk white 45

Bowl, 10" d., footed, lipped rim, Paneled
Grape patt., milk white **77**

Bowl, 12" oval, footed, lipped rim, Paneled
Grape, milk white **95**

Bowl, sherbet, Paneled Grape patt., milk
white **16**

Bowl/nut dish, 6 1/2" oval, Paneled Grape
patt., No. 49, milk white **18**

Box, cov., Rabbit on eggs, milk white
w/painted eggs, 7" **55**

Box, cov., Santa in Sleigh, milk white
w/painted decoration **34**

Butter dish, cov., American Hobnail, milk
white **38**

Butter dish, cov., Paneled Grape patt.,
milk white, 1/4 lb. **30**

Cake salver, skirted rim, bell footed, Paneled Grape patt., No. 59, milk white,
11" d. **60**

Cake salver, skirted square, footed,
Beaded Grape patt., milk white, 11" d. **67**

Cake stand, Beaded Grape patt., footed,
milk white, 9 1/2" sq. **70**

Cake stand, Beaded Grape patt., footed,
milk white, 11" sq. **108**

Candelabra, triple branch, skirted, Paneled
Grape patt., No. 90, milk white, pr. **530**

Candle lamp, two-part, milk white
stemmed base, blue satin shade w/Mary
Gregory decoration **55**

Candleholders, Della Robbia patt., clear
w/colored staining, low, pr. **25**

Candlestick, single light, Beaded Grape
patt., milk white, 4" h. **16**

Lotus Single Candlestick

Candlestick, single light, Lotus patt.,
green, 9" h. (ILLUS.) **40**

Candlestick, single light, Spiral wrap
around square base, black, 7" h. **32**

Candlestick, single light, two-handled, Mis-
sion patt., No. 1015, clear, 7" h. **28**

Candlestick, three-light, Lotus patt., green
satin **56**

Candlesticks, Beaded Grape patt., milk
white, 4" sq., pr. **16**

Candlesticks, Old Quilt patt., milk white,
4" h., pr. **18**

Candlesticks, Paneled Grape patt., milk
white, 4", pr. **21**

Candy container, novelty, model of clock,
green **15**

Candy dish, cov., Della Robbia patt., No.
DR-17, pastel stained fruit **32**

Candy dish, cov., English Hobnail patt.,
green **38**

Candy dish, cov., Thousand Eye patt.,
clear **69**

Candy dish, cov., three-footed, Paneled
Grape patt., No. 103, milk white **20**

Candy dish, footed, crimped rim, Water-
ford patt., No. 31, clear w/ruby stain **39**

Candy dish, cov., square, Old Quilt patt.,
milk white, 6 1/2" h. **27**

Candy jar, cov., footed, Paneled Grape
patt., No. 26, milk white, 6 1/2" h. **26**

Candy jar w/domed cover, footed, Della
Robbia patt., No. 17, milk white, 1/2 lb.,
7" h. **42**

Celery vase, Paneled Grape patt., milk
white **35**

Celery vase, footed, Paneled Grape patt.,
milk white, 6" h. **39**

Celery vase, footed, pinched rim, Beaded
Grape patt., milk white, 6 1/2" h. **16**

Champagne, Princess Feather patt., pink **18**

Champagne, Thousand Eye patt., clear **35**

Cheese dish w/domed cover, Old Quilt
patt., milk white, 4 1/2" h. **45**

Chocolate box, cov., round, Paneled
Grape patt., milk white, 6 1/2" d. **50**

Cigarette box, cov., Beaded Grape patt.,
milk white, 4 x 6" **25**

Cocktail, round footed, English Hobnail
patt., clear, 3 oz. **8**

Cocktail, square footed, English Hobnail
patt., clear, 3 oz. **8**

Compote, cov., 5" h., square, low footed,
Old Quilt patt., milk white **22**

Compote, cov., 7" h., footed, Paneled
Grape patt., milk white **33**

Compote, open, 4 1/2" d., 6" h., ruffled rim,
Paneled Grape patt., milk white w/pansy
decoration No. 34 .... **30**

Compote, open, 9" sq., footed, Paneled
Grape patt., milk white **40**

Compote, open, 6" d., Della Robbia patt.,
clear w/colored staining **25**

Compote, open, footed, crimped & ruffled,
Waterford patt., No. 32, clear w/ruby
stain **119**

Console set: bowl & pr. of candlesticks;
Thousand Eye patt., clear, 3 pcs. **145**

Cordial, footed, Waterford patt., No. 5,
clear w/ruby stain, 1 oz. **49**

Cordial, English Hobnail, square base,
clear, 3 3/4" h. **12**

Creamer, Paneled Grape patt., milk white,
6 1/2 oz. **13**

Creamer & cov. sugar bowl, Paneled
Grape patt., milk white, pr. **45**

Creamer & open sugar bowl, Della Rob-
bia patt., clear w/colored staining, pr. **25**

Creamer & open sugar bowl, individual,
Paneled Grape patt., milk white, pr. **25**

Creamer & open sugar bowl, Maple Leaf
(Bramble) patt., milk white, pr. **28**

Creamer & sugar bowl, American Hobnail
patt., milk white, pr. **26**

Creamer & sugar bowl, Thousand Eye patt., clear, pr. 110
Cruets, English Hobnail patt., milk white, 6 1/2" h., set of 2 30
Cruets w/original stopper, Paneled Grape patt., milk white, pr. 38
Cup, Paneled Grape patt., milk white 8
Cup & saucer American Hobnail patt., milk white 18
Cup & saucer Beaded Edge patt., milk white 12
Cup & saucer, English Hobnail patt., milk white 16
Cups & saucers, English Hobnail patt., milk white, 8 sets 65
Decanter w/stopper, American Hobnail, milk white 42
Egg cup, American Hobnail, clear, 4 1/2" h. 42
Fairy lamp, two-part, Thousand Eye patt., Brandywine blue 28
Flowerpot, Paneled Grape patt., milk white, 4 1/4" h. 30
Fruit cocktail w/underplate, Paneled Grape patt., milk white, 3 1/2", 2 pcs 18
Goblet, American Hobnail patt., clear, 6" h. 16
Goblet, American Hobnail patt., milk milk, 6" h. 9
Goblet, Beaded Grape patt., round, footed, clear, 8 oz. 24
Goblet, Della Robbia patt., stained dark colors, 6" h. 48

English Hobnail Goblet

Goblet, English Hobnail patt., round base, clear, 6" h. (ILLUS.) 12
Goblet, English Hobnail patt., square base, clear, 6" h. 9
Goblet, Paneled Grape patt., clear, 6" h. 19
Goblet, Paneled Grape patt., ruby, 6" h. 29
Goblet, water, footed, Beaded Grape patt., milk white, 9 oz. 11
Goblet, water, Paneled Grape patt., No. 14, milk white, 8 oz. 14
Goblet, wine, Della Robbia patt., milk white, 4 3/4" h. 16
Goblet, wine, Della Robbia patt., stained dark colors, 4 3/4" h. 52
Goblet, wine, Paneled Grape patt., clear, 4" h. 18

Goblet, wine, Paneled Grape patt., milk white 20
Goblet, wine, Paneled Grape patt., ruby, 4" h. 29
Goblets, stemmed, Paneled Grape patt., milk white, set of 8 80
Gravy boat & liner, Paneled Grape patt., milk white 40
Ivy ball vase, footed, cupped rim, Paneled Grape patt., milk white 38
Jardiniere, Paneled Grape patt., milk white, 5" h. 18
Jardiniere, Paneled Grape patt., milk white, 6 1/2" h. 20
Marmalade dish w/ladle, cov., English Hobnail patt., milk white, 5 1/2", 2 pcs. 25
Mayonnaise dish, underplate & ladle, Paneled Grape patt., milk white, 3 pcs. 28
Mint compote, flat, footed, Waterford patt., No. 19, clear w/ruby stain, 5 1/2" d. 59
Mint compote, footed, crimped rim, Waterford patt., No. 34, clear w/ruby stain 49
Model of butterfly, No. 2, green satin, small 18
Model of owl, on two stacked books, cobalt carnival, 3 1/2" h. 26
Model of owl w/glass eyes, dark blue, 5 1/2" h. 35
Model of Pouter Pigeon, apricot mist, 2 1/2" h. 35
Model of Pouter Pigeon, clear, 2 1/2" h. 25
Model of sleigh, milk white w/holly decoration, No. 1872 30
Model of slipper, grandma's, blue satin w/white decoration 18
Nappy, round, Paneled Grape patt., milk white, 4 1/2" d. 9
Nappy, round, handled, Paneled Grape patt., milk white, 5" d. 14
Novelty, model of a straw hat, milk white w/decoration, 4 1/2" 38
Novelty, model of a top hat, English Hobnail patt., milk white, 3" h. 10
Pickle dish, Paneled Grape patt., oval, milk white, 8" l. 13
Pitcher, 7 1/4" h., American Hobnail, milk white 68
Pitcher, 8 1/2" h., Old Quilt patt., ruby carnival 89

Rocker Pattern Covered Pitcher

Pitcher, cov., Rocker patt., No. 101, clear
(ILLUS.).. 80
Pitcher, milk, Paneled Grape patt., milk
white, small 18
Pitcher, No. 31, Paneled Grape patt., milk
white, 1 pt.. 36
Pitcher, water, 8 1/2" h., Old Quilt patt.,
milk white 38
Planter, Paneled Grape patt., milk white,
6 x 9".. 35
Plate, 10 1/2" d., English Hobnail patt.,
green... 28
Plate, 7" d., Beaded Edge patt., milk white 7
Plate, 7" d., Beaded Edge patt., No. 64-2
fruit decoration 11
Plate, 8 1/2" d., round, English Hobnail
patt., milk white 10
Plate, 8" d., English Hobnail patt., green............ 12
Plate, dinner, 10 1/2" d., Beaded Grape
patt., milk white 22
Plate, lattice border, black w/white enamel
Mary Gregory decoration 38
Plate, Three Kittens, milk white 45
Plate, Three Owls, milk white 48
Plate, 8" d., Princess Feather patt., pink 12
Punch bowl & base, bell-shaped, Princess
Feather patt., clear..................................... 280
Punch bowl & base, bell-shaped, Princess
Feather patt., purple carnival 450
Punch bowl, base & underplate, Colonial
Paneled patt., black.................................... 340
Punch cup, Paneled Grape patt., milk
white, 2 1/2" h. 19
Punch set: 11" d. bowl, base, ladle & 24
cups; Paneled Grape patt., milk white,
the set 550
Relish dish, three-part, Beaded Grape
patt., milk white, 9 1/2" d. 58
Salt & pepper shakers, footed, Princess
Feather patt., clear, pr.................................. 28
Salt & pepper shakers, footed, Paneled
Grape patt., milk white, 4 1/4" h., pr.............. 25
Salt & pepper shakers w/original tops,
Beaded Grape patt., milk white, pr................ 15
Sherbet, American Hobnail patt., white,
3 3/4".. 14
Sherbet, Princess Feather patt., pink
opaque 15
Snack tray, Thousand Eye patt., clear, 2
pcs... 59
Sugar bowl, cov., lacy edge, footed, Pan-
eled Grape patt., No. 45, milk white 27
Sugar bowl/spooner, cov., Paneled Grape
patt., milk white 43
Tidbit, two-tier, center-handled, Paneled
Grape patt., milk white 55
Tumbler, bell-rimmed, Paneled Grape
patt., milk white, 6" h. 16
Tumbler, footed, Beaded Edge patt., milk
white... 16
Tumbler, iced tea, Della Robbia patt.,
stained dark colors, 6" h............................... 24
Tumbler, iced tea, English Hobnail patt.,
clear, set of 3.. 25
Tumbler, iced tea, English Hobnail patt.,
round base, clear, 6" h. 14
Tumbler, iced tea, Old Quilt patt., milk
white, 5 1/4" h., 11 oz.................................. 16

Tumbler, juice, Paneled Grape, clear,
4 3/4" h.. 24
Tumbler, water, footed, Old Quilt patt., milk
white, 8 oz. 10
Vase, bud, American Hobnail, lilac opales-
cent 28
Vase, miniature, jack-in-the-pulpit shape,
pink satin w/white "snow flower" decora-
tion 22
Vase, 9" h., fan-type, octagonal-shaped
foot, Beaded Grape patt., milk white 12

Paneled Grape Milk Glass Vase

Vase, 11 1/2" h., bell-rimmed, footed, Paneled Grape patt., milk white (ILLUS.) 45
Vase, 14" h., Paneled Grape patt., milk
white... 55
Vase, 15" h., Paneled Grape patt., milk
white... 26

WESTON GLASS

Weston, West Virginia is a major center of mouth-blown, handmade glass. An interconnected number of companies produced glass here from the 1920s until the 1980s. Over the years they had overlapping ownership, shared orders and co-mingled molds and shapes. Color production peaked in the 1930s with very limited use of color after the summer of 1940. Colors included ruby, Ritz or cobalt blue, topaz, rose pink, green, black amethyst and crystal. Decorating shops were part of the operations. Companies included Weston Glass, West Virginia Glass Specialty, Louie Glass and others. Products are often indistinguishable. Glass continues to be made in Weston.

Candlesticks, footed, ruby w/platinum lat-
tice decoration, pr....................................... $80
Cocktail, hourglass-shaped, light blue
Frost Nip decoration w/platinum,
2 3/8" h.. 22
Cocktail, hourglass-shaped, royal-cobalt
blue, 2 3/8" h. 8
Cocktail, No. 742 barbell-form, cobalt blue
w/platinum bands 220

Cocktail, No. 742 barbell-form, green Frost Nip decoration w/platinum on clear **85**

Cocktail shaker, cov., lady's leg form w/stainless metal high-heel holder, cobalt blue **1,200**

Lady's Leg Cocktail Shaker

Cocktail shaker, cov., lady's leg form w/stainless metal high-heel holder, ruby (ILLUS.) **1,600**

Cocktail shaker, cov., Long Feller No. 741, bands of blue Frost Dip decoration **120**

Cocktail shaker, cov., Long Feller No. 741, ruby w/platium lattice decoration **180**

Compote, open, No. 1100, ruby bowl w/platinum lattice decoration, clear foot **64**

Dish, cov., figural, model of an apple w/stem finial on the cover, clear, 9" d **46**

Goblet, water, No. 400, green octagonal single bead stem, green foot, pink bowl **22**

Ice bucket, No. 1 paneled, glass ears w/metal bail handle, green **34**

Jam jar, cov., cobalt blue w/platinum trim **56**

Jar jar, cov., Czecko Ringed design, pink **54**

Night set: bottle & cup; No. 2 bell-shaped, rose pink, 2 pcs. **38**

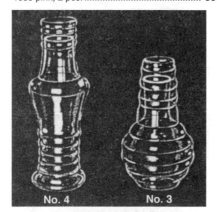

Weston-Louie Night Sets

Night set: bottle & cup; No. 3 ringed design, rose pink, 2 pcs. (ILLUS. right) **58**

Night set: bottle & cup; No. 4 tall corset shape, green, 2 pcs. (ILLUS. left) **48**

Weston Chico Pattern Pitcher

Pitcher, Chico, ovoid ringed body, cobalt blue w/applied clear handle (ILLUS.) **85**

Pitcher, cov., No. 1108, three-ringed base, applied handle, green **78**

Pitcher, green Frost Nip decoration w/black silhouette pixies **89**

Pitcher, Harpo No. 453, three rings, cobalt blue w/applied clear handle **85**

Pitcher, Modernistic Deco style, flat-sided w/applied green handle, 60 oz. **140**

Pitcher, Semper design, cobalt blue w/clear reeded handle **80**

Pitcher w/ice lip, Groucho oval, black amethyst w/clear applied reeded handle **120**

Pitcher w/ice lip, Groucho oval, cobalt blue w/clear applied reeded handle **95**

Salt & pepper shakers, No. 1001, balus-trade shape, pink, pr. **32**

Tumbler, five-ringed, cobalt blue **9**

Tumbler, Modernistic, flat-sided, green, 9 oz. **22**

Tumbler, Modernistic, flat-sided, pink, 12 oz. **26**

Urn, No. 20, cobalt blue, two applied clear handles, 10" h. **78**

Urn, No. 20, ruby w/platinum band, two applied clear handles, 10" h. **110**

Urn, Semper shape, cobalt blue w/two applied clear reeded handles, 10" h. **94**

Urn, three-ringed lower portion, black ame-thyst w/two applied clear reeded handles **85**

Vase, ruby body w/platinum bands, clear foot **78**

Vase, Semper shape, cobalt blue **65**

Vase, 10" h., Modernistic Deco design, flat-sided, pink **85**

Vase, 10" h., No. 20, no handles, black amethyst **42**

Vase, 13" h., No. 23 balustrade shape, black amethyst **42**

WRIGHT (L.G.) GLASS COMPANY

This firm, operating from 1938 until its liquidation in 1999, was a wholesaler of reproductions of Victo-rian-era glass and pressed pattern glass and nov-elty items such as covered animal dishes. Wright owned some original moulds, but the vast majority of the glass was produced for Wright by Fenton, Viking or Westmoreland from new moulds commis-sioned by Wright. A recent book, The L.G. Wright Glass Company, *by Measell and Roetteis, provides a comprehensive history of the company and its products and also pictures more than 1900 pieces of Wright glass in color.*

Animal covered dish, Frog, blue **$45**
Animal covered dish, Horse, amber................ **35**
Animal covered dish, Rooster, Amberina......... **45**

Wright Turkey Covered Dish

Animal covered dish, Turkey, purple slag
(ILLUS.)... **55**

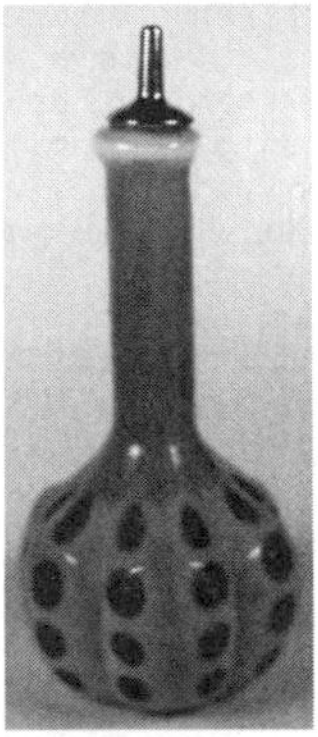

Wright Coin Spot Barber Bottle

Barber bottle, fluted form, cranberry opalescent Coin Spot patt. (ILLUS.) **225**
Barber bottle, fluted form, cranberry opal-
escent Fern patt. **165**
Basket, Panel Grape patt., blue opalescent
w/crystal handle **195**
Butter dish, cov., Argonaut patt., blue
opalescent.. **100**

Wright Chocolate Argonaut Butter Dish

Butter dish, cov., Chocolate glass, Argo-
naut patt. (ILLUS.).. **125**
Butter dish, cov., Eye-Winker patt., ruby........... **75**
Compote, cov., Eye-Winker patt., green,
large **75**

Compote, cov., Stipple Star patt., amber,
large **95**
Compote, open, crimped rim, Princess
Feather patt., blue **35**
Compote, open, Eye-Winker patt., amber,
large **60**
Creamer, Argonaut patt., blue opalescent **45**

Cranberry Beaded Curtain Creamer

Creamer, Beaded Curtain patt., cranberry
w/crystal handle (ILLUS.) **145**

Wright Cherry Decorated Creamer

Creamer, Cherry patt., red, green & gold
decoration (ILLUS.) **25**

Opalescent Coin Dot Creamer

Creamer, cranberry opalescent Coin Dot
patt. (ILLUS.).. **110**

Creamer & cov. sugar bowl, Stipple Star
patt., ruby, pr. **120**

Moon and Star Wright Cruet

Cruet w/original stopper, Moon and Star
patt., amber, crystal stopper (ILLUS.) **135**

Opalescent Coin Dot Finger Bowl

Finger bowl, crimped edge, cranberry
opalescent Coin Dot patt. (ILLUS.) **95**
Goblet, Eye-Winker patt., amber........................ **25**

Wright Herringbone Goblet

Goblet, Herringbone patt., ruby (ILLUS.) **40**
Goblet, Mirror and Rose patt., ruby **40**
Goblet, Panel Grape patt., blue opalescent **40**

Wright Princess Feather Goblet

Goblet, Princess Feather patt., amber
(ILLUS.)... **30**
Goblet, Princess Feather patt., blue.................. **28**

Wright Sawtooth Pink Goblet

Goblet, Sawtooth patt., pink (ILLUS.)................ **25**
Novelty, hand vase, amber **145**

L.G. Wright Hand Vase Novelty

Novelty, hand vase, emerald green
(ILLUS.)... **125**

Pitcher, Carnival glass, God & Home patt., purple **175**

Pitcher, Eye-Winker patt., ruby **85**

Wright Inverted Thumbprint Pitcher

Pitcher, milk, amethyst Inverted Thumbprint patt. (ILLUS.) **100**

Opalescent Drapery Pattern Pitcher

Pitcher, milk, cranberry opalescent Drapery patt. (ILLUS.) **300**

Opalescent Spiral Pattern Pitcher

Pitcher, milk, cranberry opalescent Spiral patt. (ILLUS.) **275**

Pitcher, Panel Grape patt., blue opalescent..... **145**

Pitcher, tankard, Beaded Curtain patt., milk glass w/green interior **550**

Rare Sample Coin Dot Pitcher

Pitcher, Topaz opalescent Coin Dot patt., applied crystal handle, sample item only (ILLUS.) **650**

Salt shaker w/metal lid, Argonaut patt., blue opalescent **25**

Salt shaker w/metal lid, Mirror and Rose patt., green **30**

Eye-Winker Sauce Dish

Sauce dish, Eye-Winker patt., blue (ILLUS.) **20**

Beaded Curtain Peach Blow Spooner

Spooner, Beaded Curtain patt., peach blow (ILLUS.) **90**

Wright Cranberry Sugar Shaker

Sugar shaker w/metal lid, cranberry Inverted Thumbprint patt. (ILLUS.).............. **125**

Carnival God & Home Tumbler

Tumbler, Carnival glass, God & Home patt., purple (ILLUS.)...................................... **55**

Mirror and Rose Pattern Wine

Wine, Mirror and Rose patt., emerald green (ILLUS.).. **40**
Wine, Mirror and Rose patt., pink....................... **30**

Moon and Star Opalescent Wine

Wine, Moon and Star patt., flared rim, Topaz opalescent (ILLUS.) **125**
Wine, Stipple Star patt., amethyst **25**

Wright Stipple Star Wine

Wine, Stipple Star patt., blue (ILLUS.)................ **25**

Panel Grape Blue Wine

Wine glass, Panel Grape patt., blue (ILLUS.)... **30**

Glossary of Selected Glass Terms

Applied—A handle or other portion of a vessel which consists of a separate piece of molten glass attached by hand to the object. Most often used with free-blown or mold-blown pieces but also used with early pressed glass.

Banana stand—A dish, usually round, with two sides turned-up to form a valley and resting atop a pedestal base. A banana bowl is usually an oblong or boat-shaped bowl with deep sides. Popular form in late Victorian pattern glass.

Bar lip—A style of lip used on early pressed and mold-blown decanters where a thick ring of applied glass forms the rim of the piece.

Berry bowl—A small dish, most often round, used to serve individual helpings of ripe berries but also used for ice cream or other desserts. It was usually part of a set which included a large (master) berry bowl and several small ones. A popular form in pressed glass.

Celery vase—A tall vase-form vessel, often with a pedestal base, used to serve celery in the Victorian era. It was a common pressed glass piece used in most homes.

Crimping—A method of decorating the rims of bowls and vases. The glass worker used a special hand tool to manipulate the nearly-molten pressed or blown glass and form a ribbon-like design.

Crystal—A generic term generally used today when referring to thin, fine quality glass stemware produced since the early 20th century. Derived from the Italian term cristallo referring to delicate, clear Venetian blown glass produced since the 14th century.

Egg cup—A small footed cup, sometimes with a cover, that was meant to hold a soft-boiled egg at breakfast. Most commonly found in early pressed flint glass patterns of the 1840-70 era.

Elegant glass—A modern collector's term used when referring to the better quality 20th century glasswares of such companies as Heisey, Cambridge or Fostoria. Meant to differentiate these wares from the less expensive Depression glass of the same era.

Epergne—A French term used to describe a special decorative vessel popular in the 19th century. It generally consists of one or more tall, slender trumpet-form vases centering a wide, shallow bowl base. The bowl base could also be raised on a pedestal foot. It sometimes refers to a piece with a figural pedestal base supporting several small bowls or suspending several small baskets. Also made from silver or other metals.

Etching—A method of decorating a piece of glass. The two main types are acid etching and needle etching. In acid etching a piece is covered with an acid-resistant protective layer and then scratched with a design which is then exposed to hydrofluoric acid or acid fumes, thus leaving a frosted design when the protective layer is removed. Needle etching is a 20th century technique where a hand-held or mechanized needle is used to draw a fine-lined design on a piece. Ornate repetitive designs were possible with the mechanized needle.

Fire-polishing—A process used to finish early American mold-blown and pressed glass where a piece is reheated just enough to smooth out the mold seams without distorting the overall pattern.

Flint glass—The term used to refer to early 19th century glass which was produced using lead oxide in the batch, thus producing a heavy and brilliant glass with a belltone resonance when tapped. When first developed, powdered flints were used instead of lead oxide, hence the name. Nineteenth century American glassmakers used "flint" to describe any quality glass, whether or not it was made with lead.

Galleried rim—A form of rim most often used in early free-blown or mold-blown glass objects, usually sugar bowls. The rim is turned-up around the edge to form a low shelf or gallery which will support the cover.

Knop—Another term for 'knob,' usually referring to a finial on a lid or a bulbous section on the stem of a goblet or wine glass.

Marigold—The most common color used in Carnival glass, generally a bright iridescent orange.

Milk white glass—Also known as milk glass; an opaque solid white color popular in the late 19th century for some glass patterns, novelties and animal covered dishes. Glassmen referred to it as opal (o-pál).

Mold-blown—A method of glass production where a blob of molten glass (called a "gather") is blown into a patterned mold and then removed and further blown and manipulated to form an object such as a bottle.

Novelty—A pressed glass object generally made in the form of some larger item like a hatchet, boat or animal. They were extremely popular in the late 19th century and many were meant to be used as match holders, toothpick holders and small dresser boxes.

Opal—Pronounced o-pál, this was the term used by 19th century glassmen to describe the solid white glass today known as milk glass.

Pattern glass—A term generally referring to the popular pressed glass tablewares produced from the mid-19th century into the early 20th century.

Pontil mark—The scar left on the base of a free-blown, mold-blown and some early pressed glass by the pontil or punty rod. The hot glass object was attached at the base to the pontil rod so the glassworker could more easily handle it during the final shaping and finishing. When snapped off the pontil a round scar remained which, on finer quality pieces, was polished smooth.

Pressed glass—Any glass produced by a pressing machine. First widely produced in the 1820s in a limited range of pieces, by the turn of the 20th century it was possible to produce dozens of different objects by mechanical means.

Rose bowl—A decorative small spherical or egg-shaped bowl, generally with a scalloped or crimped incurved rim, which was designed to hold rose petal potpourri or a bouquet of small roses. It was widely popular in the late 19th century and was produced in many pressed glass patterns as well as more expensive art glass wares such as satin glass.

Scalloping—A decorative treatment used on the rims of plates, bowls, vases and similar objects. It was generally produced during the molding of the object and gave the rim a wavy or ruffled form.

Sheared lip—A type of lip sometimes used on early American free-blown or mold-blown pieces, especially bottles and flasks. It refers to the fact that the neck of the piece is snipped or sheared off the blow pipe.

Sickness—A term referring to cloudy staining found in pressed or blown glass pieces, especially bottles, decanters and vases. It is caused when a liquid is allowed to stand in a piece for a long period of time causing a chemical deterioration of the interior surface. Generally it is nearly impossible to remove completely.

Spall—A shallow rounded flake on a glass object, generally near the rim of a piece.

Spill holder—Also called a 'spill,' is a small vase-form glass holder used in the 19th century to hold spills. The spill was a rolled up thin tube of paper which had been placed under an oil lamp during filling to catch any drips or 'spills' of oil. Once rolled up it could be used as a punk to light lamps. What collectors today call spill holders were produced mainly in flint glass in the 1850s and 1860s, however, research shows that the manufacturers listed them as spoon holders, not spills, a term that doesn't appear until the 1870s.

Spooner—A vase or goblet-form glass piece which was meant to hold a bunch of spoons at the center of a table. It was part of the table set common in Victorian pattern glass.

Stemware—A general term for any form of drinking vessel raised on a slender pedestal or stemmed base.

Strap handle—An early form of applied handle on glass objects. It is a fairly thick ribbon of glass generally terminating at the base with a decorative squiggle or curlique. It is flattened where later applied handles are round.

Table set—A matching set of four pieces commonly produced in late 19th century pressed pattern glass. The set included a spooner (spoon holder), creamer, covered sugar bowl and covered butter dish.

Vaseline—A greenish yellow color of glass which was popular in Victorian pressed and blown glass. It was named by collectors for its resemblance to vaseline petroleum jelly. In original glass company catalogs or advertisements this color was simply called "canary" (canary yellow).

Waste bowl—A small, deep bowl commonly part of a ceramic tea set, but also produced in glass. It was made to hold the dregs from the bottoms of tea cups or the teapot.

Whimsey—A glass or ceramic novelty item. Generally in Victorian glass it is a free-blown or mold-blown object, often made by a glassworker as a special present and not part of regular glass production. Glass shoes, pipes and canes are examples of whimseys.

Appendix I
Glass Collectors' Clubs

Art & Decorative Glasswares

American Cut Glass Association
P.O. Box 482
Ramona, CA 92065-0482

Antique & Art Glass Salt Shaker
    Collectors' Society
2832 Rapidan Trail
Maitland, FL 32751-5013

Czechoslovakian Collectors Guild
    International
P.O. Box 901395
Kansas City, MO 64190-1395

Mount Washington Art Glass Society
P.O. Box 24094
Fort Worth, TX 76124-1094

Paperweight Collectors' Association
P.O. Box 40
Barker, TX 77413-0040

Vaseline Glass Collectors, Inc.
P.O. Box 125
Russellville, MO 65074

Wave Crest Collectors Club
P.O. Box 2013
Santa Barbara, CA 93120

The Whimsey Club
Lon Knickerbocker
2 Hessler Ct.
Dansville, NY 14437

Other Types of Glass

AKRO AGATE

Akro Agate Collector's Club, Inc.
Roger Hardy
97 Milford St.
Clarksburg, WV 26301

CAMBRIDGE

National Cambridge Collectors
P.O. Box 416
Cambridge, OH 43725-0416

CANDLEWICK

National Candlewick Collector's Club
6534 South Ave.
Holland, MI 43528

CARNIVAL

American Carnival Glass Association
9621 Springwater Lane
Miamisburg, OH 45342

Collectible Carnival Glass Association
2100 South Fairway Dr.
Joplin, MO 64804

Heart of America Carnival Glass
4305 W. 78th St.
Prairie Village, KS 66208

International Carnival Glass Association
P.O. Box 306
Mentone, IN 46539-0306

New England Carnival Glass Club
% Eva Backer, Membership
12 Sherwood Rd.
West Hartford, CT 06117-2738

Canadian Carnival Glass Association
12 Dalhousie Crescent
London, Ontario CANADA N6G 2H7

DEPRESSION

National Depression Glass Association
P.O. Box 8264
Wichita, KS 67209-0264

20-30-40's Society, Inc.
P.O. Box 856
LaGrange, IL 60525-0856

Western Reserve Depression Glass Club
5168 Lake Vista Dr.
Solon, OH 44139

Canadian Depression Glass Association
119 Wexford Road
Brampton, Ontario CANADA L6Z 2T5

DUNCAN & MILLER

National Duncan Glass Society
P.O. Box 965
Washington, PA 15301

FENTON

Fenton Art Glass Collectors of America
P.O. Box 384
Williamstown, WV 26187

National Fenton Glass Society
P.O. Box 4008
Marietta, OH 45750-4008

FINDLAY
Collectors of Findlay Glass
P.O. Box 256
Findlay, OH 45839-0256

FIRE-KING
Fire-King Collectors Club
1406 E. 14th St.
Des Moines, IA 50316

FOSTORIA
The Fostoria Glass Society of America
P.O. Box 826
Moundsville, WV 26041-0826

GREENTOWN
National Greentown Glass Association
P.O. Box 107
Greentown, IN 46936-0107

HEISEY
Heisey Collectors of America
169 W. Church St.
Newark, OH 43055

IMPERIAL
National Imperial Glass Collector's
   Society
P.O. Box 534
Bellaire, OH 43906

MILK GLASS
National Milk Glass Collectors Society
% Helen Storey
46 Almond Dr.
Hershey, PA 17033-1759

MORGANTOWN
Old Morgantown Glass Collectors' Guild
P.O. Box 894
Morgantown, WV 26507-0894

Morgantown Collectors of America, Inc.
% Jerry Gallagher
420 1st Ave. N.W.
Plainview, MN 55964-1213

PATTERN
Early American Pattern Glass Society
P.O. Box 266
Colesburg, IA 52035

PHOENIX & CONSOLIDATED
Phoenix & Consolidated Glass
   Collectors
41 River View Dr.
Essex Junction, VT 05452

STRETCH GLASS
Stretch Glass Society
P.O. Box 901
Hampshire, IL 60140

TIFFIN
Tiffin Glass Collectors' Club
P.O. Box 554
Tiffin, OH 44883-0554

WESTMORELAND
National Westmoreland Glass
   Collectors' Club
P.O. Box 100
Grapeville, PA 15634

Westmoreland Glass Society
1144 42nd Ave.
Vero Beach, FL 32960

Special Glass Clubs

Antique & Art Glass Salt Shaker
   Collector's Society
2832 Rapidan Trail
Maitland, FL 32751-5013

Marble Collectors' Society of America
P.O. Box 222
Trumbull, CT 06611-0222

National Marble Club of America
440 Eaton Rd.
Drexel Hill, PA 19026-1205

National Reamer Collectors Association
% Deborah Gillham
47 Midline Ct.
Gaithersburg, MD 20878-1996

National Toothpick Holder
   Collectors' Society
P.O. Box 417
Safety Harbor, FL 34695-0417

International Perfume Bottle Association
3314 Shamrock Rd.
Tampa, FL 33629

General Glass Clubs

Art Glass Discussion Group
405 Lafayette Ave.
Cincinnati, OH 45220

Historical Glass Museum
1157 N. Orange, Box 921
Redlands, CA 92373

Glass Research Society of New Jersey
1501 Glasstown Rd.
Millville, NJ 08332-1566

National American Glass Club
P.O. Box 8489
Silver Spring, MD 20907

Appendix II
Museum Collections of American Glass

Many local and regional museums around the country have displays with some pressed glass included. The following are especially noteworthy.

New England

Connecticut: The Frank Chiarenza Museum of Glass, Meriden; Wadsworth Atheneum, Hartford.

Maine: Jones Gallery of Glass and Ceramics (June—October), Sebago; Portland Museum of Art, Portland.

Massachusetts: Old Sturbridge Village, Sturbridge; Sandwich Glass Museum (April—November), Sandwich.

New Hampshire: The Currier Gallery of Art, Manchester.

Vermont: Bennington Museum (March—November), Bennington.

Mid-Atlantic

Delaware: Henry Francis du Pont Winterthur Museum, Winterthur.

New Jersey: Museum of American Glass, Wheaton Village, Millville.

New York: Corning Museum of Glass, Corning; Cooper-Hewitt Museum, The Smithsonian Institution's National Museum of Design (by appointment), New York; Metropolitan Museum of Art, New York; New-York Historical Society, New York.

Pennsylvania: Historical Society of Western Pennsylvania, Pittsburgh; Philadelphia Museum of Art, Philadelphia; Westmoreland Glass Museum, Port Vue.

Southeast

Florida: Lightner Museum, Saint Augustine; Morse Gallery of Art (Tiffany glass), Winter Park.

Louisiana: New Orleans Museum of Art, New Orleans; Ruby Stain Museum, New Orleans (large private collection of ruby-stained and other pattern glass, by appointment only)

Tennessee: Houston Antique Museum, Chattanooga.

Virginia: Chrysler Museum of Norfolk, Norfolk.

Washington, D.C.: National Museum of American History, Smithsonian Institution.

West Virginia: The Huntington Galleries, Inc., Huntington; Oglebay Institute—Mansion Museum, Wheeling; West Virginia Museum of American Glass, Weston.

Midwest

Indiana: Greentown Glass Museum, Greentown; Indiana Glass Museum, Dunkirk.

Michigan: Henry Ford Museum, Dearborn

Minnesota: A.M. Chisholm Museum, Duluth.

Ohio: Cambridge Glass Museum, Cambridge; Milan Historical Museum, Milan; National Heisey Glass Museum, Newark; Toledo Museum of Art, Toledo.

Wisconsin: John Nelson Bergstrom Art Center and Mahler Glass Museum, Neenah.

Southwest and West

California: Los Angeles County Museum of Art, Los Angeles; Wine Museum of San Francisco and M.H. de Young Museum, San Francisco.

Texas: Mills Collection, Texas Christian University, Fort Worth, MSC Forsyth Center Galleries, Texas A & M University, College Station.

AMERICAN PRESSED
GLASS & BOTTLES
INDEX